NEW CAR BUYING GUIDE 1996 EDITION

The Editors of Consumer Reports Books with Bill Hartford

Consumer Reports Books
A Division of Consumers Union
Yonkers, New York

Published by Consumers Union of United States, Inc., Yonkers, New York 10703.

Library of Congress Catalog Card No.: 88-15006

ISBN: 0-89043-846-3

ISSN: 1044-3045

Design by Joseph DePinho

Page composition by Peter Cusack

First printing, July 1996

This book is printed on recycled paper. 

Manufactured in the United States of America.

New Car Buying Guide 1996 Edition is a Consumer Reports Book published by Consumers Union, the nonprofit organization that publishes *Consumer Reports*, the monthly magazine of test reports, product Ratings, and buying guidance. Established in 1936, Consumers Union is chartered under the Not-for-Profit Corporation Law of the State of New York.

The purposes of Consumers Union, as stated in its charter, are to provide consumers with information and counsel on consumer goods and services, to give information on all matters relating to the expenditure of the family income, and to initiate and to cooperate with individual and group efforts seeking to create and maintain decent living standards.

Consumers Union derives its income solely from the sale of *Consumer Reports* and other publications. In addition, expenses of occasional public service efforts may be met, in part, by nonrestrictive, noncommercial contributions, grants, and fees. Consumers Union accepts no advertising or product samples and is not beholden in any way to any commercial interest. Its Ratings and reports are solely for the use of the readers of its publications. Neither the Ratings, nor the reports, nor any Consumers Union publications, including this book, may be used in advertising or for any commercial purpose. Consumers Union will take all steps open to it to prevent such uses of its material, its name, or the name of *Consumer Reports*.

CONTENTS

INTRODUCTION

Shopping for a new car—or a new vehicle? *Consumer Reports New Car Buying Guide, 1996 Edition* keeps *car* in the title even though chances are good the wheels you may be interested in this year are not on a car.

In this *Guide*, we've got reports on other vehicles that may be on your shopping list, vehicles that people are buying in increasing numbers: minivans, sport-utility vehicles (SUV's), and pickup trucks.

We've been testing minivans and SUVs since they were introduced, and this year we've added tests on pickup trucks to the *New Car Buying Guide*. The term "car" is somewhat generic, as it includes all types of personal passenger vehicles.

At *Consumer Reports* we recognize that a new-car buyer needs guidance in purchasing such a highly technological product, one that most manufacturers peddle with a blatant appeal to the emotions. Buying a new car is a down-to-earth, practical matter. It's an important decision and involves a long-term commitment. The latest ads and television commercials would have you believe that buying a new car is a simple short-term commitment: "Yours for only $199 a month!" "No down payment!" And that driving a new family car is simply a matter of making a monthly rental payment.

But the truth is that whether you lease or buy a brand-new car today, you are making a major financial decision that will affect your pocketbook for several years. Anyone in the market for a new car is faced with making a selection based on more than the outlay of dollars to be budgeted monthly.

To make an informed decision on what new car to drive, consumers must consider not only the sticker price and financing arrangement—or the terms of the leasing contract—but also how well a car is built and designed to do what it is supposed to do. Size, performance, safety, reliability, fuel economy, and other attributes are all important factors when shopping for a new car.

For guidance about making such a major buying decision—one of the single most expensive purchases that many consumers make—*Consumer Reports* has, since 1936, anonymously bought and tested new cars and published reports evaluating them as regularly as manufacturers have introduced the latest models to the marketplace. No other car-testing organization can match Consumers Union's (CU's) reputation for unbiased recommendations, authoritative judgments, and reliable Ratings that regularly appear in the articles in *Consumer Reports*. Now, consumers in the market for a new car can turn to *New Car Buying Guide*, which each year presents CU's new-car test reports in one comprehensive car-buying reference.

Based on the results of CU's automobile testing and on statistical analysis of over 600,000 cars, minivans, pickups, and sport-utility vehicles, *New Car Buying Guide* provides a complete overview of today's new-car market. It gives all the information needed to buy the best vehicle—from how to choose a reliable model that suits your needs and fits your budget, to how to negotiate with the dealer for the best price.

How to use this book

Novice and seasoned new-car buyers should read chapter 1, Dealing with the Dealer, first. It shows you step-by-step how to negotiate the best deal on a new car—whether you're buying or leasing.

Chapter 2, How to Choose a Safe Car, will give you our analysis of the results of the latest government crash tests and information about important safety mechanisms in new cars.

In chapter 3, Child Safety Seats, we describe the proper way to install and use child-restraint seats. The results of our tests of more than two dozen safety seats are given in a Ratings chart that will help you to choose among them. All states require that infants and children be buckled into an approved child-safety restraint. Some of these seats may be integrated into the backseats of several vehicles now on the market.

Chapter 4, Safety Equipment, covers practical safety tactics and equipment to help protect you and your car if your vehicle suddenly becomes disabled.

In chapter 5, Buying Tires, we dispel a few myths about tires and include Ratings for many popular tires for sport-utility vehicles, pickup trucks, family sedans, and performance cars. The tires on the car have a great effect on ride, handling, and performance. Although it is not always possible to specify the tires you want mounted on the wheels of your new car, it is important to have a knowledge of tire design, Ratings, and manufacturers.

Chapter 6, How to Buy Auto Insurance, will inform you about the many decisions you will have to make regarding insurance coverage. An explanation of the types of coverage in an insurance policy and tips on how to shop for insurance will help you get the best buy. Our Ratings chart of three dozen insurers evaluates companies' strengths and weaknesses.

Chapter 7, Choosing the Right

Options, can help you equip a car sensibly and economically.

In chapter 8, How *Consumer Reports* Tests Cars, you'll learn about the rigorous tests we put each car through before deciding on its Rating.

Use the chapters to research, comparison shop, and narrow down your choices to models that are suited to your needs and likely to provide you with reliable transportation.

About the reports

Chapter 9, Summary Judgments of the 1996 Cars, contains reports on over 100 new cars. We provide detailed reports and Ratings for cars we've tested recently. Although the tested car may be a model from an earlier year, a car reported on in detail is essentially the same as the corresponding 1996 model. Other cars are given brief overviews, either because we haven't tested the car or because our test findings may no longer be valid. For example, we may not yet have had a chance to test a new model, or the manufacturer may have made major engineering changes since we last tested a particular car.

The prices listed in each report can help you find cars in your price range and compare prices of different models.

Chapter 10, Facts and Figures, provides technical data that can also help when you are considering and comparing models. Not included in Facts and Figures is any reference to the latest information now included with new cars in the showroom—the percent of domestic and imported content. Where parts come from is not a factor in *Consumer Reports* evaluation of a new car.

For all cars, predicted reliability Ratings and judgments are based on our analysis of the responses to CU's 1995 Annual Questionnaire, the complete results of which are shown in chapter 11, which contains our Frequency-of-Repair report, 1988–95.

Chapter 12 lists manufacturers' telephone numbers in case you wish to reach them for any reason.

Before you visit the dealer

New Car Buying Guide is designed to put the odds of finding a good car at a good price in your favor. Thumb your way through it, read it, use it to evaluate various cars and to start your comparison shopping. Most important, read it carefully before you test drive a car, talk to a salesperson, or attempt to negotiate a deal.

1

DEALING WITH THE DEALER

If our readers' experiences are any guide, nine out of ten new-car buyers are ultimately satisfied with the deal they got from their dealer. Why, then, does buying a car so often evoke emotions usually reserved for root-canal work?

For one thing, whereas dealers for some makes satisfy more than nine in ten of their customers, dealers for other makes leave fewer customers happy.

If you buy a *Toyota* or *Mazda*, you're about four times more likely to be dissatisfied with the deal than if you buy a *Saturn* or *Infiniti*. The chart on page 4, drawn from responses to our 1995 Annual Questionnaire, gives the specifics.

For another thing, the inevitable haggling over price creates friction, even if the haggling eventually results in a satisfactory deal.

For example, nearly one in ten readers told us that the dealer wasn't straightforward about the price. Other readers were dissatisfied because the salesperson was discourteous or ill-informed. And some said they weren't happy because the dealer pressured them to buy extra equipment or services, or because the final price included costs they hadn't known about before they closed the deal.

Despite such pitfalls, you can negotiate effectively with the dealer—if you know how. Arm yourself with knowledge and an organized plan, and you'll stand the best chance of getting the car you want, equipped to your liking, at a fair price.

The steps to a deal

One: Narrow your choices

Decide what size and type of vehicle suits your needs. Don't fall in love with any one car: Consider at least two or three makes and models, and don't be afraid to switch.

Case in point: Bahij Jada, a Californian we talked with, wanted to buy a minivan. "We wanted a Dodge Caravan," he says, "but they all had either more equipment on them than we wanted, or a lot less. The dealers wouldn't move on price. Then I called a Nissan dealer and literally bought a Quest by fax that same afternoon. We did pretty well, but you still have to do your homework."

Two: Learn the cost

You need to find out what the dealer paid for the car—the wholesale, or "invoice," price. On average, the dealer cost is 90 percent of the manufacturer's suggested retail price (MSRP), also known as the sticker price, but it can be as little as 80 percent or as much as 96 percent.

The Summary Judgments of the new cars, beginning on page 47, include cost factors you can use to gain some idea of the wholesale price.

You can get a better idea of dealer cost from printed price guides available at bookstores, newsstands, or your local library or bank. But the guides may not be current, because prices change frequently throughout the year, as do various "factory incentives"—the short-term discounts or rebates so often trumpeted in ads.

You can obtain up-to-date price information from the Consumer Reports New Car Price Service (see inside back cover). For a fee, this service will provide you with a printout that lists the wholesale and retail prices of a car and its various options, and also give information on current rebate offers. (Other pricing services include AAA's AutoEase and CarBargains.)

Whatever the source, make a worksheet to price each vehicle.

- Write down the make, model, and trim line. List each option or options package you want, by name and manufacturer's code number (you'll find that information on the price information printouts).
- Note in two columns the wholesale and retail price for the basic car and each extra-cost option. Add the destination charge to both columns (it's a fixed charge, and dealers take no markup on it). Total your columns, and subtract any factory-to-dealer rebate from the wholesale column. The difference between the final wholesale and retail prices represents the room you have to bargain.

Three: Start to bargain

Bring your worksheet to the dealership. Present your figures to the salesperson and ask for the lowest markup over dealer cost the dealership will accept. If your figures are challenged, ask to see documentation showing that they are wrong.

The dealership may include a "conveyance" or "documentation" fee in the final price. It's a largely arbitrary charge, purportedly to cover the cost of preparing the paperwork, and can range from about $50 to $300 or more. You probably won't be able to negotiate the fee away, so consider it part of the price—and a reason to choose one dealer over another.

Throughout the negotiations, always bargain up from the invoice price, not down from the sticker price. And keep the negotiations simple: Don't discuss trade-ins, leases, or financing until you reach a firm price for the new car.

You may come to terms quickly. That's what happened to Jennifer Moll, who wanted a *Honda Civic*. The salesperson at a Greenwich, Conn., dealership "quickly offered me a great-sounding price," she says. "He invited me to check it with other Honda dealers. I did, but not only were they higher-priced, the people I talked to weren't so nice. I went back to the Greenwich dealer."

Four: Play the endgame

You will probably be made to wait for lengthy periods while the salesperson ferries the deal to the dealership's sales manager. Sometimes the long waits are a tactic designed to wear you down. Stay calm. You can't negotiate well if you are angry or anxious.

You don't have to say how much you're willing to pay, and you should never say, "I want to pay X dollars a month"—that only gives the salesperson reason to structure a loan over a longer period to make it seem more reasonable. (In fact, you'll wind up paying *more* for the car because the longer loan term increases the amount of interest you'll pay.) As a rule, it's best to take the shortest-term loan you can afford, to hold down the interest cost and thus reduce the overall cost of ownership.

Don't be rushed into making a decision immediately. A deal that's good today should be good tomorrow as well. Be completely frank about your willingness to shop elsewhere. If you feel you're getting a runaround, get up and leave.

After you've agreed on a price, you may be passed on to a "business manager," ostensibly to close the deal. Be wary. This individual may try to sell you undercoating, rustproofing, fabric protection, etching of the vehicle identification number on the windows, or a costly extended warranty. Refuse them all, since they are worthless, overpriced, or both.

What's the bottom line?

How much over invoice must you spend? A lot depends on supply and demand. For a brand-new model in tight supply or for a luxury car with low sales, you may have to pay the sticker price or close to it. Otherwise, paying $300 to $500 over invoice is reasonable.

Once you have a firm price, you can talk about leasing or financing. If you have a trade-in, find out how much it's worth. You can call the Consumer Reports Used Car Price Service (1-900-466-0500; the cost is $1.75 per minute, and the typical call lasts five minutes or more). Also check printed guides, such as the "N.A.D.A. Official Used Car Guide" or the "Kelley Blue Book"; many bank loan officers have a copy of those guides.

Dealers and manufacturers sometimes offer low loan rates as a sales incentive. Those rates may seem attractive, but you have to calculate the final cost of that loan versus any alternatives. For instance, does a low "teaser" rate apply only if you pay the full sticker price, or is it offered even after you've beaten down the price? Don't jump at the dealer's terms without first checking local bank or credit-union rates.

Read the fine print

Always read the sales contract carefully. One Texan we spoke with learned that lesson the hard way. "All I wanted was a rate quote on a loan," says Marvin Rau. "Instead, they took me into a room and ran lots of paperwork past me, which they had me sign. I left a deposit and took the truck home to show it to my wife. We decided we didn't want the truck, but when I brought it back, the dealer said I'd already bought it." (Rau eventually managed to return the truck and get his deposit back.)

Also, be sure the contract really is a sales contract, if you're buying the car. People sometimes believe they're buying a car only to find that the dealership has maneuvered them into a lease agreement instead. Be sure, too, that an officer at the dealership signs the contract.

Do you hate to haggle?

Many people find haggling over price a distasteful process. Here are some alternatives.

No-haggle dealers

GM's Saturn Corporation popular-

Dealer Satisfaction

The brand of car you buy can affect your happiness with the deal. According to our readers who responded to questions on our Annual Questionnaire about car-buying satisfaction, some dealers just do it better. And, as the table shows, the better dealers aren't necessarily those carrying the most popular or the most expensive cars.

Average and range of satisfaction with dealers are based on more than 136,000 new-car purchases, as described in responses to our 1995 Annual Questionnaire. Percentages for a brand are the averages of models with 100 or more responses. Data are adjusted for the age of the buyer (older buyers tend to be more satisfied than younger ones).

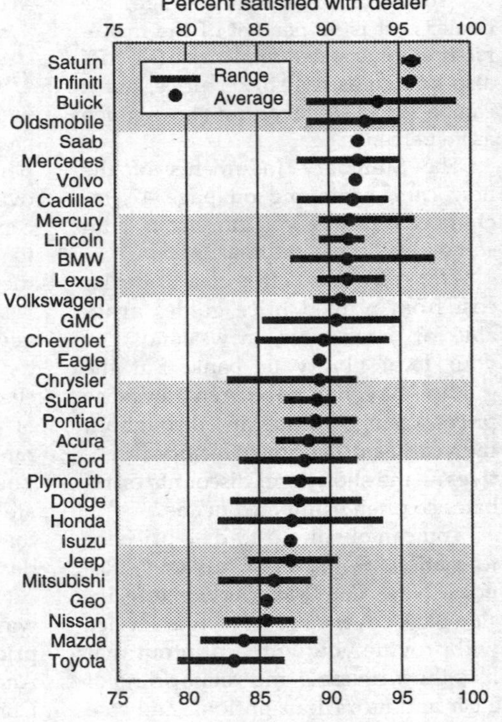

ized the practice of selling cars for a fixed, take-it-or-leave-it price. The practice has won quite a few devoted customers. Now, perhaps 5 percent of dealers nationwide have a no-haggle pricing policy; many others have a "no-haggle" price on a few specific models.

The policy does make it easy to come to terms with the dealer. However, our engineers' experience in buying cars for our testing program has shown that a no-haggle price isn't necessarily the lowest price available on that model.

Auto-buying services

These firms do all or part of the negotiating for you. You explain exactly what you're looking for, and the service contacts one or more dealers in your area and negotiates a price. Sometimes you pay the service a flat fee ($50 is typical); at other times the service receives its fee or commission from the dealer.

Unfortunately, you can't be sure how good a deal a buying service turns up unless you research prices on your own. We don't think you should use a buying service as your sole source of price information.

Local buying services are listed in the Yellow Pages under Automobile Brokers. Two services that operate nationally are:

- Auto Insider (800-446-7433). This is a free service that provides the names of local dealers who have agreed to provide discounts. But we have found that the discounts vary; in addition, you have to visit the dealer in person to find out the price.
- CarBargains (800-475-7283). This service, run by the nonprofit Center for the Study of Services in Washington, D.C., charges a flat $150 fee for quote sheets from at least five local dealers who agree to sell you a car for a certain amount over the factory-invoice price. If you also order a printout from a pricing service, you'll know ahead of time how attractive a discount you're being offered.

On-line shopping

It's now possible to car-shop by computer, using one of the major on-line services or the Internet:

- Subscribers to America Online,

CONSIDERING A LEASE? AVOID THE POTHOLES

Newspaper ads touting "low, low monthly rates" make leasing a car seem enticing. Is it any wonder that so many would-be new-car buyers, reeling from sticker shock, grab the lease deals auto manufacturers and dealers are offering? Today, more than 30 percent of the new cars rolling off dealer lots are leased.

Leasing appeals to so many people largely because of low up-front costs. Buy a $20,000 auto with a 20 percent down payment and 6 percent sales tax, and your initial cost will be $5200; you could lease the same car for about $400 in up-front charges.

But leasing isn't as good a deal as the tempting ads make it seem. In the long run, leasing often costs more. After the typical 36-month lease ends, the lease customer owns nothing while the buyer still has a car worth thousands of dollars. Even if the monthly loan payments for a car run substantially more than the monthly lease payments, the owner will invariably come out several hundred dollars ahead of the lease customer.

If you're still tempted to lease, keep the following basics in mind:

- The first step is to negotiate the price as if you were buying the car. Although lease ads imply a set monthly rate, the lower the price, the lower your monthly payments will be.
- Read the advertising fine print. The most attractive terms are often available only if you pay a "capitalized cost reduction"—the money you must put down to qualify for the low payments touted in the ad. Further, those payments are usually a come-on available only on stripped-down models. Expect to pay more if you want a car with extra features or a larger-than-standard engine.
- Be sure you can live within the lease restrictions. Most dealers limit you to between 12,000 and 15,000 miles of driving a year. Clock any more and you could be charged as much as 25 cents a mile.
- Ask what protections you'll have to cover repairs or damage. Make sure the manufacturer's warranty covers the entire term of the lease and the number of miles you're likely to drive.

A standard lease contract requires you to pay for "excess wear and tear"; ask the dealer to spell out what that means. If you don't, you risk paying steep repair bills when the lease is up.

Make sure, too, that the lease includes "gap insurance." If the car is stolen or totaled, gap insurance will pay the difference between what you owe on the lease and what the car is worth—a difference that can amount to thousands of dollars.

- Know what the car's residual value will be. Leasing companies base the monthly payments on an estimate of the car's "residual," or ultimate resale, value. You can often buy the car at that price when the lease is up (although lately, an increasing number of the contracts we've seen do not give this option). If you want to end the lease early, you'll have to pay the difference between the car's estimated value and the total monthly payments you've made to that point. That often amounts to all the remaining payments you'd owe to the lease's expiration.
- Take your time before you sign. Ask to take home a copy of the lease contract and scrutinize it closely. Sizing up a leasing deal is complicated because contract terms vary widely from state to state and even dealer to dealer.

Watch out for extra charges, such as fees for conveyance, disposition, and preparation. Those are pure dealer profit and can be negotiated.

New national rules, due this spring from the Federal Reserve Board, will require all car leases to use standardized terminology. That should make comparison-shopping for auto leases much simpler. Until then—and probably after, too—buckle up. You're on your own.

CompuServe, or Prodigy can sign up with AutoVantage for as little as $1 for a three-month trial period (the normal fee is $49).

Among other offerings, AutoVantage promises to negotiate a discount price for you at any of about 1000 dealers nationwide. You then use a toll-free telephone number to place an order.

- Auto-By-Tel is a free service that promises to find you a new car at a wholesale price through a nationwide network of 1200 dealers. You can find this service on CompuServe (as "Autobytel") or Prodigy ("Auto-by-tel"), or on the World Wide Web at *http://www.autobytel.com.*

You need to have done all your homework first, but then you simply fill in blanks on an ordering screen. You're supposed to request a quote only if you're serious about buying the car.

2

HOW TO CHOOSE A SAFE CAR

What's the safest car? That's a question often asked by our readers—and, unfortunately, one that can't be answered precisely. The science of car safety is still far from cut-and-dried.

But even if we can't tell you which car will best protect you and your family under all conditions, we can tell you which important features and performance factors to look for.

Why air bags are essential

Combined with a safety belt, the air bag is one of the most effective safety features. More than a quarter of all cars on the road have at least one air bag. Our advice: Look for a car with dual air bags. That should be easy; dual air bags are standard in most 1996 cars.

The government estimates that air bags have saved about 1000 lives since they were introduced. And the Insurance Institute for Highway Safety (IIHS), an insurance industry group, predicts that the number of lives saved will soon increase to about 4000 per year as air bags become more widespread. Consider, too, the countless serious injuries that air bags have prevented; more than half a million air bags have deployed so far.

Conventional air bags are effective in a frontal impact but not in a side or rear crash or in a rollover. That's why safety belts remain vital. Belts and air bags work very well together.

Some reports indicate that air bags have done more harm than good in a few cases. But it's important to keep those isolated cases in perspective.

The National Highway Traffic Safety Administration (NHTSA) estimates that more than a dozen small children have been killed by air bags. Three fatalities involved a rear-facing infant carrier, where the baby's head was directly in the path of the rapidly inflating air bag. That risk is an additional reason to install any child safety seat in the rear seat.

In a sports car or pickup truck without a usable rear seat, use a forward-facing safety seat if the vehicle has a passenger's air bag. (The 1996 *Ford Ranger* and *Mazda* B-Series and 1997 *Ford F-150* pickups have a switch to disable the passenger's air bag when you use an infant carrier.)

Another dozen or so fatalities involved drivers. The evidence suggests that most were either not wearing their safety belt or were sitting very close to the steering wheel. A belt helps keep you properly positioned so the air bag can safely do its job. You should also adjust the driver's seat as far back as you comfortably can.

Air bags have also caused some injuries. But the IIHS estimates that fewer than 1 percent were serious.

Next after head-on crashes, side impacts kill the most people—about 9000 per year—and a few automakers now offer side air bags. The 1995 *Volvo 850* was first to have them, and Mercedes-Benz and BMW are offering them in some new models. Next year, Ford and GM will introduce side air bags in some high-end models. Eventually, BMW will offer an additional side air bag for the head.

How telling are crash tests?

The most comprehensive crash-test data available to consumers come from the government. For the past 17 years, the NHTSA has been running cars head-on into a barrier at 35 mph, with high-speed cameras and instrumented test dummies recording results. Each vehicle is scored on the extent of likely "injuries" to the safety-belted dummies.

We analyze the NHTSA data independently and assign our own scores (see the table on pages 10–12). The best score, ⊖, indicates that a belted human occupant most likely would have survived the crash with little or no injury. The worst score, ●, indicates virtually certain serious injury or death. Cars have become more crashworthy over the years; today, most score ○ or better—quite good for a severe crash.

These barrier crash tests simulate a head-on collision between two cars of the same size and weight. Thus, you couldn't predict how a tiny car—say, a *Geo Metro*—would fare against a large car—say, a *Lincoln Town Car*—by looking at the test results. In a two-car head-on collision, the larger car is likely to be safer.

Further, the NHTSA's frontal crash tests say little about how a car would fare in an angle, side, or rear crash or a rollover. But models that did well in the frontal crash tests have had a significantly lower overall fatality rate than models that did poorly.

In Europe, offset crash testing, which involves only part of the car's front, is preferred. Europeans argue that, on the road, offset crashes are far more common than full-frontal crashes. We think our government should add offset tests to its program.

Last year, the IIHS put 14 cars through those tough offset tests, with 40 percent of the car's front striking a crushable barrier at 40 mph (see box on page 8). The 1995 *Chevrolet Lumina, Ford Taurus,* and *Volvo 850* performed especially well; the *Chevrolet Cavalier, Mitsubishi Galant, Chrysler Cirrus,* and *Nissan Maxima* performed poorly. Of the 1996 models tested, the *Ford Taurus* did very well; the *Toyota Avalon* was in mid-pack.

The government is also phasing in a new side-impact standard, since side crashes can be especially deadly. The standard specifies a test that simulates a crash in which a car traveling at 15 mph is broadsided by another going 30 mph. To satisfy the safety standard, the entire car must be reinforced from roof to floor. The "side-impact claim" column in our safety table notes which 1996 models claim to meet that standard. (By 1997, all passenger cars must comply.)

TOUGH CRASH TESTS ON POPULAR SEDANS

Up to now, the only information on how cars behave in a collision has come from the National Highway Traffic Safety Administration (NHTSA), which has been crash-testing cars for the past 17 years. But this year, the Insurance Institute for Highway Safety (IIHS) staged a different—and in many ways tougher—series of crash tests on 14 sedans.

The government and IIHS tests complement each other. Here's how they differ:

• The government crashes cars into a rigid barrier, so the car absorbs all the forces. The IIHS used a honeycomb barrier that crushes, absorbing some of the crash forces just as one car does when it hits another.

• The government crashes cars at 35 mph. The IIHS uses 40 mph.

• The government crashes its cars head-on into the barrier. The IIHS staged offset-barrier crashes. Only the left side of the car—40 percent of the front end—hits the barrier. Since an offset crash concentrates the crash forces over a smaller frontal area, it's an especially severe test of a car's ability to crush progressively without intruding on passenger space. A full-frontal crash puts more emphasis on the car's air bags and safety belts.

The IIHS graded the sedans largely on these factors:

Structure

The most important scoring factor. A car's structure should absorb crash energy effectively, without severely deforming the passenger compartment. But in some cars, the dashboard was pushed back considerably, the doors jammed shut, or the floor panel or center console buckled, trapping the driver dummy's feet or legs.

Restraints

How well the safety belt and air bag controlled the driver dummy's movement and prevented contact with hard interior surfaces.

Injury measurements

Analysis of the forces recorded by instruments on the test dummy's head, neck, chest, legs, and feet, estimating the severity of the "injuries."

The IIHS plans to crash-test the redesigned 1996 *Ford Taurus* soon, with other models to follow. We've long urged the NHTSA to add similar tests to its schedule.

INSURANCE INDUSTRY CRASH-TEST DATA

The key results from 40-mph crash tests conducted by the Insurance Institute for Highway Safety on 14 midsize sedans. In ranking the cars, the IIHS used the following scale: **G** = Good, **A** = Acceptable, **M** = Marginal, **P** = Poor.

				Injury Measures			
Make and model	**Overall**	**Structure**	**Restraints**	**Head/neck**	**Chest**	**Left leg**	**Right leg**
Chevrolet Lumina	G	G	G	G	G	G	G
Ford Taurus	G	G	G	A	G	G	G
Volvo 850	G	A	G	G	G	G	G
Toyota Camry	A	A	G	A	G	A	G
Subaru Legacy	A	A	G	G	G	P	G
Honda Accord	A	A	G	G	G	P	A
Mazda Millenia	A	M	G	G	G	P	G
Saab 900	M	P	M	G	G	G	A
Ford Contour	P	M	G	G	G	P	P
Volkswagen Passat	P	M	P	G	G	P	G
Chevrolet Cavalier	P	P	P	A	G	P	G
Mitsubishi Galant	P	P	P	G	G	P	A
Chrysler Cirrus	P	P	M	G	G	P	P
Nissan Maxima	P	A	P	M	G	P	P

Avoiding a crash

No matter how carefully you drive, sooner or later you'll have to swerve or brake abruptly. Your car should respond quickly and predictably to its steering, and it should stop short and straight, without skidding. The Summary Judgments, starting on page 47, include highlights of our handling and braking assessments. They also include the date of our original report, so you can research a model in more detail.

Several features—antilock brakes, traction control, and a new one called yaw control—can also help you keep your car safely under control.

Antilock brakes

An antilock brake system (ABS) uses a computer to prevent the wheels from locking up and skidding in a hard stop. By pulsing the brakes many times per second, ABS lets you stop shorter on slippery roads and steer while braking. New-car buyers should pass up any model not equipped with this vital safety feature.

ABS has recently garnered some negative publicity. A study by the insurance industry three years ago suggested that ABS reduces neither the number nor the cost of auto accidents. Two recent NHTSA studies reported mixed results: ABS significantly reduced frontal collisions on wet roads, and it cut down on fatalities to pedestrians and bicyclists. But for some reason, cars that had ABS were involved disproportionately in run-off-the-road accidents.

Those findings are surprising and disturbing, because ABS is clearly superior in controlled tests. *Consumer Reports* has tested well over 100 ABS-equipped cars on our test track to date. In our 1995 tire tests on wet pavement, our test car stopped from 60 mph about 70 feet shorter, on average, with the ABS working than with the ABS disabled.

A study commissioned by the auto industry and released earlier this year puts ABS in a much better light. That study looked at some 43,000 accidents of all kinds, including minor ones. Although the overall fatality rate was the same for cars with and without ABS, the overall accident rate for ABS-equipped cars was about 10 percent lower—and on slippery roads, it was almost 20 percent lower—with commensurate reductions in injuries.

As for the increase in off-road crashes reported in the NHTSA studies, we can only conjecture. Possibly, some people in ABS-equipped cars managed to steer around an obstacle rather than hit it, but then lost control. Some people may have overestimated the benefits of ABS and driven less cautiously. And some people undoubtedly don't use ABS properly. With antilock brakes, you shouldn't pump the brake pedal on slippery pavement; just mash the pedal and hold it down. When the ABS makes the brake pedal pulsate and chatter, don't panic and let up on the brakes.

Traction control

This useful option can help keep the drive wheels from spinning, especially on slippery roads. Traction control is nice to have in front-wheel-drive cars, and a godsend in rear-wheel-drive cars.

But beware: All traction-control systems are not created equal. Low-speed systems work only up to about 25 mph. A powerful engine can easily overpower such a system.

All-speed traction control is much more sophisticated. It not only helps you get started on slippery pavement, but it can prevent loss of control if you accelerate too hard in a turn. To make sure you get all-speed traction control, check the manufacturer's sales literature or the owner's manual.

Yaw control

This promising innovation sprang from ABS technology. When a car loses traction in a curve and starts to swing sideways (yaw), the ABS computer selectively brakes a wheel, helping the driver regain control. BMW and Mercedes-Benz are already phasing in such systems.

SAFE-DRIVING TIPS

Whatever kind of car you drive, some basic safety strategies can help keep you out of harm's way.

- **Find a good driving position.** Position the seat so you can just hang your wrist over the top of the steering wheel when you extend your arm. Adjust the head restraint so it's directly behind but not touching your head. Hold the wheel symmetrically, at about 3 and 9 o'clock, so you can steer left or right quickly and precisely. If you drape your arm over the top of the wheel, the air bag can break your arm or push it into your face if it deploys.
- **Go with the flow.** Keep up with traffic if conditions permit. A wide disparity in speeds is dangerous.
- **Be a loner.** Avoid clumps of cars on the highway so you're not involved in someone else's accident.
- **Keep track of traffic.** Look far down the road, and keep your eyes moving to spot any problems before you reach them. Check your mirrors frequently.
- **Think ahead.** Keep thinking of possible traffic emergencies, and plan escape routes.
- **Don't be a left-lane hog.** The left lane is a passing lane, not a "fast" lane. Don't try to block speeders; leave the policing to the police.
- **Signal!** Signal lane changes as well as turns.
- **Wait to turn left.** When you're stopped in traffic, waiting to turn left, keep the wheels aimed straight ahead until the way is clear. If you wait with the wheels cut to the left, someone could hit you from behind and push you into oncoming traffic.
- **Help 'em merge.** If you're in the right lane of a multilane highway, you can help entering traffic merge safely and smoothly by temporarily moving over a lane if traffic permits.
- **Brake at the right time.** Slow down to a safe speed before you enter a turn. Hard braking in mid-corner can upset the car's balance.
- **Try the ABS.** If your car has an antilock brake system, the pedal's vibration and rumbling noise could startle you the first time. Don't wait for an emergency; find a deserted, slippery road or empty parking lot and hit the brakes hard enough to actuate the ABS so you'll know what it feels like.
- **Protect your night vision.** Don't stare at approaching headlights. If you're being blinded, focus on the right shoulder of the road.
- **Catch some Z's.** Don't drive when you're sleepy. If your eyes tend to stay focused on one spot, that's a danger sign. Pull over as soon as you find a safe place and nap for a few minutes.

1996 Cars: Crash Protection Judgments

As published in the April 1996 issue of *Consumer Reports*.

Crash protection scores are based on CU's analysis of data from 35-mph barrier crash tests conducted by the National Highway Traffic Safety Administration. Tests simulate a head-on crash with another vehicle of similar size and weight that's traveling at the same speed. Instrumented, safety-belted driver and passenger dummies record crash forces. Our analysis assesses the likelihood of various levels of injury. Results of this test are very specific; they don't predict how well passengers will fare in other kinds of crashes. Scores are missing for many models because the government tests a limited number of cars each year and because of changes in car design—most often, the addition of an air bag—since the tests were run.

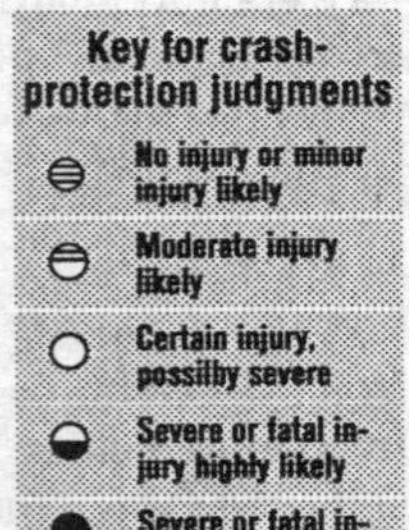

Key for crash-protection judgments
No injury or minor injury likely
Moderate injury likely
Certain injury, possilby severe
Severe or fatal injury highly likely
Severe or fatal injury certain

Injury claim rates give an idea of how well cars protect passengers in real-world accidents. They're based on the frequency of insurance claims made for each model, compared with all vehicles (**overall**) and with cars of that type (**for type**). In general, passengers in big cars fare better than small cars, but some small cars (the *Geo Prizm*, for example) did better than other small cars. Judgments are based on data from the Highway Loss Data Institute, an insurance-industry organization. Again, data are not available for many cars because of recent redesigns.

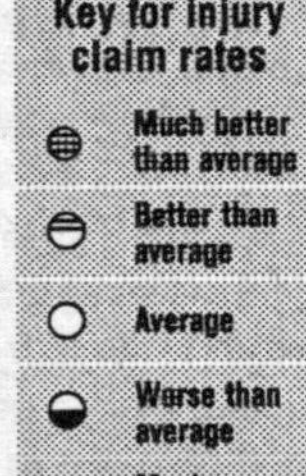

Safety equipment is what's available, as specified by manufacturers. "Daytime lights" are daytime running lights. "Optional" means the equipment is available at extra cost. "Varies" means that availability varies by trim line.

Some automakers now make a **side-impact claim** for their cars, meaning the car meets a new government safety standard being phased in that requires improved side-impact protection. All passenger cars are required to comply with this standard by 1997.

Throughout, **NA** means the information is not available—the car wasn't tested or tested recently, or data were unusable.

Make and model	Crash protection		Injury claim rate		Safety equipment					Side-impact claim
	DRIVER	PASSENGER	OVERALL	FOR TYPE	DRIVER AIR BAG	PASSENGER AIR BAG	ANTILOCK BRAKES	TRACTION CONTROL	DAYTIME LIGHTS	
Acura CL (1997)	NA	NA	NA	NA	Standard	Standard	Standard	No	No	✓
Acura Integra	⊖	○	○	⊜	Standard	Standard	Varies	No	No	—
Acura RL (1997)	NA	NA	NA	NA	Standard	Standard	Standard	Optional	No	✓
Acura SLX	NA	NA	NA	NA	Standard	Standard	Standard	No	No	—
Acura TL	NA	NA	NA	NA	Standard	Standard	Standard	Varies	No	✓
Audi A4	⊖	⊜	NA	NA	Standard	Standard	Standard	No	No	✓
Audi A6	⊜	⊜	⊖	⊜	Standard	Standard	Standard	No	No	✓
BMW 3-Series	⊖	⊖	○	○	Standard	Standard	Standard	Optional	No	✓
BMW 318ti	NA	NA	NA	NA	Standard	Standard	Standard	Optional	No	✓
BMW 5-Series	NA	NA	⊖	⊖	Standard	Standard	Standard	Varies	No	✓
BMW 740iL	NA	NA	⊜	⊜	Standard	Standard	Standard	Optional	No	✓
BMW Z3	NA	NA	NA	NA	Standard	Standard	Standard	Optional	No	✓
Buick Century	⊜	○	⊖	⊜	Standard	No	Standard	No	No	—
Buick Le Sabre	NA	NA	⊜	⊜	Standard	Standard	Standard	Varies	No	[1]
Buick Park Avenue	NA	NA	⊜	⊜	Standard	Standard	Standard	Optional	No	—
Buick Regal	NA	NA	⊖	⊜	Standard	Standard	Standard	No	No	✓
Buick Riviera	NA	NA	NA	NA	Standard	Standard	Standard	Optional	No	✓
Buick Roadmaster	NA	NA	⊜	⊜	Standard	Standard	Standard	No	No	✓
Buick Skylark	NA	NA	○	○	Standard	Standard	Standard	Standard	No	—
Cadillac De Ville	NA	NA	⊜	⊜	Standard	Standard	Standard	Standard	Standard	✓
Cadillac Eldorado	NA	NA	⊖	⊜	Standard	Standard	Standard	Standard	Standard	✓
Cadillac Fleetwood	NA	NA	⊜	⊜	Standard	Standard	Standard	Standard	Standard	✓
Cadillac Seville	NA	NA	⊜	⊜	Standard	Standard	Standard	Standard	Standard	✓
Chevrolet Astro	NA	NA	⊖	⊖	Standard	Standard	Standard	No	No	—
Chevrolet Beretta	NA	NA	◒	◒	Standard	No	Standard	No	Standard	—
Chevrolet Blazer	○	●	NA	NA	Standard	No	Standard	No	Standard	—
Chevrolet C/K	NA	NA	⊖	⊜	Standard	No	Standard	No	Standard	—
Chevrolet Camaro	⊜	⊜	○	⊖	Standard	Standard	Standard	Varies	No	✓
Chevrolet Caprice	⊖	◒	⊖	⊖	Standard	Standard	Standard	No	No	✓
Chevrolet Cavalier	○	○	NA	NA	Standard	Standard	Standard	Varies	Standard	✓
Chevrolet Corsica	○	●	◒	◒	Standard	No	Standard	No	Standard	—
Chevrolet Corvette	NA	NA	⊖	⊜	Standard	Standard	Standard	Standard	No	—
Chevrolet Lumina	⊜	⊜	NA	NA	Standard	Standard	Varies	No	No	✓
Chevrolet Lumina van	NA	NA	⊖	⊜	Standard	No	Standard	Optional	No	—
Chevrolet Monte Carlo	⊖	⊖	NA	NA	Standard	Standard	Standard	No	No	✓
Chevrolet S-Series	◒	●	○	○	Standard	No	Standard	No	Standard	—
Chevrolet Suburban	NA	NA	⊜	⊜	Standard	No	Standard	No	Standard	—
Chevrolet Tahoe	⊖	○	⊜	⊜	Standard	No	Standard	No	Standard	—
Chrysler Cirrus	◒	NA	NA	NA	Standard	Standard	Standard	No	No	✓
Chrysler Concorde	⊖	⊖	⊖	⊖	Standard	Standard	Standard	Optional	No	✓
Chrysler LHS	⊖	⊜	⊖	⊖	Standard	Standard	Standard	Standard	No	✓
Chrysler Sebring	⊜	⊜	NA	NA	Standard	Standard	Standard	No	No	✓
Chrysler Sebring Convertible	NA	NA	NA	NA	Standard	Standard	Optional	No	No	✓
Chrysler Town & Country	○	⊖	NA	NA	Standard	Standard	Standard	No	No	✓
Dodge Avenger	⊜	⊜	NA	NA	Standard	Standard	Varies	No	No	✓
Dodge Caravan	NA	NA	NA	NA	Standard	Standard	Standard	No	No	✓
Dodge Dakota	⊜	⊖	⊖	⊖	Standard	No	Optional	No	No	—

Make and model	Crash protection		Injury claim rate		Safety equipment					Side-impact claim
	DRIVER	PASSENGER	OVERALL	FOR TYPE	DRIVER AIR BAG	PASSENGER AIR BAG	ANTILOCK BRAKES	TRACTION CONTROL	DAYTIME LIGHTS	
Dodge Grand Caravan	○	⊖	NA	NA	Standard	Standard	Standard	No	No	✓
Dodge Intrepid	⊖	⊖	⊖	⊖	Standard	Standard	Optional	Optional	No	✓
Dodge Neon	⊖	⊖	NA	NA	Standard	Standard	Optional	No	No	✓
Dodge Ram	⊜	◒	⊖	⊖	Standard	No	Optional	No	No	—
Dodge Stratus	◒	NA	NA	NA	Standard	Standard	Optional	No	No	✓
Eagle Summit	NA	NA	NA	NA	Standard	Standard	Varies	No	No	—
Eagle Summit Wagon	NA	NA	NA	NA	Standard	Standard	Optional	No	No	—
Eagle Talon	⊖	⊜	NA	NA	Standard	Standard	Optional	No	No	—
Eagle Vision	⊖	⊖	⊖	⊖	Standard	Standard	Varies	Optional	No	✓
Ford Aerostar	NA	NA	○	○	Standard	No	Varies	No	No	—
Ford Aspire	⊖	⊖	NA	NA	Standard	Standard	Optional	No	No	—
Ford Bronco	⊜	⊜	⊖	⊖	Standard	No	Standard	No	No	—
Ford Contour	⊜	○	NA	NA	Standard	Standard	Optional	Varies	No	✓
Ford Crown Victoria	NA	NA	⊖	⊖	Standard	Standard	Optional	Optional	No	✓
Ford Escort	⊖	○	◒	⊖	Standard	Standard	Varies	No	No	—
Ford Explorer	⊖	⊜	⊖	⊖	Standard	Standard	Standard	No	No	—
Ford F-Series (1997)	NA	NA	NA	NA	Standard	Standard	Optional	No	No	✓
Ford Mustang	⊜	⊖	◒	○	Standard	Standard	Optional	No	No	—
Ford Probe	⊜	⊜	◒	○	Standard	Standard	Optional	No	No	—
Ford Ranger	⊖	⊜	○	○	Standard	Optional	Varies	No	No	—
Ford Taurus	⊖	⊖	NA	NA	Standard	Standard	Optional	No	Optional	✓
Ford Thunderbird	⊜	⊜	○	⊖	Standard	Standard	Standard	Optional	No	✓
Ford Windstar	⊜	⊜	NA	NA	Standard	Standard	Standard	Optional	No	✓
GMC Jimmy	○	●	NA	NA	Standard	No	Standard	No	Standard	—
GMC Safari	NA	NA	⊖	⊖	Standard	Standard	Standard	No	No	—
GMC Sierra C/K	NA	NA	⊖	⊜	Standard	No	Standard	No	Standard	—
GMC Sonoma	◒	●	○	○	Standard	No	Standard	No	Standard	—
GMC Suburban	NA	NA	⊜	⊜	Standard	No	Standard	No	Standard	—
GMC Yukon	⊖	○	⊜	⊜	Standard	No	Standard	No	Standard	—
Geo Metro	⊖	⊖	NA	NA	Standard	Standard	Optional	No	Standard	✓
Geo Prizm	NA	NA	◒	⊖	Standard	Standard	Optional	No	Standard	—
Geo Tracker	NA	NA	◒	●	Standard	Standard	Optional	No	Standard	—
Honda Accord	⊖	○	○	○	Standard	Standard	Varies	No	No	✓
Honda Civic	NA	NA	NA	NA	Standard	Standard	Varies	No	No	✓
Honda Civic del Sol	NA	NA	○	⊖	Standard	Standard	Varies	No	No	—
Honda Odyssey	⊖	⊖	NA	NA	Standard	Standard	Standard	No	No	✓
Honda Passport	⊖	○	○	◒	Standard	Standard	Varies	No	No	—
Honda Prelude	NA	NA	◒	○	Standard	Standard	Varies	No	No	—
Hyundai Accent	○	⊖	NA	NA	Standard	Standard	Optional	No	No	✓
Hyundai Elantra	NA	NA	NA	NA	Standard	Standard	Varies	No	No	✓
Hyundai Sonata	○	○	NA	NA	Standard	Standard	Varies	No	No	✓
Infiniti G20	NA	NA	○	○	Standard	Standard	Standard	No	No	—
Infiniti I30	NA	NA	NA	NA	Standard	Standard	Standard	No	No	✓
Infiniti J30	⊖	○	○	⊖	Standard	Standard	Standard	No	No	—
Infiniti Q45	NA	NA	⊖	⊖	Standard	Standard	Standard	Optional	No	—
Isuzu Hombre	NA	NA	NA	NA	Standard	No	No	No	No	—
Isuzu Oasis	⊖	⊖	NA	NA	Standard	Standard	Standard	No	No	✓
Isuzu Rodeo	⊖	○	○	◒	Standard	Standard	Varies	No	No	—
Isuzu Trooper	NA	NA	⊖	○	Standard	Standard	Varies	No	No	—
Jaguar XJ6	NA	NA	⊖	⊖	Standard	Standard	Standard	Optional	No	✓
Jeep Cherokee	⊖	○	⊖	○	Standard	No	Optional	No	No	—
Jeep Grand Cherokee	NA	NA	⊖	⊖	Standard	Standard	Standard	No	No	✓
Jeep Wrangler (1997)	NA	NA	NA	NA	Standard	Standard	Optional	No	No	—
Land Rover Discovery	NA	NA	NA	NA	Standard	Standard	Standard	No	No	—
Lexus ES300	NA	NA	⊖	⊜	Standard	Standard	Standard	No	No	—
Lexus GS300	○	○	○	◒	Standard	Standard	Standard	Optional	No	✓
Lexus LS400	NA	NA	⊜	⊜	Standard	Standard	Standard	Optional	No	✓
Lexus LX450	NA	NA	NA	NA	Standard	Standard	Standard	No	No	—
Lexus SC400/SC300	NA	NA	⊖	⊜	Standard	Standard	Standard	Optional	No	✓
Lincoln Continental	NA	NA	NA	NA	Standard	Standard	Standard	Optional	No	✓
Lincoln Mark VIII	NA	NA	⊖	⊜	Standard	Standard	Standard	Optional	No	✓
Lincoln Town Car	NA	NA	⊖	⊜	Standard	Standard	Standard	Optional	No	✓
Mazda 626	NA	NA	○	○	Standard	Standard	Standard	Varies	No	✓
Mazda B-Series	NA	NA	○	○	Standard	Standard	Optional	No	No	✓
Mazda MPV	NA	NA	NA	NA	Standard	Standard	Varies	No	No	—
Mazda MX-5 Miata	NA	NA	○	⊖	Standard	Standard	Standard	No	No	—
Mazda MX-6	NA	NA	○	⊖	Standard	Standard	Optional	No	No	✓
Mazda Millenia	⊜	⊜	NA	NA	Standard	Standard	Optional	No	No	—
Mazda Protegé	○	◒	NA	NA	Standard	Standard	Standard	Varies	No	✓
Mazda RX-7	NA	NA	⊖	⊜	Standard	Standard	Varies	No	No	✓

Make and model	Crash protection		Injury claim rate		Safety equipment					Side-impact claim
	DRIVER	PASSENGER	OVERALL	FOR TYPE	DRIVER AIR BAG	PASSENGER AIR BAG	ANTILOCK BRAKES	TRACTION CONTROL	DAYTIME LIGHTS	
Mercedes-Benz C-Class	⊖	⊖	NA	NA	Standard	Standard	Standard	Varies	No	✓
Mercedes-Benz E-Class	NA	NA	⊖	○	Standard	Standard	Standard	Standard	No	✓
Mercury Cougar	⊜	⊜	○	⊖	Standard	Standard	Optional	Optional	No	✓
Mercury Grand Marquis	NA	NA	⊖	⊖	Standard	Standard	Optional	Optional	No	✓
Mercury Mystique	⊜	○	NA	NA	Standard	Standard	Optional	Varies	No	✓
Mercury Sable	⊖	⊖	NA	NA	Standard	Standard	Optional	No	Optional	✓
Mercury Tracer	⊖	○	◒	⊖	Standard	Standard	Varies	No	No	—
Mercury Villager	NA	NA	⊖	⊜	Standard	Standard	Standard	No	No	—
Mitsubishi 3000GT	NA	NA	○	⊖	Standard	Standard	Varies	No	No	—
Mitsubishi Diamante	NA	NA	⊖	⊖	Standard	Standard	Standard	Optional	No	—
Mitsubishi Eclipse	⊖	⊜	NA	NA	Standard	Standard	Optional	No	No	✓
Mitsubishi Galant	○	⊖	◒	◒	Standard	Standard	Optional	No	No	✓
Mitsubishi Mirage	NA	NA	NA	NA	Standard	Standard	No	No	No	—
Mitsubishi Montero	NA	NA	NA	NA	Standard	Standard	Varies	No	No	—
Nissan 200SX	NA	NA	NA	NA	Standard	Standard	Optional	No	No	✓
Nissan 240SX	○	⊖	NA	NA	Standard	Standard	Optional	No	No	✓
Nissan 300ZX	NA	NA	○	⊖	Standard	Standard	Standard	No	No	—
Nissan Altima	⊖	⊖	◒	◒	Standard	Standard	Optional	No	No	—
Nissan Maxima	⊖	○	◒	◒	Standard	Standard	Optional	No	No	✓
Nissan Pathfinder	NA	NA	NA	NA	Standard	Standard	Optional	No	No	—
Nissan Quest	NA	NA	⊖	⊜	Standard	Standard	Varies	No	No	—
Nissan Sentra	⊖	⊖	NA	NA	Standard	Standard	Optional	No	No	✓
Nissan Truck	NA	NA	○	◒	Standard	No	Varies	No	No	—
Oldsmobile 88	NA	NA	⊖	⊖	Standard	Standard	Standard	Varies	Standard	—
Oldsmobile 98	NA	NA	⊜	⊜	Standard	Standard	Standard	Optional	Standard	—
Oldsmobile Achieva	NA	NA	○	○	Standard	Standard	Standard	Varies	Standard	—
Oldsmobile Aurora	○	○	NA	NA	Standard	Standard	Standard	Standard	Standard	✓
Oldsmobile Bravada	○	●	NA	NA	Standard	No	Standard	No	Standard	—
Oldsmobile Ciera	⊜	○	⊖	⊜	Standard	No	Standard	No	No	—
Oldsmobile Cutlass Supreme	NA	NA	⊖	⊜	Standard	Standard	Standard	No	No	✓
Oldsmobile Silhouette	NA	NA	⊖	⊜	Standard	No	Standard	Optional	Standard	—
Plymouth Breeze	◒	NA	NA	NA	Standard	Standard	Optional	No	No	✓
Plymouth Grand Voyager	○	⊖	NA	NA	Standard	Standard	Optional	No	No	✓
Plymouth Neon	⊖	⊖	NA	NA	Standard	Standard	Optional	No	No	✓
Plymouth Voyager	NA	NA	NA	NA	Standard	Standard	Optional	No	No	✓
Pontiac Bonneville	⊜	○	⊖	⊖	Standard	Standard	Standard	Optional	Standard	—
Pontiac Firebird	⊜	⊜	○	⊖	Standard	Standard	Standard	Varies	No	✓
Pontiac Grand Am	NA	NA	○	○	Standard	Standard	Standard	Varies	Standard	—
Pontiac Grand Prix	⊖	○	⊖	⊜	Standard	Standard	Optional	No	Standard	✓
Pontiac Sunfire	○	○	NA	NA	Standard	Standard	Standard	Varies	Optional	✓
Pontiac Trans Sport	NA	NA	⊖	⊜	Standard	No	Standard	Optional	No	—
Range Rover	NA	NA	NA	NA	Standard	Standard	Standard	Standard	No	✓
Saab 900	⊖	⊖	⊖	⊖	Standard	Standard	Standard	Varies	Standard	✓
Saab 9000	NA	NA	⊜	⊜	Standard	Standard	Standard	Varies	Standard	—
Saturn	⊜	⊜	NA	NA	Standard	Standard	Optional	Varies	Standard	✓
Saturn SC	NA	NA	○	⊖	Standard	Standard	Optional	Varies	No	—
Subaru Impreza	NA	NA	◒	○	Standard	Standard	Optional	No	No	✓
Subaru Legacy	⊜	⊖	○	○	Standard	Standard	Varies	Varies	No	✓
Subaru SVX	NA	NA	⊖	⊜	Standard	Standard	Standard	No	No	✓
Suzuki Esteem	NA	NA	NA	NA	Standard	Standard	Optional	No	Standard	✓
Suzuki Sidekick	NA	NA	◒	●	Standard	Standard	Optional	No	Standard	✓
Suzuki Swift	⊖	⊖	NA	NA	Standard	Standard	Optional	No	Standard	✓
Suzuki X90	NA	NA	NA	NA	Standard	Standard	Standard	No	Standard	✓
Toyota 4Runner	NA	NA	NA	NA	Standard	Standard	Varies	No	No	—
Toyota Avalon	⊜	⊜	NA	NA	Standard	Standard	Optional	No	No	✓
Toyota Camry	⊜	⊜	○	○	Standard	Standard	Varies	No	No	✓
Toyota Celica	NA	NA	◒	○	Standard	Standard	Optional	No	No	—
Toyota Corolla	⊖	⊜	◒	○	Standard	Standard	Optional	No	No	—
Toyota Land Cruiser	NA	NA	⊜	⊜	Standard	Standard	Standard	No	No	—
Toyota Paseo	NA	NA	●	◒	Standard	Standard	Optional	No	No	✓
Toyota Previa	NA	NA	⊖	⊖	Standard	Standard	Optional	No	No	—
Toyota RAV 4	NA	NA	NA	NA	Standard	Standard	Optional	No	No	—
Toyota Supra	NA	NA	NA	NA	Standard	Standard	Standard	Varies	No	—
Toyota T100	⊖	⊜	NA	NA	Standard	No	Optional	No	No	—
Toyota Tacoma	NA	NA	NA	NA	Standard	No	Optional	No	No	—
Toyota Tercel	○	⊖	NA	NA	Standard	Standard	Optional	No	No	✓
Volkswagen Golf	○	○	NA	NA	Standard	Standard	Varies	Varies	Standard	✓
Volkswagen Jetta	○	○	◒	⊖	Standard	Standard	Varies	Varies	Standard	✓
Volkswagen Passat	⊖	⊖	NA	NA	Standard	Standard	Varies	Varies	Standard	✓
Volvo 850	⊜	○	⊖	⊜	Standard	Standard	Standard	Optional	Standard	✓
Volvo 960	NA	NA	⊖	⊜	Standard	Standard	Standard	No	Standard	✓

3

CHILD SAFETY SEATS

Jennifer L. Metcalf of Fort Dodge, Iowa, says she'll never underestimate the value of a properly installed child safety seat. It saved the life of her newborn son Evan.

On a rainy November morning, mother and son were traveling on a fast two-lane secondary road. The temperature was dropping and, when Jennifer pulled out to pass a car, her sedan hit a patch of ice. The car spun, hit a ditch, and rolled over. It landed upright, with both sides smashed, all the windows shattered, and the roof over the passenger seat crushed. Motorists who stopped to help seemed astonished to see Jennifer emerge from the car with Evan in her arms. He suffered only a cut nose. Without the safety seat, he would have been tossed around in the car—perhaps even thrown from it—and severely if not fatally injured.

Events like the one above have led all states to require all infants and small children to ride in a safety seat. Every manufacturer must certify that its seats meet government standards, which include protection in a head-on crash.

Yet despite the laws and standards, automobile accidents remain the leading cause of death for children under age five in the United States. The National Highway Traffic Safety Administration (NHTSA) estimates that some 700 children die in car crashes each year; another 60,000 to 70,000 are injured.

Parents who *don't* use a safety seat shoulder the blame for many of those deaths and injuries. According to NHTSA, about 80 percent of adults now buckle up. But the usage rate for child safety seats is only about 65 percent. Other parents unwittingly contribute to death and injury statistics by failing to install and use the safety seat properly.

Faulty safety seats may also contribute to the toll. Our crash tests of 25 safety seats turned up three unsafe models—the *Century 590* and *Evenflo On My Way 206*, for infants, and the *Kolcraft Traveler 700*, for infants and small children. Those three seats are more likely than others to fail when used in certain ways, even if properly installed. We have judged them Not Acceptable.

As we were preparing this report for publication, Evenflo independently issued a recall of the *On My Way 206* (see the box on page 14). We have asked Century and Kolcraft to recall their unsafe seats, too.

Reliable information on the brands and models of safety seats involved in accidents isn't readily available. So we don't know if injuries or deaths have been associated with the seats we judged Not Acceptable. Further, we don't know how many of those safety seats are currently in use. But, according to NHTSA, approximately 200,000 *On My Way 206* infant seats are affected by the Evenflo recall.

The other 22 safety seats we tested provided an adequate level of protection in our tests. Any of them would make a suitably safe choice.

Testing for safety

In our past reports on child safety seats, we took statements of compliance with the federal standard as assurance of their safety. This time, we crash-tested the seats ourselves to find out how well they perform in trials that were similar to, but in some cases slightly tougher than, the ones the government specifies.

We used "sled tests" that simulate a 30-mph head-on crash into a fixed barrier. The tests were done under our direction by a contract laboratory that also does safety testing for many manufacturers.

Following manufacturers' instruc-

LATEST FEDERAL STANDARDS

Last year, the National Highway Traffic Safety Administration announced tougher certification criteria for safety seats. The new tests are similar in many ways to the ones we used.

Key parts of the new NHTSA requirements include:

- The use of a 20-pound dummy, representing a typical nine-month-old, for infant seats and convertible seats in their rear-facing position. Seats that meet the new standard can be labeled for use by infants up to 22 pounds, the weight of a typical one-year-old. The standard was set to encourage the practice of having infants ride in the rear-facing position until they reach their first birthday.
- Certification tests for booster seats now parallel our tests—using a dummy representing a three-year-old and one representing a six-year-old.

The new criteria took effect in January 1996 for add-on safety seats, and will take effect in September 1996 for seats built into cars and minivans.

tions, we installed each safety seat securely on an automobile seat attached to a test sled, then harnessed a crash-test dummy snugly into the seat. High-speed cameras tracked the movement of the dummy and safety seat. After the crash, we examined the seat's structural integrity.

We tested the three types of seats available:

• Infant seats, typically labeled for babies up to 20 pounds—about the weight of a nine-month-old.

• Convertible seats, used facing rearward for babies until they're a year old and facing forward for children to age four or so. They are typically labeled for use with children up to about 40 pounds.

To test their safety for toddlers, we used the same dummy the manufacturers use to meet government standards—a 33-pound model, comparable with a three-year-old. To test safety for infants, we tested representative designs from each manufacturer using the "nine-month-old" dummy. Similarly designed models (see Ratings footnotes) should perform the same.

• Booster seats, designed for that in-between age when a child is too big for a convertible seat but too small to use safety belts. They're used either with an attached shield or harness to restrain a child or without the shield or harness to boost a child up so the vehicle's lap-and-shoulder belts fit properly.

We tested with both the "three-year-old" dummy and a 47-pound one representing a typical six-year-old.

The problems we found

Infant seats

The Not Acceptable *Century* and *Evenflo* consist of a detachable base and a carrier. According to the instructions, the base can remain installed in the vehicle and the carrier snapped into and out of it. Or, the carrier can be strapped in alone, using the vehicle's belts. We tested both ways.

In our sled tests, the *Century 590* performed well when used without its base. But when tested with the base and using the "nine-month-old" dummy, the force of the impact separated the carrier and dummy from the base. We repeated the test on three new samples. The same failure occurred with two; with the other, the carrier rotated backward enough to compromise an infant's safety. In a final test with a "six-month-old" dummy, the seat's performance was acceptable, but just marginally.

We had given the *Century 590* high marks in past reports, based solely on its convenience, assuming that the federal standard ensured its safety. We were disturbed by its unexpectedly poor crash-test performance.

In contrast to the *Century*, the *Evenflo On My Way 206* remained secure when used with its base in tests with the "nine-month-old" dummy. But when tested *without* its base, the carrier broke at one of the hook-ups for the vehicle belt. That left one side of the carrier—with the dummy strapped inside—unsecured from the bench seat. A second test yielded the same result. In one test with the "nine-month-old" dummy and another with the "six-month-old" dummy, the shell cracked but did not break in the belt hook-up area.

Convertible seat

When tested in the rear-facing position with the "nine-month-old" dummy, the *Kolcraft Traveler 700* performed safely. It failed our safety tests when we used the "three-year-old" dummy with the seat facing forward, as it would be for a small child. The seat's buckle failed, releasing both harness and dummy. As the dummy hit the shield, it broke away. In one test, the dummy was left hanging from the seat's harness straps. In another, it was ejected from the seat.

Booster seats

Century advises against using its booster seats with the shield or harness for children over 45 pounds, so we didn't test Century's seats that way. In contrast, Fisher-Price recommends using the shield on its booster with children over 40 pounds but not with smaller children, contrary to the advice of safety experts. We tested that model both ways with both the "three-year-old" and "six-year-old" dummies.

Overall, all four boosters provided very good protection when used without the shield and with the vehicle's safety belts.

But results differed when we tested with the shields. The *Gerry Double Guard* and *Fisher-Price* no-back models provided only fair to poor protection with the "six-year-old" dummy. The two *Century Breverra* high-back boosters provided better upper-body protection than the no-back booster seats.

Which harnesses are safest?

Our tests also allowed us to evaluate the effectiveness of the various harness systems used in convertible seats.

The five-point harness provided the

A MAJOR RECALL

Shortly before we went to press, Evenflo voluntarily recalled its *On My Way 206* infant seat. The company's tests show that, in a crash under certain conditions, the seat may crack when used without its base. Seats made between May 7, 1994, and May 31, 1995, are affected.

The company has set up a toll-free number—800-225-3056—for consumers who own the infant seat. Callers will hear a recording that says there have been no reports of cracks in actual usage and no injuries reported. The message states that the seat is safe to use with its base. Based on our tests, we concur. Callers can obtain a "no-tools-required retrofit kit" at no charge. We have ordered a kit and will report on its effectiveness later this year.

We're glad that Evenflo has recalled this seat. Historically, however, such recalls are seldom completely effective. The company can readily notify only those owners who filled out and mailed in registration cards. If you know anyone who owns an *On My Way 206*, tell them about the recall.

best protection against head injury. The overhead-shield design provided less protection than either the five-point harness or the T-shield models.

Selecting a seat

Choosing the right safety seat goes a long way toward making your child safer and more comfortable. And the more convenient the seat is to use, the more likely it is to be used every time your child is in the car. Here we list the types of seats, variations in harness designs, and good points and drawbacks of each.

Convertible seats

Which children? For babies up to one year old, a convertible seat can be mounted in a rear-facing position. For children up to about 40 pounds, the seat can be installed in a forward-facing position. You can choose among three types of restraint:

5-point harness. This type of restraint uses five straps—two at the shoulders, two at the legs, one at the crotch. It provides the best protection against head injury for all children, and the best fit for small infants.

Good point: Easy to buckle and unbuckle.

Drawbacks: Straps can get in the way when you put the child in the seat.

T-shield: This type uses a plastic, T-shaped yoke that buckles into the seat at the crotch, connected to a pair of harness straps. It provides good protection.

Good points: Easy to move out of the way when seating the child. Usually easy to buckle and unbuckle.

Drawbacks: A small infant's head may not clear the shield.

Overhead shield: This type has a padded, tray-like shield that swings down over the child's head.

Good points: Generally easy to use. Some shields are adjustable to fit a smaller child or to accommodate bulky winter clothing.

Drawbacks: Doesn't protect against head injury as well as other designs. A small infant's head may not clear the shield. Shield may block your view of the buckle.

Infant seats

Which children? Best choice for newborns and small infants. Seats for infants face rearward in a semireclined position to help support baby's head, neck, and back.

Good points: All of these double as a baby carrier. Some come with a detachable base that remains installed in the vehicle.

Drawbacks: None.

Booster seats

Which children? Those too big for a convertible seat, too small for the vehicle's belts.

Good points: High-back boosters used with their harness and shield are effective for smaller kids who may not remain seated unless confined. High-back boosters and no-back models can be used without the shield to make the child sit high enough to use the vehicle's safety belts; that's best with children old enough to understand the importance of staying seated and buckled up.

Drawbacks: In our tests, no-back, shielded boosters did not protect well, especially with a larger dummy.

Built-in seats

Which children? Those over one year and 20 pounds. Some GM, Ford, Chrysler, and Volvo models offer an optional safety seat that is integrated into the rear seat. Typically uses a five-point harness, and converts to a booster.

Good points: No installation. Can't dislodge in a crash. Places a child farther away from the front seats, reducing the risk of head injury.

Drawbacks: Lacks head support for sleeping child. (But designs for some new cars will recline.)

Safety-seat alternatives?

Safety vest

The *All Our Kids Travel Vest 602* ($43) proved difficult to fit to a child

---

BUCKLING DOWN THE INSTALLATION

Installing a safety seat can't be left to instinct or logic. It's important to refer to the section on safety-seat installation in your vehicle owner's manual and heed all the instructions that come with the safety seat you buy. If the information in either manual isn't clear, call the automaker, the safety-seat manufacturer, or both.

Safety-belt snafus The center rear seat is the safest place to install a child safety seat. In most vehicles, the center lap belt will hold a safety seat securely. But some lap belts are too short to cover a sizable safety seat, especially if it has to be rear-facing. In some cars, the distance between belt anchors may be insufficient to fit a safety seat.

Along with those problems, we had difficulty threading safety belts through some seats. Lap-and-shoulder belts pose an assortment of problems. You may need a locking clip, a supplemental buckle, or a replacement belt.

Fit, form, and frustration Deeply contoured seats and some bucket seats make secure installation of a safety seat difficult or even impossible. Some cars have a raised center rear seat; a safety seat installed there is likely to slide around and wobble. We found that the safety seats' instructions were usually reasonably helpful in explaining how to cope with oddities of car-seat design.

About air bags If you and the child are usually the car's only occupants, you may prefer to install an infant seat in the front. Generally, that's fine—but not if the car has a passenger-side air bag. (Only a few vehicles have an air bag that can be disabled.) When triggered, an air bag will strike the back of the infant seat, dealing a violent blow to the baby's head. Experts recommend moving the passenger seat as far back as possible to minimize the risk of injury when a child in a forward-facing convertible seat or booster rides in front.

HOW TO LOCK THE WEBBING OF AN ELR LAP BELT WITH A HEAVY-DUTY LOCKING CLIP

The object is to achieve a snug belt fit so the child restraint can be firmly anchored. First, place the child restraint on the seat of the vehicle and secure it with the belt as you normally would. Then pull all the webbing from the retractor, using chalk to mark the surplus. Do this close to the retractor so the clip won't interfere with routing the belt. Finally, release the buckle and tie off the webbing as shown in Steps 1 to 4, following the arrows. The size of the loop will, of course, vary. Chalk marks notwithstanding, this will have to be done by trial and error until you get the belt to fit tightly around the restraint.

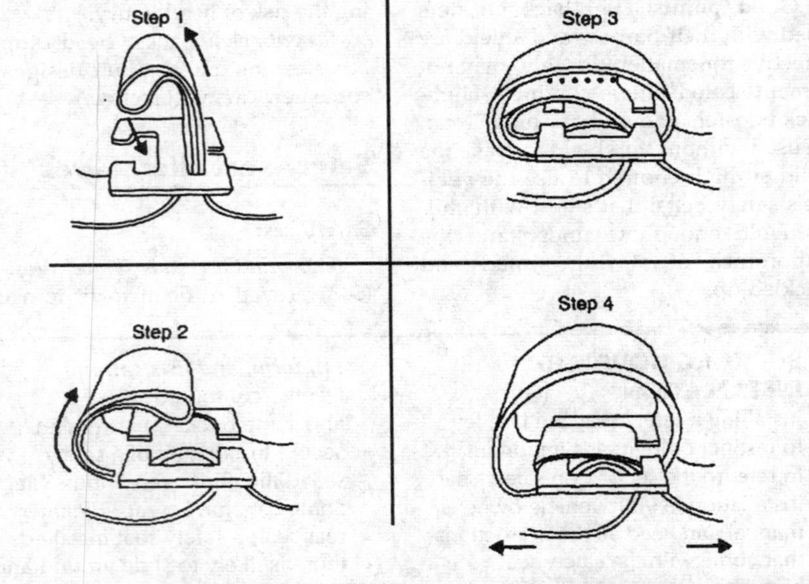

and to our test vehicles. Worse, half the samples we bought came with an incorrectly threaded harness, a problem that wasn't obvious and not clarified by the instructions. Even after we threaded the straps according to the photo on the box, the vest was just fair in our crash tests.

In March 1995, the *All Our Kids Travel Vest* models 600 and 602 were recalled due to a flammability problem. If you own one of those vests, return it to the company: 1540 Beach St., Montabello, Calif. 90640, for fire-retardant treatment.

Traveling infant bed

The *Cosco Dream Ride Ultra* 02-719, $63, can be used as a conventional infant seat or as a traveling bed for premature infants and others who must lie flat. As a bed, the *Dream Ride* performed well in three of four crash tests. In one test, however, it partially released from the safety-belt hook-up. It performed poorly as an infant seat. It tipped too far backward and increased the risk of injury.

Safety seats plus

The *Safeline Sit 'n' Stroll* and the *Century 4-in-1 System* convert from safety seat to stroller. When we covered their prowess as strollers in a July 1994 report, we favored the *Century*—but it incorporates the Not Acceptable *Century 590* safety seat. The *Safeline* proved to be a safe child seat, but not a particularly convenient one. As a stroller, it didn't negotiate curbs very well, its brakes were hard to use, and its handle was too low for tall adults. Converting it from safety seat to stroller, with a child weighing 20 pounds or more, would require considerable strength.

Different cars, different belts

The installation of a child safety seat will vary depending on the vehicle's belt system, and may even require special adapters. The information that follows will be helpful in dealing with different installations.

Lap-only belts

Lap belts in center rear seats are the most likely to allow you to anchor a child restraint tightly. (The center rear is also regarded as the safest spot in a vehicle.) Most can be easily tightened by pulling on the free end of the belt webbing. Even so, the belt may loosen if the buckle rests at an angle on the child-restraint frame or belt slot. Check by pulling forward on the child restraint after the belt is tightened. If the belt loosens, check the child-restraint instructions, as well as the vehicle owner's manual, for possible solutions, or move the restraint to another seat.

Lap belts in outboard seats of pre-1989 model cars probably have retractors that lock the webbing every inch or so. These belts are tightened by feeding the webbing into the retractor. But lap belts in some vehicles do not lock except when a crash occurs. This will be discussed later.

Combination lap-and-shoulder belts

Shoulder belts are now required in back as well as front outboard seats. There are two basic kinds of combination lap/shoulder belts. One allows the lap belt to be locked; the other may not, at least for now.

Government safety rule. Under a federal regulation that went into effect September 1995, lap belts in passenger cars must be capable of tightly securing child restraints, without the need of ". . . attaching any device to the seat belt webbing." This requirement will ultimately make locking clips (see Figure 3.4), now needed in many vehicles to secure a child restraint tightly, a thing of the past. It isn't always obvious that belts can be made to lock, so you should know what to look for and how to adapt the belt system you have.

Belts that lock. Some combination lap-and-shoulder belts have latch plates that allow the webbing to move

ADD-ONS MAKE SAFETY BELTS MORE COMFORTABLE

When it comes to safety belts, one size does not fit all. Children and short adults often find the shoulder belt uncomfortable—it's mounted too high or too far back in many cars and so cuts annoyingly across the neck. As a result, some people wear the belts incorrectly—or they don't wear the belt at all.

We recently tested two add-on devices designed to make a shoulder belt accommodate people of below-average height. Not only did we ask staffers with children to assess the comfort and convenience of these shoulder-belt adjusters, we also did our own version of a 30-mph crash test to find out if the product affected safety.

The *Child-Safer* ($25, from Westech U.S.A., Inc., 800-934-4646) is a two-foot-long piece of hard plastic with slots for both the lap and shoulder belts. The *SafeFit* (sold at Toys 'R' Us, Wal-Mart, and other retailers for about $13) is a padded nylon sleeve through which you pass the lap-and-shoulder belt.

Neither device works with separate lap-and-shoulder belts or with motorized automatic belts; they're designed only for the "three-point" belts found on many cars. The *Child-Safer* claims to fit people between 38 and 60 inches in height; the *SafeFit* claims to fit small adults and children who have outgrown a child restraint but aren't big enough for a safety belt.

Neither product takes the place of a conventional child-safety seat. The *Child-Safer* claims to work in conjunction with a booster seat, however.

With either product, it's important to be sure the safety belt still fits occupants properly: The lap portion should go across the lap and the shoulder belt diagonally across the middle of the chest. If the add-ons don't allow the belt to fit that way, they shouldn't be used.

Federal safety standards don't cover these shoulder-belt adjusters, but the manufacturers say the products have been tested for safety. Both the *Child-Safer* and *SafeFit* worked as they should in our crash tests.

We adapted the federal safety test for child restraints, belting a dummy the size of a six-year-old into a rear seat mounted on an air-powered sled. Instruments on the dummy and high-speed cameras recorded the peak crash forces and the dummy's forward movement in each crash.

The *Child-Safer* requires a few inches of slack in the shoulder belt, so it allowed the dummy to move farther forward than did the *SafeFit*. But in all the tests, the dummy's movement and the forces it sustained were within acceptable criteria.

The *SafeFit* was easier to use than the *Child-Safer*. Staffers who used them judged the *SafeFit* sleeve easier to install, more comfortable, and better fitting. Most panelists needed about 20 minutes to figure out how to route the belts through the proper slots in the *Child-Safer*. The *SafeFit* could be put in place much more quickly; and because it slides along the belt, it allows a range of adjustments. The *Child-Safer* allows only three slots for the shoulder belt.

The best protection remains the standard safety belt alone. The *Child-Safer* and the *SafeFit* aren't ideal, though they can help make an otherwise ill-fitting belt comfortable. We favor the *SafeFit*, for its convenience and price.

in one direction (to tighten the lap belt), but not the other. Once buckled, the lap portion stays tight. To release the webbing, the latch plate must be tilted (Figures 3.1 and 3.2).

Belts that don't lock. Many vehicles have belts with free-sliding latch plates that do not incorporate a locking mechanism in the latch (Figure 3.3). The belt stays loose during normal driving but would lock in a sudden stop.

The mechanism that locks the belt is called an emergency locking retractor, or ELR. This type of belt may not hold a child restraint tightly, unless you know what to do.

Locking clips. The lap portion of an ELR belt can be locked with a special metal locking clip (Figure 3.4). Install the child restraint as instructed by the manufacturer, and tighten the lap portion. Next, clamp the lap and shoulder portions together at the latch plate. The lap belt will now stay tightly secured (Figure 3.5). All child restraints are sold with these locking clips along with instructions on how to install them.

Switchable retractors. Late-model vehicles may have "switchable" retractors, converting a nonlocking ELR into an automatic locking retractor, or ALR. An ALR locks every inch or so and will

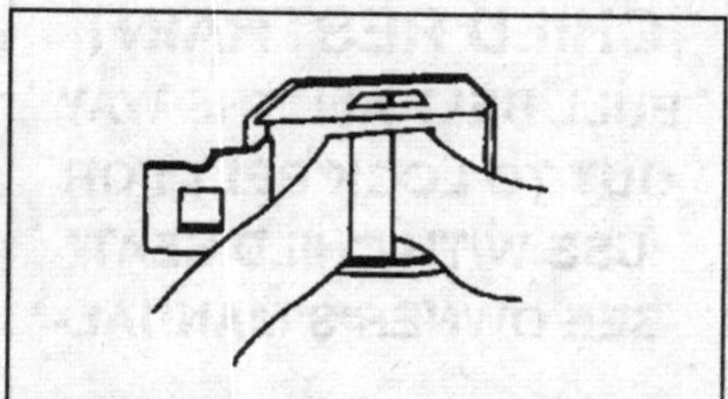

Figure 3.1 Locking bar

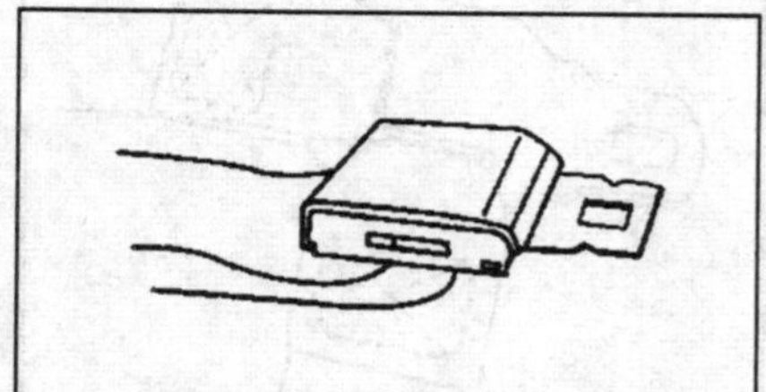

Figure 3.2 Belt locked (webbing parallel)

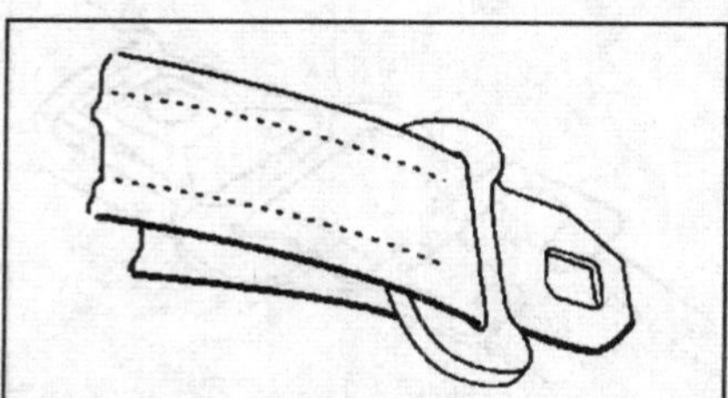

Figure 3.3 Free-sliding latch plate

keep a child restraint firmly anchored.

Continuous loop belts with a free-sliding latch plate incorporate the switching mechanism at the shoulder end. Where the lap and shoulder belt are individually sewn to the latch plate (Figure 3.6), each belt has its own retractor and the switching mechanism is built into the lap belt.

If the retractors in your vehicle are switchable, a label on the belt will usually tell you about it (details can be found in the vehicle owner's manual). To switch, all you do is pull the belt all the way out and then let it rewind. Listen for a click signaling that the webbing is rewinding from an ELR to an ALR. It takes only a second or two to switch back and forth. When not used for a child restraint, the ELR mode is recommended.

It's worth pulling on the belt to see if it has a switchable retractor even if there is no label telling you about it. And always look for information in the vehicle owner's manual. Some manufacturers give instructions on the belts themselves (see Figure 3.7).

Lap belts that do not lock. If you find that lap-only belts or combination lap-and-shoulder belts that have each belt portion separately sewn to the latch plate cannot be switched, all is not lost. You can tie off the surplus belt webbing so you are left with a shorter lap belt of the exact length needed to secure the child restraint tightly.

This has to be done correctly, so follow the instructions in your vehicle owner's manual very carefully.

Special heavy-duty locking clips. In order to shorten a lap belt, you will need a special heavy-duty locking clip. Do not confuse a regular locking clip that comes with a child restraint with the extra-strong locking clips that are obtainable only from auto dealerships. The two can look virtually identical, so don't try telling them apart by appearance. The wrong clip could bend in a crash and release the tied-off webbing.

If you are not sure, it's best to get another one from your auto dealership. Put a small dab of colored paint on your heavy-duty clip, so you'll always be able to identify it and prevent possible mix-ups.

Automatic belts

Front seats may have "automatic" belts, designed to wrap around the occupant without any action on his or her part. There are several types, but none is suitable for securing a child restraint.

When combination lap-and-shoulder belts are attached to the door, you must have a special lap belt installed for securing a child restraint. The belt is obtainable from your dealership. For more information, consult your vehicle owner's manual. (General Motors provides the belt free of charge and also compensates dealers for the cost of installation.)

Another type of "automatic" belt consists of a shoulder belt and a separate "manual" lap belt. The shoulder belt wraps around you as you close the door, or it moves into position on a motorized track. Some of the lap belts lock, others are switchable (see the section "Switchable Retractors"), so you may not encounter this problem.

In some cars a nonlocking lap belt can be replaced by one that locks. Look for information in the vehicle owner's manual. There may be a label on the belt itself that explains what must be done. If you are stuck with a nonlocking lap belt, there is a way of shortening it so it will secure a child restraint tightly. Use a "heavy duty" locking clip as explained earlier (see the section "Special Heavy-Duty Locking Clips") and follow the steps illustrated.

Front seats could pose an additional hazard: The belt buckle can be too far forward to secure a child restraint safely. A "supplemental child buckle" may be needed that will clip into an eye bolt farther back, in line with the seat cracks. Again, read the labels on vehicle belts. They carry lifesaving information.

Incompatibility: Other problems with vehicle belts and seats

In many newer cars, belts come out of the seat cushion from one to several inches in front of the base of the seatback. This configuration improves lap-belt fit for adults and also for children who are tall enough to use the vehicle belt system by keeping the belt flat on the lap.

Installing child restraints in such seats, however, poses difficult and in some cases insurmountable problems. Whether or not you can tightly secure a restraint with such belts depends somewhat on the child-restraint belt-path geometry and the shape of the seat cushion. Each combination is different.

In extreme cases, usually in smaller sports cars, seat cushions may be

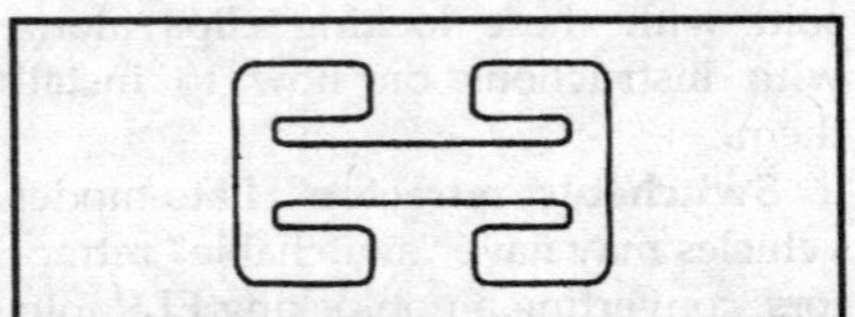

Figure 3.4 Locking clip

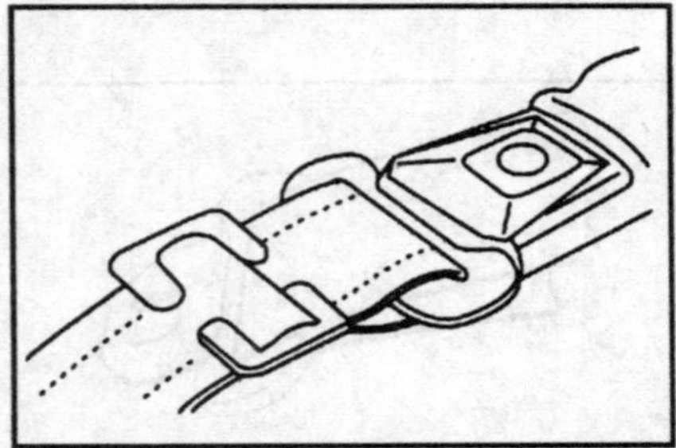

Figure 3.5 Lap and shoulder belts locked together

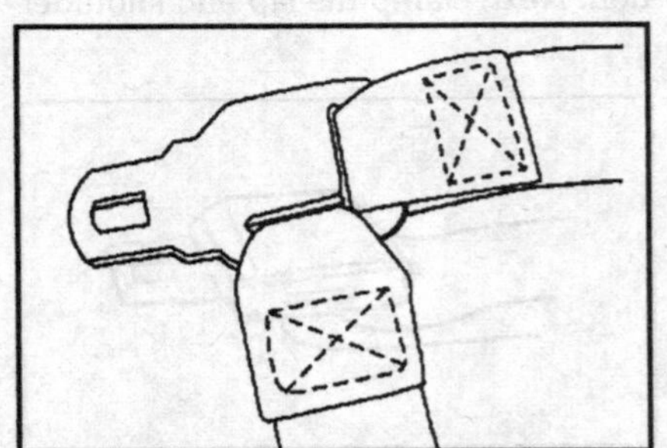

Figure 3.6 Shoulder and lap portions sewn to latch plate

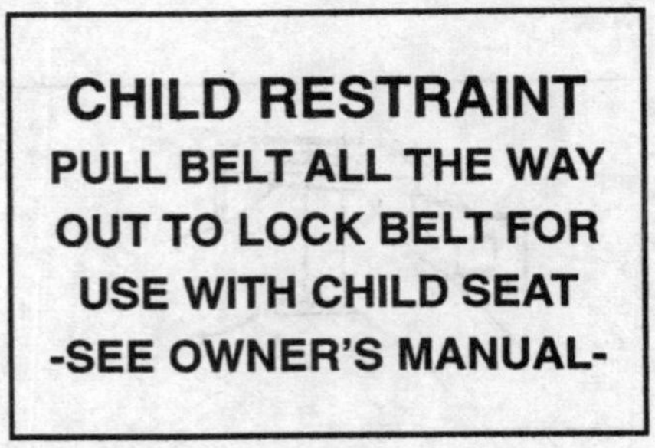

CHILD RESTRAINT
PULL BELT ALL THE WAY OUT TO LOCK BELT FOR USE WITH CHILD SEAT
-SEE OWNER'S MANUAL-

Figure 3.7

deeply dished out but narrower than your child restraint, belts may be as much as 10 inches forward of the seatback, and buckles may be on a long, stiff stalk. All of these features make child-restraint installation difficult, if not impossible.

What can be done? When you are in the market for a new or used car, check the rear seats. Try installing your child restraint(s) before making a decision. Some restraints may fit better than others, and some rear seats may not accommodate child restraints at all.

Use of a top tether strap will improve stability and is now recommended by some automakers.

Another problem you may encounter in front seats as well as in rear seats of smaller cars is that the child restraint simply does not fit into the available space. Try installing the restraint forward and facing rear.

Until the infant weighs at least 20 pounds and is one year old, the rear-facing orientation is a must. The only solution to this dilemma is to place the infant *facing rear* in the backseat. When you are driving with a newborn, or an infant who has medical problems, another adult should ride with the infant in the back seat.

For children who are old and large enough to use a forward-facing restraint, the air bag is not expected to pose a hazard, but the National Highway Traffic Safety Administration recommends that the vehicle seat be moved as far away from the instrument panel as is possible.

Built-in child restraints

For children over one year old, installation problems can be avoided with built-in or "integrated" child restraints. These restraints are only forward-facing and fold out of the vehicle seatback when needed. When folded back up, the seat can be used by an adult.

FIXES FOR UNSAFE SAFETY SEATS?

In late 1995 we judged three child safety seats Not Acceptable because they failed our crash tests. We have since tested retrofits offered for two seats, which owners can install to make those seats safer. The third manufacturer continues to maintain that its seat is safe, despite mounting evidence to the contrary. Here's the latest:

Kolcraft: Now safer

The *Kolcraft Traveler 700* can be used facing rearward for infants, facing forward for toddlers. In our crash tests, the buckle assembly and overhead shield broke when the seat was forward-facing. Such a failure could eject a child from the seat. Kolcraft will provide a replacement buckle to owners of some 100,000 *Traveler 700* seats made between November 1994 and August 1995; call 800-453-7673.

The replacement buckle assembly held tight in our follow-up crash test. But the harness straps slipped on impact, so the test dummy's upper body wasn't restrained quite as well as we'd like. Nonetheless, parents who have installed the replacement buckle can feel confident that the buckle and shield will stay intact.

Evenflo: Ineffective fix

The *Evenflo On My Way 206* consists of an infant carrier and base. You can keep the base strapped in the car and pop the carrier in and out to transport the baby, or use the carrier alone as a safety seat. The *206* failed our tests when used without its base. The carrier broke where the safety belt hooks into it, so it was no longer secured to the car. Evenflo voluntarily devised a retrofit kit to solve the problem, offering the kit to owners of some 200,000 *On My Way 206* seats; call 800-225-3056.

The retrofit is supposed to reinforce the area where the safety belt threads through the carrier. But in our follow-up crash test, although the safety belt continued to hold the carrier, the reinforcements dislodged and the carrier cracked in the same general area as in our first test. Therefore, we still recommend using the *Evenflo On My Way 206* only *with* its base, and securing the base with the car's safety belt.

Evenflo has supposedly discontinued the *On My Way 206*. Its replacement, the *On My Way 207*, performed well in our safety tests.

People who already own a *206* can get reinforcements to improve its safety. Those reinforcements were also on seats packaged as *207s* that we found at several retailers.

But reinforcements are not part of the *On My Way 207*. On the ones we found, the box said *207* and a sticker on the seat said *207*. But each was, in fact, a relabeled *On My Way 206* with the reinforcements.

If you buy a *207*, be sure it's the real thing. If it has the reinforcements, take it back and exchange it.

Century: Still a problem

Century continues to deny that its *Century 590* infant seat has a safety problem. In our tests, the *590* performed well *without* its base. When tested with the base, the carrier and dummy were ejected, and the base broke in three out of four runs. In the fourth run, the carrier rotated backward enough to compromise an infant's safety.

The manufacturer has launched a publicity campaign to discredit our findings. But other tests also point to a safety problem. At our urging, the National Highway Traffic Safety Administration began its own technical evaluation and crash-tested the *590*; the base cracked much the way it did in our tests. In a different test, run by the Canadian government, the carrier was ejected from the base.

Following publication of our original report, several class-action lawsuits were filed against Century. And we have also learned of an accident in which a nine-week-old infant was ejected from the vehicle while still strapped to the *590* carrier, which broke away from its base. The infant was unharmed.

Our advice remains: Don't use the *590* with its base. We still believe Century should voluntarily recall the *590*. Failing that, the NHTSA should order a recall.

When children have outgrown child restraints

Vehicle lap-and-shoulder belts rarely fit a child who has outgrown a child restraint. Ideally, the lap belt should go over the upper thighs, and the shoulder portion should cross the collarbone and follow a straight line to the buckle. Until the child is tall enough, the shoulder belt might go across the face or throat, and the lap belt might ride up around the waist. Such poor fit increases the risk of injury. A booster seat can bridge the gap. There are two kinds.

Shield boosters

Use a shield booster if only lap belts are available in the rear seat of your vehicle. Many different models are on the market. Some require the lap belt to go over the shield, whereas on others the lap belt threads through the base. Do not use a shoulder belt with a shield booster unless the manufacturer *specifically* recommends it.

Belt-positioning boosters

If your vehicle has lap-and-shoulder belts in the rear seat, raising the child up on a "belt-positioning" booster can help keep the belts in the right position. Worn correctly, with the lap belt low and snug and the shoulder belt close to the chest, this system is believed to provide more effective crash protection than a shield booster.

Some shield boosters convert to belt-positioning boosters with the removal of the shield. This conversion should only be done if specifically allowed by the manufacturer.

Seatbacks

To reduce the chance of whiplash injury, make sure your child's ears are below the top of the vehicle seatback or head restraint. This will ensure that the head is supported during a crash. Some boosters are available with backrests. In addition to increasing comfort, letting the child rest his or her head against the sides of the booster seat would protect the child's neck in vehicles with low seatbacks.

Vehicle safety belts alone

You can stop using a booster when the lap belt stays down below the hips and does not ride up around the waist, and the shoulder belt comes down without crossing the child's face or throat. If the shoulder belt rubs against the neck, a soft cloth or collar between the belt and the neck will make it more comfortable. Devices to deflect the shoulder belt away from the neck are on the market, for use by both older children and small adults. General Motors has introduced a "comfort guide" in some of its models (recommended for ages six to ten), which allows a child to use the shoulder belt by keeping it away from the face and neck. It's available in rear seats only.

Front seats in a number of automobiles have adjustable shoulder-strap attachment points, which can be lowered and raised for correct belt fit. These may also be in rear seats of present production vehicles. Look for this feature when shopping for a new car.

Never tuck the shoulder belt under the arm. In a crash the belt may crush the child's ribs and increase the chance of "submarining" (sliding under the belt), which could cause severe abdominal and spinal injuries.

Placing the shoulder belt behind the child's back, a practice recommended in the past, should be done only in an emergency, when the child too small for a lap-and-shoulder belt must ride in such a position and no booster seat is available. Although a lap belt alone does not provide optimal protection at any age, it is still believed to be better than no restraint at all. Encourage your child to sit fully upright against the seatback. Slouching prevents good belt fit.

A final admonition: Your own good judgment isn't enough, and you could make a bad mistake. It's far more complex than it seems. Pay careful attention to information on belt labels, con-

---

MORE ON UNSAFE SAFETY SEATS

The government and the manufacturers of the child safety seats that did poorly in our recent tests have been active since we released our findings. Here's the latest:

Companies' actions

• **Kolcraft.** The National Highway Traffic Safety Administration announced a recall of *Kolcraft Traveler 700* child safety seats, citing "recent media reports" that raised questions about the seat's effectiveness. About 100,000 seats are affected by the recall.

In tests performed by Kolcraft after the company learned of our findings, the manufacturer claimed that failures did occur "on occasion" when the *Traveler 700* was crash-tested at speeds above those specified by the government. The failures occurred in models made after November 1, 1994, when the company redesigned the seat.

People who bought a *Traveler 700* made after November 1, 1994, and mailed in the registration card will automatically receive a replacement buckle assembly. Owners who did not register their safety seats can call 800-453-7673 to request the new buckle. It will also fit seats made before November 1, 1994.

Kolcraft announced its replacement-buckle program about a month after we released our crash-test findings. We applaud the company for acting in a timely and responsible manner.

• **Century.** The *Century 590* infant seat failed our crash tests; as a result, the NHTSA is conducting its own defect investigation. The manufacturer, however, continues to deny that there are safety problems with the *Century 590*. In our tests, the seat failed to provide protection when used with its base. It works fine when installed directly onto the vehicle seat without its base.

• **All Our Kids.** This company made the *All Our Kids Travel Vest*, recalled due to a flammability problem. The company recently went out of business and is no longer responding to phone calls.

What's ahead?

We petitioned the NHTSA to upgrade its test standards and procedures for safety seats. The agency is considering whether to make the changes we asked for.

sult the vehicle owner's guide, and follow the instructions that come with your child restraint.

For more information

On recalls

Call NHTSA's Auto Safety Hot Line (800-424-9393). Be ready to provide the brand name, model number, and manufacturing date, all found on the seat itself.

On other baby products

Our *Guide to Baby Products* offers buying advice and testing information on cribs, high chairs, strollers, and more. Call 515-237-4903.

WHERE TO CALL

Child safety seats

Century	800-837-4044
Cosco	800-544-1108
Evenflo	800-233-5921
Fisher Price	800-432-5437
Gerry	800-626-2996
Kolcraft	800-453-7673
Safeline	800-829-1625

Recommendations

Nearly all the seats we tested kept their test dummies safe even in slightly stricter tests than those currently mandated by the government. Except for the three Not Acceptable seats, any model we tested would be a good choice, provided it fits your vehicle. The clear choices are:

- **Infant seat:** the top-rated *Century 565*, A Best Buy at $35.
- **Convertible seat:** the *Century 1000 STE Classic*, A Best Buy at $53. (If you can't find that *Century*, look first at the higher-rated models that use a five-point harness. That design offers somewhat better protection than a T-shield or an overhead shield.)
- **Booster seat:** Any tested model can safely be used without its shield or harness to position a child to wear vehicle safety belts. For younger children who may not stay put: the *Century Breverra Premiere 4885* or *4880* (used with the harness or shield), each about $60.

If you own the Not Acceptable *Century 590*, throw away the base. If you own the Not Acceptable *Evenflo On My Way 206*, use it only with its base and call the manufacturer for information about the recall. Owners of the Not Acceptable *Kolcraft Traveler 700* can use the seat safely in the rear-facing position. When it's time to switch it to the forward-facing position, scrap the *Kolcraft* and replace it with a different model.

All safety seats come with a registration card. Fill it out and mail it in, so you can be contacted if the seat is the subject of a recall.

For the typical SAFETY seat, expect . . .

- Adequate protection in a 30-mph head-on crash
- Fully assembled product, with adequate instructions
- Locking clip for use with vehicle safety belts, if needed
- Removable, machine-washable pads
- Mail-in registration card, so you can be notified of a manufacturer's recall
- 1-year warranty

Notes on the table

Price is the estimated average, based on a national survey, for the seat in the fabric tested. (In the Features column, the tested fabric is listed first.) An * indicates the price we paid.

Harness. Infant seats have a V-shaped harness (**V**). Convertible seats use either a 5-point harness (**5PT**), a T- shield (**TS**), or an overhead shield (**OH**). One booster seat has a swing-out shield (**SS**) that allows access to the seat.

Safety scores are based on the seats' performance in our tests simulating a 30-mph head-on crash. Column headings list the "age" of the dummies we used, the seats' orientation (front- or rear-facing), and (for boosters) whether we used the seats' harness or shield or lap-and-shoulder belts like those found in real vehicles.

Convenience. Ease of use includes the effort involved in getting a child in and out of the seat, buckling up and unbuckling, and ease of adjusting the harnesses and straps. With infant seats, portability was also a factor. To judge ease of installation, we placed the safety seats in three cars of differing sizes, seat types, and belt configurations, using a side and center rear seat (the smallest car didn't have a center seating position). We also assessed the instructions and the ease of removing the pad covers for washing.

Weight is rounded to the nearest pound. For infant seats that are installed in a base, we give the weight for the carrier alone and (in parentheses) for the carrier and base.

Space is the minimum width required to fit the seat within a set of vehicle safety belts. For infant seats, figures in parentheses are for the seat alone, without the base; for convertible seats, figures in parentheses are for rear-facing installation.

Comments cover good and bad points of installation and convenience, notable findings from our crash-tests.

Features. Accessories and available fabrics, plus numbers for similar models. They may have different fabrics and features, but they have the same harness system and shell and should perform the same as the ones we tested.

RATINGS Safety Seats

As published in the September 1995 issue of *Consumer Report*

Brand and model	Price	Harness	Safety			
INFANT SEATS			9-mo.			
Century 565, **A BEST BUY**	$*35	V	⊖			
Kolcraft Rock'n Ride 13100	30	V	⊖			
Gerry Guard With Glide 627	56	V	⊖			
■ **NOT ACCEPTABLE** *When used* ***with*** *the base, the following seat may not provide*						
Century 590 (4595)	62	V	— [1]			
■ **NOT ACCEPTABLE** *When used* ***without*** *the base, the following seat may not*						
Evenflo On My Way 206 [2]	65	V	— [3]			
CONVERTIBLE SEATS			3-yr. front facing	9-mo. rear facing		
■ *The following models are judged suitable for small infants as well as larger infants*						
Century 1000 STE Classic, **A BEST BUY**	53	5PT	⊖	[4]		
Century SmartMove 4710	128	5PT	⊖	⊖		
Evenflo Trooper 229	77	5PT	⊖	[5]		
Cosco Touriva 02514	68	5PT	⊖	[6]		
Kolcraft Auto-Mate 13225	58	5PT	○	⊖		
Safeline Sit'n'Stroll 3240X	140	5PT	○	⊖		
■ *The following models are judged less suitable for small infants, but suitable for*						
Century 2000 STE	65	TS	⊖	[4]		
Evenflo Scout 225	63	TS	⊖	[5]		
Evenflo Champion 224	64	OH	⊖	⊖		
Century 5500 STE Prestige	90	OH	○	⊖		
Gerry Guard SecureLock 691	*97	OH	○	⊖		
Century 3000 STE	77	OH	○	⊖		
Cosco Touriva 02045	*90	OH	○	[6]		
Cosco Touriva 02014	*60	OH	○	○		
Evenflo Ultara I 235	90	OH	○	⊖		
■ **NOT ACCEPTABLE** *In the* ***forward-facing position****, the following seat may*						
Kolcraft Traveler 700 13405	60	OH	—	— [7]		
BOOSTER SEATS			3-yr. +shield	3-yr. +belts	6-yr. +shield	6-yr. +belts
Century Breverra Premiere 4885	58	5PT	⊖	⊖	— [8]	⊖
Century Breverra 4880	60	TS	⊖	⊖	— [8]	⊖
Fisher-Price T-Shield A09196	42	TS	○ [9]	⊖	◒	⊖
Gerry Double Guard 675	60	SS	○	⊖	●	⊖

[1] *Without base, score is* ⊖.
[2] *Mfr. has initiated a voluntary recall of this model. Call 800 225-3056.*
[3] *With base, score is* ○.

Convenience				Weight	Space	Comments	Features
EASE OF USE	INSTALLATION	INSTRUCTIONS	CLEANING				
⊖	○	⊖	⊜	6 lb.	4 in.	Requires installation with each use. Indicator helps you position seat properly.	Converts to rocker or glider. Poly/cotton (or terry cloth).
⊖	⊖	⊜	◒	6	14	Requires installation with each use. Nonremovable vinyl pad covers must be spot-cleaned. When exposed to hot sun, vinyl could get very hot.	Vinyl. **Similar:** 13102,13802.
⊖	○	⊖	⊜	8	14	Requires installation with each use. May not fit vehicle with short safety belts. Vehicle belts can be difficult to weave through the safety seat. Hard-to-adjust harness straps. Slightly uncomfortable handle.	Converts to rocker or glider. Comes with harness pads. Velour (or poly/cotton). 90-day warranty. **Similar:** 628.
sufficient protection in a crash.							
⊖	○	⊖	⊜	6 (10)	15 (14)	Carrier released from base in our safety tests. Without base, requires installation with each use. Indicator helps you position seat properly.	Canopy. Poly/cotton (or velour). **Similar:** 590 (4593, 4597).
provide sufficient protection in a crash.							
⊖	○	⊖	⊜	8 (11)	15 (14)	Carrier released from sled in our safety tests, when tested without its base.	Canopy. Poly/cotton. Has unique carrier handles.
and small children.							
⊖	○	⊖	⊜	9	10 (up to 16)	Rear-facing, requires installation with each use and may not fit vehicle with short safety belts. Two-position latch opening allows better fit.	Velour (or terry cloth). **Similar:** 1500 STE Prestige
○	○	⊖	⊜	17	16 (16)	More reclined rear-facing position than most convertibles. Seat moves to upright position on impact, to protect infant. May not fit in small cars or other vehicle seats because of wide base. Hard-to-operate reclining mechanism.	Comes with infant head-support cushion. Velour.
⊖	○	⊖	⊖	9	11 (up to 14)	Vehicle safety belt may interfere with buckle on safety seat in rear-facing position.	Top-tether kit free from mfr. Has support cushion for infants. Velour.
⊖	⊖	⊜	○	8	10 (15)	Pad covers not machine-washable.	Velour (or poly/cotton). **Similar:** 02545, 02564, 02584.
⊖	○	○	○	9	up to 11 (16)	Harness-adjustment dials, although locked for our tests, let straps slip somewhat. Rear-facing, requires installation with each use and may not fit vehicles with short safety belts. Nonremovable pad covers must be spot-cleaned.	Comes with pillow. Velour. **Similar:** 13204, 13205, 13224.
○	●	○	○	14	up to 18 (18)	Requires installation with each use. May not fit some vehicles because of wide base. When rear-facing, may not fit vehicles with short safety belts. Does not recline. Awkwardly placed safety-belt pathway may restrict child's movement. Belts could be dislodged by child if they aren't tight. Hard-to-adjust harness straps.	Converts to stroller. 6-mo. warranty. Velour. **Similar:** 3240 S
large infants and small children.							
⊖	○	⊖	⊜	10	10 (up to 16)	Rear-facing, requires installation with each use and may not fit vehicles with short safety belts. Exposed metal near latch; when exposed to sun, could get hot enough to cause a burn. Two-position latch opening allows better fit.	Velour. **Similar:** 2500 STE Prestige.
⊖	○	⊖	⊖	10	11 (up to 14)	Vehicle safety belt may interfere with buckle on safety seat in rear-facing position.	Top-tether kit free from mfr. Poly/cotton (or velour).
⊖	○	⊖	⊖	10	11 (up to 14)	Vehicle safety belt may interfere with buckle on safety seat in rear-facing position.	Top-tether kit free from mfr. Velour (or poly/cotton).
⊖	○	⊖	⊖	13	10 (up to 16)	Rear-facing, requires installation with each use and may not fit vehicles with short safety belts. Two-position latch allows better fit. Exposed metal near latch; when exposed to sun, could get hot enough to cause a burn.	Adjustable shield, lower-back support pad, and mud guard. Velour.
⊖	⊖	⊖	◒	13	up to 14 (up to 17)	More reclined rear-facing position than most convertibles. Pad covers hard to remove, not machine-washable. Hard-to-operate reclining mechanism.	Automatic harness straps; unique buckle takes getting used to. Redesigned, sold as "One Click." Velour (or poly/cotton). 90-day warranty.
⊖	○	⊖	⊖	12	10 (up to 16)	Rear-facing, requires installation with each use and may not fit vehicles with short safety belts. Exposed metal near latch; when exposed to sun, could get hot enough to cause a burn. Two-position latch opening allows better fit.	Comes with pillow. Velour. **Similar:** 3500 STE Prestige.
⊖	⊖	⊜	○	10	10 (15)	Pad covers not machine-washable.	Adjustable shield, built-in pillow. Velour (or poly/cotton). **Sim:** 02044, 02054, 02055, 02064, 02065, 02244, 02344.
⊖	⊖	⊜	○	10	10 (15)	Pad covers not machine-washable.	Velour. **Similar:** 02034.
⊖	◒	⊖	◒	12	17 (16)	May not fit some vehicles because of wide base. Vehicle belt may interfere with buckle on safety seat in rear-facing position. Overhead shield may not adjust tightly for small child. Easy-to-adjust reclining mechanism. Hard-to-remove pads.	Adjustable shield. Top-tether kit available free from mfr. Poly/cotton (or velour). **Similar:** Premier 235.
not provide sufficient protection in a crash.							
○	○	◒	○	11	up to 11 (16)	Buckle failure released harness and dummy in our tests. Instructions error may lead to incorrect harness usage for infants. Rear-facing, requires installation with each use and may not fit vehicles with short safety belts.	Velour. **Similar:** 13404, 13424, 13425.
○	◒	⊜	⊜	9	up to 13	Vehicles belts may be difficult to weave through the safety seat.	High-back style. Velour (or poly/cotton). **Similar:** Sport 4890.
⊖	◒	⊜	⊜	8	up to 13	Vehicles belts can be difficult to weave through the safety seat.	High-back style. Poly/cotton (or velour).
⊜	○	○	⊜	6	up to 15	Requires installation with each use when shield is used and then may not fit vehicles with short safety belts.	Backless style. Requires some assembly. Mud guard. Velour. No written warranty.
◒	◒	○	○	9	up to 15	Tools needed to remove shield. Shield could pinch child or installer when being lowered. Nonremovable pad covers must be spot-cleaned.	Backless style. Velour (or poly/cotton). 90-day warranty. **Similar:** 676.

4 *Not tested rear-facing. Should perform similarly to Century 3000 STE.*
5 *Not tested rear-facing. Should perform similarly to Evenflo Champion 224.*
6 *Not tested rear-facing. Should perform similarly to Cosco Touriva 02014.*
7 *Rear-facing, score is* ⊖.
8 *Mfr. advises against using shield with children over 45 lb.*
9 *Mfr. advises against using shield with children under 40 lb.*

4

SAFETY EQUIPMENT

A flat tire or a breakdown that sidelines your car puts you in harm's way. According to the National Highway Traffic Safety Administration, hundreds of people die every year when motorists plow into parked vehicles. No doubt some of those cars had been parked because of trouble on the road. An average driver approaching your car at 60 mph needs about 200 feet to stop. If a hill or curve conceals your presence, the margin of safety may be smaller, even if your car's emergency flashers are on. Thus some sort of auxiliary warning device should be standard gear in every car.

Here's our advice on the best type of warning device to use.

Fusée flares: Bright in fog

Like triangle reflectors, flares can be placed as far from the car as necessary, and they don't require electric power. These powder-filled tubes produce a small, bright red flame when they're struck like a match.

Although widely used, flares have a numbers of drawbacks:

- Flares didn't command our attention as well as triangles did. Their light comes from one small source and isn't very conspicuous at a distance. The light could be mistaken for a taillight. A flare does have an edge in heavy fog: It creates a large red-cloud effect.
- A flare's light may not last until help arrives.
- Flares produce gagging fumes and smoke and pose a fire hazard near dry brush or combustible materials.
- Flares should be replaced about every three years for maximum effectiveness, according to one manufacturer.

Some flares have a wire stand that keeps the burning end off the ground. Others stand vertically when you push a spike into the ground. Spiked flares won't tip over, but they can be all but impossible to drive into concrete or asphalt. If you can't drive the flare into the ground, you'll have to lay it on its side. It will lose some of its visibility that way, and it may roll away. (One 15-minute flare we bought had a plastic tab around its cap to prevent rolling.) Even if you do manage to plant a spiked flare, it could flatten another car's tire if you don't remove the spike when you leave.

Flares sell for a few dollars apiece and most commonly come in 15- and 20-minute versions. Thirty-minute versions are available, but they may be hard to find.

Flashing lights: None too bright

These lights, which typically mount magnetically on the roof, resemble the flasher on an emergency vehicle. They draw power form the car's cigarette-lighter socket, so they won't work in every emergency.

Up close, the flashes emanating from these lights may seem bright enough. But from a couple of hundred feet away, even the better lights we tested were no more visible than our car's own emergency flashers. If you could place one of these flashing lights 100 feet from the car, it might provide a useful warning, but the cord on the tested model was only 10½ feet long.

Flashlights: Dim bulbs

Add a couple of blinking bulbs to a flashlight, put a word like "hazard" on the package, and you have a product that might almost pass as a roadside emergency signal. Don't be taken in. We bought such lights and lanterns and tested them as warning signals. They provided virtually no light from a distance. A flashlight can be invaluable in an emergency, but not to warn motorists.

Emergency gear: A basic list

Something as minor as a shard of glass can disable a car without warning. Assuming you don't have a cellular phone on board and so can't call for help immediately, you'll need to carry other equipment to keep a brief delay from becoming a major interruption. The following list, by no means exhaustive, should serve as a rough guide to what you need. All the equipment is readily available at auto-parts shops, hardware stores, and pharmacies.

Essentials

No driver should be without a first-aid kit, which should include a variety of bandages. Of the two *Johnson & Johnson* kits we examined, the *First Aid Kit 8155*, available at most pharmacies, was better stocked than one targeted for use in a car.

The American Red Cross also sells a well-stocked first-aid kit. Contact your local Red Cross chapter for ordering information.

A flat tire can be one of the simplest things to fix, provided you have a lug wrench and a working jack to make the change. Be sure the spare is ready to be called into service—check its pressure when you check the pressure of the other tires.

If the battery conks out, booster cables enable a passing motorist to give you a jump start. If you drive in a cold climate, we recommend a hefty, four- or six-gauge set of cables. For added reach, get a 16-foot version.

Other essentials include a flashlight and spare change for telephone calls. You might also want to carry a white towel or pillowcase; it can protect clothing if you have to crawl under the car, and it can serve as a warning flag.

WHAT TO DO IF YOU HAVE A FLAT TIRE

No, we're not going to tell you how to use a jack. You can read about that in your car owner's manual. But we are going to suggest you practice using that jack on a sunny day, in the safety of a level driveway or a quiet parking lot, rather than on the shoulder of a crowded highway on some cold and rainy night. (In some new cars, we find the jack installed so tightly that it can't be removed without tools. Some wheel lugs may be hard to loosen, too.)

We're also going to advise you on what simple items to carry to make tire-changing safer and less frustrating. And, most important, we'll provide some tips that could help you avoid a deadly accident when a tire goes flat.

Some people may not be strong or healthy enough to change a flat themselves. For them, a car phone could be worthwhile. And for a woman traveling alone, especially at night or in a lonely area, staying in the car and keeping the doors locked may be wise, as long as the car is off the road. If someone stops to help, roll down the window just enough to ask the Good Samaritan to call the police or road service.

Surviving a blowout

A tire rupture—an abrupt loss of air—is rare these days, but it can happen. If you have a blowout—or even a "slowout," a gradual loss of air—the car may start to swerve. Your first instinct may be to release the accelerator and hit the brakes, but that would only make the car harder to control.

Instead, keep your foot steady on the accelerator and grip the steering wheel as firmly as you can, keeping as straight a course as possible. When you're sure you have the car under control, ease your foot off the accelerator and gently steer onto the shoulder, well off the road. If there's no safe, level spot to pull over, turn on your hazard flashers and keep limping along until you find one—but keep your speed down, or the flat tire could twist itself right off the wheel. You'll ruin the tire by driving on it, but that's better than becoming a traffic fatality.

If you can't get the car to a safe spot, get out and stand well behind the car, away from traffic, and wait for help. A white cloth tied to the antenna or door handle is a universal distress signal.

Be prepared

When you check the air in your car's tires, don't forget the spare. Few things are more frustrating than starting to change a flat and discovering that the spare is flat as well.

Items to keep in your car include a flashlight with fresh batteries; a one-foot-square piece of $^3/_4$ inch plywood to keep the jack from sinking into soft dirt or mud; a wheel chock to keep the car from rolling off the jack; and a set of reflective hazard triangles—more visible than flares. When you're stuck in or near a traffic lane, set up the triangles to guide traffic around your car.

Other handy items: coveralls to protect your good clothes; a piece of carpeting to kneel on; work gloves—or some waterless mechanic's hand cleaner and a few paper towels; and small change, in case a phone is near.

When you bring the flat to a garage for repair, make sure it's fixed right. Some mechanics simply plug the hole from outside. A proper repair requires removing the tire from the wheel and checking the inside for damage. Also, the hole should be patched from inside as well as plugged from outside. A puncture on or near the sidewall can't be fixed; you must replace the tire.

Basic tools

You may not be handy with tools, but a passing Good Samaritan might be. Keep these tools in a small pouch or tackle box in the trunk: pliers, screwdrivers (both flat and Phillips head), open-end wrenches, electrical tape and duct tape, a wire hanger, and a pocketknife.

Extra security

If you're willing to go the extra mile—possibly on foot—carry an empty *red* container specifically designed to hold gasoline, along with a siphon. Be sure the container is completely empty after you use it; air it out for a few minutes, then cap it before you put it back in the trunk. When you get home, air the container outdoors until the gasoline fumes have dissipated.

A blown fuse can disable taillights or even prevent the car from running. Keep a few replacement fuses in the glove box. Check the car's owner's manual for the size of fuses you need and the location of the fuse box.

You may never need to use a fire extinguisher, but you may want to keep one on board for an added sense of security. Be sure you buy one with an Underwriters Laboratories rating of at least 1A, 10B, C. (These letters and numbers, standard coding on fire extinguishers, denote a unit that can handle small fires of all types.)

Triangle reflectors: Best choice

Compared with emergency flares or warning lights, triangles have several advantages: They're reusable, and they don't require electrical power. You can place them hundreds of feet from the car, and they can sit in the trunk for years without losing their effectiveness.

The U.S. Department of Transportation (DOT) requires interstate truck drivers to carry triangles and has a standard governing their performance and design. The standard requires, among other things, that triangles be highly reflective, 17 to 22 inches on the side, with a stable base. Models meeting the standard carry a certification statement or the letters DOT. As you might expect they look and perform pretty much alike, and, in our tests, they outperformed a brand (since discontinued) that didn't meet the standard.

We tested each triangle's visibility by viewing it from distances of 100, 200, 300, and 400 feet. We put the triangles in front of a parked car so we could compare them to the car's flashers. For night tests, we aimed a car's low-beam headlights at the triangles from the same distances. All the triangles that conform to the government standard invariably appear brighter than the car's flashers.

Once deployed, a triangle should stand up to wind gusts and to vibrations from passing traffic. All the ones we tested have a weighted base and proved quite stable.

To be effective at night, a triangle must be placed perpendicular to the traffic flow. Turn it more than a few degrees from that position and its visibility drops off sharply.

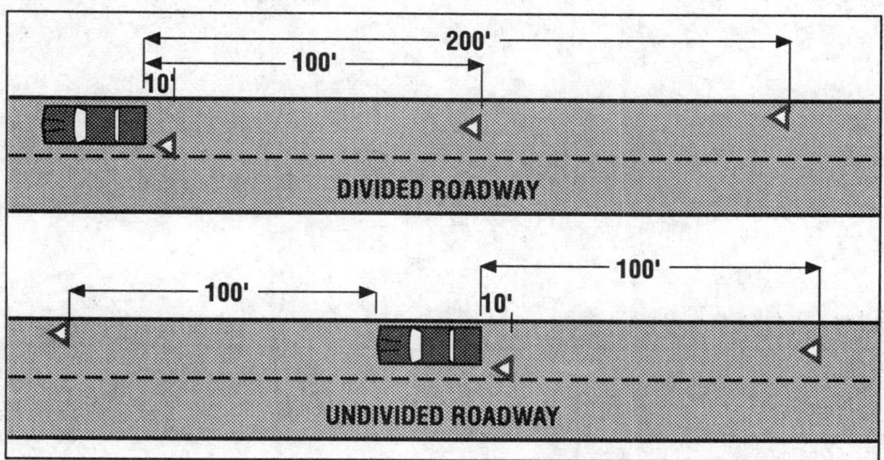

Figure 4.1 Positioning Triangles and Flares *Our suggestion for best placement: On divided highways and larger undivided roads, put all three devices behind the car, at distances of 10 feet (about four paces), 100 feet, and 200 feet, arranged to guide oncoming traffic around your car. On an undivided road, position the devices as shown: One 100 feet in front of the car, another 100 feet behind, and a third, 10 feet behind the car.*

You should have at least three triangles on hand so you can position them both to alert other drivers and to help guide them safely around your vehicle. (See Figure 4.1.) Don't take our advice as ironclad, however. Let common sense and road conditions guide you.

5

BUYING TIRES: THREE EASY STEPS

If you're confused about shopping for car tires, you're not alone. Tire makers seem to go out of their way to snow you with jargon, arcane codes and indexes, and similar names for dissimilar tires. And relying on a tire dealer for advice is risky: The salesperson may not know the product—or may steer you toward the most profitable or slowest-selling line.

Unfortunately, there's no simple way to tell a good tire from one that's not so good. Over the years, our tests have shown that neither brand nor price is an accurate gauge of quality. In fact, some of the most expensive tires we've tested have performed worse than some of the cheapest.

Before shopping for tires, then, it pays to learn a few basics. This chapter will help you decide when it's time to replace your old tires. And it will advise you about the kind of tire that's best for your car and your style of driving, and tell you where you can find the best price and widest selection.

We will also tell you which tires excelled in our tests. Our latest tests include 10 models designed specifically for pickup trucks and sport-utility vehicles, a rapidly growing market; details and Ratings start on page 32. And we'll discuss, on page 31, the various kinds of passenger-car tires that we tested previously and that are still available.

Step 1: When to buy

You may not think about replacing tires until they grab your attention by failing a safety inspection or, worse yet, skidding on wet pavement or blowing out. But checking your tires regularly for excessive wear and obvious damage is safer.

Check at least monthly. Even a new tire can develop a deep cut, or a bulge or bubble that signifies internal damage—and imminent failure. If you've driven on your tires for more than 20,000 miles or so, check the depth of the tread regularly. A nearly bald tire is treacherous on slick roads, and the skimpy layer of rubber provides little protection from road hazards.

Checking the tread depth is simple. All passenger-car and light-truck tires have built-in tread indicators that tell you at a glance if too little tread is left. Ordinarily, the indicators are virtually invisible; but when the tire is badly worn, they show up as bars running across the tread at regular intervals.

To monitor tread depth before it sinks to the bare minimum, use a tread-depth gauge, an inexpensive and easy-to-use syringe-like tool sold by tire dealers and auto-parts stores. The gauge is marked in thirty-seconds of an inch; 2⁄32 is the legal limit in most states, but you should replace the tire before that. (To make tires last longer, rotate them from front to back periodically, as recommended in the car owner's manual.)

Step 2: What to buy

That depends on how you drive. Every tire is a compromise. A model that delivers maximum grip in hard turns and during braking, for example, may ride noisily and hard, and may wear out quickly. And one that rides quietly may not grip well in snow or mud.

Your first instinct may be to go for the same tires that came on your car or truck. But that may not be your best choice. Automakers meet strict government fuel-economy standards in part by equipping their new cars with tires that roll especially easily—and thus eke out an extra fraction of an mpg. Automakers also tend to look for tires that ride softly, to make a brief test drive at the dealership more appealing. But the automaker's priorities needn't be yours. You may be willing to sacrifice a bit in some areas for better traction, say, or longer tread life.

Most tires sold today are all-season tires, designed to perform reasonably well in dry weather, rain, and snow, although without excelling in any area. The all-season category includes several subcategories.

Basic all-season tires

Basic all-season tires are standard equipment on most new family sedans. Consider that type if long tread life, a comfortable ride, and budget price are all-important. If you sometimes drive in snow, make sure the tire has "M+S" (mud and snow) on the sidewall. You can tell a basic all-season tire by the speed rating imprinted on its sidewall—an S or a T, or sometimes no letter at all. (See "speed rating" in the box on page 30.)

All-season touring tires

All-season touring tires are hyped by the industry as premium quality. But in practice, even manufacturers can't agree on a definition. Goodyear, which claims to have coined the term, once defined the breed as a "performance tire with manners." So-called touring tires are generally more expensive than basic all-season tires (although there's considerable overlap), but we haven't noted significant differences, overall. Most touring tires carry an S or a T speed rating.

All-season performance tires

All-season performance tires are a

relatively new category. Consider them if you drive aggressively. Such tires offer superior braking and cornering, but at the expense of shorter tread life and, often, a harder and noisier ride. If they have an M+S rating, they retain one advantage of basic all-season tires: decent traction in snow. Performance tires have a squat, wide profile and an H speed rating.

Ultra-high-performance tires provide the ultimate in handling and braking on wet and dry pavement, but they ride harshly and wear out quickly, and they tend to be hopeless in snow. Such tires are very wide and squat and generally have a V or Z speed rating.

Light-truck tires

Light-truck tires are available for general road use, on/off road, and off-road. The off-road type has the chunkiest, most aggressive tread for better traction off the pavement. Light-truck tires also come in regular-load and, for hauling heavy cargo, extra-load types. We tested on/off-road, regular-load tires.

Snow tires

Snow tires are your best bet for mountainous areas with heavy snowfall—better than any all-season tires. But they ride noisily and grip relatively poorly on dry roads, so remove them for the summer.

Step 3: How to buy

Selling tires is a highly competitive business. Sales are common, and list prices are meaningless, so it's up to you to find the best price.

Check ads in newspapers and car magazines. Phone several sources and compare prices. Don't forget to check the price of balancing, and ask whether mounting is included. Find out, too, whether a road-hazard warranty comes with the tires.

Before the tires are installed, make sure they're the right model and size. Check the date of manufacture (see the box below), and refuse a tire that's more than two or three years old. If you're buying fewer than four tires, make sure the mechanic replaces the right ones.

Tires are sold in several different types of outlets. Here's what to expect from each:

Tire dealers

About half of all buyers shop at

DECODING A TIRE

Have you ever wondered what all those cryptic numbers and letters on a tire's sidewall mean? Here's your personal decoder that explains the most important items:

Size and shape

Typically, the tire size looks something like P185/70R14. The "P" means a passenger-car or light-truck tire; "LT" means a tire for light-truck use only. (Some tires omit that.) The next three digits tell you how wide the tire is, in millimeters (here, 185 mm). Large and high-performance cars tend to have wide tires, greater than 200 mm. The two digits after the slash are the "aspect ratio"—the ratio of the height of the sidewall to the tire width. Here, the sidewall height is 70 percent of the width, or about 130 mm. Performance tires tend to have a low aspect ratio—usually 60 or less—and a squat appearance. The "R" simply means radial ply—a design used for virtually all tires. The two digits at the end are the diameter of the wheel, in inches.

Speed rating

Some tires have an additional letter either within the size designation, before the "R" (185/70SR14, say) or just after the wheel diameter; such letter codes reflect the maximum speed the tire is certified to sustain. Conventional tires may carry an S (112 mph) or T (118 mph) speed rating, or none at all. Most performance tires carry an H (130 mph); ultra-high-performance tires, a V (149 mph), Z (149-plus), W (168 mph) or Y (186 mph). A high speed rating is generally an indication of a tire designed more for sporty driving than for comfort or economy.

Treadwear rating

This is a measure of how well a tire's tread will wear, compared with a "reference" tire graded at 100. Theoretically, a tire with a wear index of 450 (relatively high) should last three times as long as one with an index of 150 (relatively low). Tire makers conduct the tests themselves, so view such numbers skeptically. Still, they're the only available guide for comparing tread life.

Traction and temperature

Scores are for government tests for stopping on a wet surface and resisting the effects of high temperatures. A is best, C is worst. Look for at least a B.

Date of manufacture

Every tire has a Department of Transportation serial number—something like DOT DBUA A44 414 GCD 415. The last three digits tell you the week and year the tire was made; thus, 415 indicates the 41st week of 1995. Don't buy a tire that's more than two or three years old.

Maximum pressure

The tire's highest safe inflation pressure, in pounds per square inch (for example, 35 PSI MAX PRESS). It's best to follow the inflation recommendations in the car owner's manual. In any case, don't exceed the maximum listed on the tire. (And don't trust the garage's air pump; they're notoriously inaccurate. Buy an inexpensive tire gauge.)

these stores, which offer a wide selection of brands, models, and sizes and, usually, knowledgeable salespeople. If they don't have what you want in stock, they can generally get it for you within a few days.

Service stations

Your local garage will probably be very accommodating if you're a regular customer. But it may offer limited stock, and the staff may not be knowledgeable about tires. If the garage doesn't stock the model you want, ask to have it ordered.

Department stores, warehouse clubs, and auto-parts stores

The quality and selection vary at chain stores such as Costco, Sam's Club, and Sears. If you do find premium name-brand tires at such outlets, be sure to check the prices against those of other tire dealers.

Mail-order houses

These outlets generally offer the lowest prices and a very wide selection. Look for their ads in auto buff magazines. Most have a toll-free number. Delivery generally takes only a few days, and you can have the tires shipped directly to your garage.

Passenger-Car Tire Ratings

All-season performance tires (tested for January 1995)

All 11 models in this group are still available. We tested size P205/60R15 tires, which fit many midsize and large cars. Test car: Pontiac Bonneville SSEi.

The Dunlop D60 A2 was the overall tire of choice here: It scored at or near the top in every braking and cornering test, without compromise in ride or noise. Treadwear rating: 280. Dunlop's ads say the *D60 A2* has been improved. The current average price is $80.

The *Goodyear Eagle Aquatred* also performed very well, overall, but it droned. And at $150 average, it's pricey. Treadwear rating: 260.

The *Yokohama Avid MD-H4* ($94) braked well; it's particularly good for cars without antilock brakes. Treadwear rating: 300.

The *BF Goodrich Comp T/A HR4* ($94) is good for cars without antilock brakes, and it cornered best in the group. Treadwear rating: 360.

The *Bridgestone Potenza RE 92* ($100), *Pirelli P4000 Super Touring* ($103), *General XP2000 II* ($75), *Firestone Firehawk GTA* ($80), and *Michelin XGT H4* ($108) were unexceptional.

The *Michelin MXV4 Green X* ($125) was near the bottom in wet braking. Its name suggests ecological benefits; it did, in fact, show low rolling resistance, which should benefit fuel economy. So did the *Goodyear Eagle GA* ($160)—but it was the most expensive tire in this group, and the lowest rated, overall.

Basic all-season tires (tested for February 1994)

Seven of the ten tire models in this group are still available. We tested size P185/70R14 tires, which fit popular models such as the *Toyota Camry* and Honda Accord and many compact Detroit models. Test car: Mazda 626.

The impressive *Bridgestone Turanza S* has been renamed *Turanza T* ($73 average price). It excelled in wet and dry braking with ABS, but its wet-braking performance with the ABS disconnected was disappointing. Treadwear rating: 420.

The *BF Goodrich The Advantage* ($60) distinguished itself in wet cornering, but its braking was mediocre. Treadwear rating: 300.

The *Sears Roadhandler Plus 70* ($70), *Firestone FR680* ($61), *Michelin XH4* ($81), and *Goodyear Invicta GS* ($87) had middling scores, overall. The *General Ameri-Tech ST* ($57) generally disappointed us.

WHERE TO CALL

Tires

BF Goodrich	800-847-3435
Bridgestone	800-367-3872
Cooper	800-854-6288
Dunlop	800-548-4714
Firestone	800-543-7522, ext. 3788
General	800-847-3349
Goodyear	800-321-2136
Kelly Springfield	800-638-5112
Michelin	800-847-3435
Pirelli	800-327-2442
Sears	contact local store
Yokohama	800-366-8473

Recommendation

These tires were impressive. They could corner and brake almost as well as the all-season performance tires we reported on last year, except in one test: braking on wet pavement with ABS. In that test, even the best model in this group performed no better than the worst model in the all-season performance-tire group. Surprisingly, despite their aggressive tread designs, the light-truck tires weren't much noisier.

There wasn't all that much difference, overall, from the best to the worst tires in this group. Nevertheless, several models stood out. The *Dunlop Radial Rover*, A Best Buy, performed the best in all our braking tests and among the best in cornering and handling. It rode well and had good steering feel. And at an average price of $83, it's relatively inexpensive. For most light-truck owners, we see little reason to consider any tire model except the *Dunlop*.

We tested two *Michelin* models. The *LTX A/T* ($114), an on/off-road tire, behaved well overall. The *LTX M/S* ($105) is designed more for on-road use; we included it to see the difference. Not surprisingly, the *M/S* was the most like a passenger-car tire, quiet and comfortable. And it performed well in wet braking and wet cornering. But the two *Michelin* models earned the same overall score in our tests.

Finally, we were surprised that the *Goodyear Wrangler Aquatred* ($120) didn't excel in our wet-pavement tests, and that the *Goodyear Wrangler Radial* ($100)—a very big seller—was the worst of the group.

Notes on the Ratings

These tires are logical replacements on vehicles such as the Jeep Grand Cherokee (which we used as our test car), Ford Explorer, Chevrolet C/K pickup, and Ford F-Series pickup. We bought standard-load, on/off-road tires in size P235/75R15. Prices are the estimated average, based on a recent national survey.

We tested for stopping distance on dry pavement from 60 mph (the average was 139 feet). On wet pavement, we tested from 40 mph with the Jeep's antilock-brake system (ABS) working (average: 72 feet), and then we repeated the tests with the ABS turned off (average: 93 feet).

To see how well the tires grip during both wet and dry cornering, we drove around our skid pad faster and faster until the Jeep could no longer hold its circular path. We also drove around our one-mile handling circuit, where we evaluated how well the tires responded to the steering and how well they warned the driver as they were about to lose their grip. And we drove on each set of tires for several hundred miles on a variety of public roads so we could evaluate the tires' steering response and ride comfort under normal driving conditions.

We checked rolling resistance—how long it took the Jeep to coast down from 40 mph, and how fast it was going at the end of a specified distance. The farther it rolled, the better the fuel economy should be. We recorded and analyzed the noise level inside the car on both smooth and coarse pavement at 30 mph. And we've listed each model's treadwear rating—a rough indicator of tire life.

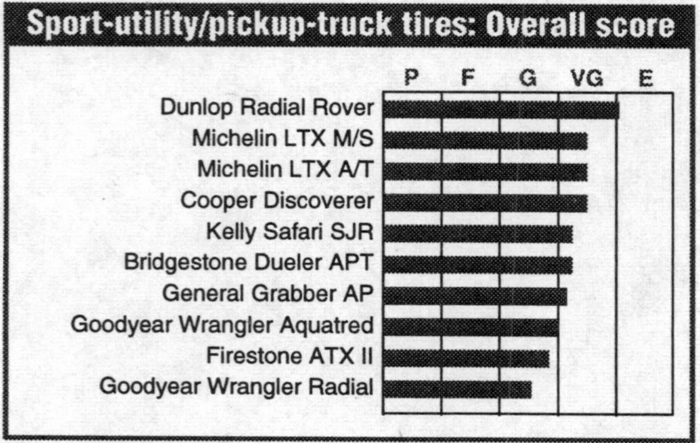

RATINGS

As published in the January

Dunlop Radial Rover ($83)
A Best Buy

Slightly outperformed the rest in braking, and among the best in dry and wet cornering. Safe and responsive handling and a comfortable ride. Highest treadwear rating in this group.

Braking:
60 mph, dry pavement .....137 feet
40 mph, wet with ABS........69 feet
wet without ABS ....87 feet
Cornering: dry pavement..........◍
wet pavement ....◓
Handling ....◓
Noise: smooth road ....◓
coarse road.............................○
Ride ....◍
Rolling resistance......................◓
Treadwear rating 440

Bridgestone Dueler APT ($85)

A performance-oriented tire, with a noisy, harsh ride. Very nimble and responsive, and second best in wet and dry braking. But doesn't grip as well as some on the wet skid pad. Worst in rolling resistance. Available only from Sears.

Braking:
60 mph, dry pavement .....137 feet
40 mph, wet with ABS........70 feet
wet without ABS ....90 feet
Cornering: dry pavement..........◍
wet pavement .... ○
Handling ....◍
Noise: smooth road ....◓
coarse road.............................○
Ride ....◒
Rolling resistance......................○
Treadwear rating 300

SUV and pickup-truck tires

1996 issue of *Consumer Reports.*

Michelin LTX M/S ($105)

A good wet-weather performer with ABS, and very comfortable—softer and quieter than the others.

Braking:	
60 mph, dry pavement	142 feet
40 mph, wet with ABS	71 feet
wet without ABS	96 feet
Cornering: dry pavement	⊜
wet pavement	◓
Handling	◓
Noise: smooth road	⊜
coarse road	○
Ride	⊜
Rolling resistance	⊜
Treadwear rating	400

Michelin LTX A/T ($114)

Among the quietest tires on smooth pavement. Otherwise, average in most respects.

Braking:	
60 mph, dry pavement	139 feet
40 mph, wet with ABS	70 feet
wet without ABS	93 feet
Cornering: dry pavement	⊜
wet pavement	○
Handling	◓
Noise: smooth road	⊜
coarse road	○
Ride	◓
Rolling resistance	◓
Treadwear rating	400

Cooper Discoverer ($85)

Showed strongest grip in dry cornering. Very predictable as it's about to lose its grip. Especially quiet on smooth pavement.

Braking:	
60 mph, dry pavement	138 feet
40 mph, wet with ABS	74 feet
wet without ABS	93 feet
Cornering: dry pavement	⊜
wet pavement	◓
Handling	⊜
Noise: smooth road	⊜
coarse road	○
Ride	○
Rolling resistance	◓
Treadwear rating	400

Kelly Safari SJR ($80)

Long stopping distances without ABS. Noisy on smooth pavement, relatively quiet on coarse.

Braking:	
60 mph, dry pavement	139 feet
40 mph, wet with ABS	72 feet
wet without ABS	96 feet
Cornering: dry pavement	⊜
wet pavement	◓
Handling	⊜
Noise: smooth road	◓
coarse road	○
Ride	○
Rolling resistance	⊜
Treadwear rating	320

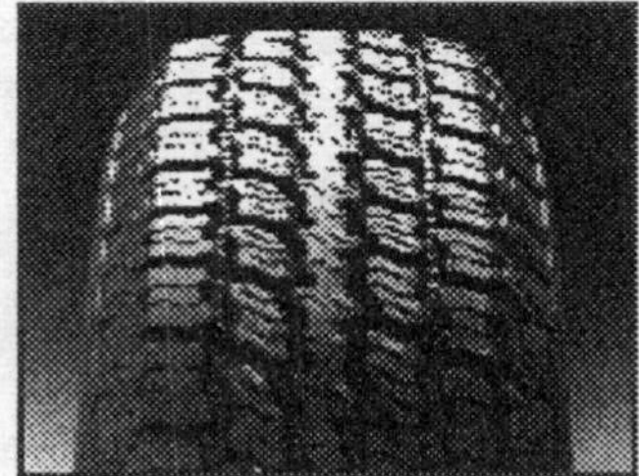

General Grabber AP ($84)

Cornered well on dry pavement, adequately on wet. Responds fairly slowly to steering. Reasonably quiet, but ride is only so-so.

Braking:	
60 mph, dry pavement	138 feet
40 mph, wet with ABS	72 feet
wet without ABS	95 feet
Cornering: dry pavement	⊜
wet pavement	○
Handling	◓
Noise: smooth road	⊜
coarse road	○
Ride	◒
Rolling resistance	◓
Treadwear rating	Not available

Goodyear Wrangler Aquatred ($120)

One of the longest wet stoppers with ABS; one of the shortest without ABS. In cornering, loses grip progressively rather than abruptly.

Braking:	
60 mph, dry pavement	142 feet
40 mph, wet with ABS	74 feet
wet without ABS	91 feet
Cornering: dry pavement	⊜
wet pavement	○
Handling	⊜
Noise: smooth road	◓
coarse road	◒
Ride	○
Rolling resistance	⊜
Treadwear rating	360

Firestone ATX II ($87)

Consistently scored at the bottom in cornering tests. Not an especially comfortable ride. Scored well in rolling resistance.

Braking:	
60 mph, dry pavement	139 feet
40 mph, wet with ABS	74 feet
wet without ABS	94 feet
Cornering: dry pavement	◓
wet pavement	○
Handling	○
Noise: smooth road	◓
coarse road	○
Ride	◒
Rolling resistance	⊜
Treadwear rating	Not available

Goodyear Wrangler Radial ($100)

A disappointing tire. Worst in wet braking, mediocre in dry braking and wet cornering. Not much steering feel, but handles precisely. Noisiest tire of the bunch.

Braking:	
60 mph, dry pavement	141 feet
40 mph, wet with ABS	76 feet
wet without ABS	97 feet
Cornering: dry pavement	⊜
wet pavement	○
Handling	⊜
Noise: smooth road	◓
coarse road	●
Ride	○
Rolling resistance	◓
Treadwear rating	300

6

HOW TO BUY AUTO INSURANCE

Americans spent an average of $638 per car on auto insurance in 1993, the latest year for which data are available. If you were paying that much for a TV or a camera, you'd certainly shop around. Yet, with auto insurance, most people don't. When we asked our readers last spring whether they had shopped around the last time they bought or renewed insurance, six out of ten said they had not.

Two things make it difficult to shop for auto insurance: Companies can charge widely different prices for similar coverage, and the quality of service is impossible to judge—until you're unfortunate enough to be in an accident. This report offers help on both counts.

When it comes to cost, it's hard to avoid doing some legwork; you'll have to call different companies, describe your driving history, and get their quotes. But you'll get much more useful information if you know what to ask, and if you know precisely what kind of coverage you need. This report gives you that guidance, with tips for different kinds of consumers, from older drivers to newly licensed teens.

When it comes to service, the Ratings on pages 38–39 remove the mystery. The Ratings show what nearly 34,000 of our readers throughout the country thought about their treatment by 36 companies. They tell you which companies pay claims promptly and which ones might leave you waiting for a check while your car sits at the repair shop. The recommendations on page 37 guide you toward a handful of companies with low prices and good service. If another company offers a good deal, the Ratings let you check its service, too.

Before you begin shopping, you should understand a basic rule: Insurance isn't meant to cover every dent and scratch. That kind of coverage would cost you plenty. Like other kinds of insurance, auto insurance is best used to protect yourself against expenses you could not otherwise afford.

To keep premiums reasonable, buy the coverage you really need and accept a high deductible. Depend on the insurance company only for major losses.

That way, it's relatively easy to tailor your coverage for optimum savings. As the table on pages 40–41 shows, auto insurance actually includes several different kinds of coverage, each with its own price, or premium. You can buy less or more of each, depending on your needs.

Avoiding catastrophes

The most necessary coverage against financial ruin is bodily-injury liability insurance. It pays for the other person's medical treatments, rehabilitation, or funeral costs when you're found at fault in an auto accident. It's mandatory in most states and the District of Columbia, and desirable everywhere.

Bodily-injury liability and its companion coverage, property-damage liability, are sold with monetary limits—the limit of what the insurance company will pay after each accident. Each state requires drivers to have liability coverage up to certain specified limits. In Utah, for example, the required coverage is $25,000 per person, $50,000 per accident, and $15,000 for property damage per accident. (Liability coverage is sometimes expressed in the policy as a string of numbers: for example, 25/50/15.)

In many parts of the country, however, the state requirements don't come close to covering potential losses. If a court ruled you owed more, you might have to dip into your other assets. So it makes sense to buy more coverage. That extra insurance often isn't expensive; you pay the most for the first dollars of coverage.

An umbrella policy is a more cost-effective way to buy liability coverage; it pays for losses above and beyond what's protected by auto and homeowner's insurance. A $1-million umbrella policy typically costs about $200 a year.

Sweating the small stuff

Whereas most people may find it worthwhile to buy more liability insurance than they now have, many should carry *less* collision and comprehensive insurance. Collision pays for the repair of your car or replacement of its market value when it collides in an accident or rolls over, regardless of who was at fault. Comprehensive—sometimes called "other than collision" in the policy—pays for similar replacement after theft or for the repair of damage caused by other events, such as fire, flood, and windstorm. Both coverages carry deductibles.

The bigger the deductible you're willing to live with, the cheaper the coverage. In general, we recommend a minimum collision deductible of $250 or $500. If you have a moderately priced car more than five years old, you can save more money by dropping collision and comprehensive entirely. Most likely, the car's value has dropped so much that you wouldn't get much from the insurer if the car were totaled or stolen.

Zeroing in on price

Which insurers should you consider? Obviously, price is the primary consideration. Before shopping, find out if your state insurance department offers free comparisons of auto-insurance prices; as the box on page 39 shows, 36 states offer such guides. Most guides show what a number of insurers would charge for different types of driver in various regions in the state. Few guides are up-to-date, and the examples probably won't match your exact situation. But they can give you an idea of whether a company charges drivers like you more or less than average in your region.

Consumers in California, Florida, New Jersey, New York, Pennsylvania, and Washington can take advantage of CU's new Auto Insurance Price Service. Callers to the service's 800 number receive a list comparing up to 25 of the least expensive policies for their particular situation, including service Ratings and shopping tips. Subscribers in those three states should see the inside front cover for details.

Whether you use a phone service or call companies, agents, or brokers, get as many quotes as possible. Insurers don't always offer identical coverages; for instance, one might offer $250,000/$500,000 in bodily injury liability, while another might offer $300,000/$500,000. Still, try to compare similar coverages.

If a company isn't listed in the Ratings, call your state insurance department for its record of consumer complaints. If complaints against a company are frequent relative to other carriers, seek another insurer.

Before you switch

Even if you can find a better price, leaving your current company isn't always wise. Insurers often reward longtime customers with discounts and accident-forgiveness programs. Liberty Mutual Insurance Company, for instance, waives surcharges on minor accidents for customers who have remained with the company, accident-free, for five years.

What's more, signing with a new company can be difficult. Families with teenage drivers have a particularly daunting time; rates for young males can be more than triple the base adult rate because teens historically have severe and costly accidents.

Christine and Mark Ahasic of Brooklyn, N.Y., discovered that after they placed their 17-year-old son, Mark, on their policy last year. The six-month coverage for their 1993 Eagle Vision jumped to $1883 from $1061. But after shopping extensively, they found that their original insurance carrier, Allstate, still had the best price because of the discounts it offers long-term customers and holders of auto/home-insurance packages. After Mark Jr. went off to college in Illinois, the Ahasics got a 20-percent discount that applies to students without cars who live over 100 miles from home.

One frustration for consumers is that companies offering lower prices can be quite restrictive. For example, United Services Automobile Association and its sister carrier, USAA Casualty, offer competitive rates in many parts of the country. But they accept only active or retired military officers and their current and former dependents.

Although other insurers don't limit their sales according to occupation or demographics, that doesn't mean their arms are open. If you've had more than one accident or moving violation recently, you may have trouble finding coverage with any company except the one assigned to you through your state's assigned-risk or high-risk pool.

High-risk pools work the same way in most states. Private insurers must cover a certain number of "risky" drivers, based on their share of the auto-insurance market. These drivers pay very high rates. Once you're in the pool, you're usually stuck there for three years, the minimum amount of time it takes to clear a driving record. As your record improves, start shopping private companies. Companies that sell "nonstandard" coverage to "risky" drivers can be cheaper than assigned risk. You may even qualify for an intermediate-priced, "standard" policy. Some states are helping drivers leave the high-risk pool; starting this December in Texas, for instance, insurers must offer their standard rates to their high-risk pool customers who have been ticket- and accident-free for three years.

What if you're one of the millions of adult drivers outside the high-risk plan, with no violations or accidents in the past three years? Sometimes, insurers offer new clients with a good driving record their standard rate, which may be reduced to the least expensive "preferred" rate after they've been with the company a few years. Others offer the preferred rate right away. But it doesn't hurt to do what Felicia Hsieh of Coral Springs, Fla., does: Always ask for the preferred rate. "They don't give it to me until I ask," she notes.

Questions, questions

In most states, insurance applicants can expect a barrage of questions that seem to have nothing to do with cars—including how long they've worked at their current job, whether they own their home, whether they smoke, even their level of schooling. That process, called underwriting, may determine whether you'll get coverage, and if you do, how much you'll pay.

Not all underwriting is legitimate. A 1994 study by the Texas Office of the Public Insurance Counsel showed that many insurers used illegal guidelines, based on marital status and nationality, to restrict coverage. Nearly one in five had restrictions on new applicants between ages 65 and 75, regardless of their driving ability. Texas law prohibits companies from dropping drivers with a limited number of not-at-fault accidents, but the study found that insurers made it hard for such drivers to get new coverage.

If you're not accepted, ask why. If it's a mistake on a credit record, for instance, try to get it fixed and apply again. Find out, too, what standards the company requires. Even if the agent says your only resort is the assigned-risk pool, call a few more companies. Insurers often differ on underwriting standards. Some will ask for five years of driving experience, others for only three.

Getting accepted for coverage doesn't put you in the clear. In most states, insurers have the right to cancel you for any reason within the first 60 days of coverage. They may cancel your policy, for example, if they find that you've lied about your record of accidents or violations.

After 60 days of coverage, you can't be dropped in most states. But there are notable exceptions. If, after an accident, the insurer finds you misrepresented information—not listing a teenage driver on the policy, for instance—it may pay the claim but cancel further coverage. If a member of your household has a driver's license suspended, you could say good-bye to your insurance as well. Even a late payment can jeopardize your coverage.

Consider the car

Other factors won't disqualify you from coverage but can add hundreds of dollars to your premium. Owning a luxury or performance car, for instance: You'll pay a lot for insurance if you drive a Chevrolet Corvette or a Porsche. Less glamorous models also can be costly if they're stolen frequently for parts. The Honda Accord sedan ranks among the "most wanted" by car thieves, according to the National Insurance Crime Bureau. A 30-year-old would pay State Farm $1032 a year—6 to 7 percent of the Accord's base price—to insure it in suburban Chicago with a standard policy.

A model's safety story counts, too. If it has antilock brakes and air bags, has done well in crash tests, and has generated low bodily-injury claims, it will cost less to insure relative to other models. For instance, Continental Insurance Company charges virtually the same to insure a 1992 Geo Storm and a much more expensive 1994 Volvo 850 sedan because the Volvo has a better safety record.

What about service?

Once you're covered, what are your chances of getting good service? It depends on the insurer. According to our readers, service varies significantly, particularly with respect to claims handling.

When some 34,000 readers answered auto-insurance questions on our 1994 Annual Questionnaire, they told us that promptness in claims handling was the single most significant factor in deciding how much they liked a company's service. (Our definition of prompt is a payment that arrives less than 30 days after the claim is filed.)

Among the best companies for prompt claims handling were Erie Insurance Exchange, Citizens Insurance Company of America, Hartford Casualty Insurance Company, and Amica Mutual Insurance Company. Those companies delayed payment only about 6 percent of the time. Conversely, two of the slowest companies—20th Century Insurance Company and New Jersey Manufacturers Insurance Company—delayed payment 21 and 17 percent of the time, respectively.

For the most part, however, readers were paid promptly. Seventy percent said they got their check within 14 days of filing their claim. Not that there weren't hassles. Fourteen percent of readers cited at least one problem regarding claims. They complained most frequently about difficulty in reaching an agent or company representative, and about disagreement over the amount of damages.

Who has the best service?

The best way to ensure satisfaction after an accident is to shop for coverage among the companies near the top of our Ratings. First on the list is Amica Mutual Insurance Company, which has topped our Ratings five consecutive times. In 1995, it received an overall score of 95 out of 100 from our survey of its customers. The company at the bottom of the Ratings, Metropolitan Property and Casualty Insurance Company, earned a score of 78, where 80 means "very good" service. Nearly a quarter of Metropolitan's customers mentioned at least one claims problem.

The reasons for Amica's high ranking abound. In addition to its low percentage of late payments, Amica doesn't push policyholders to use specific garages. It requires just one estimate. And checks go out within two days after the claim amount is established.

Amica's drawback is inaccessibility. In some regions, even applicants with spotless records can't get a toehold unless they are referred by current policyholders. The company also prefers applicants with driving records free of any accidents or violations in the previous three to five years. Nevertheless, Amica has accepted a fair number of *Consumer Reports* readers in the past. In 1992, 12,630 readers called the company for quotes; it took on 3386 of those who applied.

Just behind Amica in the Ratings are United Services Automobile Association, USAA Casualty Insurance Company, and Cincinnati Insurance Company. All were high-rated when we last covered auto insurance in 1992.

Amica, United Services, and USAA are called "direct writers." Customers who call an 800 number or visit such a company's offices deal with employees, not commission agents or brokers. Direct writers often offer very competitive rates because they don't pay commissions, which can add 5 to 15 percent to the premium.

Among insurers that pay commissions, those using "exclusive" agents may be less expensive than those using independent agents. Commissions for exclusive agents are generally lower.

Report that accident?

Even a good insurer will charge more to drivers who cost it money. At many insurers, one at-fault accident that costs the company $400 to $500 can result in three years of substantial surcharges. More than one can mean nonrenewal.

Twelve percent of readers told us they decided not to file a claim with their insurer at some point in the past three years for fear it would raise their premium. As a result, they paid an average of $300 out of pocket. But that's probably less than they would have spent on three years of surcharges.

When you report an accident, keeping good records can speed the claims process. Obtain the names and addresses of all drivers, passengers, and witnesses, as well as appropriate li-

(continued on page 42)

RATINGS Auto insurance

As published in the October 1995 issue of *Consumer Reports.*

Listed in order of overall score

Notes on the table

Ratings are based on responses to CU's 1994 Annual Questionnaire. Almost 34,000 readers told us about the service they received on their most recent auto-insurance claim since January 1, 1991, as well as the nonclaims service they received during the period. Results reflect the experiences of our readers, not necessarily those of all auto-insurance policyholders. An * after a name indicates a direct writer or a company that deals with exclusive agents, not independent agents or brokers. **Overall score** is based on readers' overall judgments of how well their insurance company handled their claim. We used a six-point scale: 100 = excellent, 80 = very good, 60 = good, 40 = fair, 20 = poor, 0 = very poor. The median company rating was 84. Each insurer received at least 179 responses. Differences of less than about five points are not meaningful. **Claims problems** reflects the percentage of policyholders from each company who said they had experienced one or more of the following: difficulty reaching an agent or company representative; delay in handling a claim or paying out

Company	Overall score (0–100)	Claims problems	Nonclaims problems	Payment delays (%)	Where sold
Amica Mutual*		⊖	⊜	6	National
United Services Auto. Assn. (USAA)*		⊖	⊜	7	National
USAA Casualty*		○	⊜	7	National
Cincinnati		⊜	⊖	7	Midwest, Southeast
Erie Ins. Exchange		⊖	⊖	6	Midwest, East
National General*		○	⊖	8	National
Erie Ins. Co.		⊖	⊖	7	Midwest, East
Auto-Owners		○	○	8	Midwest, Southeast, Southwest
Citizens Ins. Co. of America		⊖	◒	6	Mich., Ind.
Hartford Ins. Co. of the Midwest*		○	○	9	National
New Jersey Manufacturers*		○	⊜	17	N.J., Pa.
State Automobile Mutual*		○	○	7	Midwest, Southeast
Nationwide Mutual Fire*		○	⊖	8	National
Hartford Casualty		○	○	6	National
Government Employees Ins. Co. (GEICO)*		○	○	10	National
State Farm Mutual Auto.*		○	○	9	National
State Farm Fire & Casualty*		○	○	9	National
American Family Mutual*		○	○	9	Midwest, Southwest, West
Nationwide Mutual*		○	○	9	National
Auto Club Ins. Assn.*		○	◒	9	Mich.
Continental [1]		○	○	16	National
SAFECO Ins. Co. of America		○	○	16	National
GEICO General*		○	○	11	National
Hartford Underwriters*		◒	○	14	National
Liberty Mutual Fire*		○	○	11	National
Allstate*		○	◒	11	National
Horace Mann*		◒	●	12	National
California State Auto. Assn.*		◒	○	13	Calif., Nev.
Liberty Mutual*		○	◒	13	National
Prudential Property & Casualty*		◒	●	13	National
20th Century Ins.*		●	○	21	Calif.
Travelers Indemnity		◒	◒	14	National
Allstate Indemnity*		●	◒	16	National
Farmers Ins. Exchange*		○	◒	16	Mainly west of the Mississippi
Aetna Casualty & Surety		●	◒	14	East of the Mississippi
Metropolitan Property and Casualty		●	○	16	National

[1] *Now called Continental Casualty Co.*

the agreed-upon settlement; disagreement over the dollar amount of damages, who was at fault, or what the policy covered; rude treatment; complicated procedures; and other, unspecified problems. The average company had complaints from 14 percent of surveyed policyholders. **Nonclaims problems** reflects the percentage of policyholders who said they had experienced one or more of the following: unfairly large rate increases; not enough information from the company about changes in coverage and other issues; poor service when changing coverage; difficulty contacting the company or agent; unclear explanation of coverage; late or incorrect billing; and other unspecified problems. The average company had complaints from 23 percent of surveyed policyholders. **Payment delays** is the percentage of policyholders with settled claims who said they didn't get their total payment within 30 days of filing. Policyholders received late payments 10 percent of the time from the average company. **Where sold** indicates in which states or regions a company sells its coverage. "National" means that the company sells coverage in most states. Few companies sell in all 50 states. **Who's eligible** shows which drivers the company is willing to insure. "Anyone" means any driver with a valid driver's license may apply.

Who's eligible
Anyone
Current or retired military officers
Dependents of USAA customers
Anyone
Anyone
Mainly members of some associations and employees of some companies.
Anyone
Anyone
Anyone
In most states, AARP members only
State employees; employees of N.J. Business & Industry Assn. members
Anyone
Anyone
Anyone
Government employees
Anyone
Anyone
Anyone
Anyone
Auto-club members ($37 a year to join)
Anyone
Anyone
Anyone
In most states, AARP members only
Anyone
Anyone
Anyone
Auto-club members ($41 a year to join)
Anyone
Anyone
Anyone
Mainly members of some associations
Anyone
Anyone
Anyone
Anyone

HELP FROM YOUR STATE

Every state and the District of Columbia provide telephone numbers so residents can call with auto-insurance questions and complaints. States in boldface provide auto-insurance shopping guides; most guides offer price comparisons by region or individual county. The 800 numbers are accessible only in-state.

State	Phone number	State	Phone number
Alabama*	334-269-3550	**Missouri**	800-726-7390
Alaska	907-269-7900	**Montana**	800-332-6148
Arizona	602-912-8444	**Nebraska***	402-471-2201
Arkansas	800-852-5494	**Nevada**	800-992-0900
California	800-927-4357	New Hampshire	800-852-3416
Colorado	303-894-7499	**New Jersey**	800-446-7467
Connecticut	203-297-3867	New Mexico	800-947-4722
Delaware	800-282-8611	**New York**	800-342-3736
District of Columbia	202-727-8000	North Carolina	800-662-7777
		North Dakota	800-247-0560
Florida	904-922-3132	**Ohio**	800-686-1526
Georgia	404-656-2070	Oklahoma	405-521-2828
Hawaii	808-587-1234	**Oregon**	503-378-4484
Idaho	800-721-3272	**Pennsylvania**	717-787-2317
Illinois+	217-782-4515	**Rhode Island**	401-277-2223
Indiana	800-622-4461	**South Carolina**	800-768-3467
Iowa	515-281-5705	South Dakota	605-773-3563
Kansas	800-432-2484	Tennessee	800-342-8385
Kentucky	502-564-3630	**Texas**	800-252-3439
Louisiana	800-259-5300	**Utah**	800-439-3805
Maine	207-624-8475	**Vermont**	802-828-3301
Maryland	800-492-6116	**Virginia**	800-552-7945
Massachusetts*	617-521-7777	**Washington**	800-562-6900
Michigan	517-373-0240	**West Virginia**	800-642-9004
Minnesota	800-657-3602	**Wisconsin**	800-236-8517
Mississippi	800-562-2957	**Wyoming***	800-438-5768

*Shopping guide has no price comparisons.
+ Database with some price comparisons available at some public libraries.

AUTO INSURANCE: WHAT TO BUY, HOW MUCH TO BUY, AND . . .

Type of coverage	What it pays for	Whom it compensates
Bodily injury liability Required in most states	Medical, rehabilitation, and funeral costs if a member of your household is found at fault. Also, legal costs and settlements for nonmonetary losses (pain and suffering).	The other driver; the other driver's passengers; passengers in your car; pedestrians whom you or members of your household injure.
Property-damage liability Required in most states	Repair and replacement of vehicles and any other property you or members of your household damage in an accident.	Owners of the damaged property who are not members of your household.
Medical-payments coverage; also called "med pay" Usually optional	Medical, rehabilitation, and some funeral costs. Also pays limited compensation for services needed during convalescence.	Your household members, regardless of fault; passengers with insufficient health insurance. (They could also collect under bodily injury liability.) Household members injured by a motor vehicle as pedestrians.
Personal-injury protection Mandatory in states with no-fault insurance; optional in some others	A broader form of med pay, PIP pays medical and funeral costs; also a portion of lost wages and the costs of in-home assistance, regardless of fault.	You and members of your household.
Uninsured- and underinsured-motorist coverage Mandatory in many states	Medical costs, rehabilitation, funeral costs, and/or losses from pain and suffering resulting from an accident caused by a hit-and-run driver, or by a driver without insurance or without enough insurance.	You and members of your household, while riding in a car, as bicyclists, or as pedestrians.
Collision Optional	Repair of auto damaged in a collision or rollover, regardless of fault. Reimburses car's market value—minus the deductible—when car is totaled.	You and members of your household.
Comprehensive Optional	Repair of auto damage from windstorms, flood, fire, vandalism, and some other events. Reimburses market value of car or car parts—minus the deductible—after a theft.	You and members of your household.
Other, optional coverages		
Glass breakage	Covers comprehensive deductible when cracked glass needs replacement.	You and members of your household.
Rental reimbursement	Car rental while your car is being fixed after an accident.	You and members of your household.
Towing	Towing after an accident or if a car breaks down.	You and members of your household.
Uninsured-motorist property damage	UMPD pays for damage to your property by someone without insurance, or without enough insurance to pay your costs.	You and members of your household.

The choices	We recommend
Coverage limits can be as low as your state minimum requirement and as high as $500,000 per person and $1 million per accident.	If you have a home, bank accounts, and a reasonably well-paying job, buy at least $100,000 per person, $300,000 per accident. Buy the minimum required by your state only if you have few assets and a low-paying job.
You can buy various limits, from the state minimums to $100,000.	At least $50,000 on each car. State minimum requirements—as low as $5000—often won't cover repairs to, or replacement of, a lot of cars today.
For a few dollars a year, you can buy coverage in increments of $1000 or $5000, up to $25,000. There's no deductible.	At most, $5000 per car for people with good health insurance. Your health plan probably covers you and your household already. If you aren't covered elsewhere—or have huge health-insurance copayments and deductibles—you may want to buy more to cover what your health insurance won't cover.
A basic coverage is required, usually with upper limits. You may be able to buy more. In some states, PIP coverage includes a deductible.	If you have good health, life, and disability coverage, buy only state minimum requirement.
Limits similar to those of bodily injury liability. Most states say you can't buy more of this coverage than you buy of liability insurance.	In densely populated states where lots of people drive uninsured, this coverage is essential. Buy at least $100,000 per person and $300,000 per accident, where such limits are offered.
Deductibles range from $50 to $2500 per accident. Higher deductibles cost less.	At least a $250 deductible. Consider dropping entirely on low- and midprice cars five or more years old.
Deductibles range from $0 to $2500. Higher deductibles cost less. Some insurers won't offer deductibles higher than a certain amount.	At least a $250 deductible. Consider dropping entirely on low- and midprice cars five or more years old.
Usually costs 15 to 20 percent of the comprehensive premium, with no deductible.	Where offered, skip this coverage if it's more than a few dollars a year.
Typically $15 to $25 a year. Pays about $15 per day for up to 30 days.	Buy this if you have only one car and no alternative transportation.
One available coverage, typically pays up to $50 per tow. Costs about $5 per car per year.	Join an auto club that offers towing among its services. You'll get better value.
UMPD has no deductible and is far cheaper than collision because it covers less.	Where offered, buy this only if you don't have collision.

. . . HOW TO SAVE

After you determine what coverage you need and compare prices among companies that provide the best service (see Ratings), ask for applicable discounts. Some may already be included in the premium.

- Auto/homeowners package: Both policies must be with the same company.
- Multicar: Policy must include at least two cars.
- Good driver/renewal: No claims or tickets for at least 36 months.
- Passive restraints: Automatic safety belts, air bags, or both.
- Antilock brakes.
- Antitheft devices: An approved device can be installed before or after the car's purchase.

For parents of teenage drivers:

If your teenagers don't own cars, name them on your policy as occasional operators of your least-expensive cars. If they do own cars, cover them under your policy; otherwise, they will most likely go into the very costly state high-risk pool. Some people put their teenagers who own their own cars on separate insurance policies to shield themselves from liability. But lawyers we consulted say that parents might still be held liable in some states. More tactics:

- Check into discounts. Driver's education could qualify; so could a good academic record.
- If the young driver goes to school more than 100 miles away—without a car—another discount may apply.

Young singles on their own:

Avoid performance or "turbo" cars. A turbo engine can add more than 10 percent to your premium.

- Be aware that if a roommate has had tickets or accidents, your insurance rates could be affected, even if you never lend out your car.
- Tie the knot: Married males under 30 pay the same premiums as older drivers.

Older people:

If you're 50 or older, take a defensive-driving course that's approved by your state motor-vehicle department; completion may earn you a 5- to 15-percent discount off most coverages. In some states, discounts are available for all drivers. (You may also be able to reduce your motor-vehicle points.)

Travelers:

If your policy covers collision, reject the costly collision-damage waiver when you rent a car. (Your credit-card company may also provide that coverage free.)

- If you don't own a car but rent a lot, consider a nonowner liability policy for $200 to $300 a year.
- If you'll be away a long time without your car, drop collision and liability for that period. Your state may require you to garage the car and surrender the license plates, however.

Commuters:

If you drive a just few miles to public transportation, ask for a mileage discount. If you carpool, check for yet another discount.

cense-plate numbers and insurance-identification numbers. Photograph the damage. Copy all paperwork. And keep track of accident-related expenses—lost wages, telephone bills, rental-car payments—for later reimbursement.

Soon after you call the insurer, an adjuster or appraiser will call to see your car at home or in the shop. Don't authorize repairs until the car is inspected, or you could find yourself footing the bill.

If the other driver was clearly at fault in an accident that damaged property only, you might be able to retrieve your collision deductible. Ask your insurance company to go after the other driver's company for reimbursement.

Recommendations

Look first to the direct writers and exclusive-agency companies from our survey. In the Ratings, those insurers have asterisks after their names. The high-rated ones are likely to offer very good service at competitive prices. You can find their phone numbers in the Yellow Pages or through the 800 operator.

To identify low-priced companies, obtain a copy of your state's auto-insurance price comparison, where available. For more quotes, call a handful of agents and brokers recommended by friends.

When you call insurers or their representatives, remember to ask for the discounts mentioned on page 41. Try to obtain quotes from at least three companies. Then check our Ratings to see which of the less expensive companies rated highest for service.

7

CHOOSING THE RIGHT OPTIONS

Yesterday's luxury option often becomes today's standard equipment: Many 1996 models come with items once considered deluxe. Air-conditioning and automatic transmission, for instance, are part of the deal for most cars these days. But you'll still have to pay extra for many of the newest features—if you decide they're worth it.

Options are sold two ways: one by one, with a price for each, or as part of a package ("Preferred Equipment Group"). Packages can be good deals if you want most of the items. On some imported cars, desirable options like antilock brakes are available in theory but in practice come only on cars equipped with expensive frills such as leather seats.

Here's a guide to options available today. ✓ indicates a recommended option—one that we think adds significantly to safety or comfort and convenience.

Transmission • engine

Automatic transmission. Standard in most vehicles; costs up to $1450 as an option. Reduces driver fatigue in traffic. Overdrive gear and lockup torque converter improve fuel economy. Today's automatics are practical even with a small engine. Some models now have a 5-speed automatic. **Recommendation:** Manual transmissions usually deliver better fuel economy, but automatics are much easier to drive.

Optional engine. Getting more horsepower adds $110 to $1425. A larger engine gives you more power and better acceleration, of course, and usually less noise at highway speeds, but typically worsens fuel economy. May be available only with other equipment upgrades. **Recommendation:** Most base engines are adequate in passenger cars. Light trucks, minivans, and sport-utility vehicles may benefit, especially for trailer-towing.

Brakes • drive train • suspension

✓ **Antilock brakes.** Standard in many vehicles, $500 to $1160 if an option. Rapid on-off pulsing of the brakes lets you maintain control during hard stops and stop shorter on slippery roads. To use, don't pump the brakes, just stomp and steer. **Recommendation:** Highly recommended safety item.

✓ **Traction control.** Standard on some cars, $175 to $1950 as an option. Improves traction and directional stability on slippery roads, though not as effectively as all-wheel drive. Sophisticated systems work at all speeds; others, typically, below 25 mph. **Recommendation:** Worthwhile, especially in rear-wheel-drive cars.

All-wheel drive. Costs $1000 to $3890 where it's not standard. Greatly improves traction and directional stability in snow and mud. Full-time all-wheel drive, which requires no driver action to engage, also improves handling on dry roads. Selectable all-wheel drive is almost as easy to use. Part-time four-wheel drive can't be used on dry roads. **Recommendation:** Makes a vehicle more sure-footed but reduces fuel economy, and it's costly to repair.

Limited-slip differential. $95 to $505. Improves traction on slippery roads, but can cause the driving wheels to slip to the side. **Recommendation:** Traction control or all-wheel drive does the job better.

Adjustable ride control. $100 to $2200. Theoretically lets you tailor the ride and handling to driving conditions. **Recommendation:** More gimmick than benefit.

Automatic level control. $175 to $910. Adjusts height of rear suspension to keep car level regardless of load. **Recommendation:** Useful if you often carry a full load or tow a trailer.

Air bags • cruise control • seats

✓ **Air bags.** Standard in all cars and most other passenger vehicles, especially for driver's side; $400 as an option on a few trucks. Markedly reduces chances of serious injury or death in frontal crash, though safety belts are still needed for full protection. **Recommendation:** A must for both front seats.

✓ **Adjustable steering column.** $130 to $235. Lets you position steering wheel comfortably; eases access to driver's seat. Some have power tilt and telescoping and a memory feature. **Recommendation:** Especially useful for cars with more than one driver.

Cruise control. $175 to $395. Helps you stay within speed limit; may reduce driver fatigue and improve fuel economy. But can lull the driver into inattention. Practical only where traffic is light. **Recommendation:** Best for those who do a lot of long-distance driving.

Power seat. $175 to $955. Adjustable for comfort and driver visibility. Convenience of controls varies. Some cars also have power for the front passenger seat. Memory feature remembers settings for several drivers. **Recommendation:** A big help in cars with low front seats.

Leather upholstery. $490 to $1675. Looks and feels luxurious, but is often slippery and clammy. Without a seat heater ($225 to $580 additional), leather feels cold in winter. **Recommendation:** Durable and easier to clean than cloth, but an indulgence.

Windows • locks • mirrors

✓ **Rear-window defroster.** $70 to $330, but standard in most cars. Keeps the rear window clear of fog, frost, and snow. **Recommendation:** Worth getting.

✓ **Rear-window wiper/washer.** $120 to $280, but standard in many vehicles. Clears grime from rear window of wagons, hatchbacks, sport-utility vehicles, and vans. **Recommendation:** Worthwhile for those vehicles.

✓ **Central locking system.** $25 to $440. Lets you lock and unlock all doors at once, inside or out, with a remote control. Variations abound. The best design depends on your comfort level where you travel. Possible nuisances: automatic systems that don't let you open your door from inside; systems that automatically unlock all the doors when the car is put in Park (as on many General Motors cars). **Recommendation:** A convenience that soon can seem indispensable; especially worthwhile where security is a concern.

✓ **Power mirrors.** $70 to $140. More than a convenience, they contribute to safety by making the mirrors easy to adjust. **Recommendation:** Especially useful for cars with more than one driver.

Power windows. $250 to $330. Some give you one-touch lowering of driver's window and driver's control of all windows. Lock-out feature reduces hazard to children. Switches can be confusing and hard to find at night. **Recommendation:** An indulgence, perhaps, but after you've lived with power, five turns of a window crank can seem a burden.

Air-conditioning • phone • sound system

✓ **Air-conditioning.** $520 to $1950, but standard on many vehicles. Add $100 to $200 for automatic temperature control. Improves comfort, reduces outside noise, and prevents window fogging year-round. Reduces fuel economy, particularly in stop-and-go traffic. Costly to repair. **Recommendation:** A must in the South and Southwest, and very nice anywhere. Just try to sell a used car without it.

Theft-deterrent system. $100 to $585 gets you some combination of alarms, flashing lights, honking horns, and autosound systems that becomes useless if yanked loose. May deter theft and reduce your insurance rates, but false alarms disturb the neighbors; alarms are widely ignored in most cities. **Recommendation:** Worthwhile, but cheaper ones are available as aftermarket devices.

Autosound system. $25 to $2075, depending on components and features. CD or tape player lets you listen to what you like. The best systems approach room acoustics. But the costlier the system, the more tempting to thieves. **Recommendation:** Strictly a matter of personal preference.

Cellular phone. $650 to $950. Lets you call police, ambulance, or tow truck—or just tell someone you'll be late. Hands-free operation is preferable while driving. Monthly and per-call charges are dropping. **Recommendation:** Regular cellular phones will work, but those designed specially for cars allow hands-free use. Some models come prewired for them.

Electronic instrument-panel display. $245 to $490. Large digital speedometer may be easy to read. But often, these designs are more confusing than analog versions. **Recommendation:** A fix for something not broken.

Trip computer/vehicle monitor. $200 to $440; often packaged with electronic instrument-panel display. This gadget displays fuel use, miles to empty, and such. The monitor may provide warnings of a burned-out taillight, needed engine service, etc. **Recommendation:** Expensive replacement for pencil and paper. When a bulb burns out, display goes blank.

Child seat • sunroof • spare

Integrated child seat. $100 to $250. More expensive than many seats sold separately, but no fumbling or difficulty installing it correctly. When not deployed, it may reduce comfort for passenger in its place. **Recommendation:** Worthwhile for families with small children.

Sunroof/moon roof. $350 to $1700. Generally, a sunroof lets light in only when open; a moon roof is like a window (with shade) in the roof. Improves ventilation, brightens the interior. Usually reduces headroom. Noisy when open. **Recommendation:** Go ahead, but check headroom.

Conventional spare. $80 to $260. Adds a fifth (full-size) tire to the rotation. Harder to handle than limited-service spare, but no speed or distance restriction. **Recommendation:** Worthwhile if there's room in the trunk, but not very common anymore.

Not worth the money

Extended-service contract. Cost varies. Extends manufacturer's warranty, which typically runs for three or four years. **Recommendation:** May be worthwhile for an unreliable model—but you wouldn't want to buy one of those anyway.

Dealer "packs," or add-ons. Cost varies. Packs include dealer-installed rustproofing, pinstripes, paint and upholstery preservatives, etc. At best, they're unnecessary or no better than aftermarket products you apply yourself. Improperly applied rustproofing can hasten corrosion. **Recommendation:** A waste of money.

8

HOW CONSUMER REPORTS TESTS CARS

One of the unique and important aspects of our auto-testing program is how we get the cars we test. Unlike other cars magazines, we buy all our cars anonymously from dealers, just as you would. That way, we're sure of getting a typical production model rather than a borrowed "press car" carefully prepared by the manufacturer.

We report on a group of cars nearly every month—more than 40 cars each year. They include mostly practical family sedans, with a smattering of luxury cars, sporty coupes, pickup trucks, sport-utility vehicles, and vans.

Our auto engineers and other staffers take turns using each car for everyday driving until the car is broken in. Then our engineers and technicians put the cars through several thousand miles of formal tests at our test facility in East Haddam, Connecticut, and on public roads, to find out things you couldn't possibly learn during a brief test drive at the dealership. The combined results of that research form the basis of our reports.

We group our findings into four basic categories: performance, comfort, convenience, and fuel economy. But safety is a central theme running throughout all our tests.

One aspect of safety is a car's ability to protect its occupants in a crash. To inform you about that, we interpret government crash-test results and note the availability of vital safety equipment such as air bags and proper safety belts.

Another aspect of safety is a car's ability to avoid a crash altogether—a composite of elements such as acceleration, handling, braking, and cockpit design. A poor driving position, for example, is not only uncomfortable; it can also cause premature fatigue, reducing your concentration and preventing you from reacting quickly and effectively in an emergency. Tall drivers should have room to stretch out, and short drivers should be able to see the road without craning. We check whether the seat and steering column provide sufficient adjustment for a comfortable reach to the steering wheel and pedals, and whether all controls are easy to use and all displays are easy to see.

A complete physical

To make sure each car is a typical sample, we inspect its vital parts as soon as we take delivery. Using a 50-item checklist, we go over the fluid levels, engine tuning, headlight aim, and much more to make sure they're within the manufacturer's specifications. If we find a major defect, we let the dealer repair it. After the car is broken in, we inspect it again.

Changing places

Our engineers drive each group of cars in convoy five times around a 30-mile course, switching cars after each lap. As they drive over the smooth highways and rutted rural roads, they tape-record their judgments of ride, handling, seat comfort, driving position, noise, and other factors.

Dropping the anchor

We run our braking tests on both wet and dry pavement. Clearly, the shorter the stop, the better. But stops should also be straight, without swerving, even in our test where the pavement is more slippery on one side of the car than on the other. Cars with antilock brakes enjoy a considerable advantage in all our wet-pavement braking tests. One of our tests consists of ten consecutive stops from 60 mph to check the brakes' resistance to "fade"—overheating and loss of effectiveness—which might occur during continuous hard braking.

Silence is golden

Our engineers drive each car at specified speeds on smooth and coarse pavement while a tape recorder registers the noise level. We also record the noise level during full-throttle acceleration. Our audio engineers then analyze the tape in our electronics lab. In addition, we factor in our test drivers' subjective judgments about the intensity and quality of the noise. A noisy car is not only unpleasant; it can cause driver fatigue and dangerous lapses in judgment.

How fast?

A car should have enough power to merge safely onto a highway, keep up with traffic on uphill stretches, and pass safely on a two-lane road. A car's speedometer is rarely dead-on accurate, so we use sophisticated electronic test gear during our acceleration runs—a computer inside the car to record the test data on a tape, and an electronic sensor that scans the pavement with a beam of light. The sensor provides precise data on the car's speed, elapsed time, and distance traveled.

Pushing the limits

Our handling tests at the track tell us not only how quickly a car can negotiate a sharp curve or make a fast lane change, but also how the car behaves when pressed beyond its cornering ability. Emergency handling becomes critically important if you have to swerve around a child who runs out from between parked cars, or if you misjudge a curve and enter it too quickly. A "forgiving" car responds controllably and predictably to a typical driver's instinctive actions, while a "twitchy" car may require the skill and reflexes of a seasoned test driver.

9

SUMMARY JUDGMENTS OF THE 1996 CARS

Years ago, everyone waited eagerly each fall for the new-car introductions. To build up the excitement, car transporters unloaded in the dead of night, and dealers veiled their showroom windows.

But those were simpler times. Now, automakers introduce their new models throughout the year, preview them on TV months in advance, and sell them as soon as they roll off the truck. That's because the auto industry has become too competitive for traditional model cycles. The gestation period for a new car, from drawing board to production line, has dropped from five or six years to three, and automakers must time their introductions to use their production capacity most efficiently. Also, advertising has become sophisticated enough to draw car buyers all year long.

Planned obsolescence

The result hasn't been good for consumers. In fact, buying a car has become even more confusing and nerve-racking than ever before.

Nowadays, even if you buy a brand-new car as soon as it's introduced, it may become obsolescent—last year's used car—within weeks. The barely changed 1997 *Buick LeSabre*, for instance, was introduced this past January, leaving the 1996 version a scant few months of life. The 1997 *Ford F-150* pickup truck, new from the ground up, is already selling alongside the 1996 model. The 1997 *Acura RL*, which replaces the *Legend*, is also in the showrooms, as is the new *Acura CL*. The 1997 *Jeep Wrangler* and 1997 replacements for the aging *Ford Escort* and *Mercury Tracer* should be out soon.

Augmenting this proliferation of new models is an age-old marketing technique called "rebadging"—pinning a new name on an existing model. Carmakers use rebadging as a quick way to build their model lineup without going through the expensive and time-consuming process of designing and testing a new product.

In 1994, for example, Honda found itself without an entry in the hot sport-utility-vehicle market. Rather than take the time to design and develop its own sport-utility vehicle (SUV), Honda made a deal with Isuzu: It created the *Honda Passport* simply by pinning its own badge on the *Isuzu Rodeo*.

The problem is that people who buy a *Passport* on the strength of Honda's reputation for quality and reliability will actually be getting an *Isuzu* model that hasn't been as reliable as most *Honda* models. This year, rebadging also turned the *Isuzu Trooper* into the *Acura SLX*, as well as the *Honda Odyssey* into the *Isuzu Oasis*.

A variation on that theme includes models that spin off other models from the same maker. The *Infiniti I30*, for example, is a gussied-up *Nissan Maxima* at a higher price. (Infiniti is Nissan's prestige line.) Under its skin, the *Lexus ES300* looks a lot like the *Toyota Camry*, and the pricey *Toyota Land Cruiser* is much like the even pricier *Lexus LX450*. (Lexus is Toyota's prestige line.)

Domestic automakers have been doing the same thing for years. Most *Chryslers*, *Dodges*, and *Plymouths* are basically the same, as are corresponding *Ford* and *Mercury* models—although they may differ in equipment and price. General Motors, too, has had more than its share of *Buicks*, *Chevrolets*, *Oldsmobiles*, and *Pontiacs* that are similar under the skin.

Knowing which models are similar can expand your options. If you can't get a good deal on a *Dodge Caravan*, for example, you can shop for the similar *Plymouth Voyager*.

Trucks come on strong

Perhaps the hottest automotive news remains the superheated market for sport-utility vehicles—although we often wonder why. Compared with sedans, SUVs are clumsy and hard to get into, and they tend to guzzle fuel (see box on page 48). But they offer a large cargo area, a commanding view of the road, and the all-weather capability of four-wheel drive. For more and more car buyers, the benefits of an SUV seem to outweigh the drawbacks.

SUV lineups are expanding both up and down the price scale. Several luxury automakers—Infiniti, Lincoln, Mercedes-Benz—are introducing new models in the $40,000-to-$50,000 range. At the same time, small new models from Toyota and Suzuki have joined the *Geo* and basic *Jeep* models in the under-$20,000 range. The big, expensive SUVs tend to give you little comfort at a high price, whereas the inexpensive little ones can become really unpleasant on anything more than a short trip.

Pickup trucks are another rapidly growing segment of the car market—although, again, they're not the right choice for everyone. So far, Ford's full-sized F-Series pickup has been the best-selling vehicle of any type, whether car or truck. Our preliminary glimpse of the new 1997 model leaves us impressed. The *Ford* has become even more carlike than before, to attract more buyers looking for a workhorse replacement for their car or minivan.

In this book we've added pickups

to our roundup. And in the coming months, we plan to test even more pickups and SUVs.

The best of the best

Much of the latest crop of autos and light trucks appears to be competent and sophisticated—and, arguably, the safest ever. But several models deserve special mention. Here are our picks of the very best in five basic categories:

Best family sedan

For competent family transportation at a moderate price, don't look any further than the *Toyota Camry* (see page 130). In overall performance, it ranks with cars costing thousands more. The *Camry* is also available in a coupe and wagon (see page 131). And it's been exceptionally reliable for years.

Best inexpensive car

That has to be the new *Honda Civic* (see page 59), a far more polished design than you'd expect for the price. It matches the very best small cars in ride, seating comfort, and fuel economy. And it has been very reliable.

Best sport-utility vehicle

The *Ford Explorer* (see page 156) outscores its competition mainly because it's the least trucklike. Its interior is roomy and versatile, and it offers full-time selectable four-wheel drive as an option.

Highest-mileage car

Among cars with a gasoline engine, the 1996 *Toyota Tercel* (see page 69) with a manual four-speed transmission recorded the best fuel economy in our recent tests: about 39 mpg, overall. If the highest possible mileage is your ultimate goal, then the *Volkswagen Golf* with the new direct-injection TDi diesel engine is the car of choice. But diesels aren't for everyone. They are noisier, idle roughly, and are not very performance-oriented.

Most fun to drive

That depends on your definition of fun. If you enjoy driving a car that's small and nimble, with quick and accurate steering, a responsive and throaty engine, and a precise manual shifter, it's easy to fall in love with the two-seater *Mazda MX-5 Miata* (see page 80). Some of our test-drivers thought the small new *BMW 318ti* hatchback was also fun to drive.

Best regardless of price

The luxurious and meticulously finished *Mercedes-Benz* E-Class, now represented by the redesigned *E320*, wins out. Its predecessor, tested in 1994

THE TROUBLE WITH SUVS

Scientists are reaching a consensus that the Earth is warming and that human activities are part of the cause. Atmospheric levels of carbon dioxide are increasing—and more CO_2 means the atmosphere will retain more of the sun's energy. And despite growing concern over global warming, CO_2 emissions are continuing to increase. Some of America's favorite vehicles—sport-utility vehicles (SUVs) and other light trucks—are partly to blame.

SUVs and trucks are selling briskly. But these vehicles, with their big, gas-guzzling engines, all burn more fuel than comparable passenger cars. The more fuel a vehicle burns, the more CO_2 it produces. That's largely why vehicle emissions now account for a third of all CO_2 emissions, and why they are growing at a faster rate than any other source.

The popularity of SUVs also explains why the average fuel economy of U.S. vehicles has declined steadily since 1987. That lower fuel economy affects your pocketbook, too. If you buy, say, a *Ford Explorer* over a *Ford Taurus*, you can expect to pay nearly 30 percent more each year for fuel—$1100 versus $850 in 15,000 miles of typical driving.

The United States has pledged to reduce carbon-dioxide emissions to 1990 levels by the end of this decade. Fulfilling that pledge will largely depend on individual choices—including the choice of what to drive. SUVs have qualities that many people want: four-wheel drive, lots of cargo room, and plenty of space for passengers. But they also tend to handle ponderously and deliver a bouncy ride. By contrast, minivans offer many of the same good qualities SUVs do, plus slightly better fuel economy; they may well be a better choice.

Here comes trouble: The top graph at the right shows how sales of light trucks (including SUVs) have climbed, at the expense of passenger cars. The second graph shows the effect of booming truck sales on fuel economy. In short, vehicles in the United States are burning more fuel and spewing more carbon dioxide into the atmosphere.

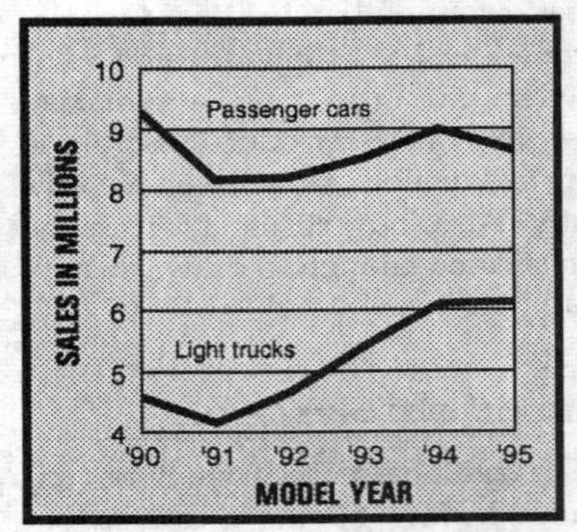

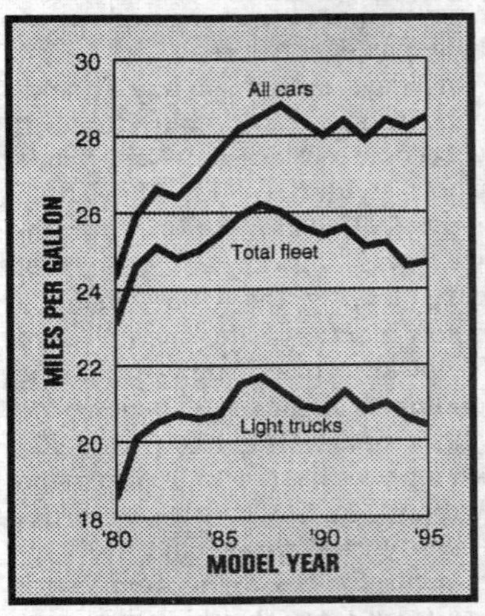

scored highest of any car in our tests—mainly because of its ability to balance several often-conflicting demands. It accelerated splendidly without using too much fuel. And it combined responsive handling with a quiet and composed ride. Its base price has been lowered to $43,500. But even so, with many fine cars available for half as much, few people will find the *E320* worth its high cost.

Cars of all sizes

On the pages that follow we list over 100 models, divided into eight groups, as discussed below. Within each group the cars are listed in alphabetical order.

Small Cars

Generally the cheapest to buy and run, with the most nimble handling, but some also provide only marginal room, comfort, and crash-resistance. Typically, the rear seat is suitable for occasional short-term use at best, and the ride is relatively harsh.

Sports/Sporty Cars

Specialized and performance oriented two-door versions of small and compact cars.

Compact Cars

Practical transportation for a small family.

Midsize Cars

Larger coupes and sedans, offering more room than most compact cars for about the same money.

Large Cars

The largest domestic models, most having a full six-passenger capacity.

Minivans

A roomier alternative to the nearly extinct station wagon.

Sport-Utility Vehicles

Originally clones of the military's jeep, designed for off-road driving, but increasingly used as sporty runabouts and family wagons.

Pickup Trucks

They have been steadily migrating from farms and contractors' shops to city streets and suburban driveways. Pickup trucks are best when carrying truly bulky items, such as an upright refrigerator, or messy loads like loose mulch, firewood, or compost.

About the reports

We provide detailed reports and Ratings for cars we've tested recently. Although the tested car may be a model from an earlier year, a car reported on in detail is essentially the same as the corresponding 1996 model. Other cars are given brief paragraphs, either because we haven't tested the car or because our test findings may no longer be valid. *Note:* The date of original publication appears at the end of each detailed report because some 1996 models may have slightly different fuel economy and engine behavior from the tested car. Predicted reliability for all cars is based on our analysis of the responses to CU's 1995 Annual Questionnaire, the complete results of which are shown in the Frequency-of-Repair charts.

The cars that we recommend are marked with a ☑. Those cars should perform well and be relatively trouble-free, we believe. Consider those models first. Not all recommended models performed equally well in our tests, but all should be better than average in their size and price class, and all should be at least reasonably reliable. A make or model that's described in a brief paragraph but that is not marked isn't necessarily a poor performer. We simply may not have any recent experience with that model, or it may have a poor reliability record.

Price range is the sticker price from the cheapest model with no options to the most expensive model trim line with automatic transmission and air-conditioning. Prices are current as of February 1, 1996. Note, however, that many automakers have had price increases since then, while the *New Car Buying Guide* was being prepared for publication.

Cost factor notes the approximate percentage of the sticker price that is the dealer's cost; by multiplying the sticker price by the cost factor, you can figure about how much the dealer paid and how much room there is left for bargaining.

For precise information on both list price and dealer's cost for the basic car and for every available option, we recommend that you order a printout from our New Car Price Service (see inside back cover) for those cars you expect to shop for seriously.

Depreciation is our judgment of how well a new model will keep its value. It's based on the difference between a model's original sticker price and its resale value over the past three years. (Consequently, our depreciation judgment is not available for models that have been around for less than three years.)

As automotive design has improved from year to year, we have made our Ratings criteria more and more demanding to keep pace. In January 1993, we made some changes in the way we score the vehicles we test. To make the reports in this book comparable to one another, we've updated earlier auto tests to reflect our new scoring methods. Thus, test results that would have earned a ⊜ in previous years might now earn only a ○ or a ◒. In addition, we've added, eliminated, combined, and redefined certain factors.

We continue to use an absolute scale to score all types of vehicles, using the same standards for all, because we believe that all vehicles licensed for use as family transportation on public roads should perform competently in our most important tests.

Remember, the five-point Ratings scale for the test reports ranges from excellent ⊜ to very good ⊖ to good ○ to fair ◒ to poor ●. The five-point Ratings scale for predicted reliability ranges from much better than average ⊜ to better than average ⊖ to average ○ to worse than average ◒ to much worse than average ●.

SMALL CARS

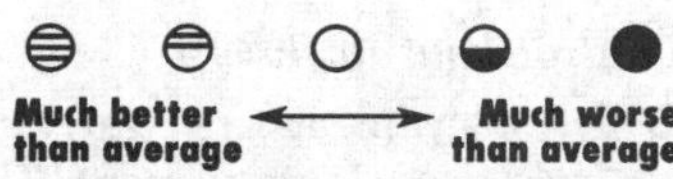

With few exceptions, these models provide transportation on a budget. Typical sticker prices for small cars range from $8000 to $12,000; some sporty versions run more. These models serve nicely as second cars or for running errands. Their small dimensions and light weight make them maneuverable in tight spots and frugal with fuel. But most are cramped inside, and their ride is, for the most part, noisy and harsh. Many claim seating accommodations for five—and in almost every case that's overoptimistic. Generally, even two adults are crowded in the rear seat and will be uncomfortable on a long drive.

Recommended models of small cars are the *Acura Integra*, the *Chevrolet Cavalier/Pontiac Sunbird*, the *Geo Prizm/Toyota Corolla*, the *Honda Civic*, the *Nissan Sentra*, the *Mazda Protegé*, and the *Subaru Impreza*.

Acura Integra LS ✓

***Price range:** $16,460–$20,980*
***Cost factor:** 88%*
Depreciation: ⊖

Overview

An impressive mix of performance and practicality. Seating is tight, but the ride and handling are competitive.

Acceleration

⊖ The 1.8-liter Four revs freely and performs briskly. The VTEC Four in the *GS-R* version would provide even more power without a significant loss of fuel economy, but it requires Premium fuel.

Transmission

⊜ The five-speed manual shifts crisply, and its gearing strikes a good balance between performance and economy. A four-speed automatic is optional except in *GS-R* versions.

Economy

⊖ Should average about 30 mpg on Regular fuel.

Routine handling

⊜ The sedan feels light and agile on country lanes, but the body leans noticeably in turns. The car maintains its composure well in ripply curves, and the steering is accurate and quick, although a little light.

Emergency handling

⊖ The *Integra* plows a bit when pressed hard; lifting off the accelerator quickly tightens the car's path. The car threaded through our avoidance maneuver nimbly, but mediocre tire grip limited the speed it could attain.

Braking

○ Stops from 60 mph took 142 feet on dry pavement, a long 170 feet on wet pavement. Initially, the *Integra* veered slightly in our wet divided-pavement test, but then it quickly straightened out.

Ride, normal load

⊖ The supple suspension soaks up broken pavement, transmitting only muted kicks. It controls pitching even on pavement heaves.

Ride, full load

⊖ Ride is hardly affected.

Noise

○ Road noise is intrusive, as is engine noise at high revs.

Driving position

⊖ Despite low seats that lack a height adjuster, even very short drivers can see clearly over the hood. The clutch pedal has a long travel; short-legged drivers who moved the seat forward found that their knees bumped the steering column when they operated the pedals. Six-footers will find adequate legroom and ample headroom in front.

Front seating

⊖ Good, firm support.

Rear seating

◒ The rear seat barely holds two six-footers, and three average-size men sitting abreast are a crowd. Headroom and toe space are both tight.

Access

○ Getting in and out is difficult because the frameless windows curve in and the door opening is awkwardly shaped.

Climate system

⊖ The powerful system delivers lots of heated or cooled air, but the recessed temperature slide and fan switch are awkward to grasp.

Controls and displays

⊖ The instruments are clear, but some controls need improvement. The two tiny horn buttons, on the spokes of the steering wheel, are hard to find in a hurry; we prefer a large horn control in the hub of the steering wheel. Also, the switch for the fog lights is hidden at the rear of the center console.

Trunk

○ We were able to pack four Pullman cases and one weekend bag, or a folded wheelchair, with room left over. The one-piece rear seatback can fold down to expand the trunk. The compact spare leaves ample room in its well for stashing small articles. Acura recommends a towing limit of 1000 pounds.

Safety

The upper anchor on the front safety belts is adjustable for comfort. The rear three-point belts are difficult to buckle and require a locking clip to secure a child seat. Our bumper-basher damaged both bumpers. Repair estimates: $840 front, $700 rear.

In government crash tests, the driver fared better than the passenger.

Predicted reliability

⊜ The *Integra* has an excellent reliability record.

Based on a November 1994 report.

Chevrolet Cavalier LS ✓

Price range: $10,500–$17,500
Cost factor: 93%
Depreciation: NA

Overview

This new design is a vast improvement over the unfavorable original, and offers proof that General Motors—Detroit's sleeping giant—can get a car right if it tries.

Acceleration

○ The 2.2–liter Four provides a competent mix of Acceleration and fuel economy. It isn't as smooth, however, as the engines in the *Mazda Protegé* and *Nissan Sentra*.

Transmission

⊖ The smooth-shifting three-speed automatic transmission includes a locking torque converter, so it performs much like a four-speed. A five-speed manual transmission is standard on the base and *Z24*, but not available in the *LS*.

Economy

⊖ Respectable fuel economy—about 26 mpg overall.

Routine handling

⊖ The *Cavalier's* steering is fairly quick. There was noticeable body roll when cornering in routine driving, even more in hard test-track turns.

Emergency handling

○ The car showed a mild tendency to plow ahead. The *Cavalier's* tail wagged when we forced the car through our avoidance maneuvers, but that was easy to control.

Braking

⊖ Stopping distances were quite short on a dry track, rather long on a wet one. The car stopped straight in our wet split-surface tests. The brake pedal, too sensitive in ordinary stops, requires increased effort in a series of hard stops.

Ride, normal load

○ Not bad for a small sedan: compliant on most roads, rising and falling choppily on bumpy back roads.

Ride, full load

○ A full load makes the ride feel firmer and, for rear-seat riders, bouncy.

Noise

○ The *Cavalier* is relatively quiet inside, but the engine is noisy when revved.

Driving position

⊖ Even without height adjustable seats, our shortest driver could see over the hood. Tall drivers had too little legroom.

Front seating

⊖ The *Cavalier* offers reasonable accommodations, as small cars go. The front seats feel resilient and comfortable for a while. But a long drive may leave its mark in your lower back and shoulders. The aforementioned height adjustment for the front seats is sorely missed.

Rear seating

○ The rear bench seat accommodates three tall passengers, but not very comfortably. The cabin narrows substantially at the top, so the heads of passengers sitting near the doors graze the roof pillars.

Access

○ The low seats and sloping roof line conspire to make access more clumsy than it should be, but at least the doors open fairly wide.

Climate system

⊜ The climate system works well. The air conditioner switches on automatically in Defrost to clear windows on steamy days. The rear defroster concentrates extra heat in the center, so that part of the window clears very quickly.

Controls and displays

⊜ All controls are clearly labeled and easy to use. The steering wheel has a height adjustment.

Trunk

○ The trunk holds four Pullman cases and one weekend bag, or a folded wheelchair, with room left over. The folding rear seatback makes room for more. (Neither the seatback nor the remote trunk release, standard in the *LS*, can be locked.) Small objects fit around the compact spare that stows under the floor. A full-size tire doesn't fit in the well. The trunk's short opening interferes with loading.

Safety

The front safety belts have an adjustable upper anchor for a comfortable fit. The rear seatback has guides to position the shoulder belts on small adults or children who are too big for a safety seat. All belts will secure a child safety seat, but some safety seats may not fit properly in the rear. The front seat's adjustable head restraints provide whiplash protection even when fully lowered. There are no rear-seat head restraints.

In our basher tests, the car's bumpers suffered what appeared to be minor cosmetic damage—a slight crack near the rear license plate. Most owners probably wouldn't bother with the repair. If they did, the $502 estimate, due to hidden damage, might change their minds.

Government crash tests showed that both driver and passenger dummies received possibly severe "injuries."

Predicted reliability

○ Expect average reliability for the *Cavalier* and similar *Pontiac Sunbird.*

Based on a June 1995 report.

Dodge Neon Highline

Price range: *$9,495–$12,700*
Cost factor: *92%*
Depreciation: *NA*

Overview

The *Neon* needs lots of improvement to join the top ranks of small sedans.

Acceleration

○ Strangely, this *Neon,* with the 2.0-liter, 132-hp Four, is considerably slower than the one we tested in 1995. The optional 150-hp Four with dual overhead camshafts doesn't feel much more responsive.

Transmission

○ The three-speed automatic is at least partly to blame for the slow acceleration; most modern automatics have four speeds. The transmission shifts smoothly enough, but the economy gearing makes the engine labor during acceleration at moderate speeds.

Economy

○ Expect to average only about 26 mpg.

Routine handling

⊖ The *Neon* handles safely but not nimbly. The tires grip well, and the body leans only moderately in corners, but the steering feels heavy and rubbery.

Emergency handling

⊖ Weaving through our avoidance maneuver was fairly easy, but the *Neon* felt bulkier than it really is.

Braking

○ Braking performance was about average, but the antilock system tends to activate prematurely.

Ride, normal load

◒ The *Neon* jitters stiffly even on smooth roads. Bumpy roads transmit hard, jerky jolts to the occupants.

Ride, full load

● A full load makes the suspension compress fully and crash and bang on every major bump.

Noise

○ The 2.0-Four sounds harsh during acceleration. The optional 150-hp Four with dual overhead camshafts is just as noisy.

Driving position

⊖ Six-foot drivers will find just enough legroom. Short drivers may wish they could sit a little higher. The height adjustment for the steering wheel, packaged with cruise control, is a worthwhile option.

Front seating

⊖ Interior space is probably the *Neon's* best feature. The small front seats are generally comfortable, although lower-back support could be better.

Rear seating

◒ Three six-footers can just fit in the rear; knee room is abundant, but toe space is tight, and the sloping roof pillars limit the outside passengers' headroom. The rear seat is too firm—downright hard in the middle. The seatback offers no side or lower-back support.

Access

○ Access front and rear is average for a small sedan.

Climate system

⊖ The climate-control system works well. Its four rotary knobs are illuminated at night. In most cars, you shut off the fan by turning the knob counterclockwise. In the *Neon,* the center position is off; you twist clockwise for more heated air, counterclockwise for more air-conditioned air.

Controls and displays

⊖ Controls and displays are fine for the most part, and the horn is where you want it, in the center of the steering wheel. The *Highline* lacks a tachometer. The headlight knob is low, and only the front windows are power-operated; the rears crank manually.

Trunk

◒ The trunk is small. The opening is short, less than ten inches front to back, but the sill is cut fairly low to ease loading. Folding the split rear seatback takes a firm tug on the two tabs. Neither the inside trunk release nor the rear seatback sections can be locked; anyone who gets into the cabin has access to the trunk.

Safety

The *Neon's* shoulder belts have adjustable upper anchors. The belts can secure a child seat without a special clip. Fully lowered, the front head restraints are too low. And they don't lock when raised, so they could be forced downward in a crash. The nonadjustable head restraints are also too low. Our bumper basher didn't damage the front or rear bumpers.

In a recent government crash test, the 1996 *Neon* did much better than the 1995 model; both the driver and passenger dummies suffered only moderate "injuries."

Predicted reliability

● According to our latest reader survey, the *Neon* had serious reliability problems in 1995, its first model year, with nearly twice the problems of the average 1995 car. The major trouble spots were body and electrical problems.

Based on a March 1996 report.

Dodge Neon Sport

Price range: $9,495–$12,500
Cost factor: 92%
Depreciation: NA

Overview

The *Neon's* power train feels crude, the brakes are so-so, and the ride is harsh and noisy. If all that doesn't dissuade you, consider the *Neon's* first-year reliability record—one of the worst in our survey of owners.

Acceleration

⊖ The optional 2.0-liter, 150-hp Four with dual overhead camshafts provides ample acceleration.

Transmission

⊖ The five-speed manual transmission doesn't shift precisely. Our *Sport* supposedly had performance-oriented gear ratios, but it was hard to tell. Still, the car is more responsive with the manual transmission than with the optional three-speed automatic.

Economy

⊖ We averaged 30 mpg, overall. The standard 2.0-liter, 132-hp Four with a single camshaft is just as noisy but less powerful.

Routine handling

⊖ The *Neon* corners fairly nimbly, with little body roll, but it doesn't feel quite as agile as a comparable *Nissan 200SX SE-R* or *VW Golf GTI*. The handling is responsive, but the steering feels heavy and rubbery.

Emergency handling

⊖ At the track, the *Neon* felt steady in sweeping turns and secure and predictable in our avoidance maneuver.

Braking

○ Stopping distances were about average in our braking tests, but the brake pedal felt a little touchy. Our car pulled slightly to the left during hard stops.

Ride, normal load

◒ The ride is jittery and choppy, even on good roads. Bumps elicit sharp jolts.

Ride, full load

◒ A full load reduces the choppiness a little but worsens the impact.

Noise

◒ Occupants endure unceasing road rumble and engine boom. At high revs, the engine sounds loud.

Driving position

⊖ The driving position suited all our testers. The seat is high enough, legroom is adequate for tall people, and even a five-footer can see well over the hood. The height of the steering wheel can be adjusted. The carpeted wheel housing makes only a so-so left footrest.

Front seating

⊖ The front seats are a bit lumpy, but they provide good support, particularly at the sides.

Rear seating

◒ The rear seat is fairly spacious, with enough knee and headroom for two tall people. Toe space under the front seats is cramped, though. Three tall people can fit, but not happily.

Access

○ A particularly narrow passage makes climbing into the rear a trial.

Climate system

⊖ The climate-control system works well, but the controls could be better. To use the air conditioner for defrosting, you must turn the fan knob from one of the heat settings all the way through the Off position to one of the air-conditioning settings. A simple On/Off switch for the air conditioner would have simplified matters.

Controls and displays

⊖ The gauges are clear, most controls are easy to operate, and the horn is in the center of the steering-wheel hub, where it belongs. The headlight knob is low and hard to see, and the ignition lock has an annoying release button for the key. Power door locks are standard. Remote keyless entry is optional.

Trunk

◒ The size of the trunk is adequate, and the split rear seatback can be folded down to provide more luggage room. A folded wheelchair can fit in the trunk.

Safety

The height of the shoulder-belt anchors isn't adjustable. The belts can secure a child safety seat without a separate clip. A built-in child seat is optional in all but the base coupe and sedan versions.

The front head restraints don't lock firmly in a raised position, but they're just high enough to protect an average-size adult when they're lowered. The rear restraints are too low. Our bumper basher caused no damage front or rear.

A 1996 *Neon* sedan did fairly well in government crash tests. The driver and passenger dummies suffered only moderate "injuries."

Predicted reliability

● The *Neon* had serious reliability problems in its first year, according to our most recent owner survey. The problem rate was more than twice the average for all 1995 models.

Based on a May 1996 report.

Eagle Summit ES

Price range: *$10,090–$13,334*
Cost factor: *95%*
Depreciation: *NA*

Overview

Bum brakes take this model out of the competitive running.

Acceleration

⊖ Accelerates briskly, but the 1.8-liter Four does not always idle smoothly.

Transmission

⊖ Five-speed manual shifts smoothly.

Economy

⊜ About 34 mpg in mixed driving.

Routine handling

⊖ Safe but not crisp. The tires squeal even during moderate cornering, and the front end tends to plow ahead in hard turns.

Emergency handling

○ Plows easily in avoidance maneuvers and then wags its tail somewhat.

Braking

●/○ (without/with antilock brakes) Without antilock brakes, the car needed 171 feet to stop from 60 mph on a dry track. On wet pavement, it skidded 244 feet—the worst performance we've seen since we started doing wet-braking tests in mid-1991. The car veered sharply and started to spin in our wet divided-pavement test. The similar *Mitsubishi Mirage* that we check-tested had antilock brakes; it stopped satisfactorily under all conditions, but it is unlikely you will find a car with antilock brakes.

Ride, normal load

○ Rides firmly and absorbs most ride motions well. Rough, patched pavement elicits stiff kicks and some choppiness. The *Summit* jitters less than the *Toyota Corolla* or *Geo Prizm* on the highway.

Ride, full load

○ Generally more pleasant.

Noise

○ Moderate noise from road and wind.

Driving position

⊖ Seat-height adjuster and optional tilt steering column help most drivers find a comfortable position. Legroom is adequate for tall drivers, and headroom is generous. Short drivers can see out well, but they may not be able to floor the clutch pedal unless they position the seat too close to the accelerator.

Front seating

⊖ Firm, generally satisfactory support. Tall people may find that the seatbacks press into their shoulders; reclining the seatbacks more than usual helps a little.

Rear seating

◓ Barely holds two six-footers. But three average-size men may feel less cramped than in some other small sedans.

Access

○ Difficult in rear because of narrow door openings.

Climate system

⊜ Versatile system quickly furnishes plenty of heated or cooled air; you must close the outboard dash vents for full airflow to the floor or windshield. A two-position Bilevel setting adjusts the airflow to favor the dash or floor vents.

Controls and displays

⊖ Major controls are easy to see and grasp, but some minor switches are either hidden or awkward to operate. The radio sits low, and it lacks contrast. The instruments are easy to read, but the speedometer is marked only in 20-mph increments.

Trunk

○ Holds four Pullman cases, or a folded wheelchair, with room left over. Folding the split rear seatback expands the trunk. Small articles fit easily in the large well surrounding the compact spare.

Safety

Buckling the rear three-point belts takes both hands—and you need a locking clip to hold a child safety seat. The center rear lap belt may not work with some child seats. The right front lap belt can secure a child seat without a clip. The bumper basher did $65 worth of damage to the front bumper, while the rear needed a total bumper replacement, estimated at $708.

Government crash test results were not available.

Predicted reliability

⊖ Above-average reliability record.

Based on an August 1993 report.

Eagle Summit Wagon

Price range: *$14,499–$16,374*
Cost factor: *92%*
Depreciation: ○

This cross between a small station wagon and a very small van is tall and boxy; it has a single sliding door and a high front seating position that offers a commanding view. The 2.4-liter Four (the engine of choice) delivers energetic acceleration. Handling, though, comes up a bit short. The ride is quiet and comfortable, and cargo space is abundant compared with that of other small wagons. The *Eagle*

Summit and *Wagon* are built by Mitsubishi.

Predicted reliability ⊖

Ford Aspire

Price range: *$8790-$9,405*
Cost factor: *94%*
Depreciation: NA

Overview

This successor to the late *Ford Festiva* feels sluggish and ungainly. At least it's stingy with fuel.

Acceleration

◒ The 1.3-liter Four's acceleration is leisurely on the straightaway, agonizingly slow uphill.

Transmission

⊖ The five-speed manual is geared for economy. Be prepared to downshift a lot to keep up with highway traffic. A three-speed automatic is optional.

Economy

⊜ With the manual transmission, expect to average about 36 mpg.

Routine handling

◒ The *Aspire* handles clumsily and is reluctant to change direction. With the standard manual steering, the car is tiring even to drive around town.

Emergency handling

◒ The body leans sharply in turns; the steering becomes increasingly heavy and the wheel requires additional twirling in midturn. With a car this small, swerving between the traffic cones in our avoidance maneuver shouldn't have been such a chore.

Braking

○ Stopping distances from 60 mph were a bit long—46 feet on dry track, 165 on wet—and the car weaved somewhat as it slowed. That's unusual with antilock brakes. The car veered to the right in our wet divided-pavement tests but eventually straightened out.

Ride, normal load

○ The *Aspire's* ride is choppy under the best of circumstances.

Ride, full load

◒ Ride becomes unpleasant when the car carries a full load of people and luggage. Rear-seat riders suffer on bumpy back roads. Road rumble, suspension thumps, and wind noise add to the unpleasantness.

Noise

○ The engine sounds strained when you rev it.

Driving position

⊖ Tall drivers have ample headroom but too little legroom. They may also be annoyed by the built-in head restraints, which force them to slouch forward, and by the short seat cushions, which lack much thigh support. The nonadjustable steering wheel is high in relation to the seat.

Front seating

⊖ The front seats are nicely shaped, comfortably firm, and relatively high off the floor.

Rear seating

◒ The rear seat is built for two, but they had better not be too tall. The short seat cushion doesn't support long legs, and the seatback is too erect for comfort.

Access

○ For a small car, getting in and out of front and rear seats is fairly easy.

Climate system

○ The system is simple and effective. The rear-window defroster clears fog quickly, but it's slow to clear frost. The rear-window wiper is a worthwhile option, even though it's noisy.

Controls and displays

⊖ The small horn buttons on the spokes of the steering wheel are hard to find in an emergency, and the climate controls could be closer at hand. The *Aspire* has Ford's overly complex radio—a design the automaker should rethink.

Trunk

◒ The luggage area holds three Pullman cases and one weekend bag, or a folded wheelchair, with room left over. Folding the rear seatbacks provides ample room for outsize cargo. A removable security panel is optional. A compact spare is all that's available. Tall people need to watch out for the sharp corners of the open hatch lid. Ford advises against towing a trailer with the *Aspire*.

Safety

All but short occupants were comfortable with the safety belts. A child safety seat can go in any seating position without a locking clip. Our low-speed basher tests left the bumpers undamaged.

Both driver and passenger dummies fared well in government crash tests.

Predicted reliability

Insufficient data. The *Aspire* needs more time on the road to establish a reliability history.

Based on an October 1994 report.

Ford Escort

Price range: *$11,430–$12,480*
Cost factor: *NA*
Depreciation: *NA*

For 1997, there will be a new version of Ford's top-selling "subcompact." The redesigned *Escort* will have a new body, dashboard, chassis and suspension upgrades, and a slightly revised engine. The *Escort* comes in two body styles—a four-door sedan and wagon—

and will be about four inches longer. Suspension changes are aimed at giving the *Escort* a firmer ride that is more similar to its European counterparts. Standard safety features include dual air bags and childproof door locks. The *Mercury Tracer* is similar.

Predicted reliability

New model, no data.

Geo Metro LSi (two-door and four-door)

Price range: *$8,380–$9,730*
Cost factor: *93%*
Depreciation: ●

Overview

Although completely redesigned, the *Metro* remains too small, seriously underpowered, and unpleasant on long trips. We tested two *Metros*: the four-cylinder LSi four-door with a three-speed automatic and the three cylinder two-door hatchback LSi with a five-speed manual transmission.

Acceleration

◒ (four-door)/● (two-door) The 1.0-liter Three and the 1.3-liter Four both accelerate weakly. Uphill stretches slow the car noticeably. So do extra passengers, or even just turning on the air conditioner. And you don't get back in fuel economy what you give up in performance.

Transmission

○/⊖ The manual transmission shifts well; the automatic shifts abruptly at times.

Economy

⊖/⊖ The three-cylinder engine, mated to a five-speed manual transmission, averaged 35 mpg—no better than the mileage of the more powerful *Hyundai Accent* and *Toyota Tercel*. The four-cylinder engine and three-speed automatic combination netted 29 mpg—decent but unexceptional.

Routine handling

○/⊖ The hatchback handles a bit better than the sedan, although neither is as nimble as a small car should be. The sedan leans more than the hatchback in corners, and its power steering feels slow and numb.

Emergency handling

○/○ Both versions of the *Metro* negotiated our avoidance maneuver adequately but not crisply.

Braking

○/◒ Our hatchback, which lacked antilock brakes, swerved to the side on both dry and wet pavement. It veered alarmingly in our divided-pavement test. Antilock brakes helped the sedan stop straight, if rather long, in all our tests, but we had to tromp hard on the brake pedal in both cars.

Ride, normal load

◒/◒ Both *Metros* offers a stiff, choppy ride. Sharp bumps deliver harsh impacts, and the suspension crashes and bangs.

Ride, full load

◒/◒ A full load worsens matters a bit.

Noise

◒/◒ Both *Metros* drum up plenty of engine noise.

Driving position

○/○ Tall people will find the cockpit cramped, except for headroom. The seat is low, and five-footers may not see well over the hood.

Front seating

○/○ The small front seats provide generally satisfactory support. The forward-leaning head restraints bothered some test drivers.

Rear seating

◒/◒ The rear seat is designed to hold just two passengers, and none too comfortably at that. Six-footers just fit. The cushion is too low, the seatback too erect.

Access

○/○ Getting into the front seat is fairly easy in both the two-door and the four-door. Accessing the rear is a little more challenging, but the hatchback's front passenger seat helps by scooting well forward.

Climate system

⊖/⊖ Plenty of heated or cooled air rushes from the *Metro's* climate-control system. The fan is noisy, though, and airflow to the rear is minimal.

Controls and displays

⊖/⊖ Most instruments are easy to see, but some controls are poorly placed. The horn switches, on the spokes of the steering wheel, are hard to find in a hurry. The switch for the rear defroster is hidden, and the radio is too low, too far, and needlessly complex.

Trunk

◒/● The four-door's trunk holds four Pullman cases (or a folded wheelchair) with room left over. Folding the fifty-fifty split rear seatback makes even more luggage room. The hatchback can take just two Pullman cases unless you fold down its one-piece seatback. The sedan's low-hanging trunk lid and latch pose a hazard to someone loading the trunk.

Safety

Neither *Geo* version has adjustable shoulder-belt anchors. A child safety seat is easy to install in the outer rear positions without a locking clip. The rear seat lacks head restraints, and the top of the seatback barely reaches the center of an adult's back. Our bumper basher caused severe damage: $693 in the front, $606 in the rear.

The new *Metro* did fairly well in the government's 35-mph crash test—but note that it's one of the lightest cars on the road. Since most cars are heavier, it is likely to fare much worse in a real-world collision with another car.

Predicted reliability

○ The new *Metro* has an average reliability record.

Based on a September 1995 report.

Geo Prizm LSi ✓

Price range: $12,495–$13,145
Cost factor: 94%
Depreciation: ⊖

Overview

The latest model provides a bigger body and retains the old virtues, including decent performance, careful finish, and the promise of reliability.

Acceleration

⊖ The 1.8-liter Four delivers lively performance.

Transmission

⊜ The tested five-speed manual makes a nice compromise between performance and economy.

Economy

⊜ Expect to average about 33 mpg.

Routine handling

⊖ The *Prizm* feels more agile than the similar *Toyota Corolla.* The body rolls a bit less in corners, and the steering provides crisper response.

Emergency handling

○ Lifting off the accelerator during hard cornering makes the rear end wag abruptly, requiring quick correction.

Braking

○ Quite short stops in wet and dry tests, although the car veered a little to the left. Stops were straight in the wet divided-pavement test, where the surface is slicker under the left wheels than under the right.

Ride, normal load

○ Never a punishing ride, although large bumps make their presence known a bit more forcefully than in the *Corolla.*

Ride, full load

○ A full load tranquilizes the ride a bit.

Noise

○ Engine buzzes during acceleration.

Driving position

⊖ A bit more cramped than the *Corolla's;* the optional sunroof robs some headroom in either model. The angle of the driver's seat cushion lacks adjustment. Short drivers must move the seat uncomfortably close to the accelerator so they can floor the clutch pedal, but they can see out well.

Front seating

⊖ Firm, generally satisfactory support, although tall people may wish for more thigh support.

Rear seating

◒ The rear seat looks like that in the *Corolla,* but it feels tighter. It's just wide enough to hold three average-size men, but not very comfortably. Tall people need more knee and headroom.

Access

○ Wide front-door openings and a tilt steering column ease front access, but small rear openings, tight foot clearance, and inward-curving door frames impede access to the rear.

Climate system

⊜ Versatile system quickly furnishes plenty of heat or cooling, but you must close the outboard dash vents for maximum airflow to the floor and windshield. The four-speed fan runs fairly quietly.

Controls and displays

⊜ Most are logical and easy to use. The round climate-control knobs are easier to use than the slides in the *Corolla.* The radio sits low and is rather complicated to operate. The instruments are clear.

Trunk

○ Holds four Pullman cases and two weekend bags, or a folded wheelchair, with room left over. Folding the split-rear seatback expands the luggage room. Small articles can fit into an unfinished bin or in the well around the compact limited-service spare. The trunk, unlike that of the *Corolla,* is not secure from thieves who get into the passenger compartment; the rear seatbacks don't lock. Beware of the blunt latch that protrudes from under the open trunk lid.

Safety

A driver-side air bag supplements comfortable three-point belts with adjustable shoulder-belt anchors. Buckling the three-point belts in the rear requires both hands—and you need a locking clip to secure a child safety seat. The *Prizm* fared almost as poorly as did the *Corolla* in our 3- and 5-mph bumper-basher tests. Damage estimates: $65 front, $806 rear.

Government crash-test results were unavailable for the *Prizm,* but a similar *Toyota Corolla* protected both the passenger and driver quite well.

Predicted reliability

⊜ Previous *Prizms,* like their *Toyota Corolla* cousins, have been very reliable.

Based on an August 1993 report.

Honda Civic EX ✓

Price range: $12,080–$15,150
Cost factor: 90%
Depreciation: ○

Overview

The *Civic* coupe, like the sedan, delivers a supple ride and a nice combination of performance and fuel economy. *Civics* have a long history of excellent reliability.

Acceleration

⊖ Even with the top-of-the-line VTEC Four, you have to rev the engine hard to tap its power.

Transmission

⊖ The gearing in the manual transmission is biased toward economy. The optional automatic is one of the best available in any small car.

Economy

⊜ Expect to average about 34 mpg with the 1.6-liter VTEC Four and five-speed manual transmission. The base 1.6-liter Four is also thrifty, and fairly responsive.

Routine handling

⊖ The *Civic* handles soundly but not crisply. The tires squeal, and the body leans sharply during cornering.

Emergency handling

○ Modest tire grip and fairly slow steering response limited the *Civic's* performance in our avoidance maneuver.

Braking

⊖ The brakes felt good in normal driving, and they performed well on our track.

Ride, normal load

⊖ The *Civic* has the supple and quiet ride of a larger car. Even bumpy roads deliver only muted kicks and small, taut pitches.

Ride, full load

○ A full load stiffens the ride.

Noise

⊖ Some road noise enters the cabin.

Driving position

⊖ Legroom is adequate for six-footers. The height of the seat isn't adjustable, but even short drivers see well over the hood.

Front seating

⊖ The front seats are quite comfortable; some of our testers wanted a bit more lower-back support.

Rear seating

◒ In the rear, headroom is skimpy, especially in the center. Room for legs and toes is also tight.

Access

○ Wide doors ease front-seat access—if you have room to open the door fully. As in most coupes, rear access is awkward. To ease the way, the right front seat scoots forward when it's folded—but then it doesn't slide back automatically to its former setting.

Climate system

⊜ The climate-control system works well, but the temperature-control slide feels stiff. The air conditioner engages automatically in Defrost, but you must turn it off manually to change to the Heat or Vent mode.

Controls and displays

⊖ Controls are well designed except for the hard-to-find horn buttons on the steering-wheel spokes.

Trunk

○ The trunk is fairly roomy, and the rear seatbacks fold down for still more cargo. But releasing the seatbacks is an awkward task. A folded wheelchair can fit in the trunk.

Safety

The safety belts can secure a child safety seat without a separate clip. But the preferred center-rear position is too narrow for some child seats. The front head restraints are high enough to protect an average-size adult even when they're fully lowered, and they lock in any of several raised positions. The rear head restraints can protect only short adults.

Our bumper basher creased both bumpers. Repair estimates ran to $464 front, $453 rear.

The government crash-tested a 1996 *Civic* sedan head-on into a barrier at 35 mph earlier this year. Both driver and passenger dummies were well protected—the passenger dummy especially so.

Predicted reliability

⊜ We expect the newly designed *Civic* to prove exceptionally reliable, like its predecessors.

Based on a May 1996 report.

Honda Civic LX ✓

Price range: $10,350–$16,480
Cost factor: 90%
Depreciation: ○

Overview

If you want a small car, you won't go wrong with the *Honda Civic.*

Acceleration

○ Acceleration is more than adequate. The fancier *EX* version's more powerful VTEC (valve timing electronically controlled) Four provides even more power, but the *EX* costs $1230 extra.

Transmission

⊖ The new four-speed transmission is arguably the best automatic in any small car, always selecting the right gear at the right time. One quibble: When you shift from Park to Drive, the shifter tends to slip past the normally used D4 position and into D3, which locks out fourth gear. A five-speed manual is standard equipment.

Economy

⊖ With the *LX*'s 1.6-liter Four, you can expect to average about 31 mpg.

Routine handling

⊖ The steering requires just the right effort, and it's responsive. The tires grip well, and the car feels sure-footed even in challenging, bumpy turns.

Emergency handling

⊖ Even when pushed to its limits on our test track, the *Civic* carved confidently through fast turns and around the traffic cones marking our avoidance maneuver course.

Braking

○ By contemporary standards,

stops were somewhat long on both wet and dry pavement. In our wet divided-pavement test, where the track is slicker under one side of the car than under the other, the *Civic* veered but didn't spin out—not bad for a car without antilock brakes. A *Civic* with antilock brakes that we check-tested brakes much better: It stayed straight in our divided-pavement test and stopped 18 feet shorter from 60 mph on wet pavement.

Ride, normal load

⊖ The *Civic* provides a remarkably supple, absorbent ride for a small car. On broken pavement, you feel only a few muted, rubbery kicks, and the highway ride is steady and composed.

Ride, full load

○ A full load degrades the ride a bit.

Noise

○ The cabin stays fairly hushed most of the time, but the engine roars when you accelerate, and the tires thrum on coarse pavement.

Driving position

⊖ The cockpit suited all our test drivers. Legroom is adequate for six-footers, and the low dash lets five-footers see well over the hood.

Front seating

⊖ The small front seats provide generally good, firm support, although a bulge in the middle of each seatback bothered some testers.

Rear seating

○ The rear seat is adequate and comfortable, and provides decent support for two, but it's tight for three.

Access

○ Front and rear access are average for a small four-door sedan.

Climate system

⊜ The climate-control system works well, but the temperature-selector slide feels cheap and imprecise. The air conditioner engages automatically in Defrost mode, but you must turn it off manually when you change to Heat or Vent mode.

Controls and displays

⊖ The controls are exemplary except for the horn buttons, on the steering wheel spokes, which are hard to find in a hurry. The gauges are easy to read.

Trunk

○ The *Civic's* trunk is especially roomy, and the split rear seatback can fold down for even more luggage room. But the seatback releases on the rear package shelf and in the trunk are hard to reach. A folded wheelchair can fit in the trunk. A full-size spare can fit in the trunk.

Safety

The front shoulder belts have adjustable upper anchors. You don't need a special clip to secure a child seat, but the center-rear position may be too narrow for some models. The adjustable front-seat head restraints are high enough even for tall occupants, and they lock in their raised positions. The rear seat's low built-in restraints may not protect tall passengers. The headlights lit the road especially well. Our bumper basher, in its series of 3- and 5-mph blows, creased both bumpers. Repair estimate: $464 front, $453 rear.

Both driver and passenger dummies were well protected in government crash tests.

Predicted reliability

⊜ The *Civic* should be exceptionally reliable.

Based on a March 1996 report.

Hyundai Accent (two-door and four-door)

Price range: *$8,285–$9,295*
Cost factor: *94%*
Depreciation: *NA*

Overview

It's neatly packaged and well equipped for its price, but reliability remains a key question. We tested both the base four-door *Accent* with an automatic transmission and the two-door L with a five-speed manual.

Acceleration

◒ (four-door)/○ (two-door) The 1.5-liter Four accelerates adequately with the four-speed automatic transmission and even better with the five-speed manual.

Transmission

○/⊖ The manual shifts easily; the automatic could be smoother.

Economy

⊖/⊜ Expect to average about 35 mpg with the manual, 28 mpg with the automatic.

Routine handling

⊖/⊖ Our hatchback's manual steering required a lot of muscle, so power steering is a must.

Emergency handling

⊖/○ The sedan's power steering and wider tires improved handling and helped the car thread our avoidance maneuver at a respectable pace.

Braking

○/○ Both *Accents* stopped fairly well from 60 mph in our dry braking tests, but on wet pavement the hatchback took more than 200 feet—a good 30 feet farther than average for small cars we've tested lately. Despite the lack of antilock brakes, both *Accents* stopped nearly straight in our wet divided-pavement test, in which the road is slicker under one side of the car than under the other.

Ride, normal load

◒/◒ The suspension damps the sharpest road bumps fairly well, but smaller pavement flaws make the ride stiff and choppy. The sedan jitters even on smooth roads. The hatchback rides less nervously.

Ride, full load

◒/◒ In both the sedan and hatchback, a full load quells the motions.

Noise

○/○ The *Accent* isn't too noisy, as small cars go, but road and wind noise and engine hum often intrude.

Driving position

⊖/⊖ The *Accent* offers more front legroom than a *Toyota Tercel* or *Geo Metro,* but not quite enough for a tall person. Headroom is generous. None of the cars in this group offer height adjustments for the seat or the steering wheel, but even a five-footer could see well over the *Accent's* hood.

Front seating

⊖/⊖ The front seats provide reasonable support.

Rear seating

◒/◒ Three six-footers can fit in the rear, but it's a snug fit.

Access

○/○ Front access is easy, particularly in the hatchback. When you fold the hatchback's front seatback, the seat scoots fully forward. Access to the sedan's rear is easier still, although foot and head clearances are tight.

Climate system

⊖/⊖ The climate system works well. You can switch on the air conditioner in any mode to dehumidify the cabin.

Controls and displays

⊖/⊖ The temperature controls are too low. And the horn switches, on the spokes of the steering wheel, are hard to find quickly. Aside from that, the controls are generally well placed.

Trunk

◒/○ With the hatchback's security panel in place, luggage space is about the same as in the sedan: Both models can take four Pullman cases (or a folded wheelchair). But folding the hatchback's rear seat allows much more room for luggage. The sedan's rear seatback doesn't fold.

Safety

The front shoulder belts have an adjustable upper anchor for a comfortable fit. Buckling the rear belts takes both hands. You need a locking clip to secure a child seat in the rear, and the ends of the center lap belt are too close together to accommodate many child seats in that position. The rear head restraints are barely high enough to protect average-size people from whiplash injury. Our cars escaped undamaged from our 3- and 5-mph bumper-basher tests.

In government crash tests, the driver was likely to suffer certain injury, possibly severe. The passenger was likely to suffer moderate injury.

Predicted reliability

Insufficient data. Previous *Hyundais* have suffered from especially poor reliability. Hyundai says its new model is much improved, but we suggest waiting at least a year before buying.

Based on a September 1995 report.

Hyundai Elantra

***Price range:** $10,899–$13,799*
***Cost factor:** 90%*
***Depreciation:** NA*

The *Elantra* has been redesigned for 1996. It is available in both a four-door sedan and a five-door wagon. In size and price, it fits between the new *Accent,* Hyundai's basic small car, and the *Sonata,* Hyundai's midsize sedan. The exterior is exceptionally nondescript, but the underpinnings are up-to-date, the interior is well laid out, and it comes with lots of standard equipment. The *Elantra* must complete with well-established small cars like the *Honda Civic, Toyota Corolla,* and *Dodge/Plymouth Neon.* Reliability has been a problem for Hyundai, so caution is advised for the first year or so.

Predicted reliability

No data, new model.

Mazda Protegé ES ✓

***Price range:** $11,695–$14,695*
***Cost factor:** 93%*
Depreciation: ○

Overview

The *Protegé* offers a roomy interior, an efficient and refined power train, pleasant handling, and a good ride. Reliability should be good, too.

Acceleration

○ The *ES* version's 1.8-liter Four delivers ample performance. The 1.5-liter Four that's standard in *DX* and *LX* models is slightly less powerful but thriftier.

Transmission

⊖ The four-speed automatic transmission usually shifted smoothly. It can start off in second gear, an asset on slippery surfaces. An On/Off button lets you choose between using overdrive or locking it out. A five-speed manual transmission is available on all models.

Economy

⊖ Expect about 26 mpg.

Routine handling

⊖ The *Protegé* corners with a moderate amount of body roll. Strong tire grip and fairly quick steering inspire confidence.

Emergency handling

⊖ In hard test-track turns, easing off the accelerator subdued the sedan's tendency to plow straight ahead. The car felt safe and predictable in abrupt avoidance maneuvers.

Braking

⊖ Stops were reliably short on dry roads, longer on wet roads, and perfectly straight in our wet split-surface tests, where the pavement under one side of the car is slicker than under the other.

Ride, normal load

○ The ride feels jittery at times, but it's never harsh. The cheaper *LX* model has a slightly more comfortable ride.

Ride, full load

○ A full load of passengers and luggage makes the ride somewhat stiffer on back roads, more tranquil on highways.

Noise

○ Inside, the *Protegé* is reasonably quiet, but coarse pavement causes some tire noise. The engine becomes vocal when revved, but it sounds polished rather than harsh.

Driving position

⊖ All drivers felt at home behind the wheel, thanks to simple but effective seat and steering-wheel adjustments.

Front seating

⊖ The front bucket seats feel hard at first, but you soon notice only that they provide very good support.

Rear seating

○ The rear seat fits three tall occupants, but isn't kind to any of them.

Access

⊖ It's relatively easy to get in and out of the *Protegé*.

Climate system

⊜ The climate system responds quickly to changes in setting. The air conditioner runs on any setting, but it doesn't kick in automatically in Defrost to keep windows fog-free on damp days. (To maximize airflow to the windshield, you have to close the dash vents near the doors.) If you forget to shut off the rear-window defroster, it will be on when you restart the car.

Controls and displays

⊖ Most controls are easy to reach and use, but the climate controls can be difficult to adjust while driving.

Trunk

○ The trunk holds four Pullman suitcases and one weekend bag, or a folded wheelchair, with room left over. Either or both rear seatbacks can be folded to expand cargo room. Small items can be stored around the compact spare tire, under the trunk floor. A full-service tire fits in the well, but Mazda doesn't offer one for the *Protegé*. Loading the trunk is easy, but watch out for the latch protruding from the open lid. The remote trunk release and the seatbacks can be locked to secure the trunk.

Safety

The front safety belts have an adjustable upper anchor, to help fit short and tall people. Very short buckles make the rear belts a bit hard to snap on. The lap-and-shoulder belts need a locking clip to hold a child safety seat in place. Safety seats that requires a top tether are a problem: Mazda doesn't provide an anchor. The front-seat head restraints are adequately tall even when lowered. Those in the rear seat are too low, and they aren't adjustable.

Dents inflicted by our bumper basher required $451 in repairs to the front bumper, $419 to the rear.

Government crash tests indicate certain injury; possibly severe for the driver, and even worse for the passenger.

Predicted reliability

⊖ Expect very good reliability.

Based on a June 1995 report.

Mercury Tracer

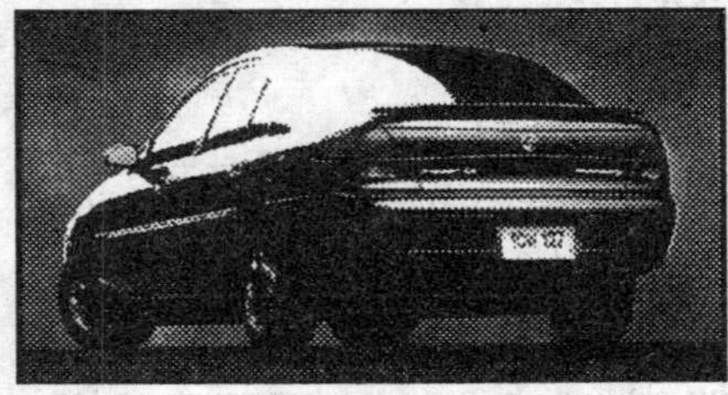

Price range: $11,560–$12,635 (est.)
Cost factor: NA
Depreciation: NA

The *Tracer*, cousin to the *Ford Escort*, is redesigned for 1997. Expect a new body, dashboard, chassis and suspension upgrades, and a slightly revised engine. The *Tracer* comes in two body styles—a four-door sedan and wagon—and will be about four inches longer. Suspension changes are aimed at giving the *Tracer* a firmer ride that is more similar to its European couterparts. Standard safety features include dual air bags and childproof door locks.

Predicted reliability

New model, no data.

Mitsubishi Mirage

Price range: $9989–$12,850
Cost factor: 91%
Depreciation: ○

See EAGLE SUMMIT.

Nissan Sentra GXE

Price range: $11,499–$15,229
Cost factor: 92%
Depreciation: ◒

Overview

The *Nissan Sentra*, while a new design, is not an innovative one. The old *Sentra* was a good-tempered little car with a Milquetoast personality. The new version is about the same.

Acceleration

○ The 1.6-liter Four runs smoothly and delivers adequate acceleration, but it isn't as quick as the engines in competing models.

Transmission

⊖ The four-speed automatic transmission downshifts too often in routine driving. You'll find yourself glancing at the shifter to make sure it's in the right gear. A little more horsepower or lower gearing would help. The cruise control had some trouble holding a set speed. A five-speed manual transmission is available.

Economy

Slightly better than cars in this class—about 28 mpg overall.

Routine handling

The *Sentra* goes where it's pointed, but without the typical small-car enthusiasm. The steering borders on sluggish, and the body rolls markedly in turns.

Emergency handling

The car plowed ahead stubbornly in hard test-track turns. Mediocre tire grip slowed our speed through the accident-avoidance course.

Braking

Stopping distances were about average. The car veered slightly but finally stopped straight in our wet divided-pavement tests.

Ride, normal load

The suspension deals with most road irregularities quite well, but it bounds over dips and swells in the road.

Ride, full load

When the *Sentra* is fully loaded, the ride turns bouncy.

Noise

The cabin is fairly hushed, except when the engine is revved—and most drivers will rev it often to get up to speed, climb hills, and pass other cars.

Driving position

Most drivers should be at home behind the controls, although legroom is a bit tight for tall people. The thin steering wheel isn't very pleasant to grip.

Front seating

The front bucket seats provide good, firm support in all the right places.

Rear seating

Three average-size people fit in the rear, in typical small-car discomfort. Occupants over six feet tall have to sit near the doors; the raised middle perch limits headroom.

Access

Getting in and out of the rear seat is a bit of a struggle.

Climate system

The climate system does what it's supposed to do, although too much air flows to the windshield when the system is set for Heat. The air conditioner does not automatically engage in Defrost. Unlike many cars in this price class, the *Sentra* lacks ducts that direct heat to the rear seat. The rear defroster has a fifteen-minute timer.

Controls and displays

The car's controls are well thought out and very easy to operate; the displays, simple and legible. The power switch for the driver's window is lighted, a thoughtful touch.

Trunk

The trunk holds four Pullman suitcases, or a folded wheelchair, with room left over. The divided rear seatbacks fold to expand capacity.

Safety

Adjustable upper anchors make the front safety belts comfortable for just about everyone. The rear belts require two hands to buckle up. They can secure a child safety seat, but because the buckles are forward of the seatback, it can be difficult to tighten the belts around some child safety seats. Larger safety seats placed in the center of the seat may block access to the outboard buckles. Even when fully lowered, the front-seat head restraints provide good whiplash protection. The built-in rear-seat head restraints are just high enough to protect occupants of average height.

Our bumper basher pushed both bumpers out of alignment and dented them slightly. The rear bumper mounts were damaged, too. The repair estimates: $424 front, $380 rear.

Both the driver and passenger dummies escaped serious "injuries" in government crash tests.

Predicted reliability

The redesigned *Sentra* has been very reliable.

Based on a June 1995 report.

Plymouth Neon

Price range: *$9445–$12,700*
Cost factor: *92%*
Depreciation: *NA*

See DODGE NEON.

Pontiac Sunfire GT

Price range: *$11,504–$17,734*
Cost factor: *92%*
Depreciation: *NA*

Overview

In the tested two-door *GT* version, the *Sunfire* is a quick car for its class, but its handling is far from sporty. The four-door version with automatic transmission is much better, overall.

Acceleration

The *GT's* gutsy 2.4-liter Four accelerates impressively.

Transmission

The five-speed manual transmission is well matched to the engine, but it doesn't shift crisply. Three- and four-speed automatics are optional.

Economy

Fuel economy is mediocre; expect to average about 25 mpg.

Routine handling

The *Sunfire* handles smooth and wide curves well enough, even though the body leans considerably. Cornering on bumpy or wavy pavement tends to make the car lurch, and the steering isn't precise enough to handle sharp bends gracefully.

Emergency handling

○ The *Sunfire* wants to plow straight ahead in hard turns. It lost its grip fairly easily in our emergency avoidance maneuver.

Braking

⊖ Braking was competent.

Ride, normal load

○ On the highway, the ride is fairly tranquil except for some side-to-side rocking. But bumps elicit strong kicks and pitching and make the front of the body shake.

Ride, full load

◓ A full load makes matters worse.

Noise

○ The engine's gruff, whiny sound gets tiring.

Driving position

○ The driver's seat is too low and too close to the pedals and steering wheel. The wheel can be adjusted for height, but the seat can't, and our five-foot-tall tester had trouble seeing over the hood.

Front seating

⊖ The large front seats provide only average support.

Rear seating

◓ The rear seat has poor headroom. With three average-size people crowded abreast, the outside passengers' heads touch the inward-curving roof pillars.

Access

○ After folding the right front seatback, you can make it scoot forward to ease entry to the rear seat—but that takes a hard shove. The seat remembers its former position when you slide it back, but the seatback doesn't remember its angle.

Climate system

⊜ The climate-control system has convenient rotary knobs, but the heat comes slowly. Rear passengers get ample airflow, thanks to ducts under the front seats. The rear defroster doesn't clear the top and bottom of the glass.

Controls and displays

⊜ The major controls are well designed, and the horn control is conveniently located in the center of the wheel. The power-window switches, on the center console, are lit at night, a useful feature. Power door locks and a keyless-entry transmitter are worthwhile factory options.

Trunk

◓ The trunk is reasonably roomy, and the rear seatback can be folded for more luggage room. A folded wheelchair can fit in the trunk.

Safety

Several drivers complained that the shoulder belt rode up on their neck (the height of the shoulder-belt anchors isn't adjustable). The belts can secure a child seat without a separate clip. The adjustable front head restraints are high enough to protect an average-size adult, but they don't lock firmly; your head can knock down the restraint in a rear-end crash. The rear head restraints are too low to be effective. Daytime running lights, an effective safety feature, are standard. Our bumper basher did no damage.

When the government crash-tested the *Sunfire's* twin, the *Chevrolet Cavalier* sedan, both the driver and passenger dummies suffered certain "injury," possibly severe.

Predicted reliability

○ The redesigned *Sunfire* and similar *Chevrolet Cavalier* have had an average reliability record.

Based on a May 1996 report.

Saturn SL1

Price range: $10,495–$12,895
Cost factor: 87%
Depreciation: ⊖

Overview

Even with the redesign, this *Saturn* is still not quite up to date.

Acceleration

○ The *SL1*'s 1.9-liter engine accelerates well but is noisy.

Transmission

○ The four-speed automatic shifts smoothly enough, but it often "hunts" annoyingly between gears and delays downshifts. Selecting the Performance rather than the Economy mode helps only a little. A five-speed manual transmission is standard.

Economy

⊖ Expect to average about 29 mpg. The *SL2's* more powerful engine would average about 27 mpg.

Routine handling

⊖ The *Saturn* threaded through our avoidance maneuver predictably but not quickly. The steering feels somewhat heavy and provides little road feel.

Emergency handling

○ In fast corners, the *Saturn* plows ahead strongly. The body leans heavily, and the front tires squeal and heel over onto their sidewalls. As a result of our handling tests, both front tires' sidewalls were badly scalloped and one tire wore through to the steel wires of the belt.

Braking

○ The brakes work well enough, but when the antilock feature kicks in, the pedal chatters strongly. That might make some drivers ease off the brakes just when they shouldn't.

Ride, normal load

○ On the highway, the ride is tolerable but not entirely controlled. Bumps provide firm kicks and snappy jostling.

Ride, full load

○ A full load softens the ride somewhat.

Noise

○ The engine is noisy, especially during acceleration—and it's a nasty, raspy noise at that.

Driving position

○ The driver's seat is low, perhaps too low for some short drivers. You have to move up to an *SL2* to get a height adjustment. Legroom is cramped for six-footers. The steering wheel adjusts for height but not for reach. Tall drivers had to recline the seatback excessively to get far enough away from the wheel.

Front seating

○ The small front seats are comfortably firm, but the cushions are a bit short for optimum thigh support.

Rear seating

◒ The rear bench is not a happy place for adults. The cushions are too low, the back is too erect, and space is tight.

Access

○ Getting in and out takes some agility, especially in the rear. Three six-footers can squeeze in only if they're slim.

Climate system

⊜ The climate-control system provides ample airflow front and rear, although the controls are hard to grasp. When the heater is in Defrost mode, you have to switch on the air conditioner manually.

Controls and displays

○ The gauges are easy to read, day or night. The horn buttons, on the spokes of the steering wheel, are poorly placed and inconvenient, and the turn-signal lever obscures the panel-lighting switch.

Trunk

◒ The split rear seatback can fold for more luggage room, but neither the remote lid release nor the rear seatback can be locked. The optional keyless-entry transmitter can pop open the trunk lid—a small convenience you appreciate more and more over time.

Safety

As with some other GM products, the front lap-and-shoulder belts are a little difficult to buckle. You don't need a special clip to install a child seat. The nonadjustable front head restraints are amply high, but the rear ones are too low for most adults. The *Saturn* has daytime running lights, a useful safety feature. But the lights, which use the headlight high beams, are very bright and aimed high—a problem for the driver of the car in front. Our bumper basher left the car unscathed.

In government crash tests, the driver and passenger were very well protected.

Predicted reliability

⊖ Previous *Saturns* have had the best reliability record of any domestic model. On the basis of our latest survey, we predict a better-than-average record for the 1996 model.

Based on a March 1996 report.

Saturn SL2 and Station Wagon

Price range: $10,495–$12,895
Cost factor: 87%
Depreciation: ⊖

All *Saturns* (except the sporty *SC*) were redesigned last year, with substantial body and interior refinements. However, their engines still produce too much noise, vibration, and harshness. Still, *Saturns* remain very popular and have a fine reliability history.

Predicted reliability ⊖

Subaru Impreza L ✓

Price range: $13,495–$18,195
Cost factor: 91%
Depreciation: ◒

Overview

Proper equipment makes a big difference when choosing as *Impreza*. We'd opt for any version with bigger tires and antilock brakes.

Acceleration

○ The 1.8-liter Four stumbled occasionally during the first mile or two after a cold start.

Transmission

⊖ Digging much power out of the engine isn't easy; the five-speed manual gearbox in the *L* model lacked crispness and the clutch grabbed, making the car shudder at times. (The automatic transmission in the *LS* we checked actually feels more responsive.) A convenient "hill holder" clutch feature keeps the car from rolling back when starting off uphill.

Economy

⊖ Expect to average about 29 mpg.

Routine handling

⊖ Despite its fairly soft suspension, the *Impreza L* doesn't lean all that much during cornering. The nicely weighted steering responds quickly.

Emergency handling

○ In hard cornering, the *Impreza* plows ahead somewhat, but it grips the pavement quite well. The check-tested, *LS* version, with wider tires, handles more nimbly and crisply than the *L*.

Braking

◒/⊖ (without/with antilock brakes) The *L* version, without antilock brakes, stopped adequately—in 146 feet—in braking tests from 60 mph on dry pavement. But the distance stretched to 220 feet on wet pavement, and the car spun out in our wet split-pavement braking test, where the surface is slicker under the left wheels than under the right ones. By contrast, the *Impreza LS*, with antilock brakes, stopped 30 percent shorter (in 153 feet) on the wet track. And it stopped absolutely straight in the wet divided-pavement braking test.

Ride, normal load

⊖ Smooth and gentle on the highway, although bad roads provoke some jitters and kicks.

Ride, full load

○ A full load evens the ride a bit on good roads but makes the suspension kick harder on patched or broken pavement.

Noise

○ Annoying clicks emanate from the electrical relays in the dash. The clutch pedal also clicks, and road roar is significant. The engine growls more in the *L* version with manual transmission than in the *LS* with automatic.

Driving position

⊖ Six-footers may find the legroom to the accelerator just adequate. To floor the clutch pedal, short drivers may need to move the seat too close to the accelerator. Despite the low front seats, even short drivers can see out well.

Front seating

⊖ Very good support.

Rear seating

◒ The rear seat can barely hold two six-footers or three average-size men, and they need more side and lower-back support.

Access

○ Intrusive windshield pillars and doorposts hinder access, though a tilt steering column can increase thigh clearance. Getting in and out of the rear takes dexterity.

Climate system

⊖ Plenty of heated or cooled air is available, but air leaks from the outboard dash vents. The fan is fairly noisy. The rear-window defroster works adequately but lacks a timer.

Controls and displays

⊖ The instruments are clear enough, but the speedometer is marked off only in 20-mph increments. The tiny horn buttons are hard to find in an emergency, and the steering wheel obstructs the ignition switch, rear defroster, and power mirror control.

Trunk

○ Holds four Pullman cases or a folded wheelchair with room left over. The *L* version's rear seatback is fixed; you need to move up to the *LS* version to get folding seatback sections. The trunk lacks cubbies or bins, but a few small items can fit in the well around the compact spare.

Safety

Dual air bags supplement the comfortable three-point front safety belts, which have adjustable shoulder anchors. The three-point belts require a locking clip to secure a child safety seat. Some child seats may be hard to install in the center rear.

The government has yet to crash-test an *Impreza*.

Predicted reliability

⊜ The *Impreza* has compiled an excellent reliability record.

Based on an August 1993 report.

Suzuki Esteem GLX

Price range: $11,599–$13,699
Cost factor: *95%*
Depreciation: *NA*

Overview

It's functional and workmanlike—no more, no less.

Acceleration

○ The 1.6-liter Four accelerates well enough.

Transmission

⊖ The optional four-speed automatic sometimes bumps into gear. A five-speed manual is standard equipment.

Economy

⊖ Overall mileage is respectable: about 29 mpg.

Routine handling

⊖ Cornering is safe but unenthusiastic, and the steering feels vague and unresponsive around the straight-ahead position.

Emergency handling

○ The car tends to run wide in tight, fast turns, and the small, 13-inch tires don't grip well. Still, the *Esteem* threaded our avoidance maneuver safely, without any nasty surprises.

Braking

○ Stops were straight and reasonably short in our braking tests, but after ten consecutive stops we needed to press harder on the brake pedal to stop the car. Such brake fade is uncommon nowadays.

Ride, normal load

○ The *Esteem's* ride is nervous and busy; uneven pavement elicits short, choppy pitching motions.

Ride, full load

◒ A full load worsens the ride somewhat.

Noise

○ The engine sounds harsh when it's revved, and it moans even at steady highway speeds.

Driving position

○ Tall drivers may find the legroom too limited. And short drivers may have trouble seeing the road ahead; the steering wheel is high, and it lacks a height adjustment.

Front seating

⊖ The small front seats give good, firm support, and they cradle occupants especially well during cornering.

Rear seating

O Three six-footers just fit in the rear; space for head and toes is tight.

Access

O Access is decent for a car this size.

Climate system

⊖ The climate-control system works well, but the temperature slide is stiff. Ducts direct air to the rear.

Controls and displays

⊖ The gauges are easy to read, but the horn buttons, on the spokes of the steering wheel, are hard to find in a hurry. The cruise-control buttons are crowded onto the windshield-wiper lever. The remote release tabs for the trunk lid and fuel door are easy to confuse because they're close together on the floor and similarly shaped.

Trunk

◒ The trunk is deep but fairly small, and the opening is short front to back. You can stash a few small items in the well around the spare. Neither the trunk release nor the rear seatback can be locked to secure your luggage from someone with access to the cabin. The split rear seatback can fold down to make more room for luggage.

Safety

The *Esteem's* front shoulder belts have adjustable anchors. The angle of the inboard ends makes the front safety belts hard to buckle. And the belts retract with a vengeance: The tang can strike the door glass if you let go too soon. You don't need a special clip to install a child safety seat. The adjustable front-seat head restraints are high enough even when they're fully lowered, and they lock in a raised position. The nonadjustable rear head restraints are marginal. Our bumper basher left both bumpers unharmed.

The government hasn't scheduled a crash test of the *Esteem* for this year.

Predicted reliability

New model, no data. Since the *Esteem* is a new model, we can't predict its reliability.

Based on a March 1996 report.

Suzuki Swift

Price range: $8,999–$10,209
Cost factor: 93%
Depreciation: O

See GEO METRO.

Toyota Corolla ✓

Price range: $13,288–$15,058
Cost factor: 89%
Depreciation: ◒

Overview

Except for a slightly softer ride and a higher sticker price, the *Corolla* is similar in most ways to the *Geo Prizm*—with both maintaining superb reliability records.

Acceleration

O Adequate performance from the 1.8-liter Four with automatic transmission, but in cars of this size we prefer the extra zip and fuel economy provided by a manual gearbox.

Transmission

⊖ Even though we prefer the manual (see page 58 for a test of the *Geo Prizm*), the automatic shifts smoothly.

Economy

⊖ Expect to average about 30 mpg with the automatic transmission, 33 mpg with the manual.

Routine handling

⊖ Safe and predictable but less nimble than the *Prizm*.

Emergency handling

O The body rolled sharply, and the front end plowed in hard turns on the track and in our avoidance maneuver.

Braking

O The antilock brakes stopped the *Corolla* quite short from 60 mph on both wet and dry pavement, but the car veered a little to one side. It also weaved a bit in our difficult wet divided-pavement test, where the surface is slicker under the left wheels than under the right ones.

Ride, normal load

O The suspension damps out the biggest road irregularities, but the ride feels jiggly on the highway. Broken pavement produces firm kicks.

Ride, full load

O A full load irons out some of the nervousness.

Noise

O The engine booms unpleasantly during acceleration.

Driving position

⊖ Drivers of various sizes can get comfortable behind the *Corolla's* controls and see out well.

Front seating

⊖ Good, firm support. Long-legged drivers should find plenty of thigh support, but they may wish the seat cushion were longer. The optional sunroof makes headroom a premium.

Rear seating

◒ The rear seat can barely hold two six-footers or three average-size men. With three abreast, the seatback twists outboard passengers inward.

Access

O Wide doors and a tilt steering column ease front access. Small rear doors, inward curving door frames, and sharply slanted roof pillars hamper rear access.

Climate system

⊖ The system puts out plenty of warmed or cooled air, but you have to shut the outboard dash vents for full airflow to the floor or windshield. The rear-window defroster works well but lacks a timer to turn it off.

Controls and displays

⊖ Easy-to-use controls and clear instruments are typical of *Toyotas,* and the *Corolla* is no exception. Switches for the power windows and locks are lighted at night, a nice touch. But the climate-control slides are awkward. We prefer the *Prizm's* rotary controls.

Trunk

○ The trunk can hold four Pullman cases and two weekend bags, or a folded wheelchair, with room left over. You can fold the split rear seatback to expand the trunk. Small items can fit in a bin under the floor of the trunk or in the well around the limited-service spare.

Safety

Dual air bags supplement the comfortable front safety belts, which have a convenient height adjuster for the shoulder portion. Buckling the rear three-point belts takes both hands, but at least the belts fit comfortably. Any of the three-point belts can secure a child safety seat if you use a locking clip. Our bumper basher damaged both bumpers in simulated 3- and 5-mph tests—a disappointment, since previous *Toyotas* have done well in those tests. The repair estimates: $527 front, $486 rear.

Government crash tests indicated that the passenger dummy fared better than the driver.

Predicted reliability

⊜ *Toyotas* in general, and the *Corolla* in particular, have been very reliable.

Based on an August 1993 report.

Toyota Corolla DX Wagon ✓

Price: $15,058
Cost factor: 89%
Depreciation: ◒

Overview

This perennial good performer among small models provides decent all-round performance, versatility, and distinguished reliability.

Acceleration

○ The 1.8-liter Four provides ample get-up-and-go, but not without considerable noise during hard acceleration.

Transmission

⊖ The tested electronically controlled four-speed automatic has a button on the shifter that lets you lock out fourth gear during towing, or when you want to keep the transmission from shifting back and forth on uphill stretches. A five-speed manual is available.

Economy

⊖ Expect to average about 28 mpg with the automatic.

Routine handling

⊖ The car holds its course obediently and leans only moderately in turns. The steering feels precise, although a bit short on road feel.

Emergency handling

○ Remains secure, and predictable, if not very crisp during abrupt maneuvers.

Braking

⊖ The wagon stopped well from 60 mph—shorter and straighter than its sedan counterpart on dry pavement, and just about as well on wet pavement. In the challenging wet divided-pavement test, in which the asphalt is slicker under the left wheels than under the right, the wagon veered only slightly.

Ride, normal load

⊖ Rides fairly comfortably for a small car—at least when lightly loaded.

Ride, full load

○ Full load of passengers and luggage makes the wagon pitch, kick, and bounce its rear end.

Noise

○ The engine booms even during moderate acceleration, and road roar and wind noise are present at highway speeds.

Driving position

⊖ Short drivers sit too low to see well over the hood.

Front seating

⊖ Reasonably comfortable, although long-legged people may find thigh support lacking.

Rear seating

◒ Rear seat is tight, especially for three.

Access

⊖ Fairly easy in front, but tight foot clearance is a problem in back.

Climate system

⊖ Provides plenty of warmed or cooled air wherever it's needed. You must close the outboard dash vents to direct maximum airflow to the floor or windshield. To keep the rear window clear in messy weather, you need the optional rear wiper.

Controls and displays

⊜ Most controls are logical and easy to use, but those for the climate-control system are confusing. Displays could not be clearer.

Cargo area

◒ The 28-cubic-foot cargo area is slightly larger than that of the *Saturn* and *Ford Escort* wagons, and is easy to load and unload. To expand the cargo area, you swing the rear seat cushion forward against the front seatbacks and then fold down the rear seatback to form a flat floor. Tall people should beware of the sharp latch protruding from the open lid. Maximum payload is 930 pounds; trailer-towing capacity is 1500 pounds. The *Corolla* comes with a compact spare, but the well has room for a full-size tire. A small covered bin behind the left rear wheel can hold small items, and a removable vinyl blind can cover the cargo area.

Safety

The comfortable front safety belts, with a height adjuster for the shoulder belts, are supplemented by dual air bags. The rear three-point belts need a locking clip to secure a child safety seat. The rear head restraints are too low to be effective in preventing whiplash. In our 3- and 5-mph hydraulic bumper-basher tests, both bumpers suffered extensive damage. Repair estimates were $539 for the front, $354 for the rear.

As with the *Corolla* sedan, government crash tests indicated that the passenger dummy fared better than the driver.

Predicted reliability

⊜ The *Corolla* has enjoyed a first-rate history of reliability.

Based on a September 1993 report.

Toyota Tercel (four-door and two-door)

Price range: $10,348–$11,908
Cost factor: 92%
Depreciation: ○

Overview

The *Toyota Tercel* is exceptionally reliable but overpriced and underequipped, and its smooth, efficient power train can't make up for a cramped, noisy cabin. We tested two *Tercels*: the four-door DX with an automatic transmission and the base two-door with a four-speed manual.

Acceleration

○ (4-door)/⊖ (2-door) The *Tercel's* drive train is its best feature. The 1.5-liter Four feels strong with either the base car's four-speed manual transmission or the *DX's* four-speed automatic.

Transmission

⊖/⊖ The manual shifts crisply; the automatic, smoothly and quickly.

Economy

⊜/⊜ The manual-transmission version averages 39 mpg, the automatic 32. (Like the *Geo Metro* and *Hyundai Accent*, the *Tercel* uses regular gasoline.) Squeezing extra miles out of a gallon of gas is the *Tercel's* forte.

Routine handling

⊖/○ In either configuration, the handling feels unresponsive. The body leans, and the tires squeal easily during cornering. The two-door model's manual steering feels vague in the straight-ahead position and heavy during cornering. The four-door's very light power steering gives the driver little road feel.

Emergency handling

○/○ Both cars felt fairly secure through our avoidance maneuver, although the body leaned sharply and the tail wagged a bit.

Braking

◒/◒ Braking distances ran fairly long even on a dry track. On a wet track, the cars slewed to the side and needed nearly 200 feet to stop from 60 mph. Both cars spun out in our wet divided-pavement test. Neither had antilock brakes.

Ride, normal load

○/○ The *Tercels* provide a veneer of isolation on smooth roads, but sharp bumps crash through virtually unfiltered, and the rear suspension often compresses fully with a thud.

Ride, full load

◒/◒ A full load makes the ride even worse.

Noise

○/◒ The DX is a shade quieter inside than the base model, but both admit plenty of road, wind, and engine noise.

Driving position

○/○ Headroom is plentiful, and five-footers can see well over the hood, but front legroom is especially tight for tall people. The accelerator is too lightly sprung. Since there's nothing to brace your foot against, cramps threaten your right leg on long trips.

Front seating

○/○ The front seats provide generally good, firm support. The base car's vinyl upholstery feels sweaty in summer and chilly in winter. The *DX's* cloth upholstery feels much better.

Rear seating

●/● The rear bench is cramped even for two average-size adults, let alone three. Space for knees and feet is tight, and headroom is adequate only in the outboard positions. The cushion is too low and hard in the middle.

Access

○/○ Access to the front seats is fairly easy. Climbing into the rear is awkward, particularly in the four-door.

Climate system

⊖/⊖ The *Tercel* lacks vents for defogging the side windows, an unusual omission these days. The rear heater ducts provide moderate airflow.

Controls and displays

⊜/⊖ The major controls are easy to use.

Trunk

◒/◒ The trunk can hold four Pullman cases (or a folded wheelchair) with room left over. The base version's rear seatback doesn't fold, but an options package in our *DX* version includes a sixty-forty split seatback. Watch your head when you load luggage; the open trunk lid hangs low, and its latch is fairly sharp.

Safety

The four-door *DX* has adjustable shoulder-belt anchors; the two-door doesn't. The rear safety belts are fairly easy to use. You can easily secure a child safety seat in any seating position without a locking clip. The rear head restraints are barely high enough to protect average-size people. Our bumper-basher's 3- and 5-mph impacts damaged the front bumper to the tune of $455. In the rear, the bumper pushed up one taillight and creased the fender. The repair estimate: $689.

Our analysis of the government's crash test of a 1995 *Tercel* indicates that the driver dummy suffered certain injury, possibly severe, while the passenger dummy fared quite well.

Predicted reliability

⊜ Like many *Toyotas*, the *Tercel* has enjoyed an excellent reliability record for many years.

Based on a September 1995 report.

Volkswagen Golf GL

***Price range:** $13,150–$19,975*
***Cost factor:** 92%*
Depreciation: ○

Overview

While the *Golf* is a fine performer overall, reliability problems prevent us from recommending this model.

Acceleration

○ The lively 2.0-liter Four feels particularly responsive at low engine speeds but loses its punch at high speeds. In a check-test of the similar *Jetta* with the optional four-speed automatic transmission, we found performance sluggish.

Transmission

⊜ The nicely geared five-speed manual shifts precisely.

Economy

⊖ Fuel economy should average about 30 mpg.

Routine handling

⊜ The car feels agile and sporty on winding country roads. It cornered swiftly and precisely through sweeping turns at our test track, although it leaned sharply.

Emergency handling

○ The *Golf* lifted a rear wheel well off the pavement in our sharp back-and-forth avoidance maneuver, a trait that's unusual but not unsafe.

Braking

⊖ Our early-production *Golf* has four-wheel disc brakes; later versions come with drum brakes in the rear. Our car stopped fairly short from 60 mph—in 137 feet on dry pavement, 154 feet on wet pavement. The car veered to one side in our divided-pavement tests, but it straightened out in the end.

Ride, normal load

⊖ The car provides a supple ride for one or two passengers.

Ride, full load

○ When fully loaded, the ride deteriorates and the suspension clanks—especially on shabby roads.

Noise

○ Wind noise predominates on the highway.

Driving position

⊖ Tall drivers who like to sit high may run out of head- and legroom because raising the seat also moves it forward.

Front seating

⊖ Provides good, firm support.

Rear seating

○ The rear seat has room for two six-footers, three in a pinch, but lumpy wings and a bulge along the top of the seatback compromise comfort.

Access

⊖ Skimpy foot room hampers access; the doors' sharp corners are menacing.

Climate system

⊖ Warmed or cooled air is generally well distributed front and rear. Air leaks from dash vents, regardless of mode setting. Bilevel delivers the same air temperature to the face and the feet, instead of cooler air above, warmer below.

Controls and displays

⊖ The horn controls are buttons on the spokes of the steering wheel; we prefer to have the horn control in the hub of the wheel, where it's easy to find in a hurry. The complicated windshield-wiper control works the front wipers, the rear wiper and—with a quick flick—the window washer. Flick slowly and the washer just dribbles. The rear-window wiper has only an intermittent setting; a continuous setting would be useful in a downpour. Reflections obscure the instruments on sunny days.

Trunk

◒ The trunk holds little more than three Pullman cases and one weekend bag, or a folded wheelchair, but folding the split rear seatback provides a lot more room. You can hide a few small articles in the well around the compact spare. The *Golf* can tow a 1000-pound trailer.

Safety

The *Golf* has dual air bags and lap-and-shoulder belts front and rear. You need a locking clip to secure a child safety seat—a significant fact omitted from the owner's manual. The clutch pedal lacks a safety switch to prevent the engine from starting when the clutch is engaged. Our bumper basher didn't harm the bumpers.

Both driver and passenger dummies received possibly severe "injuries" in government crash tests.

Predicted reliability

◒ Reliability is below average.

Based on an October 1994 report.

Volkswagen Golf GTI

***Price range:** $16,000–$19,685*
***Cost factor:** 92%*
Depreciation: ○

Overview

Though the *Golf GTI* handles with finesse, it falls short in acceleration. The hatchback configuration gives it a decisive edge in cargo room.

Acceleration

○ The 2.0-liter Four accelerates adequately. The *VR6* version, a step up from the *GTI*, has a smooth, 172-hp V6, but adds several thousand dollars to the bottom line.

Transmission

⊖ The five-speed manual transmission shifts smoothly enough, but it feels vague at times. Getting into reverse requires moving the lever left and forward; we prefer the more usual right-and-backward motion. A four-speed automatic is available.

Economy

⊖ Expect to average about 27 mpg.

Routine handling

⊜ The *Golf GTI* is fun to drive, even if it isn't quick. It glides smoothly and crisply from one bend to the next.

Emergency handling

⊖ Although the body leans quite a bit in hard turns, the tires grip well. A rear tire sometimes lifted off the track when negotiating hard corners, but that's far less alarming than it may look.

Braking

⊜ The *GTI* braked well.

Ride, normal load

○ Ride motions are frequent but mostly mild.

Ride, full load

○ A full load actually improves the ride.

Noise

⊖ The main sounds inside are a muted engine hum and a bit of wind rush at highway speeds.

Driving position

⊖ Short drivers enjoy a commanding view ahead, but tall drivers must sit low because raising the seat moves it forward. The steering wheel doesn't adjust for height.

Front seating

⊖ The front seats are firm and nicely shaped. An awkward rotary knob adjusts the angle of the seatback.

Rear seating

○ Two six-footers fit easily in the rear, three if they're slim.

Access

⊖ The front seatbacks fold far forward to ease access to the rear.

Climate system

○ The climate-control system works well and has easy-to-use rotary knobs.

Controls and displays

○ The controls take some getting used to. The horn buttons, on the spokes of the steering wheel, are hard to find quickly, and the windshield wiper stalk isn't clearly labeled. The Off position for the wipers is between Intermittent and Low speed, and it's easy to spritz the rear window when you want to only wipe it. The gray-on-black labels are hard to discern. Sunlight casts annoying reflections on the gauges.

Trunk

○ The space behind the rear seat is fairly roomy. With the split rear seat folded, the *Golf* hatchback can swallow a lot of cargo. A folded wheelchair can fit in the trunk.

Safety

A "pre-tensioner" on the safety belts automatically takes up any slack in the webbing in a crash. The *Golf* has a height adjustment for the front shoulder-belt anchors. You don't need a separate clip to install a child safety seat—but many child seats may be too broad to fit in the preferred center-rear position. The front head restraints are high enough for an average-size adult even when they're fully lowered; but they don't lock when raised, so they wouldn't help tall occupants much. The rear seats don't have head restraints. Daytime running lights, an effective safety feature, are standard equipment. Our bumper basher left the rear unscathed but did $577 worth of damage in front.

When the government crash-tested a *Jetta* in 1994, both the driver and passenger dummies suffered certain, possibly severe "injuries." The *Golf* claims to comply with the 1997 dynamic side-impact safety standard.

Predicted reliability

◒ The *Golf* and its sedan cousin, the *Jetta*, haven't been all that reliable in the past few years. We predict worse-than-average reliability for the *GTI*.

Based on a May 1996 report.

Volkswagen Jetta III

Price range: $14,250–$20,610
Cost factor: 91%
Depreciation: ○

Overview

Performance is sprightly and the handling is generally crisp, but a bouncy ride tempers the comfortable seats. Reliability has been disappointing.

Acceleration

⊖ The *GLX* version comes with an exceptionally smooth and responsive 2.8-liter V6. Lower trim lines have a 2.0-liter Four, which also performs nicely but not as powerfully. Accelerating the V6 hard makes the steering pull to the right.

Transmission

⊜ The five-speed manual shifts smoothly, and its gear ratios complement the engine. A four-speed automatic is optional.

Economy

○ Fuel economy is only about 23 mpg.

Routine handling

⊜ Steering is quick, precise, and nicely

weighted, with excellent feedback. The body leans moderately during hard cornering, but the car holds the road well.

Emergency handling

⊖ The *Jetta* sailed through our avoidance maneuver in a steady, predictable manner.

Braking

⊖ The car stopped from 60 mph in 134 feet on dry pavement, in 156 feet on wet pavement. It weaved slightly in our wet divided-pavement test, but it quickly straightened out.

Ride, normal load

○ The *Jetta* soaks up mild bumps reasonably well at low speeds. But the ride becomes unsettled at highway speeds, with buoyant pitching and unpleasant up-and-down and sideways motions.

Ride, full load

◒ Noticeably worsens; impacts become harsher, and bumps often fully compress the rear suspension.

Noise

⊖ The cabin is very quiet.

Driving position

⊖ Multiple adjustments help most drivers get comfortably situated. Legroom and headroom under the optional sunroof are adequate for six-footers. Tall drivers may have to sit low because the seat moves forward as it rises, reducing legroom.

Front seating

⊖ Good, firm support. Effective heaters are standard equipment in both front seats.

Rear seating

○ Just about accommodates three six-footers, as long as they're slim.

Access

⊖ Front and rear access are good.

Climate system

⊖ Works powerfully, but the dash vents leak some air in all modes. The rear defroster lacks a timer to shut it off.

Controls and displays

⊖ The instruments are clear at night, but reflections sometimes cause problems in the daytime. Some controls are confusing or hard to find. For example, the horn buttons are on the spokes of the steering wheel rather than in the hub, and the power switches for the rear windows are on the instrument panel—an unusual location. Finding the Off position for the windshield wipers is tricky. The passenger-side air bag usurps the glove compartment.

Trunk

⊖ The large trunk can hold five Pullman cases and one weekend bag, or a folded wheelchair, with room left over. The split rear seat can tumble and fold to expand the trunk. The compact spare takes up its entire well, leaving no room for hiding small items.

Safety

Dual air bags are standard. The front safety belts have adjustable upper anchors, but our short driver found the belt too close to her neck even with the anchor fully lowered. The rear three-point belts also have an adjustable anchor. They need a locking clip to secure a child seat—important information that's omitted from the owner's manual. Our bumper basher did no damage to the front or rear.

Both the driver and passenger dummies received possibly severe "injuries" in government crash tests.

Predicted reliability

◒ The *Jetta* has a below-average reliability record.

Based on a November 1994 report.

SPORTS/SPORTY CARS

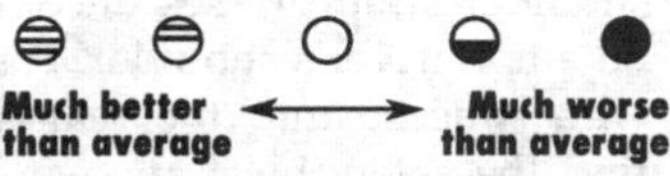

By our definition, a sporty car is simply a two-door coupe or convertible with a performance image. But that definition encompasses many disparate designs. Some sporty models are based on sedans, but with greater emphasis on acceleration and handling than on economy and comfort. The *Mazda MX-6*, for example, is related to the *Mazda 626* compact-size sedan, but its sleeker body and tighter suspension set it apart.

A few sporty models, such as the *Mitsubishi 3000GT*, *Mazda MX-5 Miata*, and *Nissan 300ZX*, are unadulterated sports cars with a strong bias toward performance at the expense of practicality. Such cars usually have an unusually harsh, noisy ride, minimal trunk room, and a vestigial rear seat or no seat at all. Fuel economy also becomes secondary in many sports cars.

Our recommended models are the *Acura Integra*, the *Honda Prelude*, the *Mazda MX-5 Miata*, the *Nissan 200SX*, the *Nissan 300ZX*, the *Saturn SC*, the *Subaru SVX*, the *Toyota Celica*, and the *Toyota Supra*.

Acura Integra GS-R 

Price range:* *$16,460–$20,980
Cost factor:* *88%
Depreciation:

Overview

Combining nimble handling and zesty engine response with impressive fuel economy *and* high predicted reliability makes for a fine all-around package.

Acceleration

The standard engine in the *GS-R* version is a 1.8-liter VTEC Four. It serves up vigorous acceleration while revving freely to its unusually high, 8000-rpm redline.

Transmission

The five-speed manual shifts crisply, and its gear ratios are well chosen for lively performance. Even when the *Integra* is cruising at highway speeds in fifth gear, the engine revs fairly high.

An automatic transmission is not available in the *GS-R*.

Economy

Expect to average about 30 mpg on Premium fuel. The non-VTEC 1.8-liter engine in other versions runs on Regular fuel.

Routine handling

The steering provides decent road feel, and the car stays well planted in bumpy turns. During hard cornering at our track, it displayed a slight tendency to plow ahead—easily corrected by letting up on the accelerator.

Emergency handling

The *Integra* threaded through our avoidance maneuver crisply and confidently.

Braking

Antilock brakes stopped the car short and straight in all our braking tests.

Ride.

Ride is a bit on the stiff side; rough pavement elicits jiggles, kicks, and some rocking motions. It's also taut and busy on expressways, but it remains well controlled.

Noise

Quite a lot of road noise enters the cabin. The engine makes a sporting sound when revved.

Driving position

Most people should be able to find a good driving position despite the low driver's seat, which can't be raised. Six-footers will find just enough legroom and adequate headroom. Even short drivers can see well over the hood.

Front seating

The front seats provide good, firm support—perhaps too firm for some people. The seatbacks are shaped to cradle occupants during hard cornering.

Rear seating

Forget the rear seat; knee room is skimpy, and headroom is atrocious.

Access

Access to the front seats is just adequate.

Climate system

The climate-control system takes a bit of fiddling but works well, despite a stiff temperature slider and rather noisy fan. Although the rear defroster works slowly, it eventually gets the job done. The rear-window wiper is useful in wet weather, but it lacks a continuous setting.

Controls and displays

The instruments are clear, and most controls are easy to reach, but the layout is flawed.

Trunk

The trunk holds three Pullman cases and one weekend bag, or a collapsed wheelchair, with room left over. The split rear seatback can be folded to expand the luggage area. The *Integra* comes only with a compact spare.

Safety

Putting on the front safety belts requires a long reach backward, and the shoulder strap presses uncomfortably on a tall driver's shoulder. Passengers who squeeze into the rear seat will find the safety belts awkward to put on. Also, the lap portion rides too high, on the abdomen. Securing a child safety seat requires a locking clip. Our bumper basher's 3- and 5-mph blows damaged the rear bumper to the tune of $554. The front survived unscathed.

The driver was better protected than the passenger in government crash tests.

Predicted reliability

⊖ The *Integra* continues to have an excellent reliability record.

Based on a June 1994 report.

BMW 318ti

Price range: *$20,560*
Cost factor: *89%*
Depreciation: *NA*

The rear-wheel-drive *318ti* is the newest addition to BMW's smallish 3-Series line. The hatchback coupe is several inches shorter than the regular *318.* As with other *BMWs,* the emphasis is on sports car–like driving (complete with rear-wheel drive) rather than luxury, although the *318ti* comes with a wealth of standard equipment.

Predicted reliability

No data, new model.

BMW Z3

Price: *$28,750*
Cost factor: *85%*
Depreciation: *NA*

This stylish new roadster, built in BMW's new plant in Spartanburg, S.C., is based on components from 3-Series *BMW* sedans. It's often compared with the *Mazda Miata,* although the *BMW* is a little larger (big enough inside for six-footers) and several thousand dollars costlier. It makes its debut with a 1.9-liter Four, and a 2.8-liter inline Six will be available later this year.

Predicted reliability

No data, new model.

Chevrolet Camaro

Price range: *$14,990–$24,490*
Cost factor: *92%*
Depreciation: ○

Overview

The *Camaro/Firebird* twins continue the muscle car tradition of big V8s, rear-wheel drive, and poor reliability.

Acceleration

⊖ The tested V6 and optional four-speed automatic transmission was not at all pokey, but once we sampled the effortless thrust of the V8 (see the *Firebird* test on page 84), our smaller-engined *Camaro* felt sluggish and harsh.

Transmission

⊖ The optional four-speed automatic shifts smoothly. A five-speed manual is standard.

Economy

◒ Not as bad as with the V8. Expect about 19 mpg with the V6.

Routine handling

⊖ Too wide to be truly nimble, but corners with minimum body roll. Tires gripped well, but the rear end sometimes skipped out in bumpy turns.

Emergency handling

⊖ Inspires confidence in tricky situations. The car's bulk made it difficult to weave through the accident-avoidance course, but it held the track firmly and responded quickly to steering inputs.

Braking

⊖ Braked very well, but not as impressively as the *Firebird.*

Ride

○ A reasonably comfortable ride for a sporty model. It's fairly smooth on the turnpike. As the road deteriorates, the ride becomes jerky but not really harsh.

Noise

○ The V6 runs more quietly overall than the *Firebird's* V8, but the engine sounds unpleasantly rough during acceleration. Wind occasionally hissed past the rear hatch.

Driving position

⊖ Comfortable for drivers of all sizes. The height adjuster on the optional six-way power seat lets the driver see well over the long hood. The view to the rear and over the shoulder is poor, and the car's front and rear ends are invisible to the driver. Headroom is generous; legroom is adequate for six-footers, but a wide transmission tunnel forces the accelerator too far to the left.

Front seating

⊖ Bucket seats cradle occupants nicely.

Rear seating

● Regard the rear buckets as seating for emergencies only. Knee room is too tight for most adults, and high front seatbacks and wide roof pillars make passengers feel claustrophobic.

Access

○ Watch your face; the unframed, inward-curving door windows are hard to see. And pay attention to the weak door detents; if they let go, the door can close on your hand or leg. Rear access is abominable.

Climate system

⊖ Supplies plenty of warmed or cooled air and distributes it evenly. Fan sounds noisier than that of the *Firebird*.

Controls and displays

○ Controls are within easy reach and logically arranged. Unfortunately, you have to fumble for either of the two little pads on the steering wheel to sound the horn. Climate controls are unlit, so you can't see the settings at night.

Trunk

◒ Trunk is shallow toward the front of the car, deep toward the back. It can hold three Pullman cases, or a folded wheelchair with room left over. Folding the rear seatback—no easy chore—affords extra cargo room. Lifting heavy items over the trunk's high sill into the deep rear well is a challenge. Hinged security panel hides cargo. Compact spare resides under cover behind right rear wheel housing. Towing limit is 1500 pounds.

Safety

Dual air bags supplement the front safety belts. Reaching them is a long stretch, as in most two-door cars. The remote upper anchors make the shoulder belts ride uncomfortably on the occupant's neck. The front passenger's belt requires a locking clip to secure a child's safety seat. The rear belts don't require a clip, but the seating positions may be too narrow for some child safety seats. Our low-speed bumper-basher tests inflicted minimal damage.

Both driver and passenger dummies were well protected in government crash tests.

Predicted reliability

◒ Reliability improved slightly, although it's still worse than average.

Based on an October 1993 report.

Chevrolet Corvette

Price range: $37,225–$45,060
Cost factor: 85%
Depreciation: ◒

Overview

America's only native sports car delivers blazing power, secure braking, crisp handling, and dismal reliability. This is the last year for the current generation *Corvette*.

Acceleration

⊖ Very fast: 0 to 60 mph in 5.5 seconds. A quarter-mile in 14.1 seconds, reaching a speed of 103 mph.

Transmission

⊖ Shifting of the six-speed manual feels heavy but precise. To save fuel, a computer automatically glides the shifter from first gear directly into fourth when you shift at fairly low speed and low engine revs. It's hard to see from the position of the shifter what gear you're in. But with such tremendous torque on hand, it almost doesn't matter; you could do 55 mph in any of the five top gears. At 60 mph in sixth gear, the engine loafs along at about 1380 rpm. That's barely above idle speed.

Economy

● Not exactly a commuter's delight: about 17 mpg in mixed driving—on Premium fuel.

Routine handling

⊖ Smooth but not nimble. The *Corvette's* size and weight make it a bit awkward to steer. On bumpy roads, the tires don't stay firmly planted on the pavement. It's not a car you can thread easily in and out of traffic.

Emergency handling

⊖ Crisp and very quick, with only slight tail wag when the tires began to let go.

Braking

⊖ The antilock brakes functioned superbly.

Ride

◒ The Sport and Performance settings on the electronically controlled suspension stiffen the ride, giving control at the expense of comfort. On the softer Tour setting, winding roads that are less than glassy smooth make the car bound; on rough roads, a tall driver's head might bang against the glass top.

Noise

◒ At highway speeds, the road and wind noises intrude. The power train booms loudly at 55 mph in sixth gear.

Driving position

○ With seats pushed all the way back, the seatback can't recline enough to accommodate tall drivers. Short drivers are too close to the accelerator pedal when the seat is adjusted so they can depress the clutch pedal; with the accelerator at a comfortable distance, the clutch pedal is too long a stretch. Drivers can't see well over the long hood, even with the six-way power seat raised.

Front seating

⊖ Firm, well-padded support.

Access

● Awkward to get in and out.

Climate system

⊖ The optional automatic climate-control system nicely maintains the chosen temperature. It's unobtrusive—except after the car has sat in the hot sun. Then, a loud torrent of air blows in until the temperature stabilizes. The side-window defoggers, rear-window defroster, and heated outside mirrors work very well.

Controls and displays

⊖ Major controls are logical. Push buttons call up digital readouts for various computer functions. The shifter partly blocks access to the radio. All the displays are clear and easy to read.

Trunk

● Two Pullman cases and a couple of

weekend bags. Deploying the security blind halves the luggage room. A locking bin behind the passenger seat can hold valuables. But *Corvettes* are not exactly known to have large cargo areas.

Safety

Dual air bags supplement three-point belts that are comfortable but tricky to buckle. Our bumper basher tore the rear bumper's plastic covering. Repair estimate was $493.

The government has not yet crash-tested a *Corvette.*

Predicted reliability

● The *Corvette's* reliability is poor. A new *Corvette* is scheduled to go into production next year.

Based on a September 1992 report.

Chrysler Sebring

Price range: *$16,441–$24,675*
Cost factor: *92%*
Depreciation: *NA*

This sporty coupe and its cousin, the *Dodge Avenger,* were designed by Chrysler and are built in Illinois by Mitsubishi. We'd choose the 2.5-liter Mitsubishi V6 over the noisy Chrysler 2.0-liter Four. Handling is competent. The chassis absorbs big bumps well, but little pavement flaws transmit firm kicks. The front seats provide quite good support. Three adults fit tightly in the rear seat. Some minor controls are poorly placed, but the gauges are clear. The trunk is large, and the rear seatback can be folded. This year a convertible joins the line. Its underpinnings have more in common with the *Cirrus,* a good, up-to-date midsize sedan. Expect nicely laid-out controls and an interior that's roomy for a convertible.

Predicted reliability ○

Dodge Avenger ES

Price range: *$14,040–$18,121*
Cost factor: *92%*
Depreciation: *NA*

Overview

In our test of midsize coupes, which included the *Buick Riviera, Chevrolet Monte Carlo Z34,* and *Ford Thunderbird LX,* the *Avenger* had the best design. Reliability has been average.

Acceleration

○ The V6 delivers good performance. The base version's Four is noisy and less responsive.

Transmission

⊖ The four-speed automatic shifts smoothly. A five-speed manual is standard equipment with the Four, but unavailable with the V6.

Economy

○ Expect to average about 22 mpg in mixed driving with the V6.

Routine handling

⊖ The *Avenger* feels nimble in routine twists and turns, but its large turning circle makes parking more work than it should be.

Emergency handling

⊖ Handling felt nimble and responsive in our avoidance maneuver, thanks to the fairly quick steering and the tires' strong grip. The front end tended to plow ahead a bit in hard turns at our test track.

Braking

⊖ Stops were short and straight on dry pavement, a bit long on wet pavement. The *Avenger* stopped fairly straight in our test on wet divided pavement, where the road surface is more slippery under one side of the car than under the other.

Ride, normal load

○ The *Avenger* has a relatively pleasant highway ride, but small pavement flaws jar the occupants a bit.

Ride, full load

○ A full load of passengers helps smooth out the rough spots.

Noise

○ The incessant whir of the tires detracts from the ride.

Driving position

⊖ You can adjust the height of the lumbar support by raising or lowering the seat cushion; the cushion moves, but the seatback stays put. Short drivers couldn't see out well even with the seat fully raised, and some tall drivers complained that the adjustable steering column didn't lift far enough to clear their thighs. With the seat adjusted fairly far back, the buckled safety belt blocked the seatback adjuster.

Front seating

⊖ The front seats provide firm support, but a little more contouring along the sides would cradle occupants better. A bulge in the upper part of the seatback annoyed some of our testers.

Rear seating

◒ Three tall people can squeeze into the rear seat for a short jaunt, but two average-size people are the practical limit for longer trips.

Access

○ Getting in and out is fairly easy—if you have room to open the large doors all the way. The driver's seatback is designed to return to its previous position after being folded for access to the rear seat, but the feature often misses the mark.

Climate system

○ The climate-control system distributes air unevenly, and its fan is noisy. A single button switches on the air conditioner in any mode. An Economy setting saves fuel when it's not too hot. You must close the vents on the doors by hand to direct maximum airflow to the windshield or floor. The rear defroster doesn't cover enough of the glass.

Controls and displays

⊖ Most controls and gauges are simple and straightforward. But the small horn buttons, on the spokes of the steering wheel, are hard to find in a hurry. There's no indicator to tell you when the fog lights are on.

Trunk

⊖ The trunk holds five Pullman suitcases or a folded wheelchair with room left over. Folding the split seatback extends the cargo room. (You can lock the seatback and the remote trunk release for security.) A removable cargo net stabilizes tippy items like grocery bags.

Safety

Adjustable upper anchors on the front safety belts are an unusual and welcome detail in a coupe. Head restraints front and rear protect against whiplash. In our 3- and 5-mph bumper-basher tests, the front bumper was damaged very slightly; the repair estimate was $43.

An *Avenger* protected its safety-belted dummy "occupants" well in recent government 35-mph crash tests.

Predicted reliability

○ Expect reliability to be about average.

Based on a July 1995 report.

Eagle Talon

Price range: $14,059–$20,271
Cost factor: 93%
Depreciation: ○

The *Talon* and similar *Mitsubishi Eclipse* were redesigned for 1995. They are made in Illinois by Mitsubishi. The standard engine is a Chrysler-built 2.0-liter Four that powers the *Neon;* it needs lots of revving before it produces much power. More expensive trim lines get a more powerful Mitsubishi 2.0-liter turbocharged Four. The *Talon* is available with either front- or all-wheel drive.

Predicted reliability ●

Ford Mustang

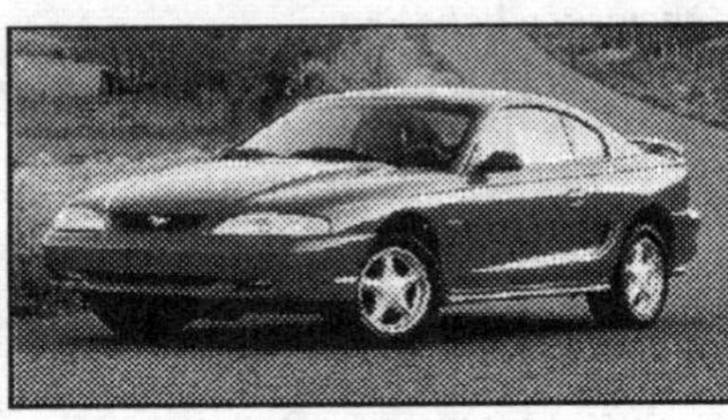

Price range: $15,180–$23,495
Cost factor: 91%
Depreciation: ◒

Overview

Nostalgia and stylistic flourishes can't make up for the *Mustang's* overall mediocrity. We tested the V8-powered *GT* and V6 *Mustangs*.

Acceleration

⊜/⊖ (*GT/V6*) The base 3.6-liter V6 feels sluggish. Even the V8 falls well short of the *Camaro* and *Firebird* V8s.

Transmission

⊖/⊖ With either engine, the four-speed automatic shifts slowly and prematurely into fourth, making the engine lug. A five-speed manual is available.

Economy

●/○ Expect to average about 22 mpg with the *Mustang* V6 and about 18 mpg with the V8, both on Regular fuel.

Routine handling

⊖/⊖ Both *Mustangs* bounce and hop on rippled curves. The *GT* rolls less in corners, thanks to its stiffer suspension and wider tires, but neither version feels particularly sporty.

Emergency handling

⊖/⊖ In hard cornering at our track, both *Mustangs* plowed ahead until the front tires regained their grip, but they negotiated our avoidance maneuver steadily and securely.

Braking

⊖/⊖ The *Mustangs,* with their antilock brakes, stopped quite short and straight, but both exhibited too much nosedive.

Ride

◒/◒ Expect a jerky, active ride in either version. The V6's ride motions are larger and more rubbery than those of the *GT*.

Noise

○/⊖ The engines sound coarse and strained during acceleration, and the V6 idles noisily. The *GT* suffers from tire noise as well.

Driving position

⊖/⊖ Some testers complained that they had to recline the seat too much to get far enough from the steering wheel. Legroom is adequate for tall people, and headroom is ample. Our five-foot-tall tester had no trouble seeing over the hood. The accelerator is a bit too far left, and the skimpy footrest is too close to the driver.

Front seating

○/○ Neither *Mustang's* front seats feel especially comfortable or supportive.

Rear seating

●/● The rear seat is no place for adults.

Access

◒/◒ Climbing in and out of the front isn't too awkward.

Climate system

⊖/⊖ The climate-control system works well, although it lacks a Bilevel mode.

Controls and displays

⊜/⊜ The radio is hard to use, as is usual in *Fords*. We also dislike the placement of the power-seat switch, on the front of the seat; the fog-light switch, at the rear of the center console; and the rear defroster control, which is hidden to the left of the steering wheel.

Trunk

●/◒ The trunk holds three Pullman

cases plus three weekend bags—or two plus two with the *GT*'s trunk-mounted Mach 460 sound system. A folded wheelchair can also fit in the cargo area. The rear seatbacks can be folded. A narrow trunk opening and high sill make loading awkward. The spare is a compact.

Safety
The front safety belts easily slip out of their front seatback guides, which is an annoyance, and putting on the belts requires a long reach backward. The rear belts' lap strap tends to ride too high, on the abdomen. You can secure a child safety seat in any position without a locking clip, but some child seats may not fit the contours of the rear seat cushion. Our bumper basher caused no damage either front or rear.

Government crash tests showed that both the passenger and driver dummy fared well, with the driver slightly better.

Predicted reliability
◒ Expect reliability to be below average.

Based on a June 1994 report.

Ford Probe GT

***Price range:* $13,930–$16,450**
***Cost factor:* 92%**
***Depreciation:* ○**

Overview
Handles with precision, accelerates with verve, and even provides respectable luggage capacity. But reliability has lagged.

Acceleration
⊖ Seamless and responsive.

Transmission
⊜ Manual/◒ Automatic The five-speed shifts precisely through well-chosen ratios. The optional automatic (see *Mazda MX-6*, page 80) shifts harshly.

Economy
○ Using recommended Premium fuel, expect to average about 24 mpg.

Routine handling
⊜ Flawless handling and precise tracking.

Emergency handling
⊜ Smooth and predictable. Excellent grip from *Goodyear Eagle VR50* tires.

Braking
⊖ Competent.

Ride
◒ Stiff and jittery over all types of roads. Lots of kicks and thumps.

Noise
○ Fairly quiet at light throttle, but throaty exhaust snarl is heard during acceleration. Road noise comes through as a low-frequency rumble.

Driving position
⊜ With optional power driver's seat and tilt steering column, even short drivers can get comfortable and see easily over the hood.

Front seating
○ Uneven support from seatbacks bothered some testers.

Rear seating
● Fine for packages or small children.

Access
○ Less than graceful due to low seats, low roofline, and high and broad doorsills.

Climate system
⊖ Lacks Bilevel setting, but quiet fan distributes airflow evenly from all vents.

Controls and displays
⊜ All controls are within easy reach. Horn buttons, on steering wheel spokes rather than hub, are hard to find in an emergency.

Trunk
○ Room for four Pullman cases and two weekend bags. Trunk expands when rear seatback halves are folded down.

Safety
Dual air bags are standard equipment. No damage to the front or rear bumpers from our bumper basher.

Excellent results from government crash tests.

Predicted reliability
◒ Reliability has not improved from last year.

Based on a January 1993 report.

Honda Civic del Sol Si

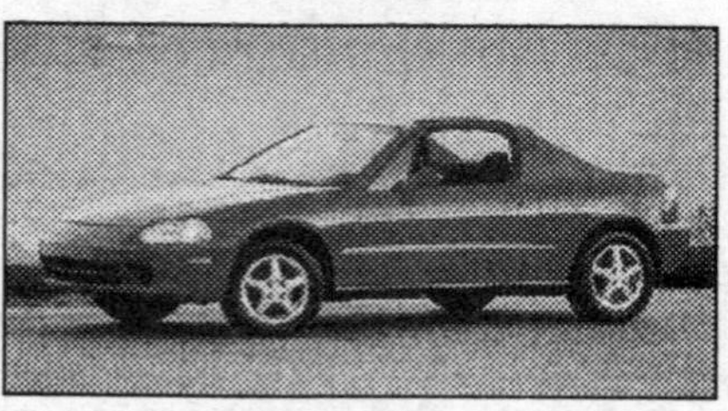

***Price range:* $14,930–$19,400**
***Cost factor:* 90%**
***Depreciation:* ⊖**

Overview
A disappointment. The *del Sol* simply lacks the driving excitement of a good sporty car.

Acceleration
○ Responsive, and slightly faster than the *Mazda Miata*, but it doesn't feel or sound as sporty.

Transmission
⊖ Shifts stiffly when cold. Although it smooths out when it warms up, it never feels crisp. It's geared for economy rather than performance, and the travel of the clutch pedal is too long. A four-speed automatic is optional.

Economy
⊜ Expect about 32 mpg overall.

Routine handling
⊖ Steering feels reasonably responsive, but not sporty, in routine driving. The body rolls moderately during cornering.

Emergency handling

⊖ Easy to control in accident-avoidance tests. Its front end plowed a bit in very hard turns, and then its tail went into a slow-motion slide.

Braking

◒ Stops from 60 mph were a bit long on a dry track and very long on a wet track. Antilock brakes would have helped, but they aren't available. The car veered to one side in the wet divided-pavement test.

Ride

○ A busy ride, and the body flexes and creaks even when the roof is in place. With the roof removed, the body twists, squeaks, and shakes considerably.

Noise

◒ Rattles and squeaks, engine drone, and tire hum add up to a noisy ride.

Driving position

○ Most drivers felt as if they were sitting on the floor, and short drivers especially had trouble seeing over the hood. The wide rear roof pillars create blind spots toward the rear. Tall drivers found ample head- and legroom. When drivers position the seat so they can reach the accelerator comfortably, they must stretch to fully depress the clutch pedal.

Front seating

⊖ The bucket seats provide firm support, perhaps too firm for some people.

Access

◒ Getting in and out requires agility when the roof is on. When it's off, you must remember to dodge the corner of the windshield frame.

Climate system

⊜ Works well, but you must close the dash vents manually for maximum heat to the floor or windshield. The side windows fog up in damp, cold weather. You can lower the rear window to improve ventilation.

Controls and displays

○ The horn buttons, on the spokes of the steering wheel, are hard to find in a hurry. So is the ignition switch, under the steering wheel. Climate controls are convenient push buttons, but their indicator lights—and most of the displays—disappear in bright sunlight.

Trunk

○ Even with the roof stored in the trunk there is room for two Pullman cases. Without the roof, the trunk held four Pullmans and a weekend case, or a folded wheelchair. Small items can fit in the well around the compact spare, and other storage nooks abound inside the car. The *del Sol* isn't designed to tow a trailer.

Safety

Dual air bags supplement the three-point belts, which are difficult to snap into their buckle because it's wedged low between the seat and the center console. Some child seats may not fit in the narrow passenger's seat, and those that do require a locking clip. The bumper basher broke a fog lamp mount; the repair cost was $18.

The government has not crash-tested a *del Sol*.

Predicted reliability

○ The reliability of the *del Sol* has remained average.

Based on an October 1993 report.

Honda Prelude Si 

Price range: *$19,690–$25,880*
Cost factor: *89%*
Depreciation: ⊖

Overview

A happy blend of performance and handling, but the interior layout could be better.

Acceleration

⊖ Not quite as fast as most sports cars, but very lively.

Transmission

⊜ Smooth and accurate, with well-matched gear ratios.

Economy

○ About 26 mpg overall, with recommended Premium fuel.

Routine handling

⊜ The five-speed manual is smooth, with quick, precise, and nicely weighted steering.

Emergency handling

⊖ Competent, with a bit of tail wag.

Braking

⊖ Respectable stopping distances.

Ride

◒ Well controlled, but replete with small jerks, kicks, and jiggles on bumpy roads.

Noise

○ Some wind and road noise.

Driving position

⊖ Should suit most drivers, but depressing the clutch pedal requires a stretch.

Front seating

⊖ Firm and comfortable, with large side bolsters support in hard cornering.

Rear seating

● Tight head- and knee room, and almost no room for feet.

Access

◒ Very awkward.

Climate system

○ Outboard dash vents have to be shut to get effective heating and side-window defrosting—a nuisance.

Controls and displays

○ Scattered operating controls, and tiny spoke buttons for horn.

Trunk

● Two Pullman cases and two weekend bags.

Safety

Dual air bags supplement front three-point belts. No damage to front or rear bumpers from our basher.

The government has not crash-tested a *Prelude.*

Predicted reliability

⊜ Has proven to be extremely reliable.

Based on a January 1993 report.

Mazda MX-5 Miata 

Price range: *$18,950–$23,530*
Cost factor: *89%*
Depreciation: ⊖

Overview

A spiritual successor to the British sports cars of the 1950s and 1960s, this two-seater has been far more reliable. A crisp transmission and quick, precise steering make the *Miata* fun to drive. Although the cabin is small and typically noisy, the *Miata* should be on your sports car wish list.

Acceleration

○ The 1.8-liter Four provided invigorating acceleration, and its feel and sound are pure vintage sports car.

Transmission

⊜ Crisp, quick shifts from the five-speed manual. The optional four-speed automatic would take much of the fun out of driving this car.

Economy

⊖ Expect about 29 mpg overall.

Routine handling

⊜ Nimble and precise, with steering so quick and direct that the steering wheel feels almost like an extension of your body.

Emergency handling

⊜ The car's instant response and strong grip made it a natural in the twisty turns of the test track. It handled accident-avoidance maneuvers quickly and neatly; making the tail slide out requires deliberate mishandling by the driver.

Braking

⊖ Stopped straight and reasonably short from 60 mph on a dry track, but stops could have been shorter on wet pavement. The car weaved initially but then stopped straight in the divided-pavement test, in which the pavement is more slippery under one side of the car than the other.

Ride

◒ Stiff and nervous, like the old English roadsters. It can be tiring on long trips and uncomfortable on rough back roads. The car's body flexes slightly whether the convertible top is up or down but feels more solid with the optional hardtop in place.

Noise

◒ As with most convertibles, engine noise and exhaust drone are ever present, and wind noise predominates with the cloth top raised. The hardtop amplifies the sound of the tires on coarse pavement.

Driving position

○ Short drivers may find the seat cushion too low for a good view over the hood. Tall drivers who adjust the seat all the way back must sit bolt upright, since there's no clearance for reclining the seatback.

Front seating

⊖ Good, firm support for most drivers, but a bit more padding wouldn't hurt. The interior shortchanges tall occupants in lower back and thigh support, but headroom is ample even with the hardtop in place.

Access

◒ It takes agility to hurdle the high doorsills while ducking under the low roof. The tiny and awkward outside door handles accommodate only one finger.

Climate system

⊜ Provides plenty of heat, keeping the cabin comfortable even when the top is down in cool weather. The air conditioner works well, too. Turning on the fan switch activates the rear defroster in the optional hardtop for ten minutes.

Controls and displays

⊖ The controls need cleaning up. The horn buttons, in the spokes of the steering wheel, are hard to find in an emergency. The radio has myriad cryptic controls and buttons, too many to manage while watching the road, but no simple On/Off control. All the displays are logical, well laid out, and easy to read.

Trunk

● This is a not a car to take on a long trip. Plan to travel light; the tiny trunk holds only one weekend bag. And no towing, for obvious reasons.

Safety

Dual air bags supplement the safety belts. Tall occupants felt trapped by the pressure of the shoulder belt. Short occupants complained that it rode uncomfortably across the neck. You'll need a locking clip to secure a child safety seat, and some safety seats may not fit into the narrow bucket seat. The bumper basher shifted the plastic bumper, which required a $40 realignment.

The passenger fared better than the driver in government crash tests.

Predicted reliability

⊜ The *Miata* has enjoyed an excellent reliability record.

Based on an October 1993 report.

Mazda MX-6 LS

Price range: *$19,095–$21,648*
Cost factor: *89%*
Depreciation: ○

Overview

It's less sporty and a bit more softly sprung than the *Ford Probe,* which is also made at *Mazda's* Flat Rock, Michigan, plant. Avoid the automatic transmission—unfortunately, we didn't.

Acceleration

⊖ Would be more responsive with the five-speed manual.

Transmission

⊜ Manual/◒ Automatic Automatic downshifts abruptly into first gear when accelerating from low speed, and it thumps through other gears.

Economy

○ About 24 mpg overall on recommended Premium fuel, the same as with the manual transmission.

Routine handling

⊜ Almost as nimble as the *Probe,* although its suspension is slightly softer.

Emergency handling

⊖ Competent, smooth, and predictable.

Braking

⊖ Performed well on dry and wet pavement.

Ride

◒ Bumps cause firm kicks, taut rocking, choppy pitching, and hood shake.

Noise

○ Tires contribute the only prominent noise.

Driving position

⊜ Tilt steering column and power adjustments (optional) make position perfect for any size driver.

Front seating

⊜ Supportive, comfortable, prominently bolstered, and adjustable for lumbar support.

Rear seating

● Not hospitable for adults.

Access

○ Low roof, low seats, high doorsills, and prominent bolsters make access awkward.

Climate system

○ Ample and even air distribution, but the fan is noisy.

Controls and displays

⊖ Horn buttons on steering-wheel spokes are hard to locate to punch in an emergency. Climate controls work well, but the air-conditioning push button doesn't depress far enough, making it difficult to tell whether it is on or off.

Trunk

○ Four Pullman cases and two weekend bags fit easily, and split rear seatback folds for long cargo.

Safety

Dual air bags with three-point belts. Our bumper basher caused no damage front or rear.

The government has not crash-tested an *MX-6,* but the similar *Ford Probe* was tested and protected both the driver and passenger very well.

Predicted reliability

◒ Reliability has slipped.

Based on a January 1993 report.

Mazda RX-7

Price: *$37,800*
Cost factor: *89%*
Depreciation: ◒

Overview

Cast as a return to the pure sports car, the *RX-7* looks and feels the part. Comfort is not part of the script. Because of slow sales and a generally declining market for sports cars, this is likely to be the *RX-7's* last year.

Acceleration

⊜ Fierce—0 to 60 mph in 6 seconds.

Transmission

⊜ Five-speed manual is well matched to the engine. The shift pattern is short, and the action of the shifter feels precise.

Economy

● About 18 mpg overall.

Routine handling

⊜ Handles twisty, narrow roads with aplomb. It's nimble and precise, but on high-crowned or bumpy roads, the car tends to dart about.

Emergency handling

⊜ Sped through our avoidance-maneuver course at 60.5 mph, beating the 1992 *Dodge Stealth's* record by 1 mph.

Braking

⊜ Record breaking: only 119 feet to a stop from 60 mph.

Ride

● Whether the road is smooth or bumpy, every pebble and seam announces itself.

Noise

◒ Loud road noise on coarse roads and tire noise on smooth roads intrude into the cabin.

Driving position

○ This sports car has a cockpit that is cramped for even average-size people. With the accelerator a comfortable distance away, you have to stretch to floor the clutch pedal.

Front seating

⊖ Narrow buckets seats provide good, firm support, especially in hard cornering.

Access

◒ Narrow footwells and very low seats and roof make access especially awkward.

Climate system

⊖ Versatile system that quickly provides ample warm or cool air.

Controls and displays

○ Placement could be better. Horn buttons on steering wheel spokes are easy to bump. Wiper lever is cluttered (it works the front and rear wipers), and is hidden by the steering wheel when the front wipers are on. Instrumentation is complete, but reflections occasionally obscure the chrome-rimmed gauges.

Trunk

● One Pullman case or a couple of weekend bags, because resonator duct for the optional Bose sound system takes up almost half the trunk space.

Safety

Tension of shoulder belts is uncomfortably high. Seat cushion may be too narrow for some child seats. Driver visibility is good. No damage to front or rear bumpers from our bumper basher.

The government has not crash-tested an *RX-7.*

Predicted reliability

Insufficient data.

Based on a September 1992 report.

Mitsubishi 3000GT

***Price range:** $30,690–$64,000 (est.)*
***Cost factor:** 82%*
Depreciation: ○

In its sportiest form, the *3000GT* is loaded with techno-gadgets. Trim lines range from the 222-hp base model with front-wheel drive on up to the 320-hp VR-4, with twin turbochargers, four-wheel steering, electronically adjustable suspension, and all-wheel drive. The latter version gives good cornering grip, exceptionally short stops, and powerful acceleration. The car is fast, but it's too heavy and wide to feel nimble. The rear seat is just for show. A *Spyder* convertible with a retractable hardtop is also available.

Predicted reliability ○

Mitsubishi Eclipse

***Price range:** $14,436–$24,990*
***Cost factor:** 87%*
Depreciation: ○

The *Eclipse* and similar *Eagle Talon* were redesigned in 1995. They're made in Illinois by Mitsubishi. The standard engine is the Chrysler-built 2.0-liter Four that powers the *Neon;* it needs lots of revving before it produces much power. More expensive trim lines get a more powerful Mitsubishi 2.0-liter turbocharged Four. The *Eclipse* comes with either front- or all-wheel drive. A convertible version was introduced this year.

Predicted reliability ●

Nissan 200SX SE-R

***Price range:** $12,449–$16,069*
***Cost factor:** 91%*
***Depreciation:** NA*

Overview

The sporty *SE-R* version of the *200SX* offers a zesty and refined power train and capable handling and braking.

Acceleration

⊖ The 2.0-liter Four delivers lively performance.

Transmission

⊜ The five-speed manual transmission shifts crisply, and its well-chosen ratios complement the engine. A smooth-shifting four-speed automatic transmission is available

Economy

⊖ Expect to average about 28 mpg. The base 1.6-liter Four is less responsive but uses less fuel.

Routine handling

⊜ The *SE-R* feels sporty to drive. Its crisp cornering, with minimal body roll and good tire grip, inspires confidence. The steering responds quickly enough, but it doesn't communicate as much road feel as we'd like.

Emergency handling

⊖ The *SE-R* threaded through our avoidance maneuver quickly and securely.

Braking

⊜ The exemplary brakes stopped the car short and straight in all our braking tests.

Ride, normal load

○ The ride feels firm and tightly controlled on good roads, but bumpy roads elicit short, stiff motions.

Ride, full load

○ A full load does little harm on smooth surfaces, but it worsens the ride considerably on poor roads.

Noise

○ The cabin screens out most road and wind noise. The engine sounds loud at high revs, but it's a sporty sound that some people may like.

Driving position

○ The front seats are fairly low, and they can't be raised. Tall drivers found the accelerator too close and thigh support wanting. Even our medium-size drivers had too little legroom when they moved the seat forward far enough to fully depress the clutch pedal. Our shorter drivers couldn't see forward well.

Front seating

⊖ Although the front seats are small, they provide good, firm support.

Rear seating

◒ Misery for two adults.

Access

○ The right front seat scoots forward when its seatback is folded, but it doesn't return to its earlier position when it's pushed back.

Climate system

⊖ The climate-control system works well, but its fan is noisy.

Controls and displays

⊖ The controls are well designed, and the horn control is in the center of the wheel, where it belongs. Minor complaints include a tiny, awkward push button that releases the ignition key and a power door-lock switch that's not labeled clearly.

Trunk

◒ Folding the split rear seatback adds cargo room, but when the trunk is open, the lid hangs low enough to menace your head. What's worse, the latch has a sharp protrusion. The trunk-release tab, on the floor between the driver's seat and the door, is hard to reach.

Safety

All the safety belts can secure a child safety seat without a separate clip. In the center of the rear seat, the buckles are too close together to accommodate some child seats. The front head restraints are high enough to protect an average-size adult even when they're lowered, but the rear head restraints could protect only a short adult. Our bumper basher dented both bumpers and bent their reinforcements. Repair estimates: $401 front, $405 rear.

In the government's frontal crash tests of the *Nissan Sentra*, the sedan version of the *200SX*, the driver and passenger dummies sustained moderate "injuries."

Predicted reliability

⊖ We expect the *200SX* to be very reliable.

Based on a May 1996 report.

Nissan 240SX

Price range: $18,359–$22,249
Cost factor: 89%
Depreciation: ○

Redesigned in 1995, the *240SX* remains a rear-wheel-drive coupe. It competes with front-drive models such as the *Acura Integra Coupe* (see page 73) and *Toyota Celica* (see page 86). The 2.4-liter Four offers adequate if noisy acceleration. The *240SX* provides fine handling and a reasonably comfortable ride.

Predicted reliability
Insufficient data.

Nissan 300ZX Turbo 

Price range: $37,439–$44,679
Cost factor: 87%
Depreciation: ⊖

Overview
Although it's everything a sports car should be—very fast with razor-sharp handling—it's also remarkably smooth and easy to drive.

Acceleration
⊖ Blazing acceleration without any noticeable turbo lag: 0 to 60 mph in 6.1 seconds, and a quarter mile in just 14.6 seconds, reaching 98 mph.

Transmission
⊖ Shifts crisply and precisely. Well-chosen gear ratios provide plenty of pickup in every gear.

Economy

● Expect 21 mpg overall.

Routine handling
⊖ Almost perfect. Its four-wheel steering makes cornering especially precise and well balanced.

Emergency handling
⊖ Very steady. Excellent tire grip, minimal body roll, and smooth steering give crisp and quick response.

Braking
⊖ Antilock brakes provide short, straight stops.

Ride
◒ The electronically controlled suspension offers two settings. Even in the Touring mode, the softer of the two, the ride won't let you forget you're in a sports car. In Sport mode, the ride worsens, becoming harder and more jittery.

Noise
◒ Except for a low-frequency throb on uneven pavement, the *300ZX* is commendably quiet inside for a sports car.

Driving position
○ Pedal placement could be better: When the seat is back far enough to allow adequate legroom to the accelerator, the driver has to stretch to fully depress the clutch pedal. Some drivers may find the steering wheel too high or too close, and you can't adjust it.

Front seating
⊖ Bucket seats provide good, firm support.

Access
◒ Nimbleness is required.

Climate system
⊖ The fully automatic climate control system unobtrusively maintains the chosen temperature. Ample air from numerous ducts. Defogging and defrosting worked well front, side, and rear, as did the heated mirrors.

Controls and displays
⊖ Easy to reach, as they are all grouped tightly under the steering wheel, but

hard to see. Two small horn buttons blend into the steering wheel spokes. Instruments are clear and easy to read.

Trunk

○ Cargo bay is roomy for a sports car; it holds three Pullman cases and two weekend bags with room to spare.

Safety

Besides dual air bags, the *300ZX* has three-point safety belts anchored to the door. The inboard ends are so short that buckling up is awkward. The foglight lens suffered damage during the bumper-basher test. The replacement light was $125.

The government has not crash-tested a *300 ZX.*

Predicted reliability

○ We predict an average repair record—better than most for this type.

Based on a September 1992 report.

Pontiac Firebird Trans Am

***Price range:** $15,614–$27,364*
***Cost factor:** 91%*
Depreciation: ⊖

Overview

The best and worst of the old muscle car breed: balanced rear-wheel drive handling and strong acceleration, but terrible reliability.

Acceleration

⊜ The V8 provides effortless thrust.

Transmission

⊜ The optional transmission automatic shifts smoothly. We check-tested a V8 with the six-speed manual that's standard with the V8 and found it slightly notchy but accurate, and well suited to the engine.

Economy

● The V8 increases fuel bills by about 30 percent over a similar *Firebird V6*—because it delivers fewer mpg and because the manufacturer recommends that it be fueled with Premium.

Routine handling

⊜ The car is too wide to be truly nimble, but it corners with minimal body roll. The wide tires gripped the road exceptionally well. Steering felt a bit smoother, quicker, and more precise than that of the *Camaro.*

Emergency handling

⊖ Inspires confidence in tricky situations. The car's bulk made it difficult to weave through the accident-avoidance course, but it held the track firmly and responded quickly to steering inputs.

Braking

⊜ The *Firebird* stopped in 118 feet from 60 mph on dry pavement—matching the record held by the *Volvo 850* sedan. The *Firebird* also stopped short on wet pavement. The wet-track test (where the pavement is more slippery under one side of the car than the other) proved only a small challenge; the *Firebird* weaved slightly, then straightened out.

Ride

○ A reasonably comfortable ride for a sporty model. The *Firebird* feels stiffer than the *Camaro.* The car reacts tautly to every tiny road irregularity. Its ride is well controlled but almost punishing at times.

Noise

○ Performance enthusiasts may like the V8's deep rumble and exhaust drone, although the attendant wind rush and loud tire thumps are less gratifying.

Driving position

⊖ Comfortable for drivers of all sizes. The view to the rear and over the shoulder is poor, and the car's front and rear ends are invisible to the driver. Headroom is generous; legroom is adequate for six-footers, but a wide transmission tunnel forces the accelerator too far to the left.

Front seating

⊖ Buckets cradle occupants nicely. Power adjustments are for lower back support and spread of the wing bolsters. Manual adjustment sets angle of the seat cushion.

Rear seating

● Regard the rear buckets as seating for emergencies only. Knee room is too tight for most adults, and high front seatbacks and wide roof pillars make passengers feel claustrophobic.

Access

○ It helps to be young and supple. Watch your face; the unframed, inward-curving door windows are hard to see. And pay attention to the weak door detents; if they let go, the door can close on your hand or leg. Rear access is dreadful.

Climate system

⊜ Supplies plenty of warmed or cooled air and distributes it evenly.

Controls and displays

⊖ Controls are within easy reach and logically arranged. The horn control perches conveniently in the center hub of the steering wheel, along with the air bag. Climate controls are unlit, so you can't see the settings at night. Important displays are easy to read.

Trunk

◒ The trunk is shallow toward the front of the car, deep toward the back. It can hold three Pullman cases, or a folded wheelchair with room left over. Folding the rear seatback, which is no easy chore, affords extra cargo room. Lifting heavy items over the trunk's high sill into the deep rear well is a challenge. Hinged security panel hides cargo. Compact spare resides under cover behind right rear wheel housing. Towing limit is 1500 pounds.

Safety

Dual air bags supplement the front safety belts. Reaching them is a long stretch, as in most two-door cars. The remote upper anchors make the shoulder belts ride uncomfortably on the occupant's neck. The front passenger's belt requires a locking clip to secure a child's safety seat. The rear belts don't require a clip, but the seating positions may be too narrow for some child safety seats. Our low-speed bumper-basher tests inflicted minimal damage, knocking a fog lamp out of alignment.

Crash protection for driver and passenger has been admirable in government tests.

Predicted reliability

● *Firebirds* have wretched reliability records.

Based on an October 1993 report.

Saturn SC2

***Price range:** $12,195–$13,295*
***Cost factor:** 87%*
Depreciation: ⊖

Overview

This domestic model matches the overall performance of its Japanese competition and has been a reliable performer as well.

Acceleration

⊖ Very quick.

Transmission

⊜ Five-speed manual shifted competently through well-chosen gear ratios. Finding reverse, however, often required a struggle, and the clutch sometimes engaged abruptly.

Economy

⊖ Impressive 30 mpg overall.

Routine handling

⊜ Nimble and precise on smooth roads, but the front tires danced a bit on bumpy pavement. The car wandered somewhat on the highway, especially in crosswinds. Steering is nicely weighted and gives good feel for the road.

Emergency handling

⊖ No difficulties with accident-avoidance maneuvers, but the *Saturn's* quick steering and tendency to slide its tail made it feel a bit twitchy. Bumps in the pavement and hard acceleration nudged the front end off its line through turns.

Braking

⊜ The optional antilock brakes worked well.

Ride

◒ Quite stiff. On poor roads, the ride became almost punishing at times.

Noise

○ The engine buzzes and vibrates when revved, but at steady speeds the *SC* is very quiet for its class.

Driving position

⊖ Suited all but tall drivers, who wanted more headroom and thigh support. Wheel housing makes an uncomfortable footrest. A handwheel at the side of the seat cushion to move seat forward as well as up is difficult to operate.

Front seating

○ Some testers felt squeezed by the prominent wing bolsters.

Rear seating

● Unpleasant for most living creatures.

Access

◒ Low seats and low roof make access awkward, and annoying motorized safety belts don't help. In rear, a challenge getting in or out.

Climate system

⊖ Furnishes plenty of heating or cooling, but the heater and windshield defroster were slow to produce. There are no side-window defoggers, and the rear-window defroster must be shut off manually.

Controls and displays

⊜ Full instrumentation is clear and easy to read. Turn-signal lever moves stiffly, and switches for the power door locks lack labels. Manual control for the driver's outside mirror requires a long reach. Climate system's Mix setting is unmarked, and small indicator for the rear-window defroster hides behind the steering-wheel rim. Lighted arrow that tells you when to upshift is annoying and unnecessary.

Trunk

○ Three Pullman cases and three weekend bags. Split rear seatback folds sixty-forty. Neither the rear seatback nor the remote trunk-lid release can be locked.

Safety

The *SC* has dual air bags as standard equipment. No damage front or rear by our bumper basher.

The government has not crash-tested a *Saturn SC*.

Predicted reliability

⊖ *Saturns* have compiled a better-than-average reliability record. Expect a redesign next year.

Based on a July 1992 report.

Subaru SVX

***Price range:** $29,995–$35,495*
***Cost factor:** 90%*
Depreciation: ●

Overview

As a sporty coupe, it's an able although not spectacular performer—and with the available all-wheel drive it's almost practical.

Acceleration

⊖ Ample, at 8.8 seconds 0 to 60 mph.

Transmission

⊜ The four-speed automatic shifts smoothly.

Economy

● Expect about 19 mpg.

Routine handling

⊜ Feels very stable. While all-wheel drive provides excellent traction, the *SVX* lacks the precise handling of truer sports cars.

Emergency handling

⊖ Body rolled noticeably. Steering effort is a bit light.

Braking

⊖ Antilock brakes do an excellent job.

Ride

○ Comfortable for a sports coupe—smooth on good roads, just a bit stiff and busy on bumpy ones.

Noise

⊖ Surprisingly quiet inside; almost as pleasant as a good family sedan.

Driving position

⊖ Thanks to the tilting and telescoping steering wheel and optional eight-way power seat, all but the tallest people should find a comfortable driving position.

Front seating

⊖ Bucket seats need a bit more side support.

Rear seating

● For adult transportation only when there's no other option.

Access

○ Relatively easy.

Climate system

⊖ Automatic climate-control system quickly furnishes plenty of warmed or cooled air. Fresh air from the dash vents can't be warmed, and there are no ducts to the rear seats.

Controls and displays

⊖ Aside from the two tiny horn buttons on the steering wheel spokes, the controls are generally well designed. However, the automatic Up feature on the driver's power window is hazardous. If it's activated accidentally, the glass will squeeze anything in its way as it tries to close. Instruments are easy to see and read.

Trunk

○ Roomy for a sports coupe; folding rear seatback expands it farther. Four Pullman cases and a weekend bag fit with ease.

Safety

Dual air bags are standard. No damage front or rear from our bumper basher.

The government has not crash-tested an *SVX*.

Predicted reliability

Insufficient data.

Based on a September 1992 report.

Toyota Celica GT 

Price range: $16,958–$24,178
Cost factor: 87%
Depreciation: ○

Overview

This well-rounded design offers hatchback versatility, sporty handling, and high fuel economy. It should prove exceptionally reliable as well.

Acceleration

⊖ The *GT* version, with its 2.2-liter Four, accelerates decently, although it's notably slower than the *Acura Integra*. *ST* versions have a 1.8-liter Four that's even less responsive.

Transmission

⊜ The five-speed manual shifts accurately but not as crisply as the *Integra's*. A four-speed automatic is optional.

Economy

⊖ Expect about 28 mpg overall.

Routine handling

⊜ With the optional sport suspension, the *Celica* corners confidently, with restrained body roll. The steering is quick but lacks crispness. The tires grip well in hard cornering, and backing off the accelerator easily mitigates the car's slight tendency to plow ahead.

Emergency handling

⊖ The *Celica* threaded cleanly through our avoidance maneuver.

Braking

⊖ The antilock brakes generally performed well, although wet stops were a trifle long. In our difficult wet divided-pavement test, where the asphalt is slicker under the left wheels than under the right, the *Celica* veered to one side and then straightened out.

Ride

○ Even with its optional sport suspension, the *Celica* rides better than most sporty coupes, smoothing out the jiggles and softening the kicks on secondary roads. Rough pavement causes small, taut pitches and vertical jiggles. The ride is busy but well controlled on the highway.

Noise

○ Considerable road noise and tire roar penetrate the cabin. The engine drones unpleasantly.

Driving position

⊖ Most drivers should be able to find a good driving position. Legroom is adequate for tall drivers, but the glass sunroof robs precious headroom. With the seat raised, even short drivers should see well over the hood.

Front seating

⊖ The front seats provide good, firm support, especially along the sides of the seatback. The optional leather upholstery is perforated and not too slippery.

Rear seating

● Save the rear seat for packages.

Access

◒ Climbing into the front takes agility; climbing into the rear takes acrobatic skill.

Climate system

⊖ The climate-control system quietly furnishes plenty of warmed or cooled air. The rear-window wiper is useful in wet weather; it has both continuous and intermittent settings.

Controls and displays

⊜ The displays are clear and easy to read. The horn button is integrated with the driver-side air bag in the center of the steering wheel, as it should be. Other controls are easy to reach and use as well.

Trunk

◒ The *Celica's* trunk is roomy for a small hatchback, but the sill is high. We could pack three Pullman cases and two weekend bags, or a folded wheelchair. Folding the split rear seatback expands the luggage room. The *Celica* comes with a compact spare. The open hatch is menacing to a tall person's head.

Safety

Putting on the front safety belts requires a long reach backward, and both the front and rear shoulder belts press uncomfortably on the shoulder of an adult. All of the belts can secure a child safety seat without a locking clip, but some child seats won't fit the deep pockets of the rear cushions properly. Our bumper basher did no damage front or rear.

The government has not crash-tested a *Celica.*

Predicted reliability

⊜ The *Celica* has excellent reliability.

Based on a June 1994 report.

Toyota Paseo

Price: *$13,038*
Cost factor: *89%*
Depreciation: ○

The newly redesigned *Paseo* may look sporty, but it's built on the underpinnings of the humdrum *Tercel.* The *Paseo* typifies a small car with its stiff and choppy ride. The steering feels light, but the engine at least delivers decent performance—although not quite sports car–like. Consider the rear seat merely a shelf for packages (it's too small to really be taken seriously). The trunk is reasonably roomy for such a small car. The controls and displays are simple, clear, and logical—in the typical *Toyota* fashion.

Predicted reliability ⊜

Toyota Supra Turbo ✓

Price range: *$38,600–$41,000*
Cost factor: *84%*
Depreciation: ○

Overview

In its quickest and most expensive form, the *Supra* is designed to go from here to there at triple the speed limit. The *Supra* still maintains its position as a top-rated sports car, even when its ranks are thinning.

Acceleration

⊜ The 320-hp, 3.0-liter Six with twin-turbos provides blistering acceleration: 0 to 60 mph in 5.9 seconds.

Transmission

⊜ The six-speed manual and limited-slip differential, along with traction control, transfer power to massive ultralow-profile rear tires. For 1996, the *Supra Turbo* is available only with an automatic transmission.

Economy

○ Expect about 22 mpg overall on Premium fuel.

Routine handling

⊜ The steering is quick but lacks much feel.

Emergency handling

⊜ At our track, we had merely to point the *Supra* from corner to corner. Only the width of its body limited the speed through our avoidance maneuver.

Braking

⊜ Antilock brakes halted the *Supra* from 60 mph in just 114 feet on dry pavement—the best performance of any car we've tested. The *Supra* stopped short and straight in our wet-braking tests as well.

Ride

◒ Ride is especially harsh—the price you pay for a car that handles like a race car.

Noise

○ Very prominent at all speeds.

Driving position

⊖ The low driver's cushion impedes the view of the hood.

Front seating

⊖ Firm front seats provide strong support.

Rear seating

● The rear seat is far too cramped for adults, and the pockets in the rear cushion are too narrow for a child seat.

Access

◒ Climbing in and out requires agility.

Climate system

⊖ The system works well.

Controls and displays

⊜ Controls and displays are very good, with the usual quality feel from *Toyota.*

Trunk

● The trunk is extremely shallow.

Safety

Dual air bags are standard.

The government has not crash-tested a *Supra.*

Predicted reliability

⊖ The *Supra* has an above-average reliability record.

Based on a June 1994 report.

COMPACT CARS

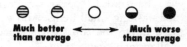

⊜ ⊖ ○ ◒ ●

Much better than average ⟷ **Much worse than average**

In both size and comfort, this category is a distinct step up from the small sedans. The best and most practical compact models can accommodate three adults relatively comfortably in the rear seat.

Some compacts are very pricey. Although the least expensive domestic models start at just over $12,000, the costliest European models—*Saab 900* and *BMW* 3-Series convertibles—penetrate the $30,000 luxury-car barrier.

Compact models deliver worse fuel economy than the small sedan. The U.S.-made compacts are better suited to an automatic transmission, whereas most imports work well with either a manual or automatic.

Recommended models are the *BMW* 3-Series, *Ford Contour/Mercury Mystique, Infiniti G20, Mazda 626, Mitsubishi Galant, Nissan Altima, Subaru Legacy,* and *Volkswagen Passat*.

Audi A4

Price: *$26,500*
Cost factor: *88%*
Depreciation: *NA*

Overview

The five-speed manual is the transmission of choice here. The lazy automatic hobbles this spirited sedan—the best *Audi* we've tested in years.

Acceleration

⊖ The 2.8-liter V6 provides plenty of power.

Transmission

○ The five-speed automatic transmission that we tested makes the car feel sluggish unless you floor the accelerator. Although it shifts very smoothly, it upshifts prematurely, which makes the engine lug. And it shifts down reluctantly on uphill inclines. The standard five-speed manual seems to be the way to go with the shared *VW/Audi* 2.8-liter V6.

Economy

◒ The *A4* averaged about 22 mpg, overall, on Premium fuel.

Routine handling

⊜ The *A4* has a distinctly European sports-sedan character, with quick and precise handling. It feels stable in corners; the body leans very little, and the steering generally requires just the right amount of effort.

Emergency handling

⊖ The car tended to run wide in our emergency avoidance maneuver, where we press cars to their cornering limits, but it remained safe and controllable. The extra-cost Quattro all-wheel-drive option would have given not only better traction on snow and ice but better handling under all conditions as well.

Braking

⊖ The brakes feel a bit grabby in gentle stops, but they're powerful.

Ride, normal load

○ The firm suspension and low-profile tires stiffen the ride so you feel more of the small bumps and minor irregularities in the road.

Ride, full load

⊖ The ride improves with a full load of people and luggage aboard.

Noise

⊖ The interior of the *A4* is very quiet at highway speeds.

Driving position

⊜ A power seat with many adjustments and a steering column that tilts and telescopes should help almost anyone find a comfortable driving position.

All but the tallest drivers will find plenty of head- and legroom, and even short drivers can see well over the hood.

Front seating

⊜ The leather-covered front seats are firm and comfortable. The driver gets power adjustments; the passenger, manual controls. Seat heaters, a welcome addition, come with the extra-cost All Weather Package, which also includes a heated lock for the driver's door.

Rear seating

◒ The rear seatback is too erect, and the cushion is too flat. Two can sit there in moderate comfort, but space is tight for three.

Access

⊖ Access is very good front and rear.

Climate system

⊜ The automatic system performs flawlessly, and it includes a pollen filter. The manual switches, should you need them, are confusing and are mounted a bit too low.

Controls and displays

○ Our major complaint with the controls is the stubby headlight lever between the steering wheel and turn-signal lever. You can easily turn off the headlights while signaling for a left turn. Daytime reflections can badly obscure the speedometer and other gauges.

Trunk

⊖ The trunk is spacious, with nooks for stashing small items. And you can fold down the split rear seatback for still more luggage room.

Safety

The *A4* has two air bags, as well as "pre-tensioners" that take up slack in the safety belts in a crash. The head restraints don't lock in a raised position; when lowered, they're just adequate for average-size adults. The belt anchors in the center of the rear seat may be too close together to accommodate some child seats, but the automatic-locking lap belt makes it easy to mount any child seat that fits. Our hydraulic bumper basher inflicted $450 worth of damage to the front of the car, $671 to the rear.

The *A4* performed well in a recent government crash test.

Predicted reliability

New model, no data.

Based on a February 1996 report.

BMW 3-Series 

***Price range:** $25,950–$41,390*
***Cost factor:** 84%*
Depreciation: ○

Overview

This responsive and agile sedan is long on driving fun but short on rear-seat comfort and trunk space. It's available as a two-door coupe, convertible, or four-door sedan.

Acceleration

⊖ Our tested four-door *325i*, with its 2.5-liter Six, felt responsive but is not quite as quick as its competition, like the *Mercedes-Benz C280* and *Volvo 850 Turbo*. For 1996, a 2.8-liter Six replaces the 2.5.

Transmission

⊜ The optional four-speed automatic transmission enhances the sedan's sporty feel. You can shift to 3 instead of D for maximum performance, or switch to manual mode to hold first, second, or third gear. The optional traction-control system works wonders on the rear wheels under slippery conditions. A five-speed manual is standard.

Economy

○ Relatively good at 24 mpg overall, on Midgrade fuel as recommended by BMW.

Routine handling

⊜ Precise handling like a sports car and tenacious grip make the driver feel very much in control at all times.

Emergency handling

⊜ The sedan breezed through avoidance maneuvers.

Braking

⊖ Stopping distances from 60 mph were shorter than average: 131 feet on dry pavement, 145 feet on wet pavement. The car stopped straight in our wet divided-pavement test.

Ride, normal load

⊖ The ride is firm but generally smooth and comfortable.

Ride, full load

⊖ Compliant and never unsettling on rough roads, even with a full load of people and luggage aboard.

Noise

⊖ Very good sound insulation adds to the interior comfort.

Driving position

⊜ An array of useful power adjustments make it easy to select the perfect position.

Front seating

⊜ Good, firm support in all the right places. We like the grainy, "grippy" leather upholstery, but the seat heaters warmed slowly.

Rear seating

◒ The rear seat is cramped for three adults. Even two tall adults will wish for more knee and headroom.

Access

⊖ Front access is very good; rear, a little less so.

Climate system

⊜ The system is versatile; separate controls let the driver and front passenger set different temperatures.

Controls and displays

⊖ Well designed and close to the driver, but several controls such as the fog-light switch and panel-light control are hidden from view. A short driver couldn't see the levers for the windshield wipers and cruise control. The tiny indicator lights for the air-conditioning, air recirculation, and rear defroster are too dim to be seen in daylight.

Trunk

◒ Three Pullman cases and two weekend bags, or a folded wheelchair, just about fill the relatively small trunk. A short trunk opening makes loading and unloading large items difficult. Convenient extras in the trunk include a small storage bin, tie-down loops, and an emergency tool kit on the underside of the trunk lid. A full-size spare is standard. Folding seatbacks that allow more room for cargo are an option. Trailer towing is not recommended.

Safety

The front and rear safety belts are comfortable and convenient. All but the center rear lap belt require a locking clip to secure a child safety seat, a significant detail the owner's manual fails to mention. The bumpers haven't been a strong point on this model, but our 1994 car fared better than our 1992 car in our bumper-basher tests. The front bumper and grille suffered $451 worth of damage; the rear bumpers, $458. The automaker claims that the *325i* meets the 1997 dynamic side-impact standard.

Both the driver and passenger dummies fared very well in government crash tests.

Predicted reliability

⊖ *BMW* 3-Series models have achieved a better-than-average reliability record.

Based on an August 1994 report.

Buick Skylark Gran Sport

Price range: $15,491–$17,701
Cost factor: 96%
Depreciation: ◒

Overview
An adequate car, but for a new, pricey model, adequate just isn't good enough.

Acceleration
⊖ Very responsive.

Transmission
⊜ Three-speed automatic usually shifted smoothly, but it shifted into and out of lockup too often at highway speeds.

Economy
◒ Expect about 21 mpg overall.

Routine handling
⊖ With the adjustable ride control on Auto or Soft, the front suspension crashed and banged on bumps; we used the Sport setting.

Emergency handling
⊖ Good speed through the avoidance course, but the steering felt slow and the body leaned a lot. Behavior was better in steady-speed turns.

Braking
⊖ Standard antilock brakes performed well.

Ride, normal load
○ We couldn't get a comfortable ride at any setting: Auto gave a busy ride punctuated by thumps and kicks; Soft gave a queasy, bounding ride; and Sport made the ride stiff and choppy.

Ride, full load
◒ The suspension bottomed on big bumps.

Noise
⊖ The *Skylark* was very quiet and provided a hushed cabin even on the highway.

Driving position
○ The steering wheel is canted toward the driver's left shoulder; raising the seat for good visibility over the hood places the head too close to the roof and windshield pillar.

Front seating
⊖ Satisfactory, but the seats lack thigh support for taller riders.

Rear seating
◒ Unfriendly in every way.

Access
◒ Inward-curving window frames threaten riders getting in and out of the car.

Climate system
⊜ The heater was powerful but slow to deliver.

Controls and displays
⊖ Mostly easy to operate, but power door locks are infuriating: They lock automatically when starting in Drive, the switches are unlighted, and their hair-trigger action makes its too easy to lock yourself out. The various gauges are blocked out by the steering wheel or driver's hands on the wheel.

Trunk
○ Four Pullman cases and two weekend bags fit easily. Split rear seatback folds to extend trunk. Watch out for sharp corners on open trunk lid.

Safety
Dual air bags are standard. At front, bumper basher shifted grille upward and broke a mounting tab. Replacing grille cost $91. Rear was undamaged.

The government has not crash-tested a *Skylark* recently.

Predicted reliability

○ Expect only average reliability.

Based on a June 1992 report.

Chevrolet Beretta

Price range: $13,490–$16,690
Cost factor: 92%
Depreciation: ◒

This is the last year for the *Beretta.* This pseudo-sporty coupe version of the humdrum *Chevrolet Corsica* sedan offers no surprises, good or bad. The V6 is a better choice than the weak and noisy Four. The low front seats make it hard to see over the hood. Although the displays are clear, the controls are awkward, and the climate-control system is weak. Within the GM family, the new *Pontiac Sunfire* (see page 63) is a better choice. Otherwise, the *Honda Civic* coupe (see page 58) is a far better choice.

Predicted reliability
○ Reliability has been average.

Chevrolet Corsica

Price: $14,385
Cost factor: 93%
Depreciation: ◒

Overview
Archetypal rental car, undistinguished in performance and handling. Will be replaced by the brand new *Chevrolet Malibu* this fall.

Acceleration

○ Weak acceleration from the 2.2-liter Four. The 3.1-liter V6 would provide more power at the expense of a few miles per gallon.

Transmission

⊜ The three-speed automatic with lockup occasionally shifted abruptly.

Economy

○ Expect about 25 mpg average.

Routine handling

○ Queasy and vague steering, and the steering wheel shook slightly; in turns, the car leaned heavily and tried to plow straight ahead.

Emergency handling

○ Slow, but controllable in accident-avoidance tests. In hard turns, the front end plowed, the tires screamed, and the car heeled over hard.

Braking

○ The car took longer than average to stop, despite its antilock brakes.

Ride, normal load

○ Became a bit busy at times but was never harsh.

Ride, full load

◒ About the same, although the suspension bottomed occasionally.

Noise

⊖ The engine sounded particularly noisy at highway speeds. The optional V6 is likely to be quieter.

Driving position

○ As in other GM compacts, the wheel angles toward the left of the driver. Neither short nor tall drivers could see well over the hood, despite an inclined track that raises the seat as it slides forward.

Front seating

○ Would have been quite comfortable if not for a firm bolster at the top of each seatback that forced occupants to slouch.

Rear seating

◒ Tall riders found enough room but not enough support in the low rear seat.

Access

○ High and wide doorsills, low seats, and intrusive doorposts must be contended with. In the rear, tight foot clearance is the major obstacle.

Climate system

○ Below-freezing temperatures challenged the heater, and warm-up was slow. The fan became quite noisy at its higher speed settings.

Controls and displays

○ Horn buttons on the steering-wheel spokes are hard to find in a hurry. The automatic transmission selector doesn't interlock with the brake pedal; when you shift out of Park, the car could take off faster than you expect. Rotary climate controls are positioned low, are stiff to operate, and are too far from the driver. Contrast of displays are a bit weak in daytime but otherwise easy to read.

Trunk

◒ Four Pullman cases and two weekend bags with room to spare. Split fold-down rear seat is part of the Comfort Convenience Package.

Safety

Only a driver-side air bag is standard. No damage front or rear from our bumper basher.

The driver dummy fared better than the passenger in government crash tests.

Predicted reliability

○ The *Corsica* has an average reliability record, as does its coupe version, the *Chevrolet Beretta.*

Based on a June 1992 report.

Chrysler Cirrus

Price range: $17,560–$19,490
Cost factor: 92%
Depreciation: NA

Overview

This model combines a roomy interior with good, solid overall performance. Like other recently introduced Chrysler models, it has more problems than the average car.

Acceleration

⊖ The 2.5-liter V6 provides lively acceleration.

Transmission

⊜ The four-speed automatic shifts very smoothly. A manual transmission isn't offered.

Economy

○ Expect about 22 mpg on Regular fuel.

Routine handling

⊖ The *Cirrus* corners well, and the body leans only modestly. The steering is neither too heavy nor too light, but it could be more responsive.

Emergency handling

⊖ During hard turns at our test track and in our avoidance maneuvers, the *Cirrus* tended to run wide, but its handling remained stable and predictable.

Braking

○ The *Cirrus* needed 145 feet to stop from 60 mph on a dry track and 167 feet on a wet one—an unimpressive performance. After repeated stops, the brakes overheated, chattered, and temporarily lost some of their effectiveness.

The car stopped straight on our wet divided pavement, where the road is more slippery under one side of the car than the other.

Ride, normal load

⊖ The *Cirrus's* ride feels taut and well controlled.

Ride, full load

⊖ A full load doesn't affect the ride much.

Noise

⊖ The cabin is usually quiet, although the suspension thrums annoyingly on rough pavement.

Driving position

⊖ Thanks to the optional eight-way power seat and tilt steering column, nearly anyone should be able to find a good driving position. Tall people enjoy more than enough head- and legroom, and even short people can see out easily.

Front seating

⊖ The large individual front seats provide good, firm support. We also liked the *LXi's* leather upholstery; it's perforated and not slippery.

Rear seating

⊖ The rear seat is the most spacious of any in this class, with ample room for three six-footers. Niggling complaints include the absence of a center armrest and narrow door armrests.

Access

⊖ The family-size *Cirrus* provides very good access to both front and rear seats.

Climate system

⊜ The system is powerful and versatile. You can select air-conditioning in any mode, and it comes on automatically in Mix and Defrost modes, where it's needed to clear condensation from the inside of the glass.

Controls and displays

⊜ The controls are easy to operate, and their layout is first-rate. The displays are clear and well lit at night. The headlights don't measure up, though. The low-beam pattern is poor, and the high beams lack sufficient brightness and range.

Trunk

⊖ The roomy trunk can hold five Pullman cases and one weekend bag, or a folded wheelchair—and much more when the rear seatback is folded down. You can stash small items in the well around the compact spare, and the well can hold a full-size tire that has gone flat. The *Cirrus* can tow a 1000-pound trailer, according to Chrysler.

Safety

The safety belts are comfortable and easy to use, and you can secure a child safety seat without a special locking clip. You can order a built-in child seat for the center rear. The *Cirrus's* bumpers emerged virtually unscathed from our hydraulic bumper basher's 3- and 5-mph blows.

The driver suffered severe "injuries" in recent government crash tests. Passenger results were not available.

Predicted reliability

● Reliability has been poor.

Based on a March 1995 report.

Dodge Stratus

***Price range:** $14,460–$16,110*
***Cost factor:** 92%*
***Depreciation:** NA*

Overview

The *Stratus* falls too far short of the competition; we recommend that you adopt a wait-and-see approach to this new sedan.

Acceleration

○ The optional 2.4-liter Four accelerates adequately, but it sometimes surges and stumbles. It doesn't run as smoothly as Chrysler's 2.5-liter V6, nor is it even as economical.

Transmission

⊖ The four-speed automatic shifts smoothly.

Economy

◒ In mixed driving, expect to average about 20 mpg with the 2.4-liter Four versus 22 mpg with the 2.5-liter V6, on Regular fuel.

Routine handling

⊖ The *Stratus* corners well, although it's not as agile or precise as the *Ford Contour* or *Mercury Mystique.*

Emergency handling

○ Remains fairly predictable.

Braking

○ In our braking tests on dry and wet pavement, the *Stratus* stopped straight but fairly long, and the brakes temporarily lost some effectiveness after a series of ten moderate stops from 60 mph. Such brake "fade" might be a problem only under the most severe condition—mountain driving or trailer towing—but it's uncommon in contemporary cars.

Ride, normal load

○ The ride is firm but well controlled on most roads.

Ride, full load

○ A full load doesn't have much effect on the ride, one way or the other.

Noise

○ Road rumble on coarse pavement and wind noise at highway speeds penetrate the passenger compartment.

Driving position

⊖ Legroom is adequate for six-foot drivers, and even five-foot drivers can see out well.

Front seating

⊖ The front seats are large and roomy, and they give good support all around.

Rear seating

⊖ Three tall people have ample room, although the seat itself could be shaped and padded a bit better.

Access

⊖ Good access both front and rear.

Climate system

⊖ To stay cool on really hot days, you have to run the air conditioner full blast. And in cold weather, the rear-window defroster takes its time.

Controls and displays

⊜ Clear, well-lit instruments complement the first-rate controls.

Trunk

⊖ The trunk is big, and you can fold down the rear seatback for still more luggage room.

Safety

The safety belts are comfortable and easy to use, and you don't need a cinch clip to secure a child seat. A built-in child seat in the center rear position is a $100 option. The *Stratus* emerged from our 3- and 5-mph bumper-basher tests virtually unscathed. The *Stratus's* headlight pattern is poor on low beam, and the high beams have a short range.

In the government's 35-mph barrier crash test of a 1995 *Stratus*, the driver dummy received serious "injuries." That's especially disquieting for a new model. Data for the passenger dummy were lost.

Predicted reliability

The *Stratus* continues Chrysler's woeful pattern of poor reliability problems with new models.

Based on a December 1995 report.

Ford Contour GL 

Price range: $13,785–$16,170
Cost factor: 92%
Depreciation: NA

Overview

Forget the old insipid *Ford Tempo*. This new design is an impressive replacement.

Acceleration

○ The base 2.0-liter Four performs adequately but idles roughly. The engine stumbled and occasionally stalled when first starting out in cool weather, a rare phenomenon since fuel injection replaced the carburetor years ago.

Transmission

⊖ The four-speed automatic shifts smoothly most of the time. It can start in or hold second gear if necessary, and it has a push button that can lock out fourth gear. It shifts more often and more conspicuously on the highway when matched with the Four, compared to when it's teamed with the optional V6. We ran a brief check-test of a car with a five-speed manual transmission. The ratios were well chosen, and the transmission shifted smoothly. The optional traction control works smoothly at all speeds.

Economy

○ Expect to average about 26 mpg on Regular fuel.

Routine handling

⊖ The *Contour GL*, with its base suspension and tires, handles pleasantly. But during cornering, it leans more than the stiffer-riding *Mercury Mystique LS*. The car responds nimbly, quickly, and precisely to the steering.

Emergency handling

○ At our track, the base *Contour* ran a bit wide during hard cornering, but it remained stable and forgiving. It negotiated our avoidance maneuver safely and securely.

Braking

○ The *Contour* needed 148 feet to stop from 60 mph on a dry track, 158 feet on wet pavement—a mediocre showing. The brakes initially feel touchy, but they respond smoothly, without grabbing. The car stopped straight in our wet divided-pavement test.

Ride, normal load

⊖ The standard suspension in the base *Contour* delivers a very good ride, better than either the *Mystique LS's* or the *Chrysler Cirrus's*. The *Contour* controls ride motions well and absorbs flaws in the pavement resiliently.

Ride, full load

⊖ A full load doesn't affect the suspension much.

Noise

○ Road noise is excessive. The four-cylinder engine sounds harsh and gruff, especially when it's revved up.

Driving position

⊖ All *Contours* (and *Mystiques*) were supposed to come with a tilt steering column—but Ford deleted the feature in early-production cars, including ours, without reducing the price. Lacking both an adjustable wheel and a height adjustment for the seat, our *Contour* didn't provide an optimal driving position for some drivers—especially for our five-foot driver, who had trouble seeing over the hood. Tall drivers will find enough legroom and more than enough headroom. The left footrest is comfortable, too.

Front seating

⊖ The individual front seats feel soft, but they provide good, firm support except for the lower back.

Rear seating

○ The rear seat is cramped. The base *Contour's* rear seatback doesn't fold down, and its rear seat isn't as comfortable as the folding seat in the *Mystique LS*, especially for three. Head- and knee room are barely adequate for six-footers, and passengers must sit erect with no side support for the torso. The folded center armrest makes a lumpy seatback for the middle passenger.

Access

⊖ Access is good front and rear.

Climate system

⊖ The system includes a replaceable pollen-dust filter, unique in this class. You can't select air-conditioning in every mode, but it goes on automatically in Mix and Defrost. The heater and defroster work well, with easy adjustment and a fairly quiet fan.

Controls and displays

⊖ For the most part, controls are nicely designed. Lighting of the controls is excellent. Nighttime illumination includes not only all the door-mounted switches, but even the interior door handles on all four doors. The instruments are clear. The *Contour's* switches for the power windows are awkwardly located—vertically on the door panel, rather than more horizontally, as in the *Mystique*. Also, the *Contour's* rear-window defroster is hidden behind the steering wheel, and the power-mirror control, too, hides behind the wheel. The switch for the power locks is far back on the door panel, where it's awkward to reach.

Trunk

○ The roomy trunk can swallow five Pullman cases and a weekend bag, or a folded wheelchair, with room left over. The optional split rear seatback in the high-line version folds easily to expand cargo room. You can hide a few small articles in the well around the compact spare.

Safety

The three-point safety belts incorporate a switchable retractor that lets you secure a child seat without a special locking clip. Most child seats won't fit properly in the center of the rear seat; the safety-belt buckles are too close together. Ford claims the bumpers can withstand a 5-mph impact without damage. But our basher inflicted enough damage to the rear to require replacement of the bumper.

In government crash tests, the driver was well protected; the passenger suffered certain "injuries."

Predicted reliability

○ Expect average reliability.

Based on a March 1995 report.

Infiniti G20 

Price range: *$23,800–$26,500*
Cost factor: *85%*
Depreciation: ⊖

Overview

Here's proof that a sedan can be practical without being stodgy, plus the *G20's* reliability has been excellent. And Infiniti sales and service staffers seem to be unusually courteous.

Acceleration

○ The 2.0-liter Four, with just 140 horsepower, provides ample acceleration.

Transmission

⊖ The five-speed manual transmission shifts smoothly, and its gear ratios complement the engine.

Economy

⊖ Expect about 29 mpg on Regular fuel.

Routine handling

⊖ The *G20* negotiates winding country roads with agility, and the body stays level in wide, sweeping turns. The steering, however, could give more feedback.

Emergency handling

○ The car plowed ahead only minimally in hard turns at our test track. It negotiated our avoidance maneuver respectably, with just a bit of tail wag, which our drivers found quite easy to correct.

Braking

⊖ The *G20* needed 136 feet to stop from 60 mph on dry pavement—an average performance. It stopped straight in our tough wet divided-pavement test, where the road is more slippery under the left side of the car than under the right.

Ride, normal load

⊖ The car delivers a firm and tightly controlled ride, yet it soaks up dips and ripples in the pavement nicely.

Ride, full load

⊖ Ride characteristics are maintained with a full load.

Noise

⊖ Wind and road noise is particularly well suppressed. The only notable intrusion is engine noise at high revs.

Driving position

⊖ Multiple seat adjustments and a tilt steering column provide a good driving position for almost anyone. Six-footers have adequate legroom and ample headroom under the optional sunroof. Five-footers can see clearly over the hood.

Front seating

⊖ Good, firm support.

Rear seating

○ Holds three tall people, as long as they're slim. The left and right portions of the seatback provide too little support for the lower back, forcing passengers to slouch forward.

Access

⊖ Getting in and out is quite easy.

Climate system

⊖ System works well and unobtrusively. Air vents are properly located and the fan is quiet.

Controls and displays

⊖ The instruments are clear, but some of the driver's controls are poorly placed. The switches for the power seat require an awkward reach back along the side of the seat, and the power switches for all but the driver's window are tucked away on the center console, obscured by the bulky, overhanging armrest. You must push an annoying button to release the ignition key. The horn buttons, located on the wheel spokes, aren't easy to find in a hurry.

Trunk

○ The generous trunk can swallow five Pullman cases and one weekend bag, or a folded wheelchair, with room left over. A split folding rear seatback comes only with the optional Touring Package.

Safety

The comfortable front safety belts have adjustable upper anchors and a pretensioning system. The rear three-point belts are a bit difficult to buckle and require a locking clip to properly secure a child seat. Our bumper basher, which simulates 3- and 5-mph front and rear collisions, did $638 worth of damage to the front bumper and grille and $363 damage to the rear.

The government has not crash-tested a *G20*.

Predicted reliability

⊖ The *G20* has consistently scored well above average in reliability, according to our reader surveys.

Based on a November 1994 report.

Mazda 626 LX 

Price range: *$15,495–$22,795*
Cost factor: *90%*
Depreciation: ○

Overview

Mazda's 626—with either a Four or V6—is a well-rounded and high-rated family sedan.

Acceleration

○ Adequate performance from the 2.0-liter Four. A smooth-running V6 is available for those who want better acceleration.

Transmission

⊖ The optional four-speed automatic nearly always shifts smoothly. A Hold feature lets you shift it like a manual, or start off and hold it in, say, second gear—especially useful on slippery or hilly roads. A five-speed manual is standard.

Economy

○ Expect to average about 25 mpg on Regular fuel.

Routine handling

⊖ The body leans quite a bit during cornering, but the car holds the road well even in bumpy turns. The steering feels too light; it could provide more feedback.

Emergency handling

⊖ In emergency maneuvers, the *626* handles safely and predictably enough, but it lacks the *Honda Accord's* crisp feel.

Braking

⊖ Stops were straight and fairly short in all our braking tests—even in our demanding wet divided-pavement test.

Ride, normal load

⊖ The *626* has a commendably compliant ride, the best in a group test including three of its comfortable-riding competitors: the *Toyota Camry*, *Honda Accord*, and *Mitsubishi Galant*. Rough pavement produces just muted kicks and an occasional shift from side to side. On the highway, the *626* feels less taut than either the *Camry* or *Accord*.

Ride, full load

⊖ Except for slightly firmer kicks, a full load has no effect on the quality of the ride.

Noise

⊖ The *626* produces more road noise than the *Camry* and *Accord*. Some thrumming from the engine also finds its way into the cabin, but it's fairly unobtrusive.

Driving position

⊖ The driver's seat has an adjuster for the angle of the cushion, but not for height; most of our drivers would have preferred to sit a bit higher. Nevertheless, even our five-foot-tall tester could easily see over the hood. Six-footers had adequate legroom and ample headroom even with the optional sunroof. Drivers both tall and short appreciated the comfortable, nicely placed left footrest.

Front seating

⊖ The cloth-covered seats are nicely shaped and provide firm and generally satisfactory support. Some testers complained of too little lower-back support and thin seat padding.

Rear seating

○ The rear bench seat felt more cramped than the *Camry's*, especially for three adults. In the outboard positions, tall passengers will find adequate headroom and plenty of knee room. The center of the cushion is higher than the sides, and the center of the seatback protrudes considerably, so a middle passenger must perch unsteadily far above and ahead of the passengers on either side.

Access

⊖ Getting in and out is straightforward front and rear.

Climate system

⊜ The system evenly distributes plenty of warmed or air-conditioned air, but the outboard dash vents leak some air in Heat, Mix, and Defrost modes. The center dash vents can draw in outside air directly, and their motorized vanes can oscillate to shift the airflow back and forth.

Controls and displays

⊜ All instruments are clear and easy to read. The only major deficiency among the controls is the placement of the horn buttons—on the spokes of the steering wheel, rather than the center hub. The buttons are hard to find quickly, especially if the steering wheel is not at dead center.

Trunk

⊖ Five Pullman cases and one weekend bag, or a folded wheelchair, fit into the roomy trunk with room to spare. The split rear seatback can easily be folded down to expand the cargo area. A compact spare is the only type available. The owner's manual advises against towing a trailer.

Safety

The *626* has dual air bags. All belts are comfortable to wear, and the upper anchors of the front shoulder belts have adjustable upper anchors. You need a locking clip to secure a child seat with any of the shoulder belts. The front head restraints are high enough to afford whiplash protection even when they're fully lowered. The integral rear restraints aren't high enough for tall passengers. The bumpers emerged unscathed from their 5-mph encounters with our bumper basher.

The *626* did an excellent job of protecting both driver and passenger dummies in a government crash test.

Predicted reliability

○ Expect an average reliability record.

Based on a January 1994 report.

Mercury Mystique LS 

Price range: $14,330–$15,705
Cost factor: 90%
Depreciation: ◒

Overview

Forget the old, dull *Mercury Topaz.* The *Mercury Mystique* is thoroughly up-to-date.

Acceleration

○ The optional 2.5-liter V6 accelerates smoothly and powerfully. The engine stumbled and occasionally stalled when first starting out in cool weather, a rare phenomenon since fuel injection replaced the carburetor years ago.

Transmission

⊜ The four-speed automatic shifts smoothly most of the time. It can start in or hold second gear if necessary, and it has a push button that can lock out fourth gear. We ran a brief check-test of a car with a five-speed manual. The ratios were well chosen, and the transmission shifted smoothly. The optional traction control works effectively at all speeds.

Economy

○ Expect to average about 23 mpg on Regular fuel.

Routine handling

⊜ Thanks to its sporty suspension and performance tires, the *Mystique* negotiates winding country roads on a par with the best sports sedans. Quick and lively steering response makes the car feel especially agile.

Emergency handling

⊖ The *Mystique LS* felt very sporty on the track, gripping the pavement tenaciously. It confidently sailed through our avoidance maneuver, posting the highest speed in its test group, which included the *Ford Contour GL, Chrysler Cirrus LXi,* and *Honda Accord LX.*

Braking

○ The *Mystique* stopped from 60 mph on a dry track in 140 feet, on a wet track in 165 feet—a mediocre showing. The brakes initially feel touchy, but they respond smoothly, without grabbing. The car stopped straight in our wet divided-pavement test.

Ride, normal load

○ The *Mystique* feels hard and busy on rough roads. Ruts and ripples make the car snap and pitch.

Ride, full load

○ A full load doesn't affect the suspension much.

Noise

○ Road noise is excessive, but the V6 snarls satisfyingly.

Driving position

⊖ The *Mystique* was supposed to come with a tilt steering column—but Ford deleted the feature in early-production cars, including ours, without reducing the price. But the power seat adjuster makes the driving position adaptable for most drivers. Tall drivers will find enough legroom and more than enough headroom. The left footrest is comfortable, too. We liked the feel of the *Mystique LS's* thick leather-upholstered steering wheel.

Front seating

⊖ The individual front seats feel soft, but they provide good, firm support except for the lower back. Although the optional leather upholstery isn't perforated, it's loosely gathered and not slippery.

Rear seating

○ The rear seat is cramped. But the folding seat in the *Mystique LS* is more comfortable than the rear seat (with nonfolding seatback) in the base *Contour,* especially for three. Head- and knee room are barely adequate for six-footers, and passengers must sit erect, with no side support for the torso. The folded center armrest makes a lumpy seatback for the middle passenger.

Access

⊖ Access is good front and rear.

Climate system

⊜ The system includes a replaceable pollen/dust filter, unique in this class. You can't select air-conditioning in every mode, but it goes on automatically in Mix and Defrost. The heater and defroster work well, with easy adjustment and a fairly quiet fan.

Controls and displays

⊜ For the most part, the controls are nicely designed. Lighting of the controls is excellent. Nighttime illumination includes not only all the door-mounted switches, but even the interior door handles on all four doors. The instruments are clear. The power-mirror control hides behind the steering wheel, and the switch for the power locks is far back on the door panel, where it's awkward to reach.

Trunk

⊖ The roomy trunk can swallow five Pullman cases and a weekend bag, or a folded wheelchair, with room left over. The optional split rear seatback in the high-line version folds easily to expand cargo room. You can hide a few small articles in the well around the compact spare.

Safety

The three-point safety belts incorporate a switchable retractor that lets you secure a child seat without a special locking clip. Most child seats won't fit properly in the center of the rear seat; the safety-belt buckles are too close together. Ford claims the bumpers in the *Mystique* can withstand a 5-mph impact without damage. But our basher inflicted enough damage to the front of the *Mystique* to require replacement of the bumper. The estimate: $681.

In government crash tests, the driver was well protected; the passenger suffered certain "injuries."

Predicted reliability

○ Reliability has been average.

Based on a March 1995 report.

Mitsubishi Galant LS

Price range: $14,421–$20,866
Cost factor: 87%
Depreciation: ○

Overview

The *Galant* is an extremely competent car, scoring only a notch below the excellent *Toyota Camry* and *Honda Accord.*

Acceleration

○ The 2.4-liter Four in the tested *LS* delivers lively performance (but not up to that of the *Honda Accord's* VTEC Four).

Transmission

○ The four-speed automatic shifts smoothly most of the time. Its "Fuzzy Logic" feature senses when the car is going uphill or downhill and shifts accordingly. It usually works well, but sometimes it downshifts prematurely, even on short downgrades. (A five-speed manual is standard on the *S* version.)

Economy

○ Expect to average about 24 mpg on Regular fuel.

Routine handling

⊖ The *Galant's* steering provides better road feel than the steering of the other cars with which it was tested: *Toyota Camry, Honda Accord,* and *Mazda 626.* But the car isn't quite as agile as the *Accord.*

Emergency handling

⊖ Handling remained safe and controllable throughout our avoidance maneuver, despite the car's slight tendency to wag its tail.

Braking

○ The *Galant* stopped short and straight on wet and dry pavement, but it veered slightly in our wet divided-pavement test.

Ride

⊖ Ride was smooth enough on good roads, but even minor pavement flaws caused firm kicks and jolts. A full load subdues the kicks and jiggles a bit.

Noise

○ The *Galant* transmits more road noise than do the other cars, and the engine resonates unpleasantly at about 2500 rpm.

Driving position

⊖ Several seat adjusters help most drivers get comfortably situated behind the controls. Legroom to the accelerator is a bit tight for long-legged drivers. Even with the seat fully raised, headroom under the sunroof remains sufficient for all but the tallest drivers. Our five-foot-tall tester had no trouble seeing over the hood. The left footrest is fairly comfortable.

Front seating

⊖ Some of our testers found the *Galant's* seats too thinly padded and lacking sufficient support for the lower back.

Rear seating

○ The contoured rear bench is a little lower and less supportive than those of the three competing models previously mentioned. Two tall rear passengers will find sufficient headroom and knee room, and three average-size adults can sit without undue pinching. But the folded armrest makes a poor backrest for the center passenger.

Access

⊖ Front and rear, access poses no difficulty.

Climate system

⊜ The versatile and effective system furnishes plenty of warmed or cooled air, but the outboard dash vents leak some air in the Heat, Mix, and Defrost modes. A two-position Bilevel mode can bias more airflow from either the dash or the floor vents.

Controls and displays

⊜ The instruments are clear, but the levers for the turn signal and wipers obscure some minor controls, and some labels lack sufficient contrast.

Trunk

⊖ Swallows five Pullman cases and a weekend bag, or a folded wheelchair, with room left over. The one-piece rear seatback can fold down to expand cargo capacity. You can hide small items around the compact spare or in a shallow tray behind it. The open trunk lid and its blunt latch menace the head of anyone much taller than five feet. *Mitsubishi* advises against towing a trailer with the *Galant.*

Safety

The *Galant* has dual air bags. The front shoulder belts have adjustable upper anchors. The rear three-point belts require two hands to buckle, but they're generally comfortable to wear. The shoulder belts have special retractors that let you secure a child safety seat without a locking clip. The adjustable front head restraints are high enough to afford whiplash protection even when they're lowered all the way. The integral rear head restraints are barely high enough to protect an average-size adult. Our hydraulic bumper basher dented the plastic front bumper (repair estimate: $496) but left the rear one unharmed.

In government crash tests, the passenger dummy fared better than the driver.

Predicted reliability

○ Reliability has improved to average this year.

Based on a January 1994 report.

Nissan Altima SE

Price range: $15,649–$20,999
Cost factor: 88%
Depreciation: ○

Overview

We liked our sport-oriented *SE* better than the top-of-the-line *GLE* we tested in 1993. But we think the less expensive *GXE* is the best value. Reliability to date has been outstanding.

Acceleration

⊖ The 2.4-liter Four provides spirited performance, but it's not as smooth as the smaller Four in the *G20* from Nissan's Infiniti division.

Transmission

⊜ The five-speed manual shifts competently, although not as crisply as that of a competitor, the *Acura Integra*.

An automatic is optional.

Economy

⊖ Expect to average about 28 mpg overall on Regular fuel.

Routine handling

⊖ The *Altima* handles soundly overall, although it lacks the agility of the most nimble sport sedans. It leans somewhat in turns, and the tires squeal sooner than those of the other cars in this group.

Emergency handling

⊖ When pressed to its limits, the car plows ahead a little. But it remained steady in our avoidance maneuver.

Braking

⊖ The antilock brakes stopped the car from 60 mph in 132 feet on dry pavement, 149 feet on wet pavement. The car stopped straight in our wet divided-pavement test.

Ride, normal load

○ The ride is busy and firm, with stiff jiggles and snaps on broken pavement.

Ride, full load

○ A full load worsens the ride a little.

Noise

⊖ The cabin is fairly quiet; a little wind and road noise manages to come through, and the engine sounds gruff at high revs.

Driving position

⊖ The driver's seat is low and lacks a height adjuster. Even so, short drivers can see out well. The height of the steering wheel is adjustable. Tall drivers will find plenty of headroom but sparse legroom. Flooring the clutch pedal requires a stretch.

Front seating

⊖ The front seats provide generally good, firm support except under the thighs. The optional, nonperforated leather upholstery is slippery and feels like vinyl.

Rear seating

○ Three six-footers have just enough room in the rear seat—as long as they're slim. Headroom is marginal, especially in the center, and toe space under the front seats is tight. With three riding abreast, the shape of the seatback tilts outboard occupants toward the center.

Access

○ Entering and exiting the front or rear requires average effort.

Climate system

⊜ The climate-control system works well enough, but the dash outlets are too low for optimal air distribution.

Controls and displays

⊖ The instruments are clear, and most controls are well laid out. But the horn buttons, on the spokes of the steering wheel, are hard to find in a hurry. You must push an annoying button to release the ignition key. Two switches control the driver's power window: one for "one touch" down, and the other for normal use. Other automakers combine those functions in one button.

Trunk

○ The trunk can hold five Pullman cases, or a folded wheelchair, with room left over. The rear seatback doesn't fold down, but a pass-through port behind the armrest lets you carry long objects such as skis inside the car. The compact spare leaves no room in its well for concealing small items. The *Altima* can tow a 1000-pound trailer, according to Nissan.

Safety

The front safety belts are comfortable, and their upper anchors are adjustable for height. You can secure a child seat in any position without a locking clip. Our basher knocked the front bumper off kilter and creased the rear bumper. Repair estimates: $477 front, $470 rear.

Both the driver and passenger were well protected in government crash tests.

Predicted reliability

⊜ The *Altima* has an excellent record for reliability.

Based on a November 1994 report.

Oldsmobile Achieva

Price range: *$13,495–$16,495*
Cost factor: *94%*
Depreciation: ◒

Overview

In performance, handling, and ride, our basic *Achieva* was an underachiever. The *Achieva* is available in both two-door and four-door body styles.

Acceleration

○ More sound than fury from revving the engine.

Transmission

⊖ Three-speed automatic with lockup sometimes shifted abruptly.

Economy

○ Expect about 24 mpg overall.

Routine handling

○ Steering felt vague and slow, and car tended to plow straight ahead during cornering. We had to make constant small steering corrections to maintain course.

Emergency handling

○ In avoidance maneuvers, the car plowed, tires squealed, and steering felt lifeless.

Braking

○ Braking distances with the antilock brakes were only slightly longer than those of the *Skylark* and *Grand Am,* largely because of narrower tires on the *Achieva.*

Ride, normal load

○ Rode stiffly, shuddering over ridges and patches on highways. Ride became worse on back roads.

Ride, full load

◒ With an added full load, suspension slammed onto its stops repeatedly.

Noise

⊜ Ran quietly at steady speeds, but the engine was noisy when revved.

Driving position

⊜ Too low for a good view ahead. Steering wheel is too high and canted toward driver's left shoulder, and its thin rim is uncomfortable to grasp. We missed a power driver's seat option.

Front seating

⊜ Firm, comfortable support.

Rear seating

◒ Tall riders found just enough head- and knee room. Most riders wanted more lower-back support, and long-legged riders wanted more thigh support.

Access

◒ High and wide doorsills and lower seats conspire to impede access. In the rear, tight foot clearance and inward curve of door frames interfere with access.

Climate system

⊜ Took a while to furnish adequate heat; cool air arrived promptly. Fan was noisy in Defrost, and side-window defogging was weak.

Controls and displays

⊜ Resemble those in the *Skylark,* right down to the annoying automatic door locks. Thumbwheels for operating vents would benefit from labels to indicate open and closed positions. Instruments are positioned in good view, but daytime reflections clouded their readings.

Trunk

⊜ Four Pullman cases and two weekend bags. Remote trunk-release tab, like those in other GM compacts, felt flimsy (ours stopped working soon after buying the car).

Safety

Dual air bags are standard. When the passenger seat is moved forward, the floor-mounted inboard buckle for the door-mounted safety belt slips out of reach. No damage to front or rear bumpers from our basher.

The government has not crash-tested an *Achieva* with dual air bags.

Predicted reliability

◒ Reliability has been below average.

Based on a June 1992 report.

Plymouth Breeze

***Price:** $14,060*
***Cost factor:** 92%*
***Depreciation:** NA*

See DODGE STRATUS.

Pontiac Grand Am GT

***Price range:** $13,499–$15,499*
***Cost factor:** 92%*
Depreciation: ⊜

Overview

This popular compact is reasonably priced and scored well in some tests, but it falls down badly in ride and rear seat comfort.

Acceleration

⊜ The optional V6 isn't as quick as we thought, but its a better choice than the noisy Four.

Transmission

⊜ The automatic performed well; a five-speed manual is available only with the four.

Economy

◒ Expect about 20 mpg overall.

Routine handling

⊜ The tires grip well in turns, but the front end bounces disconcertingly on undulating pavement.

Emergency handling

⊜ Feels a bit clumsy during hard cornering, but the tail remains securely planted.

Braking

⊜ Stops from 60 mph were straight and reasonably short on wet and dry pavement. The car also stopped straight in the wet divided-pavement test, but the antilock brakes made the brake pedal pulse annoyingly.

Ride, normal load

○ The car rocks mildly on good roads, and the ride feels rubbery. The bouncing of the front end on undulating roads degrades the ride as well as the handling.

Ride, full load

○ With a full load, ride worsens significantly, and the rear suspension all too easily compresses with a jolt.

Noise

⊜ The car squeaks, rattles, and groans on rough pavement, the exhaust growls constantly, and wind noise must be endured at highway speeds.

Driving position

⊜ Optional power driver's seat accommodates most physiques comfortably. With the seat raised, even short drivers can see well over the hood.

Front seating

⊖ The front seats provide generally good, firm support, although tall people could use more thigh support.

Rear seating

○ Headroom is skimpy, and sitting three abreast is a squeeze.

Access

● Mostly miserable.

Climate system

⊖ Provides adequate heat and cooling and distributes it evenly, but it takes a while to get going.

Controls and displays

⊖ The instruments are clear and easy on the eyes, but some controls are badly designed. The levers for the turn signals and wipers feel clumsy, and the switches for the power windows, on the center console, don't operate intuitively. The door locks engage automatically as soon as you put the car in gear, but they don't unlock automatically when you shift into Park; we found that feature annoying. The radio is one of the most user-friendly ones we've seen lately.

Trunk

○ Four Pullman cases and a weekend bag, or a folded wheelchair, fit in the trunk with room to spare. Split folding seatbacks expand the trunk but don't lock. The trunk lacks cubbies or bins.

Safety

The *Grand Am* has dual air bags. The bumper basher inflicted $98 in damage to the front, $726 to the rear. Securing a child safety seat up front requires a special lap belt from the dealer. In the rear, you can secure a child seat without a locking clip. Special retaining straps help position the rear shoulder belts properly for older children.

The government has not crash-tested a *Grand Am* with dual air bags.

Predicted reliability

○ The *Grand Am* has a repair record that's about average.

Based on a June 1993 report.

Saab 900 SE V6

Price range: $23,995–$42,495
Cost factor: 89%
Depreciation: ○

Overview

Although it remains quirky, the *Saab 900* is thoroughly modern. Respectable performance, generous list of standard equipment, and relatively low price make it a bargain within this segment.

Acceleration

⊖ Smooth acceleration from the 2.5-liter V6. A 150- and 185-horsepower Four are also available.

Transmission

⊖ The optional four-speed automatic doesn't shift as smoothly as it should in a car of this class. Normal, Sport, and Winter settings change the shifting characteristics to suit the circumstances. The Winter setting provides starts in third gear; shifting returns to normal when the car reaches 50 mph. The traction-control system effectively limits front wheel spin. A Five-speed manual is standard with the Four

Economy

○ About 22 mpg, overall, on Regular fuel.

Routine handling

⊖ The *900* corners surefootedly, with restrained body roll, even in abrupt maneuvers. The steering provides good feedback during driving, but some may find it a bit heavy during parking.

Emergency handling

⊖ Imparted a feeling of confidence in abrupt maneuvers.

Braking

⊖ Stopped in 131 feet from 60 mph on dry pavement, 155 feet on wet pavement. It stopped straight in our wet divided-pavement test.

Ride, normal load

○ The ride feels taut most of the time, even on smooth roads.

Ride, full load

○ Same taut ride even with a full load of passengers and luggage.

Noise

⊖ The inside is quiet; only a bit of wind noise penetrates at highway speeds, and the V6's snarl reminds you that this is a sports sedan.

Driving position

⊖ Most drivers find a position that suits them well.

Front seating

⊖ Both power-operated front seats have a wide range of adjustments, and the driver's seat can "memorize" three positions. Both seats are firm and generally supportive, though a bit shy on side support. Leather upholstery and seat heaters are standard equipment.

Rear seating

○ Consider this a four-passenger car. Three adults in the rear seat are one too many.

Access

⊖ Quite good front and rear.

Climate system

○ The system's automatic setting doesn't work well. Drivers can count on cold feet all winter, because the puny vents under the dashboard don't deliver. Raising the temperature above 70 degrees doesn't warm the feet much, but it does overheat the passengers. Despite its 10 speed settings, the fan doesn't move much air on the Auto setting, so the cabin becomes stuffy. Adjusting the fan manually improves matters. The Bilevel feature is reversed: Warmer air flows from the dash vents than from the floor vents.

Controls and displays

○ The redesigned *Saab* has modernized controls and displays, but inconveniences still abound. The horn controls—two small buttons on the spokes of the steering wheel—are our biggest criticism. We much prefer a horn control in the center of the steering wheel.

Trunk

⊖ The hatchback design gives the *Saab* an edge over comparable sedans when it's time to haul cargo. The trunk holds five Pullman cases and a weekend bag, or a folded wheelchair, with ease—and the rear seatbacks can fold for even more cargo room. A full-size tire would fit in the well, but only a compact spare is available. Towing is limited to a 2000-pound trailer with brakes, or a 1000-pound trailer without brakes.

Safety

The front safety belts have an adjustable anchor for the shoulder strap. The rear seat has three-point safety belts for all three passengers. A locking clip is needed to secure a child safety seat in any seating position. Built-in booster seats are optional for the rear outboard positions. The front and rear head restraints are high enough to provide whiplash protection. Our basher didn't leave a mark on the *Saab's* bumpers.

Both the driver and passenger were well protected in government crash tests.

Predicted reliability

◒ Reliability is below average.

Based on an August 1994 report.

Subaru Legacy LS AWD

Price range: $16,495–$25,495
Cost factor: 90%
Depreciation: ◒

Overview

There is much to recommend about the *Legacy*. The sophisticated and unobtrusive all-wheel-drive system is a desirable extra. We tested the four-door *LS*.

Acceleration

○ The 2.2-liter Four delivers adequate acceleration, but the *Legacy* isn't as quick as some of its competition with V6s like the *Nissan Maxima* and *Volkswagen Passat*.

Transmission

⊖ The tested four-speed automatic shifts quite smoothly. A five-speed manual is available in some versions. The all-wheel-drive option performs flawlessly.

Economy

○ Expect to average about 23 mpg on Regular fuel.

Routine handling

⊜ The *Legacy* easily carves through twisty roads. The steering feels precise and requires just the right amount of effort. At the track, the car tended to run slightly wide in hard turns; easing off the accelerator quickly brought it back on course.

Emergency handling

⊖ The *Legacy* negotiated our avoidance maneuver quickly, although it wagged its tail a bit.

Braking

⊜ The car stopped impressively short from 60 mph—in just 125 feet on a dry track, 153 feet on a wet track. Braking was perfectly straight in our challenging wet divided-pavement test, where the pavement is slicker under one side of the car than under the other.

Ride, normal load

⊖ The ride is taut but compliant. The worst bumps produce only muted kicks.

Ride, full load

⊖ A full load doesn't hurt the ride at all.

Noise

⊖ The cabin remains quiet at cruising speeds.

Driving position

⊜ Thanks to a height adjuster on the driver's seat and a tilt steering column, almost any driver can get comfortable. Six-footers have more than enough head- and legroom, and five-footers can see nicely over the hood. The left footrest is comfortable, if a bit too close.

Front seating

⊖ The cloth-covered front seats provide good, firm support.

Rear seating

⊖ The contoured rear seat can hold three slim six-footers in reasonable comfort. The folded center armrest makes a tolerable though narrow seatback.

Access

⊖ Good access front and rear.

Climate system

⊖ The versatile system provides plenty of cooled or heated air, and enough of that air reaches the rear seat to keep passengers comfortable. The fan is fairly quiet and free of drafts. The rear-window defroster lacks a timer and must be switched off manually.

Controls and displays

⊜ The tiny horn buttons on the spokes of the steering wheel are hard to find when you need them. Aside from that, the controls and displays are easy to use.

Trunk

○ The trunk can accept four Pullman cases and two weekend bags, or a folded wheelchair, with room left over. In all but the base sedan, the split rear seatback can fold down to make more cargo space. You can stash a few small items out of sight in the well around the compact spare tire. Maximum trailer-towing capacity is 2000 pounds.

Safety

The front safety belts are convenient and comfortable, with adjustable upper anchors. In the rear, the three-point belts are a bit hard to buckle around adults, but they can easily secure a child safety seat without a separate locking clip. The car survived 3- and 5-mph blows from our hydraulic bumper basher with no damage.

In government crash tests, the driver dummy fared better than the passenger dummy.

Predicted reliability

⊜ Excellent reliability record.

Based on a February 1995 report.

Subaru Legacy Outback Wagon

***Price:** $21,995*
***Cost factor:** NA*
***Depreciation:** NA*

Overview

It's not as tough as it looks. Get the regular *Legacy AWD* wagon instead.

Acceleration

○ The optional 2.5-liter Four accelerates well.

Transmission

⊖ The four-speed automatic shifts smoothly enough. A five-speed manual is available with the standard 2.2-liter base engine. Its permanent all-wheel-drive system is good in snow, but not for serious off-roading.

Economy

◒ Expect to average about 21 mpg with the 2.5, on Premium fuel. The standard 2.2-liter Four averages about 23 mpg on Regular.

Routine handling

⊖ The *Outback* doesn't handle as well as the regular *Legacy*.

Emergency handling

○ It leans considerably and fishtails a little in hard turns.

Braking

⊖ Straight, fairly short stops.

Ride, normal load

○ The ride isn't as supple as the Regular *Legacy*.

Ride, full load

○ A full load doesn't affect the ride all that much.

Noise

⊖ Not particularly noisy.

Driving position

⊜ Tall drivers have ample headroom and adequate legroom. Short drivers can see out well.

Front seating

⊖ The front seats are supportive but hard.

Rear seating

⊖ The rear seat is also hard, but roomy. Three tall, slim people can fit back there.

Access

⊖ Fairly easy to get in and out.

Climate system

⊜ The climate-control system is powerful.

Controls and displays

⊜ The major controls and displays are exemplary.

Cargo area

○ The *Outback's* 31-cubic-foot usable cargo volume isn't all that large for a medium-size wagon. Payload capacity is 900 pounds. The rear seat can fold flat, and a low sill eases loading.

Safety

With its dual air bags, adjustable front shoulder-belt anchors, and claimed dynamic side-impact protection, the *Outback* has all the current safety items. The adjustable front head restraints are fine; the rear seat lacks head restraints. All the seats can hold a child safety seat without a locking clip. The center-rear belt is too short for the largest child seats. Our bumper basher caused damage to both the front and rear bumpers.

In a government crash test of a 1995 *Legacy* sedan, both the driver and passenger dummies fared well.

Predicted reliability

⊜ *Legacys* have an excellent reliability record.

Based on a June 1996 report.

Volkswagen Passat GLX ✓

***Price range:** $18,430–$22,320*
***Cost factor:** 90%*
***Depreciation:** NA*

Overview

The redesigned version is better than the old, combining a pleasant ride with competent, responsive handling. Opt for the five-speed manual transmission instead of the automatic.

Acceleration

⊖ When pressed, the 2.8-liter V6 performs spiritedly.

Transmission

○ On moderate hills, the tested four-speed automatic downshifts reluctantly and with a jerk. You must hold in the button on the shifter to get past Neutral—and then the shifter will move all the way to "2." The five-speed manual is a better choice.

Economy

◒ Expect to average about 20 mpg on Regular fuel.

Routine handling

⊜ The *Passat* handles very responsively. The steering provides lots of road feel. During hard cornering, the car leaned somewhat, but its tires gripped tenaciously.

Emergency handling

⊖ The *Passat* was quick through our avoidance maneuver, faster than such competition as the *Subaru Legacy* and *Nissan Maxima*.

Braking

⊖ The *Passat* braked from 60 mph in 132 feet on a dry track, 154 feet on a wet track. It stopped straight in our wet divided-pavement test. The brake pedal requires a bit too much effort in moderate stops.

Ride, normal load

⊖ The *Passat* rides firmly, but it effectively soaks up most ripples and ruts.

Ride, full load

⊖ A full load makes the ride feel just a bit stiffer.

Noise

⊖ The cabin is reasonably quiet except for wind noise.

Driving position

⊖ A height adjustment on the seat and a tilt steering column help almost everyone find a comfortable driving position. Even six-footers have ample legroom and enough headroom. All, including our five-foot driver, appreciated the commanding view over the hood.

Front seating

⊜ The front seats provide good, firm support. Both seats have manual adjustments for height and lumbar support.

Rear seating

⊖ The high, contoured rear seat provides good support even for three adults.

Access

⊖ Access to the rear is unusually easy.

Climate system

⊖ The versatile system offers air-conditioning in all modes. Airflow is strong and fairly quiet. The dash vents leak air when the system is in the Heat or Defrost mode. In Bilevel mode, the air should be cooler from the upper vents than from the lower vents—but in the *Passat*, it isn't.

Controls and displays

⊖ The horn buttons, on the spokes of the steering wheel, are hard to find quickly. The wiper controls are confusing, and the switches for the rear windows are inconvenient for the driver to reach. The gauges and the labels for the switches lack contrast during the day. If you leave a window or the sunroof open, you can close it from the outside by turning the key in the door lock.

Trunk

⊖ The roomy trunk can swallow five Pullman cases and one weekend bag, or a folded wheelchair, with room left over. Trailer-towing capacity is 2000 pounds with a manual transmission, 1000 pounds with an automatic.

Safety

Daytime running lights and dual airbags are standard. The *Passat's* other safety features include automatic safety-belt pre-tensioners, which instantly take up slack during a crash. Unfortunately, the passenger-side air bag crowds out the glove compartment. The rear three-point safety belts can secure a child seat without a locking clip. Our bumper basher inflicted damage to the tune of $745 in front, $556 in the rear.

The driver and passenger dummies both fared well in government crash tests.

Predicted reliability

○ The *Passat's* reliability has been average.

Based on a February 1995 report.

MIDSIZE CARS

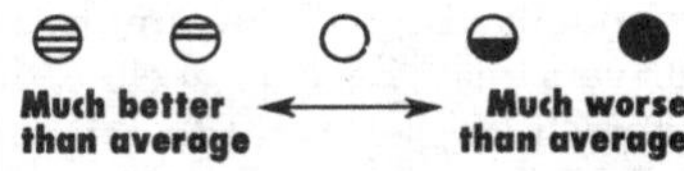

The midsize car category includes many family sedans, but also coupes, station wagons, and one luxury hatchback (the *Saab 9000*) are on the list. The models are larger than compacts, usually seating five in reasonable comfort. Some claim six-passenger capacity.

Recommended models in this broad category include the *Acura TL, BMW* 5-Series, *Buick Regal, Chevrolet Lumina, Honda Accord, Infiniti I30, Infiniti J30, Infiniti Q45, Lexus ES300, Lexus GS300, Lexus LS400, Lexus SC400/SC300, Lincoln Mark VIII, Mazda Millenia, Mercedes-Benz* E-Class, *Nissan Maxima, Saab 9000, Toyota Avalon, Toyota Camry, Volvo 850,* and *Volvo 960.*

Acura CL

Price range: *$22,110–$28,000 (est.)*
Cost factor: *89%*
Depreciation: *NA*

This fairly upscale coupe was introduced earlier this year as a 1997 model. It's based on the *Honda Accord Coupe* and offers the *Accord's* powerful 2.2-liter "VTEC" Four. A 3.0-liter V6 will appear late this year, but only with an automatic transmission. Either engine is a good choice. The *CL* should perform much like an *Accord,* with good handling and a refined, quiet ride, but it's a bit small inside. Honda is confident enough of its keyless-entry system to omit a key lock on the trunk lid.

Predicted reliability

⊜ Reliability is predicted to be excellent.

Acura RL

Price: *$41,000–46,000 (est.)*
Cost factor: *86%*
Depreciation: *NA*

The *RL* replaces the *Legend,* which has served as the flagship of Honda's luxury *Acura* line since 1986. The *RL* is a bit bigger than the *Legend,* and it offers a roomy and well-laid-out interior. The 3.5-liter V6 should provide sprightly performance. You can also expect a quiet ride. The *RL* is priced in the $40,000 range, where it must compete with formidable competitors such as Mercedes-Benz's new *E320* and BMW's newly redesigned 5-Series.

Predicted reliability

⊜ Should continue the fine *Honda/Acura* tradition.

Acura 2.5 TL ✓

Price range: *$27,900–$35,500*
Cost factor: *87%*
Depreciation: *NA*

Overview

The flavor is vanilla—although a premium grade vanilla, to be sure. This car is competent, but it holds no surprises.

Acceleration

⊖ The 2.5-liter, five-cylinder engine feels strong.

Transmission

⊖ The four-speed automatic shifts smoothly most of the time, and it's nicely matched to the *2.5TL's* engine.

Economy

○ Expect to average about 23 mpg, overall, on Premium fuel.

Routine handling

⊖ The *TL* handles competently, but the body leans quite a bit in sharp turns. The variable-effort power steering feels too light at low speeds and a bit heavy at highway speeds, but it's responsive.

Emergency handling

○ The *TL* generally behaves well during hard cornering, but it fishtailed a little in our emergency avoidance maneuver.

Braking

⊖ Stops were straight and reasonably short in all our braking tests.

Ride, normal load

⊖ On the road, the *TL* feels longer and wider than it is; it gives a firm yet supple ride.

Ride, full load

⊖ A full load doesn't affect the ride.

Noise

⊖ The cabin was hushed except on coarse pavement.

Driving position

⊖ Some of our drivers couldn't find an

ideal position despite the seat adjustments and tilt steering wheel. The driver gets power adjustments on the seat; the passenger makes adjustments manually. Legroom is ample, but tall drivers may have to recline the seat more than they want to for adequate headroom. Five-footers can easily see over the hood.

Front seating

⊖ The front seats, upholstered in leather, feel supportive. Seat heaters are standard in the costlier *Acura 3.2TL*, unavailable in the *2.5TL*.

Rear seating

⊖ The rear seat is comfortable for two but a bit tight for a middle passenger.

Access

⊖ Rear entry and exit require some agility because of narrow door openings, large doorsills, and tight foot clearance.

Climate system

⊜ The automatic system works simply and effectively in Auto mode. However, its manual-control switches are small, unlabeled, and unlit.

Controls and displays

⊖ Most of the major controls and displays are close to ideal. But the small horn switches on the spokes of the steering wheel are hard to find in a hurry, and the turn-signal lever completely hides the master cruise-control and fog-light switches.

Trunk

○ The rear seatback doesn't fold down, but the trunk is roomy. A small port lets you slide long, narrow items such as skis through the trunk and into the passenger compartment. The hinges of the trunk lid drop when the trunk is closed; they could crush any luggage that's placed underneath.

Safety

The *2.5TL* has air bags for both driver and passenger, and lap-and-shoulder safety belts with adjustable upper anchors. The front head restraints can be locked in their raised positions. Even when they're lowered, they're high enough to provide proper protection against whiplash. The built-in rear head restraints are also high enough. Our bumper basher caused no damage.

The government has not yet crash-tested the *Acura TL*.

Predicted reliability

⊜ Previous *Acura* models have had an exemplary reliability record, and we predict that the *TL* will be very reliable as well.

Based on a February 1996 report.

Audi A6

Price range: *$32,300–$34,000*
Cost factor: *88%*
Depreciation: ●

This replacement for the *Audi 100* received an exterior face-lift in 1995. The last time we tested this model, we found many faults, from idiosyncratic placement of controls to a mediocre ride and sluggish acceleration. Audi says it has remedied the most serious shortcomings. Audi has also juggled the list of options. You can now add all-wheel drive (Quattro option) to the base car, for instance. Audi provides all scheduled maintenance for three years or 50,000 miles.

Predicted reliability

Insufficient data.

BMW 5-SERIES 

Price range: *$37,900–$49,900*
Cost factor: *84%*
Depreciation: ◒

The redesigned 5-Series cars are new this year and hit the showroom floors as 1997 models. Improvements in refinement and safety make these fine cars even better. The 5-Series leaves the impression of pure precision. Handling should be nimble and accurate. The new models are a little roomier inside than their predecessors and come with side-impact air bags. Expect a firm but supple ride and a quiet cabin with comfortable and supportive seats. Clear displays compliment easy-to-reach controls, and the trunk is roomy. Traction control, a godsend in winter, will be standard equipment.

Predicted reliability ⊖

Buick Century

Price range: *$16,720–$19,406*
Cost factor: *94%*
Depreciation: ○

Overview

An average reliability record is this antiquated model's sole claim to fame. In overall performance, it doesn't come close to its major competitors.

Acceleration

○ The optional 3.1-liter V6 accelerates adequately.

Transmission

⊖ The four-speed automatic shifts smoothly most of the time.

Economy

○ Expect to average about 22 mpg on Regular fuel.

Routine handling

◒ Every little twist and turn in the road makes the *Century* lean heavily and squeal its tires. The steering feels slow and almost detached from the front wheels. In sharp turns at our test track, the tires lost their grip early, and the car plowed ahead stubbornly.

Emergency handling

◒ The car negotiated our test-track avoidance maneuver safely, but its handling felt reluctant, clumsy, and uncertain.

Braking

○ The *Century* stopped from 60 mph in 144 feet on dry pavement, 155 feet on wet pavement—a below-average braking performance. It pulled strongly to one side in our difficult wet divided-pavement test.

Ride, normal load

○ Below about 30 mph on rural roads, the *Century* holds out the promise of a comfortable ride. But at higher speeds, the promise goes unfulfilled. The ride feels queasy and spongy, with hopping, wallowing, and bouncing in bumpy curves. The suspension often extends or compresses fully with a jolt. Even on smooth highways, the front end rises and falls unceasingly.

Ride, full load

○ A full load makes the ride even worse.

Noise

⊖ There's very little road or tire noise, but wind noise is pronounced even at modest speeds.

Driving position

○ The height-adjustable steering wheel and optional power driver's seat should help most drivers get comfortable, although long-legged drivers will wish for more legroom. Even without fully raising the seat, our five-foot driver could see quite easily over the hood.

Front seating

⊖ The cloth-covered split-bench front seat comfortably accommodates two adults. Support is mostly good and firm, though we wished for more side support, especially when we went through turns.

Rear seating

◒ The rear seat is worse than the rear seat in many much smaller cars. It feels tight even for average-size adults, much less for six-footers.

Access

○ Entry and exit require average effort.

Climate system

⊖ The system works well and has a full complement of modes, but its controls require a long reach. The air conditioner comes on automatically in the Bilevel and Defrost modes. The heater warms up quickly, the temperature is easy to modulate, and the fan runs fairly quietly. Rear passengers must do with less than their share of heat, though, and the rear defroster works slowly.

Controls and displays

● The instrument panel and operating controls are archaic and inconvenient. The power seat switches are awkwardly placed on the front of the cushion. The hazard flasher is completely hidden, and the horn buttons are hard to find quickly. The doors lock automatically when you shift the transmission into gear, but they don't unlock automatically until you turn off the ignition switch—a persistent irritation. The shiny metalwork over most of the buttons and knobs creates annoying reflections in the gauges. Like the *Chevrolet Lumina,* the *Century* lacks a daytime "pass-to-flash" feature.

Trunk

⊖ The trunk holds five Pullman cases and two weekend bags, or a folded wheelchair, with room left over. Trailer-towing capacity is 1000 pounds —or 2000 pounds with a factory-installed heavy-duty cooling option—according to Buick.

Safety

The *Century* lacks a passenger-side air bag, and it retains GM's awkward and uncomfortable door-mounted safety belts. The owner's manual says you need a locking clip to secure a child safety seat, but actually you don't— at least not in the rear. To mount a child seat in the front, you'll need a special lap belt installed by the Buick dealer. Our bumper basher caused some slight dings, too minor to repair.

In government crash tests, the driver dummy fared better than the passenger.

Predicted reliability

○ The *Century* has an average reliability record.

Based on a January 1995 report.

Buick Regal Gran Sport 

Price range: $19,445–$21,800
Cost factor: 91%
Depreciation: ◒

Overview

The *Buick,* as equipped, rides smoothly and quietly. It also has established a solid reliability record.

Acceleration

⊖ A 3.8-liter V6—standard in the *Regal Limited* and *Gran Sport*—is worth the extra money when shopping for the *Regal Custom* (a 3.1-liter V6 is standard). The larger V6 provides plenty of torque without sacrificing fuel economy.

Transmission

⊖ The four-speed automatic shifts very smoothly.

Economy

◒ Expect about 20 mpg overall, on Regular fuel.

Routine handling

⊖ The tires squeal too easily during cornering, but the solid-feeling steering and modest body roll are reassuring.

Emergency handling

○ The sedan ran wide in tight turns at our test track, and it felt sloppy in our accident-avoidance maneuvers.

Braking

⊖ The *Buick* required 138 feet to stop

from 60 mph on dry pavement, and 150 feet on wet pavement. It veered slightly in our challenging wet divided-pavement test.

Ride, normal load

⊖ The car rode comfortably and very quietly on smooth highways. The suspension soaked up large road imperfections nicely, but it kicked a bit over broken pavement.

Ride, full load

⊖ Loading the car fully challenged the suspension, enlarging the ride motions and sharpening the kicks.

Noise

⊖ Impressively quiet at highway speeds.

Driving position

⊖ The optional power adjuster on the driver's seat and the height adjuster on the steering column should allow most people to find a comfortable driving position.

Front seating

⊖ The seats initially felt more comfortable than those in the *Pontiac Grand Prix* and *Oldsmobile Cutlass Supreme* sedans. Perhaps it was the resiliency of the cloth upholstery, or some extra padding, that made the seatbacks feel less misshapen. But the lack of real support became apparent in time, and our backs soon began to ache.

Rear seating

○ The rear seat is roomy enough for tall people and wide enough for three average-size adults. It's high and well padded, but it doesn't provide enough back or thigh support.

Access

⊖ Large door openings ease access.

Climate system

⊜ Quickly provides lots of warmed or cooled air and distributes it evenly. Our car had the heavily promoted dual climate-control system, which allows the driver and front passenger to adjust the temperature independently. It works well.

Controls and displays

⊖ The horn control is conveniently placed in the center of the steering wheel. But that's about the only modern design in the controls. As with many older GM models, the *Regal* headlights lack a "flash-to-pass" feature. The flush-mounted door locks are balky, and the buttons for the windshield and rear defrosters are easy to confuse. The instruments are small and scattered all over the panel, and the steering wheel blocks the battery-voltage and oil-pressure displays. Fortunately, the *Buick's* displays and most of the controls are nicely illuminated at night.

Trunk

⊖ The trunk is as roomy as that of the *Pontiac Grand Prix,* but it lacks the port that allows skis or other long narrow objects to fit inside the car. Maximum trailer towing capacity is 1000 pounds with the 3.1-liter V6, 2000 pounds with the 3.8-liter V6.

Safety

The *Regal* has dual air bags. You must request a special lap belt from the dealer to secure a child safety seat in the right front seat (the belt and installation are free). You'll need a special clip to secure a safety seat in the rear outboard positions. The built-in rear head restraints are too low to be effective. Our bumper basher damaged both bumpers, resulting in repair estimates of $458 in front, $348 in the rear.

Government crash-test results were not available.

Predicted reliability

○ Expect overall reliability.

Based on a February 1994 report.

Buick Riviera

***Price:** $29,475*
***Cost factor:** 89%*
***Depreciation:** NA*

Overview

While achieving a pillowy, ultraquiet ride, the *Riviera* sacrifices too many other important qualities.

Acceleration

⊖ The optional supercharged 3.8-liter V6 delivers outstanding acceleration.

Transmission

⊜ The four-speed automatic shifts almost imperceptibly. The all-speed traction-control system, an option, uses the brakes and engine effectively to keep the front wheels from spinning.

Economy

● Expect about 17 mpg overall. Buick says that the *Riviera* can use Regular fuel, but that Premium improves performance.

Routine handling

○ The *Riviera* feels ponderous on winding back roads and clumsy in tight quarters. Its body leans considerably during cornering, and the steering wheel feels lethargic and imprecise.

Emergency handling

○ The car feels unwieldy in abrupt maneuvers.

Braking

⊖ The *Riviera* always stopped short and straight, even in our test on wet divided pavement, but the brakes were difficult to modulate. The brake pedal required significantly more effort after repeated stops in our fade test.

Ride, normal load

⊖ In the old Buick tradition, the *Riviera* rides smoothly and quietly on the highway, but it bounds over crests and dips on back roads.

Ride, full load

⊖ A full load of people and luggage doesn't affect the ride significantly.

Noise

⊜ The *Riviera* offers an ultraquiet ride.

Driving position

○ Few drivers felt truly comfortable behind the wheel; when they raised the seat to see out well, they complained of too little headroom. (The sunroof robs some headroom, but finding a *Riviera* without that option may be difficult.) When our shortest driver raised the seat and adjusted the seatback to see out, she felt too close to the steering wheel. The low windshield hampers the driver's view of overhead signs.

Front seating

⊖ The front seats are well padded, but their side support isn't strong enough. Both front seats have power adjustments.

Rear seating

○ Headroom is skimpy in the rear seat as well. There's enough shoulder room for three adults, but the folded center armrest doesn't offer proper back support. Knee room is generous.

Access

○ Access front and rear is average in the coupe.

Climate system

⊖ The automatic climate-control system offers separate temperature controls for the driver and front passenger, but distribution is spotty. On the Heat setting, both the driver and passenger have cold feet. It takes a lot of fumbling with several individually adjustable dashboard vents to eliminate drafts. Airflow to the rear seat is generous and more evenly distributed. The air conditioner engages automatically when the climate system is set to the Defrost mode.

Controls and displays

○ The radio and climate controls require a very long stretch. Vital displays such as the speedometer and turn-signal indicators can be hidden from view.

Trunk

⊖ The rear seatback doesn't fold, but the roomy trunk can hold five Pullman cases and three weekend bags with a little room left over. A folded wheelchair fits easily. The spare-tire well won't accept a full-size tire. A switch in the glove compartment can disable the remote trunk release for security. Also, a separate key operates the glove compartment and the trunk's outside lock—handy when you leave the car with a parking attendant.

Safety

The front safety belts are neither convenient nor comfortable, and their design allows extra slack to form during a crash. Even worse, the design allows the wearer to add even more slack to relieve pressure. In the rear, "comfort guides" help position the safety belts properly on small adults and large children. The buckle end of the center lap belt is too long to use with some child safety seats. The front and rear head restraints are just high enough to protect average-size adults. Our 3- and 5-mph bumper-basher tests severely damaged the *Riviera's* bumpers, tearing the covers, bending the impact bars, and loosening a parking light.

The *Riviera* has yet to be crash-tested by the government.

Predicted reliability

○ The *Riviera* has an average reliability record.

Based on a July 1995 report.

Cadillac Eldorado

***Price range:** $39,995–$42,995*
***Cost factor:** 87%*
Depreciation: ●

Overview

It's even cushier than the *Lincoln Mark VIII,* but the power of the Northstar V8 challenges its front-wheel-drive chassis. The "active" electronic suspension is designed to react to various road conditions.

Acceleration

⊜ Fastest of the luxury coupes with a 6.8-second 0-to-60-mph time. The traction control is hard put to prevent the potent V8 from spinning the front wheels. Traction in snow is excellent.

Transmission

⊜ Four-speed automatic shifts smoothly at all times.

Economy

● Not thrifty: about 15 mpg in mixed driving, on Premium fuel.

Routine handling

⊖ Compared with other luxury coupes, it feels cumbersome. The body rolls noticeably during cornering, the tires squeal, and the steering feels unresponsive. The suspension reaches the top and bottom of its travel on sharp bumps.

Emergency handling

○ The body wallows in hard turns. In avoidance maneuvers, the car initially plows ahead and then wags its tail.

Braking

⊖ The car stopped fairly short and straight, but the nose dived considerably during hard stops.

Ride, normal load

⊖ It feels superficially comfortable, at least on good roads. On back roads, the suspension absorbs a series of bumps nicely, but the impacts of isolated bumps pass through to the occupants.

Ride, full load

⊖ With a full load, ride is smoothed and side-to-side motions are quelled.

Noise

⊖ Some road and wind noise penetrates, but generally quiet inside.

Driving position

⊖ Power driver's seat and tilt steering column help most people find a comfortable position, and even tall people have ample legroom. Even drivers who raise their seat fully found plenty of headroom in the tested car, which did not have the optional glass sunroof. But the steering wheel is too close. That's a problem especially for short drivers; when they raise the seat, they must also move it forward to reach the pedals. Wide rear pillars add to a driver's blind spots.

Front seating

⊖ The large seats seem cushy, but they don't provide quite enough support. Both are power operated. The leather upholstery doesn't "breathe." The optional seat heaters work very well.

Rear seating

◒ Two adults fit, but not all that comfortably. It's not a place to sit for very long. Three sitting abreast would be very uncomfortable indeed.

Access

○ Easy enough in front if the long doors can open fully, but watch out for the frameless window glass. Getting into the rear seat takes dexterity.

Climate system

⊖ The fully automatic system works almost perfectly: You select the temperature and the system does the rest. One complaint: You can't select Bilevel or Vent mode. The heated mirrors and rear defroster work quickly.

Controls and displays

○ The instruments are clearly labeled and easy to read, but some controls are poorly placed. The steering wheel blocks the view of the trip computer and climate-control system, and the hazard flasher lurks under the steering column. The radio has knobs for volume and tuning, a welcome feature that's rare these days.

Trunk

⊖ Enormous trunk can easily hold five Pullman cases and a weekend bag, or a folded wheelchair.

Safety

Dual air bags and three-point belts are standard. The shoulder belt chafes the neck of some drivers. It's easy to mount a child safety seat up front, but the rear-seat buckle ends are too short; it takes a contortionist to latch those belts or install a child safety seat in the rear. The bumper basher inflicted an estimated $152 in damage in front and $56 in the rear.

The government has not crash-tested an *Eldorado*.

Predicted reliability

● The *Eldorado* reliability record is poor. The *Seville* is just as bad but even more expensive.

Based on a July 1993 report.

Cadillac Seville STS

***Price range:** $42,995–$47,495*
***Cost factor:** 87%*
Depreciation: ●

Overview

Again, GM's strong Northstar V8 outpowers the competition, but the chassis needs more sophistication to cope with the engine's power and compete with the world's best luxury sedans. Unfortunately, most *Cadillacs*, GM's premier line, have faltered in reliability.

Acceleration

⊖ Despite its weight, the *STS* accelerates faster than most luxury cars, going from 0 to 60 mph in only 6.9 seconds.

Transmission

⊖ Four-speed automatic shifts smoothly. With so much power driving the front wheels, the traction-control system is essential—and effective.

Economy

● Only 17 mpg on Premium fuel.

Routine handling

⊖ Feels fairly crisp in routine driving.

Emergency handling

○ The car plowed ahead a bit in avoidance maneuvers, but the tires gripped well.

Braking

⊖ Stops were short and straight.

Ride, normal load

⊖ Rides smoothly enough on the highway, but, despite the *STS's* "road-sensing" active suspension, irregularities in the road elicit frequent snappy motions and firm kicks. Broken pavement turns the ride choppy.

Ride, full load

⊖ With a full load, the car maintains a smooth highway ride.

Noise

⊖ Although hardly noisy inside, it's not as hushed as a *Lexus* or *Infiniti*. There's some wind noise on the highway and road noise on coarse pavement, plus body squeaks. The throaty roar of the V8 engine makes itself known on a regular basis.

Driving position

⊖ The roomy cockpit offers plenty of legroom for six-footers, but the optional sunroof robs valuable headroom. Short drivers need more elevation than the seat allows to see well over the hood.

Front seating

⊖ Large, soft, leather-covered front seats feel voluptuous. Both are power operated and provide generally well-placed support. The leather upholstery is perforated. The optional front-seat heaters worked well.

Rear seating

○ Deeply sculpted rear bench seats two or three in moderate comfort.

Access

⊖ A fairly low roof and steeply raked windshield pillars make access to the front seats somewhat more difficult than in other luxury cars such as the *Lexus* and the *Infiniti*. And, when you open the door, annoyingly weak checks can allow the door to bounce back at you. A low backseat and broad, high sills somewhat hamper access to the rear.

Climate system

⊖ The fully automatic system works well. It even routes some air to the windshield to keep it clear in damp weather. Plenty of air gushes from the front vents (the fan is a little noisy on its highest speed, though). Rear-seat passengers can adjust their own ventilation, which includes a fan in the rear of the center console.

Controls and displays

⊖ The basic controls are well designed, and the instruments are clear, but the steering wheel blocks part of the climate-control display and the trip computer. The climate display shows the outside temperature, a nice touch that buyers of luxury cars have come to expect.

Trunk

○ Fully carpeted and ample for a family of four. It holds four Pullman cases and two weekend bags, or a folded wheelchair, with room left over. The compact spare tires stores under the trunk floor, and small objects can fit behind it.

Safety

The *Cadillac* is equipped with dual air bags and GM's two-retractor belt system. The upper anchor is adjustable for height. The short buckles on the rear three-point belts are hard to latch. A child safety seat can fit in any position without a locking clip, but it's tough to strap one into the center rear position. Our bumper basher damaged the cover on both bumpers. Repair estimate: $693 front, $653 rear.

The government has not crash-tested a *Seville*.

Predicted reliability

● *Seville* continues Cadillac's woeful reliability record.

Based on a November 1993 report.

Chevrolet Lumina LS ✓

Price range: *$16,355–$18,055*
Cost factor: *90%*
Depreciation: ◒

Overview

Thanks to a complete redesign for 1995, the *Lumina* is much more modern—and it's much more competitive.

Acceleration

○ The 3.1-liter V6 accelerates adequately. Those who want more performance can choose a 3.4-liter V6 with dual overhead camshafts (DOHC).

Transmission

⊜ The four-speed automatic shifts very smoothly.

Economy

◒ Expect about 21 mpg overall on Regular fuel with the 3.1-liter V6.

Routine handling

⊖ The *Lumina* handles competently but uninspiringly in normal driving. The body leans in hard turns, and the steering feels numb. If you lift your foot off the accelerator too suddenly during a hard turn, the tail wags unsettlingly.

Emergency handling

○ The *Lumina* felt sloppy in our avoidance maneuver.

Braking

○ The *Lumina* needed more than the average distance to stop from 60 mph: 144 feet on a dry track, 161 feet on a wet track. It pulled slightly in our dry-pavement tests, but it stopped straight in our challenging wet divided-pavement test.

Ride, normal load

⊖ The *Lumina* generally rides nicely, even over sharp bumps. On the highway, the car sometimes bobs slowly.

Ride, full load

⊖ A full load makes the ride more buoyant and somewhat less comfortable.

Noise

⊜ The *Lumina* is very quiet inside. Road noise is virtually nonexistent, wind noise is subdued, and the engine is inaudible except during acceleration.

Driving position

⊖ The tilt wheel and optional power seat help tailor the driving position for virtually any physique. Short drivers can see well over the hood. The parking-brake linkage infringes on the left footrest.

Front seating

⊖ The cloth-covered split-bench front seat can hold two comfortably. The padding is a bit thin in spots. Excessive play in the seatback recliners allows the seatbacks to rattle and rock annoyingly. Individual front seats are optional.

Rear seating

⊖ The rear seat is merely adequate for three six-footers, if they're slim.

Access

⊖ Access to front and rear seats is easy.

Climate system

⊜ The system is top-notch. The controls work very smoothly, the fan is fairly quiet, and the air conditioner, heater, and defroster are strong and virtually free of drafts.

Controls and displays

⊜ The instrument panel shows good design and attention to detail. The controls are logically arranged and easy to use, and most are lit at night. Most cars today have a daytime "flash-to-pass" feature—but several GM models, including the *Lumina*, still lack this useful safety feature.

Trunk

⊖ The trunk is ample for full family service. We were able to pack five Pullman cases, or a folded wheelchair, with room to spare. The owner's manual is mum on trailer-towing capacity, but a sales brochure says it's 1000 pounds.

Safety

You won't need a locking clip to secure a child safety seat in any seating position. The rear seat incorporates comfort guides to align the belts properly on children or short adults. The rear head restraints are too low to protect most adults from whiplash. Our bumper basher left the car's front and rear bumpers undamaged.

Both the driver and passenger dummies were well protected in government crash tests.

Predicted reliability

○ We predict an average reliability record.

Based on a January 1995 report.

Chevrolet Monte Carlo Z34

Price range: $17,255–$19,455
Cost factor: 91%
Depreciation: NA

Overview

The *Z34* isn't the sporty coupe it pretends to be. The basic *LS* version is a better package for less money.

Acceleration

⊖ The 3.4-liter V6 accelerates well but is very thirsty, averaging only about 18 mpg overall. The *LS's* 3.1-liter V6 is more fuel efficient but still responsive.

Transmission

⊜ The four-speed automatic shifts very smoothly.

Economy

● Expect about 18 mpg overall with the 3.4-liter V6.

Routine handling

⊖ The *Monte Carlo* jerks and bobs on the dips and crests of country roads. The steering is none too quick, and it gives little feel of the road. Stronger tire grip would have improved handling in our track tests.

Emergency handling

○ The car felt sloppy in hard turns, first plowing ahead and then wagging its tail. It negotiated our avoidance maneuver rather slowly.

Braking

○ The antilock brakes aren't up to snuff. Stopping distances were relatively long. The car pulled to one side on dry pavement, although it stopped commendably straight in our wet split-surface tests. The brake pedal felt spongy and required significantly more effort than most modern braking systems.

Ride, normal load

○ The *Z34* feels stiff on small bumps, bouncy on large ones—the worst of both worlds.

Ride, full load

○ A full load makes matters worse.

Noise

⊖ Wind whistle and road noise aren't bothersome, but the engine and exhaust growl, while sporty, can be tiring.

Driving position

⊖ Room for head and legs is ample even for tall drivers. And short drivers can see out well, thanks to the range of adjustment in the power seat. You can also adjust the height of the steering column.

Front seating

○ The front seats feel lumpy, with bulges in the wrong places.

Rear seating

◒ Two six-footers can squeeze into the rear seat, but three shouldn't try. In the center position, headroom is barely adequate for a person of average height. The seat feels lumpy and uncomfortable. You have to duck under the front safety belts when you get in and out.

Access

○ Access is easy as long as you have room to open the door fully. Do so carefully; the door checks are weak, and the door can bounce back at you.

Climate system

⊜ The climate-control system provides good airflow throughout the cabin, but the heater takes a while to warm up.

Controls and displays

⊜ The controls and displays are nicely designed. One thing we miss is a "flash-to-pass" headlight control, a safety feature most cars have these days.

Trunk

⊖ The trunk can hold five Pullman cases and one weekend bag, or a folded wheelchair, with room left over. The rear seatbacks can fold for more luggage room. The *Monte Carlo's* two separate keys, one for the ignition and the other for the doors and trunk, would make sense when you leave the car with an attendant—except that you can't lock either the seatbacks or the remote trunk release. The spare-tire well won't hold a full-size spare.

Safety

The front safety belts are neither easy to put on nor comfortable to wear. You can adjust the position of the shoulder belt by moving the head restraint; even so, the belt remains too low for tall people. The lap belt often rides up onto the abdomen. A "comfort guide" helps position the rear belts properly on large children and small adults, but the belts seem to work better and more easily with child safety seats than with people. The front head restraints are amply high; those in the rear are too low to provide good whiplash protection. Our bumper basher tore the rear bumper's plastic cover in two places near the license plate. Most owners wouldn't have bothered fixing the damage—especially when they learned that the repair would cost $600.

The safety-belted driver and passenger dummies in a 1995 *Chevrolet Monte Carlo* suffered moderate "injuries" in the government's 35-mph crash test.

Predicted reliability

◒ Reliability has been below average.

Based on a July 1995 report.

Ford Taurus LX

Price range: *$17,995–$22,000*
Cost factor: *91%*
Depreciation: *NA*

Overview

This model is new from the ground up—but the more things change, the more they stay the same. The sporty SHO version is also new this year.

Acceleration

⊖ The new 3.0-liter Duratec V6 is based on the V6 in the *Ford Contour,* but it's larger and more powerful. It accelerates smoothly and responsively. The less-responsive base 3.0-liter V6, with 55 fewer hp, should perform satisfactorily, with about the same fuel economy.

Transmission

⊖ The four-speed automatic transmission shifts smoothly, but not as smoothly as the *Toyota Camry's* and *Buick LeSabre's,* for example. A button lets you lock out fourth gear—useful in hilly terrain to keep the transmission from shifting back and forth between third and fourth gears. And you can start off in second gear for better traction on slippery roads.

Economy

◒ Expect about 21 mpg.

Routine handling

⊖ Despite a new engine, transmission, suspension, and steering assembly, the *Taurus's* overall driving experience hasn't changed as dramatically as the styling. The *Taurus* corners crisply, and it leans less than other comparable cars, such as the *Honda Accord, Toyota Camry,* and *Buick LeSabre.* The steering responds fairly quickly, but the variable-effort power steering sometimes becomes disconcertingly heavy in sharp turns and too light during parking.

Emergency handling

○ The *Taurus* negotiated our avoidance maneuver predictably and safely, although the tires could have gripped better.

Braking

○ Stops were straight, but not all that short, in our braking tests on wet and dry pavement.

Ride, normal load

⊖ The ride feels firm and smooth on secondary roads, but the *Taurus* lacks the suppleness of a *Camry* or *Accord* on bumps. The highway ride is firm and settled.

Ride, full load

⊖ A full load doesn't bother the *Taurus's* ride.

Noise

⊖ Wind noise enters the passenger compartment at highway speeds.

Driving position

⊖ The adjustable power driver's seat and tilt steering column help almost any driver to get comfortable behind the wheel. Legroom and headroom are ample for tall drivers, and even short drivers can see easily over the hood.

Front seating

⊖ The front seat cushions are comfortably firm, but the seatbacks lack enough side and lower-back support.

Rear seating

⊖ In the rear, room for head and shoulders is lacking, particularly when three sit abreast.

Access

⊖ Very good access front and rear.

Climate system

⊜ Manual or automatic, the climate-control system works very well. It automatically dehumidifies and filters the air, and ducts under the front seats route air to the rear.

Controls and displays

⊜ The dashboard of the new *Taurus* brings all switches within easy reach of the driver. But it takes all of 22 buttons to work the sound system. If you choose the optional automatic climate-control system, you get another 12 buttons for various forms of manual override. That's far too many, especially when compared with just the three easy-to-use rotary knobs and one button for the manual climate-control system.

Trunk

○ Folding the rear seatback adds luggage space to the roomy trunk. The open trunk lid hangs low, so watch your head.

Safety

The *Taurus* has dual air bags and front safety belts with an adjustable upper anchor. Even the center rear position has a lap-and-shoulder belt. The front-seat head restraints don't lock when they're raised, but they're high enough even when they're lowered. Our bumper basher made only a minor crease in the rear bumper, but the repair estimate was $502.

Recent government crash tests of the new *Taurus* showed fairly good results for both driver and passenger.

Predicted reliability

No data, new model. The *Ford Taurus* and its twin, the *Mercury Sable,* are too new to have compiled a reliability record. Previous models were about average in reliability.

Based on a January 1996 report.

Ford Thunderbird LX

Price: *$17,485*
Cost factor: *91%*
Depreciation: ◒

Overview

This traditional rear-wheel-drive design still holds its own in competition with more modern models.

Acceleration

⊖ The optional V8 is powerful, the standard V6 less responsive. The supercharged V6 has been dropped.

Transmission

⊖ The four-speed automatic shifts smoothly, but it's slow to downshift.

Economy

◒ Expect about 20 mpg overall with the V8.

Routine handling

⊖ The body doesn't lean much in sharp turns. The *Thunderbird's* steering feels overly light and provides too little feedback, but it's quick. The car plows stubbornly ahead in hard turns until you back off the accelerator pedal.

Emergency handling

○ The car behaved well in our avoidance-maneuver test.

Braking

⊖ Braking was quite good on dry pavement and about average on wet pavement. The car stopped straight in our test on wet pavement. Some vibration in the brake pedal is normal when antilock brakes are working, but the *Thunderbird's* pedal vibrates more than usual; that could frighten an inexperienced driver into letting up on the brakes in an emergency.

Ride, normal load

○ On the highway the ride feels unsettled, and on back roads the suspension reacts sharply to flaws in the pavement.

Ride, full load

○ A full load consisting of passengers and luggage actually calms the ride.

Noise

⊖ The interior is quiet except when the engine is revved.

Driving position

⊖ The seat and steering column adjustments provide a comfortable driving position for most people.

Front seating

⊖ The front seats feel soft and enveloping—almost confining.

Rear seating

○ Three average-size adults have room enough in the rear seat, but headroom is inadequate for anyone much taller than 5 feet 10 inches. Support for thighs and the lower back is in short supply.

Access

○ Access to the front and rear seats is easy enough if you have room to open the long, heavy doors fully.

Climate system

⊜ The climate-control system is semiautomatic; it operates the fan automatically after you set the temperature and air-distribution mode. With the system on Automatic and Defrost, the air conditioner comes on and the fan switches to its highest speed to keep the windows clear in humid weather. The heater warms the front seat area quickly, but the rear-seat passengers must wait patiently for the heat to trickle through the ducts.

Controls and displays

⊜ There's nothing fussy about the main controls and displays. But the radio that Ford has used for several years is a nuisance.

Trunk

○ The trunk holds five Pullman suitcases or a folded wheelchair and then some. There's room around the compact spare to stash a few small items, but a full-size tire won't fit in the well. Keep your head down while you're loading or unloading the trunk. When the trunk is open, the lid hangs low and its lip is sharp.

Safety

Front-seat occupants have to reach back for the safety belts. On some people, the belts rode too high, over the abdomen. The rear belts fit adults reasonably well, but they're awkward to use with a child safety seat; the buckles are spaced inconveniently, and the belts require a locking clip. The rear seat lacks head restraints. The car did well in our low-speed basher test: Some paint peeled off the front bumper when the plastic cover flexed, but the bumper wasn't dented.

Both driver and passenger dummies were very well protected in government crash tests.

Predicted reliability

◒ Expect below-average reliability.

Based on a July 1995 report.

Honda Accord EX V6 

Price range:* *$15,100–$25,100
Cost factor:* *88%
Depreciation: ○

Overview

The new V6 is smooth and fast, but the old Fours provide better value.

Acceleration

⊖ Although the smooth 2.7-liter V6 delivers ample acceleration, it doesn't respond to the accelerator as quickly as do comparable cars in this class, such as a *Toyota Camry, Ford Taurus,* or *Buick LeSabre.* The 2.2-liter VTEC Four is a little noisier than the V6, but it accelerates virtually as well, delivers better fuel economy, and drops the car's price by a few thousand dollars.

Transmission

⊖ The four-speed automatic transmission shifts smoothly, but it takes a moment to downshift when you want more acceleration. A five-speed manual is not available with the V6.

Economy

◒ Expect to average about 21 mpg.

Routine handling

⊖ The V6 version feels more front-heavy and less nimble than the sprightly four-cylinder *EX* we tested previously.

The body leans noticeably in corners. Although the steering doesn't respond quickly, it feels smooth and nicely weighted.

Emergency handling

⊖ Strong tire grip helps curb the *Accord's* tendency to run wide in tight, fast corners. The car negotiated our emergency avoidance maneuver quickly and ably.

Braking

⊖ The car stopped straight in our braking tests, but wet stops were a little longer than average.

Ride, normal load

⊖ What strikes you immediately is the *Accord's* solid, refined feel. The ride is particularly smooth on expressways, but even rough pavement doesn't faze it.

Ride, full load

⊖ A full load doesn't faze the ride either.

Noise

⊖ Cabin isolation from wind, road, and engine noise is very good.

Driving position

⊜ A tilt steering column and eight-way power seat should let most drivers get comfortable. Legroom and headroom are fine, but very tall drivers may wish for more room across the knees. The driver's seat has an adjustable lumbar bulge, which we found to be too high and too firm.

Front seating

⊖ The front seats give good support, and they hold occupants firmly in place during cornering.

Rear seating

○ The rear seat cushion is low. With three sitting there, the center passenger must perch precariously and uncomfortably on the raised portion of the seat. (The *Accord* is a little narrower than a *Camry* or *Taurus*, but this is hardly noticeable except when three passengers sit in the rear seat.)

Access

⊖ Very good front and rear.

Climate system

⊜ The manual climate-control system is effective and simple to use. Ducts under the front seats direct air to the rear.

Controls and displays

⊜ The controls are first-rate except for the small, hard-to-find horn buttons. The instrument cluster displays the transmission gears you select.

Trunk

○ The trunk is a bit smaller than some of the competition, but you can fold down the one-piece rear seatback to expand the luggage room. When the trunk lid is open, watch out for the latch.

Safety

Dual air bags and safety belts with an adjustable anchor provide front-seat crash protection. The adjustable front head restraints lock in position, so they shouldn't be knocked down in a crash. The rear head restraints are too low to protect most adults against whiplash. Our bumper basher inflicted damage that was hard to see but costly to repair. Estimates were $470 in front, $600 in rear.

In government crash tests, the driver dummy came out fairly well, but the passenger dummy suffered severe "injuries."

Predicted reliability

⊜ The *Accord* has been among the most trouble-free cars for many years. We expect the 1996 models to follow suit.

Based on a January 1996 report.

Hyundai Sonata GLS

***Price range:** $13,849–$17,849*
***Cost factor:** 89%*
***Depreciation:** NA*

Overview

Although the latest model is noticeably improved, it still needs more polishing to be competitive. And the previous model's dismally poor reliability calls for caution.

Acceleration

○ The 3.0-liter V6 sounds raucous during acceleration.

Transmission

⊖ The four-speed automatic shifts smoothly enough most of the time. But in the early 1995 versions, a severe jerk accompanies shifts from Reverse to Drive while the car is stopped. A manual transmission is available only with the four-cylinder engine.

Economy

◒ Expect about 21 mpg overall, on Regular fuel.

Routine handling

⊖ The *Sonata's* body leans noticeably in turns, and the tires squeal even during mild cornering. The steering feels overly light, and the car tends to run wide in hard turns.

Emergency handling

○ Felt sloppy but not unsafe in our avoidance maneuver.

Braking

⊖ The car needed 135 feet to stop on a dry track from 60 mph, and 158 feet to stop in the wet. It stopped reasonably straight in our wet divided-pavement test.

Ride, normal load

○ Bumpy roads elicit snaps, jolts, and stiff jiggles. Even on a smooth highway, the car finds and transmits tiny bumps that other cars in the same class don't seem to notice.

Ride, full load

○ A full load worsens the ride a bit.

Noise

⊖ The cabin remains fairly quiet inside.

Driving position

⊖ A height adjuster on the seat and a tilt steering column help most people find a comfortable driving position. Six-footers will find adequate head- and legroom, and five-footers can see out well.

Front seating

⊖ The cloth-covered front seats provide generally good, firm support, but the padding runs thin in spots, and the lumbar support feels lumpy. Both the front and rear seatbacks lack full support.

Rear seating

○ The rear seat is snug for three six-footers, and the middle passenger is uncomfortable. Two passengers, however, have adequate comfort.

Access

⊖ Front and rear access are good.

Climate system

⊜ The system is versatile and powerful, and the fan is fairly quiet. The air conditioner doesn't come on automatically in the Defrost mode, as it does in competing cars such as the *Nissan Maxima* and *Subaru Legacy*.

Controls and displays

⊖ The *Sonata's* tiny horn buttons, on the spokes of the steering wheel, are hard to find in a hurry. The radio sits inconveniently low, but the gauges are clear.

Trunk

⊖ The trunk accepts five Pullman cases or a folded wheelchair, with room left over. Maximum trailer-towing capacity is 2000 pounds.

Safety

The *Sonata* has adjustable upper anchors on the front shoulder belts. It also has switchable retractors front and rear, which allow a child safety seat to be secured without a special clip. Despite claims of 5-mph bumpers, our bumper basher put large dents in both bumpers. Repair estimates: $493 front, $439 rear.

Both the driver and passenger dummies would have suffered certain "injuries" in government crash tests.

Predicted reliability

Insufficient data. We cannot predict the reliability of the new *Sonata*. But previous *Hyundais* have had poor reliability records.

Based on a February 1995 report.

Infiniti I30 ✓

***Price range:** $28,420–$34,180*
***Cost factor:** 86%*
***Depreciation:** NA*

Overview

It's a "designer" version of the *Nissan Maxima*, with an extra $5000 worth of status. See page 125 for a full report on the *Maxima*.

Acceleration

⊖ The 3.0-liter V6 is the car's best feature. It revs with silky smoothness, accelerates briskly, and mates with the four-speed automatic transmission.

Transmission

⊜ Very smooth-shifting automatic. A five-speed manual is available—which is rare for a luxury/sports sedan.

Economy

○ Expect to average about 23 mpg, overall, on Premium fuel.

Routine handling

⊖ The *I30* doesn't stand out in handling. The body leans considerably during cornering, and the overly light steering gives the driver little feel of the road. The car goes where you aim it, but not as crisply as the *Audi A4*, for example.

Emergency handling

○ The *I30* was slow through our emergency avoidance maneuver, which consists of sharp lane changes left and right, but the handling remained predictable.

Braking

⊖ Stopping distances were about average in our braking tests on wet and dry pavement, although the pedal felt a bit spongy after repeated stops. The car stopped straight in our challenging test on wet divided pavement, where the road is much more slippery under one side of the car than under the other.

Ride, normal load

⊖ The *I30* absorbs most road bumps nicely, although damaged pavement can deliver firm kicks.

Ride, full load

○ A full load of passengers quells some of the large body motions but stiffens the ride a bit.

Noise

⊖ The cabin is commendably quiet, no matter what.

Driving position

⊖ Our testers gave the driving position mixed reviews. Some found it nearly ideal. Some wanted to sit higher. And others complained that the steering wheel was too long a reach in relation to the pedals. Even our five-foot tester could see easily over the hood, but the high rear deck made backing up difficult for her. The driver gets power seat adjustments; the passenger, manual adjustments.

Front seating

⊖ The front seats provide good, firm support everywhere except at the sides. To get heated seats, you have to buy an "enhanced traction" package, with a limited-slip differential. We passed it up.

Rear seating

⊖ The deeply shaped rear seat coddles two adults, but adding a center passenger forces the other two out of their comfortable position. Several testers wished for more lower-back support.

Access

⊖ Access front and rear is very good.

Climate system

⊜ The automatic climate-control system works just about flawlessly, but the rear defroster sometimes took 15 minutes or more to clear the rear window. The side mirrors aren't heated.

Controls and displays

⊜ The layout of the controls is virtually perfect.

Trunk

○ The rear seatback doesn't fold, but a small port behind the rear center armrest lets skis or other long, narrow items extend through the trunk into the passenger compartment. The remote trunk release, on the driver's-door armrest, can be triggered accidentally while the car is moving.

Safety

The front compartment has two air bags plus safety belts with adjustable upper anchors. The front and rear head restraints are amply high even when fully lowered, and they lock in any position. Our car emerged unscathed from our hydraulic bumper-basher's 3- and 5-mph blows.

The government hasn't crash-tested an *I30*. When the similar *Nissan Maxima* was crash-tested last year, the driver dummy probably escaped with only moderate "injuries," while the passenger dummy's "injuries" were certain and possibly severe.

Predicted reliability

⊜ The *I30* is too new to have a reliability record, but the *Maxima* has held up well. We predict the *I30* will be very reliable as well.

Based on a February 1996 report.

Infiniti J30 ✓

Price range: $39,920–$41,000
Cost factor: 84%
Depreciation: ●

Overview

Plush comfort for two, but rear seating and handling precision get short shrift.

Acceleration

⊖ Smooth and responsive acceleration from the V6 driving the rear wheels.

Transmission

⊜ Very smooth shifting.

Economy

◒ Expect about 20 mpg, on Premium fuel.

Routine handling

⊖ Pleasant handling on dry roads but noticeable lean in tight turns. The steering, while quite responsive, isn't as crisp as it could be. The tires break loose fairly easily on slippery surfaces; we'd like to see electronic traction control in a rear-wheel-drive car of this class.

Emergency handling

○ Respectable times in the avoidance-maneuver test, but tail wag was tricky to control. Hard cornering under power was steady.

Braking

⊜ Excellent stopping: 122 feet on dry track and 143 feet on wet track, from 60 mph. The antilock brakes work unobtrusively.

Ride, normal load

⊜ A gentle ride over all kinds of roads.

Ride, full load

⊖ With full load aboard, the ride generally remains good, although bumps and ruts send tremors through the body.

Noise

⊖ Engine is virtually inaudible except during hard acceleration, and tire noise is subdued.

Driving position

⊖ Eight-way power seat and tilt wheel can accommodate just about any physique, though legroom is skimpy for tall people. Raising the seat lets short drivers see out nicely.

Front seating

⊜ Leather seats are nicely padded and offer good lower-back support. With leather, seat heaters are especially helpful in cold climes; but they're not available, even at extra cost.

Rear seating

◒ Deeply sculpted rear bench holds two people in minimal comfort; room for heads and knees is marginal at best. With three sitting abreast, the middle passenger perches uncomfortably on a raised bolster.

Access

⊖ Good, but watch curved door frames. In rear, low roof and narrow opening make getting in and out a challenge.

Climate system

⊜ Works very well. Its only fault is a tendency to concentrate too much warmed air on the driver's right foot.

Controls and displays

⊜ All the major controls are laid out logically. Instruments carry clear labels. One quibble: The fancy analog clock, with its gold-on-white face, is hard to read.

Trunk

◒ Holds only three Pullman cases and a weekend bag, and sill is high.

Safety

Comfortable front lap-and-shoulder belts are supplemented with dual air bags. Height of shoulder-belt anchors is adjustable. Rear lap-and-shoulder belts are a bit difficult to buckle. A rearward-facing infant carrier should not be used in the right front seat of the *Infiniti*—or any car equipped with a passenger-side air bag. No damage front or rear from our bumper basher.

In government crash tests, the driver "dummy" was better protected than the passenger.

Predicted reliability

⊜ The *J30* has an excellent reliability record.

Based on a May 1993 report.

Infiniti Q45

Price range: *$52,400–$59,350*
Cost factor: *83%*

Overview

Sedans don't get much better than this, which is also true for the *Lexus LS400*.

Acceleration

⊖ Lively acceleration from the 4.5-liter, 32-valve V8.

Transmission

⊜ The four-speed automatic always shifts smoothly. The traction-control system cuts power at the slightest hint of wheel spin. It can be switched off if desired.

Economy

● Expect to average 17 mpg on Premium fuel.

Routine handling

⊖ Capable handling for a car of its size. The all-weather tires squeal early, though. (The base *Q45* comes with performance tires that are less apt to squeal.)

Emergency handling

○ Hard cornering at the test track made the *Infiniti* plow a little and then wag its tail slightly. Somewhat weak tire grip limited speed through our avoidance maneuver.

Braking

⊖ Brakes performed well on both wet and dry pavement.

Ride, normal load

⊜ Well damped whether with or without active suspension. Broken pavement and sharp bumps produce little jiggles and well-muted kicks.

Ride, full load

⊖ With a full load, the car hardly knows the difference.

Noise

⊜ Little noise intrudes from outside. The engine makes only a muffled moan, and wind noise is practically inaudible.

Driving position

⊜ Seat and steering-wheel adjustments can tailor the cockpit to suit nearly anyone. Even short drivers should be able to see well over the hood, and tall ones will find adequate room. The driver's seat has a two-position memory that recalls the position not only of the seat but the steering wheel, head restraint, and mirrors. The seat controls are awkward. When you remove the ignition key, the seat moves back and the wheel moves forward to help you get out; insert the key and the seat moves up.

Front seating

⊜ Both front seats offer firm support —maybe too firm for some—and have power adjustments. The leather is not perforated, but the seat heaters work well.

Rear seating

○ Two adults can get comfortable in the sculpted seat, but a third occupant must perch on a raised center section. Toe space is a bit tight.

Access

⊖ Easy getting in and out, front and rear.

Climate system

⊜ Automatic system, with separate vents for the rear seat, works superbly. But the air conditioner fan could be quieter.

Controls and displays

⊖ Major controls are easy to operate, but some minor switches are hard to use. The power window switches are scattered, some on the doors, some on the center console. You must press a tiny annoying button to remove the ignition key, and the *Infiniti 's* trademark gold-toned analog clock becomes unreadable in dim light.

Trunk

⊖ Fully carpeted trunk swallows five Pullman cases and a weekend bag, or a folded wheelchair, with room left over. A compact spare is provided. Maximum trailer-towing capacity is only 1000 pounds.

Safety

Safety belts with pre-tensioners and adjustable shoulder-belt anchors, plus dual air bags, protect front-seat occupants. The rear three-point belts require two hands to buckle. A child safety seat can be secured in any seating position without a locking clip.

The government has yet to crash-test a *Q45*.

Predicted reliability

⊜ A stellar repair record has kept it a top choice for luxury car buyers.

Based on a November 1993 report.

Jaguar XJ6

Price range: *$56,320–$66,270*
Cost factor: *84%*
Depreciation: ●

Jaguar freshened up this rear-wheel-drive model's styling for 1995, and the engine and suspension received some tweaks. The 4.0-liter inline Six delivers smooth and powerful acceleration. The *XJ6* carves neatly through twisting country roads and remains predictable while negotiating tight turns. The ride is soft and well mannered. The once-chaotic control layout has been markedly improved. The front seats are nicely shaped but the cockpit is cramped, and legroom is inadequate for tall drivers. The rear accommodates three adults in comfort.

Predicted reliability

Insufficient data.

Lexus ES300 ✓

Price: $32,400
Cost factor: 85%
Depreciation: ○

Overview

The *Lexus ES300* combines *Camry* performance and reliability with a pleasant, quiet ride and many comforts.

Acceleration

⊖ The 3.0-liter V6 provides smooth lively acceleration, just as it does in the bigger *Toyota Avalon*.

Transmission

⊜ The four-speed automatic shifts smoothly. The transmission offers a choice between power and economy shifting patterns.

Economy

◒ Expect to average about 22 mpg. Toyota says you can use Regular fuel or Premium for "improved performance."

Routine handling

⊖ The *ES300* behaves much like the *Camry* in routine driving—competent but not exciting. Steering response is fairly quick. Could use more feedback, especially at lower speeds.

Emergency handling

○ In hard turns, easing off the accelerator controls the car's tendency to plow straight ahead. The *ES300* ran through our avoidance course willingly, with just a hint of tail wag.

Braking

⊖ Stopping distances on wet pavement were just a bit long—167 feet. Stops on dry pavement and in our divided-pavement test—where the road under one side of the car is slicker than the road under the other side—were short and straight.

Ride, normal load

⊖ A pleasant, quiet ride helps passengers feel isolated from the world outside.

Ride, full load

⊖ The ride is a bit stiffer when the car is fully loaded, but it's not uncomfortable.

Noise

⊖ We noticed wind noise at highway speeds.

Driving position

⊖ Most drivers can find a comfortable position at the height-adjustable steering wheel. Both front bucket seats have power-operated adjustments. The seat cushion can be moved independently of the seatback, so you can position the height of the lower-back support. On the driver's seat, the prominence of the lower-back support is adjustable too.

Front seating

⊖ The optional leather upholstery is so slippery that passengers slide about, especially in hard turns. Take the cloth upholstery—if you can find a *Lexus* that has it.

Rear seating

○ Three adults fit in the rear seat—if one is less than 5-feet, 9-inches tall and willing to sit in the middle. The bench seat isn't shaped well, so all three passengers are likely to complain after only a short while.

Access

⊖ The hard-to-see unframed rear windows can be hazardous to your face and eyes when entering the car.

Climate system

⊜ The automatic climate-control system is similar to the one in the *Toyota Avalon* and *Mazda Millenia*, but we found that we needed to set the temperature rather high to create a comfortable level of warmth inside the car.

Controls and displays

⊖ The controls are generally well designed, but we constantly confused the knobs for temperature setting and radio volume. The lighted gauges sometimes faded out in bright sunlight.

Trunk

○ The trunk easily holds five Pullman suitcases and one weekend case, or a folded wheelchair. It will hold skis and other long, slender items, too, thanks to a small port behind the rear-seat armrest. You can lock the port for security. The well for the full-service spare tire has room for a few small items.

Safety

The front safety belts have adjustable upper anchors that make them fit well. All the safety belts can secure a child safety seat, but installing one in the center seat blocks access to the buckles for the outboard belts. The rear-seat headrests are barely tall enough to protect average-size occupants, and they aren't adjustable. Those in front adjust to a variety of heights.

The car came through our bumper-basher tests unscathed. The *Lexus ES300* is not on the government's crash-test schedule for this year.

Predicted reliability

⊜ The *ES300* has maintained a top-notch reliability record since its introduction.

Based on a May 1995 report.

Lexus GS300 ✓

***Price:** $45,700*
***Cost factor:** 85%*
Depreciation: ○

Overview

The *GS300*, although slightly smaller than the *Lexus LS400*, is just about as comfortable overall—and it delivers better fuel mileage. Reliability for the *GS300* has been exceptional.

Acceleration

⊖ Although the 3.0-liter Inline Six accelerates energetically, the *Lexus's* acceleration times are slower than some of its competition.

Transmission

⊜ The electronically controlled automatic transmission shifts extremely smoothly under all conditions. It offers a choice of Power or Normal modes, which change the shift points appropriately. The optional traction-control system does a fine job when driving at any speed.

Economy

◒ Expect about 21 mpg overall on Premium fuel.

Routine handling

⊖ The *Lexus* handles soundly but lacks knife-edge precision. The body rolls a bit during cornering, and the steering, while quick enough, feels overly light. The car wants to plow ahead a little in tight turns.

Emergency handling

○ In our emergency lane-change maneuver, the aforementioned plowing tendency suddenly turned to tail wag, requiring swift correction.

Braking

⊖ The *Lexus* stopped short and straight in all our braking tests.

Ride, normal load

⊖ The *GS300* fairly floats over rough pavement, and bumps cause only gentle jiggles. Uneven surfaces, however, elicit soft but pronounced rocking motions.

Ride, full load

⊖ Kicks become a bit firmer.

Noise

⊜ The *Lexus* is almost eerily quiet.

Driving position

⊜ Multiple power-seat and steering-column adjustments help almost any driver get comfortable. The windshield header limits tall drivers' view of overhead traffic lights. Short drivers can see over the hood well.

Front seating

⊜ The individual front seats give good, firm support all around, but the optional leather upholstery feels a bit slippery. Memory settings aren't available for the driver's seat; they should be. The optional seat heaters are effective, although a little slow to warm. Front legroom is more than adequate, but tall people will find that the sunroof infringes on headroom when the seat is raised. The left footrest is very comfortable.

Rear seating

⊖ The deeply sculpted rear seat accommodates two in exceptional comfort, but a middle passenger has to perch too high. The sunroof is also a problem for tall passengers in the center rear.

Access

⊜ Wide door openings and a steering wheel that moves up and forward make front entry easy. Wide rear doors help in back.

Climate system

⊜ The fully automatic climate-control system works nearly flawlessly.

Controls and displays

⊜ The controls are a model of logical design, and the displays are exceptionally clear—a lesson in world-class ergonomics. One quibble: The releases for the trunk, fuel-filler door, and hood are buried under the left side of the dash.

Trunk

○ The plushly carpeted trunk is somewhat small but certainly adequate for a family of four. We fit four Pullman cases and two weekend bags in the trunk with room left over. A folded wheelchair just fits. The rear seatback doesn't fold down. A full-service spare resides in a well in the trunk floor. Access to the trunk could be better; the opening is narrow front to back, and a high sill makes loading awkward. The recommended towing limit is 2000 pounds.

Safety

The *Lexus* comes with dual air bags and safety-belt pre-tensioners that instantly take up slack in the belt during a crash. The outboard three-point belts have switchable retractors so you can cinch up a child seat without using a separate locking clip. Our basher did minor cosmetic damage to both bumpers; some owners might not bother to fix it. But the repair estimates came to $736 front and $807 rear.

Both the driver and passenger dummies would have suffered certain "injuries" in government crash tests.

Predicted reliability

⊜ The *GS300* has proven very reliable.

Based on a May 1994 report.

Lexus LS400

***Price:** $52,900*
***Cost factor:** 84%*
Depreciation: ○

The flagship of Toyota's luxury-car division is one of the world's finest luxury sedans. Its 1995 redesign left the outside looking similar, but a longer wheelbase provides more interior room. The engine is also a little stronger, and the *LS400* shed 200 pounds, so the performance feels a little livelier. This model combines a sophisticated rear-wheel-drive power train with a lush, quiet, leather-wrapped interior. The *LS400* continues to emphasize quietness and road isolation.

Predicted reliability ⊖

Lexus SC400 ✓

Price range: *$43,400–$52,400*
Cost factor: *85%*
Depreciation: ⊖

Overview

The emphasis is on sporty performance, but with no sacrifice in luxury and comfort for the front-seat occupants. A slightly cheaper, six-cylinder version, the *SC300*, is also available.

Acceleration

⊜ The smooth and refined 4.0-liter V8 accelerates with authority. Zero-to-60 mph takes 7.8 seconds. Engine response starts slowly, then builds rapidly.

Transmission

⊜ Four-speed automatic shifts extremely smoothly. The traction-control system keeps the rear wheels from spinning at any throttle setting, but the standard-equipment "performance" tires don't grip well in snow.

Economy

◒ Expect a bit over 19 mpg in mixed driving, on Premium fuel.

Routine handling

⊜ The *Lexus* carves through winding country roads with the agility of a sports car. It feels very secure and precise, even at cornering limits, and the body hardly leans.

Emergency handling

⊜ Faster and smoother threading through avoidance maneuvers than any other luxury coupe.

Braking

⊜ The antilock brakes stop short and straight on both wet and dry pavement, with no instability in the difficult wet divided-pavement test, where one side of the track is slicker than the other.

Ride, normal load

⊖ A taut, well-controlled ride. The car cruises with aplomb on highways; its ride worsens on bumpy roads, where the suspension transmits muted kicks and quick, short pitching motions.

Ride, full load

○ With a full load, the ride is firmer with busier motions.

Noise

⊖ Very quiet on expressways except for tire thump on tar strips.

Driving position

⊖ Power seat and tilt/telescoping steering column allow most people to find a comfortable driving position. Very short drivers may not see well over the hood, and tall people may lack headroom under the optional glass sunroof.

Front seating

⊖ Good, firm support, but leather upholstery is slippery and the optional seat heaters warm slowly. Both front seats are power adjustable.

Rear seating

◒ Designed to seat only two people—if they're jockey-size.

Access

○ The doors don't open as wide as most, but their hinges move the leading edge away from the body. That allows extra foot clearance when the door can't open fully .

Climate system

⊜ Works superbly. Select temperature and it automatically controls fan speed, distribution of heat or cooling, and air source. The heated mirrors clear frost quickly; the rear-window defroster works slowly.

Controls and displays

⊖ An Auto setting automatically turns on the headlights when the light level drops, but there's no indicator to tell you that lights are on. The knobs for radio volume and inside temperature are easily confused. And the climate-control and radio displays lack contrast. The fluorescent instrument displays are clear, though.

Trunk

◒ Smallest of the luxury coupes, holding just three Pullman cases and a weekender. A folded wheelchair won't fit.

Safety

The front restraint system includes dual air bags and three-point safety belts with a convenient belt positioner. The rear seat has two three-point belts. You can mount a child safety seat front or rear without a locking clip, but the indentations in the rear seat may be too narrow for some child seats. Our 3- and 5-mph bumper-basher tests inflicted internal damage, which wasn't readily visible. Repair estimates ran to $611 in front and $149 in rear.

The government has yet to crash-test this model.

Predicted reliability

⊖ Reliability has slipped slightly.

Based on a July 1993 report.

Lincoln Mark VIII 

Price: *$39,650*
Cost factor: *88%*
Depreciation: ●

Overview

An excellent ride and impressive engine performance are the coupe's strong points.

Acceleration

⊜ The sophisticated 4.6-liter V8 provides exhilarating power; the car accelerates to 60 mph in 7.2 seconds.

Transmission

⊖ The electronically controlled four-speed automatic usually shifts smoothly, but at times it bumps into gear or delays its shifts. The traction assist is not as effective as the *Lexus's* more sophisticated traction-control system. It works only at low speeds, and a heavy right foot can easily overwhelm it.

Economy

● In mixed driving, we averaged nearly 19 mpg, on Premium fuel.

Routine handling

⊖ The steering feels too light around town, but the *Lincoln* is surprisingly agile for such a large and heavy car.

Emergency handling

○ Plows ahead a little in abrupt maneuvers, but quick response from the throttle and steering tames that tendency.

Braking

⊖ The car always stops straight and fairly short. The pedal pulses annoyingly against the driver's foot when the antilock system engages.

Ride, normal load

⊜ The suspension uses air cushions instead of springs. It provides a steady and serene ride, soaking up major road irregularities and transmitting only very gentle pitches and muted jiggles.

Ride, full load

⊖ With a full load, the ride is hardly affected. Mild shaking and flexing of the body on rough roads are all that stand in the way of ride perfection.

Noise

⊖ You can hear the wind but little road or tire noise, at highway speeds.

Driving position

⊖ Suits most drivers well, although six-footers may want more headroom under the optional glass sunroof and perhaps a bit more legroom to the pedals. Raising the seat lets short drivers see well over the hood, but then, to reach the pedals, they may have to sit too close to the steering wheel.

Front seating

⊖ Good, firm support, although the cushions tend to concentrate a bit too much pressure under the thighs. Both the driver's and front passenger's seats provide full power adjustment. The smooth leather upholstery is slippery. Seat heaters would be welcome in cold weather, but they're not available even as an option.

Rear seating

◒ The rear seat has safety belts for three, but even two passengers are a squeeze; room for head, knees, and toes is skimpy, and the center position is simply too tight for an adult.

Access

⊖ Fairly easy provided there's enough room for the large doors to swing open fully.

Climate system

⊖ The automatic system quietly furnishes plenty of warmed or cooled air front and rear. The fan holds off too long after the engine starts up, though, and then it cranks up with a whoosh. The rear defroster works slowly and clears only a narrow band.

Controls and displays

⊜ Most controls are easy to see and reach, although the radio's controls could stand improvement.

Trunk

○ The trunk is fairly shallow but can hold four Pullman cases and three weekend bags, or a folded wheelchair, with room left over.

Safety

Front restraints include dual air bags and three-point safety belts. Grasping the belt's tang requires a long reach back, and the shoulder portion rides uncomfortably across a short person's neck. In the rear seat, the lap portion of the three-point belts tends to ride too high. You need a locking clip to secure a child safety seat. Don't place a rear-facing infant seat in the right front seat of the *Lincoln* (or of any car equipped with a passenger-side air bag). Our bumper basher damaged the front bumper and headlight mountings to the tune of $108; the rear escaped damage.

The government has not crash-tested a *Mark VIII*.

Predicted reliability

○ Merely average.

Based on a July 1993 report.

Mazda Millenia S 

Price range: *$27,525–$35,595*
Cost factor: *87%*
Depreciation: *NA*

Overview

The spunky yet refined *Millenia* offers responsive acceleration and a comfortable ride.

Acceleration

⊖ The supercharged 2.3-liter V6, standard in the tested *S* version, initially feels subtle but then quickly becomes robust.

Transmission

⊖ The four-speed automatic doesn't shift as smoothly as the transmissions in competitive cars such as the *Toyota Avalon, Lexus ES300,* and *Oldsmobile Aurora*. A "hold" feature lets drivers select and hold gears like a manual transmission. Electronic traction control, standard on *S* models, works well.

Economy

◒ Expect to average about 22 mpg on Premium fuel.

Routine handling

⊖ The *Millenia* grips the road well, but the body leans noticeably when cornering, especially in tight turns. The smooth steering conveys a fair amount of road feel.

Emergency handling

⊖ On the test track, the *Millenia* ran through our avoidance maneuvers confidently and quickly.

Braking

⊖ Stops were consistently short and straight.

Ride, normal load

⊖ The suspension masks all kinds of ripples, ruts, and ridges in road surfaces.

Ride, full load

⊖ Even with a full load on board, the ride remains comfortable.

Noise

⊖ The car is quiet inside, but we noticed some tire noise on coarse pavement. The engine is silent when cruising, rich-sounding when revved.

Driving position

⊖ The driver's seat has power controls for seat height and tilt. Headroom under the sunroof and legroom are tight for tall drivers.

Front seating

⊜ The bucket seats provide good, firm support for most occupants, but tall drivers could use more thigh support. Both seats have power adjustments to move them forward and back and to adjust the seatback angle. Heaters, included in the 4-Seasons Package, warmed the leather upholstery on cold days.

Rear seating

O This car has a decidedly unluxurious rear seat. It does hold three six-foot-tall occupants—but just barely.

Access

⊖ The low seat, high and broad door sills, and snug foot clearance make it a bit hard for passengers to get in or out.

Climate system

⊜ The automatic climate-control system has many attributes, but maintaining a constant temperature isn't one of them. The system features a fuel-saving economy setting for the air-conditioning.

Controls and displays

⊜ Most controls are clearly labeled and easy to use. But at night, it's literally a stab in the dark figuring out which switch does what among the many window and lock controls on the driver's door. Lighted controls would be a major improvement. An On indicator for the fog lamps would be useful, too. The radio is a long reach for the driver, and its multifunction controls are hard to figure out when driving.

Trunk

O The *Millenia's* trunk holds five Pullman cases or a folded wheelchair with room left over. The narrow trunk opening—just 12 inches from front to back—makes loading or unloading cargo an annoyance. It can be more than annoying if your head hits the trunk lid or its unfriendly latch. A compact spare tire is standard, but a full-size tire will fit in the trunk well. Do not use the *Millenia* as a towing vehicle.

Safety

The front safety belts have adjustable shoulder-belt anchors. The front passenger belt and the three-point belts in the outboard rear seats require a locking clip to secure a child safety seat. Further, the car lacks a tether anchor that some child seats require.

In our bumper-basher test, however, the bumper covers had to be replaced and the reinforcements realigned. And because the bumpers blend into the car's body, some of the body as well as the bumpers need paint. The repair estimates came to $840 for the front, $802 for the rear.

The *Millenia* performed very well in recent government crash tests.

Predicted reliability

⊜ Excellent reliability.

Based on a May 1995 report.

Mercedes-Benz C280

Price range: *$29,900–$35,250*
Cost factor: *87%*
Depreciation: *NA*

Overview

The small *Mercedes* may be the entry-level model for this high-priced nameplate, but it's luxuriously appointed throughout. Reliability, however, has been disappointing.

Acceleration

⊖ The *C280* accelerated from 0 to 60 mph in just 8.2 seconds—within one second of the quick *Volvo 850 Turbo's* time.

Transmission

⊜ The four-speed automatic engages slowly from Park, but it shifts smoothly once the car is under way. It doesn't permit starts in second or third gear, so starting out on slippery pavement could be tricky without optional traction control.

Economy

◒ The 2.8-liter Six should average about 20 mpg; Premium fuel is recommended. The *C220's* 2.2 liter Four is more economical but less responsive.

Routine handling

⊜ Responsive and secure. Easing off the throttle controls the tendency of the front end to run wide in hard turns.

Emergency handling

⊖ We noted a mild tail wag in abrupt maneuvers, but that, too, was easy to control.

Braking

⊜ Braking is excellent on dry pavement, very good on wet pavement. The car stopped straight in our wet divided-pavement test.

Ride, normal load

⊖ Feels supple and well damped on inconsistent back roads.

Ride, full load

⊖ There is deterioration in ride with a full load.

Noise

⊖ The *C280* is the quietest of the cars we tested together in a group of four: the *Volvo 850 Turbo, BMW 325i,* and *Saab 900 SE*. Wind noise is especially well suppressed.

Driving position

⊖ Most people should be comfortable behind the wheel, but tall drivers may have to tip the seat back to gain enough legroom.

Front seating

⊖ Both front seats enjoy a full range of power adjusters. The vinyl upholstery feels hard—and cold in winter, hot in summer. Leather is an expensive option. Seat heaters are a worthwhile investment.

Rear seating

○ Roomy and reasonably comfortable for two, but three's a crowd.

Access

⊖ Easy front and rear.

Climate system

○ Automatic climate-control systems are supposed to be "smart." The one in the *Mercedes* isn't. The thermostat is off by about 10 degrees, so you have to drop the temperature setting manually to about 60 degrees to cool the car in hot weather. In cold weather, manual operation warms the car and clears the windshield faster than automatic operation. The car has an unusual winter-weather feature: a Rest setting that circulates residual engine heat to keep the interior warm for about a half hour after the engine is shut off.

Controls and displays

⊖ Most controls are straightforward, but reflections sometimes spoil the otherwise clear displays. *Mercedes* models have had an oil-pressure gauge for decades. Leaving it out of this new model lessens the value of the car.

Trunk

○ The trunk holds four Pullman cases and one weekend bag, or a folded wheelchair, with room left over. The trunk opening is short. Folding rear seatbacks, which allow expansion of the trunk area, is an option. Trailer towing is not recommended. A full-service spare is standard equipment.

Safety

Power-operated head restraints are a novel feature on the front seats. Retractable head restraints are an option for the rear seat. The owner's manual fails to mention the need for a locking clip to secure a child seat with the shoulder belts. The center rear lap belt doesn't require a clip. The *C-Class* models lack childproof rear door locks, a penny-wise and pound-foolish cost cut.

The *C280* fared poorly in our low-speed bumper-basher tests. The front bumper was pushed back, damaging the grille, surrounding sheet metal and body structure behind the bumper. The repair estimate for the front end was $818. Damage to the rear bumper totaled $494.

Crash protection results from the government produced good protection ratings for both the driver and passenger "dummies."

Predicted reliability

◒ The C-Class has been below average.

Based on an August 1994 report.

Mercedes-Benz E-Class ✓

Price range: $39,900–$49,900
Cost factor: 87%
Depreciation: ◒

The civilized E-Class is a lovely car to drive. It combines spirited acceleration with acceptable fuel economy, precise handling with a luxurious ride. This year's redesign added a touch more interior space, making the car feel significantly roomier. Refinements to the suspension and steering further improve the fine handling. Side-impact air bags are standard. A new family of engines and a station wagon are due next year.

Predicted reliability ⊖

Mercury Cougar

Price: $17,430
Cost factor: 91%
Depreciation: ○

See FORD THUNDERBIRD.

Mercury Sable

Price range: $18,995–$22,355
Cost factor: 91%
Depreciation: NA

See FORD TAURUS.

Mitsubishi Diamante

Price: $35,250
Cost factor: 80%
Depreciation: ◒

Although it's a capable car, the *Diamante* doesn't stand out against such high-line competitors as *BMW* and *Volvo*. Acceleration is strong only at illegal speeds. The four-speed automatic transmission usually shifts smoothly. The *Diamante* handles competently but not nimbly. The ride is well controlled and quiet. The front seats are comfortable; the rear seat is tight even for two. A redesign is due next year.

Predicted reliability ⊖

Nissan Maxima GXE 

Price range: $20,999–$26,279
Cost factor: 88%
Depreciation: ○

Overview

Although it's still a fine car, the latest redesign seems to have cut corners, compromising the seat comfort, ride, and handling.

Acceleration

⊖ The 3.0-liter V6 accelerates impressively, yet it delivers respectable fuel economy.

Transmission

⊜ Sometimes the four-speed automatic downshifts abruptly. A five-speed manual is available only in the *GXE* and *SE*.

Economy

○ Expect about 24 mpg, overall—but on Premium fuel.

Routine handling

⊖ The *Maxima* feels ponderous during cornering. Overly light steering gives little road feel, imparting a feeling of uncertainty. But the car grips the road well.

Emergency handling

○ The *Maxima* tended to run wide and plow straight ahead during hard cornering at our track, but it negotiated our avoidance maneuver competently.

Braking

⊖ The *Maxima* braked from 60 mph in 133 feet on a dry track, 158 feet on a wet track. It stopped straight in our wet divided-pavement test.

Ride, normal load

○ Bumpy roads cause firm jiggles, quiet rocking, and annoying flexing of the body. Some bumps make even the steering column shake. The ride improves on the highway, however.

Ride, full load

○ A full load makes the ride firmer and more jittery.

Noise

⊖ The cabin is fairly quiet except for a little road and wind noise.

Driving position

⊖ Despite the tilt steering column and the many adjustments offered by the power seat, our testers couldn't find a comfortable driving position. While tall people have enough leg- and headroom, the low seat cushion doesn't support the thighs sufficiently. That and an accelerator that's too lightly sprung make for a sore right leg after prolonged driving. Our five-foot driver would have liked to sit higher, although she could see out well enough.

Front seating

⊖ The cloth-covered front seats generally give good, firm support. The driver's seat has an adjustable lumbar bulge. Leather seats are available in both the *SE* and *GLE* models.

Rear seating

⊖ The low rear bench doesn't give long-legged passengers sufficient thigh and lower-back support. Three slim six-footers can fit.

Access

⊖ Front and rear access is good.

Climate system

⊜ The system is versatile, powerful, and quiet. The Bilevel mode is supposed to provide cooler air from the upper vents than from the floor vents, but both airstreams in the *Maxima* seem to be the same temperature.

Controls and displays

⊜ Controls and displays are logical and easy to use, a typical *Maxima* trademark.

Trunk

○ We could pack five Pullman cases or a folded wheelchair into the trunk with room left over. There's room in the well around the spare to hide small items. The rear seatback doesn't fold down. Instead, there's a small pass-through port for long objects like skis. Maximum trailer-towing capacity is 1000 pounds.

Safety

The *Maxima's* up-to-date safety roster includes adjustable upper anchors for the front safety belts. Also switchable retractors front and rear let you secure a child safety seat without a separate locking clip. Despite Nissan's claim of 5-mph bumpers on the *Maxima*, our bumper basher caused $683 in damage in front, $892 in the rear.

The driver fared better than the passenger "dummy" in government crash tests.

Predicted reliability

⊜ *Maximas* have been exceptionally reliable.

Based on a February 1995 report.

Oldsmobile Aurora

Price: $34,860
Cost factor: 93%
Depreciation: NA

Overview

The *Aurora* suffers from an uncomfortable ride, poor visibility, low fuel economy, and heavy-handed performance.

Acceleration

⊖ The 4.0-liter V8 feels responsive and smooth.

Transmission

⊜ The four-speed automatic shifts very smoothly. The traction-control system keeps the front wheels from spinning excessively under slippery conditions.

Economy

● The car's weight takes a toll on fuel economy. Expect about 17 mpg, overall, on Premium fuel.

Routine handling

⊖ The *Aurora* feels cumbersome on winding roads and requires too much steering correction in sharp corners. Parking is a chore because of the car's wide turning circle.

Emergency handling

○ Our driver's hands and arms had to move quickly to thread the car through our avoidance course. The heavy steering gives the driver little road feel.

Braking

⊖ Stops were short and straight in all our braking tests. The brake pedal pulsed strongly when the antilock brake system was working.

Ride, normal load

○ Harsh impacts and strong rocking motions were the norm on bumpy roads.

Ride, full load

○ With a full load, sharp kicks became abrupt snaps. At highway speeds, the car rose and dove over undulations in the road. Our car came with *Michelin MXV-4* tires, intended for optimum handling characteristics. The standard *Goodyear Eagle GA* tires are supposed to provide a gentler ride. We found that they made the ride less harsh.

Noise

⊜ The *Aurora* emitted some squeaks and rattles, despite its much-touted rigid body. Wind noise at highway speeds was disturbing.

Driving position

○ The firm but somewhat lumpy front bucket seats have the usual assortment of power adjustments, plus separate adjustments for middle- and lower-back support. But despite prolonged fiddling with the seat and steering column controls, most drivers were dissatisfied.

Front seating

⊖ Everyone found the cockpit claustrophobic.

Rear seating

○ The rear seat accommodates three six-footers, but only those sitting by the doors will be comfortable.

Access

○ Getting in and out is not what it should be in a car of this size.

Climate system

⊜ The automatic climate system, with separate controls for the driver and front passenger, is nearly ideal.

Controls and displays

⊖ The many controls take some getting used to, but they do work well. All are illuminated at night. The steering wheel hides several switches, including the trunk release. Worse, the trunk release is carelessly designed: If you don't flip a switch to lock it out, it's active even when the car is moving. Glare from the upper instrument panel obscured the windshield when we were driving into the sun.

Trunk

○ The trunk easily holds five Pullman cases or a folded wheelchair. Skis fit, but the part that accommodates them doesn't lock. The trunk's narrow opening and high, broad sill make access difficult.

Safety

The front safety belts are fairly awkward to use and uncomfortable to wear, especially if you're tall. The *Aurora* needs adjustable shoulder-belt anchors, like those in most other cars today. The front belts have a "comfort zone" feature that can allow several inches of slack to be added, compromising safety. The rear lap-and-shoulder belts can hold a child safety seat without a locking clip. The buckle on the center lap belt is too long to thread through some child seats. The bumpers held up well against our basher.

Government crash-test results show that driver and passenger dummies would suffer certain "injury," possibly severe.

Predicted reliability

◒ Worse than average.

Based on a May 1995 report.

Oldsmobile Ciera

Price range: $13,995–$16,955
Cost factor: 94%
Depreciation: ●

See BUICK CENTURY.

Oldsmobile Cutlass Supreme

Price range: *$17,455–$20,160*
Cost factor: *94%*
Depreciation: ◒

Overview

Moderate price, a new dash and dual air bags aren't enough to redeem this aging and uninteresting model. The *Cutlass Supreme* will be replaced next year by the *Oldsmobile Intrigue.*

Acceleration

⊖ The 3.1-liter V6 performs well and provides adequate fuel economy. The 3.4-liter V6 isn't worth the extra money.

Transmission

⊜ Very smooth automatic shifting.

Economy

◒ About 20 mpg, overall, on Regular fuel.

Routine handling

○ Tight turns require more cranking of the steering wheel than they should; the body leans considerably, and the suspension tops and bottoms disconcertingly in bumpy curves.

Emergency handling

○ In hard turns at the track, the car felt sloppy and plowed stubbornly. It threaded through our avoidance course steadily, although not very crisply.

Braking

⊖ Stopping distances from 60 mph measured a respectable 133 feet on dry pavement, 151 feet on wet pavement. The *Oldsmobile* stopped reasonably straight in our tough wet divided-pavement test.

Ride, normal load

○ Feels sloppy and poorly controlled on smooth roads, and stiff and unyielding on bumpy roads—the worst of both worlds.

Ride, full load

○ A full load overtaxes the rear suspension, making it kick on broken pavement and compress fully on sharp bumps.

Noise

⊖ Creaks and rattles detract from an otherwise quiet ride.

Driving position

⊖ We recommend the optional power adjuster for the driver's seat. That and a height adjuster for the steering column provide a comfortable driving position for people of most sizes.

Front seating

○ The front seats are like those in the *Pontiac Grand Prix,* which is to say that several drivers complained of a backache after less than an hour's ride. Weak side support and fairly slippery leather upholstery forces front occupants to struggle to stay in position when the car changes direction.

Rear seating

○ The rear seat is nowhere as comfortable as it looks. It's low and flat—and practically devoid of back and side support. The hard wing bolsters on the seatback twist outboard passengers inward, and the folded center armrest serves as a far-from-perfect seatback.

Access

⊖ Large door openings ease access.

Climate system

⊖ Delivers ample warmed or cooled air. But rather than provide proper ventilation at face level, the low dash vents create drafts.

Controls and displays

○ Most controls are awkward to use. The headlight switch isn't close at hand, and it's hard to get the fingers around it. The hood release is on the floor, where you'd expect to find the trunk release. The power-window switches on the driver's door are poorly angled. The headlights lack a "flash-to-pass" feature. The steeply slanted displays are hard to read; some are tiny, and some are hidden by the steering wheel.

Trunk

⊖ Like the trunks of the *Buick Regal Gran Sport* and *Pontiac Grand Prix,* the *Olds* trunk is capable of holding five Pullman suitcases and a weekend case, or a folded wheelchair, with room to spare. Anyone who gets inside the car also has access to the trunk, since the folding rear seatback and remote trunk release (under the dash) can't be locked. The sedan can tow up to 1000 pounds.

Safety

The *Oldsmobile* has dual air bags. Securing a child safety seat in the right front seat requires a special lap belt; the dealer will install it free on request. The rear head restraints are too low to be effective. The car's bumpers came through our basher assault without even a scratch.

The government has not crash-tested a *Cutlass Supreme* with dual air bags.

Predicted reliability

◒ The *Oldsmobile* has a below-average reliability record.

Based on a February 1994 report.

Pontiac Grand Prix

Price range: *$17,089–$20,851*
Cost factor: *92%*
Depreciation: ○

Overview

This aging model benefits from several improvements, including a second air bag, modernized safety belts, and an improved instrument panel.

Acceleration

⊖ The optional 3.4-liter V6 in our *GT*

version and the 3.1-liter V6 in the base version don't feel all that different in everyday driving, but the larger engine accelerates faster when pressed.

Transmission

⊜ The four-speed automatic shifts smoothly. A switch that allows starts in second gear aids traction on slippery surfaces.

Economy

● Expect about 18 mpg with the 3.4-liter V6, and 20 mpg with the 3.1.

Routine handling

⊖ The *Grand Prix,* with the "GT" options, handles better than the *Buick Regal Gran Sport* and *Oldsmobile Cutlass Supreme SL,* thanks to its quick and nicely weighted steering and minimal body roll.

Emergency handling

⊖ Quick steering gives the car an edge in avoidance maneuvers, but hard cornering can make the front end plow briefly.

Braking

⊖ The *Pontiac* stopped from 60 mph in 140 feet on a dry track, 155 feet on a wet one. Stops were straight in the tough wet divided-pavement test.

Ride, normal load

○ The car rides firmly even on the highway, and broken or patched pavement tends to unsettle the suspension.

Ride, full load

○ The jolts become harder when the car is carrying a full load, but not to the point of being unsettling.

Noise

⊖ The passenger compartment is reasonably hushed, but occupants remain aware of the engine's drone and the tires' hum.

Driving position

⊖ The optional power driver's seat and the height adjuster on the steering wheel allow drivers of almost any size to get comfortable. Without the power adjuster, the driving position is too low.

Front seating

○ The front seats look more comfortable than they feel. Back support is poorly placed. The side bolsters fail to hold occupants in place during cornering, and the slippery optional leather upholstery doesn't help.

Rear seating

○ Room for head and knees just suffices for six-footers. Even three average-size adults won't feel pinched, although the middle passenger won't like the folded armrest that serves as a seatback. Back and thigh support could be better.

Access

⊖ Large door openings ease access, despite fairly high and broad sills.

Climate system

⊜ The climate-control system works quickly and powerfully.

Controls and displays

⊜ Contemporary new instrument panel features logically arranged gauges and controls that are nicely lighted at night. About the only thing we missed is a "flash-to-pass" feature, a safety function that's sadly absent in the other GM models as well. The power door locks activate when the transmission shifts into gear and unlock when the ignition is turned off. That's inconvenient if someone wants to get out when the engine is running. The hood release is on the floor, where you'd expect the trunk release to be. The trunk release is in the glove compartment, which has a lock.

Trunk

○ Five Pullman cases and a weekend bag—or a folded wheelchair—can fit into the *Pontiac's* trunk with room to spare. A port behind the optional center armrest lets you carry skis inside the car. When the trunk lid is open, beware: Its sharp corners can gouge your head. Trailer-towing capacity is 1000 pounds.

Safety

The *Pontiac* has dual air bags and conventional front safety belts rather than the old, awkward door-mounted ones. However, there's still room for improvement; the height of the shoulder-belt anchors isn't adjustable. The rear three-point belts can secure a child safety seat without special clips. (A rear-facing infant seat shouldn't be used in front because of the air bag.) The bumpers suffered substantial damage from our basher. Repair estimates totaled $722 in front, $430 in the rear.

The driver "dummy" fared better than the passenger in government crash tests.

Predicted reliability

◒ The *Grand Prix* has a below-average reliability record.

Based on a February 1994 report.

Saab 9000 CSE 

***Price range:** $31,195–$41,195*
***Cost factor:** 87%*
Depreciation: ◒

Overview

The *Saab* offers the biggest, most versatile cargo area in its class, but you pay for that convenience by having to endure the *Saab's* stiff ride.

Acceleration

⊜ The 2.3-liter Four with optional intercooled turbocharger delivers powerful performance. The nonturbo version is a good deal less powerful. Some turbocharged engines provide a delayed response when you step down on the accelerator, but we noted no appreciable turbo lag in the *Saab.*

Transmission

⊜ The tested four-speed automatic transmission usually shifts smoothly. A five-speed manual is available on several *9000* models. The *Saab* spins its front wheels all too easily; a traction-control system comes only on the sportier *Aero* version.

Economy

◒ Expect about 21 mpg overall on Regular fuel.

Routine handling

⊜ The *Saab* handles very capably, with little body roll. Accelerating through hard turns makes it want to plow a little, but easing off the accelerator easily corrects that tendency.

Emergency handling

⊖ The *Saab* proved stable and predictable in our avoidance maneuver.

Braking

⊖ Stops were short and generally straight on both wet and dry pavement. The *Saab* veered to the right momentarily, then straightened out in our difficult wet divided-pavement test, where the surface is slicker under the left wheels than under the right.

Ride, normal load

○ The *Saab* makes sure its occupants feel every flaw in the road. Ride motions are well controlled, but the suspension announces ruts and ridges with stiff jiggles and sharp jolts.

Ride, full load

○ The ride remains just as stiff with a full load in the car.

Noise

⊖ The cabin is generally quiet, but some road and wind noise intrudes.

Driving position

⊖ The widely adjustable power seat should help most drivers get comfortable. The steering wheel neither tilts nor telescopes. Tall people will find sufficient legroom but insufficient headroom under the sunroof. Short drivers can see out well. The carpeted wheel housing makes a so-so left footrest.

Front seating

⊜ The front seats provide good, firm support. The driver's seat can "memorize" three separate seat positions. The heavily grained leather isn't slippery. Quick-acting seat heaters are standard—and welcome, especially in northern climes.

Rear seating

⊖ The rear seat would be roomy enough for three tall people if headroom were more generous. The cushion is too flat, and the center passenger must lean back against a lumpy armrest.

Access

⊜ Wide door openings help access to front and back.

Climate system

⊜ The *Saab's* fully automatic climate-control system performs extremely well in both Auto and Manual modes. Fans in the rear doors keep even those windows clear.

Controls and displays

○ The displays are generally fine. The controls could be better; it seemed that whatever we looked for was hidden by something else. It was especially easy to poke the sunroof switch when groping between the seats for the window buttons.

Trunk

⊖ The trunk can accommodate five Pullman cases and one weekend bag, or a folded wheelchair, with room left over. But with the split rear seatbacks folded, the hatchback body can swallow cargo up to 5½ feet long and 3 feet wide—very close to station wagon–size proportions. Maximum trailer-towing capacity is 2000 pounds.

Safety

The *Saab* has dual air bags and front belt pre-tensioners that instantly take up slack in a crash. Also, it claims to meet the government's 1997 side-impact safety standard. Properly securing a child seat with the three-point belts requires a separate locking clip. Despite the *Saab's* reputation for sturdiness, our bumper basher damaged the plastic cover on both bumpers. The creases aren't too noticeable—but if you're a perfectionist, you'd pay about $422 to fix the front, $530 to fix the rear.

The government has not recently crash-tested a *Saab 9000*.

Predicted reliability

⊖ The *Saab 9000* has an above-average reliability record.

Based on a May 1994 report.

Toyota Avalon XLS ✓

Price range: *$23,418–$27,448*
Cost factor: *86%*
Depreciation: *NA*

Overview

The *Avalon* is essentially a well-appointed, and larger, *Toyota Camry* with an extremely roomy back seat.

Acceleration

⊖ The 3.0-liter V6 is energetic.

Transmission

⊜ The smooth-shifting four-speed automatic offers a choice of power and normal shifting characteristics. You can turn off overdrive for trailer-towing, or switch it on for highway cruising.

Economy

○ Expect to average about 22 mpg. Toyota says Regular fuel is acceptable but recommends Premium for "improved performance."

Routine handling

⊖ This sizable car corners more eagerly than you might expect.

Emergency handling

○ When pushed into hard turns, the car tends to plow straight ahead. Easing off the accelerator corrects the problem. The steering responds quickly, but it's too light to provide much feel of the road.

Braking

⊖ Stops were comfortably short and straight in all our braking tests.

Ride, normal load

⊖ The ride is usually comfortable. The car soaks up most pavement flaws.

Ride, full load

⊖ A full load of passengers and luggage doesn't affect the ride.

Noise

⊖ The *Avalon* is very quiet inside, even though wind noise intrudes at highway speeds.

Driving position

⊜ The driving position is excellent.

Front seating

⊜ We chose bucket seats for the front (instead of the optional bench that can seat three). The seats are large and luxurious, with a multitude of power-operated adjustments to provide for occupants of all sizes and shapes. The seat cushion and the seatback can be adjusted independently, so you can position lower-back support where you need it most. The soft leather upholstery looks inviting and feels comfortable, except for an initial chill on a cold day.

Keep trips short if you choose the bench seat and ride three in front; the center passenger won't tolerate the folded armrest as a backrest for very long.

Rear seating

⊜ Even three tall passengers have room to cross their legs—or stretch—in the roomy rear seat.

Access

⊜ Getting in and out is easy at all four doors.

Climate system

⊜ The automatic climate-control system works well. It can be operated manually, too.

Controls and displays

⊜ Like most *Toyotas*, the *Avalon's* controls are pleasingly simple and easy to use. When the sun goes down, the headlights switch on automatically, but there's no indicator to show that they're on. That might lead you to think the lights are on at twilight when they aren't.

Trunk

⊖ The large trunk swallows five Pullman cases and two weekend bags (or a folded wheelchair) with room left over. But beware of the lid hinges: When the lid is closed, they can crush articles left under them. A shallow bin behind the left rear wheel housing keeps small items from bouncing about. There's also some storage room around the full-service spare tire.

Safety

The front shoulder belts have adjustable-height anchors, and are comfortable for short and tall wearers. The rear seat has three lap-and-shoulder belts; that's unusual, even in cars of this ilk. You can secure a child safety seat with any of the belts simply by pulling the belt out fully and releasing it so it locks. Toyota advises against placing a safety seat in the middle of the bench front seat. The head restraints are adequately tall.

In our bumper tests, bashes to the front bumper pushed the grille up, into the hood. The damage, hardly noticeable, would cost $544 to fix.

Both the driver and passenger dummies fared very well in government crash tests.

Predicted reliability

⊖ Expect very good reliability.

Based on a May 1995 report.

Toyota Camry LE V6 ✓

***Price range:** $16,468–$25,038*
***Cost factor:** 87%*
Depreciation: ○

Overview

It's silky-smooth and competent—and still the standard-bearer among moderately priced sedans.

Acceleration

⊖ The 3.0-liter V6 accelerates enthusiastically, but it still delivers good mileage. The base 2.2-liter Four accelerates well, too.

Transmission

⊜ The well-mated V6 engine and four-speed automatic transmission perform exceptionally smoothly. The electronic four-speed automatic offers Power and Normal modes. A five-speed manual transmission is available only with the Four.

Economy

○ Expect to average about 23 mpg with the V6, about 24 mpg overall with the Four.

Routine handling

⊖ In normal driving, the *Camry* turns into bends quite eagerly; the steering responds quickly and smoothly, and the body leans only moderately.

Emergency handling

○ In our emergency avoidance maneuver, handling was sound although unexceptional. The body leaned considerably, and the rear fishtailed a little.

Braking

⊖ The *Camry* stopped reasonably short and straight in all our braking tests, and the brake pedal felt smooth and reassuring.

Ride, normal load

⊖ The expressway ride is firm and well controlled, and rough rural roads elicit only muted jiggles and kicks.

Ride, full load

⊖ A full load makes the ride even firmer, but not to the point of discomfort.

Noise

⊖ Little noise or vibration enters the cabin.

Driving position

⊖ Manual height and tilt adjustments on the seat and a tilt steering column make it easy to find a comfortable driving position. A power driver's seat and leather upholstery are optional—and pricey. Six-footers have adequate legroom and ample headroom. Five-footers can easily see over the hood.

Front seating

⊜ The front seats are comfortable, with good, firm support.

Rear seating

⊖ The rear seat is firm and supportive, too, and it holds three tall people easily.

Access

⊖ Getting in and out is easy front and rear.

Climate system

⊜ The manual climate-control system works simply and effectively, and ducts under under the front seats route air to the rear.

Controls and displays

⊜ Everything is sensibly laid out, just where you expect to find it. The instrument cluster conveniently displays the selected transmission gear, and pressing the large center hub of the steering wheel sounds the horn—a design that's preferable to small horn buttons on the steering wheel spokes.

Trunk

⊖ The trunk is roomy, and folding the split rear seatback gains even more cargo space.

Safety

The *Camry* has dual air bags and front safety belts with an adjustable upper anchor. The front head restraints are amply high even when fully lowered, and they can be tilted forward. A positive lock prevents them from being knocked down in a crash. A series of 3- and 5- mph blows with our hydraulic bumper basher left the front and rear of the *Camry* unscathed.

In government crash tests, both the driver and passenger dummies fared very well.

Predicted reliability

⊜ The *Camry* continues to compile an excellent reliability record.

Based on a January 1996 report.

Toyota Camry wagon ✓

Price range:* *$21,608–$23,918
Cost factor:* *87%
Depreciation: ○

Overview

The *Camry* sedan has always been an excellent choice, and so is the wagon version. Reliability is superior, but the wagon's handling can be a bit tricky.

Acceleration

○ The 3.0-liter V6 in the tested *LE* version delivers satisfactory acceleration.

Transmission

⊜ The four-speed automatic shifts smoothly. The cruise control loses its memory below 25 mph or so.

Economy

◒ Expect about 21 mpg on the recommended Premium fuel. (The 2.2-liter Four runs on Regular.)

Routine handling

⊖ Most family-size station wagons aren't particularly nimble, but the *Camry* handles well in normal driving. We'd welcome more feedback from the steering. The body rolls only moderately during cornering.

Emergency handling

○ In extreme situations the tail end can become twitchy, sliding out fairly abruptly. Inflating the tires to the full-load pressures that are recommended by Toyota didn't steady the handling much.

Braking

⊜ Braking is excellent. From 60 mph, the wagon stopped in 126 feet on a dry track, 137 on wet. Stops were straight in our difficult wet divided-pavement test, where the pavement is slicker under one side of the wagon than under the other.

Ride, normal load

⊖ The *Camry* rides firmly but comfortably on all but the roughest roads.

Ride, full load

○ Smoothed out on expressways but harsher on bumpy roads.

Noise

⊖ The optional roof rack produces some wind noise. Otherwise, the ride is quiet, especially for a wagon.

Driving position

⊖ Seat adjustments and tilt steering column help most people get comfortable behind the wheel. Short drivers can see well enough over the hood, but some might prefer to sit a bit higher.

Front seating

⊖ Good, firm support. Manual adjustments are useful but hard to reach.

Rear seating

⊖ The roomy rear seat welcomes three passengers—even tall ones—but the center rider may find the seat a bit too firm on a long trip. The optional third seat is an unhappy place to be—even for kids.

Access

⊖ Front doors need stronger checks to hold them open.

Climate system

⊜ Versatile and generally effective, but it struggles to keep passengers warm when temperatures dip below about 10 degrees. You have to shut the outboard dash vents for maximum heating or defrosting, which is a nuisance.

Controls and displays

⊜ Always well designed in *Toyota* models. The wiper control seems complex at first glance, but it's clearly labeled and easy to use. Horn is sounded by pressing either the steering wheel hub (where the air bag is built in) or extensions that stretch from the hub into the steering wheel spokes, an ideal arrangement.

Cargo area

⊖ Almost as roomy as that of the boxy *Volvo 940*, and its payload capacity comes close to that wagon's also. The split second seat and optional third seat fold easily to form a long, flat cargo floor. Tie-down loops keep cargo from shifting about, and small items can fit out of sight in a plastic tub that holds the jack. The compact spare is stored out of the way, behind the right rear wheel housing. You can't get a cargo cover unless you buy the inhospitable third seat. The wagon can tow up to 2000 pounds, according to the owner's manual.

Safety

You can adjust the height of the shoulder anchors on the front safety belts. The rear belts are comfortable to wear but awkward to buckle. The front and rear head restraints are high enough to protect against whiplash. The owner's manual warns against placing a child safety seat in the optional third seat. Our car's bumpers survived our low-speed bumper-basher tests without a scratch.

In government crash tests, both the driver and passenger dummies fared very well.

Predicted reliability

Camrys have been very reliable, according to our subscribers.

Based on a September 1994 report.

Volvo 850 Turbo

Price range: *$26,125–$33,950*
Cost factor: *92%*
Depreciation:

Overview

A turbocharger makes this fine sedan even better. The interior is roomy and comfortable.

Acceleration

Very quick acceleration—0 to 60 mph in just 7.2 seconds. (Our nonturbo 1993 *850 GLT* needed 9.5 seconds to reach 60.)

Transmission

Winter, Economy, and Sport settings on the four-speed automatic vary the shift points. The Winter setting allows starts in second or third gear, improving traction on slippery roads so well that we see little need for the none-too-effective traction-control system. A five-speed manual is available only in nonturbo models.

Economy

Expect about 22 mpg on Premium fuel.

Routine handling

The steering isn't quick but is nicely weighted and imparts confidence in the car's handling. The body leans moderately during moderate cornering, more in hard turns.

Emergency handling

Excellent tire grip helped the car thread through our avoidance maneuver. Easing up on the accelerator reduces the car's tendency to run wide.

Braking

On a dry track, the *Volvo* stopped from 60 mph in 125 feet, almost as short as the 118-foot record posted by our 1993 *850 GLT*. Stops lengthened only slightly, to 139 feet, on a wet track. Stops were straight in our tough wet divided-pavement test, where the track is slicker under one side of the car than the other.

Ride, normal load

The car jiggles constantly on poor, winter-worn roads.

Ride, full load

The jiggling is worst with a full load.

Noise

The ride remains very quiet except for slight wind noise at expressway speeds and occasional tire hiss. The engine snarls when revved, a trait most fans of sports cars appreciate.

Driving position

The driver's seat offers an unusually wide range of fore-and-aft adjustments to accommodate people of nearly all sizes. Also, the steering wheel can be telescoped in and out as well as raised or lowered.

Front seating

The large, comfortably firm front seats provide especially good side support. Lower-back support is good too, but the knob that adjusts it is hard to turn. The leather upholstery is soft and not slippery, but it feels sticky on hot days. The optional seat heaters are welcome on cold days.

Rear seating

The roomy and high rear seat is nearly ideal, even in the center position, where the folded armrest serves as a seatback.

Access

Access to front and rear seats is straightforward.

Climate system

The electronic system, with separate settings for the driver and front passenger, generally works well.

Controls and displays

Most controls and displays are easy to see, read, and use. But the control for the windshield wipers is needlessly complicated and poorly labeled. The two controls for the outside power mirrors aren't labeled at all, but they work well once you find them.

Trunk

The huge trunk easily holds five Pullman cases and one weekend bag, or a folded wheelchair. One or both of the rear seatbacks can fold to expand the trunk. The tire well in the trunk is big enough for a full-size tire, but only a compact spare is available from Volvo. Towing capacity is 3300 pounds if the trailer has brakes, 1540 pounds if it doesn't.

Safety

The front seats have high head restraints, and the anchors for the shoulder belts have an adjustment for height. The rear seat has three-point safety belts and head restraints for all three passengers. The owner's manual fails to note that the safety belts require a locking clip to secure a child seat.

Our bumper basher's 3- and 5-mph blows left no mark on the front bumper, two insignificant dents on the rear bumper. Volvo claims compliance with the 1997 dynamic side-impact standard.

In government crash tests, the driver "dummy" fared much better than the passenger.

Predicted reliability

⊜ The *Volvo 850* has a much-better-than-average reliability record.

Based on an August 1994 report.

Volvo 960 ✓

Price range: *$33,960–$35,260*
Cost factor: *92%*
Depreciation: ◒

The rear-wheel-drive *960* is the lone remaining 900-Series *Volvo*. It comes with a 2.9-liter in-line Six that performs enthusiastically. Volvo has tweaked the suspension to improve both handling and ride. The front seats are pleasantly firm and nicely shaped. The rear seat is about as hospitable as they get, even for three adults. The climate-control system heats and cools superbly. The sedan has a cavernous trunk; the wagon, an exceptionally roomy cargo area. Side-impact air bags are standard this year.

Predicted reliability ○

LARGE CARS

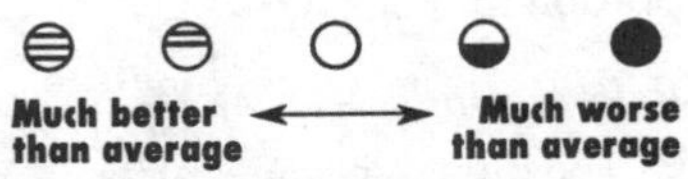

Large cars have been an endangered species since the fuel crisis of the 1970s, but the domestics that are included in this market segment retain a small, loyal following.

Large cars make good highway cruisers; they offer a soft, quiet ride and armchair-like seating accommodations for five. (Equipped with a front bench seat, they can handle six.) Although they get more miles out of a gallon of gas than they used to, they still cost a lot to fuel. The rear-wheel-drive, full-frame designs such as the *Ford Crown Victoria/Mercury Grand Marquis* twins excel in towing heavy trailers, whereas front-wheel-drive models such as the *Pontiac Bonneville* and *Oldsmobile Eighty Eight* and *Ninety Eight* make more efficient use of interior space.

Surprisingly nimble for large cars are the "LH" cars from Chrysler—the *Chrysler Concorde, Dodge Intrepid,* and *Eagle Vision.* Two V6 engines are offered, and both average about 21 mpg. Sporty handling is possible with the firmest suspension.

Recommended cars in this class include the *Chrysler Concorde, Ford Crown Victoria/Mercury Grand Marquis,* and *Pontiac Bonneville.*

BMW 740iL

Price : $62,490
Cost factor: 82%
Depreciation: ◒

This V8-powered model, redesigned last year, competes with the world's finest and costliest luxury sports sedans. The engine has grown to 4.4 liters—which makes a fast car even faster. This model handles superbly and has all the fancy interior appointments you'd expect in a car of this price. Displays are quite clear, and nearly all controls are sensibly laid out and easy to reach.

Predicted reliability

New model, no data.

Buick LeSabre

Price range: *$21,955–$25,505*
Cost factor: *91%*
Depreciation: ◒

Overview

It's the Rip Van Winkle of cars. If you loved the 1976 *LeSabre,* you'll love this one too.

Acceleration

⊖ The 3.8-liter V6 delivers lively performance.

Transmission

⊜ The four-speed automatic transmission shifts exceptionally smoothly.

Economy

◒ Expect to average a respectable 20 mpg.

Routine handling

◒ The car wants to plow straight ahead in turns. The tires don't grip well; they squeal easily during hard cornering.

Emergency handling

◒ We had to twirl the wheel a lot to horse the car through our avoidance maneuver.

Braking

◒ The *LeSabre* nosedived sharply in our braking tests. It stopped fairly straight, but it needed more than average room on both dry and wet pavement. The pedal felt spongy and hard to modulate.

Ride, normal load

⊖ The ride feels pillow-soft when you're cruising along seamless expressways in a straight line. But the *LeSabre* doesn't like to change direction; the steering feels vague and slow, and the car leans sharply and wallows through turns. Undulating secondary roads upset the car's composure. At anything above about 30 mph, the ride feels queasy and bouncy, and rutted roads transmit sharp blows to the occupants.

Ride, full load

○ A full load makes the seesaw motions worse.

Noise

⊜ The cabin is isolated from virtually all noise from outside.

Driving position

○ The tilt steering column and optional six-way power seat should help most people find a good driving position. Tall drivers have adequate legroom—and enough headroom to clear a ten-gallon hat. Short drivers should have no problem seeing out.

Front seating

○ The split bench front seat is like a

budget living room sofa: It feels soft, but it lacks support. Expect it to give you a backache. Theoretically, three can sit up front, but save the center portion for packages.

Rear seating

⊖ The plush, roomy rear seat can keep three tall adults comfortable.

Access

⊖ Access to front and rear is very easy.

Climate system

⊜ The climate-control system works well, despite a noisy fan.

Controls and displays

○ The gauges are small and the controls are dated. Glittery chromed switches clutter the door armrest. Oddly, the awkward headlight switch and separate parking-light switch are also on the door. Small warning lights stretch across the top of the dash in a groove, where they're easy to overlook. The climate-control push buttons are far from the driver and easy to confuse.

Trunk

⊖ The rear seatback doesn't fold, but the trunk is large.

Safety

The *LeSabre* has dual air bags. The front lap-and-shoulder belts have an adjustable upper anchor, but the belts are awkward to reach and buckle. The front head restraints are too low for adults, and they don't lock when raised, so they could be forced down in a crash. Our bumper basher damaged both bumpers to the tune of $316 in front, $180 in back.

Although the government hasn't crash-tested the *LeSabre,* it did crash the similar *Pontiac Bonneville* a few years ago. The driver dummy fared well, but the passenger dummy suffered what were possibly severe "injuries."

Predicted reliability

⊖ The *LeSabre's* reliability record is better than average.

Based on a January 1996 report.

Buick Park Avenue

***Price range:** $28,205–$32,820*
***Cost factor:** 89%*
Depreciation: ●

Buick's top-of-the-line sedan competes with big domestic luxury cruisers such as the *Oldsmobile Ninety Eight* and *Chrysler LHS,* with emphasis on soft ride and every imaginable power convenience. The standard, 3.8-liter V6 is quite capable of powering this large car; the Ultra version comes with a snappier supercharged V6. Next year, a new car based on the *Buick Riviera/ Oldsmobile Aurora* platform will replace the *Park Avenue.*

Predicted reliability ○

Buick Roadmaster

***Price range:** $25,560–$27,575*
***Cost factor:** 91%*
Depreciation: ◒

Overview

Smooth and quiet ride, but otherwise a rear-wheel-drive throwback to Detroit's age of dinosaurs. This is its last year.

Acceleration

○ The 5.7-liter V8 came up short.

Transmission

⊜ Very smooth shifting.

Economy

● Expect about 17 mpg overall.

Routine handling

◒ It leaned heavily as we threaded through the accident-avoidance course at necessarily slow speeds and with much sawing of the steering wheel.

Braking

◒ Antilock brakes didn't stop the car very short on a dry track, and nosediving was severe. Stops on wet pavement were relatively short.

Ride, normal load

⊜ A soft ride very isolated from the road.

Ride, full load

⊖ A full load hardly changed the ride, except that the rear suspension occasionally bottomed gently.

Noise

⊜ Very quiet.

Driving position

⊖ Optional six-way power seat and standard tilt steering column tailor position for most drivers.

Front seating

⊜ Deeply contoured, the split 55-45 bench was quite comfortable for the driver and one passenger but not hospitable for a middle rider.

Rear seating

⊖ Roomy but inflicted a closed-in feeling.

Access

◒ Weak doorstops failed to hold heavy front doors open when parked on slight upgrades. In the rear, not as easy as one would expect from a car this size.

Climate system

⊖ Worked quickly except for the windshield defroster. There are no Mix settings and no ducts to send warm air to the rear seat.

Controls and displays

⊖ Column-mounted selector for automatic transmission not interlocked with brake pedal, increasing risk of unintended acceleration. No remote control for right outside mirror, plus other annoyances. Instruments need more contrast for ease of reading.

Trunk

⊖ Roomy but high sill, protruding rear bumper, and poorly placed cargo net hamper access.

Safety

Driver-side air bag supplements lap-and-shoulder belts. Wide rear roof pillars create a nasty blind spot. Rear bumper was unscathed by our basher, but damage to the front required a $688 repair.

The government has not crash-tested a *Roadmaster.*

Predicted reliability

◒ The *Roadmaster* is a clone of the *Chevrolet Caprice,* which also has a worse-than-average repair record.

Based on a January 1992 report.

Cadillac De Ville

***Price range:** $35,995–$40,495*
***Cost factor:** 91%*
Depreciation: ●

Cadillac's best-selling model is built on a stretched version of the *Cadillac Seville* platform. It's a big, roomy, plush four-door sedan. As of this year, all versions get Cadillac's sophisticated "Northstar" aluminum 4.6-liter V8 and electronically controlled transmission and suspension. In our preliminary tests, the *De Ville* delivered a comfortable ride and handled well for such a large car.

Predicted reliability ○

Cadillac Fleetwood

***Price :** $36,995*
***Cost factor:** 91%*
Depreciation: ●

Built on the same chassis as the *Buick Roadmaster* and *Chevrolet Caprice,* the rear-wheel-drive *Fleetwood* maintains the traditional characteristics of large domestic sedans: a soft ride, a quiet and plush interior, and enough V8 muscle to haul a heavy trailer with ease. All three cars will be discontinued after the 1996 model year. You'll find plenty of interior room front and rear, plus a large trunk. You'll also find the unwieldy handling and poor fuel economy inherent in this breed.

Predicted reliability ●

Chevrolet Caprice

***Price range:** $19,905–$24,405*
***Cost factor:** 92%*
Depreciation: ◒

Overview

If a pillow-soft highway ride is all you crave in a car, consider this big, old-fashioned rear-wheel-drive highway cruiser, slated to die at the end of this model year.

Acceleration

⊖ The optional 5.7-liter V8 is very powerful but drinks gobs of fuel.

Transmission

⊜ The optional limited-slip rear axle reduces wheel spin a little on slippery roads, but it can't compete with a true traction-control system. The electronic four-speed automatic shifts very smoothly.

Economy

● Languishes at 17 mpg overall on Regular fuel.

Routine handling

⊖ The tires squeal in hard bends, but the *Chevrolet* negotiates winding roads surprisingly well with the optional Sport Suspension. The steering is rather slow and short on feel.

Emergency handling

○ At the track, the car leaned and plowed considerably in tight turns, and stepping on the throttle in mid-turn brought the tail out.

Braking

⊖ The *Caprice* brakes competently.

Ride, normal load

⊜ The car sails along the highway, absorbing pavement flaws with only tiny, muted kicks, soft pitching, and mild side-to-side jostling. The firm suspension in our car all but eliminates the queasy ride motions common to older large *Chevrolets.*

Ride, full load

⊜ Even when it's fully loaded with passengers and luggage, the car cruises majestically, its suspension easily smothering tar strips and transverse ridges.

Noise

⊜ Road noise is completely absent, and the engine is usually hushed. But when the engine is cold, the cooling fan roars like that of a school bus.

Driving position

⊖ The six-way power seat should allow most people to find a satisfactory driving position. Tall people will find plenty of room. Some drivers would have liked to sit higher, but even short people can see well over the hood. There's no left footrest.

Front seating

⊖ The split-bench front seat feels like a living room sofa, but neither the cushions nor the seatbacks provide much support. In the center position, the passenger can't avoid sitting on the safety belts.

Rear seating

⊖ Three six-footers can just fit in the rear. The high seat cushion is well padded and supportive. Toe space is tight in the center.

Access

⊖ Rather small door openings and broad sills hinder access somewhat.

Climate system

⊜ Heat from the system arrives slowly on cold mornings, but the airflow is plentiful and quiet, and the defrosters work very well.

Controls and displays

⊖ Chevrolet has vastly improved the instrumentation and controls. The horn is in the center hub of the steering wheel, where it belongs; the radio is more user-friendly; and a belted driver can reach all the controls. On the downside, the headlights lack a flash-to-pass feature; the indicator for the rear defroster is virtually invisible in the daytime; and the seat controls are crowded in with the power-window switches along the driver's armrest.

Trunk

⊖ It's large but oddly shaped, and the poorly placed optional full-service spare takes up too much usable room. Nevertheless, five Pullman cases and two weekend bags, or a folded wheelchair, can fit with ease. With the Sport Suspension, maximum trailer-towing capacity is a robust 5000 pounds.

Safety

The car has dual air bags, but it lacks adjustable shoulder-belt anchors. Securing a child safety seat requires a separate locking clip. Our bumper basher dented the front bumper and made small tears in the rear. Repair estimates: $238 front, $243 rear.

In government crash tests, the driver "dummy" fared much better than the passenger.

Predicted reliability

◒ Reliability of the *Caprice* is below average.

Based on a March 1994 report.

Chrysler Concorde

Price range: $19,445–23,375
Cost factor: 92%
Depreciation: ○

The *Chrysler Concorde* and similar *Dodge Intrepid* (see page 143) and *Eagle Vision* are roomy, well-designed triplets. However, only the *Concorde* has been reasonably reliable. The *Concorde* can comfortably hold five. The 3.3-liter V6 accelerates well. The optional 3.5-liter V6 delivers a little more punch, but with Premium fuel. Handling is nimble, but the tires are noisier than we like, and the larger V6 can sound harsh during acceleration. The headlights are weak. Most controls are well designed. Although the rear seatback doesn't fold, the trunk is sizable.

Predicted reliability ○

Chrysler LHS

Price: $30,225
Cost factor: 92%
Depreciation: NA

Overview

This is a slightly stretched, more luxuriously equipped and more expensive version of Chryser's LH triplets—the *Chrysler Concorde, Dodge Intrepid,* and *Eagle Vision.* The *LHS's* longer body provides an even roomier rear seat and trunk.

Acceleration

⊖ The 3.5-liter V6 delivers spirited performance and good fuel economy. A low-speed traction-control system keeps the wheels well planted on slippery roads at up to 25 mph.

Transmission

⊖ The electronic four-speed automatic shifts smoothly most of the time, but not quite as smoothly as the automatics in other cars of this class, such as the *Chevrolet Caprice, Ford Crown Victoria,* and *Pontiac Bonneville.* Selecting the "3" shift position raises the shift points for sportier performance.

Economy

◒ Expect about 20 mpg on required Midgrade fuel.

Routine handling

⊖ Smooth steering gives the driver plenty of road feel, and body roll is restrained, making this big *Chrysler* feel as agile as a much smaller car. Backing off the throttle easily corrects a slight tendency to plow ahead through corners.

Emergency handling

⊖ The car confidently whipped through our emergency lane-change maneuver.

Braking

⊖ Stopped short and straight in all our braking tests.

Ride, normal load

⊖ Negotiates broken country lanes with gentle, well-damped pitches and muted jiggles, and it sails along highways with slow and subdued ride motions.

Ride, full load

⊖ A full load damps the ride even more.

Noise

⊖ The interior is reasonably quiet at steady speeds, but some road rumble and harsh engine noise still penetrate the passenger compartment.

Driving position

⊜ The eight-way power seat helps drivers of nearly any size find a comfortable seating position in the roomy cockpit. But the tilt wheel should allow finer adjustment, and the left footrest is too vertical.

Front seating

⊖ Generously padded, leather-covered seats provide good support, but the manually adjustable lumbar bulge is too high and lumpy. Unfortunately, seat heaters are not available.

Rear seating

⊜ Limousinelike backseat is superb. It allows a relaxed posture, with good support for the lower back and thighs. Three tall adults can sit abreast in comfort.

Access

⊜ Front access is easy, rear access exceptionally easy.

Climate system

⊜ Automatic climate-control system works very well.

Controls and displays

⊖ Controls are well designed, logically laid out, and nicely lit at night, and the instruments are easy to read. The small horn buttons on the spokes of the steering wheel are hard to find in a hurry, though, and adjusting the climate controls or flipping the defroster switches requires a long reach.

Trunk

⊜ The roomy trunk easily holds six Pullman cases and one weekend bag, or a folded wheelchair, with room left over. Maximum trailer-towing capacity is 2000 pounds.

Safety

With its standard dual air bags, antilock brakes, and adjustable front shoulder-belt anchors, the *Chrysler* is very well equipped for safety. Also, according to the manufacturer, the car meets the 1997 government standard for side-impact protection. You can secure a child safety seat in any seating position without a locking clip. The bumpers emerged unscathed from our 3- and 5-mph hydraulic bumper-basher tests.

The passenger "dummy" fared slightly better than the driver in government crash tests.

Predicted reliability

◒ The *LHS* has an average reliability record.

Based on a March 1994 report.

Dodge Intrepid

***Price range:** $18,445–$22,260*
***Cost factor:** 92%*
Depreciation: ○

Overview

The *Dodge Intrepid* and similar *Chrysler Concorde* and *Eagle Vision* are roomy, well-designed sedans. However, only the *Concorde* has been reasonably reliable.

Acceleration

○ The base 3.3-liter V6 doesn't pin you to the seat, but it provides adequate acceleration. A larger 3.5-liter V6 (with 53 extra hp) is optional.

Transmission

⊜ The four-speed automatic shifts smoothly. The "3" position raises the shift points for better acceleration, and it locks out fourth gear—a useful feature in hilly areas or when towing a trailer.

Economy

◒ Expect about 20 mpg overall on Regular fuel. The 3.5-liter V6 delivers a little more oomph with no sacrifice in fuel mileage, but it requires Midgrade (89 octane) fuel.

Routine handling

⊖ The *Intrepid* is agile—much more so than other sedans of its size. The body remains flat in turns, and the steering feels neither too heavy nor too light.

Emergency handling

⊖ In hard turns, letting up on the accelerator quickly corrects a slight tendency of the car to plow straight ahead.

Braking

⊖ Stops from 60 mph were straight and adequately short on both wet and dry roads. The car did veer a bit in our challenging wet divided-pavement test, where the track is slicker under one side of the car than under the other.

Ride, normal load

⊖ The *Intrepid* soaks up bumps and ruts with aplomb, even on the worst roads.

Ride, full load

⊖ A full load doesn't hurt the ride much.

Noise

⊖ The interior is relatively quiet—a notable improvement over previous LH models—although coarse pavement still causes some rumble. The 3.3-liter V6 whines noticeably when revved, but it's quieter than the 3.5-liter *Intrepid* that we reported on in 1994.

Driving position

⊖ The optional power driver's seat and standard tilt steering column help drivers of virtually any size get comfortable behind the wheel. Short drivers can see well enough over the hood—but they can't see where the hood ends.

Front seating

⊖ The large, cloth-upholstered front seats offer good, firm support. A split bench is a no-cost option.

Rear seating

⊜ The *Intrepid's* rear seat is quite large, with room enough for three six-footers to spread out and cross their legs. An optional child seat built into the rear armrest forms an adequate seatback for the middle passenger.

Access

⊜ Getting in and out is very easy front and rear.

Climate system

⊜ The climate-control system is very versatile. The air-conditioning works in any mode, and it comes on automatically in Defrost and Mix modes to quickly defog the windows. The fan is strong but noisy.

Controls and displays

⊖ Most of the controls are lighted and logically laid out, but the tiny horn buttons on the steering-wheel spokes are hard to find in a hurry.

Trunk

⊖ The roomy trunk easily holds five Pullman cases and one weekend bag, or a folded wheelchair. Like similar sedans—the *Buick Century, Chevrolet Lumina,* and *Ford Taurus,* for example—the *Intrepid* lacks a folding rear seatback to expand the trunk. Maximum trailer-towing capacity is 2000 pounds.

Safety

The *Intrepid's* front safety belts have adjustable upper anchors, and all the belts can secure a child safety seat without a separate locking clip. The lap portion of the belts can be cinched for best protection. Our series of 3- and 5-mph bumper-basher tests caused no damage front or rear.

Both driver and passenger "dummies" fared well in government crash tests.

Predicted reliability

◒ According to our readers' experience, the *Intrepid's* reliability is worse than average.

Based on a January 1995 report.

Eagle Vision

Price range:* *$19,245–$23,835
Cost factor:* *92%
Depreciation: ◒

The *Eagle Vision* and similar *Chrysler Concorde* and *Dodge Intrepid* are roomy, well-designed triplets. However, only the *Concorde* has been reasonably reliable. The *Vision* can comfortably hold five. The 3.3-liter V6 accelerates well. The optional 3.5-liter V6 delivers a little more punch, but with Premium fuel. Handling is nimble. Antilock brakes are a worthwhile option. Most controls are well designed A new "Autostick" lets you shift the automatic transmission like a manual, but without a clutch. Although the rear seatback doesn't fold, the trunk is sizable.

Predicted reliability ◒

Ford Crown Victoria LX ✓

Price range:* *$20,955–$22,675
Cost factor:* *93%
Depreciation: ◒

Overview

The *Crown Victoria,* and similar *Mercury Marquis,* are solid performers. Selecting the right options further enhances their overall behavior.

Acceleration

⊖ The smooth 4.6-liter V8 performs responsively and cruises effortlessly.

Transmission

⊜ The electronic four-speed automatic shifts smoothly under all driving conditions. An optional traction-control system limits rear wheel spin at speeds below about 35 mph.

Economy

● Expect to average about 19 mpg overall on Regular fuel.

Routine handling

⊖ The Handling and Performance package reduces body roll and aids traction. With that option, the *Ford* plows ahead only moderately and grips the pavement well in hard turns, but the steering still feels far too light.

Emergency handling

○ The car negotiated our emergency avoidance maneuver predictably, if a bit clumsily.

Braking

⊖ The *Ford* stopped well—especially on dry pavement.

Ride, normal load

⊖ The car rides smoothly on the highway, and the suspension damps out rough pavement fairly well.

Ride, full load

⊖ A full load improves the ride a bit.

Noise

⊖ The cabin is quiet except for a trace of wind noise and tire hiss.

Driving position

⊖ The optional six-way power seat helps most drivers find a satisfactory position behind the controls. Legroom to the accelerator is just adequate for six-footers, and there is no comfortable place for drivers to rest their left foot.

Front seating

○ The split-bench front seat is uncomfortable, with hard, skimpy padding in the seatback and insufficient side support. There's a center lap belt, but the passenger unlucky enough to ride in the middle must straddle the split in the cushion and large transmission hump.

Rear seating

⊖ The rear bench seat is roomy enough for three six-footers to sit abreast in reasonable comfort, although toe space under the front seats is limited and there's not enough back support.

Access

⊖ Rear access is clumsy.

Climate system

⊖ The manual system provides plenty of heated or cooled air, but it lacks a Bilevel setting and ducts to the rear seats.

Controls and displays

⊖ Aside from small, hard-to-find horn switches and a radio with inconvenient, identical, flat push buttons, the *Ford's* controls are fairly easy to use. We wish the climate-control slides were illuminated. Some *Crown Victorias* have digital gauges, but we prefer the analog type. If you opt for the Performance package as well as the Preferred Equipment Group, you can pass up the digital gauges and save $520.

Trunk

⊜ The trunk easily swallows seven Pullman cases and two weekend bags, or a folded wheelchair, with plenty of room left over. Maximum towing capacity, according to the manufacturer, is 5000 pounds if you opt for either the Class III Towing package or the Handling and Performance package.

Safety

Standard equipment includes dual air bags and comfortable three-point front safety belts with adjustable upper anchors. Ford states that the *Crown Victoria* meets the government's 1997 side-impact standard. You'll need a separate locking clip to secure a child seat in any but the center seating positions. Our bumper basher left the front bumper unharmed, but it scratched and chipped some paint on the rear bumper. Repairs were estimated at $468.

Excellent results for both driver and passenger in government crash tests.

Predicted reliability

○ Expect an average reliability record for the *Crown Victoria* and similar *Mercury Grand Marquis*.

Based on a March 1994 report.

Lincoln Continental

Price: *$41,800*
Cost factor: *88%*
Depreciation: ●

The *Continental* was redesigned last year. The new model's biggest performance upgrade came with the addition of the *Lincoln Mark VIII's* powerful aluminum V8, which should finally make this car more competitive with other luxury models. The suspension uses air cushions instead of springs. The driver can select several settings for the firmness of the suspension and the effort required to turn the steering wheel. Like other *Lincolns*, this one comes fully loaded. The spacious interior accommodates five with ease, and the cabin should be very quiet. The trunk is huge.

Predicted reliability ○

Lincoln Town Car

Price range: *$36,910–$41,960*
Cost factor: *88%*
Depreciation: ●

Despite its sophisticated V8 and full complement of safety features, the *Town Car* maintains the tradition of domestic luxury turnpike cruisers. It sits on a full frame and is powered by rear-wheel drive. Expect a soft, quiet ride and seating for six. To tame the *Town Car's* tendency to wallow on bad roads, choose the "Ride Control" package.

Predicted reliability ⊖.

Mercury Grand Marquis ✓

Price range: *$21,975–$23,385*
Cost factor: *93%*
Depreciation: ◒

The *Grand Marquis* and its sibling, the *Ford Crown Victoria,* are among the last big, old-fashioned American cars, with a V8, full frame, and rear-wheel drive. The ride is serene, and a huge trunk is a further bonus. The 4.6-liter V8 cruises effortlessly. Steering response is quite good. Choose the Handling and Performance Package, with its upgraded suspension and tires, for better handling. The front bench seat is designed to hold three, but an adult won't be happy in the middle. Legroom is adequate for tall drivers. The rear seat is roomy enough for three.

Predicted reliability ○

Oldsmobile Eighty Eight

Price range: *$20,405–$26,010*
Cost factor: *94%*
Depreciation: ●

Overview

Opt for the touring suspension unless you want a softly sprung cruiser.

Acceleration

○ Responsive 3.8-liter V6.

Transmission

⊜ Very smooth shifting.

Economy

● Expect about 19 mpg overall.

Routine handling

○ Competent but not dynamic.

Emergency handling

○ Unresponsive and sloppy.

Braking

◒ Antilock brakes worked well, but nosedive was excessive. Stops on wet pavement were somewhat long.

Ride, normal load

⊖ The Oldsmible floated smoothly over most roads.

Ride, full load

○ Full load caused frequent bottoming.

Noise

⊖ Whisper quiet.

Driving position

⊖ Easy to set with six-way power seat and tilt steering column.

Front seating

⊖ Split bench with folding center armrest is best for two.

Rear seating

⊖ Would be very good with better low-back support.

Access

⊜ No problem in front, and very easy in rear.

Climate system

⊜ Automatic system's fan speed starts out too high and requires manual adjustment.

Controls and displays

○ Overdone and inefficient, including too many radio buttons and tough-to-find horn buttons. The instruments are easy to read, but the odometer needs better lighting.

Trunk

⊜ Five Pullman cases and two weekend bags leave room to spare; limited-service compact is the only spare tire you can get.

Safety

Dual air bags supplement three-point belts in front; shoulder-belt anchor can be raise or lowered for comfort. Bumpers were unscathed when struck by our bumper basher.

The government has not crash-tested an *Eighty Eight*.

Predicted reliability

○ Expect at least average reliability for the *Eighty Eight*.

Based on a January 1992 report.

Oldsmobile Ninety Eight

Price range: $28,160–$29,260
Cost factor: 94%
Depreciation: ◓

This near-twin to the *Buick Park Avenue* is Oldsmobile's biggest turnpike cruiser. It looks and feels like a traditional old-style luxury sedan, although it has a modern body design and front-wheel drive. Cars like this emphasize a soft ride and scores of power conveniences and luxury appointments. Although reliability has been good, handling tends to be sloppy and fuel economy is less than stellar. This is the last year for this model.

Predicted reliability ○

Pontiac Bonneville

Price range: $21,589–$25,804
Cost factor: 90%
Depreciation: ○

Overview

Properly equipped, the *Bonneville* has been one of GM's best all-around large sedans. We tested the sporty *SSEi* version with the powerful supercharged V6.

Acceleration

⊜ The optional supercharged 3.8-liter V6 provides lively acceleration. However, feeding such power to the front wheels makes the steering wheel twist in the driver's hands during hard acceleration.

Transmission

⊜ The electronic four-speed automatic shifts very smoothly. It offers a choice of Normal or Performance modes, the latter shifting at higher engine speeds. The car's gearing often makes the engine labor audibly at highway speeds and uphill.

Economy

● About 18 mpg on Regular fuel is nothing to brag about.

Routine handling

⊖ The car responds quite nicely to its steering, and body roll remains nicely in check during cornering. The front end initially plows ahead during hard cornering, but it quickly comes back on course.

Emergency handling

⊖ Fast steering response helped us tame the *SSEi's* tendency to wag its tail in our emergency lane-change maneuver.

Braking

⊖ The car stopped straight and short in all our wet and dry braking tests.

Ride, normal load

○ Stiff jiggles, firm jolts, and lots of squeaks and rattles mar the ride, and the suspension sometimes fully compresses on crested bumps. Even a smooth highway elicits some rocking and pitching. Switching the computer-controlled suspension from Touring to Performance improves control but makes the ride harsher.

Ride, full load

○ A full load has the same effect.

Noise

⊖ Slight wind and tire noise is not intrusive.

Driving position

⊖ The power seat allows adjustment of the driving position to suit anyone, tall or short. Although the nine power-seat buttons on the center console require prolonged study and fiddling, eventually one can find a near-perfect adjustment. Unfortunately, the system lacks a memory feature to retain those adjustments for multiple drivers.

Front seating

⊜ The nicely shaped front seats provide superb comfort. Seat heaters aren't available.

Rear seating

⊖ The rear seat accommodates three adults adequately, but the low, flat cushion is too short fore and aft and too thinly padded. Toe space is limited in the center, and the folded armrest makes a poor backrest.

Access

⊖ Easy getting in and out, front and rear.

Climate system

⊜ Works well, providing ample, quiet airflow from all vents, front and rear. Only the front defroster mode can be controlled manually.

Controls and displays

⊖ The instrument panel and controls are generally easy to see and use, but the cup holder slides out directly over the seat-adjustment buttons on the center console, making them vulnerable to spills. The headlight dimmer lacks a flash-to-pass feature. The optional heads-up display projects the car's speed digitally onto the windshield. Ours didn't agree with the reading on the speedometer.

Trunk

⊖ Holds five Pullman cases and two weekend bags, or a folded wheelchair, with room left over. The rear seatbacks don't fold down, but a port behind the armrest allows long objects like skis and poles to pass through from the trunk. The *Bonneville's* trunk includes a well-equipped road-emergency kit and a convenient built-in air compressor for pumping up tires and other inflatables. Maximum trailer-towing capacity is 1000 pounds.

Safety

The car has dual air bags and convenient three-point front safety belts with adjustable upper anchors. Switchable retractors in the three-point belts allow you to secure a child seat easily without a special locking clip. Our bumper basher left the front end unharmed but ripped the plastic cover on the rear bumper to the tune of $770.

The driver fared much better than the passenger "dummy" in government crash tests.

Predicted reliability

○ An average reliability record.

Based on a March 1994 report.

MINIVANS

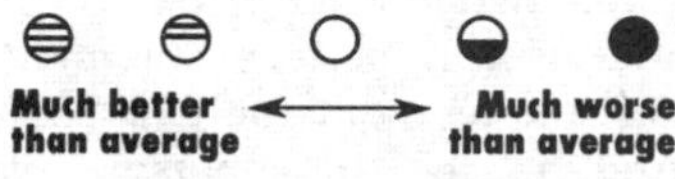

Minivans owe their popularity to their spaciousness and ease of driving. On the road, the best of the minivans feels more like a competent sedan than a truck. Their versatility also contributes to their appeal. With seating options, some can hold as many as eight adults. And by folding or removing the center and rear seats, you can increase cargo room to trucklike proportions. Don't expect sporty handling; most of these vans are clumsy in sharp turns, but many are getting better.

Our list of recommended minivans are as follows: the *Honda Odyssey/Isuzu Oasis, Mercury Villager/Nissan Quest,* and *Toyota Previa.*

Chevrolet Astro

Price range: *$19,176–$25,162*
Cost factor: *90%*
Depreciation: ○

See GMC SAFARI.

Chevrolet Lumina

Price: *$19,840*
Cost factor: *90%*
Depreciation: ○

See PONTIAC TRANS SPORT.

Chrysler Town & Country

Price range: *$24,585–$30,185*
Cost factor: *91%*
Depreciation: ○

See DODGE GRAND CARAVAN.

Dodge Caravan

Price range: *$16,615–$24,485*
Cost factor: *90%*
Depreciation: NA

Overview

All of Chrysler's minivans were completely redesigned for 1996; most notable is an optional second sliding side door on the left side, a considerable convenience.

We tested the standard-length *Dodge Caravan,* which is about 16 inches shorter than the *Grand Caravan.* It's very refined—but will it hold up well?

Acceleration

○ The 3.3-liter V6, one of four available engines, combines sufficient power with acceptable fuel economy.

Transmission

⊜ The four-speed automatic transmission shifts smoothly.

Economy

◒ Expect to average about 19 mpg on Regular fuel.

Routine handling

⊖ The *Caravan* feels nimble in normal driving. In hard cornering, though, it wants to run wide.

Emergency handling

○ It threaded our emergency avoidance maneuver safely and securely, but fairly slowly.

Braking

○ The brakes are only so-so. The *Caravan* didn't stop very short, and the brakes lost some effectiveness after repeated stops.

Ride, normal load

⊖ The *Caravan* rides as well as many sedans. Bumpy roads evoke a few muted kicks, but the highway ride is smooth.

Ride, full load

⊖ A full load actually improves the ride.

Noise

⊖ Delivers a quiet ride.

Driving position

⊖ Tall drivers will find adequate legroom and plenty of headroom, even with the seat fully elevated. Short drivers have a commanding view, although the stationary wipers are somewhat in the way.

Front seating

⊖ The soft front seats give good

support except for the lower back.

Middle seating

⊖ The *Caravan* offers seating for seven: two in front, two in the middle, and three in the rear. The middle seat has ample room for two six-footers. And if the three-person rearmost bench is unoccupied, you can mount the middle bench way back for limousinelike legroom. Captain's chairs instead of benches are optional.

Rear seating

⊖ You can remove the middle seat and replace it with the rear seat to allow five to ride with lots of luggage space behind.

Access

⊖ A low floor makes getting in and out easy, but reaching the rearmost seat requires some agility. Overall, access is easy, especially with the handy second sliding door—a worthy option.

Climate system

⊜ Our *Caravan* LE's effective climate-control system has separate temperature controls for the driver and front passenger, as well as windshield-wiper deicers and heated outside mirrors. The optional rear air conditioner isn't needed.

Controls and displays

⊜ Most controls are easy to use.

Cargo area

⊖ Cargo access is very convenient, especially with the second sliding door. The cargo area is low, flat, and carpeted. To make full use of the cargo area, you need to remove the center and rear bench seats, which is easy if you have help. The seats are heavy—89 and 106 pounds—but they have wheels to help you roll them out. Removing the seats creates 64 cubic feet of usable cargo space, plenty for most loads. (The *Grand Caravan* has about 76 cubic feet, by our measurement.) Payload capacity is 1150 pounds of people and cargo; 150 pounds of that cargo can occupy the roof rack.

Safety

Chrysler claims that its minivans meet all 1998 passenger-car safety standards. Both the front and middle-row shoulder belts have adjustable upper anchors. A child safety seat fits easily in any seat, and nicely designed built-in child seats are optional. The front head restraints are high enough. Those on the middle and rear seats need to be raised for adults—and they don't lock in position. Our bumper basher left the front unharmed; damage to the rear totaled $472.

In the government's 35-mph crash test of a 1996 *Dodge Grand Caravan*, the driver dummy sustained certain "injuries," possibly severe; the passenger dummy fared better.

Predicted reliability

New model, no data. We don't have reliability data on the redesigned *Chrysler* minivans, so we can't recommend those models yet. Previous standard-length models were average; extended models, worse than average.

Based on a July 1996 report.

Dodge Grand Caravan SE

Price range: *$17,865–$24,885*
Cost factor: *90%*
Depreciation: ***NA***

Overview

This long-wheelbase version of the *Dodge Caravan* and *Plymouth Voyager* is unusually roomy. The redesigned 1996 model converts easily from people-carrier to roomy cargo-hauler. Reliability, however, is unknown.

Acceleration

○ The optional 3.3-liter V6 in the *SE* delivers smooth and adequate acceleration. (The heavy van would overburden the base four-cylinder engine.) A stronger 3.8-liter V6 is offered in the *LE* and *ES* versions of the van.

Transmission

⊜ The four-speed automatic shifts very nicely.

Economy

● Expect to average about 18 mpg, overall, on Regular fuel.

Routine handling

⊖ The *Grand Caravan* handles well on winding country lanes; its steering is quick, and its body doesn't lean much in turns. It tended to plow ahead during hard cornering at our track, but its handling remained predictable and safe.

Emergency handling

○ It wove through our avoidance maneuver predictably but not swiftly.

Braking

○ At the track, the *Grand Caravan* stopped straight, although a bit long, on dry pavement, but quite short on wet pavement. It stopped perfectly straight in our difficult wet divided-pavement test, in which the asphalt is slicker under one side of the vehicle than under the other.

Ride, normal load

⊖ The *Grand Caravan's* suspension absorbs most pavement flaws even better than that of an excellent competing minivan, the *Ford Windstar*. But a series of irregular bumps can make the rear suspension clank. The ride is supple and well controlled on expressways.

Ride, full load

⊖ A full load makes little difference in the ride.

Noise

⊖ At driving speed, the interior of the *Grand Caravan* is quiet.

Driving position

⊖ A power seat with height adjustment is available only in the *LE* and *ES* versions. Without it, tall drivers may feel cramped, and short drivers may have trouble judging where the front of the van ends.

Front seating

⊖ The front seats give good, firm support, but the seatbacks feel a bit lumpy.

Middle seating

⊖ The middle-row bench seat holds two; even a pair of six-footers can stretch out there. A reclining seatback is a boon to comfort.

Rear seating

⊖ Three tall people can ride in comfort on the rear bench seat.

Access

⊖ Front seat access is particularly easy. The optional left sliding door greatly aids access to the center seats or cargo area, but you have to crouch and squeeze through a narrow space to reach the rear seat.

Climate system

⊜ The versatile climate-control system blows plenty of warmed or cooled air, even to the rear. (Higher trim lines offer dual left-right controls, which work well.) We chose to forgo the optional rear air conditioner, and we didn't miss it. A defroster option warms not only the side mirrors but also the place where the windshield wipers park, to help keep them from freezing up.

Controls and displays

⊜ The dashboard is close to ideal, with virtually everything within easy reach and clearly legible.

Cargo area

⊖ By our measurements, this minivan has more useful cargo space than any other front-wheel-drive model when the middle and rear seats are removed. In any of the *Chrysler* minivans, removing the middle seat and replacing it with the rear seat gives you a five-passenger vehicle with lots of cargo space—especially handy in the shorter versions. It also lets you mount three child seats directly behind the front seats, if need be. (A pair of built-in child seats for the middle seat is optional.)

Safety

You can raise or lower the upper anchors of the front- and middle-row safety belts for comfort. A child safety seat fits easily in any seating position. Our bumper basher inflicted $600 worth of damage in the rear. The front bumper itself remained unscathed, but a reinforcement was damaged to the amount of $190.

The 1996 *Grand Caravan,* when crash-tested by the government, protected the passenger better than the driver.

Predicted reliability

New model, no data. Previous *Chrysler* minivans have had average or worse-than-average reliability records. Generally, the longer-body models have been more troublesome.

Based on an October 1995 report.

Ford Aerostar 4WD

Price range: $17,820–$23,445
Cost factor: 90%
Depreciation: ○

Overview

A terrific cargo carrier. Four-wheel drive greatly improves an otherwise skittish rear-wheel-drive minivan.

Acceleration

○ Sprightly acceleration for a van.

Transmission

⊜ The four-speed automatic can downshift abruptly at times.

Economy

● Expect about 16 mpg.

Routine handling

○ Four-wheel drive provides impressive traction, and the optional limited-slip differential keeps the rear wheels from spinning. Still, normal handling feels ponderous.

Emergency handling

◒ Quick but clumsy. In hard turns, the body leaned heavily, the front wheels plowed strongly, and the tires squealed.

Braking

◒ The *Ford* has antilock brakes in the rear only. It took a long distance to stop: 165 feet from 60 mph. That's about 20 feet longer than it takes to stop a typical midsize sedan. We advise that this minivan be driven conservatively.

Ride, normal load

○ Jiggly on smooth roads and firm—bordering on choppy—on rougher roads.

Ride, full load

○ The suspension bottoms occasionally under a full load.

Noise

○ Road noise and vibration are ever-present.

Driving position

⊖ Some drivers would have liked to sit higher for a better view of the road, but the driver's seat lacks a height adjuster. The steering wheel does adjust, though.

Front seating

⊖ Quite comfortable.

Middle seating

⊖ Captain's chairs provide good side support, but weak lower-back support.

Rear seating

○ The bench accommodates three adults well.

Access

⊜ Easy getting in or out of the front. A step helps middle- and rear-seat riders climb in and out.

Climate system

○ Front and rear climate controls work well. The defroster failed to clear the lower edge of the windshield, so the wipers iced up.

Controls and displays

⊖ You can control the fan for the secondary climate system from the dash or the second seat, an intelligent design. Tiny horn buttons on the steering-wheel spokes are hard to find in an emergency. Turning on the headlights dims the brightness of the digital displays.

Cargo area

⊜ No remote hatch release, but the hatch can be left unlocked.

Safety

Driver-side air bag is standard.

The government has not recently crash-tested an *Aerostar*.

Predicted reliability

○ Expect average reliability.

Based on an October 1992 report.

Ford Windstar LX

Price range: $19,590–$23,760
Cost factor: 91%
Depreciation: NA

Overview

Longest minivan on the road with huge cargo space, the *Windstar* is one of the most refined minivans on the market, but its reliability during the first year of production was much worse than average.

Acceleration

○ A 3.8-liter V6 accelerates adequately, but the driveline shudders a little on takeoff.

Transmission

⊜ The electronic four-speed automatic shifts exceptionally smoothly. You can lock out fourth gear—a useful feature when towing. Traction control and four-wheel drive aren't available.

Economy

◒ Expect about 20 mpg, overall.

Routine handling

○ The *Windstar* feels awkward on winding roads. It needs a lot of room to turn, and the ends of the vehicle are hard for the driver to see.

Emergency handling

○ Negotiated our emergency avoidance course steadily and safely.

Braking

⊖ Stopping distances were average on dry pavement, a little long on wet. The *Windstar* stopped perfectly straight in our difficult wet divided-pavement test, where the asphalt is slicker under one side than the other.

Ride, normal load

⊖ The *Windstar* delivers the best ride of any minivan we've tested.

Ride, full load

⊖ A full load does not affect the ride.

Noise

⊖ The cabin remains commendably quiet.

Driving position

⊖ The optional power seat and tilt steering column let drivers of practically any size find a good driving position. Even short drivers enjoy a commanding view of the road ahead.

Front seating

⊖ The front seats feel spongy but provide good support.

Middle seating

○ The middle bench offers room enough for two, but its back and cushion are skimpy. (The optional pair of bucket seats are more comfortable and easier to remove.)

Rear seating

○ Three six-footers will find just enough room in the rearmost bench.

Access

⊖ A low floor eases access.

Climate system

⊜ The climate-control system and optional rear air conditioner are powerful.

Controls and displays

⊖ Most gauges are easy to see, but some minor controls are poorly placed. The radio is hard to use.

Cargo room

⊖ The *Windstar's* huge body translates into an equally huge cargo space. Payload capacity is 1360 pounds. Ford sets a towing limit of 3500 pounds.

Safety

Minivans still aren't subject to some government safety standards, but Ford claims the *Windstar* meets them all, including the 1997 side-impact requirement. The safety belts are comfortable, but they need a locking clip to secure a child safety seat. One or two built-in foldaway booster seats are optional for the middle bench. Ford's claim that the *Windstar* can withstand 5-mph impacts without damage proved only half right: Our bumper basher left the front unscathed but damaged the rear bumper to the tune of $702.

Both the driver and passenger were well protected in government crash tests.

Predicted reliability

● The *Windstar* has poor reliability.

Based on a December 1994 report.

GMC Safari SLE

Price range: $19,246–$25,877
Cost factor: 91%
Depreciation: ⊖

Overview

The *GMC Safari/Chevrolet Astro* twins are built on a decade-old truck chassis. They have a cavernous cargo room and can tow a heavy trailer, but they're also plagued with clumsy handling, an unsettled ride, and heavy fuel consumption. Plus, they've been very unreliable.

Acceleration

○ Although the *Safari*, with its 4.3-

liter V6, has good acceleration, it still feels sluggish in normal driving.

Transmission

⊜ The four-speed automatic transmission shifts very smoothly. All-wheel drive, an extra-cost option, is probably worthwhile for its extra traction.

Economy

● We averaged a disappointing 15 mpg on Regular fuel.

Routine handling

◒ Handling is imprecise and ponderous. The *Safari* wants to plow straight ahead in hard turns.

Emergency handling

◒ It negotiated our avoidance maneuver safely but not swiftly, and it fishtailed a bit.

Braking

◒ Braking was below par; stops were long. And in normal driving, the pedal feels unresponsive at first, and then overly sensitive.

Ride, normal load

○ The *Safari* never lets you forget its truck heritage. Bumpy roads cause kicking and pitching.

Ride, full load

○ A full load makes matters worse.

Noise

○ Inside, you hear a constant rumble plus lots of wind and engine noise.

Driving position

○ Front legroom is adequate fore and aft, but the bulky engine compartment infringes on foot room. The footwell is even narrower in the right front position.

Front seating

⊖ The well-padded front seats give a commanding view, but support could be better.

Middle seating

⊖ The *Safari* can seat as many as eight, with three each in the middle and rear. Three tall people can fit fairly well in the middle bench. Captain's chairs instead of benches are optional.

Rear seating

⊖ The rear bench has even more hip room for three.

Access

○ A high floor makes front access a test of agility. Climbing into the middle-row seat isn't too difficult because the sliding side door opens wide. Children may be able to clamber into the rearmost seat without moving anything out of the way, but others need to fold down the middle seatback for clearance.

Climate system

⊜ The heater warms slowly, and not enough heat reaches the front occupants' feet. The optional rear-seat heater and air conditioner work very well.

Controls and displays

⊖ The steering wheel obscures the headlight switch for some drivers. The turn-signal lever includes too many other functions—wipers and washers, mist setting, and cruise control—but no flash-to-pass feature.

Cargo area

⊜ The *Safari* has a huge amount of cargo space, but removing the rear benches is a chore. Payload capacity is 1425 pounds, 200 pounds of which can occupy the roof rack. Opening the optional three-piece rear "Dutch door" is especially inconvenient: You must release and raise the glass panel and then swing open the left and right door panels separately.

Safety

The *Safari* has dual air bags and adjustable upper anchors on the front safety belts. With the seat adjusted far back, the lap portion of the driver's belt jams in its guide; it's hard to pull out, and it tightens reluctantly around one's lap. With the middle seat removed, one of the shoulder belts just hangs in space like a pendulum. However, you can easily secure a child safety seat in any seating position. The integral front-seat head restraints are high enough. The rear restraints are adequate for average-size adults, but they don't lock in position when raised. Our bumper basher caused $950 worth of damage in front, $774 in the rear.

When the government crash-tested a 1996 *Chevrolet Astro* (a twin to the *Safari*), both the driver and passenger dummies sustained certain, possibly severe "injuries."

Predicted reliability

● Reliability has been poor. In fact, the *Safari*'s and *Astro*'s reliability record is the worst of any current minivan.

Based on a July 1996 report.

Honda Odyssey EX

Price range: $23,560–25,550
Cost factor: 88%
Depreciation: NA

Overview

It's either a small minivan or a large station wagon. And it has proved utterly reliable in its first year. A rebadged Isuzu version, called the *Oasis*, is also available.

Acceleration

○ The 2.2-liter Four labors under a heavy load or on a long upgrade.

Transmission

⊖ The four-speed automatic senses when you're going uphill or downhill and unfailingly chooses the right gear. The shifter can slip all too easily past the D4 position into D3, needlessly locking out fourth gear.

Economy

◒ Expect about 21 mpg overall, on Regular fuel.

Routine handling

⊖ The *Odyssey* handles much like the *Honda Accord*.

Emergency handling

○ The vehicle negotiated our avoidance maneuver steadily and securely. The body leaned sharply, but the tires hung on.

Braking

⊖ Stopping distances were about average for a minivan. The *Odyssey* stopped straight in our wet divided-pavement test.

Ride, normal load

⊖ The suspension is generally resilient, but bumpy pavement can make the ride feel a bit choppy.

Ride, full load

⊖ Road bumps are more pronounced.

Noise

⊖ The engine sounds noisy when revved.

Driving position

⊖ Thanks in part to the power height adjustment on the seat (available only in the tested *EX* version), most drivers fit the cockpit well. Legroom barely suffices for six-footers, though. With the power seat raised, our five-foot tester could easily see over the hood.

Front seating

⊖ The front seats feel firm and reasonably comfortable, but a bit bulgy, and thigh and side support could be better. The *EX* version seats six.

Middle seating

⊖ The individual middle seats feel much like those in the front, and their seatbacks recline a little. Room there for six-footers is ample.

Rear seating

◒ The rear seat holds two, but not as comfortably. With an optional three-person middle bench seat, the *LX* can hold seven in a pinch.

Access

⊖ Climbing into the front and middle seats is easy. Access to the rear seat is tight in the six-passenger version because the middle seats don't fold. Folding the rear bench seat leaves a flat load area.

Climate system

⊖ The climate-control system usually works well, but the air conditioner barely copes with hot, humid weather. The auxiliary rear air conditioner really earns its keep.

Controls and displays

⊖ Most controls and displays are easy to see and well laid out. The horn buttons, on the steering wheel spokes, can be hard to find in a hurry.

Cargo room

◒ The *Odyssey* has substantially less cargo volume than any other minivan, but more than a midsize station wagon. The seven-passenger configuration reduces the length of the cargo floor slightly; although the three-passenger middle bench seat can fold, it isn't removable.

Safety

Only the front safety belts have adjustable upper anchors. You can secure a child seat in the individual seats, but the bench seats' buckles may make some child seats hard to install securely.

Our bumper basher caused the front bumper to shift, and it slightly tore the rear bumper's cover. Repair estimates: $675 front and $381 to fix the minor damage to the rear.

In government crash tests, the *Odyssey* protected both the driver and passenger dummies reasonably well.

Predicted reliability

⊜ An enviable reliability record.

Based on an October 1995 report.

Isuzu Oasis ✓

Price range: $23,495–$25,990
Cost factor: 88%
Depreciation: NA

See HONDA ODYSSEY.

Mazda MPV LX AWD

Price range: $21,795–$27,895
Cost factor: 90%
Depreciation: ○

Overview

The *Mazda MPV* dates back to 1988. For 1996, the *MPV* is equipped with four conventional swing-out doors (rather than a sliding side door), dual air bags, antilock brakes, and an improved dash. Optional all-wheel drive is a plus. Otherwise, it's the same old truck, badly in need of a redesign.

Acceleration

○ The 3.0-liter V6 feels sluggish, and the weight of the *MPV* seems to overburden the engine.

Transmission

⊖ The four-speed automatic transmission shifts slowly and not too smoothly. All-wheel-drive *MPV*s have a differential lock to aid traction in severe conditions. But this van is no sport-utility vehicle, as Mazda's ads would have you believe.

Economy

● In two-wheel drive, the *MPV* averaged only 16 mpg on Regular fuel—not stellar numbers. The *MPV*'s economy would be even worse in all-wheel drive.

Routine handling

◒ The steering feels slow, vague, and rubbery, and the body leans considerably in sharp turns—so much so that the inside rear tire tends to lose traction and spin. Engaging all-wheel drive remedies that shortcoming—and, fortunately, it's a system that can remain engaged all the time. The *MPV* leaned and lurched around the turns of our test track, and its tail tended to swing out suddenly.

Emergency handling

◒ It negotiated our avoidance maneuver safely but slowly. The all-wheel drive helped a bit there, too.

Braking

○ Braking performance is about average.

Ride, normal load

◒ The *MPV* has a stiff, uncomfortable ride. Even on the highway, the ride is very firm and jiggly.

Ride, full load

◒ A full load does not improve the ride.

Noise

⊖ The interior remains fairly quiet.

Driving position

○ A five-footer can just see over the hood. Except for the generous headroom, the cockpit is cramped for a tall driver.

Front seating

⊖ The firm front seats provide some side support, but the cushions are too short and flat.

Middle seating

○ The *MPV* can seat as many as eight, with three each in the middle and rear. With all seats occupied, knee room is tight. The middle seatback can recline, a plus. Captain's chairs instead of benches are optional.

Rear seating

◒ The rear bench is barely habitable; its back can recline fully, but not partway.

Access

○ Wide left and right swing-out doors aid access to the middle seat. Wedging yourself through the narrow passage to the rear seat is difficult, but at least you can enter from either side.

Climate system

◓ The front heater fan blows plenty of warm air, but it tends to favor the driver's right foot. A rear heater is standard equipment; it warms the middle row fairly well.

Controls and displays

⊖ Most controls are easy to reach. Buttons on the spokes of the steering wheel sound the horn; we prefer the center hub for the horn control. The rear wiper control requires a rather long stretch, and the front wiper control has to share its lever with cruise-control functions.

Cargo area

● Despite the *MPV*'s generous maximum payload, 1265 pounds, cargo room is relatively small; the rear of the cargo floor is stepped up, and the middle seat isn't removable. The middle and rear seatbacks can fold, and the entire rear seat can tumble forward, but it takes diligent study of the owner's manual to figure out how to remove the rear seat.

Safety

None of the shoulder belts have adjustable upper anchors. You can secure a child safety seat in any seating position. The head restraints are marginal when lowered, but they lock in their raised position. The bumpers are largely decorative; our bumper basher made a mess of them, as well as several expensive components behind them. Damage estimates: $1237 front, $850 rear.

The government plans to crash-test an *MPV* sometime this year.

Predicted reliability

○ Expect average reliability.

Based on a July 1996 report.

Mercury Villager GS

Price range: $19,940–$26,390
Cost factor: 90%
Depreciation: ⊖

Overview

The *Mercury Villager/Nissan Quest* twins came out in 1993. They're built in Ohio by Ford and powered by Nissan's responsive 3.0-liter V6. This year, dual air bags are finally standard equipment. These minivans lack a second sliding door, and cargo room is modest.

Acceleration

○ The *Villager* accelerates well.

Transmission

⊖ The four-speed automatic transmission shifts fairly smoothly.

Economy

◒ Expect to average about 19 mpg on Regular fuel.

Routine handling

○ Handling is safe but unexceptional. The body leans a lot during hard cornering, and the steering isn't very responsive.

Emergency handling

○ The *Villager* negotiated our avoidance maneuver safely and predictably.

Braking

⊖ The *Villager* stopped reasonably well in our wet- and dry-pavement braking tests.

Ride, normal load

⊖ The *Villager* absorbs bumps in the road well and delivers a comfortable ride.

Ride, full load

⊖ A full load doesn't affect the ride much either way.

Noise

⊖ The interior remains commendably quiet, although not as quiet as a *Dodge Caravan*.

Driving position

⊖ Tall drivers found plenty of headroom but sparse legroom, and they wished the flat seat cushion offered more thigh support. (The power seat lacks an adjustment for tilt.) They also complained of a sore ankle because the accelerator is positioned awkwardly and offers too little resistance to foot pressure. Shorter drivers fared better.

Front seating

⊖ The high and resiliently padded front seats provide good support except at the sides.

Middle seating

⊖ The *Villager* offers seating for seven: two in front, two in the middle, and three in the rear. There is a two-person bench in the middle (which can be removed) and a three-person bench in the rear; both seatbacks can be reclined. Captain's chairs instead of benches are optional.

Rear seating

○ The rearmost bench is nicely padded, but three tall people have to squeeze to fit there.

Access

⊖ Access to the front seats is very easy; to the middle bench seat, not too difficult. Getting to the rearmost bench seat requires more effort.

Climate system

⊜ The heater works well after a slow start. The auxiliary heating and air-conditioning system for the rear seats also works well, but its fan is fairly noisy.

Controls and displays

○ Many minor controls are clustered tightly on the instrument panel, hidden behind the steering wheel. Both the climate controls and the radio are a fairly long reach for the driver.

Cargo area

○ The *Villager* has a smaller cargo area than, say, a *Dodge Caravan*. Removing the middle seat is tricky, and the rear seat can't be removed. But you can fold and slide the rear seat forward, way up to the front seats, for maximum cargo room—or adjust it to various positions along the track for luxuriant legroom. Payload capacity is 1290 pounds.

Safety

The *Villager* has two air bags and adjustable front shoulder-belt anchors (thankfully, the old motorized belts have been retired). The right side of the middle bench has a cumbersome safety-belt design that invites improper use. Even when the head restraints in the front and middle seats are fully lowered, they're high enough to protect average-size adults—and they lock in position when raised. You can secure a child safety seat in any seating position; nicely designed integrated child seats are available. Our bumper basher did no damage.

In government crash tests, the *Villager*'s driver dummy sustained moderate "injuries," while the passenger dummy fared worse.

Predicted reliability

○ The *Villager* and similar *Nissan Quest* have compiled an average reliability record over the past three years.

Based on a July 1996 report.

Nissan Quest

***Price range:** $20,899–$25,699*
***Cost factor:** 88%*
Depreciation: ⊖

See MERCURY VILLAGER.

Oldsmobile Silhouette

***Price range:** $21,355–$22,655*
***Cost factor:** 93%*
Depreciation: ○

See PONTIAC TRANS SPORT.

Plymouth Grand Voyager

***Price range:** $17,865-20,050*
***Cost factor:** 91%*
***Depreciation:** NA*

See DODGE GRAND CARAVAN.

Plymouth Voyager

***Price range:** $16,615–$20,790*
***Cost factor:** 91%*
***Depreciation:** NA*

See DODGE CARAVAN.

Pontiac Trans Sport

***Price:** $19,394*
***Cost factor:** 91%*
Depreciation: ○

Overview

GM's plastic-bodied minivan siblings—the *Pontiac Trans Sport, Chevrolet Lumina,* and *Oldsmobile Silhouette*—perform unimpressively, overall. They leap and bound on bumps and lean heavily in turns. Next year, an entirely new replacement should add more room, better visibility, friendlier controls, and a second sliding door.

Acceleration

○ The V6 accelerates well, but its fuel consumption is hardly competitive.

Transmission

⊜ The four-speed automatic always shifts very smoothly.

Economy

● Expect about 18 mpg overall.

Routine handling

○ The *Trans Sport* leans a lot in corners, and slow steering response makes it feel ponderous. Bumpy corners make it leap and bounce disconcertingly.

Emergency handling

○ The van felt slow and clumsy in our avoidance maneuver, and it tended to swing out its tail.

Braking

○ Even with its antilock brakes, the van took longer than average to stop from 60 mph. But it stopped straight in our wet divided-pavement test.

Ride, normal load

○ The *Trans Sport* rides smoothly on seamless roads, but broken pavement causes firm kicks and quick pitching motions. The front end bobs noticeably on undulations.

Ride, full load

○ A full load quells some of the motions.

Noise

⊖ Very little road noise penetrates the cabin, but wind noise is audible.

Driving position

○ Finding a good driving position is difficult, despite the optional power seat and tilt steering column. The steering wheel is much too close, and the driver can tell where the van's snout ends.

Front seating

⊖ The front seats provide good support, but the seatbacks feel lumpy.

Middle seating

⊖ The optional seven-passenger seating package includes three modular chairs in the center row and two more in the third row. The chairs are well padded, although not especially comfortable. Those in the second row offer ample room for three six-footers. Integral child restraints are optional for both outboard seatbacks in the second row; they deploy easily and make fairly good seatbacks when they're folded.

Rear seating

○ Seating is more cramped in the third row.

Access

⊖ Access to the *Trans Sport's* front and middle seats is particularly easy—but watch out for the sharp corner on the front doors. A narrow passage makes climbing into the third-row seat a little harder. Our *Trans Sport* has an exceptionally convenient optional power side door; a gentle tug on the handle, a touch on the keyless-entry fob, or a push on one of the two interior switches sets it gliding open or shut. The door immediately stops and reverses if it encounters any resistance, an important safety feature.

Climate system

⊜ The climate-control system furnishes ample heated or cooled air. Rear-seat passengers will appreciate the overhead cool-air vents, part of the optional rear air conditioner.

Controls and displays

○ The control layout suffers from several niggling faults. The climate-control system's many small push buttons are crammed low on the dash. The headlights lack a flash-to-pass feature—an unfortunate General Motors trait. And the doors lock automatically when you start off, but they don't unlock automatically when you stop and shift into Park.

Cargo room

○ The *Trans Sport* doesn't hold quite as much cargo as a 1994 *Plymouth Voyager.* Its cargo floor is slightly longer, but protruding wheel wells make it eight inches narrower. Removing the lightweight rear seats is easy for one person. The *Pontiac's* payload capacity is 1220 pounds. Maximum towing capacity is 2000 pounds—3000 with the optional towing package.

Safety

The *Trans Sport* has only a driver-side air bag. You can secure a child seat without a locking clip. The optional integral child seats work either as a booster, with the three-point belts, or as a toddler seat, with a built-in five-point belt. None of the rear seats have head restraints. In 3- and 5-mph encounters with our bumper basher, the reinforcements under both bumpers broke and the left headlight came loose. The repair estimates were $415 for the front end, $185 for the rear.

Government crash protection results were unavailable.

Predicted reliability

● We predict abysmal reliability records for the *Trans Sport*, *Oldsmobile Silhouette,* and *Chevrolet Lumina* minivans.

Based on a July 1994 report.

Toyota Previa LE All-Trac 

Price range: *$24,318–32,198*
Cost factor: *87%*
Depreciation: ⊖

Overview

An excellent choice as a substitute for a passenger car. The supercharged engine is now standard and should add some needed punch to the *Previa's* performance (A new *Previa,* based on the *Camry* platform, is due in 1996.)

Acceleration

◒ Acceleration is only adequate, but a full load of passengers or cargo (1235 pounds) severely taxes the engine and slows acceleration even more. Test drive one with the supercharged engine if you expect your minivan to be frequently crowded with people and/or "stuff."

Transmission

⊖ The overdrive automatic shifted too often between third and fourth gears when climbing hills.

Economy

● Expect to average about 18 mpg.

Routine handling

○ All-wheel-drive system inspires confidence on slippery surfaces. Tires grip the road well and steering feels responsive, if a bit slow.

Emergency handling

○ Abrupt maneuvers feel reasonably fast and steady, despite a lot of body lean. Good balance and strong tire grip made the *Toyota* feel relatively stable and agile in hard turns on the track.

Braking

○ The optional antilock brakes work well.

Ride, normal load

⊖ Rides like a passenger car.

Ride, full load

○ Becomes rather firm, sometimes jarring under a full load.

Noise

⊖ Quiet inside except under acceleration, when the engine throbs and vibrates.

Driving position

⊖ Since you can raise or lower the steering wheel, most drivers found a good driving position. Lanky drivers found themselves too close to the accelerator pedal; and since the driver's foot is unsupported, fatigue sets in.

Front seating

⊖ Front captain's chairs are comfortable for short and tall occupants.

Middle seating

⊖ Optional swiveling captain's chairs are comfortable.

Rear seating

◒ Flat as a bench and nearly as hard.

Access

⊖ Takes a little effort to get in and out of a high van, but handgrips on the windshield pillars are a help. In the rear, a step eases entrance.

Climate system

○ Efficient, with its separate rear air conditioner. It's difficult to direct airflow from the vents on the oddly shaped dashboard.

Controls and displays

⊖ Work well once you figure them out. Instruments are easy to read.

Cargo area

⊖ The rear seat folds out of the way, but then it blocks the driver's view to the rear. The rear hatch has no remote release, but it locks and unlocks with the power door locks.

Safety

Dual air bags supplement three-point front belts, which have adjustable upper anchors for shoulder belts.

Government crash test data were not available.

Predicted reliability

⊜ One of the best records for any minivan on the market.

Based on an October 1992 report.

SPORT-UTILITY VEHICLES

⊜ ⊖ ○ ◒ ● **Much better than average** ⟷ **Much worse than average**

It seems as if sport-utility vehicles (SUVs) are the height of fashion these days. Keep in mind, however, that they are no longer bare-bones Jeeps with minimal weather protection and trim. Most SUVs offer virtually all the comforts and conveniences of luxury sedans. With four-wheel-drive and generous ground clearance, they can churn through snow and mud—a major reason why families are turning to them as substitutes for conventional station wagons.

But don't get carried away: These models are not designed for anything as challenging as a mountain trail. Government regulations still don't require SUVs to have all of the vital protective equipment and engineering that conventional passenger cars must have (see box on page 171). However, some SUV manufacturers have been providing some of that equipment voluntarily.

Sport-utility prices range from about $12,000 for short-wheelbase vehicles such as the *Suzuki Sidekick* to over $60,000 for a *Range Rover*.

The sport-utility vehicles we recommend are the *Acura SLX/Isuzu Trooper, Ford Explorer, Jeep Grand Cherokee,* and *Lexus LX450/Toyota Land Cruiser.*

Acura SLX ✓

***Price:** $33,900*
***Cost factor:** 87%*
***Depreciation:** NA*

Although the name is new, the vehicle isn't. The *SLX* is really an *Isuzu Trooper* with minor interior cosmetic touches. We haven't tested an *SLX* yet. The *Trooper*, however, feels substantial and refined, but its weight takes a toll on acceleration. The four-wheel drive is a part-time system, but you can shift it "on the fly." Expect a roomy interior and fairly comfortable seats but only a so-so ride.

Predicted reliability ⊖

Chevrolet Blazer LT

***Price range:** $19,444–$28,546*
***Cost factor:** 91%*
Depreciation: ⊖

Overview

The redesigned *Blazer* performed much better than its predecessor, but the ride, brakes, and rear seat still fall short.

Acceleration

⊖ The 4.3-liter V6 accelerates nearly as well as the V8 in *Jeep's Grand Cherokee.*

Transmission

⊜ The four-speed automatic shifts very smoothly. A full-time four-wheel-drive system without Low range is now optional in the *LT* version, but our early *LT* has a part-time system. It has a Low range, and can shift between two- and four-wheel drive on the fly.

Economy

● Expect to average about 17 mpg.

Routine handling

○ The *Blazer* corners with some reluctance, and it requires hefty cranking of the steering wheel to make it respond. The vague steering and pronounced leaning of the body during cornering don't inspire confidence.

Emergency handling

○ The *Blazer* wanted to plow ahead in our avoidance maneuver, but its handling was predictable. In a test of the *Blazer LT, Ford Explorer Limited, Jeep Grand Cherokee,* and *Land Rover Discovery,* only the *Blazer* came with regular street tires. Off-road, those tires, plus marginal road clearance and skimpy suspension travel, got the *Blazer* stuck where the other SUVs pulled through.

Braking

◒ The brake pedal moves a long way before anything happens, and stopping distances are long. The *Blazer* stopped fairly straight in our wet-divided-pavement test.

Ride, normal load

◒ Jolts and abrupt pitching mar the ride on bumpy roads. The ride feels busy even on the highway.

Ride, full load

◒ A full load makes the body quiver and shake and the suspension bang harshly.

Noise

○ The cabin is quiet.

Driving position

⊖ The tilt steering column and power seat let most drivers get comfortable. Six-footers have ample room, and five-footers can see well over the hood. Some drivers may find the steering wheel a bit close when they adjust the seat for a comfortable reach to the accelerator.

Front seating

⊖ The front seats provide generally good, firm support except at the sides. A floor hump infringes on the front passenger's foot room. The leather upholstery isn't slippery.

Rear seating

◒ In the rear, legroom is ample for three six-footers. But the skimpy bench promotes poor posture, and the safety-belt spacing in the center is narrow for an adult. Toe space is tight.

Access

⊖ Front access is quite easy; rear access, less so.

Climate system

⊖ The manual climate-control system is versatile and effective. The air conditioner comes on in Defrost to aid defogging, and the fan is powerful. Air distribution is spotty in the rear, despite the rear ducts.

Controls and displays

⊖ Most controls are easy to find, but the driver has to stretch to reach some climate controls. The switches for the rear wiper and defroster are too low and too easily confused. The gauges are clear.

Cargo area

⊜ The cargo space is large, almost as roomy as that of the *Ford Explorer*. The payload is a bit less than that of the competition: It can carry only 1054 pounds, 200 of which can go on the roof rack.

Safety

The *Blazer* has neither a passenger air bag nor adjustable upper anchors for the front belts. The rear three-point safety belts are easy to buckle. You can easily secure a child safety seat in the outer positions without a locking clip. The front head restraints are high enough, but the rear seatbacks are low and lack restraints. The dark-tinted glass severely hampers the driver's rear view at night.

The new *Blazer* didn't do well in the government's 35-mph crash tests. The driver dummy received possibly severe "injuries"; the passenger dummy's "injuries" were judged severe or fatal. Also, the fuel tank leaked, prompting a recall.

Predicted reliability

◒ The *Blazer's* reliability record is worse than average.

Based on an August 1995 report.

Chevrolet Suburban

Price range: *$24,027–36,652*
Cost factor: *87%*
Depreciation: ⊜

This colossal SUV feels like an overgrown station wagon (like its twin, the *GMC Suburban*) that emphasizes utility over sport. Built on a full-size pickup chassis, it can seat up to nine people and tow a 10,000-pound trailer. It's available in two- and four-wheel-drive versions; expect both to be more trucklike than carlike. Climate and radio controls have been improved. Both the 5.7-liter and the mammoth 7.4-liter V8s burn a lot of gasoline. The new 6.5-liter turbodiesel V8 may make sense for *Suburban* buyers who don't own a petroleum refinery.

Predicted reliability ○

Chevrolet Tahoe

Price range: *$22,886–$35,788*
Cost factor: *88%*
Depreciation: ⊖

Formerly known as the *K-Blazer*, the *Tahoe* fills the gap between the elephantine *Suburban* and the downsized *Blazer*. It's still a good deal larger than competitors like the *Ford Explorer* and *Jeep Grand Cherokee*. The *Tahoe's* full-size pickup-truck chassis lends itself to hauling bulky cargo or towing a heavy trailer. A 5.7-liter V8 is standard; a turbodiesel V8 is optional The ride is surprisingly comfortable, and handling is reasonably secure for a vehicle of the *Tahoe's* size and weight.

Predicted reliability ◒

Ford Bronco

Price range: *$22,715–$28,540*
Cost factor: *87%*
Depreciation: ⊖

This huge four-wheel-drive sport-utility vehicle is a truck from the core outward, one that also offers various levels of interior luxury appointments. It weighs in solidly on the utility end of the sport-utility continuum, where it competes with the *Chevrolet Tahoe* and *GMC Yukon*. Its primary design is to haul a lot of gear or tow a heavy trailer. Its V8 engine delivers laughable fuel economy. A driver-side air bag and antilock brakes are standard.

Predicted reliability ●

Ford Explorer Limited 

Price range: *$18,485–$34,630*
Cost factor: *91%*
Depreciation: ⊖

Overview

The previous *Explorer* was a competent SUV. The latest redesign has made it even better. (Mercury received its own version, the *Mountaineer*, this year.)

Acceleration

○ The 4.0-liter V6 accelerates adequately. A 210-horsepower V8 is optional.

Transmission

⊖ The four-speed automatic shifts smoothly but sometimes sluggishly. A switch on the dash selects two- or four-wheel drive or four-wheel Low range. The four-wheel drive senses wheel slippage and engages automatically. The front and rear axles lock together when you select Low range.

Economy

● Expect to average about 17 mpg.

Routine handling

○ The *Explorer* leans only moderately during cornering, but the tires squeal easily. Although the steering is light, it gives some feel of the road. The *Explorer* tries to plow straight ahead in hard turns, but it's predictable. With full-time all-wheel drive, it did fairly well in our off-road tests. In the Limited version, selecting Low range raises the body two inches, helping it clear obstacles.

Emergency handling

◒ The *Explorer* was a bit slower in our avoidance maneuver than the other SUVs in our test—the *Chevrolet Blazer LT*, *Jeep Grand Cherokee*, and *Land Rover Discovery*.

Braking

○ The *Explorer* stopped straight in our wet and dry braking tests, but stops on wet pavement were long.

Ride, normal load

○ The ride is vastly improved in the latest version; it's firm and well controlled.

Ride, full load

○ Just as good as with a normal load.

Noise

○ The engine sounds harsh when pressed, but otherwise the cabin is quiet.

Driving position

⊖ The power seat and adjustable steering column let most people get comfortable. Tall drivers have plenty of room, and even five-footers can see well over the hood.

Front seating

⊖ The individual front seats give good upper and lower support, but they lack side support. The partially perforated leather upholstery isn't especially slippery or sweaty.

Rear seating

⊖ Three six-footers could fit easily in the rear seat.

Access

⊖ Large door openings, flush sills, and a low floor give relatively easy access. The running boards are a mixed blessing: handy for short people, an obstacle for tall people.

Climate system

⊖ The automatic climate-control system provides abundant airflow front and rear, although distribution is spotty at floor level. Rear passengers have their own controls for fan speed and distribution.

Controls and displays

⊖ The dashboard is well laid out, with easy-to-read gauges. The climate controls and rear-wiper control are fairly far from the driver, but the rest of the controls are easy to reach. The power-window and lock switches on the driver's door are lighted, a nice feature.

Cargo area

⊜ The cargo bay is the roomiest, compared to that of the *Blazer*, *Grand Cherokee*, and *Discovery*. It's as big as that of a small minivan. But Ford limits the total payload to less than 1000 pounds, including just 100 pounds for the roof rack. The limited-service spare hangs under the rear of the vehicle.

Safety

The front safety belts have an adjustable upper anchor, but they're a little hard to fasten. You'll need a locking clip to secure a child safety seat in all but the center rear position—and there, the buckles are too close together. A built-in child seat is optional. The front head restraints are high enough even when lowered, but the rear restraints must be raised for adults. SUVs' high bumpers don't match those on passenger cars, so we don't perform our usual bumper-basher tests on these vehicles.

In the government's 35-mph crash test of an *Explorer*, both the driver and passenger dummies fared quite well.

Predicted reliability

○ *Explorers* have compiled an average reliability record.

Based on an August 1995 report.

Geo Tracker LSi

Price range: $12,970–$15,710
Cost factor: 95%
Depreciation: ○

Overview

This model is much like the *Suzuki Sidekick*, but with a large network of Chevrolet dealers to provide service. Both are noisy, uncomfortable, and accelerate sluggishly. For a report on the *Suzuki Sidekick*, see page 164.

Acceleration

◒ The *Tracker's* 1.6-liter Four feels lethargic.

Transmission

⊖ The tested five-speed manual transmission shifts accurately. A three-speed automatic is optional in two-door models; a four-speed automatic is optional in four-doors.

The part-time four-wheel drive is unsuitable for dry roads, but its low range is especially useful for off-road use. You must stop to engage four-wheel drive. And after shifting out of four-wheel drive, you have to back up a few yards to unlock the hubs.

Economy

○ We averaged about 24 mpg with the 1.6-liter engine on Regular fuel.

Routine handling

○ The *Tracker* handles imprecisely, and its steering is slow and rubbery, but it doesn't feel especially tippy. It also leans a bit more sharply than the similar *Sidekick Sport* in turns, and it tends to wander in its lane a bit.

Emergency handling

◒ In hard turns at our track, the *Tracker* runs wide in tight corners, and its handling is generally not very tidy. It threaded through our emergency-avoidance maneuvers securely.

Braking

○ Braking performance was about average. The *Tracker's* pedal felt a little low and not very reassuring.

Ride, normal load

◒ Rode like a buckboard on bumpy roads.

Ride, full load

◒ A full load stiffens the ride a bit.

Noise

◒ Lots of wind whistle, engine buzz, and gear whine penetrate the cabin.

Driving position

○ Tall people may find the driving position awkward in both models. Legroom is tight for six-footers, and the short seat cushion gives little thigh support. Our five-foot-tall tester could see over the hood.

Front seating

○ The front seats are firm and comfortably high. The seatbacks could use more lower-back support.

Rear seating

○ The rear seat holds only two. Knee room is a little snug, but headroom and toe space are generous, and the padding is comfortably firm.

Access

⊖ Generally easy to climb in and out of, compared with most full-size SUVs.

Climate system

◒ The heater is barely adequate. The rear defroster is effective, but the side windows are slow to defrost.

Controls and displays

○ The small horn buttons are hard to find in a hurry.

Cargo area

◒ The *Tracker* has less cargo space than a small station wagon. Payload capacity is 749 pounds for our *Tracker*. Loading is convenient. Plus, you can fold down the *Tracker's* split rear seatback and tumble the seat assemblies forward to enlarge the load area. The rear cargo door easily swings open sideways a full 90 degrees, and the rear sill is flush with the cargo floor.

Safety

The *Tracker* is equipped with dual air bags, but the front shoulder-belt anchors lack a height adjustment. You can secure a child safety seat without a locking clip, but a large child seat may not fit in the narrow right front seat. The front head restraints are high enough, and they lock in position securely when they're raised. The *Tracker* has no rear head restraints. Estimates of damage to the *Tracker* from our bumper basher totaled $385 front, $949 rear.

The government has not crash-tested a four-door *Tracker*. However, a two-door *Tracker* didn't do well in its crash test.

Predicted reliability

⊖ Better-than-average reliability record.

Based on a June 1996 report.

GMC Jimmy

Price range: *$19,573–$28,179*
Cost factor: *90%*
Depreciation: ⊖

See CHEVROLET BLAZER.

GMC Suburban

Price range: *$24,027–$33,682*
Cost factor: *87%*
Depreciation: ⊖

See CHEVROLET SUBURBAN.

GMC Yukon

Price range: *$22,880–31,564*
Cost factor: *87%*
Depreciation: *NA*

See CHEVROLET TAHOE.

Honda Passport EX

Price range: *$17,990–$27,880*
Cost factor: *89%*
Depreciation: *NA*

Overview

This vehicle is simply an *Isuzu Rodeo* with a *Honda* nameplate. It falls short in handling and safety features.

Acceleration

○ The 3.2-liter V6 accelerates rather

slowly. A 2.6-liter Four is standard with the lowest-priced *DX* version—but we don't recommend it.

Transmission

⊖ The four-speed automatic shifts smoothly. The Power mode raises the shift points to deliver stronger acceleration but worse fuel economy. A Winter mode, which is of little use in a four-wheel-drive vehicle, allows starts in third gear. The part-time four-wheel-drive system shouldn't be used on dry pavement or over 50 mph; you must stop the car to engage it and back up several feet to disengage it—not the most convenient or sophisticated four-wheel-drive system.

Economy

● About 16 mpg with the 3.2-liter V6.

Routine handling

○ The steering feels slow and rubbery, and the body leans heavily in turns. The *Passport* lurched and hopped disconcertingly around tight corners at our track, but it stayed on course.

Emergency handling

◒ The vehicle didn't grip well in our avoidance maneuver.

Braking

○ Stopped straight and fairly short on a dry track. But with an antilock feature on only the rear wheels, it took all of 200 feet to stop in the wet. It veered slightly in our wet divided-pavement test.

Ride, normal load

◒ Fairly steady on good roads, but rough pavement delivers unceasing kicks, jiggles, and bounding motions.

Ride, full load

◒ The jitters increase, and the rear suspension bottoms easily.

Noise

⊖ Commendably quiet.

Driving position

⊖ The driver's seat lacks a height adjuster, but even our shortest driver could see well over the hood. Tall drivers found plenty of headroom but snug legroom.

Front seating

⊖ The front seats, which are cloth-covered, provide generally good, extra-firm support.

Rear seating

○ The split rear bench offers plenty of room but little comfort for three adults.

Access

⊖ Climbing aboard is easier than in a larger SUV, such as the gargantuan *Toyota Land Cruiser*, thanks to the lower floor, but it's still an awkward step up from the typical sedan.

Climate system

○ A powerful heater and air conditioner produce lots of warmed or cooled air, but the heater concentrates too much air on the driver's right ankle.

Controls and displays

○ The instruments are easy to read, but too many small buttons dot the dashboard and center console. Six are devoted to the windshield wipers and washers alone. The radio is mounted too low to reach easily and has tiny, illegible buttons.

Cargo room

⊖ The *Passport's* cargo volume is no bigger than that of the average station wagon. With special equipment, it can tow a 4500-pound trailer. Otherwise, towing capacity is 3500 pounds for the V6 and 2000 pounds for the four-cylinder version.

Safety

The *Passport* has dual air bags. You can secure a child safety seat without a locking clip. Even when the doughnut-shaped front and rear head restraints are lowered all the way, they're high enough to protect against whiplash. We didn't perform our usual bumper-basher tests on the *Passport*.

The passenger "dummy" fared only slightly better than the driver in government crash tests.

Predicted reliability

○ The *Passport* has compiled an average reliability record.

Based on a July 1994 report.

Isuzu Rodeo

Price range: $17,340–$27,110
Cost factor: 88%
Depreciation: ⊖

See HONDA PASSPORT.

Isuzu Trooper LS ✓

Price range: $25,360–$37,900
Cost factor: 85%
Depreciation: ○

Overview

It's more civilized than its boxy predecessor, but the four-wheel drive is a dated design.

Acceleration

○ Average get-up-and-go.

Transmission

⊖ The four-speed automatic performs well. A Winter mode lets you start off in third gear for better traction on slippery roads—but with four-wheel drive, that's not a big advantage.

Economy

● About 15 mpg in mixed driving.

Routine handling

○ Steering feels heavy and numb.

Emergency handling

◒ Handled very sloppily and leaned a lot through our avoidance course. In hard turns at the track, the tires screeched, although the car remained controllable.

Braking

○ Optional four-wheel antilock brakes on the *LS* took a bit longer than usual to stop, and nosedive was severe. But all stops were straight.

Ride, normal load

◒ Bounces, jiggles, and rocks even on smooth roads.

Ride, full load

● Springs compress fully, jolting the riders, with a full load.

Noise

⊖ Fairly quiet.

Driving position

⊖ Very good among competing SUVs. Short drivers can see out well. Some quibbles: Raising the seat is difficult when you're sitting on it; the accelerator is too far left; and the left footrest is too vertical.

Front seating

⊜ Good support except during hard cornering. Headroom is generous, and legroom is adequate for six-footers.

Rear seating

⊖ Comfortably holds two—but not three—average-size men. With three across, the center rider must lean back against the very hard folded armrest.

Access

⊖ Easy in and easy out in front, slightly less convenient in the rear.

Climate system

⊖ Puts out lots of warmed or cooled air, but too much of it reaches the driver's right foot. The mirror heaters worked well, but it's too easy to forget to shut them off. The rear wiper and washer proved useful in sloppy weather.

Controls and displays

⊖ Controls for the fog lights and rear-window defroster are too low and obscured by other equipment. Instruments are easy to read.

Cargo area

⊜ Split rear seat folds fairly simply, but securing the folded seat is a clumsy process. Maximum usable cargo volume is 43 cubic feet. A flush rear sill and skid strips on the cargo floor ease loading. Maximum payload is 1144 pounds, and maximum towing capacity is 5000 pounds.

Safety

Dual air bags are standard.

Government crash-test data were not available.

Predicted reliability

⊜ Expect much-better-than-average reliability.

Based on a November 1992 report.

Jeep Cherokee

Price range: *$14,745–$22,076*
Cost factor: *92%*
Depreciation: ⊖

A standard driver's air bag was added last year, but the basic design has changed little since 1984. The *Cherokee* handles well in normal driving and has lots of cargo room, but it remains a harsh-riding and noisy vehicle with narrow seats. The 4.0-liter Six is much stronger than the 2.5-liter Four. Although the air conditioner is powerful, the heater could be better. So could the controls and displays.

Predicted reliability ◒

Jeep Grand Cherokee 

Price range: *$24,903–$33,056*
Cost factor: *90%*
Depreciation: ⊖

Overview

The *Grand Cherokee* remains a strong, well-rounded performer with a decent ride and full-time all-wheel-drive capacity; reliability seems to have improved.

Acceleration

⊖ The optional 5.2-liter V8 accelerates briskly; it pulled our 5000-pound trailer with relative ease. The standard 4.0-liter Six performs nearly as well.

Transmission

⊖ The four-speed automatic shifts smoothly. Jeep offers three different four-wheel-drive systems—from a primitive part-time four-wheel drive to the sophisticated full-time all-wheel drive that's standard with the V8.

Economy

● Expect 15 mpg with the V8, 16 with the Six.

Routine handling

○ For an SUV, the *Grand Cherokee* hangs on reasonably well in turns, leaning only moderately. But the steering lacks feel and precision. It plows ahead a little during hard cornering, but it tightens its line easily if you let up on the accelerator. The *Grand Cherokee* proved quite capable in our off-road tests.

Emergency handling

○ It negotiated our avoidance maneuver safely but a bit sloppily, with some wagging of its tail.

Braking

○ The brakes are adequate. The *Grand Cherokee* veered a bit but then stopped straight in our wet divided-pavement test, where the surface is slicker under one side of the vehicle than under the other.

Ride, normal load

○ The *Grand Cherokee* soaks up ruts and ridges with aplomb, but it rocks rapidly from side to side on uneven pavement.

Ride, full load

○ A full load actually improves the ride slightly.

Noise

○ The cabin remains quiet.

Driving position

⊖ The power seat and tilt steering column should help most people get comfortable at the controls. All drivers will find the cockpit roomy and the view over the hood clear.

Front seating

⊖ The front seats feel soft, but they provide good, firm support. Both have six-way power adjustment. Although the optional leather seat facings aren't perforated, they're neither slippery nor clammy.

Rear seating

⊖ The rear seat easily holds three six-footers, but the seatback is too upright for comfort. Toe space is tight under the front seats.

Access

⊖ Generous door openings and a fairly low floor aid access to the ront. Climbing in and out of the rear is trickier.

Climate system

⊖ The climate-control system can run either manually or semiautomatically, and it's easy to set. Problems include dash vents that are too small and too low, a heater that takes too long to warm up, and a noisy fan.

Controls and displays

○ The control layout is dated and cluttered. The radio and climate controls are too far from the driver, and reflections often cloud the instruments. (A redesigned panel is found in 1996 models.)

Cargo area

○ The *Grand Cherokee's* usable cargo volume is the smallest when compared with the *Chevrolet Blazer, Ford Explorer,* and *Land Rover Discovery,* largely because the optional full- size spare takes up so much space. A swing-away rear tire carrier is available. The rear seats can tumble and fold for extra cargo room. Jeep allows a generous payload—1412 pounds, 150 of which can ride on the roof rack.

Safety

The safety belts are easy to use and fairly comfortable, but the anchors for the shoulder straps lack a height adjustment. The rear three-point belts incorporate a locking tang that makes it easy to secure a child safety seat. A built-in child safety seat is optional. When the front and rear head restraints are lowered, they're just high enough to protect adults.

In government crash tests, a *Grand Cherokee* protected the driver dummy fairly well, the passenger dummy less well.

Predicted reliability

○ Reliability improved to average.

Based on an August 1995 report.

Jeep Wrangler

***Price range:** $12,985–$18,753*
***Cost factor:** 90%*
***Depreciation:** NA*

This is the closest surviving descendant of the old World War II Jeep, the seed that sprouted the entire sport-utility craze. Despite the previous models' awful reliability, the *Wrangler's* popularity with the off-road set endures. The 1997 model, due in mid-1996, has been extensively redesigned. Traditional *Jeep* aficionados will rejoice: Round headlights are back. Also expect an improved chassis, with coil springs instead of leaf springs, that may provide a more forgiving ride. The dashboard has been redesigned, and dual air bags are now standard.

Predicted reliability

No data, new model.

Land Rover Discovery

***Price range:** $29,950–$36,775*
***Cost factor:** 89%*
***Depreciation:** NA*

Overview

This British model offers off-road ability, but it's clumsy and stops poorly on wet roads. It also uses too much fuel.

Acceleration

○ The small, 3.9-liter V8 gave the slowest acceleration when tested with the 4.3-liter V6 *Chevrolet Blazer*, 4.0-liter V6 *Ford Explorer*, and 5.2-liter V8 *Jeep Grand Cherokee.*

Transmission

○ The four-speed automatic doesn't downshift readily, and the shift lever is still. A five-speed manual is standard. The full-time four-wheel drive had High and Low ranges, plus a lockable center differential for added traction.

Economy

● Expect to average about 13 mpg—on Premium fuel, no less.

Routine handling

◒ Once you master the way the body leans in a turn, you can maintain a decent pace on winding roads. Steering feels a bit vague and slow in tight bends, but the *Discovery* holds its line.

Emergency handling

◒ Handling in our avoidance maneuver was disconcerting, but the vehicle never seemed on the verge of rolling over.

Braking

○ The *Discovery* stopped reasonably well from 60 mph on a dry track, but it needed 202 feet to stop on a wet track—among the worst performances we've measured in years, and truly surprising in a vehicle with antilock brakes. Stops were straight in our wet divided-pavement test.

Ride, normal load

○ The *Discovery* swallows ruts and ridges with firm but muted jolts. Uneven pavement, however, makes it rock incessantly.

Ride, full load

○ A full load quells some of the rocking.

Noise

○ The driveline whines audibly except on the highway, where tire hum and wind noise drown it out.

Driving position

○ The pedals are too close to the seat and too far left; tall people especially complained about the driving position. The steering wheel and instrument panel partly block a short driver's view of the road.

Front seating

○ The front seats feel lumpy and a bit too firm. Neither seat can be adjusted for height or tilt. The seatback lacks full side support, and the hand wheels for the recliner are low, far back, and hard to turn. The optional partially perforated leather seat facings aren't slippery.

Rear seating

⊖ The chair-high rear bench seat is roomy and fairly comfortable for three tall people. The cushion is a bit short, and the seatback is too upright. The hard, side-facing rear jump seats are fit for children only.

Access

○ A high floor makes climbing in and out a chore, particularly in the rear.

Climate system

○ The air conditioner is marginal on warm, sunny days, and keeping the cabin at a comfortable temperature requires repeated fiddling with the climate controls.

Controls and displays

○ The major controls—headlights, wipers, horn—are easy to use, but the minor controls are awful. The power-window switches, on the center console, are illogically arranged and awkward to reach. Several switches are hidden by the steering wheel, and their cryptic labels offer few clues as to their function. Reflections often obscure the gauges.

Cargo area

⊖ The cargo bay is high, but the load floor is short. The payload capacity is generous: 1483 pounds, 110 of which can go on the roof rack. A fairly low floor and flush sill ease access to the cargo area.

Safety

You can adjust the height of the front safety belts' upper anchors for comfort. The rear three-point belts are hard to buckle, and the shoulder portion rides on the neck of some occupants. Installing a child safety seat requires a locking clip, a point omitted from the owner's manual. The integral head restraints are too low for adults.

The government has no plans at present to crash-test the *Discovery*.

Predicted reliability

Insufficient data.

Based on an August 1995 report.

Lexus LX450 ✓

Price: *$47,500*
Cost factor: *85%*
Depreciation: *NA*

With the "new" *LX450*, Toyota hopes to use the snob appeal of the Lexus name to boost sales of the *Toyota Land Cruiser*. Indeed, that's what the *LX450* really is—a *Land Cruiser* with a slightly softer suspension. Under either nameplate, this big, imposing vehicle competes at the high end of the market. Acceleration is leisurely, and the ride is busy. All-wheel drive assures good traction. Five adults can fit quite comfortably. With the third–row passenger seats folded and stowed, cargo space almost rivals a minivan's.

Predicted reliability ⊖

Mitsubishi Montero LS

Price range: *$27,902–$34,971*
Cost factor: *85%*
Depreciation: ⊖

Overview

A versatile four-wheel-drive system and four-wheel anilock brakes are the pluses in this roomy SUV. Ungainly handling is a minus.

Acceleration

◒ Sluggish with the 3.0-liter V6. Opt for the optional 3.5-liter V6.

Transmission

⊖ The four-speed automatic usually shifts smoothly.

Economy

● About 15 mpg average.

Routine handling

○ It feels tippy and cumbersome, with vague, slow steering. On the highway, it tends to wander, especially in crosswinds.

Emergency handling

◒ Very sloppy on the track. It responded slowly and leaned sharply, and the tail swung out too easily. In two-wheel drive, the front end plowed stubbornly straight ahead through hard turns, and then the tail wagged abruptly. Sometimes a rear wheel lifted off the ground. Leaving the four-wheel-drive system engaged at all times improved the handling noticeably—but fuel economy will take a dive.

Braking

⊖ Fairly short stops—143 feet from 60 mph—with the standard four-wheel antilock brakes.

Ride, normal load

○ The optional adjustable shocks offer three firmness settings. The Soft setting produced a fairly gentle but floating ride. On rough roads, the Hard setting gave better ride control.

Ride, full load

● With a full load, the rear springs frequently compress fully and deliver a jolt.

Noise

○ Reasonably quiet.

Driving position

⊖ Short drivers can see well over the hood, but the accelerator is too far to the left. Tall drivers found the accelerator too close, even with the seat all the way back.

Front seating

⊜ The slippery leather front seats in our *Montero* had an adjustable suspension, as in some large trucks; it reacts *after* the vehicle goes over a bump. Some drivers liked the feature; those who didn't locked it out.

Rear seating

○ Two six-footers have ample room, but three's a crowd.

Access

⊖ Quite convenient in front. High sills and narrow foot room make rear access awkward, despite convenient grab handles on the rear doorposts.

Climate system

⊜ Quickly supplies warmed or cooled air. Controls include a two-position Bilevel setting.

Controls and displays

⊖ Major controls work well, but the switches for the power door locks and rear wiper and washer are hidden low on the dash. Gauges, with their orange-on-black markings, aren't very legible. When lowered, the tilt-column steering wheel obscures the gauges.

Cargo area

⊖ Has a high cargo bay, but usable volume is just 37 cubic feet. Rear seat is not split, but is easy to fold. The single rear door needs four feet of clearance to swing open fully. A covered conventional spare is mounted on the outside of the door, leaving more room inside for cargo; it does partially block driver's view through the rear window. Maximum trailer-towing capacity is 4000 pounds.

Safety

Dual air bags are standard. Buckling the three-point rear safety belts can be difficult.

Government crash-test data were not available for the *Montero*.

Predicted reliability

Insufficient data. The *Montero* has not yet compiled a reliability record.

Based on a November 1992 report.

Nissan Pathfinder

Price range: *$22,399–$32,129*
Cost factor: *90%*
Depreciation: *NA*

We have yet to test the new *Pathfinder*, completely redesigned this year. The new model, slightly larger than the old one, has unit-body construction instead of a full frame and is said to be far more rigid. It has a pleasing, well-laid-out interior. The old *Pathfinder* rode and handled very well for a sport-utility vehicle, and we don't expect that to change. What may change for the better is crashworthiness. The new model has dual air bags. Previous *Pathfinders* had good reliability records, as far as SUVs go.

Predicted reliability

New model, no data.

Oldsmobile Bravada

Price: *$29,505*
Cost factor: *92%*
Depreciation: *NA*

The *Bravada* is a loaded version of the *Chevrolet Blazer* and *GMC Jimmy*. The long list of standard equipment includes full-time all-wheel drive, with no low range. A driver's air bag is standard, but a passenger's air bag is still unavailable—unforgivable in a new model. Otherwise, the *Bravada* has the same strengths and weaknesses as the cheaper GM models. Expect strong acceleration and a smooth-shifting transmission. Body lean during cornering and vague steering don't inspire driver confidence. The interior is passable, and cargo room is generous.

Predicted reliability ◒

Range Rover

Price: *$55,000–$62,000*
Cost factor: *88%*
Depreciation: *NA*

The *Range Rover SE* comes with all sorts of luxury-car amenities, power everything, and leather galore, as well as a number of advanced engineering features such as sophisticated all-wheel-drive system and air suspension. When you park, the body can lower itself to ease access. Once under way, it rises again. It rises still more when you select Low range, the better to clear off-road obstructions. It rides comfortably for an SUV and handles adequately, although it doesn't accelerate briskly.

Predicted reliability

New model, no data.

Suzuki Sidekick Sport JLX

Price range: *$12,899–$18,999*
Cost factor: *92%*
Depreciation: ⊖

Overview

Crude and uncomfortable, but quite competent off-road, the *Suzuki Sidekick* is noisy and slow, with ungainly handling to boot.

Acceleration

○ The *Sidekick Sport's* 1.8-liter Four is quick for vehicles in this class..

Transmission

○ The five-speed manual transmission shifts accurately, but the clutch in our *Sidekick* made smooth shifts a challenge. A three-speed automatic is optional in two-door models; a four-speed automatic is optional in four-doors. The part-time four-wheel drive is unsuitable for dry roads, but its low range is especially useful for off-road use. You must stop to engage four-wheel drive, and after shifting out of four-wheel drive, you have to back up a few yards to unlock the hubs.

Economy

○ We averaged about 23 mpg with the 1.8 engine on Regular fuel.

Routine handling

○ The *Sidekick* handles imprecisely, and its steering is slow and rubbery, but it doesn't feel especially tippy.

Emergency handling

○ In hard turns at our track, the *Sidekick* plowed ahead slightly, then smoothly adjusted its cornering line. It threaded through our emergency-avoidance maneuvers securely and capably.

Braking

○ Braking performance was about average.

Ride, normal load

◒ Rides like a buckboard on bumpy roads.

Ride, full load

◒ A full load stiffens the ride a bit.

Noise

◒ Fairly noisy, with plenty of wind whistle, engine buzz, and gear whine penetrating the cabin.

Driving position

○ Tall people may find the driving position awkward. Legroom is tight for six-footers, and the short seat cushion gives little thigh support. Our five-foot-tall tester could see over the hood.

Front seating

⊖ The front seats are firm and comfortably high. The seatbacks could use more lower-back support.

Rear seating

○ The rear seat holds only two. Knee room is a little snug, but headroom and toe space are generous, and the padding is comfortably firm.

Access

⊖ Generally easy to climb in and out of, compared with most full-size SUVs.

Climate system

◒ The heater is barely adequate. The rear defroster is effective, but the side windows are slow to defrost.

Controls and displays

○ The small horn buttons are hard to find in a hurry. The *Sidekick's* radio controls are very inconvenient. The similar *Geo Tracker's* GM radio is designed much better.

Cargo area

◒ The *Sidekick* has less cargo space than a small station wagon. Payload capacity is 776 pounds for our *Sidekick*. Loading is convenient. In addition, you can fold down the *Sidekick's* split rear seatback and tumble the seat assemblies forward to enlarge the load area. The rear cargo door easily swings open sideways a full 90 degrees, and the rear sill is flush with the cargo floor.

Safety

The *Sidekick* comes with dual air bags, but the front shoulder-belt anchors lack a height adjustment. You can secure a child safety seat without a locking clip, but a large child seat may not fit in the narrow right front seat. The front head restraints are high enough, and they lock in position securely when they're raised. The *Sidekick's* rear head restraints are too low. Estimates of damage to the *Sidekick* from our bumper basher totaled $265 front, $637 rear.

The government has not crash-tested a four-door *Sidekick*. However, a similar two-door *Geo Tracker* didn't do well in its crash test.

Predicted reliability

⊖ The *Sidekick* has racked up a better-than-average reliability record.

Based on a June 1996 report.

Suzuki X90

Price range: *$13,499–$14,999*
Cost factor: *93%*
Depreciation: *NA*

Overview

If you have more than one friend, forget the *Suzuki X90*; it has only two seats, and interior space is tight. The standard T-bar roof gives a quasi-convertible effect.

Acceleration

○ The 1.6-liter Four accelerates adequately.

Transmission

⊖ The five-speed manual transmission shifts precisely. A four-speed automatic is optional. The part-time four-wheel drive is unsuitable for dry roads, but its low range is especially useful for off-road use. You must stop to engage four-wheel drive, and after shifting out of four-wheel drive, you have to back up a few yards to unlock the hubs.

Economy

⊖ Expect to average about 27 mpg, on Regular fuel.

Routine handling

○ The *X90* handles awkwardly in all but the gentlest turns, although well enough on good roads.

Emergency handling

○ It did reasonably well in our emergency-avoidance maneuver, but bumpy or slippery curves can make the tail wag, requiring quick steering corrections.

Braking

○ Braking is adequate, no more. We noted some reduction in brake effectiveness after repeated stops.

Ride, normal load

● It rides harshly and particularly noisily on highways. Young posteriors may tolerate the jarring ride, but our testers loathed it.

Noise

◒ Raucous engine noise, wind noise, and drive train whine make riding in the *X90* a chore.

Driving position

○ Legroom is tight for tall people, and short people may have trouble seeing over the hood.

Front seating

○ The firmly padded seats are small but comfortably high. The *X90* doesn't have a rear seat.

Access

○ Getting in and out is easy.

Climate system

○ The heater is weak, and its fan is noisy.

Controls and displays

○ Some controls, particularly those on the radio, are awkward.

Trunk

○ The *X90's* conventional trunk can hold four Pullman cases or a folded wheelchair with room left over. But when the T-top panels are removed and stowed, they usurp lots of trunk space. (They don't fit behind the seats.)

Safety

The *X90* has dual air bags and adjustable upper anchors for the shoulder belts. A child safety seat will fit easily on the passenger seat, but don't mount a rear-facing infant carrier there. The adjustable head restraints are high enough, and they lock in position securely when they're raised. Our bumper basher did no harm front or rear.

The government has no plans to crash-test the *X90*. However, a similar two-door *Tracker* didn't do well in its crash-test.

Predicted reliability

New model, no data.

Based on a June 1996 report.

Toyota RAV4

***Price range:** $14,948–$18,098*
***Cost factor:** 90%*
***Depreciation:** NA*

Overview

Nice, but almost as expensive as some larger, more useful SUVs. We tested the four-door version with AWD and a five-speed manual transmission.

Acceleration

○ The 2.0-liter Four accelerates adequately.

Transmission

⊖ The five-speed manual transmission shifts smoothly and easily. A four-speed automatic transmission is available. The full-time all-wheel-drive system works smoothly and imperceptibly. Pressing a button locks the center differential to provide even greater traction in sand or deep snow.

Economy

○ Expect to average about 25 mpg on Regular fuel with the manual transmission.

Routine handling

⊖ The *RAV4* handles much like a good conventional car. It responds quickly and nimbly to its steering, and the permanent all-wheel-drive system keeps it firmly planted on slippery pavement.

Emergency handling

○ Leans considerably and wants to plow ahead in tight, fast turns. But it felt secure and responsive in our emergency-avoidance maneuver, and in the tighter and more rigorous emergency maneuver to which we subject all SUVs.

Braking

⊖ The *RAV4* braked well in all our tests, on both wet and dry pavement.

Ride, normal load

○ The suspension absorbs road bumps quite well, and the ride is tight and well controlled on the highway. Unlike most other SUVs, the *Toyota RAV4* isn't based on a light-truck chassis. It shares components with Toyota's *Corolla, Celica,* and *Camry* passenger cars—which goes a long way toward explaining its civilized road manners.

Ride, full load

○ A full load makes the ride firmer but not uncomfortable.

Noise

○ The engine sounds a little boomy when it's revved hard, but road rumble and wind noise are muffled.

Driving position

⊖ Most people should have no problem getting comfortable behind the wheel. Legroom isn't generous, but the compartment is wide, so tall drivers should be fairly comfortable. Headroom is plentiful, and the high seating position gives a commanding view of the road ahead.

Front seating

⊖ The small front seats feel firm and supportive.

Rear seating

○ You can shoehorn three adults into the rear seat, but two people would be far happier there.

Access

⊖ Climbing into the rear through the narrow opening requires agility.

Climate system

⊖ The climate-control system works well. A Bi-level setting blows cooler air from the dash than at floor level, as is appropriate. The rear defroster also works well.

Controls and displays

⊜ The controls are easy to use.

Cargo area

◒ The *RAV4* has a big cargo area for such a small vehicle. The load floor is unusually low, the rear sill is flush, and there's no bumper to get in the way, so sliding cargo in and out is especially easy. Folding the rear seat and tumbling it forward provides added cargo room. Payload capacity is just over 900 pounds, 165 of which can occupy the roof rack. A cubby in each sidewall can conceal small valuables.

Safety

Safety equipment includes dual air bags and front shoulder belts with adjustable upper anchors. You can secure a child safety seat in any position without a locking clip, but some child seats may be too wide to fit in the recommended center-rear position. The front and rear head restraints are high enough to protect an average-size adult even when they're fully lowered, and they lock in position securely when they're raised. The *Toyota RAV4* has no bumper at all in the center rear, and the hollow plastic front "bumper" has no impact resistance to speak of. The *RAV4* makes no claims for its bumpers, so we didn't bash it. We saw no point in doing thousands of dollars in damage just to prove the obvious. (A rear bumper/trailer hitch is an extra cost dealer option that our *RAV4* didn't have.)

The government has no plans to crash-test the *RAV4* this year.

Predicted reliability

New model, no data. Like other *Toyota* models, it should be very reliable.

Based on a June 1996 report.

Toyota 4Runner

Price range: $19,488–$32,988
Cost factor: 87%
Depreciation: NA

The *4Runner* is substantially redesigned this year. We prefer the lively 3.4-liter V6 to the 2.7-liter Four. A longer wheelbase and lower floor give more cargo space and more rear-seat legroom. The four-wheel-drive system remains a part-time affair, disappointing in such a costly vehicle, and the ride is more trucklike than in upscale sport-utility vehicles from Ford and Jeep. The previous *4Runner* was extremely reliable.

Predicted reliability

New model, no data.

Toyota Land Cruiser

Price: $40,258
Cost factor: 85%
Depreciation: ⊖

Overview

Rugged construction, high ground clearance, and full-time all-wheel drive make this one of the best SUVs for on- or off-road travel.

Acceleration

○ The 4.5-liter in-line Six delivers plenty of torque at low speeds, but acceleration is leisurely at wide-open throttle.

Transmission

⊖ The four-speed automatic occasionally bumps when shifted from first to second gear. The drive train includes a sophisticated full-time all-wheel-drive system with high and low ranges.

Economy

● Not the *Land Cruiser's* strong suit: Expect to average just 14 mpg on Regular fuel.

Routine handling

○ By sedan standards, the vehicle feels ponderous on winding country roads, but it actually holds the road quite well. It plows ahead when pushed to its cornering limits, but easing up on the accelerator promptly gets it back on course.

Emergency handling

◒ The body leaned a lot in our accident-avoidance maneuver, but the *Land Cruiser* didn't feel tippy.

Braking

⊖ Stops were straight and fairly short in all our braking tests.

Ride, normal load

◒ A busy and rubbery ride regardless of the road surface. The vehicle shrugs off large road undulations, but broken pavement causes body shake.

Ride, full load

◒ A full load makes the ride more nervous.

Noise

⊖ Tire and road noises are well muted, but the drive train tends to whine incessantly.

Driving position

⊖ The driver sits tall in the saddle.

Even our five-foot driver had no trouble seeing over the hood. The steering wheel adjusts for height. Tall drivers found the headroom plentiful but the legroom snug.

Front seating

⊖ Generally good, firm support, although the cushions are a bit too short for full thigh support. Cloth upholstery is standard; leather is available in an expensive package that includes power front-seat adjusters and a third rear bench seat.

Middle seating

○ The firm, split second-row bench seat can seat three passengers in reasonable comfort, although the seatback is a bit too erect.

Rear seating

● The optional split third-row bench makes a cramped, uncomfortable perch for three.

Access

○ Even with the convenient grab handles and optional running boards, the climb to the high front and middle-row seats is difficult. You must crouch and climb to reach the rearmost bench, a task that is probably best suited for children.

Climate system

○ Versatile system provides plenty of cooled or heated air, but the heater concentrates too much air on the driver's right foot. The rear heater furnishes ample airflow to the second seat, very little to the third seat.

Controls and displays

⊜ As in other *Toyotas*, the instruments and controls are close to ideal.

Cargo room

⊜ The *Land Cruiser* is a capable and versatile cargo hauler. The second- and third-row seats can be folded out of the way easily. Payload capacity is nearly 1400 pounds.

Safety

Dual air bags are standard. The safety belts are well designed and comfortable, and you don't need a locking clip to secure a child safety seat. The front and second-row head restraints are adequately high. Those in the third row are too low when they're fully lowered.

The government has never crashed a *Land Cruiser*.

Predicted reliability

⊖ Very reliable.

Based on a July 1994 report.

HOW SAFE ARE SUVs?

Rollover is a major concern

For years the government has allowed automakers to pretend that light trucks—sport-utility vehicles, pickup trucks, and minivans—aren't used the same way as cars and therefore don't need to comply with all of the same safety standards. That era is gradually ending. Light trucks made as of September 1998 will finally have to meet the same safety standards as cars.

In truth, they already meet most of them. For instance, although dual air bags won't be required until the 1999 model year, many light trucks already have them. But some less visible safety measures, such as resistance to side impact, are showing up more slowly in trucks.

The propensity of sport-utility vehicles, particularly small models with a short wheelbase, to roll over has caused concern for many years. According to 1994 fatality figures, the latest available, small SUVs are involved in fatal rollover accidents at more than five times the rate for large passenger cars: 136 deaths per million vehicles versus 24.

For years, the National Highway Traffic Safety Administration (NHTSA) considered instituting standards that would lessen the tendency of vehicles to roll over—or at least make rollovers more survivable. In the end, the NHTSA continues to require only that SUVs have a warning label advising driver caution. Drivers of SUVs would do well to heed that warning.

Another area where light trucks don't have to measure up is bumper protection. They don't have to comply with even the weak 2½-mph passenger-car standard.In fact, they don't have to have any bumpers at all.

PICKUP TRUCKS

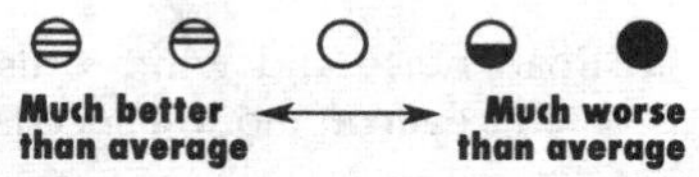

Pickup trucks are selling like crazy. In fact, the *Ford F-150* has been the best-selling vehicle (of any type) for years. Many manufacturers are making their trucks more carlike, especially in terms of the vehicle's interior appointments. Pickup trucks, much like sport-utility vehicles, are now often only used as daily transportation—most owners never use their pickup's four-wheel drive capabilities or cargo-carrying limits. We plan on testing more pickup trucks in the future. For now, we recommend only the *Ford Ranger/Mazda* B-series twins.

Chevrolet C/K

Price range: *$14,016–$24,284*
Cost factor: *87%*
Depreciation: ⊜

Chevy's full-sized pickup is designated "C" in two-wheel-drive versions, "K" in four-wheel drive. It and its twin, the *GMC Sierra,* have nicer interiors now, and the engines are a bit stronger and more refined this year, but the *C/K* is still very trucklike. It's designed for hauling large, heavy loads. Engines range from a 4.3-liter V6 up to a 7.4-liter V8 and a 6.5-liter turbodiesel. Expect a commanding view of the road and a quiet cabin. In extended-cab versions, an optional extra door on the passenger's side greatly eases loading of people or cargo.

Predicted reliability ○

Chevrolet S-Series

Price range: *$11,070–$18,215*
Cost factor: *91%*
Depreciation: ⊖

The compact "S" pickup and its twin, the *GMC Sonoma,* are a modern design—but don't expect carlike handling. (We tested a *Sonoma*—see page 171.) Isuzu gets its own version, called *Hombre.* These trucks lean a lot in corners, and the steering feels vague and heavy. The ride is stiff but quiet. The 4.3-liter V6 feels sprightly. Even with antilock brakes, stopping distances are quite long. The convenient extended-cab version has an optional side door to aid loading. The climate-control system works extremely well. Two nagging concerns: Reliability has been poor, and this truck didn't do well in government crash tests.

Predicted reliability ●

Dodge Dakota 4X2 Club Cab SLT

Price range: *$11,075–$19,713*
Cost factor: *92%*
Depreciation: ⊖

Overview

If room for people and cargo were all that mattered, the *Dakota* would rank first when compared with the *Ford Ranger XLT, GMC Sonoma SLE,* and *Toyota Tacoma LX.* But it's lifeless with the V6, and cumbersome to drive. A redesign is due for 1997.

Acceleration

○ The 3.9-liter V6 accelerates lethargically. For more power, a 5.2-liter V8 is optional.

Transmission

⊖ The four-speed automatic often hunts annoyingly between gears. A five-speed manual is available.

Economy

● Expect to average about 17 mpg on Regular fuel.

Routine handling

◒ The *Dakota* handles ponderously. The steering responds slowly and feels rubbery and uncommunicative. The body leans excessively during cornering, and the rear wheels bounce and hop in bumpy turns. A large turning circle makes parking especially ungainly.

Emergency handling

○ The *Dakota* plowed around the test track more sloppily than the *Ranger* and *Sonoma.* In our avoidance maneuver, it was clumsy and sluggish, but safe.

Braking

○ The *Dakota* turned in an average braking performance, and it came to a straight stop in our wet divided-pavement test.

Ride, normal load

◒ On poor roads, the *Dakota* snaps and bounds. The ride can become bouncy even on smooth roads.

Ride, full load

◒ A full load makes the ride worse.

Noise

○ Road noise and wind whistle are problems even at modest speeds.

Driving position

○ A five-foot driver can see out well, although the seat lacks a height adjustment. Six-footers have ample headroom and just enough legroom.

Front seating

⊖ The wide split bench front seat has adjustable lumbar support on the driver's side. The soft padding and springing give little support.

Rear seating

● The folding rear bench seat can hold three unhappy adults. It's low, flat, and skimpy.

Access

○ Front access is easy. The passageway to the rear is narrow.

Climate system

○ The heater warms up slowly, and you can't split the air between the windshield and the floor. The fan is noisy, and the small vents are too low for good distribution. The circulating mode provides only cold air. The air conditioner cools well.

Controls and displays

○ The controls are badly dated. Two hard-to-find buttons on the spokes of the steering wheel sound the horn. Our drivers often grabbed the remote-mirror lever when they wanted the headlight switch. Under some sunny conditions, reflections obscure the gauges. The climate controls are small and stiff, and the mode selector isn't lighted.

Cargo area

⊖ The cargo box is a little larger than that of the *Ranger, Sonoma,* and *Tacoma,* and the floor is conveniently low. The side rails have four stake pockets and four holes to receive tie-down hooks. Our *Club Cab* can carry a 1360-pound payload, including passengers. The rear-seat cushions fold up against the back of the cab, revealing shallow covered bins underneath. The jack resides in the right bin; the left bin can hide small articles.

Safety

A locking tang on the front passenger's safety belt allows you to secure a child safety seat without a clip. Theoretically, the rear bench seat can accommodate a child seat, but installing one is difficult because the buckle ends are too long and the center position too narrow.

In a government crash test of a 1994 regular-cab *Dakota,* the passenger dummy fared well; the driver dummy, especially well.

Predicted reliability

● The *Dakota* has proved troublesome over the years.

Based on a November 1995 report.

Dodge Ram

Price range: $13,741–$20,650
Cost factor: 88%
Depreciation: ○

All new in 1994 and much refined since then, the *Ram* still won't let you forget you're driving a truck. Handling is awkward but steady. The front seats are roomy and comfortable, and the control panel is nicely laid out. Even the regular-cab models have generous storage room behind the reclining seatbacks. Extended-cab (Club Cab) models have a rear bench seat for three but no third door. We consider the 5.9-liter V8 to be the best all-around engine — or the 5.9-liter turbodiesel Six if you plan to put in hours using the *Ram* as a work truck. Consider the massive V10 engine only if you intend on doing some serious hauling.

Predicted reliability ◒

Ford F-Series

Price range: $14,430–$25,855
Cost factor: 89%
Depreciation: NA

This has been the best-selling vehicle—car or truck—in the United States for years. The light-duty *F-150* has been completely redesigned as a 1997 model, and it looks impressive. Engines range from a 4.2-liter V6 to a 4.6-liter V8. Its interior is carlike and well laid out, with dual air bags. Four-wheel anti-lock brakes are finally available. Extended-cab models have a handy third door on the passenger's side to ease loading.

Predicted reliability

New model, no data.

Ford Ranger 4x2 Super Cab XLT ✓

Price range: $10,555–$19,890
Cost factor: 91%
Depreciation: ⊖

Overview

When you're behind the wheel, the *Ranger* feels more carlike than the three pickups it was tested with: the *GMC Sonoma, Dodge Dakota,* and *Toyota Tacoma.* Even so, it performs well as a truck.

Acceleration

⊖ The optional 4.0-liter V6 is responsive. A 2.3-liter Four and a five-speed manual transmission are standard.

Transmission

⊖ The tested four-speed automatic transmission usually shifts smoothly, but it sometimes bumps into and out of overdrive.

Economy

● You can expect to average about 18 mpg on Regular fuel with the V6 power train.

Routine handling

○ Compact pickups don't handle like cars. Their body-on-frame construction tends to flex more, blunting road feel. The *Ranger's* steering feels vague and imprecise, but it corners quite tidily for a pickup, with only moderate lean.

Emergency handling

○ Our avoidance maneuver, a rapid left-right lane change, temporarily overwhelmed the power steering, increasing the steering effort through the turns. Even so, the truck wasn't too difficult to control.

Braking

○ The *Ranger* stopped straight and fairly short in all our braking tests.

Ride, normal load

◒ The suspension absorbs big bumps fairly well. Sharp bumps deliver stiff, rubbery kicks, and uneven roads induce side-to-side rocking.

Ride, full load

◒ A full load smooths the ride a little.

Noise

⊖ The cabin is quiet except when the engine is revved.

Driving position

⊖ Without the optional six-way power seat, short drivers can't see out well. Even tall drivers might like to sit higher, but at least they'll find plenty of leg- and headroom.

Front seating

⊖ The optional bucket seats have an adjustment for the lumbar bulge and retractable bolsters for thigh support. Those seats are generally comfortable and supportive.

Rear seating

● The pair of side-facing jump seats in the rear are tiny and flimsy.

Access

○ A low floor, wide door openings, and flush sills facilitate access to the front seats. Access to the rear is awkward.

Climate system

⊖ The system provides ample cooling. Heat comes reasonably quickly too, with good airflow and even distribution.

Controls and displays

⊖ The new dashboard is attractive and well laid out. The climate controls are low and recessed, but their rotary knobs operate easily.

Cargo area

○ The six-foot cargo box is typical of compact pickups. Its load floor is conveniently low, and the tailgate is easy to remove without tools. The bed's side rails have four stake pockets, four tie-down hook holes, and provision for two-tier loading—notches for 2x6s laid across the bed. As equipped, our *Ranger* can carry 1200 pounds of people and cargo.

Safety

The front shoulder belts have adjustable upper anchors for better comfort and fit. When tested, the *Ranger* had only a driver's air bag. A passenger's air bag became optional this year, making the *Ranger* and *Mazda* B-Series the only pickups to offer one. Since a rear-facing infant carrier shouldn't be placed where an air bag could deploy, the 1996 *Ranger/Mazda* will have a switch to disable the passenger's air bag. A regular child safety seat can occupy the 1995 model's passenger seat, if you secure it with a cinch clip. Pickups aren't required to meet any bumper standards, and the bumpers on the *Ranger* are higher than those of passenger cars, so we didn't perform our usual bumper-basher tests.

The 1995 *Ranger* protected its occupants well in the government's 35-mph crash test.

Predicted reliability

○ *Rangers* have compiled an average reliability record.

Based on a November 1995 report.

GMC Sierra C/K

***Price range:** $14,086–$20,702*
***Cost factor:** 88%*
Depreciation: ⊖

See CHEVROLET C/K.

GMC Sonoma 4x2 Club Coupe

***Price range:** $11,090–$19,336*
***Cost factor:** 92%*
Depreciation: ●

Overview

The *Sonoma* performed nearly as well as the *Ford Ranger*, but reliability wasn't as good in the first year of production.

Acceleration

⊖ The optional 4.3-liter V6 is powerful. The base engine is a 2.2-liter Four; the base transmission, a five-speed manual.

Transmission

⊖ The tested four-speed automatic shifts smoothly.

Economy

● About 17 mpg on Regular fuel.

Routine handling

○ The *Sonoma* leans a bit more than the *Ranger* in corners, and it doesn't handle curves quite as neatly. A washboard road can make the rear skitter to the side.

Emergency handling

○ In hard turns, the *Sonoma* wants to plow ahead. Nevertheless, it negotiated our avoidance maneuver fairly easily and showed no nasty traits.

Braking

◒ The brake pedal needs a disconcertingly long and firm prod to make anything happen. Stops from 60 mph were a bit long in our standard wet and dry track tests. The *Sonoma* stopped fairly straight in our wet divided-pavement test, where the track is slicker under one side of the truck than under the other.

Ride, normal load

◒ The *Sonoma's* ride is firm and jiggly. On bumpy roads, the rubbery bounding and pitching can become uncomfortable. Undulations at highway speeds make the truck bounce.

Ride, full load

◒ A full load improves the ride noticeably.

Noise

⊖ The *Sonoma* would have been as quiet inside as most sedans if not for the squeaks and rattles that plagued our truck.

Driving position

⊖ Despite the lack of a seat-height adjuster, practically anyone should be able to find a good driving position and see well over the hood. Legroom is just adequate for tall people, and headroom is generous. One carp: The accelerator is too far left.

Front seating

○ The *Club Coupe* comes with two front bucket seats and a console in between. Our truck's extra-cost high-back bucket seats provide generally satisfactory support. Power adjustment isn't available.

Rear seating

● Tiny, folding jump seats are handy when needed for emergencies.

Access

○ Front seat access is easy. Nudging the passenger seatback forward folds it down and scoots the seat well forward. But even so, crawling into the back is awkward.

Climate system

⊜ The system works very well; the heat is supplied quickly and amply, and the cooling is quick and effective.

Controls and displays

⊖ The dash is fairly well laid out, with some exceptions. It's easy to hit the large headlight rocker switch instead of the interior light switch. There's no "flash-to-pass" feature. And the climate controls are too far to the right.

Cargo area

○ The six-foot cargo box has a low load floor, a quickly detachable tailgate, provision for two-tier stacking, and four tie-down anchors—but no stake pockets. With the standard heavy-duty suspension, it can carry a 1042-pound payload. An optional "smooth ride" suspension cuts 200 pounds from the *Sonoma's* payload capacity. The *Club Coupe* has a large storage area behind the front seats.

Safety

A switchable retractor on the front passenger's belt lets you install a child seat without a cinch clip. The rear jump seats have only lap belts. In government crash tests of the 1995 *Chevrolet S-10*, the *Sonoma's* twin, the passenger dummy was badly "injured" and the driver dummy was probably "killed."

Predicted reliability

● The *Sonoma* and *Chevrolet S-10* have racked up many more problems than average.

Based on a November 1995 report.

Isuzu Hombre

***Price range:** $10,999–$12,063*
***Cost factor:** 90%*
***Depreciation:** NA*

The *Hombre*, new this year, is basically a *Chevrolet* S-series pickup with different sheet metal. But whereas the *Chevrolet* is built in Louisiana, the *Hombre* is built in Brazil. It's limited to a regular cab, standard bed, and two-wheel drive. The only available power train is Chevrolet's base Four, which is barely adequate, and a five-speed manual transmission. Our concerns with this model include the subpar reliability of the *Chevrolet* S-series. And although the *Hombre* has a different body, the S pickup's poor showing in government crash tests doesn't inspire confidence.

Predicted reliability

New model, no data.

Mazda B–Series

***Price range:** $9,925–$20,715*
***Cost factor:** 90%*
Depreciation: ⊖

See FORD RANGER.

Nissan Truck

Price range: *$10,999–$19,549*
Cost factor: *92%*
Depreciation: ○

This basic compact pickup is made in Tennessee, in the same factory that produces the *Sentra.* It's available in either two- or four-wheel drive. For 1996, it finally gets a driver's air bag. The V6 has been dropped, leaving only the Four. Antilock brakes are available on the rear wheels only—an inadequate arrangement. The interior is nicely laid out, with an instrument panel that is similar to those in *Nissan* sedans.

Predicted reliability ○

Toyota T100

Price range: *$14,448–$23,578*
Cost factor: *89%*
Depreciation: ○

The *T100* is one of the few imported pickup trucks—not at all that surprising when you consider that imported trucks carry a steep 25-percent tariff. The *T100* is a full-size pickup, designed for hauling and towing. But if you expect it to do much of either, choose the V6 rather than the standard Four. Controls are easy to reach and see.

The *T100* costs quite a bit for what you get, but it has proven quite reliable.

Predicted reliability ⊖

Toyota Tacoma 4x2 Xtracab

Price range: *$12,028–$22,128*
Cost factor: *89%*
Depreciation: *NA*

Overview

A smooth and responsive power train and Toyota's history of producing reliable pickups don't make up for poor brakes, poor seating, and a flimsy cargo box.

Acceleration

⊖ The 3.4-liter V6 accelerates aggressively. The base engines are a 2.4-liter Four in two-wheel-drive models, a 2.7-liter Four with four-wheel drive. A five-speed manual transmission is standard.

Transmission

⊜ The tested four-speed automatic has well-chosen gear ratios, and it shifts smoothly.

Economy

◒ With the V6 and automatic transmission, expect to average about 21 mpg, on Regular fuel.

Routine handling

◒ The *Tacoma* changes direction reluctantly, partly because the steering is slow and numb. The rear tires break loose easily when you prod the throttle. That could provoke a skid, especially on slick or rough pavement.

Emergency handling

○ It leans a lot and tries to plow ahead in hard turns, but it threaded through our avoidance maneuver reasonably steadily.

Braking

● Don't even think of buying this truck without antilock brakes. With the non-antilock brakes in our truck, stops were especially long, and the truck slewed sideways on wet pavement. In our wet divided-pavement test, the *Tacoma* consistently spun out of control, as many vehicles without antilock brakes are apt to do.

Ride, normal load

● Even slightly bumpy pavement makes the *Tacoma* leap and bound. Minor pavement flaws elicit hard kicks, snappy pitches, and rubbery shakes, and the suspension easily runs out of travel with a thud on bigger bumps. The truck feels jittery even on smooth expressways.

Ride, full load

● A full load makes the ride worse.

Noise

⊖ The cab remains fairly quiet in expressway driving.

Driving position

○ The front seat is too low, and its height can't be adjusted. A five-footer can barely see out. Legroom for six-footers is a bit tight.

Front seating

○ The slablike split bench front seat gives little side support. The padding is firm—too firm on the seatback.

Rear seating

● The fold-down rear seats are for emergencies: The cushions are small, headroom is tight, and knee room is inadequate.

Access

○ Getting into the front is easy; the rear is a good deal more challenging.

Climate system

⊜ The system supplies abundant heated or cooled air, and it quickly clears fogged windows.

Controls and displays

⊜ The controls are logical and well arranged. The climate controls are straightforward, but they're blocked when you use the cup-holders.

Cargo area

○ The cargo box is flimsy. Tying a dirt-trail bike into the bed buckled the front of the box and dented the back of the cab as well. (We straightened the rail and reinforced it with a steel cross-beam.) The *Tacoma* has no stake pockets or provision for two-tier loading, but it provides four tie-downs. Our version of the truck is rated to carry a 1460-pound payload. The rear seat cushions fold up against the back of the cab, revealing a pair of small covered bins. Two more cubbies are built into the side walls.

Safety

You can adjust the upper shoulder-belt anchors for comfort, and you can secure a child seat in the front passenger's seat without a cinch clip. Installing a child safety seat in the rear is difficult because room is limited and the buckle ends of the safety belts are too long.

The government has yet to crash-test this truck.

Predicted reliability

Insufficient data. Previous *Toyota* pick-ups have enjoyed the best reliability record of any light truck. The *Tacoma*, too, is likely to be very reliable.

Based on a November 1995 report.

10

FACTS AND FIGURES

The tables on the following pages, as published in the April 1996 *Consumer Reports*, give mechanical specifications and body dimensions for the 1996 cars. Most of the dimensions come from our own tests and measurements; the specifications come largely from manufacturers. Throughout, **NA** means "not available."

Passengers is the maximum a car can hold, front/middle/rear, sometimes not too comfortably.

Drive tells which wheels move the car. **All-**wheel drive means the four-wheel-drive system is permanently engaged. That type is found in some sedans, sporty cars, sport-utility vehicles, and minivans. All-wheel-drive systems found in a few SUVs are **selectable** with a switch or lever. The **part-time** four-wheel-drive systems found in many trucks and sport-utility vehicles shouldn't be used on dry roads.

Fuel: Overall mileage is our own measurement, based on a realistic mix of expressway, country road, and city driving. It's available only for cars we've tested recently. **Fuel type** and **capacity** are from manufacturer's specifications.

Engines available notes displacement in liters, number of cylinders and engine type, and maximum horsepower, as specified by the manufacturer. **Transmissions available** notes **manual** or **automatic**, with the number of forward speeds. "CVT" means "continuously variable transmission." The engine/transmission versions in bold indicate the model tested to get the overall mileage.

Dimensions: Each car's **length**, **wheelbase**, and **width** are from manufacturer's data. **Turning circle** is our measurement of the clearance required by the front bumper for a U-turn. **Weight** and **percent weight front/rear** are measured on our scale, using a typically equipped car with the fuel, oil, and coolant topped off. About 50 inches from the **door top** to the ground is a reasonable minimum for easy entry by an average-size adult. **Luggage capacity** comes from government figures (not available for sport-utility vehicles, minivans, or pickup trucks).

Seating room: For three adults to sit abreast comfortably, total **front** or **rear shoulder room** should be 57 inches or more. **Front legroom** is the maximum distance from the heel of the accelerator to the base of the seatback, with the seat adjusted as far back as it will go. Drivers of average height should look for at least 40 inches. **Front** and **rear headroom** is the clearance above the head of a 5-foot 9-inch person. Zero inches means the person's head touched the roof or was even bowed by it. **Rear legroom** is measured with the front seat adjusted to provide 40 inches of legroom; adults need at least 27 inches of legroom in the rear seat to sit comfortably. (For vehicles with three seats, these measurements are for middle-row seats.)

Listed alphabetically

Make and model	Passengers	Drive	Fuel			Engines available
			OVERALL MILEAGE	TYPE	CAPACITY	
Acura CL	2/3	Front	—	Premium	17.2 gal.	2.2 Four (145 hp); 3.0 V6 (195 hp)
Acura Integra	2/3	Front	30 mpg	Regular; premium	13.2	**1.8 Four (142 hp)**; 1.8 Four (170 hp)
Acura RL	2/3	Front	—	Premium	18.0	3.5 V6 (210 hp)
Acura SLX	2/3	Part-time 4WD	—	Regular	22.5	3.2 V6 (190 hp)
Acura TL	2/3	Front	23	Premium	17.2	**2.5 Five (176 hp)**; 3.2 V6 (200 hp)
Audi A4	2/3	Front or all	22	Premium	16.4	**2.8 V6 (172 hp)**
Audi A6	2/3	Front or all	—	Premium	21.1	2.8 V6 (172 hp)
BMW 3-Series	2/3	Rear	24	Premium	17.0	1.9 Four (138 hp); **2.8 Six (190 hp)**; 3.0 Six (240 hp)
BMW 318ti	2/3	Rear	—	Premium	13.7	1.9 Four (138 hp)
BMW 5-Series	2/3	Rear	—	Premium	21.4	4.0 V8 (282 hp)
BMW 740iL	2/3	Rear	—	Premium	21.5	4.4 V8 (282 hp)
BMW Z3	2/—	Rear	—	Premium	13.5	1.9 Four (138 hp)
Buick Century	3/3	Front	22	Regular	16.5	2.2 Four (120 hp); **3.1 V6 (160 hp)**
Buick Le Sabre	3/3	Front	20	Regular	18.0	**3.8 V6 (205 hp)**
Buick Park Avenue	3/3	Front	—	Regular; premium	18.0	3.8 V6 (205 hp); 3.8 V6 supercharged (240 hp)
Buick Regal	3/3	Front	20	Regular	16.5	3.1 V6 (160 hp); **3.8 V6 (205 hp)**
Buick Riviera	3/3	Front	17	Regular; premium	20.0	3.8 V6 (205 hp); **3.8 V6 supercharged (240 hp)**
Buick Roadmaster	3/3	Rear	—	Regular	23.0	5.7 V8 (260 hp)
Buick Skylark	3/3	Front	—	Regular	15.2	2.4 Four (150 hp); 3.1 V6 (155 hp)
Cadillac De Ville	3/3	Front	—	Premium	20.0	4.6 V8 (275-300 hp)
Cadillac Eldorado	2/3	Front	15	Premium	20.0	4.6 V8 (275 hp); **4.6 V8 (300 hp)**
Cadillac Fleetwood	3/3	Rear	—	Regular	23.0	5.7 V8 (260 hp)
Cadillac Seville	3/3	Front	17	Premium	20.0	4.6 V8 (275 hp); **4.6 V8 (300 hp)**
Chevrolet Astro	2/3/3	Rear or all	—	Regular	27.0	4.3 V6 (190 hp)
Chevrolet Beretta	2/3	Front	—	Regular	15.6	2.2 Four (120 hp); 3.1 V6 (155 hp)
Chevrolet Blazer	3/3	Rear or all	17	Regular	19.0	**4.3 V6 (190 hp)**
Chevrolet C/K	3/3	Rear/part-time 4WD	—	Regular	34.0	4.3 V6 (200 hp); 5.0 V8 (220 hp); 5.7 V8 (250 hp); others
Chevrolet Camaro	2/2	Rear	19	Regular	15.5	**3.8 V6 (200 hp)**; 5.7 V8 (275 hp)
Chevrolet Caprice	3/3	Rear	17	Regular	23.0	4.3 V8 (200 hp); **5.7 V8 (260 hp)**
Chevrolet Cavalier	2/3	Front	26	Regular	15.2	**2.2 Four (120 hp)**; 2.4 Four (150 hp)
Chevrolet Corsica	3/3	Front	25	Regular	15.6	**2.2 Four (120 hp)**; 3.1 V6 (155 hp)
Chevrolet Corvette	2/—	Rear	17	Regular; premium	20.0	**5.7 V8 (300 hp)**; 5.7 V8 (330 hp)
Chevrolet Lumina	3/3	Front	21	Regular	17.1	**3.1 V6 (160 hp)**; 3.4 V6 (215 hp)
Chevrolet Lumina Van	2/3/2	Front	18	Regular	20.0	**3.4 V6 (180 hp)**
Chevrolet Monte Carlo	3/3	Front	18	Regular	17.1	3.1 V6 (160 hp); **3.4 V6 (215 hp)**
Chevrolet S-Series	3/2	Rear/part-time 4WD	17	Regular	20.0	2.2 Four (118 hp); 4.3 V6 (180 hp); **4.3 V6 (190 hp)**
Chevrolet Suburban	3/3/3	Rear/part-time 4WD	—	Regular; diesel	42.0	5.7 V8 (250 hp); 6.5 V8 turbodiesel (190 hp); 7.4 V8 (290 hp)
Chevrolet Tahoe	3/3	Rear/part-time 4WD	—	Regular; diesel	30.0	5.7 V8 (250 hp); 6.5 V8 turbodiesel (180 hp)
Chrysler Cirrus	2/3	Front	22	Regular	16.0	2.4 Four (150 hp); **2.5 V6 (168 hp)**
Chrysler Concorde	2/3	Front	21	Regular; midgrade	18.0	3.3 V6 (161 hp); **3.5 V6 (214 hp)**
Chrysler LHS	3/3	Front	20	Mid-grade	18.0	**3.5 V6 (214 hp)**
Chrysler Sebring	2/3	Front	22	Regular	15.9	2.0 Four (140 hp); **2.5 V6 (163 hp)**
Chrysler Sebring Convertible	2/2	Front	—	Regular	16.0	2.4 Four (150 hp); 2.5 V6 (164 hp)
Chrysler Town & Country	2/2/3	Front	18	Regular	20.0	**3.3 V6 (158 hp)**; 3.8 V6 (166 hp)
Dodge Avenger	2/3	Front	22	Regular	15.9	2.0 Four (140 hp); **2.5 V6 (163 hp)**
Dodge Caravan	2/2/3	Front	—	Regular	20.0	2.4 Four (150 hp); 3.0 V6 (150 hp); 3.3 V6 (158 hp); 3.8 V6 (166 hp)
Dodge Dakota	3/3	Rear/part-time 4WD	17	Regular	22.0	2.5 Four (120 hp); **3.9 V6 (175 hp)**; 5.2 V8 (220 hp)
Dodge Grand Caravan	2/2/3	Front	18	Regular	20.0	2.4 Four (150 hp); 3.0 V6 (150 hp); **3.3 V6 (158 hp)**; 3.8 V6 (166 hp)
Dodge Intrepid	3/3	Front	20	Regular; midgrade	18.0	**3.3 V6 (161 hp)**; 3.5 V6 (214 hp)
Dodge Neon	2/3	Front	26	Regular	12.5	**2.0 Four (132 hp)**; 2.0 Four (150 hp)
Dodge Ram	3/3	Rear/part-time 4WD	—	Regular	26.0	3.9 V6 (170 hp); 5.2 V8 (220 hp); 5.9 V8 (230 hp); others
Dodge Stratus	2/3	Front	20	Regular	16.0	2.0 Four (132 hp); **2.4 Four (150 hp)**; 2.5 V6 (168 hp)

Transmissions available	Dimensions								Seating room					
	LENGTH	WHEELBASE	WIDTH	TURNING CIRCLE	WEIGHT	% WEIGHT FRONT/REAR	DOOR TOP	LUGGAGE CAPACITY	FRONT SHOULDER	FRONT LEGROOM	FRONT HEADROOM	REAR SHOULDER	REAR LEGROOM	REAR HEADROOM
Man 5; auto 4	190 in.	107 in.	70 in.	NA	3065 lb.	63/37	NA	12 cu.ft.	NA	NA	NA	NA	NA	NA
Man 5; auto 4	178	103	67	39 ft.	2665	62/38	49.0 in.	12	52.0 in.	40.0 in.	4.0 in.	51.0 in.	28.0 in.	1.0 in.
Auto 4	195	115	71	NA	3700	60/40	NA	14	NA	NA	NA	NA	NA	NA
Auto 4	184	109	69	40	4365	51/49	66.0	NA	57.5	41.0	5.0	58.0	32.0	5.0
Auto 4	192	112	70	39	3278	59/41	50.0	14	55.0	43.0	3.0	53.5	28.5	2.5
Man 5; **auto 5**	178	103	68	37	3222	63/37	50.0	14	54.0	43.5	3.5	52.0	26.0	2.5
Auto 4	193	106	70	37	3405	61/39	51.5	17	56.5	44.0	2.5	56.0	31.0	3.0
Man 5; **auto 4**	175	106	67	36	3250	51/49	49.5	10	53.5	42.5	3.5	53.0	26.5	3.0
Man 5; auto 4	166	106	67	36	2790	53/47	49.5	11	54.5	40.5	4.0	52.5	27.0	2.0
Man 6; auto 4 or 5	186	105	69	38	3675	52/48	51.0	13	54.5	42.5	3.0	55.5	27.0	2.5
Auto 5	196	115	73	NA	4145	51/49	NA	13	58.5	NA	NA	58.5	NA	NA
Man 5; auto 4	159	96	67	NA	2690	52/48	NA	6	51.5	NA	NA	—	—	—
Auto 3 or **4**	189	105	69	43	3100	66/34	50.5	16	56.5	41.0	4.0	56.0	25.5	2.5
Auto 4	200	111	74	42	3450	65/35	50.5	17	59.5	42.5	6.5	59.5	32.0	4.5
Auto 4	205	111	74	42	3640	63/37	51.0	20	60.0	41.0	4.0	59.0	31.0	3.0
Auto 4	195	108	73	43	3455	64/36	50.5	16	58.0	41.5	5.0	58.5	26.5	1.5
Auto 4	207	114	75	42	3770	62/38	50.0	17	58.0	42.5	2.5	52.5	29.5	2.0
Auto 4	216	116	78	45	4195	55/45	53.5	21	64.5	41.0	5.0	65.0	30.5	4.5
Auto 4	189	103	68	41	3055	65/35	50.0	13	54.5	43.0	3.0	53.5	29.0	2.0
Auto 4	210	114	77	44	3985	62/38	50.0	20	62.0	43.0	5.0	62.5	32.5	4.0
Auto 4	202	108	76	42	3840	64/36	49.5	15	59.0	43.0	4.0	57.5	29.0	3.0
Auto 4	225	122	78	NA	4480	54/46	53.5	21	65.5	42.0	5.0	65.5	33.0	4.5
Auto 4	204	111	74	44	3935	63/37	49.5	14	59.0	43.0	3.0	57.5	31.0	2.0
Auto 4	187	111	78	44	4520	53/47	68.0	NA	64.5	41.0	4.0	67.5	33.5	4.0
Man 5; auto 3 or 4	184	103	68	39	2785	64/36	50.5	13	55.0	42.0	3.5	55.0	26.0	2.0
Man 5; **auto 4**	181	107	67	42	4180	55/45	59.5	NA	57.0	42.0	4.0	57.5	30.0	4.0
Man 5; auto 4	219	142	77	NA	3829	61/39	70.4	NA	65.0	41.0	5.0	64.0	22.5	3.0
Man 5 or 6; **auto 4**	193	101	74	43	3350	56/44	46.5	13	58.0	42.0	3.0	53.5	24.0	1.5
Auto 4	214	116	78	45	4205	55/45	52.5	20	65.5	42.0	4.5	65.5	29.0	2.0
Man 5; **auto 3** or 4	180	104	67	38	2765	64/36	50.0	14	54.5	41.0	4.5	53.5	29.0	2.0
Auto 3 or 4	184	103	68	39	2785	64/36	50.5	13	55.0	42.0	3.5	55.0	26.0	2.0
Man 6; auto 4	179	96	71	43	3380	52/48	44.0	NA	53.5	42.5	3.5	—	—	—
Auto 4	201	108	73	42	3395	64/36	51.0	16	58.0	42.5	4.5	57.0	29.5	3.5
Auto 4	192	110	75	44	3890	60/40	60.5	NA	61.5	42.0	4.5	63.5	31.5	4.0
Auto 4	201	108	72	43	3450	65/35	49.0	16	57.5	41.5	3.5	56.5	28.5	2.0
Man 5; **auto 4**	204	123	68	43	3560	61/39	58.5	NA	57.0	42.0	4.5	18.5	46.0	2.0
Auto 4	220	132	76	49	5640	48/52	67.0	NA	66.0	42.5	5.0	66.0	31.0	3.0
Auto 4	199	118	76	46	5343	52/48	66.5	NA	65.0	41.5	4.5	65.0	30.0	3.5
Auto 4	186	108	71	39	3145	64/36	48.5	14	55.0	42.0	4.0	54.0	30.0	2.0
Auto 4	202	113	74	40	3550	64/36	49.5	19	59.0	42.0	5.0	57.5	30.5	2.0
Auto 4	207	113	74	41	3605	64/36	49.0	18	59.5	43.0	5.0	58.0	34.0	3.0
Man 5; **auto 4**	187	104	70	43	3175	64/36	46.5	12	53.0	41.5	3.0	53.5	27.5	2.5
Auto 4	193	106	69	NA	3350	61/39	NA	11	55.0	NA	NA	49.0	NA	NA
Auto 4	200	119	76	42	4035	57/43	60.0	NA	62.5	40.0	5.5	64.5	30.0	5.0
Man 5; **auto 4**	187	104	69	43	3175	64/36	46.5	12	53.0	41.5	3.0	53.5	27.5	2.5
Auto 3 or 4	186	113	76	40	3985	59/41	60.0	NA	62.5	41.0	5.5	64.0	28.0	5.0
Man 5; **auto 4**	214	131	69	49	3740	59/41	59.0	NA	58.0	41.0	5.0	55.5	23.0	3.5
Auto 3 or **4**	200	119	76	42	4035	57/43	60.0	NA	62.5	40.0	5.5	64.5	30.0	5.0
Auto 4	202	113	74	41	3435	64/36	50.0	19	59.0	43.0	5.0	58.0	32.0	2.5
Man 5; **auto 3**	172	104	68	38	2600	64/36	49.5	12	53.5	41.5	5.0	52.0	29.0	2.0
Man 5; auto 4	224	135	79	48	4785	57/43	67.0	NA	66.0	41.5	5.5	67.5	23.5	4.0
Man 5; **auto 4**	186	108	71	39	3085	63/37	49.0	14	55.0	41.5	4.0	55.0	30.5	2.0

Make and model	Passengers	Drive	Fuel: Overall mileage	Fuel: Type	Fuel: Capacity	Engines available
Eagle Summit	2/3	Front	34 mpg	Regular	13.2 gal.	1.5 Four (92 hp); **1.8 Four (113 hp)**
Eagle Summit Wagon	2/3	Front or all	24	Regular	14.5	1.8 Four (113-119 hp); **2.4 Four (136 hp)**
Eagle Talon	2/2	Front or all	—	Regular; premium	16.9	2.0 Four (140 hp); 2.0 Four turbo (205-210 hp)
Eagle Vision	2/3	Front	21	Regular; midgrade	18.0	3.3 V6 (161 hp); **3.5 V6 (214 hp)**
Ford Aerostar	2/2/3	Rear or all	—	Regular	21.0	3.0 V6 (140 hp); 4.0 V6 (155 hp)
Ford Aspire	2/2	Front	36	Regular	10.0	**1.3 Four (63 hp)**
Ford Bronco	2/3	Part-time 4WD	—	Regular	32.0	5.0 V8 (199 hp); 5.8 V8 (205 hp)
Ford Contour	2/3	Front	26	Regular	14.5	**2.0 Four (125 hp)**; 2.5 V6 (170 hp)
Ford Crown Victoria	3/3	Rear	19	Regular	20.0	4.6 V8 (190 hp); **4.6 V8 (210 hp)**
Ford Escort	2/3	Front	27	Regular	11.9	1.8 Four (127 hp); **1.9 Four (88 hp)**
Ford Explorer	3/3	Rear/selectable 4WD	17	Regular	22.0	**4.0 V6 (160 hp)**; 5.0 V8 (210 hp)
Ford F-Series	3/3	Rear/part-time 4WD	—	Regular	25.0	4.2 V6 (205 hp); 4.6 V8 (210 hp)
Ford Mustang	2/2	Rear	18	Regular	15.4	3.8 V6 (150 hp); **4.6 V8 (215 hp)**; 4.6 V8 (305 hp)
Ford Probe	2/2	Front	24	Regular; premium	15.5	2.0 Four (118 hp); **2.5 V6 (164 hp)**
Ford Ranger	3/2	Rear/part-time 4WD	18	Regular	20.0	2.3 Four (112 hp); 3.0 V6 (147 hp); **4.0 V6 (160 hp)**
Ford Taurus	3/3	Front	21	Regular	16.0	3.0 V6 (145 hp); **3.0 V6 (200 hp)**; 3.4 V8 (240 hp)
Ford Thunderbird	2/3	Rear	20	Regular	18.0	3.8 V6 (145 hp); **4.6 V8 (205 hp)**
Ford Windstar	2/2/3	Front	20	Regular	20.0	3.0 V6 (150 hp); **3.8 V6 (200 hp)**
GMC Jimmy	3/3	Rear or all	17	Regular	19.0	**4.3 V6 (190 hp)**
GMC Safari	2/3/3	Rear or all	—	Regular	27.0	4.3 V6 (190 hp)
GMC Sierra C/K	3/3	Rear/part-time 4WD	—	Regular	34.0	4.3 V6 (200 hp); 5.0 V8 (220 hp); 5.7 V8 (250 hp); others
GMC Sonoma	3/2	Rear/part-time 4WD	17	Regular	20.0	2.2 Four (118 hp); 4.3 V6 (180 hp); **4.3 V6 (190 hp)**
GMC Suburban	3/3/3	Rear/part-time 4WD	—	Regular; diesel	42.0	5.7 V8 (250 hp); 6.5 V8 turbodiesel (190 hp); 7.4 V8 (290 hp)
GMC Yukon	3/3	Rear/part-time 4WD	—	Regular; diesel	30.0	5.7 V8 (250 hp); 6.5 V8 turbodiesel (180 hp)
Geo Metro	2/2	Front	29	Regular	10.6	1.0 Three (55 hp); **1.3 Four (70 hp)**
Geo Prizm	2/3	Front	33	Regular	13.2	1.6 Four (105 hp); **1.8 Four (115 hp)**
Geo Tracker	2/2	Rear/part-time 4WD	—	Regular	11.1	1.6 Four (95 hp)
Honda Accord	2/3	Front	21	Regular	17.0	2.2 Four (130 hp); 2.2 Four (145 hp); **2.7 V6 (170 hp)**
Honda Civic	2/3	Front	31	Regular	11.9	**1.6 Four (106 hp)**; 1.6 Four (113 hp); 1.6 Four (127 hp)
Honda Civic del Sol	2/—	Front	32	Regular; premium	11.9	1.6 Four (106-160 hp); **1.6 Four (125 hp)**
Honda Odyssey	2/3/2	Front	21	Regular	17.2	**2.2 Four (140 hp)**
Honda Passport	2/3	Rear/part-time 4WD	16	Regular	21.9	2.6 Four (120 hp); **3.2 V6 (190 hp)**
Honda Prelude	2/2	Front	26	Regular; premium	15.9	2.2 Four (135-190 hp); **2.3 Four (160 hp)**
Hyundai Accent	2/3	Front	28	Regular	11.9	**1.5 Four (92 hp)**
Hyundai Elantra	2/3	Front	—	Regular	14.5	1.8 Four (130 hp)
Hyundai Sonata	2/3	Front	21	Regular	17.2	2.0 Four (137 hp); **3.0 V6 (142 hp)**
Infiniti G20	2/3	Front	29	Regular	15.9	**2.0 Four (140 hp)**
Infiniti I30	2/3	Front	23	Premium	18.5	**3.0 V6 (190 hp)**
Infiniti J30	2/3	Rear	20	Premium	19.0	**3.0 V6 (210 hp)**
Infiniti Q45	2/3	Rear	17	Premium	22.5	**4.5 V8 (278 hp)**
Isuzu Hombre	3/—	Rear	—	Regular	20.0	2.2 Four (118 hp)
Isuzu Oasis	2/3/2	Front	21	Regular	17.2	**2.2 Four (140 hp)**
Isuzu Rodeo	2/3	Rear/part-time 4WD	16	Regular	21.9	2.6 Four (120 hp); **3.2 V6 (190 hp)**
Isuzu Trooper	2/3	Rear/part-time 4WD	15	Regular	22.5	**3.2 V6 (190 hp)**
Jaguar XJ6	2/3	Rear	—	Premium	23.1	4.0 Six (245 hp); 4.0 Six supercharged (322 hp)
Jeep Cherokee	2/3	Rear/selectable 4WD	—	Regular	20.2	2.5 Four (125 hp); 4.0 Six (190 hp)
Jeep Grand Cherokee	2/3	Rear or all	15	Regular	23.0	4.0 Six (185 hp); **5.2 V8 (220 hp)**
Jeep Wrangler	2/2	Part-time 4WD	—	Regular	15.3	2.5 Four (120 hp); 4.0 Six (181 hp)
Land Rover Discovery	2/3/2	All	13	Premium	23.4	**4.0 V8 (182 hp)**
Lexus ES300	2/3	Front	22	Premium	18.5	**3.0 V6 (188 hp)**
Lexus GS300	2/3	Rear	21	Premium	21.1	**3.0 Six (220 hp)**
Lexus LS400	2/3	Rear	—	Premium	22.5	4.0 V8 (260 hp)
Lexus LX450	2/3/2	All	—	Regular	25.1	4.5 Six (212 hp)
Lexus SC400/SC300	2/3	Rear	19	Premium	20.6	3.0 Six (225 hp); **4.0 V8 (260 hp)**
Lincoln Continental	3/3	Front	—	Premium	18.0	4.6 V8 (260 hp)
Lincoln Mark VIII	2/3	Rear	19	Premium	18.0	**4.6 V8 (280 hp)**; 4.6 V8 (290 hp)
Lincoln Town Car	3/3	Rear	—	Regular	20.0	4.6 V8 (210 hp)
Mazda 626	2/3	Front	25	Regular	15.5	**2.0 Four (118 hp)**; 2.5 V6 (164 hp)
Mazda B-Series	3/2	Rear/part-time 4WD	18	Regular	20.0	2.3 Four (112 hp); 3.0 V6 (147 hp); **4.0 V6 (160 hp)**
Mazda MPV	2/2/3	Rear or all	—	Regular	19.6	3.0 V6 (155 hp)
Mazda MX-5 Miata	2/—	Rear	29	Regular	12.7	**1.8 Four (133 hp)**
Mazda MX-6	2/3	Front	24	Regular; premium	15.5	2.0 Four (118 hp); **2.5 V6 (164 hp)**
Mazda Millenia	2/3	Front	22	Premium	18.0	**2.3 V6 supercharged (210 hp)**; 2.5 V6 (170 hp)
Mazda Protegé	2/3	Front	26	Regular	13.2	1.5 Four (92 hp); **1.8 Four (122 hp)**
Mazda RX-7	2/—	Rear	19	Premium	20.0	**1.3 rotary turbo (255 hp)**
Mercedes-Benz C-Class	2/3	Rear	20	Premium	16.4	2.2 Four (148 hp); **2.8 Six (194 hp)**
Mercedes-Benz E-Class	2/3	Rear	—	Diesel; premium	21.0	3.0 Six Diesel (134 hp); 3.2 Six (217 hp); 4.2 V8 (275 hp)
Mercury Cougar	2/3	Rear	20	Regular	18.0	3.8 V6 (145 hp); **4.6 V8 (205 hp)**

Transmissions available	Dimensions								Seating room					
	LENGTH	WHEELBASE	WIDTH	TURNING CIRCLE	WEIGHT	% WEIGHT FRONT/REAR	DOOR TOP	LUGGAGE CAPACITY	FRONT SHOULDER	FRONT LEGROOM	FRONT HEADROOM	REAR SHOULDER	REAR LEGROOM	REAR HEADROOM
Man 5; auto 3 or 4	174 in.	98 in.	66 in.	37 ft.	2390 lb.	62/38	48.5 in.	11 cu.ft.	54.0 in.	41.0 in.	4.5 in.	53.0 in.	26.5 in.	1.5 in.
Man 5; **auto 4**	169	99	67	38	3100	61/39	57.0	NA	55.0	40.0	2.5	55.0	29.5	5.0
Man 5; auto 4	172	99	69	41	3235	61/39	46.0	15	53.0	42.0	4.0	46.5	24.5	0.0
Auto 4	202	113	74	40	3550	64/36	49.5	19	59.0	42.0	5.0	57.5	30.5	2.0
Auto 4	190	119	72	45	4220	55/45	67.0	NA	60.0	41.0	5.0	62.5	30.0	3.5
Man 5; auto 3	156	94	66	34	2140	62/38	51.0	17	50.5	40.0	3.5	50.0	25.5	1.5
Man 5; auto 4	184	105	79	39	5005	50/50	66.5	NA	66.0	40.5	6.5	56.5	27.5	3.0
Man 5; **auto 4**	184	107	69	38	2910	65/35	51.0	14	54.0	41.0	4.0	53.0	28.5	2.0
Auto 4	212	114	78	43	4010	55/45	51.5	21	61.5	43.0	4.5	60.5	30.5	3.5
Man 5; **auto 4**	171	98	67	35	2565	61/39	49.0	17	53.0	41.0	3.5	53.5	27.5	4.5
Man 5; **auto 4**	189	112	70	40	4440	53/47	60.5	NA	56.0	42.5	3.5	56.0	29.5	5.0
Man 5; auto 4	222	139	78	NA	4400	58/42	67.0	NA	63.5	42.5	6.0	62.5	27.0	3.5
Man 5; **auto 4**	182	101	78	42	3450	58/42	49.0	10	53.5	41.5	4.5	52.0	23.0	0.0
Man 5; auto 4	180	103	70	39	2900	63/37	46.5	19	52.5	41.5	1.5	53.0	23.0	0.0
Man 5; **auto 4**	198	125	69	44	3680	60/40	59.0	NA	54.0	41.5	5.0	18.5	48.0	2.5
Auto 4	198	109	73	40	3516	64/36	50.0	16	58.5	43.0	5.5	56.0	31.5	2.0
Auto 4	200	113	73	39	3705	59/41	49.5	15	59.5	42.5	3.5	60.5	28.5	2.0
Auto 4	201	121	74	44	3940	61/39	61.5	NA	61.0	41.5	4.5	63.0	27.0	3.5
Man 5; **auto 4**	181	107	67	42	4180	55/45	59.5	NA	57.0	42.0	4.0	57.5	30.0	4.0
Auto 4	187	111	78	44	4520	53/47	68.0	NA	64.5	41.0	4.0	67.5	33.5	4.0
Man 5; auto 4	219	142	77	NA	3829	61/39	70.4	NA	65.0	41.0	5.0	64.0	22.5	3.0
Man 5; **auto 4**	204	123	68	43	3560	61/39	58.5	NA	57.0	42.0	4.5	18.5	46.0	2.0
Auto 4	220	132	76	49	5640	48/52	67.0	NA	66.0	42.5	5.0	66.0	31.0	3.0
Man 5; auto 4	199	118	76	46	5343	52/48	66.5	NA	65.0	41.5	4.5	65.0	30.0	3.5
Man 5; **auto 3**	164	93	63	35	2065	61/39	49.5	10	49.5	40.5	5.0	47.0	27.0	2.0
Man 5; auto 3 or 4	173	97	66	35	2510	61/39	48.5	13	54.5	41.5	1.5	53.0	26.0	1.0
Man 5; auto 3 or 4	143	87	64	36	2500	54/46	60.0	NA	51.5	41.0	6.0	51.0	25.5	4.5
Man 5; **auto 4**	188	107	70	41	3255	64/36	49.5	13	56.0	41.5	3.0	52.0	28.0	3.0
Man 5; **auto 4** or CVT	175	103	67	37	2440	62/38	49.0	12	52.0	42.0	5.5	51.0	28.5	3.0
Man 5; auto 4	157	93	67	33	2410	62/38	45.5	NA	51.5	42.0	3.0	—	—	—
Auto 4	187	111	71	41	3480	59/41	56.0	NA	57.5	42.0	4.0	57.5	30.5	4.0
Man 5; **auto 4**	177	109	66	40	4080	51/49	61.0	NA	56.0	40.5	2.5	55.5	33.5	3.5
Man 5; auto 4	175	100	70	39	2865	63/37	45.5	8	54.0	43.5	2.0	48.0	23.5	0.0
Man 5; **auto 4**	162	95	64	35	2290	63/37	49.0	11	52.5	40.5	3.5	51.5	27.5	2.5
Man 5; auto 4	174	100	67	NA	2700	63/37	NA	11	54.5	NA	NA	53.5	NA	NA
Man 5; **auto 4**	185	106	70	38	3095	63/37	49.5	13	58.0	42.5	4.0	56.0	30.5	3.0
Man 5; auto 4	175	100	67	39	2865	62/38	49.5	14	55.0	41.5	3.0	54.5	28.0	2.0
Man 5; **auto 4**	190	106	70	38	3195	63/37	50.0	14	57.0	42.0	3.0	56.5	30.0	2.5
Auto 4	191	109	70	40	3535	57/43	49.0	10	55.5	41.5	3.0	56.0	27.0	2.5
Auto 4	200	113	72	41	4250	58/42	50.0	15	58.0	42.5	2.5	57.0	29.0	2.0
Man 5	189	108	68	NA	2850	55/45	NA	NA	NA	NA	NA	—	—	—
Auto 4	187	111	71	41	3480	59/41	56.0	NA	57.5	42.0	4.0	57.5	30.5	4.0
Man 5; **auto 4**	177	109	66	40	4080	51/49	61.0	NA	56.0	40.5	2.5	55.5	33.5	3.5
Man 5; **auto 4**	184	109	69	40	4365	51/49	66.0	NA	57.5	41.0	5.0	58.0	32.0	5.0
Auto 4	196	113	71	42	4040	52/48	48.5	13	58.5	41.0	2.5	58.0	29.0	2.0
Man 5; auto 3 or 4	165	101	71	38	3420	57/43	58.5	NA	55.5	41.5	4.0	55.5	26.5	3.5
Auto 4	179	106	71	39	4090	57/43	60.5	NA	58.5	42.0	4.0	57.5	27.5	4.5
Man 5; auto 3	148	93	67	NA	3210	52/48	NA	NA	52.0	NA	NA	57.0	NA	NA
Man 5; **auto 4**	179	100	71	42	4535	48/52	65.0	NA	58.0	39.5	5.5	58.0	26.5	7.0
Auto 4	188	103	70	39	3400	62/38	49.5	14	56.0	42.0	1.5	55.0	28.5	2.5
Auto 5	195	109	71	38	3765	54/46	50.0	13	58.0	44.0	2.0	57.5	29.0	1.0
Auto 4	197	112	72	37	3800	55/45	51.0	14	58.0	42.5	2.0	56.5	32.5	2.0
Auto 4	188	112	76	43	5150	52/48	66.0	NA	59.0	40.5	4.0	59.0	26.5	3.0
Man 5; **auto 4**	191	106	71	39	3710	54/46	48.0	9	57.0	43.5	2.0	53.0	25.0	2.0
Auto 4	206	109	73	43	3975	62/38	51.0	18	57.0	42.0	3.5	56.5	29.5	3.0
Auto 4	207	113	75	40	3810	59/41	49.5	14	59.0	41.5	2.5	58.0	28.0	1.5
Auto 4	219	117	77	45	4055	54/46	53.0	22	62.0	41.0	4.5	62.0	31.5	3.0
Man 5; **auto 4**	184	103	69	39	2860	63/37	49.5	14	55.5	41.0	3.0	54.5	29.0	2.0
Man 5; **auto 4**	198	125	69	44	3680	60/40	59.0	NA	54.0	41.5	5.0	18.5	48.0	2.5
Auto 4	176	110	72	43	4150	56/44	64.0	NA	58.0	41.0	5.0	43.0	27.5	5.5
Man 5; auto 4	155	89	66	32	2335	52/48	43.0	NA	50.5	41.0	2.0	—	—	—
Man 5; auto 4	182	103	69	39	2865	65/35	46.0	12	54.0	42.0	2.0	49.5	23.5	0.0
Auto 4	190	108	70	42	3415	63/37	48.5	13	55.0	41.5	2.5	54.0	29.0	2.5
Man 5; **auto 4**	175	103	67	37	2630	63/37	49.5	13	54.0	41.5	5.0	52.5	30.0	3.5
Man 5; auto 4	169	96	69	37	2895	49/51	43.0	NA	52.0	42.0	1.0	—	—	—
Auto 4	177	106	68	35	3370	55/45	51.5	12	55.0	43.0	3.5	54.5	27.0	3.0
Auto 4 or 5	190	111	71	37	3585	54/46	51.5	14	55.0	45.0	4.0	55.0	31.0	3.0
Auto 4	200	113	73	39	3705	59/41	49.5	15	59.5	42.5	3.5	60.5	28.5	2.0

Make and model	Passengers	Drive	Fuel: Overall mileage	Fuel: Type	Fuel: Capacity	Engines available
Mercury Grand Marquis	3/3	Rear	19 mpg	Regular	20.0 gal.	4.6 V8 (190 hp); **4.6 V8 (210 hp)**
Mercury Mystique	2/3	Front	23	Regular	14.5	2.0 Four (125 hp); **2.5 V6 (170 hp)**
Mercury Sable	3/3	Front	21	Regular	16.0	3.0 V6 (145 hp); **3.0 V6 (200 hp)**
Mercury Tracer	2/3	Front	28	Regular	13.2	**1.8 Four (127 hp)**; 1.9 Four (88 hp)
Mercury Villager	2/2/3	Front	20	Regular	20.0	**3.0 V6 (151 hp)**
Mitsubishi 3000 GT	2/3	Front or all	—	Regular; premium	19.8	3.0 V6 (218 hp); 3.0 V6 turbo (320 hp)
Mitsubishi Diamante	2/3	Front	20	Premium	19.0	**3.0 V6 (175 hp)**
Mitsubishi Eclipse	2/2	Front or all	—	Regular; premium	16.9	2.0 Four (140 hp); 2.0 Four turbo (205-210 hp)
Mitsubishi Galant	2/3	Front	24	Regular	16.9	**2.4 Four (141 hp)**
Mitsubishi Mirage	2/3	Front	34	Regular	13.2	1.5 Four (92 hp); **1.8 Four (113 hp)**
Mitsubishi Montero	2/3/2	Selectable 4WD	15	Regular; premium	24.3	**3.0 V6 (177 hp)**; 3.5 V6 (215 hp)
Nissan 200SX	2/3	Front	—	Regular	13.2	1.6 Four (115 hp); 2.0 Four (140 hp)
Nissan 240SX	2/2	Rear	—	Premium	17.2	2.4 Four (155 hp)
Nissan 300ZX	2/—	Rear	21	Premium	18.7	3.0 V6 (222 hp); **3.0 V6 turbo (300 hp)**
Nissan Altima	2/3	Front	23	Regular	15.9	**2.4 Four (150 hp)**
Nissan Maxima	2/3	Front	24	Premium	18.5	**3.0 V6 (190 hp)**
Nissan Pathfinder	2/3	Rear/part-time 4WD	—	Regular	21.1	3.3 V6 (168 hp)
Nissan Quest	2/2/3	Front	19	Regular	20.0	**3.0 V6 (151 hp)**
Nissan Sentra	2/3	Front	28	Regular	13.3	**1.6 Four (115 hp)**
Nissan Truck	3/2	Rear/part-time 4WD	—	Regular	15.9	2.4 Four (134 hp)
Oldsmobile 88	3/3	Front	—	Regular; premium	18.0	3.8 V6 (205 hp); 3.8 V6 supercharged (225 hp)
Oldsmobile 98	3/3	Front	—	Regular	18.0	3.8 V6 (205 hp)
Oldsmobile Achieva	2/3	Front	24	Regular	20.0	**2.4 Four (150 hp)**; 3.1 V6 (155 hp)
Oldsmobile Aurora	2/3	Front	17	Premium	20.0	**4.0 V8 (250 hp)**
Oldsmobile Bravada	2/3	All	—	Regular	19.0	4.3 V6 (190 hp)
Oldsmobile Ciera	3/3	Front	22	Regular	16.5	2.2 Four (120 hp); **3.1 V6 (160 hp)**
Oldsmobile Cutlass Supreme	3/3	Front	20	Regular	16.5	**3.1 V6 (160 hp)**; 3.4 V6 (210 hp)
Oldsmobile Silhouette	2/3/2	Front	18	Regular	20.0	**3.4 V6 (180 hp)**
Plymouth Breeze	2/3	Front	—	Regular	16.0	2.0 Four (132 hp)
Plymouth Grand Voyager	2/2/3	Front	18	Regular	20.0	2.4 Four (150 hp); 3.0 V6 (150 hp); **3.3 V6 (158 hp)**; 3.8 V6 (166 hp)
Plymouth Neon	2/3	Front	26	Regular	12.5	**2.0 Four (132 hp)**; 2.0 Four (150 hp)
Plymouth Voyager	2/2/3	Front	—	Regular	20.0	2.4 Four (150 hp); 3.0 V6 (150 hp); 3.3 V6 (158 hp); 3.8 V6 (166 hp)
Pontiac Bonneville	3/3	Front	18	Regular; premium	18.0	3.8 V6 (205 hp); **3.8 V6 supercharged (240 hp)**
Pontiac Firebird	2/2	Rear	17	Regular	15.5	3.8 V6 (200 hp); **5.7 V8 (285 hp)**; 5.7 V8 (305 hp)
Pontiac Grand Am	2/3	Front	—	Regular	15.2	2.4 Four (150 hp); 3.1 V6 (155 hp)
Pontiac Grand Prix	3/3	Front	19	Regular	16.5	3.1 V6 (160 hp); **3.4 V6 (215 hp)**
Pontiac Sunfire	2/3	Front	26	Regular	15.2	**2.2 Four (120 hp)**; 2.4 Four (150 hp)
Pontiac Trans Sport	2/3/2	Front	18	Regular	20.0	**3.4 V6 (180 hp)**
Range Rover	3/3	All	—	Premium	24.6	4.0 V8 (190 hp); 4.6 V8 (225 hp)
Saab 900	2/3	Front	22	Regular	18.0	2.0 Four turbo (185 hp); 2.3 Four (150 hp); **2.5 V6 (170 hp)**
Saab 9000	2/3	Front	21	Regular	17.4	2.3 Four turbo (170-225 hp); **2.3 Four turbo (200 hp)**; 3.0 V6 (210 hp)
Saturn	2/3	Front	29	Regular	12.8	**1.9 Four (100 hp)**; 1.9 Four (124 hp)
Saturn SC	2/2	Front	29	Regular	12.8	1.9 Four (100 hp); **1.9 Four (124 hp)**
Subaru Impreza	2/3	Front or all	29	Regular	13.2	**1.8 Four (110 hp)**; 2.2 Four (135 hp)
Subaru Legacy	2/3	Front or all	23	Regular	15.9	**2.2 Four (135 hp)**; 2.5 Four (155 hp)
Subaru SVX	2/2	Front or all	19	Premium	18.5	**3.3 Six (230 hp)**
Suzuki Esteem	2/3	Front	29	Regular	13.5	**1.6 Four (98 hp)**
Suzuki Sidekick	2/2	Rear/part-time 4WD	—	Regular	14.5	1.6 Four (95 hp); 1.8 Four (120 hp)
Suzuki Swift	2/2	Front	29	Regular	10.6	**1.3 Four (70 hp)**
Suzuki X90	2/—	Rear/part-time 4WD	—	Regular	11.1	1.6 Four (95 hp)
Toyota 4Runner	2/3	Rear/part-time 4WD	—	Regular	18.5	2.7 Four (150 hp); 3.4 V6 (183 hp)
Toyota Avalon	3/3	Front	22	Regular	18.5	**3.0 V6 (192 hp)**
Toyota Camry	2/3	Front	23	Regular	18.5	2.2 Four (125 hp); **3.0 V6 (188 hp)**
Toyota Celica	2/2	Front	28	Regular	15.9	1.8 Four (110 hp); **2.2 Four (135 hp)**
Toyota Corolla	2/3	Front	30	Regular	13.2	1.6 Four (100 hp); **1.8 Four (105 hp)**
Toyota Land Cruiser	2/3/2	All	14	Regular	25.1	**4.5 Six (212 hp)**
Toyota Paseo	2/2	Front	—	Regular	11.9	1.5 Four (93 hp)
Toyota Previa	2/2/3	Rear or all	—	Regular	19.8	2.4 Four supercharged (160 hp)
Toyota RAV 4	2/3	Front or all	—	Regular	15.3	2.0 Four (120 hp)
Toyota Supra	2/2	Rear	22	Premium	18.5	3.0 Six (220 hp); **3.0 Six turbo (320 hp)**
Toyota T100	3/2	Rear/part-time 4WD	—	Regular	24.0	2.7 Four (150 hp); 3.4 V6 (190 hp)
Toyota Tacoma	3/2	Rear/part-time 4WD	21	Regular	15.1	2.4 Four (142 hp); 2.7 Four (150 hp); **3.4 V6 (190 hp)**
Toyota Tercel	2/3	Front	32	Regular	11.9	**1.5 Four (93 hp)**
Volkswagen Golf	2/3	Front	30	Regular	14.5	**2.0 Four (115 hp)**; 2.8 V6 (172 hp)
Volkswagen Jetta	2/3	Front	23	Regular	14.5	2.0 Four (115 hp); **2.8 V6 (172 hp)**
Volkswagen Passat	2/3	Front	20	Regular	18.5	1.9 Four turbodiesel (90 hp); 2.0 Four (115 hp); **2.8 V6 (172 hp)**
Volvo 850	2/3	Front	22	Premium	19.3	**2.3 Five turbo (222 hp)**; 2.4 Five (168 hp)
Volvo 960	2/3	Rear	20	Premium	20.8	**2.9 Six (181 hp)**

Transmissions available	Dimensions								Seating room					
	LENGTH	WHEELBASE	WIDTH	TURNING CIRCLE	WEIGHT	% WEIGHT FRONT/REAR	DOOR TOP	LUGGAGE CAPACITY	FRONT SHOULDER	FRONT LEGROOM	FRONT HEADROOM	REAR SHOULDER	REAR LEGROOM	REAR HEADROOM
Auto 4	212 in.	114 in.	78 in.	43 ft.	4010 lb.	55/45	51.5 in.	21 cu.ft.	61.5 in.	43.0 in.	4.5 in.	60.5 in.	30.5 in.	3.5 in.
Man 5; **auto 4**	184	107	69	39	3110	65/35	50.0	14	54.0	42.0	4.0	52.0	27.5	1.0
Auto 4	200	109	73	40	3415	64/36	50.0	16	58.5	43.0	5.5	56.0	31.5	2.0
Man 5; auto 4	171	98	67	36	2535	63/37	49.0	12	53.0	41.0	3.5	53.0	27.5	3.5
Auto 4	190	112	74	41	3900	59/41	60.0	NA	61.5	40.0	5.0	63.5	26.5	5.5
Man 5 or 6; auto 4	180	97	72	40	3805	58/42	46.0	11	56.0	43.0	3.0	44.0	20.0	1.0
Auto 4	190	107	70	43	3730	63/37	50.0	14	54.5	43.0	2.0	55.0	27.5	1.0
Man 5; auto 4	172	99	68	41	3235	61/39	46.0	15	53.0	42.0	4.0	46.5	24.5	0.0
Man 5; **auto 4**	187	104	68	38	3025	62/38	50.0	12	55.0	42.0	3.0	54.5	28.0	2.5
Man 5; auto 3 or 4	172	98	67	36	2390	62/38	49.0	11	54.0	42.0	4.5	53.0	26.0	2.0
Man 5; **auto 4**	187	107	67	44	4445	53/47	63.0	NA	56.0	40.5	5.0	56.0	30.5	3.0
Man 5; auto 4	170	100	67	39	2580	63/37	49.5	9	51.0	41.0	2.5	52.5	25.5	2.0
Man 5; auto 4	177	99	68	34	2880	55/45	46.0	9	52.0	41.5	3.5	49.5	20.0	1.0
Man 5; auto 4	170	97	71	39	3565	55/45	44.5	NA	57.0	42.0	3.0	—	—	—
Man 5; **auto 4**	181	103	67	40	3050	63/37	50.0	14	54.5	41.0	3.0	53.5	28.5	2.0
Man 5; **auto 4**	188	106	70	38	3070	64/36	50.0	15	57.0	42.0	4.5	56.5	30.5	2.5
Man 5; auto 4	178	106	69	40	4090	56/44	60.0	NA	56.5	41.5	4.0	56.5	29.0	4.0
Auto 4	190	112	74	41	3900	59/41	60.0	NA	61.5	40.0	5.0	63.5	26.5	5.5
Man 5; **auto 4**	170	100	67	38	2500	63/37	49.5	12	53.0	41.0	3.5	52.5	26.5	2.0
Man 5; auto 4	175	104	65	41	3125	56/44	57.5	NA	54.5	40.0	3.5	15.0	48.0	0.0
Auto 4	200	111	74	41	3470	64/36	50.5	18	60.0	41.5	5.0	59.0	31.0	3.0
Auto 4	206	111	75	42	3640	63/37	51.0	20	60.0	41.0	4.0	59.0	31.0	3.0
Man 5; **auto** 3 or **4**	188	103	67	39	2905	64/36	50.0	14	53.0	42.0	3.0	53.0	28.0	2.0
Auto 4	205	114	74	43	3995	63/37	50.5	16	58.0	42.0	2.0	57.5	30.5	2.5
Auto 4	181	107	67	42	4200	55/45	59.5	NA	57.0	42.0	4.0	57.5	30.0	4.0
Auto 3 or **4**	189	105	69	41	3100	66/34	50.5	16	56.5	41.0	4.0	56.0	25.5	2.5
Auto 4	194	108	71	43	3410	64/36	50.0	16	58.0	42.0	6.0	57.0	27.0	3.5
Auto 4	194	110	74	44	3890	60/40	60.5	NA	61.5	42.0	4.5	63.5	31.5	4.0
Man 5; auto 4	186	108	71	39	2930	64/36	49.5	14	55.5	41.5	3.5	54.5	30.0	2.5
Auto 3 or **4**	200	119	76	42	4035	57/43	60.0	NA	62.5	40.0	5.5	64.5	30.0	5.0
Man 5; auto 3	172	104	68	38	2600	64/36	49.5	12	53.5	41.5	5.0	52.0	29.0	2.0
Auto 3 or 4	186	113	76	40	3985	59/41	60.0	NA	62.5	41.0	5.5	64.0	28.0	5.0
Auto 4	201	111	75	43	3665	64/36	51.0	18	60.5	42.5	4.0	59.5	29.0	3.5
Man 5 or 6; **auto 4**	197	101	75	42	3545	57/43	46.5	13	58.0	41.5	3.5	53.5	24.0	1.5
Man 5; auto 4	187	103	68	42	3035	65/35	49.5	13	52.5	41.5	3.5	52.5	29.5	3.0
Auto 4	195	108	72	43	3535	65/35	50.5	16	58.0	42.0	5.0	58.0	27.5	2.5
Man 5; **auto 3** or 4	182	104	67	38	2765	64/36	50.0	13	54.5	41.0	4.5	53.5	29.0	2.0
Auto 4	192	110	74	44	3890	60/40	60.5	NA	61.5	42.0	4.5	63.5	31.5	4.0
Auto 4	186	108	74	43	4875	53/47	63.0	NA	61.0	41.0	3.0	61.0	30.0	4.0
Man 5; **auto 4**	183	102	67	37	3145	63/37	51.5	24	52.5	44.5	3.5	52.5	29.5	3.0
Man 5; **auto 4**	187	106	69	39	3275	62/38	52.0	24	58.0	42.0	3.0	57.5	31.0	1.5
Man 5; **auto 4**	177	102	67	40	2405	61/39	48.5	12	52.5	40.5	5.5	53.0	26.0	2.5
Man 5; auto 4	176	99	68	40	2420	61/39	47.0	11	53.5	42.0	3.5	52.0	22.0	0.0
Man 5; auto 4	172	99	67	37	2425	61/39	50.0	11	53.0	41.0	4.5	53.0	26.0	2.0
Man 5; **auto 4**	181	104	68	38	3040	56/44	50.0	13	54.5	42.5	3.0	53.5	30.0	3.0
Auto 4	182	103	70	39	3610	59/41	46.5	8	56.0	43.0	2.5	54.5	25.0	0.0
Man 5; **auto 4**	165	98	66	35	2290	62/38	49.0	12	52.0	41.0	4.5	51.5	27.5	2.5
Man 5; auto 3 or 4	159	98	64	36	2805	54/46	59.5	NA	51.0	42.0	5.5	50.5	26.5	4.5
Man 5; **auto 3**	149	93	63	35	1845	61/39	49.5	10	49.0	40.5	4.5	47.5	27.5	1.5
Man 5; auto 4	146	87	67	NA	2495	NA	55.0	8	49.5	41.0	4.0	—	—	—
Man 5; auto 4	179	105	67	NA	3930	55/45	63.5	NA	53.5	42.0	2.5	53.5	31.0	5.0
Auto 4	190	107	70	40	3320	62/38	51.0	15	57.0	42.5	3.5	56.5	33.0	2.5
Man 5; **auto 4**	188	103	70	38	3230	63/37	50.5	15	57.0	42.0	4.0	55.5	29.5	2.5
Man 5; auto 4	174	100	69	38	2720	63/37	46.0	16	52.5	42.5	1.0	49.0	22.5	0.0
Man 5; **auto** 3 or **4**	172	97	66	35	2540	63/37	49.5	13	54.5	40.5	4.0	54.0	25.5	2.0
Auto 4	188	112	76	43	5150	52/48	66.0	NA	59.0	40.5	4.0	59.0	26.5	3.0
Man 5; auto 4	163	94	65	36	2200	65/35	45.5	8	51.0	40.5	3.0	49.5	25.5	0.0
Auto 4	187	113	71	41	4105	54/46	63.0	NA	60.5	40.5	4.0	61.0	35.0	4.0
Man 5; auto 4	162	95	67	NA	2905	59/41	59.0	NA	53.0	40.5	5.0	52.5	25.0	4.5
Man 5; auto 4	178	100	71	39	3555	54/46	46.0	10	54.5	43.0	3.0	42.0	19.0	0.0
Man 5; auto 4	209	122	75	40	3460	59/41	NA	NA	62.0	42.0	NA	NA	NA	NA
Man 5; **auto 4**	199	122	67	46	3040	59/41	57.0	NA	54.5	41.5	5.0	53.5	24.0	0.5
Man 4 or 5; **auto** 3 or **4**	162	94	65	35	2165	63/37	48.0	9	52.0	40.0	3.5	50.5	24.0	2.0
Man 5; auto 4	160	97	67	35	2635	62/38	51.0	17	54.0	41.0	2.5	53.0	26.5	3.0
Man 5; auto 4	173	97	67	36	2955	62/38	50.5	15	53.5	42.0	2.5	52.5	27.0	2.5
Man 5; **auto 4**	182	103	68	38	3180	62/38	51.5	14	55.0	42.5	3.0	53.5	31.0	1.5
Man 5; **auto 4**	184	105	69	39	3285	62/38	49.5	14	57.0	42.0	3.0	56.0	30.5	2.5
Auto 4	192	109	69	36	3485	54/46	50.0	16	56.0	41.0	2.5	56.0	29.0	3.0

ARE CARS BECOMING MORE RELIABLE?

11

Our data, provided by millions of reader experiences over the years, show the answer is a resounding yes.

For more than 30 years, *Consumer Reports* has been tracking the reliability of automobiles based on the real-life experiences of our readers. You could buy a *Toyota* or a *Dodge* and have little trouble or lots of trouble, but it's impossible to generalize from one person's experience with one car. When you know what happened to hundreds or thousands of drivers of a specific model, however, you can say with more certainty that a *Toyota Camry* is likely to cause you less trouble than a *Dodge Neon*.

Every year, subscribers who fill out our Annual Questionnaire tell us about the car problems they have had over the previous 12 months. Their experiences form the basis of our Frequency-of-Repair records, the reports on more than 200 individual models those start on page 188. Every few years, we look back through all those data to look for trends. For this analysis, our statisticians went as far back as 1980 and compared problem rates at five-year intervals. Here's what they found.

Detroit vs. Japan and Europe

When Japanese cars entered the U.S. market 30 years ago, they proved as cheap to keep as they were to buy (a point that wasn't lost on Toyota's advertising agency). In 1980, cars built by Chrysler, Ford, and General Motors had three times the problems of the modest Japanese models. But, as the graphs on page 184 show, American automakers met that challenge: The reliability of American cars has improved dramatically since then, with the biggest improvements occurring in the 1980s. American models still aren't quite as reliable, overall, as models with foreign nameplates, but they're getting close.

Currently, Chrysler, Ford, and GM models are comparable in overall quality, averaging about 33 problems for every 100 cars. GM's *Saturn* and *Geo* models have the lowest problem rates of all the American products—fewer than 20 per 100 cars. In contrast, GM's Cadillac division has a relatively high problem rate—about 40 problems per 100 cars.

Japanese models have continued to reduce their problem rate, too. They now average about 17 problems per

RELIABILITY OF MAKES AND MODELS

The reliability of American cars has improved greatly, but overall, Japanese models are still ahead. Pickups and SUVs, once notoriously troubleprone, are now nearly as reliable as passenger cars. While the overall trends are good, particular makes and models are still problematic. Cars are listed in order of average reliability for 1995 models sold under a particular nameplate.

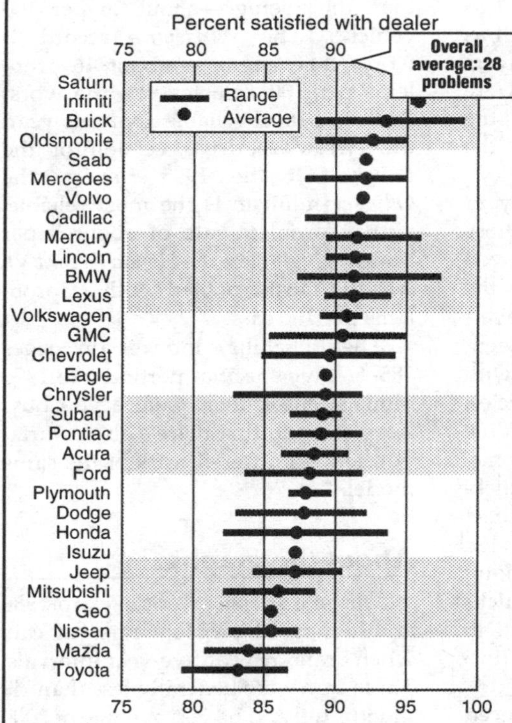

Models (▮) graphed, left to right

ACURA Legend, Integra. **INFINITI** G20, J30. **HONDA** Odyssey, Accord 4, Civic, Accord V6. **GEO** Prizm. **SUBARU** Impreza 4WD, Legacy 4WD, Legacy 2WD. **BMW** 3-Series, 5-Series. **TOYOTA** 4Runner 4WD, Camry 4, Camry V6, Pickup 4WD, Corolla, Pickup 4 2WD, T-100, Avalon. **MAZDA** Millenia, 626 V6, 626 4, Protegé. **VOLVO** 850, 850 Turbo, 960. **SATURN** SL Sedan & SW Wagon, SC Coupe. **NISSAN** Maxima, Altima, Pathfinder, Quest, Pickup 4 2WD. **EAGLE** Vision. **LEXUS** ES300, LS400, SC300/400. **LINCOLN** Town Car. **MERCEDES-BENZ** E-Class, C-Class. **CHRYSLER** New Yorker/LHS, Town & Country, Concorde, Cirrus. **OLDSMOBILE** Ciera, Cutlass Supreme, Aurora, 88, 98. **JEEP** Grand Cherokee 6 4WD, Wrangler, Grand Cherokee V8 4WD, Grand Cherokee 6 2WD, Cherokee 6 4WD. **PONTIAC** Grand Am, Grand Prix, Bonneville. **FORD** Ranger 2WD, Mustang V8, Contour, Explorer 4WD, Escort, Explorer 2WD, Thunderbird V8, Taurus, Crown Victoria, F-Series V8 4WD, F-Series 6 2WD, Aerostar 2WD, F-Series V8 2WD, Windstar. **BUICK** LeSabre, Riviera Supercharged, Riviera, Century, Regal, Park Avenue. **DODGE** Caravan, Dakota 4WD, Ram V8 & V10 4WD, Grand Caravan, Intrepid, Avenger, Ram V8 & V10 2WD, Dakota V6 2WD, Neon. **MERCURY** Villager, Grand Marquis, Cougar V8, Mystique, Sable. **PLYMOUTH** Voyager, Grand Voyager, Neon. **GMC** Sierra K1500-2500 V8, Sonoma 2WD, Jimmy 4WD. **VOLKSWAGEN** Passat, Jetta III. **CHEVROLET** Blazer 2WD, Cavalier, Suburban 4WD, Lumina, Suburban 2WD, K1500-2500 V8, Blazer 4WD, Monte Carlo, S-10 V6 4WD, S-10 4 2WD, C1500-2500 V8, Caprice, Astro 2WD, Camaro V8, S-10 V6 2WD. **SAAB** 900. **CADILLAC** De Ville, Seville.

Problem rates are shown for all models for which we had sufficient data.

100 cars. Pricey nameplates—Acura (by Honda) and Infiniti (Nissan)—are reliability leaders; more moderately priced models by Honda and Subaru aren't far behind. Other Japanese makes in the top 10 include Toyota and Mazda.

Today, European makes as a group are about as reliable as American cars, with problems turning up in about a third of the cars. *Volvos* and *BMWs* have a slightly lower problem rate—about 20 problems for every 100 cars. The reliability of *Saabs*, on the other hand, has taken a turn for the worse. In 1994, GM and Saab entered into a joint venture and introduced a new *Saab 900*, which has turned out to be quite trouble-prone.

Pickups and SUVs

In addition to passenger cars—from sporty models to sedate sedans to minivans—the Frequency-of-Repair records cover pickup trucks and sport-utility vehicles (SUVs). Pickup trucks long ago left the farm to become a second "car" in many two-car families. In recent years, SUVs have become trendy vehicles in the city as well as the country, in the Sunbelt as well as the Snowbelt. Often, however, buyers of pickup trucks and SUVs were plagued with problems, and the Frequency-of-Repair charts told the story in black and half-black dots.

That's changed. The reliability of most pickup trucks, especially those made by Ford and GM, improved greatly between 1980 and 1990, as the graphs show. Current models, on average, are about as reliable as conventional American passenger cars, with about 30 problems per 100 vehicles. The *Toyota Pickup* and *Toyota T100* stand out as the least troublesome, with about 18 problems per 100 pickups. (The graph tracks five manufacturers—General Motors, Chrysler, Ford, Nissan, and Toyota. We don't have enough data on pickup trucks from Isuzu, Mazda, or Mitsubishi to track their reliability through the 1995 model year.)

Sport-utility vehicles have reduced their problem rate even more dramatically. Now, as a group, they too are comparable with American passenger cars. Once again, a *Toyota*—the *4Runner* with four-wheel drive—stands out, with about 7 problems per 100 vehicles. And the *Chevrolet Blazer*, redesigned in 1994, now has, in its two-wheel-drive configuration, the lowest problem rate by a small margin of all *Chevrolet* models included in our analysis. As they age, however, some SUVs, including the *Jeep Cherokee*, the *Chevrolet Blazer*, and its twin the *GMC Jimmy*, become trouble-prone.

How the makes measure up

Averages provide a means of tracking trends. They don't tell you which specific model, new or used, is likely to be the more reliable—and there's a great variation, not only among one manufacturer's nameplates, but also among the models bearing each nameplate. The graph shows how the various makes fared in 1995—and how much variation there is within the makes.

For example, among the *Fords* introduced in 1995, the *Contour* is a better bet than the *Windstar*. The problem rate with the *Contour* has been better than the average—about 26 per 100 vehicles. The *Windstar's* record is worse than average—about 46 problems per 100 vehicles. It's the worst *Ford*. The most reliable *Ford* this year: the two-wheel-drive version of the *Ranger*. Of the 1995 *Hondas*, the *Odyssey* minivan is the most reliable, with a problem rate of about 5 per hundred vehicles; the *Honda Accord* V6 was the most troubled, with 21 problems per 100 cars.

The Reliability Indexes on pages 185–86 give specifics pertinent to 1996 models; check them before you buy. Keep in mind that there's also a variation among different cars of the same model.

About the graphs

Our statisticians went back to 1980 and compared problem rates of cars when brand new at five-year intervals. These cars were generally less than six months old and had an average of 3000 miles at the time when surveyed. We grouped models by the nameplate, although some are "Japanese" models

FEWER PROBLEMS

Problems in American cars dropped most in the '80s . . .

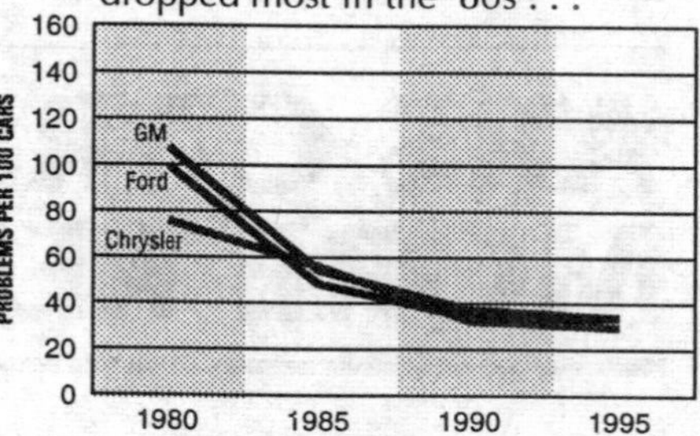

. . . but most Japanese companies reduced problems, too . . .

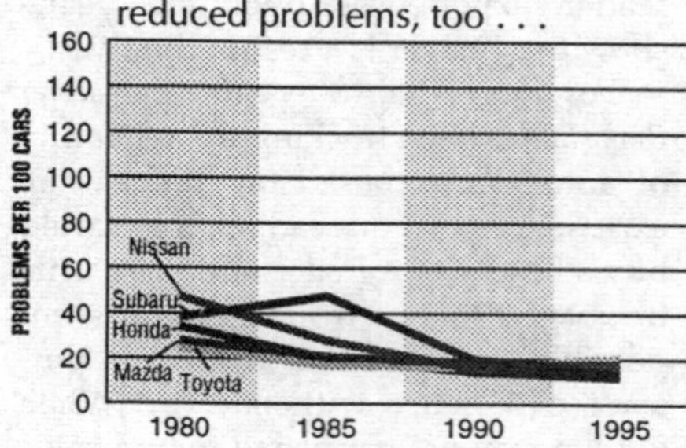

. . . while reliability of European cars stayed in between.

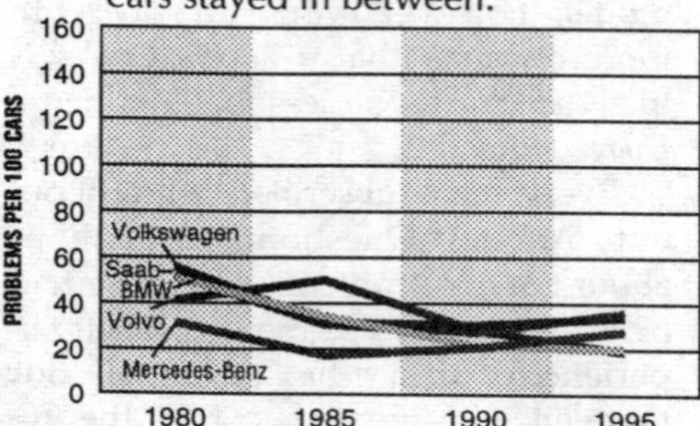

Problems in sport-utility vehicles have dropped dramatically . . .

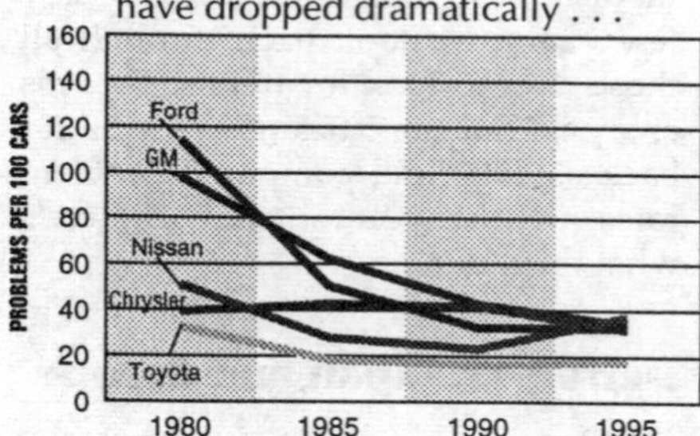

. . . as they have in pickup trucks, especially Ford and GM trucks.

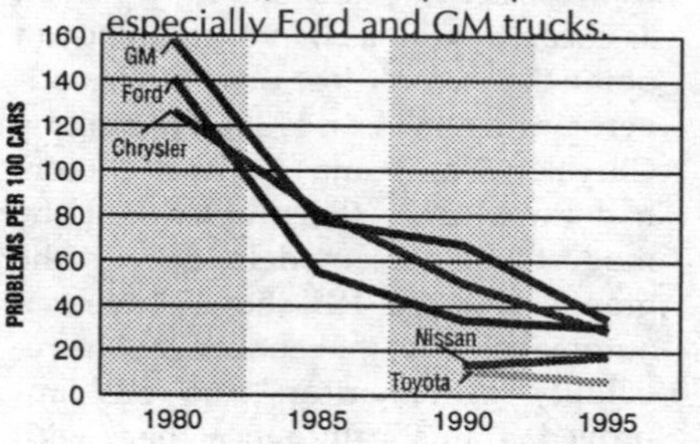

PROBLEMS PER 100 CARS
160
140
120
100
80
60
40
20
0
GM
Ford
Chrysler
Nissan
Toyota
1980
1985
1990
1995

built in the United States, some are "captive" imports (Japanese-built cars sold by domestic automakers—also called "transplants"), and some are the products of joint ventures between domestic and foreign automakers. Due to insufficient responses, not all models were covered.

1996 Cars: Reliability Indexes

As published in the April 1996 issue of *Consumer Reports,* these indexes, based on 1993–95 data, offer clues to the future.

How to read the indexes

The categories. Vehicles are listed by type. If you're not sure of a car's type, check the Summary Judgments, which begin on page 47.

The scores. Bars sum up a model's reliability history as a guide to how this year's model will fare. For details on what made a car score the way it did, see its Frequency-of-Repair record (those records start on page 188).

The benchmark. The zero line in the graphs is the average of all vehicles in our survey. Thus, the indexes directly compare reliability among all types of vehicles, from small cars to pickup trucks. Vehicles within a few points of the zero line can be considered average in reliability. Cars with identical scores and "twins"—identical cars released under two names—are listed alphabetically.

The reliability indexes are based on the Frequency-of-Repair data that apply to this year's model (that is, data from 1993 to 1995 models whose design is the same as this year's model). Indexes are based on a model's overall trouble rate, which summarizes all trouble spots for each model year. The yearly trouble rates were then compared with

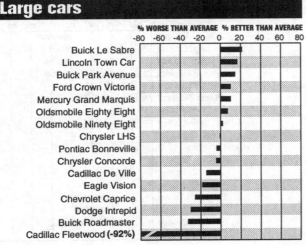

Small cars

% WORSE THAN AVERAGE % BETTER THAN AVERAGE
-80 -60 -40 -20 0 20 40 60 80

Acura Integra
Toyota Tercel
Subaru Impreza
Honda Civic
Geo Prizm
Toyota Corolla
Eagle Summit Wagon
Mazda Protegé
Saturn SL, SW
Nissan Sentra
Chevrolet Cavalier*
Pontiac Sunfire*
Eagle Summit
Mitsubishi Mirage
Mercury Tracer
Ford Escort
Geo Metro
Suzuki Swift
Volkswagen Golf
Volkswagen Jetta
Dodge Neon* **(-83%)**
Plymouth Neon* **(-83%)**

Large cars

% WORSE THAN AVERAGE % BETTER THAN AVERAGE
-80 -60 -40 -20 0 20 40 60 80

Buick Le Sabre
Lincoln Town Car
Buick Park Avenue
Ford Crown Victoria
Mercury Grand Marquis
Oldsmobile Eighty Eight
Oldsmobile Ninety Eight
Chrysler LHS
Pontiac Bonneville
Chrysler Concorde
Cadillac De Ville
Eagle Vision
Chevrolet Caprice
Dodge Intrepid
Buick Roadmaster
Cadillac Fleetwood **(-92%)**

Medium cars

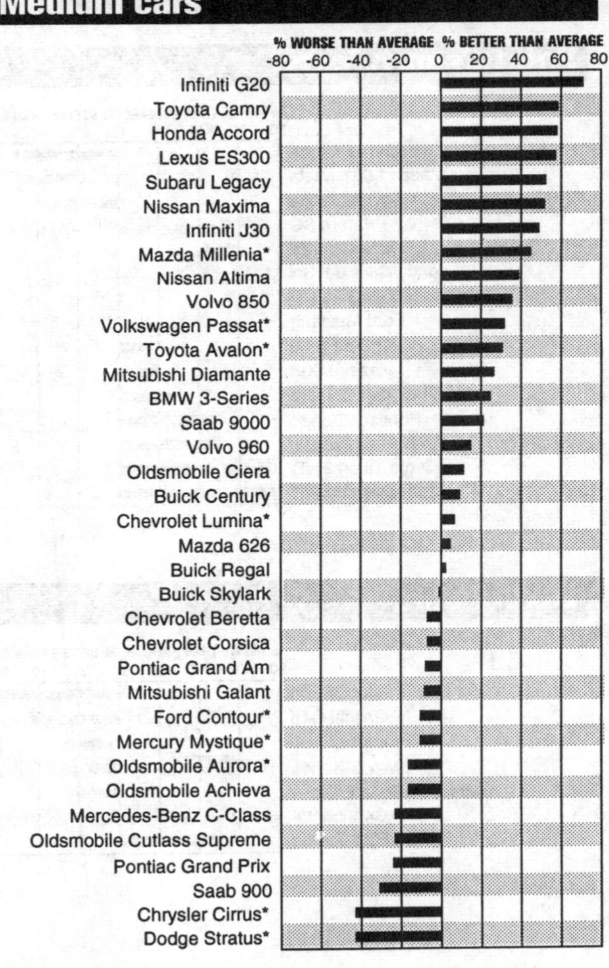

each year's average and the differences combined to create each index.

We list only models for which there were sufficient survey responses to make a judgment. Because problems with the engine, the transmission, the cooling system, and body rust are typically the most costly and difficult to fix, we weight these factors most heavily.

An * means the index is based on one model year only—because the model is new or recently redesigned, or readers didn't provide enough data on more years.

Coupes

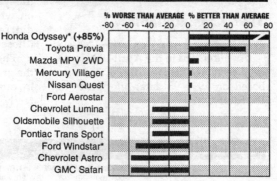

% WORSE THAN AVERAGE % BETTER THAN AVERAGE

-80 -60 -40 -20 0 20 40 60 80

Lexus SC300/400

Lincoln Mark VIII

Chrysler Sebring*

Dodge Avenger*

Buick Riviera*

Ford Thunderbird

Mercury Cougar

Chevrolet Monte Carlo*

Cadillac Eldorado

Sports/sporty cars

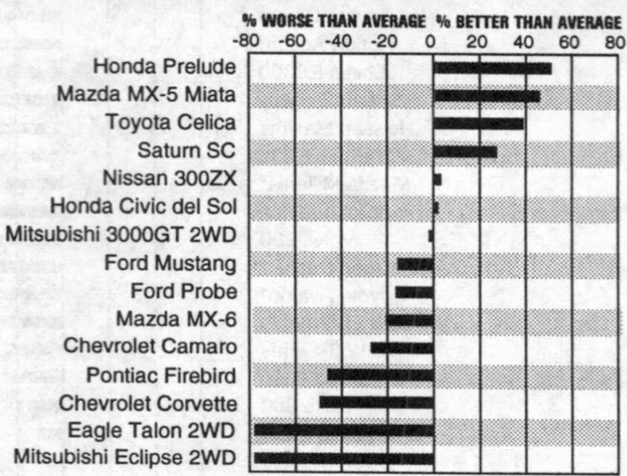

Luxury cars

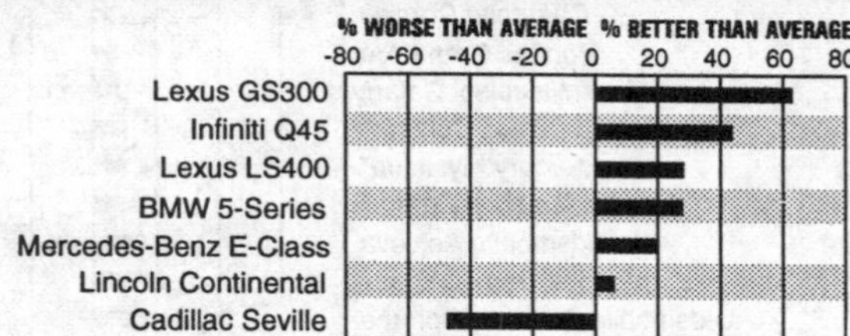

Minivans

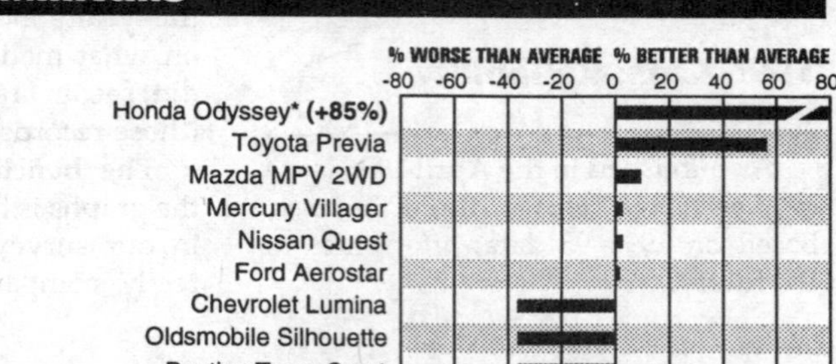

Pickup trucks

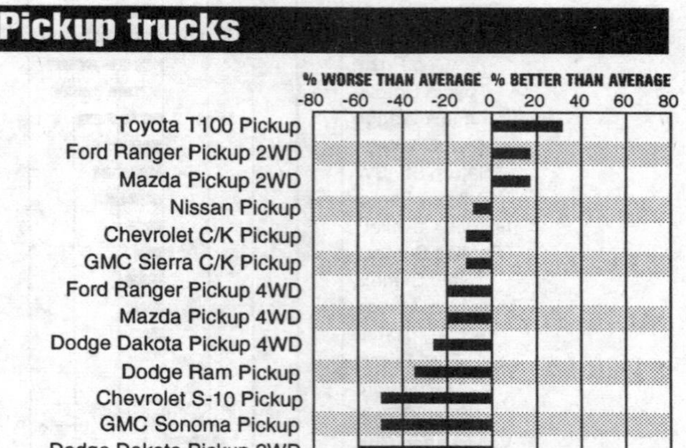

Sport-utility vehicles

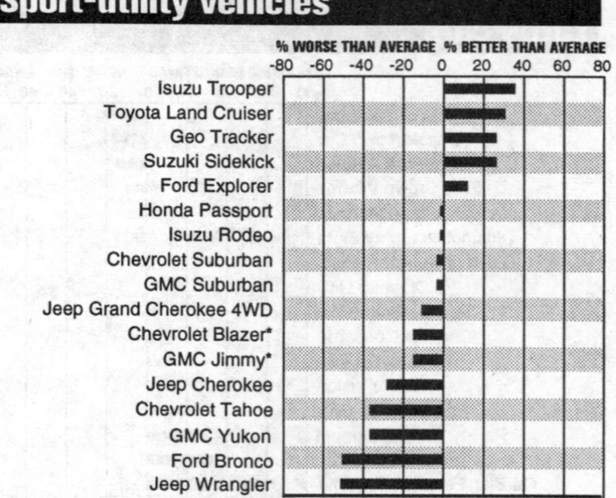

Reliability report, 1988–95

The Frequency-of-Repair charts on the following pages are a unique source of information and an invaluable resource for car buyers. The scores are based on the experiences of readers who respond to our Annual Questionnaire. This year, that represents 630,000 vehicles, including cars, minivans, pickup trucks, and sport-utility vehicles. The charts cover eight model years, 1988 through 1995.

If you're buying a used car, these charts may save you from buying someone else's problem. As any car ages, of course, things are likely to wear and break. By comparing the model year of the car you're considering with the same year's average noted in the box below, you can see how your candidate stacks up.

If you're buying a new car, our interpretations of the data that appear elsewhere in this issue—in the report on reliability trends (page 183) and the Reliability Indexes (page 185)—provide the best guidance. The charts here show what those interpretations are based on. Unless the car has been redesigned, a problem that has appeared frequently in previous versions of the car may turn up in the current year's model as well.

Follow the dots

The symbols in the charts represent the percentage of owners who have reported serious problems in each of 16 categories over 12 months (April 1994 through March 1995). Problems are "serious" when they are expensive to repair, put the car out of commission for a time, or cause a safety problem or vehicle failure.

A poor score for a particular part or category doesn't mean that a problem is inevitable. What it does mean is that a problem is more likely in that model than in most models. Nor can the data predict how many problems a particular vehicle might have. Some cars might be problem-free, others might be plagued. The key to problem rates, below, shows the percentage of cars afflicted with that problem, from the best, ⊜, 2 percent or less, to the worst, ●, nearly 15 percent or more—sometimes lots more. The data we use to create the charts are standardized to minimize differences due to varied mileage, and the symbols are on an absolute scale, so a ⊜ means the same for any trouble spot, any year, and any car.

In an older car, more problems are likely to turn up in more areas. While some older models still earn a ⊜ in some categories, a ⊖ or ○ isn't worrisome. Scores of ◒ or ● reflect too many problems, in our judgment. Have those components of the car checked out especially carefully before you buy. Low scores are of particular concern in categories such as engine and transmission, which can be difficult and costly to repair. Some 1989 to 1992 *Subarus,* for example, have an especially sorry record of engine problems. Some Chrysler products, particularly the long-wheelbase *Dodge* and *Plymouth* minivans built between 1989 and 1992, have a high incidence of problems with the automatic transmission.

Even new cars are not immune. Indeed, some problems are just as likely to turn up in a new car. Poor design or sloppy quality control, for example, may cause early problems with body hardware such as locks or windows. Electronic components usually fail early rather than late in a car's life. On a 1995 model, even a ⊖ or a ○ warrants caution. When our readers responded to our latest Annual Questionnaire, the 1995 models were generally less than six months old and had been driven an average of only 3000 miles. We think it's reasonable to expect cars that new to score ⊜ in all categories.

TROUBLE SPOTS	The Average Model							
	88	89	90	91	92	93	94	95
Engine	◒	○	○	⊖	⊖	⊖	⊜	⊜
Cooling	◒	◒	○	⊖	⊖	⊖	⊜	⊜
Fuel	○	○	○	⊖	⊖	⊖	⊜	⊜
Ignition	○	⊖	⊖	⊖	⊖	⊜	⊜	⊜
Auto. trans.	○	○	○	○	⊖	⊖	⊖	⊜
Man. trans.	⊖	⊖	⊖	⊖	⊖	⊖	⊜	⊜
Clutch	◒	◒	○	○	⊖	⊖	⊜	⊜
Electrical	●	●	●	◒	◒	◒	○	⊖
A/C	◒	◒	○	○	○	⊖	⊖	⊜
Suspension	◒	○	○	○	⊖	⊖	⊖	⊜
Brakes	●	●	●	◒	◒	○	⊖	⊜
Exhaust	◒	◒	○	○	⊖	⊜	⊜	⊜
Body rust	○	○	⊜	⊜	⊜	⊜	⊜	⊜
Paint/trim	◒	◒	○	○	○	⊖	⊖	⊜
Integrity	◒	◒	○	○	○	◒	○	○
Hardware	◒	◒	◒	◒	◒	◒	○	⊖

Key to problem rates

⊜ 2.0 % or less
⊖ 2.0 % to 5.0%
○ 5.0% to 9.3%
◒ 9.3% to 14.8%
● More than 14.8

THE "AVERAGE" MODEL

Turn to the Frequency-of-Repair chart for any car you're considering and compare its scores with the average for the same year. That gives you a sense of whether a car's problems are the ones to be expected with age or something more serious. As the average chart shows, many cars have brake problems by the time they're three or four years old. But if you compare the *Ford Bronco* or *Taurus SHO* against this chart, you'll see that they have had more than their share of brake problems.

Electrical problems and hardware failures (windows, locks, seat mechanisms) are fairly common in newer cars. But some late-model GM vehicles—the *Chevrolet Camaro, Astro* van and some sport-utility vehicles—are especially prone to hardware problems, as well as to suffering from leaks, rattles, and squeaks.

How to read the Frequency-of-Repair charts

Make and model Unless otherwise stated, includes all body, engine, and drive types.

Asterisk We didn't get enough responses to evaluate this trouble spot.

Blank square The car lacked this type of transmission in this year.

Insufficient data We didn't receive enough responses to evaluate that year's model.

Blank column The model wasn't made that year.

Mazda MX-5 Miata	88	89	90	91	92	93	94	95
			⊜	⊜	⊜	⊜	⊜	Insufficient data
			⊜	⊜	⊜	⊜	⊜	
			⊜	⊜	⊜	⊜	⊜	
			○	⊖	○	⊖	⊜	
				*	*	*	*	
			⊜	⊜	⊜	⊜	⊜	
			⊖	⊖	⊜	⊜	⊜	
			◒	◒	○	○	⊖	
			⊖	⊜	⊜	⊜	⊜	
			⊜	⊜	⊜	⊜	⊜	
			⊖	⊜	⊖	⊜	⊜	
			⊖	⊜	⊖	⊜	⊖	
			⊜	⊜	⊜	⊜	⊜	
			○	⊜	○	⊖	○	
			○	○	○	○	○	
			○	○	○	⊖	⊜	

What the trouble spots include

- **Engine** Pistons, rings, valves, block, heads, bearings, camshafts, gaskets, turbocharger, cam belts & chains, oil pump.
- **Cooling** Radiator, heater core, water pump, thermostat, hoses, intercooler & plumbing.
- **Fuel** Choke, fuel injection, computer & sensors, fuel pump, tank, emissions controls, carburetion setting.
- **Ignition** Spark plugs, coil, distributor, electronic ignition, sensors & modules, timing.
- **Transmission** Transaxle, gear selector, linkage, coolers & lines; gearbox, shifter.
- **Clutch** Lining, pressure plate, release bearing, linkage & hydraulics.
- **Electrical** Starter, alternator, battery, horn, switches, controls, lights, radio & sound system, accessory motors, electronics, wiring.
- **Air-conditioning** Compressor, condenser, evaporator, expansion valves, hoses, dryer, fans, electronics .
- **Suspension** Linkage, power-steering gear, pump, coolers & lines, alignment & balance, springs & torsion bars, ball joints, bushings, shocks & struts, electronic or air suspension.
- **Brakes** Hydraulic system, linings, discs & drums, power boost, antilock system, parking brake & linkage.
- **Exhaust** Manifold, muffler, catalytic converter, pipes.
- **Body rust** Corrosion, pitting, perforation.
- **Paint/trim** Fading, discoloring, chalking, peeling, cracking; loose trim, moldings, outside mirrors.
- **Integrity** Seals, weather stripping, air & water leaks, wind noise, rattles & squeaks.
- **Hardware** Window, door, seat mechanisms; locks, safety belts, sunroof, glass, wipers.

TROUBLE SPOTS	Acura Integra 88	89	90	91	92	93	94	95
Engine	⊖	○	⊖	⊜	⊜	⊜	⊜	⊜
Cooling	⊖	⊖	⊜	⊜	⊜	⊜	⊜	⊜
Fuel	⊖	⊖	⊜	⊜	⊜	⊜	⊜	⊜
Ignition	○	○	⊜	⊜	⊜	⊜	⊜	⊜
Auto. trans.	○	○	⊖	⊜	⊜	⊜	⊖	⊜
Man. trans.	⊜	⊜	⊜	⊜	⊜	⊜	⊜	⊜
Clutch	●	◒	⊖	⊖	⊖	⊜	⊜	⊜
Electrical	◒	◒	○	○	⊜	⊖	⊖	⊜
A/C	◒	◒	⊖	⊜	⊜	⊖	⊜	⊜
Suspension	⊖	○	⊖	⊜	⊜	⊜	⊜	⊜
Brakes	◒	●	○	⊖	○	⊜	⊜	⊜
Exhaust	●	●	◒	○	○	⊜	⊜	⊜
Body rust	●	○	⊜	⊜	⊜	⊜	⊜	⊜
Paint/trim	◒	○	⊖	⊜	⊜	⊜	⊖	⊜
Integrity	○	○	○	○	⊖	○	⊖	⊖
Hardware	○	◒	○	⊜	⊜	⊖	○	⊖

TROUBLE SPOTS	Acura Legend 88	89	90	91	92	93	94	95
Engine	⊖	⊖	⊜	⊜	⊜	⊜	⊜	⊜
Cooling	⊖	⊜	⊖	⊖	⊖	⊜	⊜	⊜
Fuel	⊖	⊖	⊜	⊜	⊜	⊜	⊜	⊜
Ignition	⊜	⊜	⊖	⊜	⊜	⊜	⊜	⊜
Auto. trans.	○	⊖	⊖	⊜	⊜	⊜	⊜	⊜
Man. trans.	⊖	⊖	⊖	○	*	*	*	*
Clutch	●	●	●	◒	*	*	*	*
Electrical	◒	◒	◒	◒	◒	○	○	⊖
A/C	⊖	⊖	⊖	⊖	⊖	⊜	⊜	⊜
Suspension	○	○	○	⊖	⊖	⊜	⊜	⊜
Brakes	●	●	◒	◒	○	⊜	⊜	⊜
Exhaust	○	○	⊖	⊜	⊜	⊜	⊜	⊜
Body rust	⊖	⊖	⊜	⊜	⊜	⊜	⊜	⊜
Paint/trim	⊖	⊖	⊜	⊖	⊖	⊜	⊜	⊜
Integrity	○	○	⊖	○	⊖	○	⊖	⊜
Hardware	○	○	○	◒	○	⊜	○	⊜

TROUBLE SPOTS	Acura Vigor 88	89	90	91	92	93	94	95
Engine					⊜	⊜	⊜	
Cooling					⊜	⊜	⊜	
Fuel					⊜	⊖	⊜	
Ignition					⊖	⊜	⊜	
Auto. trans.					⊜	*	*	
Man. trans.					*	*	*	
Clutch					*	*	*	
Electrical					◒	○	○	
A/C					⊖	⊖	⊜	
Suspension					⊜	⊖	⊜	
Brakes					○	⊜	⊜	
Exhaust					⊜	⊖	⊜	
Body rust					⊜	⊜	⊜	
Paint/trim					⊜	⊜	⊜	
Integrity					○	○	◒	
Hardware					⊖	○	⊖	

TROUBLE SPOTS	BMW 3-Series 88	89	90	91	92	93	94	95
Engine	○	○	⊖	●	⊖	⊜	⊜	⊜
Cooling	◒	◒	◒	◒	⊖	⊜	⊖	⊜
Fuel	◒	◒	○	○	⊖	⊖	⊖	⊜
Ignition	○	⊖	⊜	⊜	⊜	⊜	⊜	⊜
Auto. trans.	*	*	*	*	⊖	⊜	⊖	*
Man. trans.	*	*	*	⊜	⊖	⊜	⊜	⊜
Clutch	*	*	*	⊖	⊖	⊖	⊜	⊜
Electrical	●	●	●	●	●	◒	○	⊖
A/C	●	●	○	○	○	⊖	⊖	⊜
Suspension	○	⊖	○	○	⊖	⊖	⊜	⊜
Brakes	●	●	○	○	○	○	○	⊜
Exhaust	○	⊖	⊖	○	⊖	⊜	⊜	⊜
Body rust	⊖	⊜	⊜	⊜	⊜	⊜	⊜	⊜
Paint/trim	○	⊜	⊖	⊖	⊖	⊖	⊖	⊖
Integrity	◒	⊖	⊖	⊖	○	○	◒	⊖
Hardware	◒	◒	◒	●	●	◒	◒	⊖

TROUBLE SPOTS	BMW 5-Series 88	89	90	91	92	93	94	95
Engine	⊖	○	○	○	⊜	Insufficient data	⊖	⊜
Cooling	◒	●	◒	○	⊖		⊜	⊜
Fuel	◒	⊖	○	○	◒		⊜	⊜
Ignition	⊖	⊖	⊜	⊖	⊜		⊜	⊜
Auto. trans.	○	*	⊜	*	○		⊖	⊖
Man. trans.	*	*	*	*	*		*	*
Clutch	*	*	*	*	*		*	*
Electrical	●	●	●	●	●		○	○
A/C	○	◒	⊖	⊖	⊜		⊖	⊜
Suspension	○	○	⊜	○	⊖		⊖	⊜
Brakes	●	◒	◒	◒	⊖		⊜	⊜
Exhaust	●	◒	○	⊜	⊜		⊜	⊜
Body rust	⊖	⊜	⊜	⊜	⊜		⊜	⊜
Paint/trim	○	⊜	⊖	⊖	⊖		⊜	⊜
Integrity	○	⊖	⊖	⊖	○		⊖	⊜
Hardware	◒	○	○	◒	◒		○	⊜

TROUBLE SPOTS	Buick Century 88	89	90	91	92	93	94	95
Engine	○	⊖	⊖	⊖	⊖	⊜	⊖	⊜
Cooling	◒	◒	○	◒	○	⊜	⊜	⊜
Fuel	◒	○	○	○	⊖	⊜	⊜	⊜
Ignition	○	○	⊖	⊖	⊜	⊜	⊜	⊜
Auto. trans.	○	⊖	⊜	⊖	⊖	⊜	⊜	⊜
Man. trans.								
Clutch								
Electrical	●	●	●	◒	○	○	○	⊖
A/C	○	⊖	⊖	⊖	⊖	⊖	⊖	⊜
Suspension	◒	○	⊖	⊖	⊖	⊖	⊖	⊖
Brakes	●	●	●	●	●	○	⊖	⊜
Exhaust	●	◒	◒	○	○	○	⊜	⊜
Body rust	◒	○	⊖	⊖	⊜	⊜	⊜	⊜
Paint/trim	●	◒	○	○	⊖	⊖	⊖	⊖
Integrity	○	○	○	○	○	○	◒	◒
Hardware	◒	○	○	○	⊖	⊖	◒	⊖

TROUBLE SPOTS	Buick Electra, Park Avenue & Ultra 88	89	90	91	92	93	94	95
Engine	○	⊖	⊖	⊖	⊖	⊜	⊜	⊜
Cooling	◒	○	○	○	○	⊖	⊜	⊜
Fuel	○	○	○	⊖	⊖	⊜	⊜	⊜
Ignition	○	○	◒	○	⊖	⊜	⊜	⊜
Auto. trans.	○	⊜	⊖	⊖	⊖	⊜	⊜	⊜
Man. trans.								
Clutch								
Electrical	●	●	●	●	●	●	○	○
A/C	◒	○	⊖	◒	○	⊖	⊖	⊜
Suspension	◒	○	⊖	○	⊖	⊖	⊖	⊖
Brakes	●	●	●	◒	◒	⊖	⊜	⊜
Exhaust	○	⊜	⊖	⊜	⊖	⊖	⊜	⊜
Body rust	⊖	⊖	⊜	⊜	⊜	⊜	⊜	⊜
Paint/trim	●	◒	○	○	⊖	⊜	⊜	⊜
Integrity	○	○	○	◒	◒	○	○	○
Hardware	●	◒	◒	●	◒	◒	○	⊖

TROUBLE SPOTS	Buick Estate Wagon 88	89	90	91	92	93	94	95
Engine	●	◒	○					
Cooling	◒	●	○					
Fuel	○	○	⊖					
Ignition	⊖	○	⊖					
Auto. trans.	○	◒	⊖					
Man. trans.								
Clutch								
Electrical	●	●	●					
A/C	◒	○	○					
Suspension	○	○	○					
Brakes	●	◒	●					
Exhaust	●	◒	◒					
Body rust	◒	○	◒					
Paint/trim	●	◒	●					
Integrity	◒	◒	◒					
Hardware	◒	●	●					

TROUBLE SPOTS	Buick Le Sabre 88	89	90	91	92	93	94	95
Engine	⊖	⊖	⊖	⊖	⊖	⊜	⊜	⊜
Cooling	◒	◒	○	⊖	○	⊖	⊜	⊜
Fuel	◒	◒	○	○	⊖	⊜	⊜	⊜
Ignition	○	◒	○	◒	⊖	⊜	⊜	⊜
Auto. trans.	○	⊖	⊖	⊖	⊖	⊖	⊜	⊜
Man. trans.								
Clutch								
Electrical	●	●	●	●	◒	○	⊖	⊖
A/C	○	○	○	○	○	⊖	⊖	⊖
Suspension	●	○	⊖	⊖	○	⊖	⊖	⊜
Brakes	●	●	●	●	◒	○	⊜	⊜
Exhaust	⊖	⊜	⊜	⊜	⊖	⊜	⊜	⊜
Body rust	○	○	⊖	⊖	⊜	⊜	⊜	⊜
Paint/trim	◒	◒	○	○	○	⊖	⊖	⊖
Integrity	○	○	⊖	⊖	◒	○	○	⊖
Hardware	◒	○	○	○	◒	○	○	⊖

TROUBLE SPOTS	Buick Regal 88	89	90	91	92	93	94	95
Engine	○	○	○	⊖	⊖	⊖	⊜	⊜
Cooling	◒	◒	○	⊖	⊖	⊜	⊜	⊜
Fuel	◒	◒	○	⊖	⊜	⊜	⊜	⊜
Ignition	◒	◒	⊖	⊖	⊖	⊜	⊜	⊜
Auto. trans.	◒	○	○	⊖	⊖	⊜	⊜	⊜
Man. trans.								
Clutch								
Electrical	●	●	●	●	◒	○	○	○
A/C	●	○	◒	○	○	⊖	⊖	⊖
Suspension	◒	●	○	○	⊖	⊜	⊖	⊜
Brakes	●	●	●	●	●	◒	○	○
Exhaust	⊖	○	⊜	⊜	⊖	⊜	⊜	⊜
Body rust	⊖	⊖	⊜	⊜	⊜	⊜	⊜	⊜
Paint/trim	○	○	◒	⊖	⊖	⊖	⊖	⊜
Integrity	◒	○	○	○	⊜	○	◒	○
Hardware	●	●	●	◒	◒	○	◒	○

TROUBLE SPOTS	Buick Riviera 88	89	90	91	92	93	94	95
Engine	Insufficient data	⊖	⊜	⊖	Insufficient data	Insufficient data		⊜
Cooling		○	○	○				⊜
Fuel		◒	○	⊖				⊜
Ignition		◒	◒	⊜				⊜
Auto. trans.		⊖	⊖	⊖				⊖
Man. trans.								
Clutch								
Electrical		●	●	●				○
A/C		◒	◒	◒				⊜
Suspension		○	○	○				⊖
Brakes		●	●	●				⊜
Exhaust		⊖	⊖	⊖				⊜
Body rust		⊖	⊜	⊜				⊜
Paint/trim		○	○	⊖				⊖
Integrity		○	○	⊜				○
Hardware		○	●	◒				⊖

TROUBLE SPOTS	Buick Roadmaster 88	89	90	91	92	93	94	95
Engine				Insufficient data	⊖	⊜	⊖	Insufficient data
Cooling					○	⊜	⊜	
Fuel					⊖	⊖	⊖	
Ignition					⊖	⊜	⊜	
Auto. trans.					○	⊖	⊖	
Man. trans.								
Clutch								
Electrical					●	○	◒	
A/C					●	○	⊜	
Suspension					○	○	○	
Brakes					○	⊜	⊖	
Exhaust					⊖	⊜	⊜	
Body rust					⊜	⊜	⊜	
Paint/trim					◒	○	○	
Integrity					○	◒	●	
Hardware					◒	○	●	

Buick Skylark

Trouble Spots	88	89	90	91	92	93	94	95
Engine	●	◒	○	⊖	⊜	⊜	⊖	
Cooling	●	●	○	○	◒	⊜	⊜	
Fuel	●	○	⊖	⊖	⊖	⊜	⊜	
Ignition	◒	◒	⊖	⊖	⊜	⊜	⊖	
Auto. trans.	◒	○	○	⊖	⊜	⊜	○	
Man. trans.								
Clutch								
Electrical	●	●	●	●	●	○	○	Insufficient data
A/C	◒	○	○	○	○	⊖	⊖	
Suspension	◒	○	○	○	◒	⊖	⊜	
Brakes	◒	●	●	●	●	◒	○	
Exhaust	●	●	●	◒	⊜	⊖	⊜	
Body rust	●	●	●	◒	⊜	⊜	⊜	
Paint/trim	●	●	●	◒	○	⊖	⊖	
Integrity	◒	◒	◒	◒	◒	◒	◒	
Hardware	◒	◒	◒	◒	◒	○	◒	

Cadillac Brougham, Fleetwood (RWD)

Trouble Spots	88	89	90	91	92	93	94	95
Engine	◒	●	○	⊜		⊜	⊖	
Cooling	◒	◒	○	○		⊜	⊖	
Fuel	○	○	⊖	○		⊖	⊖	
Ignition	⊖	⊖	⊖	⊖		⊖	⊖	
Auto. trans.	◒	○	◒	⊖		⊖	○	
Man. trans.								
Clutch								
Electrical	●	●	●	●	Insufficient data	●	◒	Insufficient data
A/C	●	○	○	◒		○	⊖	
Suspension	◒	○	○	○		◒	○	
Brakes	●	●	◒	○		○	○	
Exhaust	◒	○	○	○		⊜	⊖	
Body rust	⊖	⊖	○	⊜		⊖	⊜	
Paint/trim	●	◒	◒	⊖		◒	●	
Integrity	○	○	◒	○		●	●	
Hardware	◒	◒	○	●		●	●	

Cadillac De Ville, Fleetwood (FWD)

Trouble Spots	88	89	90	91	92	93	94	95
Engine	◒	○	⊖	◒	◒	○	⊖	⊖
Cooling	◒	○	⊖	⊖	○	⊜	⊜	⊜
Fuel	⊖	⊖	○	○	○	⊖	⊜	⊜
Ignition	⊖	⊖	⊖	⊖	⊖	⊜	⊜	⊜
Auto. trans.	○	⊖	⊖	○	○	○	⊖	⊖
Man. trans.								
Clutch								
Electrical	●	●	●	◒	◒	○	○	⊖
A/C	●	○	○	◒	◒	⊖	⊖	⊖
Suspension	◒	⊖	⊖	⊖	⊖	○	⊖	⊖
Brakes	●	●	●	●	◒	○	⊖	⊜
Exhaust	⊜	⊜	⊖	⊖	⊖	⊜	⊜	⊜
Body rust	⊖	⊜	⊜	⊜	⊜	⊜	⊜	⊜
Paint/trim	○	⊖	⊖	⊖	⊖	⊖	⊖	⊜
Integrity	○	○	⊖	⊖	○	○	○	⊖
Hardware	◒	○	◒	⊖	○	○	◒	○

Cadillac Eldorado

Trouble Spots	88	89	90	91	92	93	94	95
Engine	○	○	○		○	⊖	⊜	
Cooling	○	⊖	○		⊖	⊖	⊜	
Fuel	⊖	⊜	○		⊖	○	⊜	
Ignition	⊖	⊖	⊖		○	⊜	⊜	
Auto. trans.	○	⊖	○		⊜	⊖	⊖	
Man. trans.								
Clutch								
Electrical	●	●	●	Insufficient data	◒	◒	◒	Insufficient data
A/C	●	●	◒		◒	⊖	⊖	
Suspension	○	○	⊖		○	⊖	○	
Brakes	●	●	●		◒	○	⊖	
Exhaust	⊖	⊖	⊜		⊜	⊜	⊜	
Body rust	⊜	⊜	⊜		⊜	⊜	⊜	
Paint/trim	⊖	○	⊖		○	⊖	○	
Integrity	⊖	⊖	⊜		●	●	◒	
Hardware	◒	◒	○		●	●	●	

Cadillac Seville

Trouble Spots	88	89	90	91	92	93	94	95
Engine	○	○	○	○	○	⊖	○	⊖
Cooling	●	◒	⊖	○	⊖	⊜	⊜	⊜
Fuel	⊖	⊜	○	○	⊖	○	⊖	⊜
Ignition	⊜	⊖	⊖	○	⊖	⊖	⊜	⊜
Auto. trans.	○	○	⊖	⊖	⊖	○	⊖	⊖
Man. trans.								
Clutch								
Electrical	●	●	●	●	◒	◒	○	○
A/C	●	◒	◒	◒	◒	○	⊖	⊖
Suspension	○	○	○	⊖	○	○	⊖	○
Brakes	●	●	●	●	○	○	⊜	⊜
Exhaust	⊖	⊜	⊖	⊖	⊜	⊜	⊜	⊖
Body rust	⊖	⊜	⊜	⊜	⊜	⊜	⊜	⊜
Paint/trim	○	○	⊖	⊖	⊖	⊖	⊖	⊜
Integrity	◒	○	○	⊖	●	◒	◒	○
Hardware	○	◒	◒	○	◒	◒	◒	○

Chevrolet Astro Van

Trouble Spots	88	89	90	91	92	93	94	95
Engine	◒	◒	⊖	⊖	○	⊖	⊜	⊖
Cooling	◒	○	⊖	⊜	⊖	⊜	⊜	⊜
Fuel	○	○	⊖	⊖	○	○	⊜	⊖
Ignition	○	○	⊖	⊖	⊖	⊖	⊖	⊜
Auto. trans.	○	○	⊖	⊖	⊖	○	⊖	⊜
Man. trans.	*	*						
Clutch	*	*						
Electrical	●	●	●	●	◒	●	●	○
A/C	◒	●	○	○	○	○	◒	⊜
Suspension	●	◒	◒	◒	○	○	⊖	⊖
Brakes	●	●	●	●	●	●	⊖	⊖
Exhaust	◒	◒	○	○	⊖	⊜	⊜	⊜
Body rust	⊖	⊖	⊖	⊜	⊖	⊜	⊜	⊜
Paint/trim	●	●	●	◒	◒	○	○	⊖
Integrity	◒	●	●	●	●	●	●	◒
Hardware	●	●	●	●	●	●	◒	◒

Chevrolet Blazer, K-Blazer, Tahoe

Trouble Spots	88	89	90	91	92	93	94	95
Engine	○	○	⊖	⊖	○	⊖	⊖	⊜
Cooling	●	◒	○	⊖	○	⊜	⊜	⊜
Fuel	◒	○	⊖	⊖	○	⊖	⊜	⊜
Ignition	○	○	⊖	○	⊖	⊜	⊜	⊜
Auto. trans.	◒	○	⊖	⊖	○	○	⊖	⊖
Man. trans.	*	*	*	*	*	*	*	*
Clutch	*	*	*	*	*	*	*	*
Electrical	●	●	●	●	●	◒	◒	○
A/C	◒	⊖	⊖	⊖	○	⊖	⊖	⊜
Suspension	○	○	◒	◒	⊖	○	⊖	⊖
Brakes	◒	●	◒	●	●	◒	○	⊖
Exhaust	●	●	◒	○	⊖	⊖	⊜	⊜
Body rust	●	●	◒	⊖	⊖	⊖	⊖	⊜
Paint/trim	●	●	●	●	◒	○	○	⊜
Integrity	●	●	●	◒	◒	◒	◒	○
Hardware	●	●	●	●	●	◒	◒	○

Chevrolet C1500-2500 Pickup

Trouble Spots	88	89	90	91	92	93	94	95
Engine	◒	○	○	⊖	⊖	⊖	⊖	⊜
Cooling	●	○	○	⊖	⊖	⊜	⊜	⊜
Fuel	◒	○	⊖	⊖	⊖	⊖	⊖	⊜
Ignition	○	○	○	○	⊖	⊖	⊜	⊜
Auto. trans.	○	○	○	◒	◒	⊖	⊖	⊜
Man. trans.	○	⊖	⊜	⊖	○	*	*	*
Clutch	◒	●	●	◒	○	*	*	*
Electrical	●	●	●	●	◒	◒	○	○
A/C	○	◒	○	○	○	⊖	⊖	⊜
Suspension	●	◒	○	○	○	⊖	⊖	⊖
Brakes	●	◒	◒	○	⊖	⊜	⊖	⊜
Exhaust	●	●	◒	○	⊖	⊜	⊜	⊜
Body rust	○	⊖	⊜	⊜	⊜	⊜	⊜	⊜
Paint/trim	●	●	●	◒	○	○	⊖	⊖
Integrity	◒	◒	○	○	○	○	○	○
Hardware	◒	◒	○	○	○	○	○	○

Chevrolet K1500-2500 Pickup

Trouble Spots	88	89	90	91	92	93	94	95
Engine	◒	◒	○	⊖	⊖	○	⊖	⊜
Cooling	●	◒	⊖	⊖	⊖	⊖	⊜	⊜
Fuel	◒	⊖	⊖	⊖	⊖	⊖	⊜	⊜
Ignition	○	○	○	○	⊖	⊖	⊜	⊜
Auto. trans.	◒	○	○	○	○	○	⊖	⊜
Man. trans.	*	*	⊖	*	○	*	⊖	*
Clutch	*	*	●	*	○	*	○	*
Electrical	●	●	●	◒	◒	◒	○	⊖
A/C	○	○	○	○	⊖	⊖	⊜	⊜
Suspension	◒	◒	○	○	○	⊖	⊜	⊖
Brakes	●	●	●	◒	○	○	⊜	⊜
Exhaust	●	●	●	◒	○	⊖	⊜	⊜
Body rust	○	⊖	⊖	⊜	⊖	⊜	⊜	⊜
Paint/trim	●	●	●	◒	○	○	⊖	⊜
Integrity	◒	○	○	○	○	◒	○	○
Hardware	●	◒	○	○	○	○	○	○

Chevrolet Camaro

Trouble Spots	88	89	90	91	92	93	94	95
Engine	○	○		○		⊜	⊖	⊜
Cooling	●	●		◒		⊜	⊜	⊜
Fuel	●	◒		◒		⊖	⊖	⊜
Ignition	◒	◒		◒		⊜	⊜	⊜
Auto. trans.	⊖	○		⊖		⊖	⊖	⊖
Man. trans.	*	*		*		*	⊜	*
Clutch	*	*		*		*	⊖	*
Electrical	●	●	Insufficient data	●	Insufficient data	○	◒	○
A/C	◒	○		○		⊜	⊖	⊜
Suspension	◒	◒		○		⊜	⊖	⊖
Brakes	●	◒		◒		○	⊜	⊜
Exhaust	●	●		○		⊜	⊜	⊜
Body rust	◒	○		⊖		⊜	⊜	⊜
Paint/trim	●	●		●		○	○	⊖
Integrity	●	●		●		●	●	◒
Hardware	●	●		◒		◒	◒	○

Chevrolet Caprice

Trouble Spots	88	89	90	91	92	93	94	95
Engine	○	○	○	⊖	⊖	⊖	⊖	⊜
Cooling	●	◒	○	⊖	⊜	⊖	⊜	⊜
Fuel	◒	○	⊖	○	⊖	⊜	⊖	⊜
Ignition	○	⊖	⊖	◒	⊖	⊜	⊖	⊜
Auto. trans.	◒	○	⊜	⊖	⊜	⊖	⊖	⊜
Man. trans.								
Clutch								
Electrical	●	●	●	●	◒	◒	◒	○
A/C	◒	○	⊖	◒	◒	○	⊖	⊜
Suspension	⊖	○	○	○	◒	○	○	⊖
Brakes	◒	●	●	●	◒	⊖	⊖	⊖
Exhaust	●	●	◒	●	⊖	⊜	⊜	⊜
Body rust	◒	○	◒	⊖	⊜	⊜	⊜	⊜
Paint/trim	●	◒	◒	◒	○	⊖	⊖	⊖
Integrity	◒	○	○	◒	○	◒	○	○
Hardware	◒	◒	◒	●	◒	○	◒	○

Chevrolet Cavalier

Trouble Spots	88	89	90	91	92	93	94	95
Engine	◒	◒	○	○	○	⊖	⊜	⊜
Cooling	◒	◒	◒	○	○	⊜	⊜	⊜
Fuel	◒	◒	⊖	⊜	○	⊜	⊜	⊜
Ignition	◒	◒	⊖	⊖	⊖	⊖	⊖	⊜
Auto. trans.	○	○	⊖	⊖	⊜	⊖	⊖	⊜
Man. trans.	*	⊖	*	⊜	*	*	*	*
Clutch	*	◒	*	⊖	*	*	*	*
Electrical	●	●	●	●	●	◒	○	⊖
A/C	◒	○	○	○	○	⊖	⊖	⊜
Suspension	◒	○	○	○	⊖	○	⊜	⊖
Brakes	◒	●	●	●	●	◒	○	⊖
Exhaust	●	●	⊖	⊖	⊖	⊖	⊜	⊜
Body rust	●	●	◒	○	⊖	⊖	⊜	⊜
Paint/trim	●	●	●	◒	○	○	⊖	⊜
Integrity	●	●	◒	◒	◒	◒	◒	⊖
Hardware	◒	◒	○	○	●	◒	◒	⊖

Chevrolet Celebrity

Trouble Spots	88	89	90	91	92	93	94	95
Engine	○	○	⊖					
Cooling	◒	◒	●					
Fuel	◒	◒	○					
Ignition	◒	○	○					
Auto. trans.	○	○	○					
Man. trans.	*							
Clutch	*							
Electrical	●	●	●					
A/C	○	○	○					
Suspension	●	○	○					
Brakes	●	●	●					
Exhaust	●	●	●					
Body rust	●	●	○					
Paint/trim	●	●	◒					
Integrity	◒	○	◒					
Hardware	◒	○	◒					

Chevrolet Corsica, Beretta

Trouble Spots	88	89	90	91	92	93	94	95
Engine	○	○	○	○	⊖	⊖	⊖	
Cooling	◒	◒	○	○	◒	○	⊜	
Fuel	●	●	○	⊖	⊖	⊖	⊜	
Ignition	◒	◒	○	⊖	⊖	⊖	⊜	
Auto. trans.	○	⊖	⊖	⊖	⊖	⊜	⊜	
Man. trans.	⊖	⊜	*	*	*	*	*	
Clutch	●	◒	*	*	*	*	*	Insufficient data
Electrical	●	●	●	●	●	◒	○	
A/C	◒	○	○	○	○	⊖	⊖	
Suspension	◒	○	○	○	○	⊖	⊖	
Brakes	●	●	●	●	●	●	○	
Exhaust	●	●	●	⊖	⊜	⊜	⊜	
Body rust	○	○	⊖	⊖	⊜	⊜	⊜	
Paint/trim	●	●	●	◒	○	○	⊖	
Integrity	●	●	●	◒	◒	●	◒	
Hardware	●	●	●	○	◒	◒	◒	

Chevrolet Corvette

Trouble Spots	88	89	90	91	92	93	94	95
Engine						○	⊜	
Cooling						⊜	⊜	
Fuel						⊜	⊜	
Ignition						⊖	⊜	
Auto. trans.						*	*	
Man. trans.						*	*	
Clutch						*	*	
Electrical	Insufficient data	Insufficient data	Insufficient data	Insufficient data	Insufficient data	●	○	Insufficient data
A/C						○	⊜	
Suspension						⊖	⊜	
Brakes						⊖	⊖	
Exhaust						⊜	⊜	
Body rust						⊜	⊜	
Paint/trim						○	○	
Integrity						●	●	
Hardware						●	●	

Chevrolet Lumina

Trouble Spots	88	89	90	91	92	93	94	95
Engine			○	○	⊖	⊖	⊜	⊜
Cooling			○	⊖	⊖	⊜	⊖	⊜
Fuel			○	○	⊖	⊖	⊖	⊜
Ignition			○	⊖	○	⊖	⊜	⊜
Auto. trans.			○	○	⊖	⊖	⊜	⊜
Man. trans.				*	*	*		
Clutch				*	*	*		
Electrical			●	●	●	●	◒	⊖
A/C			⊖	⊖	⊖	⊖	⊖	⊜
Suspension			○	○	⊖	⊖	⊖	⊖
Brakes			●	●	●	◒	○	⊖
Exhaust			⊜	⊜	⊖	⊜	⊜	⊜
Body rust			⊖	⊜	⊜	⊜	⊜	⊜
Paint/trim			◒	○	○	⊖	⊖	⊖
Integrity			◒	◒	◒	◒	●	⊖
Hardware			●	◒	◒	○	◒	○

Chevrolet Lumina APV Van

Trouble Spots	88	89	90	91	92	93	94	95
Engine			○	⊖	⊖	⊖	⊖	⊜
Cooling			●	○	○	⊖	⊖	⊜
Fuel			⊖	⊖	⊖	⊖	⊜	⊜
Ignition			⊖	⊜	⊖	⊖	⊜	⊜
Auto. trans.			⊖	⊖	⊖	○	⊖	⊜
Man. trans.								
Clutch								
Electrical			●	●	●	●	◒	○
A/C			○	○	○	○	⊜	⊜
Suspension			○	⊖	○	○	⊖	⊜
Brakes			●	●	●	○	⊖	⊜
Exhaust			⊖	⊜	⊖	⊖	⊜	⊜
Body rust			⊖	⊜	⊜	⊜	⊜	⊜
Paint/trim			●	●	○	○	○	⊖
Integrity			◒	◒	○	◒	◒	○
Hardware			●	●	●	●	●	◒

Chevrolet Monte Carlo

Trouble Spots	88	89	90	91	92	93	94	95
Engine								⊜
Cooling								⊜
Fuel								⊜
Ignition								⊜
Auto. trans.								⊖
Man. trans.								
Clutch								
Electrical								⊖
A/C								⊜
Suspension								⊖
Brakes								⊖
Exhaust								⊜
Body rust								⊜
Paint/trim								○
Integrity								○
Hardware								⊖

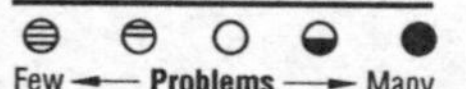

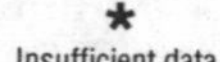

Chevrolet S-10 Blazer, Blazer (2WD)

TROUBLE SPOTS	88	89	90	91	92	93	94	95
Engine	◒	○	Insufficient data	⊖	○	○	○	⊜
Cooling	◒	○		○	⊖	⊜	⊖	⊜
Fuel	◒	⊖		⊖	○	⊖	⊖	⊖
Ignition	⊖	○		⊖	○	⊖	⊜	⊜
Auto. trans.	◒	⊜		⊜	*	⊖	⊖	⊜
Man. trans.	*	*		*	*	*	*	*
Clutch	*	*		*	*	*	*	*
Electrical	●	●		●	○	◒	●	⊖
A/C	◒	⊖		○	⊖	⊜	⊖	⊜
Suspension	○	⊖		⊖	○	⊖	⊖	⊖
Brakes	●	◒		●	●	●	◒	⊖
Exhaust	◒	○		⊖	⊜	⊜	⊜	⊜
Body rust	◒	○		○	⊖	⊜	⊜	⊜
Paint/trim	●	●		●	◒	○	⊜	⊖
Integrity	●	◒		●	◒	◒	●	○
Hardware	●	◒		●	○	●	◒	⊖

Chevrolet S-10 Blazer, Blazer (4WD)

TROUBLE SPOTS	88	89	90	91	92	93	94	95
Engine	◒	○	⊖	⊖	○	○	⊜	⊜
Cooling	●	◒	○	⊖	⊖	⊖	⊜	⊜
Fuel	○	○	⊖	⊖	○	○	⊜	⊜
Ignition	○	○	○	○	⊖	⊖	⊜	⊜
Auto. trans.	◒	⊖	○	⊜	⊖	◒	⊖	⊜
Man. trans.	*	*	*	*	*	*	*	*
Clutch	*	*	*	*	*	*	*	*
Electrical	●	●	●	●	◒	●	◒	○
A/C	◒	○	⊖	⊖	⊖	⊖	⊜	⊜
Suspension	◒	◒	○	◒	○	○	⊖	⊜
Brakes	●	●	●	●	●	●	○	⊜
Exhaust	●	◒	◒	○	⊖	⊜	⊜	⊜
Body rust	◒	●	●	◒	⊖	⊖	⊜	⊜
Paint/trim	●	●	●	●	◒	○	⊖	⊖
Integrity	◒	●	●	●	◒	●	◒	◒
Hardware	●	●	●	●	◒	◒	○	○

Chevrolet S-10 Pickup (2WD)

TROUBLE SPOTS	88	89	90	91	92	93	94	95
Engine	○	○	⊖	⊖	○	⊖	⊜	⊜
Cooling	◒	◒	○	○	⊜	⊖	⊜	⊜
Fuel	◒	○	⊖	⊖	⊖	⊜	⊖	⊜
Ignition	○	○	○	○	○	⊜	⊜	⊖
Auto. trans.	⊖	⊖	○	⊜	⊖	⊖	⊖	⊜
Man. trans.	⊖	⊖	*	⊖	⊜	⊖	○	⊖
Clutch	◒	○	*	○	○	○	○	⊖
Electrical	●	●	●	◒	◒	○	◒	○
A/C	◒	○	⊖	⊖	⊖	⊖	⊖	⊜
Suspension	○	⊖	⊖	⊖	○	⊖	⊖	⊖
Brakes	●	○	◒	○	◒	⊖	○	⊖
Exhaust	●	●	●	◒	○	⊖	⊜	⊜
Body rust	◒	◒	○	◒	⊖	⊜	⊜	⊜
Paint/trim	●	●	●	●	●	○	⊖	⊖
Integrity	●	●	◒	◒	○	○	○	○
Hardware	◒	◒	◒	◒	○	○	○	⊖

Chevrolet S-10 Pickup (4WD)

TROUBLE SPOTS	88	89	90	91	92	93	94	95
Engine	●	⊖	Insufficient data	⊖	○	Insufficient data	⊖	⊜
Cooling	◒	◒		⊖	⊖		⊖	⊜
Fuel	○	○		○	⊖		⊖	⊜
Ignition	○	⊖		◒	◒		⊖	⊜
Auto. trans.	◒	○		⊖	⊖		○	⊖
Man. trans.	*	*		*	*		*	*
Clutch	*	*		*	*		*	*
Electrical	●	●		●	◒		●	○
A/C	○	⊖		⊖	⊖		⊖	⊜
Suspension	●	●		◒	◒		⊖	○
Brakes	●	◒		◒	●		○	⊜
Exhaust	●	●		◒	⊖		⊜	⊜
Body rust	●	●		◒	○		⊜	⊜
Paint/trim	●	●		●	◒		○	⊖
Integrity	◒	●		◒	○		◒	○
Hardware	◒	●		◒	⊖		◒	⊖

Chevrolet Sportvan

TROUBLE SPOTS	88	89	90	91	92	93	94	95
Engine	◒	◒	⊖	⊖	⊖	⊜	⊖	Insufficient data
Cooling	●	◒	◒	◒	○	⊖	⊜	
Fuel	○	⊖	⊖	⊖	⊖	⊖	⊖	
Ignition	⊖	⊖	⊜	⊜	⊜	⊜	⊜	
Auto. trans.	○	○	○	⊖	○	⊖	⊖	
Man. trans.	*	*						
Clutch	*	*						
Electrical	●	●	◒	◒	◒	●	●	
A/C	◒	●	◒	◒	⊖	○	◒	
Suspension	●	◒	◒	○	○	○	⊜	
Brakes	◒	●	●	◒	●	●	○	
Exhaust	○	◒	◒	○	⊖	⊜	⊜	
Body rust	◒	◒	◒	○	⊖	⊖	⊜	
Paint/trim	●	●	●	◒	○	◒	○	
Integrity	●	●	◒	●	●	●	●	
Hardware	●	●	◒	◒	○	●	●	

Chevrolet Suburban

TROUBLE SPOTS	88	89	90	91	92	93	94	95
Engine	◒	◒	⊖	⊖	⊖	⊖	⊜	⊜
Cooling	●	●	◒	◒	○	○	⊜	⊜
Fuel	○	○	⊖	○	⊖	⊖	⊜	⊜
Ignition	⊖	○	○	⊖	⊖	⊜	⊜	⊜
Auto. trans.	○	◒	○	◒	◒	⊖	⊜	⊜
Man. trans.	*	*	*					
Clutch	*	*	*					
Electrical	●	●	●	◒	●	●	○	⊖
A/C	◒	◒	○	○	○	⊖	○	⊜
Suspension	◒	○	○	○	○	⊖	⊖	⊜
Brakes	●	●	●	●	●	○	○	⊖
Exhaust	●	◒	○	○	⊖	⊖	⊜	⊖
Body rust	●	◒	○	⊖	⊖	⊖	⊜	⊜
Paint/trim	●	●	●	◒	◒	○	⊖	⊜
Integrity	●	●	●	◒	●	◒	○	⊖
Hardware	●	●	●	◒	●	●	◒	○

Chrysler Cirrus

TROUBLE SPOTS	88	89	90	91	92	93	94	95
Engine								⊜
Cooling								⊜
Fuel								⊜
Ignition								⊜
Auto. trans.								⊖
Man. trans.								
Clutch								
Electrical								○
A/C								⊖
Suspension								⊜
Brakes								⊜
Exhaust								⊜
Body rust								⊜
Paint/trim								○
Integrity								◒
Hardware								○

Chrysler Concorde

TROUBLE SPOTS	88	89	90	91	92	93	94	95
Engine						⊖	⊜	⊜
Cooling						⊖	⊜	⊜
Fuel						⊖	⊖	⊜
Ignition						⊖	⊜	⊜
Auto. trans.						⊖	⊖	⊜
Man. trans.								
Clutch								
Electrical						◒	◒	⊖
A/C						◒	○	⊜
Suspension						⊖	⊜	⊜
Brakes						◒	○	⊖
Exhaust						⊜	⊜	⊜
Body rust						⊜	⊜	⊜
Paint/trim						⊖	⊖	⊜
Integrity						◒	◒	⊖
Hardware						◒	○	⊖

Chrysler Le Baron Sedan

TROUBLE SPOTS	88	89	90	91	92	93	94	95
Engine	●		○	○	○	⊖	⊜	
Cooling	●		○	⊖	⊖	⊜	⊜	
Fuel	◒		○	○	⊖	⊖	⊖	
Ignition	○		⊖	⊖	⊖	⊜	⊜	
Auto. trans.	○		◒	◒	⊖	⊖	○	
Man. trans.								
Clutch								
Electrical	●		◒	◒	◒	○	○	
A/C	●		○	○	⊖	⊖	⊖	
Suspension	◒		○	○	⊖	⊖	⊖	
Brakes	●		●	○	○	⊜	⊖	
Exhaust	○		⊜	●	◒	⊜	⊜	
Body rust	○		⊖	⊜	⊜	⊜	⊜	
Paint/trim	◒		○	○	⊖	⊜	⊖	
Integrity	○		○	○	○	○	○	
Hardware	◒		○	⊖	○	○	○	

Chrysler Le Baron Coupe & Convertible

TROUBLE SPOTS	88	89	90	91	92	93	94	95
Engine	●	◒	○	○	○	⊖	⊖	Insufficient data
Cooling	●	●	◒	⊖	⊖	⊜	⊜	
Fuel	◒	◒	⊖	⊖	⊖	⊖	⊜	
Ignition	○	⊖	⊖	⊜	⊜	⊜	⊜	
Auto. trans.	◒	⊖	◒	●	◒	◒	○	
Man. trans.	*	*	*	*	*	*		
Clutch	*	*	*	*	*	*		
Electrical	●	●	●	●	●	◒	○	
A/C	●	●	○	⊖	○	⊖	⊜	
Suspension	●	●	○	⊖	⊖	⊖	⊜	
Brakes	●	●	●	○	○	○	⊜	
Exhaust	○	⊜	⊜	○	⊖	⊜	⊜	
Body rust	○	○	⊜	⊜	⊜	⊜	⊜	
Paint/trim	●	●	◒	○	○	●	○	
Integrity	●	●	●	●	●	●	●	
Hardware	●	◒	●	●	●	●	◒	

Chrysler New Yorker, LHS

TROUBLE SPOTS	88	89	90	91	92	93	94	95
Engine	●	●	○	◒	◒	◒	⊖	⊜
Cooling	●	●	○	○	⊖	⊖	⊜	⊜
Fuel	●	○	○	○	○	⊜	⊖	⊜
Ignition	○	⊖	○	○	⊖	⊜	⊜	⊜
Auto. trans.	○	●	●	●	◒	○	○	⊜
Man. trans.								
Clutch								
Electrical	●	●	●	●	●	◒	◒	⊖
A/C	●	●	◒	○	◒	◒	○	⊜
Suspension	◒	◒	◒	◒	◒	○	⊖	⊜
Brakes	●	●	●	◒	◒	⊖	○	⊜
Exhaust	⊖	⊜	⊖	○	⊖	⊜	⊜	⊜
Body rust	⊖	⊖	⊖	⊜	⊜	⊜	⊜	⊜
Paint/trim	◒	○	○	⊖	○	⊜	⊖	⊜
Integrity	◒	○	○	⊖	◒	◒	◒	⊖
Hardware	●	◒	○	○	◒	○	◒	⊖

Chrysler Sebring

TROUBLE SPOTS	88	89	90	91	92	93	94	95
Engine								⊜
Cooling								⊜
Fuel								⊜
Ignition								⊜
Auto. trans.								⊜
Man. trans.								*
Clutch								*
Electrical								⊖
A/C								⊜
Suspension								○
Brakes								⊜
Exhaust								⊜
Body rust								⊜
Paint/trim								⊖
Integrity								○
Hardware								○

Chrysler Town & Country Van (2WD)

TROUBLE SPOTS	88	89	90	91	92	93	94	95
Engine			○	○	○	○	⊖	⊜
Cooling			◒	○	⊖	⊖	⊜	⊜
Fuel			○	○	⊖	⊖	⊜	⊜
Ignition			⊖	⊖	⊖	⊜	⊜	⊜
Auto. trans.			●	●	◒	◒	○	⊜
Man. trans.								
Clutch								
Electrical			●	●	●	◒	○	⊖
A/C			◒	⊖	⊖	○	⊖	⊜
Suspension			○	○	○	○	⊖	⊜
Brakes			●	●	◒	○	⊖	⊜
Exhaust			⊖	◒	⊜	⊜	⊜	⊜
Body rust			⊖	⊜	⊜	⊜	⊜	⊜
Paint/trim			◒	○	⊖	⊖	⊖	⊖
Integrity			◒	◒	◒	◒	◒	○
Hardware			●	◒	◒	◒	○	⊖

Chrysler Town & Country Van (4WD)

TROUBLE SPOTS	88	89	90	91	92	93	94	95
Engine					○	○	○	Insufficient data
Cooling					○	⊜	⊖	
Fuel					○	○	⊖	
Ignition					⊖	⊖	⊜	
Auto. trans.					●	◒	○	
Man. trans.								
Clutch								
Electrical					●	○	○	
A/C					⊖	⊖	⊖	
Suspension					○	○	⊖	
Brakes					●	◒	⊖	
Exhaust					●	⊜	⊜	
Body rust					⊜	⊜	⊜	
Paint/trim					⊖	⊖	⊖	
Integrity					●	⊖	◒	
Hardware					◒	◒	○	

Dodge Avenger

TROUBLE SPOTS	88	89	90	91	92	93	94	95
Engine								⊜
Cooling								⊜
Fuel								⊜
Ignition								⊜
Auto. trans.								⊜
Man. trans.								*
Clutch								*
Electrical								⊖
A/C								⊜
Suspension								○
Brakes								⊜
Exhaust								⊜
Body rust								⊜
Paint/trim								⊖
Integrity								○
Hardware								○

Dodge Caravan V6 (2WD)

TROUBLE SPOTS	88	89	90	91	92	93	94	95
Engine	●	●	◒	○	○	⊖	⊜	⊜
Cooling	●	●	◒	○	⊖	⊖	⊜	⊜
Fuel	●	○	◒	○	⊖	⊜	⊜	⊜
Ignition	○	⊖	⊖	⊖	⊜	⊜	⊜	⊜
Auto. trans.	◒	◒	●	◒	◒	○	⊖	⊜
Man. trans.								
Clutch								
Electrical	●	●	◒	●	●	○	○	⊖
A/C	●	◒	○	⊖	⊖	○	⊖	⊜
Suspension	◒	○	○	○	⊖	⊖	⊖	⊜
Brakes	●	●	●	●	◒	○	⊜	⊜
Exhaust	⊖	⊜	⊖	●	⊖	⊜	⊜	⊜
Body rust	○	⊖	⊖	⊜	⊜	⊜	⊜	⊜
Paint/trim	◒	◒	○	○	⊖	⊖	⊖	⊜
Integrity	◒	◒	◒	◒	◒	◒	○	⊖
Hardware	●	●	●	◒	◒	◒	○	⊖

Dodge Grand Caravan V6 (2WD)

TROUBLE SPOTS	88	89	90	91	92	93	94	95
Engine	●	●	○	○	○	○	⊖	⊜
Cooling	●	●	◒	○	⊖	⊖	⊜	⊜
Fuel	●	◒	○	○	⊖	⊖	⊜	⊜
Ignition	○	⊖	⊖	⊖	⊖	⊜	⊜	⊜
Auto. trans.	◒	●	●	●	◒	◒	○	⊜
Man. trans.								
Clutch								
Electrical	●	●	●	●	●	◒	○	⊖
A/C	●	●	◒	⊖	⊖	○	⊖	⊜
Suspension	●	◒	○	○	○	○	⊖	⊜
Brakes	●	●	●	●	◒	○	⊖	⊜
Exhaust	⊖	⊜	⊖	◒	⊜	⊜	⊜	⊜
Body rust	⊖	⊖	⊖	⊜	⊜	⊜	⊜	⊜
Paint/trim	◒	◒	◒	○	⊖	⊜	⊖	⊖
Integrity	◒	◒	◒	◒	◒	◒	◒	○
Hardware	●	●	●	◒	◒	◒	○	⊖

Dodge Grand Caravan V6 (4WD)

TROUBLE SPOTS	88	89	90	91	92	93	94	95
Engine				○	○	○	○	Insufficient data
Cooling				⊖	○	⊜	⊖	
Fuel				●	○	○	⊖	
Ignition				○	⊖	⊖	⊜	
Auto. trans.				●	●	◒	○	
Man. trans.								
Clutch								
Electrical				●	●	○	○	
A/C				⊖	⊖	⊖	⊖	
Suspension				◒	○	○	⊖	
Brakes				●	●	◒	⊖	
Exhaust				●	●	⊜	⊜	
Body rust				⊖	⊜	⊜	⊜	
Paint/trim				◒	⊖	⊜	⊜	
Integrity				◒	●	⊖	◒	
Hardware				◒	◒	◒	○	

Dodge Colt, Colt Wagon

Trouble spots	88	89	90	91	92	93	94	95
Engine	●	◒	◒	⊖	⊜	⊜		
Cooling	○	⊖	⊖	⊜	⊜	⊜		
Fuel	⊖	⊖	⊖	⊖	⊜	⊜		
Ignition	○	⊖	⊖	⊖	⊜	⊜		
Auto. trans.	○	⊖	⊖	○	○	●		
Man. trans.	⊜	⊖	⊖	⊖	⊖	⊖		
Clutch	○	⊖	⊖	⊖	⊜	⊖		
Electrical	◒	◒	○	○	○	○		
A/C	○	◒	○	○	⊜	⊜	Insufficient data	
Suspension	○	◒	○	⊖	⊜	⊜		
Brakes	●	●	◒	◒	○	○		
Exhaust	○	⊜	⊜	⊜	⊜	⊜		
Body rust	◒	⊜	⊜	⊖	⊜	⊜		
Paint/trim	○	◒	○	○	○	⊖		
Integrity	◒	◒	◒	◒	◒	○		
Hardware	○	◒	◒	○	○	○		

Dodge Dakota Pickup (2WD)

Trouble spots	88	89	90	91	92	93	94	95
Engine	○	○	○	⊜	⊖	⊖	○	⊜
Cooling	○	○	○	⊖	○	⊜	⊜	⊜
Fuel	○	○	○	○	○	⊖	⊜	⊖
Ignition	○	○	○	○	○	⊜	⊖	⊜
Auto. trans.	○	●	●	○	○	○	○	○
Man. trans.	*	*	*	*	*	⊜	*	*
Clutch	*	*	*	*	*	⊖	*	*
Electrical	◒	◒	○	◒	◒	◒	○	○
A/C	◒	◒	○	○	⊖	⊖	⊜	⊜
Suspension	○	○	○	⊖	○	○	○	○
Brakes	●	●	●	◒	◒	○	⊖	⊖
Exhaust	⊜	○	⊜	○	◒	⊜	⊜	⊜
Body rust	⊖	⊖	⊜	⊖	⊜	⊜	⊜	⊜
Paint/trim	◒	◒	○	⊖	○	⊜	⊜	○
Integrity	○	◒	◒	○	○	○	◒	○
Hardware	○	⊖	⊜	⊜	⊖	○	○	⊖

Dodge Dakota Pickup (4WD)

Trouble spots	88	89	90	91	92	93	94	95
Engine	◒	○			○	⊜	⊖	⊜
Cooling	◒	◒			○	⊖	⊜	⊜
Fuel	◒	◒			○	○	⊜	⊖
Ignition	◒	◒			○	⊖	⊜	⊜
Auto. trans.	*	*			●	◒	◒	⊖
Man. trans.	*	*			*	*	*	*
Clutch	*	*			*	*	*	*
Electrical	◒	◒			◒	○	○	⊜
A/C	*	*	Insufficient data	Insufficient data	⊜	⊜	⊖	⊜
Suspension	⊖	○			○	○	○	⊜
Brakes	●	●			◒	○	⊖	⊖
Exhaust	○	◒			◒	⊜	⊜	⊜
Body rust	○	○			⊖	⊜	⊜	⊜
Paint/trim	○	◒			⊖	⊖	⊖	⊜
Integrity	◒	⊖			○	○	◒	⊖
Hardware	○	⊖			○	○	○	⊖

Dodge Daytona

Trouble spots	88	89	90	91	92	93	94	95
Engine	●	●	◒					
Cooling	◒	●	◒					
Fuel	◒	○	◒					
Ignition	○	○	○					
Auto. trans.	*	*	○					
Man. trans.	*	*	*					
Clutch	*	*	*					
Electrical	●	●	●					
A/C	●	●	◒	Insufficient data	Insufficient data	Insufficient data		
Suspension	●	●	○					
Brakes	●	●	●					
Exhaust	⊖	⊖	⊜					
Body rust	○	◒	⊖					
Paint/trim	●	●	◒					
Integrity	●	●	◒					
Hardware	●	●	◒					

Dodge Dynasty

Trouble spots	88	89	90	91	92	93	94	95
Engine	◒	◒	⊖	⊖	○	○		
Cooling	◒	◒	○	○	⊖	⊖		
Fuel	●	○	⊖	○	⊖	⊖		
Ignition	⊖	⊖	⊖	○	⊜	⊖		
Auto. trans.	○	●	◒	◒	●	○		
Man. trans.								
Clutch								
Electrical	●	●	●	●	◒	○		
A/C	●	○	○	○	○	⊖		
Suspension	◒	◒	○	⊖	○	○		
Brakes	●	●	◒	◒	○	○		
Exhaust	⊜	⊖	⊜	●	◒	⊜		
Body rust	⊖	⊖	⊖	⊖	⊜	⊜		
Paint/trim	○	○	○	⊖	○	⊖		
Integrity	●	◒	◒	○	◒	◒		
Hardware	◒	◒	○	⊖	◒	○		

Dodge Intrepid

Trouble spots	88	89	90	91	92	93	94	95
Engine						⊖	⊖	⊜
Cooling						⊖	⊜	⊜
Fuel						⊖	⊜	⊜
Ignition						⊖	⊜	⊜
Auto. trans.						○	○	⊜
Man. trans.								
Clutch								
Electrical						◒	◒	⊖
A/C						○	○	⊜
Suspension						⊖	⊖	⊜
Brakes						◒	○	⊖
Exhaust						⊖	⊜	⊜
Body rust						⊜	⊜	⊜
Paint/trim						◒	⊖	⊖
Integrity						●	●	○
Hardware						◒	○	⊖

Dodge Monaco

Trouble spots	88	89	90	91	92	93	94	95
Engine			○	◒				
Cooling			●	●				
Fuel			◒	◒				
Ignition			◒	○				
Auto. trans.			◒	◒				
Man. trans.								
Clutch								
Electrical			●	●				
A/C			●	◒	Insufficient data			
Suspension			○	◒				
Brakes			●	●				
Exhaust			◒	◒				
Body rust			⊜	⊜				
Paint/trim			●	○				
Integrity			◒	◒				
Hardware			●	●				

Dodge Neon

Trouble spots	88	89	90	91	92	93	94	95
Engine								⊜
Cooling								⊜
Fuel								⊖
Ignition								⊜
Auto. trans.								⊖
Man. trans.								⊜
Clutch								⊜
Electrical								○
A/C								⊖
Suspension								⊜
Brakes								⊖
Exhaust								⊖
Body rust								⊜
Paint/trim								⊖
Integrity								◒
Hardware								○

Dodge Omni, America

Trouble spots	88	89	90	91	92	93	94	95
Engine	◒	◒	◒					
Cooling	◒	◒	◒					
Fuel	◒	○	○					
Ignition	○	○	⊖					
Auto. trans.	⊖	⊖	*					
Man. trans.	⊖	*	*					
Clutch	○	*	*					
Electrical	●	◒	◒					
A/C	●	●	*					
Suspension	○	○	◒					
Brakes	●	●	●					
Exhaust	⊖	⊖	⊖					
Body rust	●	◒	○					
Paint/trim	●	●	◒					
Integrity	●	●	●					
Hardware	●	◒	◒					

Dodge Ram Pickup

Trouble spots	88	89	90	91	92	93	94	95
Engine	⊖	○	⊖				⊖	⊜
Cooling	◒	◒	◒				⊜	⊜
Fuel	◒	○	◒				⊖	⊜
Ignition	○	⊖	○				⊜	⊜
Auto. trans.	○	◒	*				○	⊖
Man. trans.	*	*	*				*	*
Clutch	*	*	*				*	*
Electrical	◒	○	○				○	⊖
A/C	*	*	*	Insufficient data	Insufficient data	Insufficient data	⊖	⊜
Suspension	◒	○	⊖				○	⊖
Brakes	●	●	◒				○	⊖
Exhaust	○	●	⊖				⊜	⊜
Body rust	○	◒	◒				⊜	⊜
Paint/trim	●	●	●				○	⊜
Integrity	◒	◒	○				○	⊖
Hardware	○	○	◒				◒	⊖

Dodge Ram Van B150-250

Trouble spots	88	89	90	91	92	93	94	95
Engine	○	○	⊖	⊜	○	⊜	⊖	
Cooling	◒	◒	○	⊖	⊜	⊜	⊜	
Fuel	○	○	◒	○	⊖	○	⊜	
Ignition	◒	◒	⊖	⊖	⊖	⊜	⊜	
Auto. trans.	◒	●	●	◒	◒	○	○	
Man. trans.	*	*	*	*	*	*		
Clutch	*	*	*	*	*	*		
Electrical	●	●	◒	●	◒	◒	○	
A/C	●	●	●	◒	◒	*	⊖	Insufficient data
Suspension	◒	◒	○	◒	○	○	⊜	
Brakes	◒	●	●	●	◒	○	⊖	
Exhaust	⊖	◒	⊖	◒	⊖	⊜	⊜	
Body rust	◒	◒	○	○	⊖	⊖	⊜	
Paint/trim	●	●	●	●	◒	○	⊖	
Integrity	◒	●	◒	●	●	◒	●	
Hardware	◒	◒	○	◒	○	◒	◒	

Dodge Shadow

Trouble spots	88	89	90	91	92	93	94	95
Engine	●	●	◒	○	○	○	⊖	
Cooling	●	●	◒	○	⊖	⊜	⊜	
Fuel	◒	◒	○	○	○	⊖	⊖	
Ignition	○	○	○	⊖	⊜	⊜	⊜	
Auto. trans.	○	○	⊖	⊖	⊖	○	⊖	
Man. trans.	*	*	*	*	⊖	⊖	*	
Clutch	*	*	*	*	⊖	⊖	*	
Electrical	●	●	●	●	◒	◒	○	
A/C	●	●	●	◒	○	⊖	⊖	
Suspension	◒	●	○	○	⊖	⊜	⊖	
Brakes	●	●	●	○	⊜	⊖	⊖	
Exhaust	○	⊖	⊜	●	◒	⊜	⊜	
Body rust	○	○	⊖	⊖	⊖	⊜	⊜	
Paint/trim	●	●	◒	○	◒	◒	⊖	
Integrity	◒	◒	○	◒	◒	◒	◒	
Hardware	●	●	○	○	○	○	◒	

Dodge Spirit

Trouble spots	88	89	90	91	92	93	94	95
Engine		◒	○	○	○	⊖	⊜	⊜
Cooling		●	○	⊖	⊖	⊜	⊜	⊜
Fuel		○	○	○	⊜	⊖	⊖	⊜
Ignition		○	⊖	⊖	⊖	⊜	⊜	⊜
Auto. trans.		○	◒	◒	⊖	⊖	○	⊜
Man. trans.		*	*	*	*	*		
Clutch		*	*	*	*	*		
Electrical		●	◒	◒	◒	○	○	○
A/C		●	○	○	⊜	⊜	⊜	⊜
Suspension		◒	○	○	⊜	⊖	⊖	⊜
Brakes		●	●	○	○	⊜	⊖	⊜
Exhaust		⊖	⊜	●	◒	⊜	⊜	⊜
Body rust		○	⊖	⊜	⊜	⊜	⊜	⊜
Paint/trim		◒	○	○	⊖	⊖	⊖	⊖
Integrity		○	○	○	○	○	○	○
Hardware		○	○	⊜	○	○	○	⊖

Dodge Stealth (2WD)

Trouble spots	88	89	90	91	92	93	94	95
Engine				⊖	⊜	⊖	⊜	
Cooling				⊜	⊜	⊖	⊜	
Fuel				⊜	⊜	⊜	⊜	
Ignition				⊜	⊜	⊜	⊜	
Auto. trans.				*	*	*	*	
Man. trans.				*	○	○	*	
Clutch				*	◒	◒	*	
Electrical				○	●	◒	◒	
A/C				⊜	⊖	⊖	⊜	Insufficient data
Suspension				⊜	⊖	⊖	⊜	
Brakes				○	⊖	⊖	⊜	
Exhaust				⊜	⊜	⊜	⊜	
Body rust				⊜	⊜	⊜	⊜	
Paint/trim				◒	○	◒	⊖	
Integrity				○	◒	◒	○	
Hardware				◒	◒	◒	○	

Dodge Stratus

Trouble spots	88	89	90	91	92	93	94	95
Engine								⊜
Cooling								⊜
Fuel								⊜
Ignition								⊜
Auto. trans.								⊖
Man. trans.								*
Clutch								*
Electrical								○
A/C								⊖
Suspension								⊜
Brakes								⊜
Exhaust								⊜
Body rust								⊜
Paint/trim								○
Integrity								◒
Hardware								○

Eagle Premier V6

Trouble spots	88	89	90	91	92	93	94	95
Engine	◒	◒	○	◒				
Cooling	●	●	●	●				
Fuel	◒	○	◒	◒				
Ignition	●	◒	◒	○				
Auto. trans.	●	◒	◒	◒				
Man. trans.								
Clutch								
Electrical	●	●	●	●				
A/C	●	●	●	◒	Insufficient data			
Suspension	●	◒	○	◒				
Brakes	●	●	●	●				
Exhaust	●	●	◒	◒				
Body rust	⊖	⊖	⊜	⊜				
Paint/trim	⊖	◒	●	○				
Integrity	○	◒	◒	◒				
Hardware	●	●	●	●				

Eagle Summit (except Wagon)

Trouble spots	88	89	90	91	92	93	94	95
Engine		◒	◒	⊖	⊜	⊜		
Cooling		⊖	⊖	⊜	⊜	⊜		
Fuel		⊖	⊖	⊖	⊜	⊜		
Ignition		⊖	⊖	⊖	⊜	⊜		
Auto. trans.		⊖	⊖	○	○	●		
Man. trans.		⊖	⊜	⊜	⊖	⊖		
Clutch		⊖	⊖	⊖	⊜	⊖		
Electrical		◒	○	○	○	○		
A/C		◒	○	○	⊖	⊜	Insufficient data	Insufficient data
Suspension		◒	○	⊖	⊖	⊜		
Brakes		●	◒	◒	○	○		
Exhaust		⊜	⊜	⊜	⊜	⊜		
Body rust		⊜	⊜	⊖	⊖	⊜		
Paint/trim		◒	○	○	○	⊖		
Integrity		◒	◒	◒	◒	○		
Hardware		◒	◒	○	○	○		

Eagle Summit Wagon

Trouble spots	88	89	90	91	92	93	94	95
Engine					⊜	⊖	⊜	
Cooling					⊖	⊖	⊜	
Fuel					⊖	⊜	⊜	
Ignition					⊜	⊜	⊜	
Auto. trans.					○	⊖	⊜	
Man. trans.					*	*	*	
Clutch					*	*	*	
Electrical					○	○	○	
A/C					⊖	⊜	⊜	Insufficient data
Suspension					○	⊜	⊜	
Brakes					○	⊖	⊖	
Exhaust					⊖	⊜	⊜	
Body rust					⊜	⊜	⊜	
Paint/trim					○	⊖	⊖	
Integrity					○	◒	⊖	
Hardware					○	◒	○	

Eagle Talon (2WD)

TROUBLE SPOTS	88	89	90	91	92	93	94	95
Engine			◒	◒	◒	⊖	⊜	○
Cooling			⊖	⊖	⊜	⊖	⊖	⊖
Fuel			⊖	⊖	⊜	⊖	⊖	⊖
Ignition			⊜	○	⊜	⊜	⊖	○
Auto. trans.			○	○	⊖	*	*	*
Man. trans.			○	○	○	⊖	*	*
Clutch			○	⊖	⊖	⊜	*	*
Electrical			◒	◒	◒	○	○	◒
A/C			⊖	⊖	⊜	⊜	⊖	⊜
Suspension			⊖	⊖	⊖	○	⊜	○
Brakes			◒	◒	○	○	⊖	⊖
Exhaust			⊖	○	○	⊜	⊜	⊖
Body rust			⊜	⊜	⊜	⊜	⊜	⊜
Paint/trim			○	○	○	○	⊖	⊖
Integrity			○	○	◒	○	○	◒
Hardware			○	◒	●	◒	○	●

Eagle Vision

TROUBLE SPOTS	88	89	90	91	92	93	94	95
Engine						⊖	⊖	⊜
Cooling						⊖	⊜	⊜
Fuel						⊖	⊖	⊜
Ignition						⊖	⊜	⊜
Auto. trans.						⊖	○	⊜
Man. trans.								
Clutch								
Electrical						●	○	○
A/C						◒	○	⊜
Suspension						⊖	⊖	⊖
Brakes						◒	⊖	⊖
Exhaust						⊜	⊜	⊜
Body rust						⊜	⊜	⊜
Paint/trim						⊖	⊖	⊜
Integrity						◒	◒	⊖
Hardware						◒	○	⊜

Ford Aerostar Van

TROUBLE SPOTS	88	89	90	91	92	93	94	95
Engine	◒	○	○	◒	○	⊖	⊜	⊜
Cooling	●	●	◒	○	○	⊜	⊖	⊖
Fuel	◒	○	⊖	⊜	⊜	⊜	⊜	⊜
Ignition	○	○	⊖	⊖	⊖	⊜	⊜	⊜
Auto. trans.	●	◒	○	○	⊖	⊖	⊜	⊜
Man. trans.	*	*	*	*	*	*	*	
Clutch	*	*	*	*	*	*	*	
Electrical	●	●	●	◒	●	○	⊖	○
A/C	●	●	●	●	◒	○	⊖	⊜
Suspension	●	●	◒	○	○	○	⊖	⊜
Brakes	●	●	●	●	●	◒	⊖	⊖
Exhaust	◒	◒	◒	◒	◒	⊖	⊜	⊜
Body rust	●	●	○	⊜	⊜	⊜	⊜	⊜
Paint/trim	●	○	⊖	⊖	⊖	⊖	⊖	⊜
Integrity	●	◒	◒	○	○	○	○	○
Hardware	●	●	◒	◒	◒	◒	○	○

Ford Bronco

TROUBLE SPOTS	88	89	90	91	92	93	94	95
Engine	◒	◒	◒	○	⊖	○	⊜	
Cooling	◒	◒	◒	○	○	⊜	⊜	
Fuel	●	●	○	◒	○	○	⊖	
Ignition	○	○	○	⊖	⊖	⊜	⊜	
Auto. trans.	○	◒	◒	○	⊜	⊖	⊖	
Man. trans.	*	*	*	*	*	*	*	Insufficient data
Clutch	*	*	*	*	*	*	*	
Electrical	●	●	◒	○	●	◒	○	
A/C	●	◒	○	⊖	○	⊜	○	
Suspension	◒	●	◒	○	○	○	◒	
Brakes	●	●	●	●	●	●	●	
Exhaust	●	●	●	●	○	⊜	⊜	
Body rust	●	●	●	◒	⊖	⊖	⊜	
Paint/trim	●	●	●	◒	◒	●	○	
Integrity	●	◒	◒	◒	◒	◒	●	
Hardware	●	●	●	●	◒	◒	◒	

Ford Bronco II

TROUBLE SPOTS	88	89	90	91	92	93	94	95
Engine	◒	●	◒					
Cooling	●	●	◒					
Fuel	○	○	⊖					
Ignition	⊖	○	⊖					
Auto. trans.	◒	○	*					
Man. trans.	○	⊖	*					
Clutch	◒	◒	*					
Electrical	●	◒	◒					
A/C	●	●	●					
Suspension	○	○	⊖					
Brakes	●	◒	◒					
Exhaust	●	●	●					
Body rust	●	◒	○					
Paint/trim	●	●	●					
Integrity	◒	◒	◒					
Hardware	◒	●	◒					

Ford Club Wagon, Van

TROUBLE SPOTS	88	89	90	91	92	93	94	95
Engine	◒	◒	○	◒	○	⊖	⊜	
Cooling	●	●	◒	⊖	○	⊖	⊖	
Fuel	●	◒	○	○	◒	⊖	⊖	
Ignition	◒	○	○	⊖	⊖	⊖	⊜	
Auto. trans.	○	○	○	○	○	⊖	⊖	
Man. trans.								Insufficient data
Clutch								
Electrical	●	●	◒	◒	●	◒	○	
A/C	●	●	●	●	◒	○	○	
Suspension	●	◒	◒	◒	●	◒	○	
Brakes	●	◒	●	◒	◒	◒	◒	
Exhaust	●	●	◒	○	○	⊜	⊜	
Body rust	●	◒	◒	○	⊖	⊜	⊜	
Paint/trim	●	◒	◒	⊖	○	○	⊖	
Integrity	●	●	●	●	○	○	○	
Hardware	●	◒	○	○	◒	◒	○	

Ford Contour

TROUBLE SPOTS	88	89	90	91	92	93	94	95
Engine								⊜
Cooling								⊜
Fuel								○
Ignition								⊜
Auto. trans.								⊖
Man. trans.								⊜
Clutch								⊜
Electrical								⊖
A/C								⊜
Suspension								⊜
Brakes								⊜
Exhaust								⊜
Body rust								⊜
Paint/trim								⊖
Integrity								⊖
Hardware								○

Ford Crown Victoria, LTD Crown Victoria

TROUBLE SPOTS	88	89	90	91	92	93	94	95
Engine	○	○	⊖	⊖	⊖	⊜	⊜	⊜
Cooling	◒	◒	○	⊖	⊜	⊜	⊜	⊜
Fuel	○	○	○	⊖	⊖	⊖	⊜	⊜
Ignition	⊖	⊖	⊖	⊖	○	⊜	⊜	⊜
Auto. trans.	○	○	⊖	⊖	○	◒	⊖	⊜
Man. trans.								
Clutch								
Electrical	●	◒	●	●	◒	○	○	○
A/C	●	●	◒	○	○	⊖	⊜	⊜
Suspension	○	○	○	○	⊖	⊖	⊖	⊖
Brakes	◒	●	●	●	●	◒	○	⊖
Exhaust	●	◒	○	○	●	⊜	⊜	⊜
Body rust	○	⊜	⊖	⊖	⊜	⊜	⊜	⊜
Paint/trim	◒	○	○	⊖	⊖	⊖	⊖	⊖
Integrity	○	⊖	○	⊖	○	⊖	⊖	○
Hardware	◒	◒	◒	◒	◒	○	⊖	⊖

Ford Escort

TROUBLE SPOTS	88	89	90	91	92	93	94	95
Engine	●	◒	○	⊖	⊖	⊖	⊖	⊜
Cooling	●	◒	◒	○	⊖	⊖	⊜	⊜
Fuel	●	●	●	○	○	⊖	⊜	⊜
Ignition	◒	◒	○	⊖	⊜	⊜	⊜	⊜
Auto. trans.	●	●	○	○	⊖	⊖	⊖	⊜
Man. trans.	⊖	⊖	⊖	⊖	⊜	⊖	⊖	⊜
Clutch	○	◒	⊖	⊖	⊜	⊖	⊖	⊜
Electrical	●	●	●	●	◒	◒	○	⊖
A/C	●	●	●	●	⊖	⊖	⊜	⊜
Suspension	●	◒	◒	○	⊖	⊖	⊖	⊜
Brakes	●	●	●	●	◒	○	⊖	⊖
Exhaust	◒	◒	◒	⊜	⊜	⊜	⊜	⊜
Body rust	◒	○	⊖	⊖	⊜	⊜	⊜	⊜
Paint/trim	●	◒	○	○	⊖	⊖	⊖	⊖
Integrity	●	●	●	◒	○	○	○	○
Hardware	◒	◒	◒	◒	○	◒	○	⊖

Ford Explorer

TROUBLE SPOTS	88	89	90	91	92	93	94	95
Engine				◒	◒	⊖	⊜	⊜
Cooling				○	○	⊖	⊜	⊜
Fuel				⊖	⊖	⊜	⊜	⊜
Ignition				⊖	⊖	⊜	⊜	⊜
Auto. trans.				○	⊖	⊖	⊜	⊜
Man. trans.				○	◒	⊖	⊜	*
Clutch				○	○	⊖	⊖	*
Electrical				●	●	○	○	⊖
A/C				●	◒	⊖	⊖	⊜
Suspension				●	◒	○	⊖	○
Brakes				●	●	◒	○	⊖
Exhaust				◒	○	⊖	⊜	⊜
Body rust				⊖	⊜	⊜	⊜	⊜
Paint/trim				○	○	⊖	⊖	⊜
Integrity				○	○	○	⊖	⊖
Hardware				○	○	○	⊜	⊖

Ford F150-250 Pickup (2WD)

TROUBLE SPOTS	88	89	90	91	92	93	94	95
Engine	○	◒	○	⊖	⊖	⊖	⊜	⊜
Cooling	◒	◒	○	⊖	⊖	⊖	⊜	⊜
Fuel	◒	◒	●	●	◒	○	⊖	⊖
Ignition	○	○	○	⊖	⊖	⊖	⊜	⊜
Auto. trans.	○	○	◒	◒	○	⊖	⊖	⊜
Man. trans.	○	○	○	⊜	⊖	⊖	⊖	⊜
Clutch	◒	◒	○	○	○	◒	⊖	◒
Electrical	●	●	◒	◒	◒	○	⊖	⊖
A/C	●	◒	○	○	○	⊖	⊖	⊜
Suspension	●	◒	◒	○	⊖	○	○	⊖
Brakes	●	●	●	●	●	●	○	○
Exhaust	●	●	◒	◒	○	⊜	⊜	⊜
Body rust	◒	◒	○	⊖	⊖	⊖	⊜	⊜
Paint/trim	●	●	●	●	◒	○	⊖	⊖
Integrity	◒	◒	○	○	◒	◒	○	⊖
Hardware	◒	◒	◒	○	◒	○	○	⊜

Ford F150-250 Pickup (4WD)

TROUBLE SPOTS	88	89	90	91	92	93	94	95
Engine	◒	◒	◒	○	○	⊖	⊖	⊜
Cooling	●	◒	○	⊖	⊖	⊖	⊜	⊜
Fuel	◒	◒	◒	◒	◒	○	⊜	⊜
Ignition	○	○	○	○	⊖	⊖	⊜	⊜
Auto. trans.	◒	◒	●	●	○	⊖	⊖	⊖
Man. trans.	○	○	⊖	⊖	⊖	○	⊖	⊖
Clutch	◒	◒	○	○	⊖	◒	○	⊖
Electrical	●	●	◒	◒	◒	○	○	⊖
A/C	◒	◒	⊖	○	○	○	⊖	⊜
Suspension	●	◒	○	○	○	○	○	⊖
Brakes	●	●	●	●	●	●	◒	○
Exhaust	●	●	●	●	○	⊖	⊜	⊜
Body rust	●	◒	◒	⊖	⊖	⊜	⊜	⊜
Paint/trim	●	●	●	●	◒	○	⊖	⊜
Integrity	○	○	○	○	○	◒	○	⊖
Hardware	◒	○	○	◒	◒	◒	○	⊜

Ford Festiva

TROUBLE SPOTS	88	89	90	91	92	93	94	95
Engine	◒	○	⊖	⊖	⊜	⊜		
Cooling	⊖	⊖	⊜	⊖	⊜	○		
Fuel	○	○	⊜	⊖	⊜	⊜		
Ignition	⊖	⊖	⊖	⊖	⊜	⊜		
Auto. trans.		⊖	*	*	*	*		
Man. trans.	⊜	⊜	⊜	⊜	*	⊜		
Clutch	⊖	⊖	⊖	⊜	*	⊜		
Electrical	◒	○	○	◒	○	○		
A/C	○	○	*	*	*	*		
Suspension	○	⊖	○	⊖	○	⊖		
Brakes	●	●	●	●	◒	◒		
Exhaust	●	●	●	●	●	⊖		
Body rust	○	⊖	⊖	⊖	⊖	⊜		
Paint/trim	○	⊖	⊖	⊖	○	⊖		
Integrity	○	○	⊖	○	○	◒		
Hardware	◒	○	○	◒	⊖	●		

Ford Mustang 4 & V6

TROUBLE SPOTS	88	89	90	91	92	93	94	95
Engine	◒	⊖					⊜	
Cooling	●	◒					⊜	
Fuel	●	◒					⊖	
Ignition	◒	○					⊜	
Auto. trans.	●	◒					⊜	
Man. trans.	*	*	Insufficient data	Insufficient data	Insufficient data	Insufficient data	*	Insufficient data
Clutch	*	*					*	
Electrical	●	●					○	
A/C	●	●					⊖	
Suspension	◒	◒					⊖	
Brakes	◒	◒					⊖	
Exhaust	●	●					⊜	
Body rust	●	○					⊜	
Paint/trim	●	●					○	
Integrity	●	◒					◒	
Hardware	●	●					○	

Ford Mustang V8

TROUBLE SPOTS	88	89	90	91	92	93	94	95
Engine	○	○	⊖	⊖	⊜	⊖	⊖	⊜
Cooling	◒	○	○	⊖	⊖	○	⊜	⊜
Fuel	◒	○	○	⊖	⊖	⊖	⊜	⊜
Ignition	⊖	⊖	⊖	⊜	⊜	⊜	⊜	⊜
Auto. trans.	*	○	◒	*	*	*	○	*
Man. trans.	○	⊖	○	*	*	*	⊖	*
Clutch	◒	◒	◒	*	*	*	⊖	*
Electrical	●	●	●	◒	●	◒	○	⊖
A/C	●	●	●	◒	○	⊖	⊜	⊜
Suspension	○	○	◒	○	⊜	○	⊖	⊖
Brakes	○	○	◒	○	●	◒	⊖	⊖
Exhaust	●	○	⊖	⊜	⊜	⊜	⊜	⊜
Body rust	◒	○	⊜	⊖	⊖	⊜	⊜	⊜
Paint/trim	●	●	●	●	●	◒	○	⊖
Integrity	●	●	●	●	●	●	○	○
Hardware	●	●	●	◒	●	●	○	⊖

Ford Probe

TROUBLE SPOTS	88	89	90	91	92	93	94	95
Engine		○	⊖	⊖	⊖	⊖	⊜	⊜
Cooling		◒	○	○	○	⊜	⊜	⊜
Fuel		⊜	⊖	⊖	⊖	⊖	⊜	⊖
Ignition		⊜	⊖	⊖	⊖	⊖	⊜	⊜
Auto. trans.		◒	○	⊖	○	⊖	⊖	*
Man. trans.		⊜	⊖	⊜	*	⊜	⊜	*
Clutch		⊖	⊜	⊖	*	⊖	⊜	*
Electrical		●	●	●	◒	◒	◒	⊖
A/C		●	●	●	○	⊖	⊖	⊜
Suspension		⊖	○	○	○	⊖	⊜	⊜
Brakes		◒	◒	●	○	○	⊜	⊜
Exhaust		●	●	○	⊖	○	⊜	⊜
Body rust		⊖	⊜	⊜	⊖	⊜	⊜	⊜
Paint/trim		◒	○	◒	○	○	⊖	⊖
Integrity		◒	●	●	◒	●	●	◒
Hardware		●	●	●	◒	◒	○	○

Ford Ranger Pickup (2WD)

TROUBLE SPOTS	88	89	90	91	92	93	94	95
Engine	◒	◒	○	○	○	⊜	⊜	⊜
Cooling	◒	◒	○	⊖	⊖	⊖	⊜	⊜
Fuel	○	○	⊖	⊖	⊖	⊜	⊜	⊜
Ignition	○	○	⊖	⊖	⊖	⊜	⊜	⊜
Auto. trans.	●	○	○	⊖	⊖	⊜	⊖	*
Man. trans.	⊖	⊖	⊜	⊖	⊖	⊜	⊜	⊜
Clutch	○	○	○	⊖	⊖	⊜	⊜	⊖
Electrical	◒	●	○	○	○	○	⊖	○
A/C	●	●	●	●	○	⊖	⊖	⊜
Suspension	○	○	⊖	⊖	⊖	⊖	⊖	⊜
Brakes	◒	◒	◒	○	○	◒	◒	⊖
Exhaust	●	●	◒	◒	⊖	⊜	⊜	⊜
Body rust	◒	⊖	⊖	⊖	⊖	⊜	⊜	⊜
Paint/trim	●	●	◒	○	○	⊖	⊖	⊜
Integrity	○	⊖	○	○	○	⊖	⊖	⊖
Hardware	○	◒	○	○	○	⊖	⊖	⊜

Ford Ranger Pickup (4WD)

TROUBLE SPOTS	88	89	90	91	92	93	94	95
Engine	◒	◒	◒	○	◒	⊖	⊜	
Cooling	◒	◒	○	○	⊖	⊜	⊜	
Fuel	○	⊖	⊖	⊖	⊖	⊖	⊖	
Ignition	⊖	⊖	⊖	⊖	⊖	⊜	⊜	
Auto. trans.	◒	*	○	*	*	⊖	⊜	
Man. trans.	⊖	⊖	○	○	*	⊖	⊖	Insufficient data
Clutch	◒	○	◒	○	*	⊖	⊜	
Electrical	◒	◒	◒	○	○	○	○	
A/C	●	◒	●	●	○	⊖	⊖	
Suspension	○	○	○	○	⊖	⊖	⊖	
Brakes	●	◒	●	◒	◒	◒	◒	
Exhaust	●	●	◒	◒	⊖	⊜	⊜	
Body rust	●	⊖	○	⊖	⊜	⊜	⊜	
Paint/trim	●	◒	◒	○	○	⊖	⊖	
Integrity	◒	⊖	○	○	○	⊖	○	
Hardware	○	⊖	○	○	◒	⊖	○	

Ford Taurus 4	88	89	90	91	92	93	94	95
Engine	●	○	◒					
Cooling	●	●	◒					
Fuel	●	◒	○					
Ignition	◒	⊖	○					
Auto. trans.	●	◒	⊜					
Man. trans.	*							
Clutch	*							
Electrical	●	●	◒					
A/C	●	●	●					
Suspension	●	●	●					
Brakes	●	●	●					
Exhaust	●	◒	○					
Body rust	●	◒	⊖					
Paint/trim	●	●	⊜					
Integrity	◒	●	○					
Hardware	●	●	○					

Ford Taurus V6	88	89	90	91	92	93	94	95
Engine	◒	○	⊖	⊖	⊖	⊜	⊜	⊜
Cooling	●	●	◒	○	○	⊖	⊜	⊜
Fuel	◒	◒	○	○	○	○	⊖	⊖
Ignition	○	⊖	⊖	⊖	⊖	⊜	⊜	⊜
Auto. trans.	◒	◒	○	●	⊖	⊖	⊖	⊜
Man. trans.								
Clutch								
Electrical	●	●	●	◒	◒	◒	○	⊖
A/C	●	●	●	◒	○	○	⊖	⊜
Suspension	●	●	●	●	◒	○	⊖	⊜
Brakes	●	●	●	●	●	◒	⊖	⊖
Exhaust	⊖	⊜	⊖	⊜	⊜	⊜	⊜	⊜
Body rust	◒	◒	○	⊖	⊜	⊜	⊜	⊜
Paint/trim	●	◒	○	○	⊖	⊖	⊖	⊖
Integrity	◒	◒	○	○	◒	◒	◒	○
Hardware	◒	◒	◒	◒	○	◒	○	○

Ford Taurus SHO	88	89	90	91	92	93	94	95
Engine		⊖	⊖	⊖	⊖	⊜	⊜	
Cooling		◒	◒	◒	○	○	○	
Fuel		○	○	⊖	⊜	◒	⊖	
Ignition		⊖	○	○	⊜	⊖	⊖	
Auto. trans.						○	⊖	
Man. trans.		○	○	○	⊖	*	*	
Clutch		●	●	●	◒	*	*	
Electrical		●	●	◒	●	●	○	Insufficient data
A/C		●	●	●	◒	⊖	⊜	
Suspension		◒	◒	◒	○	◒	⊖	
Brakes		◒	●	●	●	●	○	
Exhaust		⊜	⊖	⊖	⊜	⊜	⊜	
Body rust		⊖	○	○	⊜	⊜	⊜	
Paint/trim		○	○	◒	○	⊖	○	
Integrity		◒	◒	◒	◒	●	●	
Hardware		◒	○	○	◒	◒	○	

Ford Tempo	88	89	90	91	92	93	94	95
Engine	◒	◒	◒	○	○	○	⊜	
Cooling	●	◒	◒	○	○	⊖	⊖	
Fuel	●	●	◒	◒	○	○	⊖	
Ignition	○	○	○	○	⊖	⊖	⊜	
Auto. trans.	◒	○	○	○	○	⊖	⊖	
Man. trans.	⊜	⊖	*	*	*	*	*	
Clutch	◒	◒	*	*	*	*	*	
Electrical	●	●	●	●	◒	◒	⊖	
A/C	●	●	●	◒	○	○	⊖	
Suspension	●	●	●	◒	○	⊖	⊖	
Brakes	●	●	●	●	◒	◒	○	
Exhaust	●	●	●	●	●	○	⊜	
Body rust	◒	○	⊖	⊖	⊖	⊖	⊜	
Paint/trim	●	●	◒	◒	○	○	⊖	
Integrity	●	◒	◒	◒	◒	◒	○	
Hardware	◒	◒	◒	◒	◒	◒	◒	

Ford Thunderbird V6	88	89	90	91	92	93	94	95
Engine	◒	○	⊖	⊖	⊜	⊜	⊜	
Cooling	◒	○	⊖	⊖	⊖	⊖	⊜	
Fuel	◒	○	○	⊖	⊜	⊖	⊜	
Ignition	○	⊖	⊖	⊖	⊖	⊜	⊜	
Auto. trans.	○	○	⊖	⊖	⊖	⊖	⊖	
Man. trans.		*	*	*	*	*	*	
Clutch		*	*	*	*	*	*	
Electrical	●	●	●	●	◒	○	○	Insufficient data
A/C	●	●	●	●	○	○	⊖	
Suspension	◒	◒	○	○	○	⊖	⊖	
Brakes	●	●	●	●	◒	◒	◒	
Exhaust	●	⊖	⊜	⊜	⊜	⊜	⊜	
Body rust	○	⊜	⊖	⊖	⊜	⊜	⊜	
Paint/trim	◒	◒	●	◒	◒	●	○	
Integrity	○	◒	○	○	◒	◒	○	
Hardware	◒	●	●	◒	◒	◒	○	

Ford Thunderbird V8	88	89	90	91	92	93	94	95
Engine	○			⊖	⊖	⊜	⊜	⊜
Cooling	◒			⊖	⊖	○	⊜	⊜
Fuel	◒			⊖	⊖	⊜	⊖	⊜
Ignition	⊖			○	⊜	⊜	⊜	⊜
Auto. trans.	○			○	⊖	⊜	○	⊖
Man. trans.								
Clutch								
Electrical	●			●	●	◒	○	⊖
A/C	●			●	○	⊖	⊖	⊜
Suspension	◒			○	◒	⊖	○	⊖
Brakes	●			●	●	●	◒	⊖
Exhaust	●			⊜	⊜	⊜	⊜	⊜
Body rust	○			⊜	⊖	⊖	⊜	⊜
Paint/trim	●			●	○	◒	○	⊖
Integrity	○			◒	○	◒	◒	○
Hardware	◒			◒	●	●	○	⊖

Ford Windstar	88	89	90	91	92	93	94	95
Engine								⊜
Cooling								⊜
Fuel								⊜
Ignition								⊜
Auto. trans.								⊜
Man. trans.								
Clutch								
Electrical								◒
A/C								⊜
Suspension								⊖
Brakes								◒
Exhaust								⊜
Body rust								⊜
Paint/trim								⊖
Integrity								⊖
Hardware								○

Geo Metro	88	89	90	91	92	93	94	95
Engine		○	⊖	⊖	⊖	⊖	⊜	
Cooling		⊖	⊖	⊜	⊜	⊜	⊜	
Fuel		○	○	⊜	⊜	⊖	⊖	
Ignition		⊜	⊖	⊖	⊖	⊜	⊜	
Auto. trans.		*	*	⊖	○	*	*	
Man. trans.		⊖	⊜	⊜	⊜	⊜	⊜	
Clutch		○	⊜	⊖	⊜	⊖	⊜	
Electrical		◒	◒	◒	◒	◒	○	Insufficient data
A/C		*	●	○	⊖	○	⊖	
Suspension		○	⊜	⊖	⊜	⊖	⊜	
Brakes		●	○	○	○	⊖	⊖	
Exhaust		●	●	●	⊖	⊜	⊜	
Body rust		⊖	⊖	⊖	⊖	⊜	⊜	
Paint/trim		◒	○	○	○	⊖	⊜	
Integrity		●	●	●	◒	◒	○	
Hardware		●	●	●	●	◒	○	

Geo Prizm	88	89	90	91	92	93	94	95
Engine			⊜	⊜	⊜	⊜	⊜	⊜
Cooling			○	⊖	⊜	⊜	⊜	⊜
Fuel			⊖	⊜	⊜	⊜	⊜	⊜
Ignition			⊜	⊜	⊜	⊜	⊜	⊜
Auto. trans.			⊖	⊜	⊖	⊜	⊜	⊜
Man. trans.			⊜	⊖	*	⊜	⊜	⊜
Clutch			⊖	○	*	⊜	⊜	⊜
Electrical			◒	◒	◒	○	○	⊜
A/C			⊖	⊜	⊖	⊜	⊜	⊜
Suspension			⊖	⊖	⊖	⊜	⊜	⊜
Brakes			◒	○	○	⊜	⊜	⊜
Exhaust			●	●	○	⊜	⊜	⊜
Body rust			⊖	⊖	⊜	⊜	⊜	⊜
Paint/trim			○	○	○	⊖	⊖	⊖
Integrity			●	○	⊜	○	⊖	⊜
Hardware			●	●	◒	●	○	⊖

Geo Storm	88	89	90	91	92	93	94	95
Engine			○	⊖	○			
Cooling			○	○	◒			
Fuel			○	⊜	⊖			
Ignition			○	⊖	⊖			
Auto. trans.			*	*	*			
Man. trans.			*	⊜	*			
Clutch			*	⊖	*			
Electrical			●	⊖	○	Insufficient data		
A/C			○	⊖	*			
Suspension			◒	●	⊖			
Brakes			●	●	●			
Exhaust			●	●	●			
Body rust			◒	⊖	⊜			
Paint/trim			◒	○	○			
Integrity			●	○	◒			
Hardware			●	◒	◒			

Geo Tracker	88	89	90	91	92	93	94	95
Engine		●	○	○	⊜	⊜	⊜	⊜
Cooling		⊖	⊜	⊜	⊜	⊜	⊜	⊜
Fuel		⊖	⊖	⊜	⊜	⊖	⊜	⊜
Ignition		⊖	⊜	⊜	⊖	⊜	⊜	⊜
Auto. trans.		*	*	*	*	*	⊜	*
Man. trans.		*	*	*	⊜	⊜	⊖	*
Clutch		*	*	*	⊖	⊜	⊜	*
Electrical		◒	○	○	○	○	○	⊖
A/C		*	*	*	○	⊖	⊖	*
Suspension		⊖	⊖	⊜	⊜	⊜	⊜	⊖
Brakes		●	●	◒	◒	○	⊖	⊖
Exhaust		●	●	◒	⊖	⊜	⊜	⊜
Body rust		◒	○	○	⊜	⊜	⊜	⊜
Paint/trim		○	⊖	○	○	⊖	⊖	⊜
Integrity		◒	○	○	○	◒	◒	⊖
Hardware		●	○	◒	◒	○	○	⊖

GMC Jimmy, Yukon	88	89	90	91	92	93	94	95
Engine	○	○	⊖	⊖	○	⊖	⊖	⊜
Cooling	●	◒	○	⊖	○	⊜	⊜	⊜
Fuel	◒	○	⊖	⊖	○	⊖	⊜	⊜
Ignition	○	○	⊖	○	⊖	⊜	⊜	⊜
Auto. trans.	◒	○	⊖	⊖	○	○	⊖	⊖
Man. trans.	*	*	*	*	*	*	*	*
Clutch	*	*	*	*	*	*	*	*
Electrical	●	●	●	●	●	◒	◒	○
A/C	◒	⊖	⊖	⊖	○	⊖	⊖	⊜
Suspension	○	○	◒	◒	⊖	○	⊖	⊖
Brakes	◒	●	◒	●	●	◒	○	⊖
Exhaust	●	●	◒	○	⊖	⊖	⊜	⊜
Body rust	●	●	◒	⊖	⊖	⊖	⊖	⊜
Paint/trim	●	●	●	●	◒	○	○	⊜
Integrity	●	●	●	◒	◒	◒	◒	○
Hardware	●	●	●	●	●	◒	◒	○

GMC S-15 Jimmy, Jimmy (2WD)	88	89	90	91	92	93	94	95
Engine	◒	○		⊖	○	○	○	⊜
Cooling	◒	○		○	⊖	⊜	⊖	⊜
Fuel	◒	⊖		⊖	○	⊖	⊜	⊖
Ignition	⊖	○		⊖	○	⊖	⊜	⊜
Auto. trans.	◒	⊜		⊜	*	⊖	⊖	⊜
Man. trans.	*	*		*	*	*	*	*
Clutch	*	*		*	*	*	*	*
Electrical	●	●	Insufficient data	●	○	◒	●	⊖
A/C	◒	⊖		○	⊜	⊖	⊖	⊜
Suspension	○	⊖		⊖	○	⊖	⊖	⊖
Brakes	●	◒		●	●	●	◒	⊖
Exhaust	◒	○		⊖	⊜	⊜	⊜	⊜
Body rust	◒	○		○	⊖	⊜	⊜	⊖
Paint/trim	●	●		●	◒	○	⊖	⊖
Integrity	●	◒		●	◒	◒	●	○
Hardware	●	◒		●	○	●	◒	⊖

GMC S-15 Jimmy, Jimmy (4WD)	88	89	90	91	92	93	94	95
Engine	◒	○	⊖	⊖	○	○	⊜	⊜
Cooling	●	◒	○	⊖	⊖	⊖	⊜	⊜
Fuel	○	○	⊖	⊖	○	○	⊜	⊜
Ignition	○	○	○	○	⊖	⊖	⊜	⊜
Auto. trans.	◒	⊖	○	⊜	⊖	◒	⊖	⊜
Man. trans.	*	*	*	*	*	*	*	*
Clutch	*	*	*	*	*	*	*	*
Electrical	●	●	●	●	◒	●	◒	○
A/C	◒	○	⊖	⊖	⊖	⊖	⊜	⊜
Suspension	◒	◒	○	◒	○	○	⊖	⊜
Brakes	●	●	●	●	●	●	○	⊜
Exhaust	●	◒	◒	○	⊜	⊜	⊜	⊜
Body rust	◒	●	●	◒	⊖	⊖	⊜	⊜
Paint/trim	●	●	●	●	◒	○	⊖	⊖
Integrity	◒	●	●	●	◒	●	◒	◒
Hardware	●	●	●	●	◒	◒	○	○

GMC S-15 Sonoma Pickup (2WD)	88	89	90	91	92	93	94	95
Engine	○	○	⊖	⊖	○	⊖	⊜	⊜
Cooling	◒	◒	○	○	⊜	⊖	⊜	⊜
Fuel	◒	○	⊖	⊖	⊖	⊜	⊖	⊜
Ignition	○	○	○	○	○	⊜	⊜	⊖
Auto. trans.	⊖	⊖	○	⊜	⊖	⊖	⊖	⊜
Man. trans.	⊖	⊖	*	⊖	⊜	⊖	○	⊖
Clutch	◒	○	*	○	○	○	○	⊖
Electrical	●	●	●	◒	◒	○	◒	○
A/C	◒	○	⊖	⊖	⊖	⊖	⊖	⊜
Suspension	○	⊖	⊖	⊖	○	⊖	⊖	⊖
Brakes	●	○	◒	○	◒	⊖	○	⊖
Exhaust	●	●	●	◒	○	⊖	⊜	⊜
Body rust	◒	◒	○	◒	⊖	⊜	⊜	⊜
Paint/trim	●	●	●	●	●	○	⊖	⊖
Integrity	●	●	◒	◒	○	○	○	○
Hardware	◒	◒	◒	◒	○	○	○	⊖

GMC S-15 Sonoma Pickup (4WD)	88	89	90	91	92	93	94	95
Engine	●	⊖		⊖	○		⊖	⊜
Cooling	◒	◒		⊖	⊖		⊖	⊜
Fuel	○	○		○	⊖		⊖	⊜
Ignition	○	⊖		◒	◒		⊖	⊜
Auto. trans.	◒	○		⊖	⊖		○	⊖
Man. trans.	*	*		*	*		*	*
Clutch	*	*		*	*		*	*
Electrical	●	●	Insufficient data	●	◒	Insufficient data	●	○
A/C	○	⊖		⊖	⊖		⊖	⊜
Suspension	●	●		◒	◒		⊖	○
Brakes	●	◒		◒	●		○	⊜
Exhaust	●	●		◒	⊖		⊜	⊜
Body rust	●	●		◒	○		⊜	⊜
Paint/trim	●	●		●	◒		○	⊖
Integrity	◒	●		◒	○		◒	○
Hardware	◒	●		◒	⊖		◒	⊖

GMC Safari Van	88	89	90	91	92	93	94	95
Engine	◒	◒	⊖	⊖	○	⊖	⊜	⊜
Cooling	◒	○	⊖	⊜	⊖	⊜	⊜	⊜
Fuel	○	○	⊜	⊖	○	○	⊜	⊖
Ignition	○	○	⊜	⊜	⊜	⊖	⊖	⊜
Auto. trans.	○	○	⊖	⊜	⊖	○	⊖	⊜
Man. trans.	*	*						
Clutch	*	*						
Electrical	●	●	●	●	◒	●	●	○
A/C	◒	●	○	○	○	○	◒	⊜
Suspension	●	◒	◒	◒	○	○	⊖	⊖
Brakes	●	●	●	●	●	●	⊖	⊖
Exhaust	◒	◒	○	○	⊖	⊜	⊜	⊜
Body rust	⊖	⊖	⊖	⊜	⊖	⊜	⊜	⊜
Paint/trim	●	●	●	◒	◒	○	○	⊖
Integrity	◒	●	●	●	●	●	●	◒
Hardware	●	●	●	●	●	●	◒	◒

GMC Sierra C1500-2500 Pickup (2WD)	88	89	90	91	92	93	94	95
Engine	◒	○	○	⊖	⊖	⊖	⊖	⊜
Cooling	●	○	○	⊖	⊖	⊜	⊜	⊜
Fuel	◒	○	⊖	⊖	⊖	⊖	⊖	⊜
Ignition	○	○	○	○	⊖	⊖	⊜	⊜
Auto. trans.	○	○	○	◒	◒	⊖	⊖	⊜
Man. trans.	○	⊖	⊜	⊖	○	*	*	*
Clutch	◒	●	●	◒	○	*	*	*
Electrical	●	●	●	●	◒	◒	○	○
A/C	○	◒	○	○	○	⊖	⊖	⊜
Suspension	●	◒	○	○	○	⊖	⊖	⊖
Brakes	●	◒	◒	○	⊖	⊖	⊖	⊜
Exhaust	●	●	◒	○	⊖	⊜	⊜	⊜
Body rust	○	⊖	⊜	⊜	⊜	⊜	⊜	⊜
Paint/trim	●	●	●	◒	○	○	⊖	⊖
Integrity	◒	◒	○	○	○	○	○	○
Hardware	◒	◒	○	○	○	○	○	○

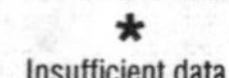

GMC Sierra K1500-2500 Pickup (4WD)

TROUBLE SPOTS	88	89	90	91	92	93	94	95
Engine	◒	◒	○	⊖	⊖	○	⊜	⊜
Cooling	●	◒	⊖	⊖	⊖	⊖	⊜	⊜
Fuel	◒	⊖	⊖	⊖	⊖	⊖	⊜	⊜
Ignition	○	○	○	○	⊖	⊜	⊜	⊜
Auto. trans.	◒	○	○	○	○	○	⊖	⊜
Man. trans.	*	*	⊖	*	○	*	⊖	*
Clutch	*	*	●	*	○	*	○	*
Electrical	●	●	●	◒	◒	◒	○	⊖
A/C	○	○	○	○	⊖	⊖	⊜	⊜
Suspension	◒	◒	○	○	○	⊜	⊜	⊖
Brakes	●	●	●	◒	○	○	⊜	⊜
Exhaust	●	●	●	◒	○	⊖	⊜	⊜
Body rust	○	⊖	⊖	⊜	⊖	⊜	⊜	⊜
Paint/trim	●	●	●	◒	○	○	⊖	⊜
Integrity	◒	○	○	○	○	◒	○	○
Hardware	●	◒	○	○	○	○	○	○

GMC Suburban

TROUBLE SPOTS	88	89	90	91	92	93	94	95
Engine	◒	◒	⊖	⊖	⊖	⊖	⊜	⊜
Cooling	●	●	◒	◒	○	○	⊜	⊜
Fuel	○	○	⊖	○	⊖	⊖	⊜	⊜
Ignition	⊖	○	○	⊖	⊖	⊜	⊜	⊜
Auto. trans.	○	◒	○	◒	◒	⊖	⊜	⊜
Man. trans.	*	*	*					
Clutch	*	*	*					
Electrical	●	●	●	◒	●	●	○	⊖
A/C	◒	◒	○	○	○	⊖	○	⊜
Suspension	◒	○	○	○	○	⊖	⊜	⊜
Brakes	●	●	●	●	●	○	○	⊖
Exhaust	●	◒	○	○	⊖	⊖	⊜	⊜
Body rust	●	◒	○	⊖	⊖	⊖	⊜	⊜
Paint/trim	●	●	●	◒	◒	○	⊜	⊜
Integrity	●	●	●	◒	●	◒	○	⊖
Hardware	●	●	●	◒	●	●	◒	○

Honda Accord

TROUBLE SPOTS	88	89	90	91	92	93	94	95
Engine	⊖	⊖	⊖	⊜	⊜	⊜	⊜	⊜
Cooling	⊖	⊖	⊜	⊜	⊜	⊜	⊜	⊜
Fuel	⊖	⊖	⊜	⊜	⊜	⊜	⊜	⊜
Ignition	⊜	⊖	○	⊖	⊜	⊜	⊜	⊜
Auto. trans.	○	⊖	⊖	⊜	⊜	⊜	⊜	⊜
Man. trans.	⊜	⊜	⊜	⊜	⊜	⊜	⊜	⊜
Clutch	◒	⊖	⊖	⊖	⊜	⊜	⊜	⊜
Electrical	◒	○	○	○	⊖	⊖	⊖	⊜
A/C	◒	◒	⊜	⊖	⊖	⊜	⊜	⊜
Suspension	○	⊖	⊖	⊖	⊜	⊜	⊜	⊜
Brakes	●	●	○	○	⊖	⊖	⊜	⊜
Exhaust	○	○	○	⊖	⊜	⊜	⊜	⊜
Body rust	○	⊖	⊜	⊜	⊜	⊜	⊜	⊜
Paint/trim	⊖	⊖	⊖	⊖	⊖	⊜	⊜	⊜
Integrity	○	⊜	○	⊖	○	○	○	⊖
Hardware	○	○	○	○	○	○	○	⊜

Honda Civic

TROUBLE SPOTS	88	89	90	91	92	93	94	95
Engine	○	⊖	○	⊜	⊜	⊜	⊜	⊜
Cooling	⊖	⊖	⊖	⊜	⊜	⊜	⊜	⊜
Fuel	○	⊖	⊖	⊜	⊜	⊜	⊜	⊜
Ignition	○	○	○	⊖	⊜	⊜	⊜	⊜
Auto. trans.	⊖	⊖	⊖	⊖	⊖	⊖	⊜	⊜
Man. trans.	⊜	⊜	⊜	⊜	⊜	⊖	⊜	⊜
Clutch	◒	○	⊖	⊜	⊜	⊜	⊜	⊜
Electrical	●	◒	◒	○	⊖	⊖	⊖	⊜
A/C	◒	◒	○	⊜	⊜	⊖	⊜	⊜
Suspension	○	⊖	⊖	⊖	⊜	⊖	⊜	⊜
Brakes	●	●	●	●	⊖	⊖	⊜	⊜
Exhaust	●	●	●	◒	⊜	⊜	⊜	⊜
Body rust	◒	⊖	⊖	⊜	⊜	⊜	⊜	⊜
Paint/trim	○	⊖	⊖	⊜	○	⊖	⊜	⊜
Integrity	○	○	○	○	○	⊖	⊜	⊖
Hardware	○	○	○	○	○	⊖	⊖	⊜

Honda Civic del Sol

TROUBLE SPOTS	88	89	90	91	92	93	94	95
Engine						⊜	⊜	
Cooling						⊜	⊜	
Fuel						⊜	⊜	
Ignition						⊜	⊜	
Auto. trans.						⊖	*	
Man. trans.						⊜	⊜	
Clutch						⊜	⊜	Insufficient data
Electrical						⊖	⊖	
A/C						⊖	⊜	
Suspension						⊜	⊜	
Brakes						⊖	⊜	
Exhaust						⊜	⊜	
Body rust						⊜	⊜	
Paint/trim						⊖	○	
Integrity						●	●	
Hardware						●	◒	

Honda CRX

TROUBLE SPOTS	88	89	90	91	92	93	94	95
Engine	⊖	⊖	⊖	⊖				
Cooling	⊖	⊜	⊖	⊜				
Fuel	⊖	⊜	⊜	⊖				
Ignition	○	⊖	○	⊖				
Auto. trans.	*	*	*	*				
Man. trans.	⊜	⊜	⊜	⊜				
Clutch	◒	○	⊜	⊖				
Electrical	◒	◒	○	⊖				
A/C	◒	○	○	○				
Suspension	⊖	⊜	⊜	⊖				
Brakes	●	◒	○	◒				
Exhaust	●	●	●	○				
Body rust	●	○	⊖	⊜				
Paint/trim	○	⊖	⊜	⊖				
Integrity	◒	○	○	⊖				
Hardware	○	○	◒	○				

Honda Odyssey

TROUBLE SPOTS	88	89	90	91	92	93	94	95
Engine								⊜
Cooling								⊜
Fuel								⊜
Ignition								⊜
Auto. trans.								⊜
Man. trans.								
Clutch								
Electrical								⊜
A/C								⊜
Suspension								⊜
Brakes								⊜
Exhaust								⊜
Body rust								⊜
Paint/trim								⊜
Integrity								⊜
Hardware								⊜

Honda Passport

TROUBLE SPOTS	88	89	90	91	92	93	94	95
Engine							⊖	⊜
Cooling							⊜	⊜
Fuel							⊜	⊜
Ignition							⊜	⊜
Auto. trans.							⊖	*
Man. trans.							⊜	*
Clutch							⊖	*
Electrical							○	⊖
A/C							⊜	⊖
Suspension							⊖	⊜
Brakes							⊖	⊜
Exhaust							⊜	⊜
Body rust							⊜	⊜
Paint/trim							⊖	⊜
Integrity							○	⊖
Hardware							○	⊜

Honda Prelude

TROUBLE SPOTS	88	89	90	91	92	93	94	95
Engine	⊖	⊖	⊜	⊖	⊜	⊜	⊜	
Cooling	⊖	⊖	⊜	⊜	⊜	⊜	⊜	
Fuel	⊖	⊜	⊜	⊜	⊜	⊜	⊜	
Ignition	⊜	⊜	⊜	⊜	⊜	⊜	⊜	
Auto. trans.	◒	⊜	*	*	⊜	*	*	
Man. trans.	⊜	⊜	⊜	⊜	⊜	⊜	*	
Clutch	●	◒	⊜	○	⊖	⊖	*	Insufficient data
Electrical	◒	◒	○	⊜	⊖	○	○	
A/C	●	○	⊖	⊖	⊖	⊜	⊜	
Suspension	◒	○	⊜	⊖	⊖	⊜	⊜	
Brakes	●	●	◒	○	⊖	⊜	⊜	
Exhaust	◒	◒	⊖	⊖	⊜	⊜	⊜	
Body rust	●	⊖	⊖	⊜	⊜	⊜	⊜	
Paint/trim	◒	⊖	⊖	⊖	⊖	○	⊖	
Integrity	○	○	⊜	⊜	○	○	⊖	
Hardware	○	○	○	⊜	○	○	⊖	

Hyundai Excel

TROUBLE SPOTS	88	89	90	91	92	93	94	95
Engine	●	●	●	◒				
Cooling	●	●	○	◒				
Fuel	◒	◒	◒	◒				
Ignition	○	◒	○	○				
Auto. trans.	●	◒	*	*				
Man. trans.	◒	◒	*	*				
Clutch	●	●	*	*	Insufficient data	Insufficient data	Insufficient data	
Electrical	●	●	●	●				
A/C	●	●	●	*				
Suspension	◒	◒	◒	○				
Brakes	●	●	◒	◒				
Exhaust	●	●	●	●				
Body rust	◒	◒	○	⊖				
Paint/trim	●	●	●	◒				
Integrity	●	●	●	○				
Hardware	●	●	●	●				

Infiniti G20

TROUBLE SPOTS	88	89	90	91	92	93	94	95
Engine				⊜	⊜	⊜	⊜	⊜
Cooling				⊜	⊜	⊜	⊜	⊜
Fuel				⊜	⊜	⊜	⊜	⊜
Ignition				⊜	⊜	⊜	⊜	⊜
Auto. trans.				⊖	⊜	⊜	⊜	⊜
Man. trans.				*	*	⊜	*	*
Clutch				*	*	⊖	*	*
Electrical				◒	○	⊖	⊜	⊜
A/C				⊖	⊖	⊜	⊜	⊜
Suspension				⊜	⊜	⊜	⊜	⊜
Brakes				⊖	⊜	⊜	⊜	⊜
Exhaust				⊜	⊜	⊜	⊜	⊜
Body rust				⊜	⊜	⊜	⊜	⊜
Paint/trim				⊜	⊖	⊜	⊜	⊜
Integrity				⊖	⊖	⊖	⊜	⊖
Hardware				◒	◒	○	⊖	⊜

Infiniti J30

TROUBLE SPOTS	88	89	90	91	92	93	94	95
Engine						⊜	⊜	⊜
Cooling						⊜	⊜	⊜
Fuel						⊖	⊜	⊖
Ignition						⊜	⊜	⊜
Auto. trans.						⊖	⊜	⊜
Man. trans.								
Clutch								
Electrical						○	⊜	⊖
A/C						⊖	⊜	⊜
Suspension						⊜	⊜	⊜
Brakes						⊖	⊜	⊖
Exhaust						⊜	⊜	⊜
Body rust						⊜	⊜	⊜
Paint/trim						○	⊜	⊖
Integrity						⊖	⊜	⊜
Hardware						◒	⊜	⊖

Infiniti Q45

TROUBLE SPOTS	88	89	90	91	92	93	94	95
Engine			⊖	⊜	⊖		⊜	
Cooling			⊜	⊜	⊜		⊜	
Fuel			○	⊖	○		⊖	
Ignition			⊜	⊜	○		⊜	
Auto. trans.			○	○	○		⊜	
Man. trans.								
Clutch						Insufficient data		Insufficient data
Electrical			◒	○	●		○	
A/C			○	⊖	⊖		⊜	
Suspension			○	○	○		⊖	
Brakes			●	●	●		⊖	
Exhaust			⊜	⊜	⊜		⊜	
Body rust			⊜	⊜	⊜		⊜	
Paint/trim			⊜	⊜	⊖		⊖	
Integrity			⊖	⊜	⊜		⊖	
Hardware			◒	◒	◒		⊖	

Isuzu Pickup 4

TROUBLE SPOTS	88	89	90	91	92	93	94	95
Engine	◒	○	⊖	⊜	○			
Cooling	○	⊖	○	⊖	⊜			
Fuel	○	◒	○	○	○			
Ignition	⊖	⊖	⊖	⊜	⊖			
Auto. trans.	*	*	*	*	*			
Man. trans.	*	⊜	⊜	*	⊜			
Clutch	*	○	⊖	*	⊖	Insufficient data	Insufficient data	Insufficient data
Electrical	○	◒	◒	○	⊖			
A/C	*	*	⊖	*	*			
Suspension	○	○	○	⊜	⊖			
Brakes	●	●	●	●	○			
Exhaust	●	●	◒	○	⊖			
Body rust	●	◒	⊖	⊖	⊜			
Paint/trim	◒	○	◒	◒	○			
Integrity	○	○	○	⊖	○			
Hardware	○	○	○	⊜	○			

Isuzu Rodeo

TROUBLE SPOTS	88	89	90	91	92	93	94	95
Engine				○	⊖	○	⊖	⊜
Cooling				○	○	⊖	⊜	⊜
Fuel				⊜	⊜	⊖	⊜	⊜
Ignition				⊖	⊜	⊖	⊜	⊜
Auto. trans.				*	*	*	⊖	*
Man. trans.				*	⊜	*	⊜	*
Clutch				*	◒	*	⊖	*
Electrical				●	◒	◒	○	⊖
A/C				○	○	○	⊜	⊖
Suspension				⊖	○	◒	⊜	⊜
Brakes				●	◒	⊜	⊖	⊜
Exhaust				◒	○	⊜	⊜	⊜
Body rust				⊖	⊜	⊜	⊜	⊜
Paint/trim				●	◒	◒	⊖	⊜
Integrity				◒	◒	○	○	⊖
Hardware				●	◒	●	○	⊜

Isuzu Trooper II, Trooper

TROUBLE SPOTS	88	89	90	91	92	93	94	95
Engine	●	●	○	○	⊖	⊖	⊜	
Cooling	●	○	⊖	◒	⊜	⊜	⊜	
Fuel	◒	○	⊖	⊜	⊖	⊜	⊜	
Ignition	⊖	⊖	⊖	⊖	⊖	⊜	⊜	
Auto. trans.	⊖	*	*	*	*	*	⊜	
Man. trans.	⊖	⊖	⊖	○	*	*	*	
Clutch	●	◒	◒	◒	*	*	*	Insufficient data
Electrical	●	◒	○	○	●	○	○	
A/C	○	○	⊖	○	⊜	⊜	⊜	
Suspension	⊖	⊖	⊖	⊖	⊜	⊜	⊜	
Brakes	●	●	●	●	⊖	⊖	⊜	
Exhaust	●	●	◒	◒	⊜	⊖	⊜	
Body rust	◒	◒	◒	○	⊜	⊜	⊜	
Paint/trim	○	○	⊖	○	⊖	⊖	⊖	
Integrity	◒	○	○	○	○	○	○	
Hardware	○	◒	○	○	◒	⊖	⊖	

Jaguar XJ6, XJS

TROUBLE SPOTS	88	89	90	91	92	93	94	95
Engine	⊖	⊖	◒					
Cooling	◒	●	○					
Fuel	○	○	◒					
Ignition	○	○	⊜					
Auto. trans.	◒	○	○					
Man. trans.								
Clutch				Insufficient data	Insufficient data	Insufficient data	Insufficient data	Insufficient data
Electrical	●	●	●					
A/C	●	●	●					
Suspension	●	●	●					
Brakes	●	●	◒					
Exhaust	⊖	○	⊜					
Body rust	●	○	○					
Paint/trim	○	○	⊜					
Integrity	○	⊖	◒					
Hardware	●	●	●					

Jeep Cherokee, Wagoneer

TROUBLE SPOTS	88	89	90	91	92	93	94	95
Engine	○	○	○	⊖	⊜	⊜	○	⊜
Cooling	◒	◒	◒	○	⊖	⊖	⊜	⊜
Fuel	◒	○	◒	⊖	⊜	⊖	⊜	⊜
Ignition	○	○	⊖	⊜	⊜	⊜	⊖	⊜
Auto. trans.	○	○	○	⊖	⊖	⊖	⊖	⊖
Man. trans.	⊖	○	○	*	*	*	⊜	*
Clutch	●	◒	●	*	*	*	⊖	*
Electrical	●	●	●	●	○	○	○	⊖
A/C	◒	○	○	○	⊖	⊜	○	⊜
Suspension	○	○	○	⊖	⊖	⊜	⊖	⊖
Brakes	●	●	●	●	○	○	⊖	⊖
Exhaust	●	●	●	●	○	⊜	⊜	⊜
Body rust	○	⊖	⊖	⊜	⊜	⊜	⊜	⊜
Paint/trim	●	●	○	○	⊖	⊖	○	⊖
Integrity	◒	●	◒	◒	◒	●	◒	◒
Hardware	●	●	◒	○	○	◒	○	○

Jeep Grand Cherokee 4WD

Trouble spots	88	89	90	91	92	93	94	95
Engine						⊖	⊖	⊜
Cooling						⊜	⊜	⊜
Fuel						⊖	⊖	⊜
Ignition						⊖	⊜	⊜
Auto. trans.						○	⊖	⊖
Man. trans.						*	*	
Clutch						*	*	
Electrical						◒	○	⊖
A/C						⊖	⊖	⊜
Suspension						○	⊖	⊜
Brakes						○	⊖	⊖
Exhaust						⊜	⊜	⊜
Body rust						⊜	⊜	⊜
Paint/trim						⊖	⊖	⊜
Integrity						◒	○	⊖
Hardware						◒	○	⊖

Jeep Wrangler

Trouble spots	88	89	90	91	92	93	94	95
Engine		◒	●	○	⊖	○	⊖	⊖
Cooling		○	○	⊜	⊖	⊜	⊜	⊜
Fuel		●	●	◒	○	●	⊖	⊜
Ignition		◒	◒	⊖	⊖	⊖	⊜	⊜
Auto. trans.		*	*	*	*	*	*	*
Man. trans.		◒	*	*	*	○	⊜	⊜
Clutch		●	*	*	*	○	⊜	⊖
Electrical	Insufficient data	●	●	◒	◒	◒	○	⊜
A/C		*	*	*	*	*	*	*
Suspension		⊖	⊖	⊖	⊖	⊖	⊜	⊜
Brakes		●	○	○	○	⊖	⊖	⊜
Exhaust		●	●	◒	○	⊖	⊜	⊜
Body rust		⊖	○	○	●	⊖	⊖	⊜
Paint/trim		⊖	○	○	◒	◒	⊖	⊜
Integrity		●	●	●	●	●	●	◒
Hardware		◒	●	◒	●	●	●	⊖

Land Rover Discovery

Trouble spots	88	89	90	91	92	93	94	95

NO DATA

Lexus ES250

Trouble spots	88	89	90	91	92	93	94	95
Engine			⊜	⊜				
Cooling			⊖	⊖				
Fuel			⊜	⊜				
Ignition			⊜	⊜				
Auto. trans.			⊜	⊖				
Man. trans.			*	*				
Clutch			*	*				
Electrical			◒	○				
A/C			⊖	⊖				
Suspension			⊖	⊖				
Brakes			○	○				
Exhaust			⊜	⊜				
Body rust			⊜	⊜				
Paint/trim			⊖	⊜				
Integrity			○	○				
Hardware			◒	◒				

Lexus ES300

Trouble spots	88	89	90	91	92	93	94	95
Engine					⊜	⊜	⊜	⊜
Cooling					⊜	⊜	⊜	⊜
Fuel					⊜	⊜	⊜	⊜
Ignition					⊜	⊜	⊜	⊜
Auto. trans.					⊜	⊜	⊜	⊜
Man. trans.					*	*		
Clutch					*	*		
Electrical					○	⊖	⊖	⊜
A/C					⊖	⊜	⊜	⊜
Suspension					⊖	⊖	⊖	⊜
Brakes					⊖	⊖	⊜	⊜
Exhaust					⊜	⊜	⊜	⊜
Body rust					⊜	⊜	⊜	⊜
Paint/trim					⊜	⊖	⊜	⊜
Integrity					⊖	⊖	⊖	○
Hardware					○	⊖	⊖	⊜

Lexus GS300

Trouble spots	88	89	90	91	92	93	94	95
Engine						⊜	⊜	
Cooling						⊜	⊜	
Fuel						⊜	⊜	
Ignition						⊜	⊜	
Auto. trans.						⊜	⊜	
Man. trans.								
Clutch								
Electrical						⊖	⊜	Insufficient data
A/C						⊜	⊜	
Suspension						⊜	⊖	
Brakes						⊖	⊖	
Exhaust						⊜	⊜	
Body rust						⊜	⊜	
Paint/trim						⊜	⊜	
Integrity						⊖	⊖	
Hardware						⊜	⊖	

Lexus LS400

Trouble spots	88	89	90	91	92	93	94	95
Engine			⊜	⊜	⊜	⊜	⊖	⊜
Cooling			⊜	⊜	⊜	⊜	⊜	⊜
Fuel			⊜	⊜	⊜	⊜	⊜	○
Ignition			⊜	⊜	⊜	⊜	⊖	⊜
Auto. trans.			⊜	⊜	⊜	⊜	⊖	○
Man. trans.								
Clutch								
Electrical			○	○	○	○	⊖	⊖
A/C			⊜	⊖	⊖	⊜	⊖	⊜
Suspension			○	⊖	⊖	⊜	⊜	⊖
Brakes			○	○	⊜	⊖	⊜	⊜
Exhaust			⊜	⊜	⊜	⊜	⊜	⊜
Body rust			⊜	⊜	⊜	⊜	⊜	⊜
Paint/trim			⊜	⊜	⊜	⊜	⊜	⊜
Integrity			⊜	⊜	⊜	⊖	⊖	⊜
Hardware			⊖	⊖	⊖	⊜	⊖	⊖

Lexus SC300/400

Trouble spots	88	89	90	91	92	93	94	95
Engine					⊜	⊜		⊜
Cooling					⊜	⊜		⊜
Fuel					⊜	⊜		⊜
Ignition					⊜	⊜		⊜
Auto. trans.					⊜	⊜		⊜
Man. trans.					*	*		*
Clutch					*	*		*
Electrical					◒	⊖	Insufficient data	⊖
A/C					⊜	⊜		⊖
Suspension					⊖	⊜		⊖
Brakes					⊜	⊜		⊜
Exhaust					⊜	⊜		⊜
Body rust					⊜	⊜		⊜
Paint/trim					⊖	⊖		⊖
Integrity					⊖	⊖		⊖
Hardware					○	⊖		⊖

Lincoln Continental

Trouble spots	88	89	90	91	92	93	94	95
Engine	●	●	◒	○	⊖	⊜	⊜	
Cooling	●	◒	○	⊖	⊜	⊜	⊜	
Fuel	◒	◒	○	⊖	⊖	⊖	⊖	
Ignition	●	○	○	⊖	⊜	⊜	⊜	
Auto. trans.	●	●	◒	●	⊖	⊖	⊜	
Man. trans.								
Clutch								
Electrical	●	●	●	●	◒	◒	○	Insufficient data
A/C	●	●	●	●	○	○	⊖	
Suspension	●	●	●	●	○	○	⊖	
Brakes	●	●	●	●	●	○	⊖	
Exhaust	○	⊖	⊖	⊖	⊜	⊜	⊜	
Body rust	⊖	⊖	⊖	⊖	⊜	⊜	⊜	
Paint/trim	○	◒	○	⊖	⊖	⊜	⊖	
Integrity	◒	◒	○	○	○	○	◒	
Hardware	●	●	●	◒	◒	◒	○	

Lincoln Mark VII

Trouble spots	88	89	90	91	92	93	94	95
Engine	⊖	⊖	○					
Cooling	○	○	⊜					
Fuel	◒	○	◒					
Ignition	⊖	⊖	⊜					
Auto. trans.	○	◒	○					
Man. trans.								
Clutch								
Electrical	●	●	●	Insufficient data	Insufficient data			
A/C	●	●	●					
Suspension	●	◒	◒					
Brakes	●	●	●					
Exhaust	●	○	◒					
Body rust	○	⊜	⊖					
Paint/trim	◒	●	○					
Integrity	○	⊖	◒					
Hardware	◒	◒	●					

Lincoln Mark VIII

Trouble spots	88	89	90	91	92	93	94	95
Engine						⊖	⊖	
Cooling						⊜	⊜	
Fuel						⊜	⊜	
Ignition						⊜	⊜	
Auto. trans.						○	⊖	
Man. trans.								
Clutch								
Electrical						●	◒	Insufficient data
A/C						⊖	⊜	
Suspension						○	⊜	
Brakes						○	⊖	
Exhaust						⊜	⊜	
Body rust						⊜	⊜	
Paint/trim						⊜	⊖	
Integrity						○	⊖	
Hardware						◒	○	

Lincoln Town Car

Trouble spots	88	89	90	91	92	93	94	95
Engine	○	○	⊖	⊖	⊜	⊜	⊜	⊜
Cooling	◒	◒	⊖	⊜	⊜	⊜	⊜	⊜
Fuel	○	○	○	⊖	⊖	⊜	⊜	⊖
Ignition	⊖	⊖	⊖	○	⊖	⊜	⊜	⊜
Auto. trans.	○	◒	○	⊖	○	○	⊖	⊖
Man. trans.								
Clutch								
Electrical	●	●	●	●	◒	○	⊖	○
A/C	●	◒	○	◒	○	⊖	⊖	⊜
Suspension	○	◒	◒	○	⊖	⊖	⊜	⊜
Brakes	◒	◒	●	●	●	○	⊖	⊖
Exhaust	●	◒	●	◒	⊖	⊜	⊜	⊜
Body rust	⊖	⊖	⊜	⊜	⊜	⊜	⊜	⊜
Paint/trim	○	◒	○	○	⊖	⊖	⊖	⊜
Integrity	○	○	○	○	○	○	○	○
Hardware	◒	●	●	●	◒	◒	○	⊖

Mazda 323

Trouble spots	88	89	90	91	92	93	94	95
Engine	◒	○	⊖	⊖	⊜			
Cooling	◒	○	⊖	⊜	⊜			
Fuel	⊖	⊜	⊖	⊜	⊖			
Ignition	○	⊖	⊖	⊜	⊜			
Auto. trans.	◒	●	⊖	○	*			
Man. trans.	⊜	⊜	⊖	⊜	*			
Clutch	⊖	○	⊜	⊜	*			
Electrical	◒	◒	○	○	◒	Insufficient data	Insufficient data	
A/C	◒	○	○	⊖	⊜			
Suspension	○	○	○	⊜	⊖			
Brakes	●	●	●	◒	⊖			
Exhaust	●	●	◒	○	⊜			
Body rust	⊖	⊖	⊖	⊖	⊖			
Paint/trim	○	○	○	⊖	○			
Integrity	○	○	◒	◒	○			
Hardware	○	◒	◒	◒	○			

Mazda 626 4

Trouble spots	88	89	90	91	92	93	94	95
Engine	○	○	⊖	⊖	⊜	⊜	⊜	⊜
Cooling	○	⊖	⊖	⊖	⊖	⊜	⊜	⊜
Fuel	⊖	⊜	⊖	⊖	⊜	⊖	⊜	⊜
Ignition	⊖	⊜	⊜	⊜	⊜	⊜	⊜	⊜
Auto. trans.	●	●	⊖	⊖	⊖	⊖	○	⊖
Man. trans.	⊜	⊜	⊜	⊜	⊖	⊖	⊜	⊜
Clutch	⊖	⊖	⊖	⊜	⊜	⊜	⊜	⊜
Electrical	◒	◒	○	○	○	○	○	⊖
A/C	◒	○	○	⊖	⊖	⊜	⊖	⊜
Suspension	○	○	⊖	○	○	○	⊖	⊜
Brakes	◒	◒	●	◒	◒	○	⊜	⊜
Exhaust	●	●	●	○	⊖	⊜	⊜	⊜
Body rust	⊜	⊜	⊜	⊜	⊜	⊜	⊜	⊜
Paint/trim	○	⊖	⊖	○	⊖	⊖	⊖	⊜
Integrity	◒	○	◒	◒	◒	●	◒	○
Hardware	●	◒	◒	◒	◒	◒	◒	⊜

Mazda 626 V6

Trouble spots	88	89	90	91	92	93	94	95
Engine						○	⊜	⊜
Cooling						⊜	⊜	⊖
Fuel						⊖	⊜	⊜
Ignition						⊖	⊜	⊜
Auto. trans.						⊖	⊖	*
Man. trans.						⊜	⊜	*
Clutch						⊜	⊜	*
Electrical						◒	○	⊖
A/C						⊖	⊜	⊜
Suspension						⊖	⊜	⊜
Brakes						◒	⊖	⊜
Exhaust						○	⊜	⊜
Body rust						⊜	⊜	⊜
Paint/trim						○	○	⊜
Integrity						●	●	⊖
Hardware						◒	●	⊖

Mazda 929

Trouble spots	88	89	90	91	92	93	94	95
Engine	◒	◒	○	○	○	○		
Cooling	○	⊖	⊖	⊖	⊖	⊜		
Fuel	○	⊜	⊜	⊖	⊜	⊖		
Ignition	⊜	⊜	⊖	⊜	⊜	⊖		
Auto. trans.	○	○	○	○	○	⊜		
Man. trans.	*							
Clutch	*							
Electrical	●	◒	◒	○	◒	○	Insufficient data	Insufficient data
A/C	○	⊜	⊜	⊖	⊖	⊖		
Suspension	○	○	⊖	⊖	⊜	⊜		
Brakes	●	●	●	●	◒	◒		
Exhaust	◒	◒	●	◒	⊖	⊜		
Body rust	⊜	⊜	⊜	⊜	⊜	⊜		
Paint/trim	○	⊖	○	⊖	○	⊖		
Integrity	⊖	⊖	○	○	○	○		
Hardware	●	◒	◒	◒	●	●		

Mazda Millenia

Trouble spots	88	89	90	91	92	93	94	95
Engine								⊜
Cooling								⊜
Fuel								⊜
Ignition								⊜
Auto. trans.								⊜
Man. trans.								
Clutch								
Electrical								⊖
A/C								⊜
Suspension								⊜
Brakes								⊜
Exhaust								⊜
Body rust								⊜
Paint/trim								⊜
Integrity								⊖
Hardware								⊖

Mazda MPV Van V6 (2WD)

Trouble spots	88	89	90	91	92	93	94	95
Engine		●	◒	◒	◒	◒		
Cooling		⊖	⊖	⊖	⊜	⊜		
Fuel		⊜	⊜	⊖	⊖	⊖		
Ignition		⊖	⊜	⊖	⊜	⊜		
Auto. trans.		○	○	○	⊖	○		
Man. trans.		*						
Clutch		*						
Electrical		◒	◒	◒	○	○	Insufficient data	Insufficient data
A/C		○	◒	⊖	⊖	⊜		
Suspension		○	○	⊖	○	○		
Brakes		●	●	●	○	⊖		
Exhaust		●	◒	⊖	⊖	⊜		
Body rust		⊜	⊖	⊜	⊜	⊜		
Paint/trim		⊜	○	○	○	⊖		
Integrity		⊖	⊖	⊖	○	○		
Hardware		●	◒	○	○	○		

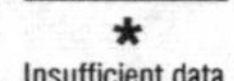

Mazda MPV Van V6 (4WD)

Trouble spots	88	89 (Insufficient data)	90	91	92	93 (Insufficient data)	94 (Insufficient data)	95 (Insufficient data)
Engine			◒	○	●			
Cooling			⊖	⊖	○			
Fuel			⊖	⊜	⊖			
Ignition			⊖	⊖	⊖			
Auto. trans.			●	◒	○			
Man. trans.			*					
Clutch			*					
Electrical			○	●	◒			
A/C			◒	○	⊜			
Suspension			◒	◒	◒			
Brakes			●	●	○			
Exhaust			◒	○	⊜			
Body rust			⊜	⊜	⊖			
Paint/trim			○	⊖	○			
Integrity			○	⊖	○			
Hardware			○	◒	◒			

Mazda MX-3

Trouble spots	88	89	90	91	92	93	94 (Insufficient data)	95 (Insufficient data)
Engine					⊖	⊖		
Cooling					⊜	⊜		
Fuel					⊖	⊜		
Ignition					⊖	⊜		
Auto. trans.					*	*		
Man. trans.					⊜	*		
Clutch					○	*		
Electrical					⊖	⊖		
A/C					○	○		
Suspension					⊖	⊜		
Brakes					⊖	⊖		
Exhaust					⊖	⊜		
Body rust					○	⊜		
Paint/trim					◒	◒		
Integrity					●	●		
Hardware					◒	◒		

Mazda MX-5 Miata

Trouble spots	88	89	90	91	92	93	94	95 (Insufficient data)
Engine			⊜	⊜	⊜	⊜	⊜	
Cooling			⊜	⊜	⊜	⊜	⊜	
Fuel			⊜	⊜	⊜	⊜	⊜	
Ignition			○	⊖	○	⊖	⊜	
Auto. trans.				*	*	*	*	
Man. trans.			⊜	⊜	⊜	⊜	⊜	
Clutch			⊖	⊖	⊜	⊜	⊜	
Electrical			◒	◒	○	○	⊖	
A/C			⊖	⊜	⊜	⊜	⊜	
Suspension			⊜	⊜	⊜	⊜	⊜	
Brakes			⊖	⊖	⊖	⊜	⊜	
Exhaust			⊖	⊜	⊖	⊜	⊖	
Body rust			⊜	⊜	⊜	⊜	⊜	
Paint/trim			○	⊖	○	⊖	○	
Integrity			○	○	○	○	○	
Hardware			○	○	○	⊖	⊜	

Mazda MX-6

Trouble spots	88	89	90	91	92 (Insufficient data)	93	94	95 (Insufficient data)
Engine	○	○	⊖	⊖		⊖	⊜	
Cooling	○	⊜	⊜	⊖		⊜	⊜	
Fuel	⊖	⊜	⊖	⊖		⊖	⊖	
Ignition	⊜	⊜	⊜	⊜		⊖	⊜	
Auto. trans.	●	●	○	*		⊖	*	
Man. trans.	⊜	⊖	⊜	⊜		⊖	*	
Clutch	⊖	⊖	⊜	⊜		⊖	*	
Electrical	◒	◒	○	○		◒	○	
A/C	○	○	⊖	⊖		⊖	⊖	
Suspension	○	○	○	⊖		⊖	⊜	
Brakes	◒	◒	◒	●		⊖	⊜	
Exhaust	●	●	◒	○		○	⊜	
Body rust	⊖	⊖	⊜	⊜		⊜	⊜	
Paint/trim	○	◒	◒	○		◒	○	
Integrity	○	◒	◒	◒		●	◒	
Hardware	●	◒	◒	◒		●	◒	

Mazda Pickup (2WD)

Trouble spots	88	89	90	91	92	93	94	95
Engine	●	○	⊖	⊖	⊖	○	⊜	⊜
Cooling	○	⊜	⊜	⊖	⊖	⊖	⊜	⊜
Fuel	◒	○	⊜	⊜	⊖	⊖	⊜	⊜
Ignition	⊖	⊖	⊜	⊖	⊖	⊖	⊜	⊜
Auto. trans.	*	*	⊜	⊖	*	*	⊖	*
Man. trans.	⊜	⊜	⊜	⊜	⊜	⊜	⊜	⊜
Clutch	○	⊖	⊖	⊜	⊜	⊜	⊜	⊖
Electrical	○	○	⊖	⊖	○	⊜	⊖	○
A/C	●	○	⊖	⊖	⊖	○	⊖	⊜
Suspension	⊜	⊖	⊜	⊖	⊜	⊖	⊖	⊜
Brakes	●	●	●	◒	⊖	⊖	◒	⊖
Exhaust	●	◒	◒	◒	⊖	⊜	⊜	⊜
Body rust	○	○	⊖	⊖	⊖	⊜	⊜	⊜
Paint/trim	○	⊜	⊖	⊖	⊖	○	⊖	⊜
Integrity	○	⊖	⊖	⊖	⊖	○	⊖	⊖
Hardware	○	⊖	⊖	⊖	⊖	⊖	⊜	⊜

Mazda Protegé

Trouble spots	88	89	90	91	92	93	94	95
Engine			⊖	⊖	⊜	⊜	⊜	⊜
Cooling			⊖	⊜	⊖	⊜	⊜	⊜
Fuel			⊜	⊖	⊖	⊜	⊜	⊜
Ignition			⊖	⊖	⊜	⊜	⊜	⊜
Auto. trans.			○	⊖	⊜	⊖	⊖	*
Man. trans.			⊜	⊜	⊜	⊖	⊜	*
Clutch			⊖	⊖	⊖	⊜	⊜	*
Electrical			◒	○	○	○	⊖	⊖
A/C			⊖	⊖	⊖	⊖	⊜	⊜
Suspension			⊖	⊖	⊖	⊜	⊖	⊜
Brakes			◒	◒	○	⊖	⊖	⊜
Exhaust			◒	○	⊜	⊜	⊜	⊜
Body rust			⊖	⊖	⊜	⊜	⊜	⊜
Paint/trim			○	○	◒	⊖	⊖	⊜
Integrity			○	○	○	⊖	○	⊖
Hardware			○	◒	◒	◒	○	○

Mercedes-Benz C-Class

Trouble spots	88	89	90	91	92	93	94	95
Engine							⊖	⊖
Cooling							⊜	⊜
Fuel							⊖	⊜
Ignition							⊜	⊖
Auto. trans.							⊜	⊖
Man. trans.								
Clutch								
Electrical							●	○
A/C							○	⊖
Suspension							⊖	⊜
Brakes							⊜	⊜
Exhaust							⊜	⊜
Body rust							⊜	⊜
Paint/trim							⊖	⊖
Integrity							⊖	⊖
Hardware							◒	○

Mercedes-Benz E-Class

Trouble spots	88	89	90	91	92	93	94	95 (Insufficient data)
Engine	◒	◒	○	○	○	⊖	⊖	
Cooling	●	◒	◒	○	○	⊖	⊜	
Fuel	◒	⊖	○	⊜	⊖	⊜	⊜	
Ignition	⊖	⊖	⊜	⊜	⊜	⊖	⊜	
Auto. trans.	○	⊖	⊜	⊖	⊖	○	⊜	
Man. trans.	*							
Clutch	*							
Electrical	●	◒	◒	◒	◒	●	◒	
A/C	●	◒	○	○	⊖	⊖	⊖	
Suspension	○	⊖	⊖	⊖	○	⊖	⊖	
Brakes	◒	◒	◒	◒	◒	◒	○	
Exhaust	○	⊖	⊖	⊜	⊜	⊜	⊜	
Body rust	⊜	⊜	⊜	⊜	⊜	⊜	⊜	
Paint/trim	⊖	⊖	⊜	⊜	⊜	⊜	⊖	
Integrity	⊖	⊜	⊖	⊖	⊖	⊖	⊖	
Hardware	◒	○	○	○	◒	◒	○	

Mercedes-Benz S-Class

Trouble spots	88	89	90 (Insufficient data)	91 (Insufficient data)	92	93 (Insufficient data)	94 (Insufficient data)	95
Engine	◒	○			○			⊜
Cooling	◒	○			⊖			⊜
Fuel	○	◒			⊖			⊜
Ignition	⊖	⊜			⊖			⊜
Auto. trans.	○	○			○			⊜
Man. trans.								
Clutch								
Electrical	◒	◒			●			○
A/C	●	○			◒			⊜
Suspension	○	⊖			●			⊖
Brakes	◒	○			○			⊜
Exhaust	⊖	⊜			⊜			⊜
Body rust	⊜	⊜			⊜			⊜
Paint/trim	⊖	⊖			⊖			⊜
Integrity	⊖	○			○			⊖
Hardware	◒	○			●			⊖

Mercury Cougar V6

Trouble spots	88	89	90	91	92	93	94	95 (Insufficient data)
Engine	◒	○	⊖	⊖	⊜	⊜	⊜	
Cooling	◒	○	⊖	⊖	⊖	⊖	⊜	
Fuel	◒	○	○	⊖	⊜	⊖	⊜	
Ignition	○	⊖	⊖	⊖	⊖	⊜	⊜	
Auto. trans.	○	○	⊖	⊖	⊖	⊖	⊖	
Man. trans.		*	*					
Clutch		*	*					
Electrical	●	●	●	●	◒	○	○	
A/C	●	●	●	●	○	○	⊖	
Suspension	◒	◒	○	○	○	⊜	⊜	
Brakes	●	●	●	●	◒	◒	◒	
Exhaust	●	⊖	⊜	⊜	⊜	⊜	⊜	
Body rust	○	⊖	⊖	⊖	⊜	⊜	⊜	
Paint/trim	◒	◒	●	◒	◒	●	○	
Integrity	○	◒	○	○	◒	◒	○	
Hardware	◒	●	●	◒	◒	◒	○	

Mercury Cougar V8

Trouble spots	88	89	90	91	92	93	94	95
Engine	○			⊖	⊖	⊜	⊜	⊜
Cooling	◒			⊖	⊖	○	⊜	⊜
Fuel	◒			⊖	⊖	⊜	⊖	⊜
Ignition	⊖			○	⊜	⊜	⊜	⊜
Auto. trans.	○			○	⊖	⊜	○	⊖
Man. trans.								
Clutch								
Electrical	●			●	●	◒	○	⊖
A/C	●			●	○	⊖	⊖	⊜
Suspension	◒			○	◒	⊖	○	⊖
Brakes	●			●	●	●	◒	⊖
Exhaust	●			⊜	⊜	⊜	⊜	⊜
Body rust	○			⊜	⊖	⊖	⊜	⊜
Paint/trim	●			●	○	◒	○	⊖
Integrity	○			◒	○	◒	◒	○
Hardware	◒			◒	●	●	○	⊖

Mercury Grand Marquis

Trouble spots	88	89	90	91	92	93	94	95
Engine	○	○	⊖	⊖	⊖	⊜	⊜	⊜
Cooling	◒	◒	○	⊖	⊜	⊜	⊜	⊜
Fuel	○	○	○	⊖	⊖	⊖	⊜	⊜
Ignition	⊖	⊖	⊖	⊖	○	⊜	⊜	⊜
Auto. trans.	○	○	⊖	⊖	○	◒	⊖	⊜
Man. trans.								
Clutch								
Electrical	●	◒	●	●	◒	○	○	○
A/C	●	●	◒	○	○	⊖	⊜	⊜
Suspension	○	○	○	○	⊖	⊖	⊖	⊖
Brakes	◒	●	●	●	●	◒	○	⊖
Exhaust	●	◒	○	○	●	⊜	⊜	⊜
Body rust	○	⊜	⊖	⊖	⊜	⊜	⊜	⊜
Paint/trim	◒	○	○	⊖	⊖	⊖	⊖	⊖
Integrity	○	⊖	○	⊖	○	⊖	⊖	○
Hardware	◒	◒	◒	◒	◒	○	⊖	⊖

Mercury Mystique

Trouble spots	88	89	90	91	92	93	94	95
Engine								⊜
Cooling								⊜
Fuel								○
Ignition								⊜
Auto. trans.								⊖
Man. trans.								⊜
Clutch								⊜
Electrical								⊖
A/C								⊜
Suspension								⊜
Brakes								⊜
Exhaust								⊜
Body rust								⊜
Paint/trim								⊖
Integrity								⊖
Hardware								○

Mercury Sable

Trouble spots	88	89	90	91	92	93	94	95
Engine	◒	○	⊖	⊖	⊖	⊜	⊜	⊜
Cooling	●	●	◒	○	○	⊖	⊜	⊜
Fuel	◒	◒	○	○	○	○	⊖	⊖
Ignition	○	⊖	⊖	⊖	⊖	⊜	⊜	⊜
Auto. trans.	◒	◒	○	●	⊖	⊖	⊖	⊖
Man. trans.								
Clutch								
Electrical	●	●	●	◒	◒	◒	○	⊖
A/C	●	●	●	◒	○	○	⊖	⊜
Suspension	●	●	●	●	◒	○	⊖	⊜
Brakes	●	●	●	●	●	◒	⊖	⊖
Exhaust	⊖	⊜	⊖	⊜	⊜	⊜	⊜	⊜
Body rust	◒	◒	○	⊖	⊜	⊜	⊜	⊜
Paint/trim	●	◒	○	○	⊖	⊖	⊖	⊖
Integrity	◒	◒	○	○	◒	◒	◒	○
Hardware	◒	◒	◒	◒	○	◒	○	○

Mercury Topaz

Trouble spots	88	89	90	91	92	93	94	95
Engine	◒	◒	◒	○	○	○	⊜	
Cooling	●	◒	◒	○	○	⊖	⊖	
Fuel	●	●	◒	◒	○	○	⊖	
Ignition	○	○	○	○	⊖	⊖	⊜	
Auto. trans.	◒	○	○	○	○	⊖	⊖	
Man. trans.	⊜	⊖	*	*	*	*	*	
Clutch	◒	◒	*	*	*	*	*	
Electrical	●	●	●	●	◒	◒	⊖	
A/C	●	●	●	◒	○	○	⊖	
Suspension	●	●	●	◒	○	⊖	⊖	
Brakes	●	●	●	●	◒	◒	○	
Exhaust	●	●	●	●	●	○	⊜	
Body rust	◒	○	⊖	⊖	⊖	⊖	⊜	
Paint/trim	●	●	◒	◒	○	○	⊖	
Integrity	●	◒	◒	◒	◒	◒	○	
Hardware	◒	◒	◒	◒	◒	◒	◒	

Mercury Tracer

Trouble spots	88	89	90	91	92	93	94	95 (Insufficient data)
Engine	◒	◒		⊖	⊜	⊖	⊜	
Cooling	◒	●		○	⊖	⊖	⊖	
Fuel	⊖	⊖		○	⊖	⊖	⊜	
Ignition	○	⊖		○	⊖	⊜	⊜	
Auto. trans.	○	○		○	⊖	⊖	⊜	
Man. trans.	⊜	⊜		⊖	*	*	*	
Clutch	◒	⊖		○	*	*	*	
Electrical	◒	◒		●	●	◒	◒	
A/C	●	●		●	⊖	⊜	⊜	
Suspension	○	○		○	○	⊖	⊖	
Brakes	●	●		◒	◒	○	○	
Exhaust	●	●		⊜	⊜	⊜	⊜	
Body rust	◒	⊖		⊜	⊜	⊜	⊜	
Paint/trim	◒	⊜		○	⊖	⊖	⊜	
Integrity	○	○		○	○	○	⊖	
Hardware	◒	○		◒	○	◒	○	

Mercury Villager Van

Trouble spots	88	89	90	91	92	93	94	95
Engine						⊜	⊜	⊜
Cooling						⊜	⊖	⊜
Fuel						⊜	⊜	⊜
Ignition						⊜	⊜	⊜
Auto. trans.						⊜	⊜	⊜
Man. trans.								
Clutch								
Electrical						◒	○	⊖
A/C						○	⊖	⊜
Suspension						⊖	⊖	⊜
Brakes						○	⊖	⊖
Exhaust						⊖	⊜	⊜
Body rust						⊜	⊜	⊜
Paint/trim						⊖	⊖	⊜
Integrity						◒	◒	○
Hardware						◒	◒	○

Mitsubishi 3000GT (2WD)

Trouble spots	88	89	90	91	92	93	94	95 (Insufficient data)
Engine				⊖	⊜	⊖	⊜	
Cooling				⊜	⊜	⊖	⊜	
Fuel				⊜	⊜	⊜	⊜	
Ignition				⊜	⊜	⊜	⊜	
Auto. trans.				*	*	*	*	
Man. trans.				*	○	○	*	
Clutch				*	◒	◒	*	
Electrical				○	●	◒	◒	
A/C				⊖	⊖	⊖	⊜	
Suspension				⊖	⊖	⊖	⊜	
Brakes				○	⊖	⊖	⊜	
Exhaust				⊜	⊜	⊜	⊜	
Body rust				⊜	⊜	⊜	⊜	
Paint/trim				◒	○	◒	⊖	
Integrity				○	◒	◒	○	
Hardware				◒	◒	◒	○	

Mitsubishi Diamante

TROUBLE SPOTS	88	89	90	91	92	93	94	95
Engine					⊖	⊖	⊖	Insufficient data
Cooling					⊖	⊖	⊖	
Fuel					⊖	⊖	⊖	
Ignition					⊖	⊖	⊖	
Auto. trans.					⊖	○	⊖	
Man. trans.								
Clutch								
Electrical					○	○	⊖	
A/C					⊖	⊖	⊖	
Suspension					⊖	⊖	○	
Brakes					◒	○	⊖	
Exhaust					⊖	⊖	⊖	
Body rust					⊖	⊖	⊖	
Paint/trim					⊖	⊖	○	
Integrity					⊖	○	⊖	
Hardware					○	◒	⊖	

Mitsubishi Eclipse (2WD)

TROUBLE SPOTS	88	89	90	91	92	93	94	95
Engine			◒	◒	◒	⊖	⊖	○
Cooling			⊖	⊖	⊖	⊖	⊖	⊖
Fuel			⊖	⊖	⊖	⊖	⊖	⊖
Ignition			⊖	○	⊖	⊖	⊖	○
Auto. trans.			○	○	⊖	*	*	*
Man. trans.			○	○	○	⊖	*	*
Clutch			○	⊖	⊖	⊖	*	*
Electrical			◒	◒	◒	○	○	◒
A/C			⊖	⊖	⊖	⊖	⊖	⊖
Suspension			⊖	⊖	⊖	○	⊖	○
Brakes			◒	◒	○	○	⊖	⊖
Exhaust			⊖	○	○	⊖	⊖	⊖
Body rust			⊖	⊖	⊖	⊖	⊖	⊖
Paint/trim			○	○	○	○	⊖	⊖
Integrity			○	○	◒	○	○	◒
Hardware			○	◒	●	◒	○	●

Mitsubishi Expo LRV

TROUBLE SPOTS	88	89	90	91	92	93	94	95
Engine					⊖	⊖	⊖	
Cooling					⊖	⊖	⊖	
Fuel					⊖	⊖	⊖	
Ignition					⊖	⊖	⊖	
Auto. trans.					○	⊖	⊖	
Man. trans.					*	*	*	
Clutch					*	*	*	
Electrical					○	○	○	
A/C					⊖	⊖	⊖	
Suspension					○	⊖	⊖	
Brakes					○	⊖	⊖	
Exhaust					⊖	⊖	⊖	
Body rust					⊖	⊖	⊖	
Paint/trim					○	⊖	⊖	
Integrity					○	◒	⊖	
Hardware					○	◒	○	

Mitsubishi Galant 4

TROUBLE SPOTS	88	89	90	91	92	93	94	95
Engine		◒	○	○	⊖	Insufficient data	⊖	⊖
Cooling		⊖	⊖	⊖	⊖		⊖	⊖
Fuel		⊖	⊖	⊖	⊖		⊖	⊖
Ignition		⊖	⊖	⊖	⊖		⊖	⊖
Auto. trans.		○	⊖	⊖	⊖		⊖	⊖
Man. trans.		⊖	⊖	⊖	*		*	*
Clutch		◒	◒	○	*		*	*
Electrical		◒	○	○	○		◒	⊖
A/C		◒	⊖	⊖	○		⊖	⊖
Suspension		⊖	⊖	⊖	⊖		⊖	⊖
Brakes		◒	○	○	○		○	⊖
Exhaust		⊖	⊖	⊖	⊖		⊖	⊖
Body rust		⊖	⊖	⊖	⊖		⊖	⊖
Paint/trim		○	○	○	⊖		⊖	⊖
Integrity		○	⊖	⊖	○		○	○
Hardware		⊖	○	⊖	○		●	○

Mitsubishi Mirage

TROUBLE SPOTS	88	89	90	91	92	93	94	95
Engine	●	◒	◒	⊖	⊖	⊖	Insufficient data	Insufficient data
Cooling	○	⊖	⊖	⊖	⊖	⊖		
Fuel	⊖	⊖	⊖	⊖	⊖	⊖		
Ignition	○	⊖	⊖	⊖	⊖	⊖		
Auto. trans.	○	⊖	⊖	○	○	●		
Man. trans.	⊖	⊖	⊖	⊖	⊖	⊖		
Clutch	○	⊖	⊖	⊖	⊖	⊖		
Electrical	◒	◒	○	○	○	○		
A/C	○	◒	○	○	⊖	⊖		
Suspension	○	◒	○	⊖	⊖	⊖		
Brakes	●	●	◒	◒	○	○		
Exhaust	○	⊖	⊖	⊖	⊖	⊖		
Body rust	◒	⊖	⊖	⊖	⊖	⊖		
Paint/trim	○	◒	○	○	○	⊖		
Integrity	◒	◒	◒	◒	◒	○		
Hardware	○	◒	◒	○	○	○		

Mitsubishi Montero

TROUBLE SPOTS	88	89	90	91	92	93	94	95
Engine		◒	○	⊖	Insufficient data	Insufficient data	Insufficient data	Insufficient data
Cooling		○	⊖	⊖				
Fuel		⊖	⊖	⊖				
Ignition		⊖	⊖	⊖				
Auto. trans.		*	*	*				
Man. trans.		*	*	*				
Clutch		*	*	*				
Electrical		○	○	○				
A/C		⊖	⊖	⊖				
Suspension		◒	○	⊖				
Brakes		●	○	●				
Exhaust		⊖	⊖	⊖				
Body rust		⊖	⊖	⊖				
Paint/trim		○	⊖	⊖				
Integrity		○	⊖	●				
Hardware		○	○	○				

Nissan 240SX

TROUBLE SPOTS	88	89	90	91	92	93	94	95
Engine		⊖	⊖	⊖	⊖	⊖	Insufficient data	Insufficient data
Cooling		⊖	⊖	⊖	⊖	⊖		
Fuel		⊖	⊖	⊖	⊖	⊖		
Ignition		⊖	⊖	⊖	⊖	⊖		
Auto. trans.		○	*	⊖	*	*		
Man. trans.		○	⊖	⊖	*	*		
Clutch		●	◒	⊖	*	*		
Electrical		◒	◒	○	○	○		
A/C		○	○	⊖	⊖	⊖		
Suspension		⊖	⊖	⊖	⊖	⊖		
Brakes		●	◒	◒	○	⊖		
Exhaust		●	◒	⊖	⊖	⊖		
Body rust		⊖	⊖	⊖	⊖	⊖		
Paint/trim		⊖	⊖	⊖	⊖	○		
Integrity		○	○	⊖	⊖	○		
Hardware		●	◒	⊖	○	○		

Nissan 300ZX

TROUBLE SPOTS	88	89	90	91	92	93	94	95
Engine	⊖	Insufficient data	○	⊖	Insufficient data	⊖	Insufficient data	Insufficient data
Cooling	◒		○	⊖		⊖		
Fuel	◒		○	○		◒		
Ignition	○		○	◒		○		
Auto. trans.	*		◒	*		*		
Man. trans.	*		⊖	⊖		*		
Clutch	*		●	●		*		
Electrical	●		●	●		◒		
A/C	○		◒	○		⊖		
Suspension	○		⊖	⊖		○		
Brakes	◒		●	●		⊖		
Exhaust	○		◒	○		⊖		
Body rust	○		⊖	⊖		⊖		
Paint/trim	◒		○	○		○		
Integrity	◒		◒	○		◒		
Hardware	◒		○	○		◒		

Nissan Altima

TROUBLE SPOTS	88	89	90	91	92	93	94	95
Engine						⊖	⊖	⊖
Cooling						⊖	⊖	⊖
Fuel						⊖	⊖	⊖
Ignition						⊖	⊖	⊖
Auto. trans.						⊖	⊖	⊖
Man. trans.						⊖	⊖	⊖
Clutch						⊖	⊖	⊖
Electrical						○	⊖	⊖
A/C						⊖	⊖	⊖
Suspension						⊖	⊖	⊖
Brakes						○	⊖	⊖
Exhaust						⊖	⊖	⊖
Body rust						⊖	⊖	⊖
Paint/trim						⊖	⊖	⊖
Integrity						○	○	⊖
Hardware						○	○	⊖

Nissan Maxima

TROUBLE SPOTS	88	89	90	91	92	93	94	95
Engine	⊖	⊖	⊖	⊖	⊖	⊖	⊖	⊖
Cooling	⊖	⊖	⊖	⊖	⊖	⊖	⊖	⊖
Fuel	○	⊖	○	⊖	⊖	⊖	⊖	⊖
Ignition	⊖	⊖	⊖	⊖	⊖	⊖	⊖	⊖
Auto. trans.	○	○	⊖	⊖	⊖	⊖	⊖	⊖
Man. trans.	◒	○	○	⊖	⊖	⊖	*	⊖
Clutch	●	●	◒	○	⊖	⊖	*	⊖
Electrical	●	◒	◒	○	○	○	⊖	⊖
A/C	◒	○	⊖	⊖	⊖	⊖	⊖	⊖
Suspension	○	⊖	⊖	⊖	⊖	⊖	⊖	⊖
Brakes	●	●	◒	●	◒	○	○	⊖
Exhaust	●	◒	⊖	⊖	⊖	⊖	⊖	⊖
Body rust	⊖	⊖	⊖	⊖	⊖	⊖	⊖	⊖
Paint/trim	○	○	⊖	○	⊖	⊖	⊖	⊖
Integrity	○	⊖	⊖	⊖	⊖	⊖	⊖	⊖
Hardware	○	◒	○	○	○	⊖	⊖	⊖

Nissan Pathfinder

TROUBLE SPOTS	88	89	90	91	92	93	94	95
Engine	⊖	⊖	⊖	⊖	⊖	⊖	⊖	⊖
Cooling	○	⊖	⊖	⊖	⊖	⊖	⊖	⊖
Fuel	○	⊖	⊖	⊖	⊖	⊖	⊖	⊖
Ignition	⊖	⊖	⊖	⊖	⊖	⊖	⊖	⊖
Auto. trans.	○	*	◒	◒	○	○	⊖	⊖
Man. trans.	⊖	⊖	⊖	⊖	⊖	⊖	⊖	*
Clutch	○	○	⊖	⊖	⊖	⊖	⊖	*
Electrical	◒	◒	○	◒	◒	◒	○	⊖
A/C	○	⊖	⊖	⊖	⊖	⊖	⊖	⊖
Suspension	○	⊖	⊖	○	○	○	⊖	⊖
Brakes	◒	◒	○	○	⊖	⊖	⊖	⊖
Exhaust	●	●	●	◒	⊖	⊖	⊖	⊖
Body rust	◒	○	⊖	⊖	⊖	⊖	⊖	⊖
Paint/trim	⊖	○	⊖	⊖	⊖	⊖	⊖	⊖
Integrity	○	○	⊖	○	⊖	○	○	⊖
Hardware	◒	◒	○	○	○	○	○	⊖

Nissan Pickup (2WD)

TROUBLE SPOTS	88	89	90	91	92	93	94	95
Engine	⊖	⊖	⊖	⊖	⊖	⊖	⊖	⊖
Cooling	○	⊖	⊖	⊖	⊖	⊖	⊖	⊖
Fuel	○	⊖	⊖	⊖	⊖	⊖	⊖	⊖
Ignition	⊖	⊖	⊖	⊖	⊖	⊖	⊖	⊖
Auto. trans.	*	○	◒	⊖	⊖	⊖	⊖	*
Man. trans.	⊖	⊖	⊖	⊖	⊖	⊖	⊖	*
Clutch	◒	○	◒	⊖	○	⊖	○	*
Electrical	◒	○	○	○	◒	○	⊖	⊖
A/C	○	○	⊖	⊖	⊖	⊖	⊖	⊖
Suspension	⊖	⊖	⊖	⊖	⊖	○	⊖	⊖
Brakes	○	○	⊖	⊖	⊖	⊖	⊖	⊖
Exhaust	◒	◒	◒	◒	○	⊖	⊖	⊖
Body rust	◒	◒	○	⊖	⊖	⊖	⊖	⊖
Paint/trim	◒	●	○	○	⊖	⊖	⊖	⊖
Integrity	⊖	⊖	⊖	⊖	○	○	○	○
Hardware	○	○	◒	○	○	○	⊖	⊖

Nissan Pickup (4WD)

TROUBLE SPOTS	88	89	90	91	92	93	94	95
Engine	⊖	⊖	○	⊖	Insufficient data	⊖	⊖	Insufficient data
Cooling	⊖	⊖	⊖	⊖		⊖	⊖	
Fuel	⊖	○	⊖	⊖		⊖	⊖	
Ignition	⊖	⊖	⊖	⊖		⊖	⊖	
Auto. trans.	*	*	*	*		*	*	
Man. trans.	*	⊖	*	⊖		⊖	⊖	
Clutch	*	○	*	○		⊖	⊖	
Electrical	◒	○	◒	○		⊖	⊖	
A/C	*	*	*	*		⊖	⊖	
Suspension	○	○	◒	○		○	○	
Brakes	◒	◒	⊖	○		⊖	⊖	
Exhaust	●	●	◒	●		⊖	⊖	
Body rust	●	●	◒	○		⊖	⊖	
Paint/trim	●	●	◒	⊖		⊖	⊖	
Integrity	○	○	⊖	○		⊖	○	
Hardware	◒	◒	◒	⊖		⊖	⊖	

Nissan Quest Van

TROUBLE SPOTS	88	89	90	91	92	93	94	95
Engine						⊖	⊖	⊖
Cooling						⊖	⊖	⊖
Fuel						⊖	⊖	⊖
Ignition						⊖	⊖	⊖
Auto. trans.						⊖	⊖	⊖
Man. trans.								
Clutch								
Electrical						◒	○	⊖
A/C						○	⊖	⊖
Suspension						⊖	⊖	⊖
Brakes						○	⊖	⊖
Exhaust						⊖	⊖	⊖
Body rust						⊖	⊖	⊖
Paint/trim						⊖	⊖	⊖
Integrity						◒	◒	○
Hardware						◒	◒	○

Nissan Sentra

TROUBLE SPOTS	88	89	90	91	92	93	94	95
Engine	◒	◒	○	⊖	⊖	⊖	⊖	Insufficient data
Cooling	◒	⊖	⊖	⊖	⊖	⊖	⊖	
Fuel	○	⊖	⊖	○	○	⊖	⊖	
Ignition	⊖	⊖	⊖	⊖	⊖	⊖	⊖	
Auto. trans.	●	◒	◒	○	⊖	⊖	⊖	
Man. trans.	⊖	⊖	⊖	⊖	⊖	⊖	⊖	
Clutch	◒	○	○	⊖	⊖	⊖	⊖	
Electrical	◒	◒	◒	○	○	○	⊖	
A/C	◒	○	○	⊖	⊖	⊖	⊖	
Suspension	◒	○	○	⊖	⊖	⊖	⊖	
Brakes	●	●	●	◒	○	○	⊖	
Exhaust	●	●	◒	○	⊖	⊖	⊖	
Body rust	◒	○	○	⊖	⊖	⊖	⊖	
Paint/trim	◒	◒	◒	○	⊖	⊖	⊖	
Integrity	◒	◒	○	○	○	○	⊖	
Hardware	◒	◒	○	○	○	○	⊖	

Nissan Stanza

TROUBLE SPOTS	88	89	90	91	92	93	94	95
Engine	○	○	⊖	⊖	⊖			
Cooling	○	⊖	⊖	⊖	⊖			
Fuel	⊖	⊖	⊖	⊖	⊖			
Ignition	○	⊖	⊖	⊖	⊖			
Auto. trans.	○	○	○	⊖	⊖			
Man. trans.	◒	*	○	⊖	⊖			
Clutch	◒	*	◒	○	○			
Electrical	●	◒	◒	○	◒			
A/C	○	○	○	⊖	⊖			
Suspension	◒	○	⊖	⊖	⊖			
Brakes	◒	●	◒	◒	◒			
Exhaust	●	●	⊖	⊖	⊖			
Body rust	⊖	⊖	⊖	⊖	⊖			
Paint/trim	○	○	○	○	⊖			
Integrity	◒	○	⊖	○	⊖			
Hardware	●	◒	○	○	○			

Oldsmobile 88

TROUBLE SPOTS	88	89	90	91	92	93	94	95
Engine	⊖	⊖	⊖	⊖	⊖	⊖	⊖	⊖
Cooling	◒	◒	○	○	○	○	⊖	⊖
Fuel	◒	○	○	○	⊖	⊖	⊖	⊖
Ignition	○	◒	◒	◒	⊖	⊖	⊖	⊖
Auto. trans.	○	○	⊖	⊖	⊖	⊖	⊖	⊖
Man. trans.								
Clutch								
Electrical	●	●	●	●	●	○	○	○
A/C	○	◒	○	○	○	⊖	⊖	⊖
Suspension	●	○	⊖	⊖	⊖	⊖	⊖	⊖
Brakes	●	●	●	●	●	○	⊖	⊖
Exhaust	⊖	⊖	⊖	⊖	⊖	⊖	⊖	⊖
Body rust	◒	⊖	⊖	⊖	⊖	⊖	⊖	⊖
Paint/trim	●	◒	○	○	○	⊖	⊖	⊖
Integrity	○	○	⊖	○	◒	○	○	○
Hardware	●	◒	◒	◒	◒	◒	○	⊖

Oldsmobile 98

TROUBLE SPOTS	88	89	90	91	92	93	94	95
Engine	⊖	⊖	⊖	⊖	⊖	⊖	⊖	⊖
Cooling	◒	○	○	⊖	○	⊖	⊖	⊖
Fuel	○	○	○	⊖	⊖	⊖	⊖	⊖
Ignition	○	○	○	○	⊖	⊖	⊖	⊖
Auto. trans.	◒	○	○	⊖	⊖	⊖	⊖	⊖
Man. trans.								
Clutch								
Electrical	●	●	●	●	●	◒	○	◒
A/C	○	◒	○	◒	○	○	⊖	⊖
Suspension	◒	⊖	○	⊖	⊖	⊖	⊖	⊖
Brakes	●	●	●	◒	◒	○	⊖	⊖
Exhaust	⊖	⊖	⊖	⊖	⊖	⊖	⊖	⊖
Body rust	⊖	⊖	⊖	⊖	⊖	⊖	⊖	⊖
Paint/trim	○	◒	⊖	⊖	⊖	⊖	⊖	⊖
Integrity	○	○	⊖	○	◒	○	◒	○
Hardware	◒	◒	◒	◒	◒	◒	◒	○

Oldsmobile Achieva

Insufficient data (95)

TROUBLE SPOTS	88	89	90	91	92	93	94	95
Engine					⊖	⊖	⊜	
Cooling					○	⊜	⊜	
Fuel					⊖	⊖	⊜	
Ignition					⊖	⊖	⊜	
Auto. trans.					⊜	⊜	⊖	
Man. trans.					*	*	*	
Clutch					*	*	*	
Electrical					◒	◒	○	
A/C					⊖	⊜	⊜	
Suspension					○	⊖	⊖	
Brakes					●	◒	○	
Exhaust					⊜	⊜	⊜	
Body rust					⊜	⊜	⊜	
Paint/trim					◒	○	⊖	
Integrity					◒	◒	◒	
Hardware					●	●	◒	

Oldsmobile Aurora

TROUBLE SPOTS	88	89	90	91	92	93	94	95
Engine								⊖
Cooling								⊜
Fuel								⊜
Ignition								⊜
Auto. trans.								⊖
Man. trans.								
Clutch								
Electrical								○
A/C								⊜
Suspension								⊜
Brakes								⊜
Exhaust								⊜
Body rust								⊜
Paint/trim								⊖
Integrity								○
Hardware								⊖

Oldsmobile Bravada

TROUBLE SPOTS	88	89	90	91	92	93	94	95
Engine				⊖	○	○	⊜	
Cooling				⊖	⊖	⊖	⊜	
Fuel				⊖	○	○	⊜	
Ignition				○	⊖	⊖	⊜	
Auto. trans.				⊜	⊖	◒	⊖	
Man. trans.								
Clutch								
Electrical				●	◒	●	◒	
A/C				⊖	⊖	⊖	⊜	
Suspension				◒	○	○	⊖	
Brakes				●	●	●	○	
Exhaust				○	⊜	⊜	⊜	
Body rust				◒	⊖	⊖	⊜	
Paint/trim				●	◒	○	⊖	
Integrity				●	◒	●	◒	
Hardware				●	◒	◒	○	

Oldsmobile Custom Cruiser Wagon

Insufficient data (92)

TROUBLE SPOTS	88	89	90	91	92	93	94	95
Engine	●	◒	○	⊖				
Cooling	◒	●	○	○				
Fuel	○	○	⊖	⊜				
Ignition	⊖	○	⊖	○				
Auto. trans.	○	◒	⊖	⊜				
Man. trans.								
Clutch								
Electrical	●	●	●	◒				
A/C	◒	○	○	◒				
Suspension	○	○	○	⊖				
Brakes	●	◒	●	◒				
Exhaust	●	◒	◒	◒				
Body rust	◒	○	◒	⊜				
Paint/trim	●	◒	●	○				
Integrity	◒	◒	◒	○				
Hardware	◒	●	●	●				

Oldsmobile Cutlass Calais

TROUBLE SPOTS	88	89	90	91	92	93	94	95
Engine	●	●	◒	◒				
Cooling	◒	●	◒	○				
Fuel	●	◒	○	⊖				
Ignition	●	◒	○	⊖				
Auto. trans.	◒	○	○	⊖				
Man. trans.	*	*	*	*				
Clutch	*	*	*	*				
Electrical	●	●	●	●				
A/C	◒	○	○	⊖				
Suspension	◒	○	○	○				
Brakes	●	●	●	●				
Exhaust	●	●	●	●				
Body rust	●	●	●	⊖				
Paint/trim	●	●	●	◒				
Integrity	◒	○	○	○				
Hardware	◒	◒	○	◒				

Oldsmobile Cutlass Ciera

TROUBLE SPOTS	88	89	90	91	92	93	94	95
Engine	○	⊖	⊖	⊖	⊖	⊜	⊖	⊜
Cooling	●	◒	◒	◒	○	⊜	⊜	⊜
Fuel	◒	◒	⊖	⊖	⊖	⊜	⊖	⊜
Ignition	◒	○	⊖	⊖	⊖	⊜	⊜	⊜
Auto. trans.	○	⊖	⊖	⊖	⊖	⊜	⊖	⊜
Man. trans.								
Clutch								
Electrical	●	●	◒	◒	○	○	○	○
A/C	○	○	⊖	⊖	⊖	⊖	⊖	⊖
Suspension	◒	○	⊖	⊖	⊖	⊖	⊖	⊜
Brakes	●	●	●	●	●	○	○	⊜
Exhaust	●	◒	◒	○	○	⊖	⊜	⊜
Body rust	●	◒	⊖	⊖	⊜	⊜	⊜	⊜
Paint/trim	●	●	◒	○	⊖	⊖	⊖	⊜
Integrity	◒	○	○	⊖	○	○	○	○
Hardware	●	◒	○	○	⊖	⊖	◒	⊖

Oldsmobile Cutlass Supreme

TROUBLE SPOTS	88	89	90	91	92	93	94	95
Engine	⊖	○	○	○	⊖	⊜	⊖	⊜
Cooling	◒	◒	○	⊖	⊖	⊖	⊜	⊜
Fuel	◒	◒	○	○	⊖	⊜	⊜	⊜
Ignition	○	◒	○	⊜	⊖	⊖	⊜	⊜
Auto. trans.	○	◒	○	⊖	⊖	⊖	⊖	⊜
Man. trans.	*	*	*	*	*			
Clutch	*	*	*	*	*			
Electrical	●	●	●	●	●	●	●	○
A/C	◒	◒	◒	○	○	⊜	⊜	⊜
Suspension	◒	◒	○	○	⊖	⊖	⊖	⊜
Brakes	●	●	●	●	●	●	●	⊜
Exhaust	○	⊖	⊖	⊜	⊜	⊜	⊜	⊜
Body rust	○	○	⊖	⊖	⊜	⊜	⊜	⊜
Paint/trim	●	●	●	◒	○	○	⊖	⊜
Integrity	●	◒	◒	○	○	◒	●	○
Hardware	●	●	●	◒	●	◒	●	⊖

Oldsmobile Silhouette Van

TROUBLE SPOTS	88	89	90	91	92	93	94	95
Engine			○	⊖	⊖	⊖	⊖	⊜
Cooling			●	○	○	⊖	⊖	⊜
Fuel			⊖	⊖	⊖	⊖	⊜	⊜
Ignition			⊖	⊜	⊖	⊖	⊜	⊜
Auto. trans.			⊖	⊖	⊖	○	⊖	⊜
Man. trans.								
Clutch								
Electrical			●	●	●	●	◒	○
A/C			○	○	○	○	⊜	⊜
Suspension			○	⊖	○	○	⊖	⊜
Brakes			●	●	●	○	⊖	⊜
Exhaust			⊖	⊜	⊖	⊖	⊜	⊜
Body rust			⊖	⊜	⊜	⊜	⊜	⊜
Paint/trim			●	●	○	○	○	⊖
Integrity			◒	◒	○	◒	◒	○
Hardware			●	●	●	●	●	◒

Plymouth Acclaim

TROUBLE SPOTS	88	89	90	91	92	93	94	95
Engine		◒	○	○	○	⊖	⊜	⊜
Cooling		●	○	⊖	⊖	⊜	⊜	⊜
Fuel		○	○	○	⊖	⊖	⊖	⊜
Ignition		○	⊖	⊖	⊖	⊜	⊜	⊜
Auto. trans.		○	◒	◒	⊖	⊖	○	⊜
Man. trans.		*	*	*	*	*		
Clutch		*	*	*	*	*		
Electrical		●	◒	◒	◒	○	○	○
A/C		●	○	○	⊖	⊖	⊖	⊜
Suspension		◒	○	○	⊖	⊖	⊖	⊜
Brakes		●	●	○	○	⊜	⊖	⊜
Exhaust		⊖	⊜	●	◒	⊜	⊜	⊜
Body rust		○	⊖	⊜	⊜	⊜	⊜	⊜
Paint/trim		◒	○	○	⊖	⊖	⊖	⊖
Integrity		○	○	○	○	○	○	○
Hardware		○	○	⊜	○	○	○	⊖

Plymouth Colt, Colt Wagon

Insufficient data (94)

TROUBLE SPOTS	88	89	90	91	92	93	94	95
Engine	●	◒	◒	⊖	⊜	⊜		
Cooling	○	⊖	⊖	⊜	⊜	⊜		
Fuel	⊖	⊖	⊖	⊖	⊜	⊜		
Ignition	○	⊖	⊖	⊖	⊜	⊜		
Auto. trans.	○	⊖	⊖	○	○	●		
Man. trans.	⊜	⊖	⊖	⊖	⊖	⊖		
Clutch	○	⊖	⊖	⊖	⊜	⊖		
Electrical	◒	◒	○	○	○	○		
A/C	○	◒	○	○	⊖	⊜		
Suspension	○	◒	○	⊖	⊖	⊜		
Brakes	●	●	◒	◒	○	○		
Exhaust	○	⊜	⊜	⊜	⊜	⊜		
Body rust	◒	⊜	⊜	⊖	⊖	⊜		
Paint/trim	○	◒	○	○	○	⊖		
Integrity	◒	◒	◒	◒	◒	○		
Hardware	○	◒	◒	○	○	○		

Plymouth Horizon, America

TROUBLE SPOTS	88	89	90	91	92	93	94	95
Engine	◒	◒	◒					
Cooling	◒	◒	◒					
Fuel	◒	○	○					
Ignition	○	○	⊖					
Auto. trans.	⊖	⊖	*					
Man. trans.	⊖	*	*					
Clutch	○	*	*					
Electrical	●	◒	◒					
A/C	●	●	*					
Suspension	○	○	◒					
Brakes	●	●	●					
Exhaust	⊖	⊖	⊖					
Body rust	●	◒	○					
Paint/trim	●	●	◒					
Integrity	●	●	●					
Hardware	●	◒	◒					

Plymouth Laser (2WD)

TROUBLE SPOTS	88	89	90	91	92	93	94	95
Engine			◒	◒	◒	⊖	⊜	
Cooling			⊖	⊖	⊜	⊖	⊖	
Fuel			⊖	⊖	⊜	⊖	⊖	
Ignition			⊖	○	⊖	⊜	⊖	
Auto. trans.			○	○	⊖	*	*	
Man. trans.			○	○	○	⊖	*	
Clutch			○	⊖	⊖	⊜	*	
Electrical			◒	◒	◒	○	○	
A/C			⊖	⊖	⊜	⊜	⊖	
Suspension			⊖	⊖	⊖	○	⊜	
Brakes			◒	◒	○	○	⊖	
Exhaust			⊖	○	○	⊜	⊜	
Body rust			⊜	⊜	⊜	⊜	⊜	
Paint/trim			○	○	○	○	⊖	
Integrity			○	○	◒	○	○	
Hardware			○	◒	●	◒	○	

Plymouth Neon

TROUBLE SPOTS	88	89	90	91	92	93	94	95
Engine								⊜
Cooling								⊜
Fuel								⊖
Ignition								⊜
Auto. trans.								⊖
Man. trans.								⊜
Clutch								⊜
Electrical								○
A/C								⊖
Suspension								⊖
Brakes								⊖
Exhaust								⊖
Body rust								⊜
Paint/trim								⊖
Integrity								◒
Hardware								○

Plymouth Sundance

TROUBLE SPOTS	88	89	90	91	92	93	94	95
Engine	●	●	◒	○	○	○	⊖	
Cooling	●	●	◒	○	⊖	⊜	⊜	
Fuel	◒	◒	○	○	○	⊖	⊖	
Ignition	○	○	○	⊖	⊜	⊜	⊜	
Auto. trans.	○	○	⊖	⊖	⊖	○	⊖	
Man. trans.	*	*	*	*	⊖	⊖	*	
Clutch	*	*	*	*	⊖	⊖	*	
Electrical	●	●	●	●	◒	◒	○	
A/C	●	●	●	◒	○	⊖	⊖	
Suspension	◒	●	○	○	⊖	⊖	⊖	
Brakes	●	●	●	○	⊜	⊖	⊖	
Exhaust	○	⊖	⊜	●	◒	⊜	⊜	
Body rust	○	○	⊖	⊖	⊖	⊜	⊜	
Paint/trim	●	●	◒	○	◒	◒	⊖	
Integrity	◒	◒	○	◒	◒	◒	◒	
Hardware	●	●	○	○	○	○	◒	

Plymouth Voyager V6 (2WD)

TROUBLE SPOTS	88	89	90	91	92	93	94	95
Engine	●	●	◒	○	○	⊖	⊜	⊜
Cooling	●	●	◒	○	⊖	⊖	⊜	⊜
Fuel	●	○	◒	○	⊖	⊖	⊜	⊜
Ignition	○	⊖	⊖	⊖	⊜	⊜	⊜	⊜
Auto. trans.	◒	◒	●	◒	◒	○	⊖	⊜
Man. trans.								
Clutch								
Electrical	●	●	◒	●	●	○	○	⊖
A/C	●	◒	○	⊖	⊖	○	⊜	⊜
Suspension	◒	○	○	○	⊖	⊖	⊜	⊜
Brakes	●	●	●	●	◒	○	⊜	⊜
Exhaust	⊖	⊜	⊖	●	⊖	⊜	⊜	⊜
Body rust	○	⊖	⊖	⊜	⊜	⊜	⊜	⊜
Paint/trim	◒	◒	○	○	⊖	⊖	⊖	⊜
Integrity	◒	◒	◒	◒	◒	◒	○	⊖
Hardware	●	●	●	◒	◒	◒	○	⊖

Plymouth Grand Voyager V6 (2WD)

TROUBLE SPOTS	88	89	90	91	92	93	94	95
Engine	●	●	○	○	○	○	⊖	⊜
Cooling	●	●	◒	○	⊖	⊖	⊜	⊜
Fuel	●	◒	○	○	⊖	⊖	⊜	⊜
Ignition	○	⊖	⊖	⊖	⊖	⊜	⊜	⊜
Auto. trans.	◒	●	●	●	◒	◒	○	⊜
Man. trans.								
Clutch								
Electrical	●	●	●	●	●	◒	○	⊖
A/C	●	●	◒	⊖	⊖	○	⊖	⊜
Suspension	●	◒	○	○	○	○	⊜	⊜
Brakes	●	●	●	●	◒	○	⊖	⊜
Exhaust	⊖	⊜	⊖	◒	⊜	⊜	⊜	⊜
Body rust	⊖	⊖	⊖	⊜	⊜	⊜	⊜	⊜
Paint/trim	◒	◒	◒	○	⊖	⊖	⊖	⊖
Integrity	◒	◒	◒	◒	◒	◒	◒	○
Hardware	●	●	●	◒	◒	◒	○	⊖

Plymouth Grand Voyager V6 (4WD)

Insufficient data (95)

TROUBLE SPOTS	88	89	90	91	92	93	94	95
Engine				○	○	○	○	
Cooling				⊖	○	⊜	⊖	
Fuel				●	○	○	⊖	
Ignition				○	⊖	⊖	⊜	
Auto. trans.				●	●	◒	○	
Man. trans.								
Clutch								
Electrical				●	●	○	○	
A/C				⊖	⊖	⊖	⊖	
Suspension				◒	○	○	⊖	
Brakes				●	●	◒	⊖	
Exhaust				●	●	⊜	⊜	
Body rust				⊖	⊜	⊜	⊜	
Paint/trim				◒	⊖	⊖	⊖	
Integrity				◒	●	⊖	◒	
Hardware				◒	◒	◒	○	

Pontiac 6000

TROUBLE SPOTS	88	89	90	91	92	93	94	95
Engine	◒	○	○	⊖				
Cooling	●	○	○	○				
Fuel	◒	◒	⊖	⊖				
Ignition	◒	◒	⊖	⊖				
Auto. trans.	○	○	⊖	⊜				
Man. trans.	*							
Clutch	*							
Electrical	●	●	●	◒				
A/C	○	○	⊖	⊜				
Suspension	◒	○	○	⊜				
Brakes	●	●	●	●				
Exhaust	●	●	●	○				
Body rust	◒	●	⊖	⊜				
Paint/trim	●	●	○	⊖				
Integrity	○	◒	⊖	⊖				
Hardware	◒	◒	⊖	○				

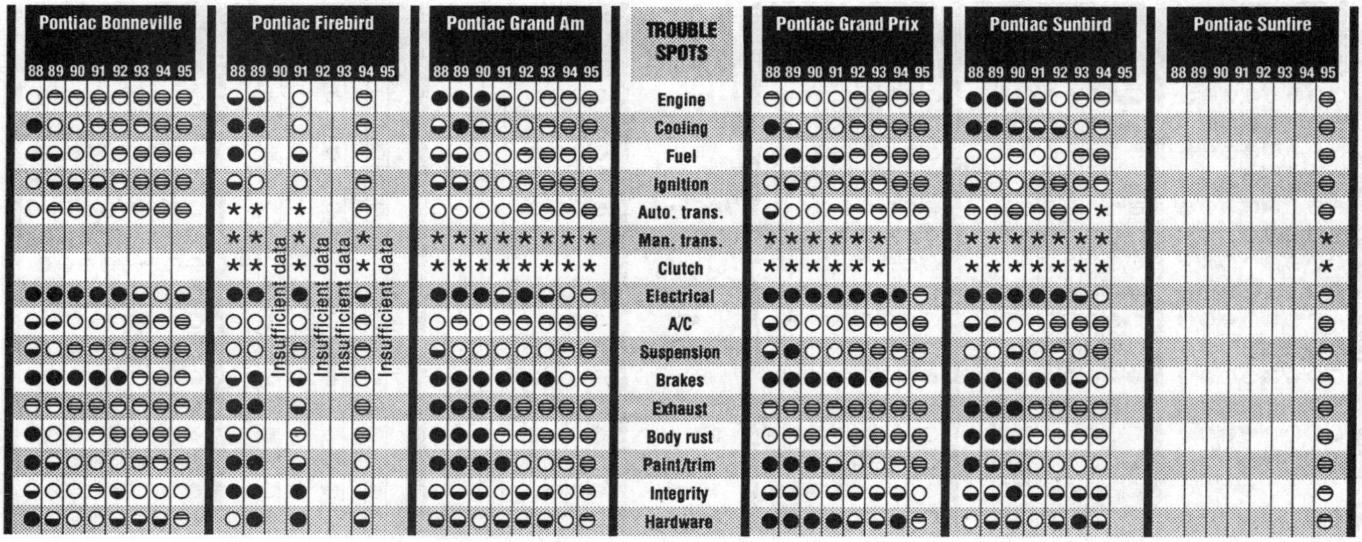

Trouble Spots	Pontiac Bonneville 88	89	90	91	92	93	94	95
Engine	○	⊖	⊖	⊜	⊖	⊜	⊜	⊜
Cooling	●	○	○	⊖	⊖	⊖	⊜	⊜
Fuel	◒	◒	○	○	⊖	⊜	⊜	⊜
Ignition	○	◒	◒	◒	⊖	⊜	⊜	⊜
Auto. trans.	○	⊖	⊖	○	⊖	⊖	⊜	⊜
Man. trans.								
Clutch								
Electrical	●	●	●	●	●	◒	○	◒
A/C	◒	◒	○	○	○	⊖	⊖	⊜
Suspension	◒	○	⊖	⊖	⊖	⊜	⊜	⊜
Brakes	●	●	●	●	●	⊖	⊜	⊖
Exhaust	⊖	⊖	⊜	⊜	⊖	⊖	⊜	⊖
Body rust	●	○	⊖	⊖	⊜	⊜	⊜	⊜
Paint/trim	●	◒	○	○	○	⊖	⊖	⊖
Integrity	◒	○	○	⊖	◒	○	○	○
Hardware	●	◒	○	○	◒	◒	◒	⊖

Trouble Spots	Pontiac Firebird 88	89	90	91	92	93	94	95
Engine	◒	◒	Insufficient data	○	Insufficient data	Insufficient data	⊖	Insufficient data
Cooling	●	●		○			⊖	
Fuel	●	○		◒			⊖	
Ignition	◒	○		○			⊜	
Auto. trans.	*	*		*			⊖	
Man. trans.	*	*		*			*	
Clutch	*	*		*			*	
Electrical	●	●		●			◒	
A/C	○	○		○			⊖	
Suspension	○	○		⊖			⊖	
Brakes	◒	●		◒			⊖	
Exhaust	●	●		◒			⊜	
Body rust	◒	○		⊖			⊜	
Paint/trim	●	●		◒			○	
Integrity	●	●		●			◒	
Hardware	○	●		●			◒	

Trouble Spots	Pontiac Grand Am 88	89	90	91	92	93	94	95
Engine	●	●	●	◒	○	⊖	⊖	⊜
Cooling	◒	●	◒	○	○	⊖	⊜	⊜
Fuel	◒	◒	○	○	⊖	⊜	⊖	⊜
Ignition	◒	◒	○	○	⊖	⊜	⊜	⊜
Auto. trans.	○	○	○	○	⊜	⊖	⊖	⊜
Man. trans.	*	*	*	*	*	*	*	*
Clutch	*	*	*	*	*	*	*	*
Electrical	●	●	●	◒	●	◒	○	⊖
A/C	○	⊖	○	⊖	⊖	⊖	⊖	⊜
Suspension	◒	○	○	○	○	○	⊖	⊜
Brakes	●	●	●	●	●	●	○	⊖
Exhaust	●	●	●	●	⊜	⊜	⊜	⊜
Body rust	●	●	●	⊖	⊖	⊜	⊜	⊜
Paint/trim	●	●	●	●	○	○	⊖	⊜
Integrity	◒	◒	◒	○	◒	◒	○	⊖
Hardware	◒	◒	○	◒	◒	◒	○	⊖

Trouble Spots	Pontiac Grand Prix 88	89	90	91	92	93	94	95
Engine	⊖	○	○	○	⊖	⊜	⊖	⊜
Cooling	●	◒	○	○	⊖	⊖	⊜	⊜
Fuel	◒	●	◒	◒	⊖	⊖	⊜	⊜
Ignition	○	◒	○	⊖	⊖	⊖	⊜	⊜
Auto. trans.	◒	○	○	⊖	⊖	⊖	⊖	⊖
Man. trans.	*	*	*	*	*	*		
Clutch	*	*	*	*	*	*		
Electrical	●	●	●	●	●	●	●	⊖
A/C	◒	○	○	○	⊖	⊖	⊖	⊜
Suspension	◒	●	○	○	⊖	⊜	⊖	⊖
Brakes	●	●	●	●	●	●	⊖	⊖
Exhaust	⊖	⊜	⊜	⊖	⊜	⊜	⊜	⊜
Body rust	○	⊖	⊜	⊖	⊜	⊜	⊜	⊜
Paint/trim	●	●	●	◒	○	○	⊖	⊜
Integrity	◒	◒	○	◒	◒	◒	◒	○
Hardware	●	●	●	●	◒	◒	●	⊖

Trouble Spots	Pontiac Sunbird 88	89	90	91	92	93	94	95
Engine	●	●	◒	◒	○	⊖	⊖	
Cooling	●	●	◒	◒	◒	○	⊖	
Fuel	○	○	⊖	○	○	⊖	⊜	
Ignition	◒	○	○	⊖	⊜	⊖	⊖	
Auto. trans.	⊖	⊖	⊜	⊖	⊜	⊖	*	
Man. trans.	*	*	*	*	*	*	*	
Clutch	*	*	*	*	*	*	*	
Electrical	●	●	●	●	●	◒	○	
A/C	◒	◒	○	⊖	⊜	⊜	⊜	
Suspension	○	○	◒	○	⊖	○	⊜	
Brakes	●	●	●	●	●	◒	○	
Exhaust	●	●	●	⊖	⊖	⊜	⊖	
Body rust	●	●	◒	⊖	⊖	⊖	⊖	
Paint/trim	●	◒	◒	○	○	○	○	
Integrity	◒	◒	●	◒	◒	◒	◒	
Hardware	○	◒	◒	○	◒	●	◒	

Trouble Spots	Pontiac Sunfire 88	89	90	91	92	93	94	95
Engine								⊜
Cooling								⊜
Fuel								⊜
Ignition								⊜
Auto. trans.								⊖
Man. trans.								*
Clutch								*
Electrical								⊖
A/C								⊜
Suspension								⊖
Brakes								⊖
Exhaust								⊜
Body rust								⊜
Paint/trim								⊜
Integrity								⊖
Hardware								⊖

Trouble Spots	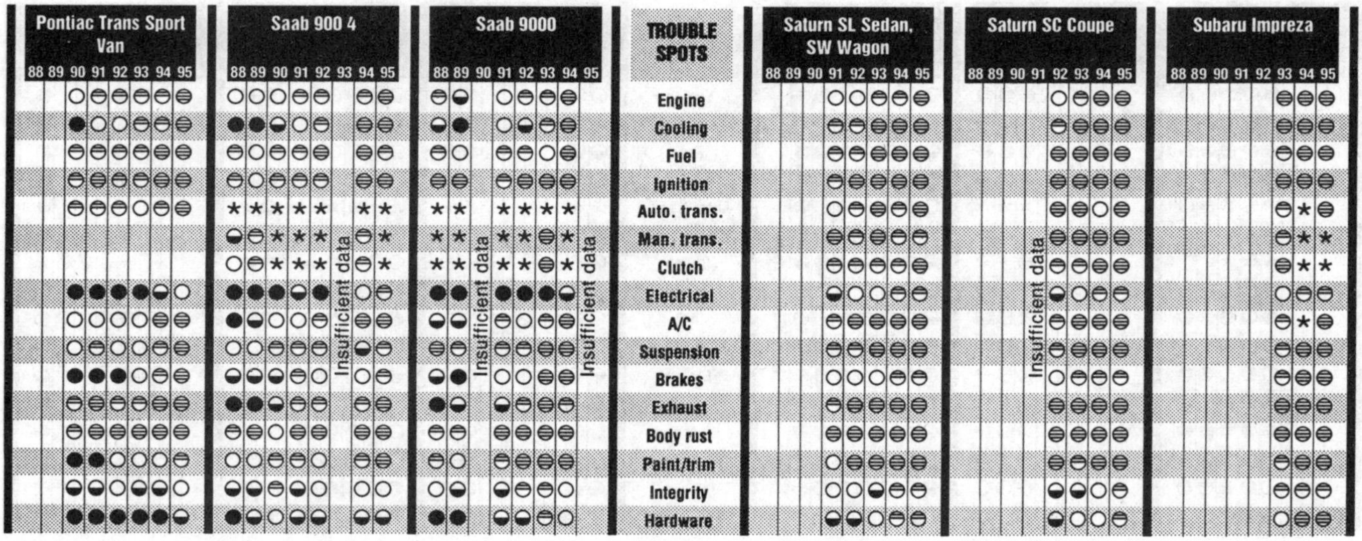 Pontiac Trans Sport Van 88	89	90	91	92	93	94	95
Engine			○	⊖	⊖	⊖	⊖	⊜
Cooling			●	○	○	⊖	⊖	⊜
Fuel			⊖	⊖	⊖	⊖	⊜	⊜
Ignition			⊖	⊜	⊖	⊖	⊜	⊜
Auto. trans.			⊖	⊖	⊖	○	⊖	⊜
Man. trans.								
Clutch								
Electrical			●	●	●	●	◒	○
A/C			○	○	○	○	⊜	⊜
Suspension			○	⊖	○	○	⊖	⊜
Brakes			●	●	●	○	⊖	⊜
Exhaust			⊖	⊜	⊖	⊖	⊜	⊜
Body rust			⊖	⊜	⊜	⊜	⊜	⊜
Paint/trim			●	●	○	○	○	⊖
Integrity			◒	◒	○	◒	◒	○
Hardware			●	●	●	●	●	◒

Trouble Spots	Saab 900 4 88	89	90	91	92	93	94	95
Engine	○	○	○	⊖	⊖	Insufficient data	⊖	⊜
Cooling	●	●	◒	○	⊖		⊜	⊜
Fuel	⊖	○	⊖	⊖	⊜		⊜	⊖
Ignition	⊖	○	⊖	⊖	⊖		⊜	⊜
Auto. trans.	*	*	*	*	*		*	*
Man. trans.	◒	⊖	*	*	*		⊖	*
Clutch	○	⊖	*	*	*		⊖	*
Electrical	●	●	●	◒	●		○	⊖
A/C	●	◒	○	○	⊖		⊜	⊜
Suspension	○	○	⊖	⊖	⊖		◒	⊖
Brakes	◒	◒	◒	⊖	○		○	⊖
Exhaust	●	●	◒	⊖	⊖		⊖	⊜
Body rust	⊖	⊜	○	⊜	⊜		⊜	⊜
Paint/trim	○	○	⊜	⊖	○		⊖	⊜
Integrity	◒	◒	⊜	◒	○		○	○
Hardware	●	◒	○	◒	◒		◒	◒

Trouble Spots	Saab 9000 88	89	90	91	92	93	94	95
Engine	⊖	◒	Insufficient data	○	⊖	⊖	⊜	Insufficient data
Cooling	◒	●		○	◒	⊖	⊜	
Fuel	⊖	○		⊖	⊖	○	⊜	
Ignition	⊜	⊜		⊖	⊜	⊜	⊜	
Auto. trans.	*	*		*	*	*	*	
Man. trans.	*	*		*	*	⊜	*	
Clutch	*	*		*	*	⊜	*	
Electrical	●	●		●	●	●	◒	
A/C	◒	◒		⊖	○	⊖	⊜	
Suspension	⊜	⊖		⊖	⊖	⊜	⊜	
Brakes	◒	●		○	○	⊜	⊜	
Exhaust	●	◒		◒	⊖	⊜	⊖	
Body rust	⊖	⊖		⊜	⊜	⊜	⊜	
Paint/trim	⊖	○		⊖	⊜	⊜	⊜	
Integrity	○	◒		◒	⊖	⊖	○	
Hardware	●	●		◒	◒	⊖	○	

Trouble Spots	Saturn SL Sedan, SW Wagon 88	89	90	91	92	93	94	95
Engine				○	○	⊖	⊖	⊜
Cooling				⊖	⊖	⊜	⊜	⊜
Fuel				⊜	⊖	⊜	⊜	⊜
Ignition				⊖	⊜	⊜	⊜	⊜
Auto. trans.				○	⊖	⊜	⊖	⊜
Man. trans.				⊜	⊖	⊜	⊖	⊖
Clutch				⊖	⊖	⊖	⊖	⊜
Electrical				◒	○	○	⊖	⊖
A/C				⊖	⊜	⊜	⊜	⊜
Suspension				⊖	⊖	⊜	⊜	⊜
Brakes				○	○	○	⊖	⊖
Exhaust				⊖	⊜	⊜	⊜	⊜
Body rust				⊜	⊜	⊜	⊜	⊜
Paint/trim				○	⊜	⊜	⊜	⊜
Integrity				○	○	◒	⊖	⊖
Hardware				◒	◒	○	⊖	⊖

Trouble Spots	Saturn SC Coupe 88	89	90	91	92	93	94	95
Engine				Insufficient data	○	⊖	⊜	⊜
Cooling					⊖	⊜	⊜	⊜
Fuel					⊜	⊜	⊜	⊜
Ignition					⊜	⊜	⊖	⊜
Auto. trans.					⊜	⊜	○	⊜
Man. trans.					⊜	⊜	⊜	⊜
Clutch					⊖	⊖	⊜	⊜
Electrical					◒	○	⊖	⊖
A/C					⊖	⊜	⊜	⊜
Suspension					⊖	⊜	⊜	⊜
Brakes					○	⊖	⊖	⊖
Exhaust					⊜	⊜	⊜	⊜
Body rust					⊜	⊜	⊜	⊜
Paint/trim					⊜	⊖	⊜	⊜
Integrity					◒	◒	○	⊖
Hardware					◒	○	○	⊖

Trouble Spots	Subaru Impreza 88	89	90	91	92	93	94	95
Engine						⊜	⊜	⊜
Cooling						⊜	⊜	⊜
Fuel						⊖	⊜	⊜
Ignition						⊜	⊜	⊜
Auto. trans.						⊖	*	⊜
Man. trans.						⊖	*	*
Clutch						⊜	*	*
Electrical						○	⊖	⊖
A/C						⊖	*	⊜
Suspension						⊖	⊜	⊜
Brakes						⊖	⊜	⊜
Exhaust						⊜	⊜	⊜
Body rust						⊜	⊜	⊜
Paint/trim						⊖	⊜	⊜
Integrity						⊖	⊖	⊖
Hardware						○	⊜	⊜

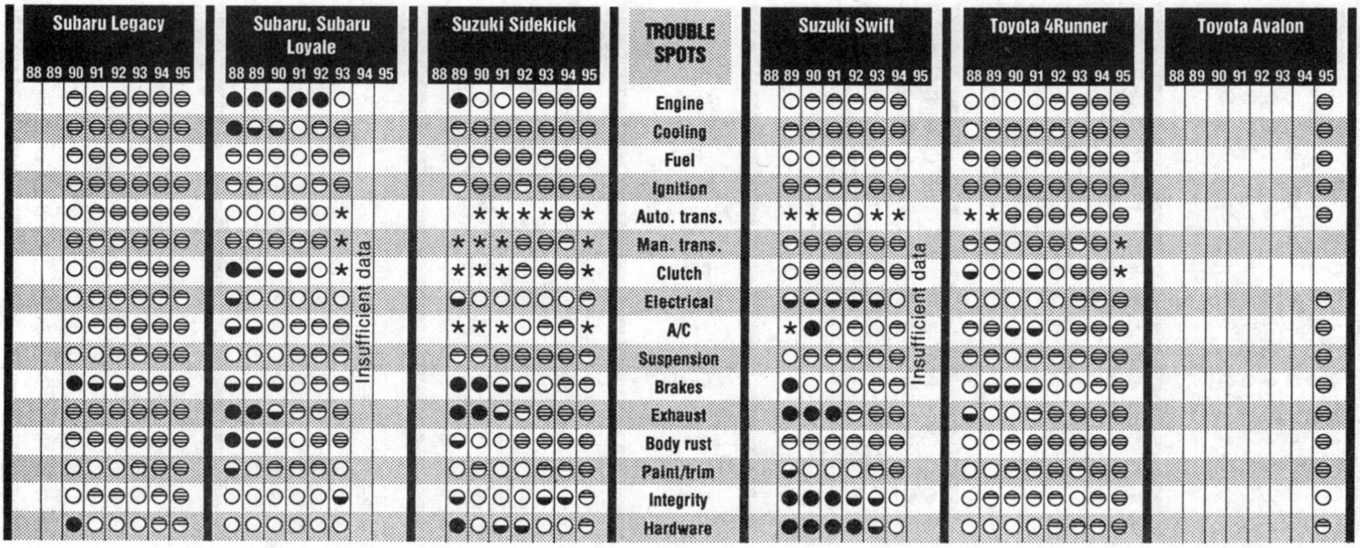

Trouble Spots	Subaru Legacy 88	89	90	91	92	93	94	95
Engine			⊖	⊜	⊜	⊜	⊜	⊜
Cooling			⊜	⊜	⊜	⊜	⊜	⊜
Fuel			⊖	⊜	⊖	⊜	⊜	⊜
Ignition			⊖	⊜	⊜	⊜	⊜	⊜
Auto. trans.			○	⊖	⊜	⊜	⊜	⊜
Man. trans.			⊜	⊖	⊖	⊜	⊜	⊜
Clutch			○	○	⊖	⊖	⊜	⊜
Electrical			○	⊖	⊖	⊖	⊖	⊖
A/C			○	⊖	⊖	⊜	⊜	⊜
Suspension			○	○	⊖	⊖	⊜	⊜
Brakes			●	◒	◒	⊖	⊖	⊜
Exhaust			⊜	⊜	⊜	⊜	⊜	⊜
Body rust			⊖	⊜	⊜	⊜	⊜	⊜
Paint/trim			○	○	○	⊖	⊜	⊜
Integrity			○	⊖	⊖	○	⊖	⊜
Hardware			●	○	○	○	⊖	⊖

Trouble Spots	Subaru, Subaru Loyale 88	89	90	91	92	93	94	95
Engine	●	●	●	●	●	○	Insufficient data	
Cooling	●	◒	◒	○	⊖	⊜		
Fuel	⊖	⊖	⊖	○	⊖	⊖		
Ignition	⊖	⊖	○	○	⊖	⊜		
Auto. trans.	○	○	○	⊖	○	*		
Man. trans.	⊜	⊖	⊜	⊖	⊜	*		
Clutch	●	◒	◒	◒	○	*		
Electrical	◒	○	○	○	○	○		
A/C	◒	◒	○	⊖	⊖	⊖		
Suspension	○	○	○	⊖	⊖	⊖		
Brakes	◒	◒	◒	○	⊖	⊖		
Exhaust	●	●	◒	⊖	⊖	⊜		
Body rust	●	◒	◒	○	⊜	⊜		
Paint/trim	◒	○	⊖	⊖	⊖	○		
Integrity	○	○	○	○	○	◒		
Hardware	○	○	○	○	○	○		

Trouble Spots	Suzuki Sidekick 88	89	90	91	92	93	94	95
Engine		●	○	○	⊜	⊜	⊜	⊜
Cooling		⊖	⊜	⊜	⊜	⊜	⊜	⊜
Fuel		⊖	⊖	⊜	⊜	⊖	⊜	⊜
Ignition		⊖	⊜	⊜	⊖	⊜	⊜	⊜
Auto. trans.			*	*	*	*	⊜	*
Man. trans.		*	*	*	⊜	⊜	⊖	*
Clutch		*	*	*	⊖	⊜	⊜	*
Electrical		◒	○	○	○	○	○	⊖
A/C		*	*	*	○	⊖	⊖	*
Suspension		⊖	⊖	⊜	⊜	⊜	⊜	⊖
Brakes		●	●	◒	◒	○	⊖	⊖
Exhaust		●	●	◒	⊖	⊜	⊜	⊜
Body rust		◒	○	○	⊜	⊜	⊜	⊜
Paint/trim		○	⊖	○	○	⊖	⊖	⊜
Integrity		◒	○	○	○	◒	◒	⊖
Hardware		●	○	◒	◒	○	○	⊖

Trouble Spots	Suzuki Swift 88	89	90	91	92	93	94	95
Engine		○	⊖	⊖	⊖	⊖	⊜	Insufficient data
Cooling		⊖	⊖	⊜	⊜	⊜	⊜	
Fuel		○	○	⊖	⊖	⊖	⊖	
Ignition		⊜	⊖	⊖	⊖	⊜	⊜	
Auto. trans.		*	*	⊖	○	*	*	
Man. trans.		⊖	⊜	⊜	⊜	⊜	⊜	
Clutch		○	⊜	⊖	⊖	⊖	⊜	
Electrical		◒	◒	◒	◒	◒	○	
A/C		*	●	○	⊖	○	⊖	
Suspension		○	⊖	⊖	⊖	⊖	⊜	
Brakes		●	○	○	○	⊖	⊖	
Exhaust		●	●	●	⊖	⊜	⊜	
Body rust		⊖	⊖	⊖	⊖	⊜	⊜	
Paint/trim		◒	○	○	○	⊖	⊜	
Integrity		●	●	●	◒	◒	○	
Hardware		●	●	●	●	◒	○	

Trouble Spots	Toyota 4Runner 88	89	90	91	92	93	94	95
Engine	○	○	○	○	⊖	⊜	⊜	⊜
Cooling	○	⊖	⊖	⊖	⊖	⊜	⊜	⊜
Fuel	⊖	⊜	⊜	⊖	⊜	⊜	⊜	⊜
Ignition	⊜	⊜	⊜	⊜	⊜	⊜	⊜	⊜
Auto. trans.	*	*	⊜	⊜	⊜	⊖	⊜	⊜
Man. trans.	⊖	⊖	○	⊜	⊜	⊖	⊜	*
Clutch	◒	○	○	◒	○	⊜	⊜	*
Electrical	○	○	○	○	○	⊖	⊜	⊜
A/C	⊖	⊜	◒	◒	○	⊜	⊜	⊜
Suspension	⊖	⊖	○	⊖	⊖	⊖	⊜	⊜
Brakes	○	◒	◒	◒	○	○	⊖	⊜
Exhaust	◒	○	○	⊖	⊜	⊜	⊜	⊜
Body rust	○	○	⊖	⊜	⊜	⊜	⊜	⊜
Paint/trim	○	○	⊖	⊜	⊜	⊖	⊜	⊜
Integrity	○	⊖	⊖	⊖	⊖	○	⊖	⊜
Hardware	○	○	○	○	⊖	⊖	⊜	⊜

Trouble Spots	Toyota Avalon 88	89	90	91	92	93	94	95
Engine								⊜
Cooling								⊜
Fuel								⊜
Ignition								⊜
Auto. trans.								⊜
Man. trans.								
Clutch								
Electrical								⊖
A/C								⊜
Suspension								⊜
Brakes								⊜
Exhaust								⊜
Body rust								⊜
Paint/trim								⊜
Integrity								○
Hardware								⊖

⊜	⊖	○	◒	●
Few ←		Problems		→ Many

* Insufficient data

Toyota Camry

TROUBLE SPOTS	88	89	90	91	92	93	94	95
Engine	○	⊖	⊖	⊖	⊜	⊜	⊜	⊜
Cooling	⊖	⊖	⊜	⊜	⊜	⊜	⊜	⊜
Fuel	⊖	⊖	⊜	⊜	⊜	⊜	⊜	⊜
Ignition	○	⊖	⊜	⊜	⊜	⊜	⊜	⊜
Auto. trans.	⊜	⊖	⊖	⊜	⊜	⊜	⊜	⊜
Man. trans.	⊖	⊖	⊖	⊜	⊜	⊜	⊜	*
Clutch	○	○	⊖	⊖	⊖	⊜	⊜	*
Electrical	●	◒	◒	◒	○	⊖	⊖	⊜
A/C	⊖	⊖	⊖	⊜	○	⊜	⊜	⊜
Suspension	○	○	⊖	⊖	⊖	⊖	⊜	⊜
Brakes	◒	◒	◒	◒	○	○	⊜	⊜
Exhaust	●	●	◒	⊜	⊜	⊜	⊜	⊜
Body rust	◒	○	○	⊜	⊜	⊜	⊜	⊜
Paint/trim	◒	○	⊖	⊖	⊖	⊖	⊜	⊜
Integrity	○	○	⊖	⊖	⊖	⊖	○	⊖
Hardware	○	○	○	○	○	⊖	⊜	⊜

Toyota Celica

TROUBLE SPOTS	88	89	90	91	92	93	94	95
Engine	◒	⊖	⊖	⊖	⊜	⊜	⊜	Insufficient data
Cooling	○	⊖	⊖	⊜	⊜	⊜	⊜	
Fuel	⊖	⊖	⊜	⊜	⊜	⊜	⊜	
Ignition	○	⊜	⊜	⊜	⊜	⊜	⊜	
Auto. trans.	⊖	⊖	⊜	⊜	⊜	⊜	⊜	
Man. trans.	⊖	⊜	⊜	⊜	⊜	*	⊖	
Clutch	○	○	○	⊜	⊜	*	⊜	
Electrical	●	◒	◒	◒	⊖	⊖	⊜	
A/C	○	⊖	●	◒	○	⊖	⊜	
Suspension	○	⊖	⊖	⊖	⊜	⊜	⊜	
Brakes	●	◒	○	⊖	⊖	⊜	⊜	
Exhaust	●	●	⊜	⊜	⊜	⊜	⊜	
Body rust	○	○	⊜	⊜	⊜	⊜	⊜	
Paint/trim	◒	○	⊜	○	⊖	⊖	⊖	
Integrity	○	⊖	○	○	⊖	○	○	
Hardware	○	○	○	○	○	○	⊜	

Toyota Corolla

TROUBLE SPOTS	88	89	90	91	92	93	94	95
Engine	○	⊖	⊖	⊜	⊜	⊜	⊜	⊜
Cooling	○	○	⊖	⊖	⊜	⊜	⊜	⊜
Fuel	⊖	⊖	⊜	⊜	⊜	⊜	⊜	⊜
Ignition	⊖	⊖	⊜	⊜	⊜	⊜	⊜	⊜
Auto. trans.	⊜	⊖	⊜	⊜	⊜	⊜	⊜	⊜
Man. trans.	⊜	⊜	⊜	⊜	⊜	⊜	⊜	⊜
Clutch	○	⊖	⊖	⊖	⊜	⊜	⊜	⊜
Electrical	◒	○	◒	◒	○	○	⊖	⊖
A/C	○	⊖	⊖	⊖	⊜	⊜	⊜	⊜
Suspension	⊖	⊖	⊖	⊖	⊖	⊖	⊜	⊜
Brakes	●	●	○	○	⊖	⊖	⊜	⊜
Exhaust	●	●	●	●	○	⊜	⊜	⊜
Body rust	○	⊖	⊖	⊜	⊜	⊜	⊜	⊜
Paint/trim	○	⊖	⊖	⊖	⊖	⊖	⊖	⊜
Integrity	○	○	○	⊖	⊖	○	○	⊖
Hardware	○	○	○	◒	○	◒	○	⊖

Toyota Cressida

TROUBLE SPOTS	88	89	90	91	92	93	94	95
Engine	◒	◒	○	⊜	Insufficient data			
Cooling	●	○	⊖	○				
Fuel	○	⊖	⊖	⊖				
Ignition	○	⊜	⊜	⊜				
Auto. trans.	⊖	⊜	⊜	⊖				
Man. trans.								
Clutch								
Electrical	●	◒	◒	◒				
A/C	●	●	◒	○				
Suspension	○	⊖	⊖	⊖				
Brakes	◒	◒	◒	◒				
Exhaust	◒	○	⊖	⊜				
Body rust	○	⊜	⊖	⊜				
Paint/trim	○	⊖	⊜	⊖				
Integrity	○	⊖	⊖	⊖				
Hardware	○	○	⊖	⊜				

Toyota Land Cruiser

TROUBLE SPOTS	88	89	90	91	92	93	94	95
Engine	Insufficient data	○	Insufficient data	⊖	Insufficient data	Insufficient data	⊜	Insufficient data
Cooling		◒		⊜			⊜	
Fuel		○		⊖			⊜	
Ignition		⊜		⊜			⊜	
Auto. trans.		⊖		⊜			⊖	
Man. trans.								
Clutch								
Electrical		○		⊖			○	
A/C		○		○			⊜	
Suspension		⊜		⊜			⊖	
Brakes		◒		●			○	
Exhaust		◒		○			⊜	
Body rust		○		⊜			⊜	
Paint/trim		○		⊖			⊖	
Integrity		⊖		⊖			○	
Hardware		⊖		○			⊖	

Toyota Pickup

TROUBLE SPOTS	88	89	90	91	92	93	94	95
Engine	⊖	⊖	⊖	⊖	⊜	⊜	⊜	⊜
Cooling	◒	○	○	○	⊜	⊜	⊜	⊜
Fuel	⊖	⊖	⊖	⊜	⊜	⊜	⊜	⊜
Ignition	⊜	⊜	⊜	⊜	⊜	⊜	⊜	⊜
Auto. trans.	○	⊖	○	⊜	⊜	⊜	⊜	*
Man. trans.	⊜	⊖	⊜	⊜	⊜	⊜	⊜	⊜
Clutch	◒	○	⊖	⊖	⊖	⊖	⊜	⊜
Electrical	○	○	⊖	⊖	⊖	⊜	⊖	⊖
A/C	○	⊖	⊖	⊜	⊖	⊜	⊜	⊜
Suspension	⊖	⊖	⊖	⊖	⊖	⊖	⊜	⊖
Brakes	◒	○	○	○	⊖	⊖	⊜	⊖
Exhaust	●	◒	○	⊖	⊜	⊜	⊜	⊜
Body rust	●	⊖	⊖	⊜	⊜	⊜	⊜	⊜
Paint/trim	○	⊖	⊖	⊖	⊖	⊜	⊖	⊜
Integrity	⊖	⊖	⊖	⊖	⊖	⊖	○	⊜
Hardware	⊖	⊖	⊖	⊖	○	⊖	⊖	⊜

Toyota Previa Van

TROUBLE SPOTS	88	89	90	91	92	93	94	95
Engine				⊜	⊜	⊜	⊜	⊜
Cooling				⊜	⊜	⊜	⊜	⊜
Fuel				⊜	⊜	⊜	⊜	⊜
Ignition				⊜	⊜	⊜	⊜	⊜
Auto. trans.				⊜	⊜	⊜	⊜	⊜
Man. trans.				*	*	*		
Clutch				*	*	*		
Electrical				●	○	○	⊖	⊖
A/C				●	○	⊖	⊜	⊜
Suspension				⊖	⊖	⊜	⊜	⊜
Brakes				○	○	⊖	⊜	⊜
Exhaust				⊜	⊜	⊜	⊜	⊜
Body rust				⊜	⊜	⊜	⊜	⊜
Paint/trim				⊖	⊜	⊜	⊜	⊜
Integrity				○	⊜	⊖	⊜	⊖
Hardware				◒	○	○	⊖	⊜

Toyota T100 Pickup

TROUBLE SPOTS	88	89	90	91	92	93	94	95
Engine						⊜	⊜	⊜
Cooling						⊜	⊜	⊜
Fuel						⊜	⊜	⊜
Ignition						⊜	⊜	⊜
Auto. trans.						*	*	*
Man. trans.						⊜	*	*
Clutch						⊜	*	*
Electrical						⊖	⊜	⊜
A/C						⊜	⊖	⊜
Suspension						○	⊖	⊖
Brakes						⊜	⊖	⊜
Exhaust						⊜	⊜	⊜
Body rust						⊜	⊜	⊜
Paint/trim						⊖	⊖	⊜
Integrity						⊖	○	○
Hardware						○	○	⊜

Toyota Tercel

TROUBLE SPOTS	88	89	90	91	92	93	94	95
Engine	◒	◒	○	⊜	⊜	⊜	⊜	Insufficient data
Cooling	◒	○	⊖	⊖	⊜	⊜	⊜	
Fuel	◒	◒	◒	⊜	⊜	⊜	⊜	
Ignition	⊖	⊖	⊖	⊜	⊜	⊜	⊜	
Auto. trans.	○	⊖	⊖	⊜	⊜	⊜	⊜	
Man. trans.	⊖	⊖	⊖	⊜	⊜	⊜	⊜	
Clutch	◒	⊖	⊖	⊜	⊜	⊜	⊜	
Electrical	◒	◒	◒	⊖	⊖	⊖	⊖	
A/C	◒	○	⊖	⊖	⊖	⊖	⊖	
Suspension	⊖	⊖	⊖	⊜	⊜	⊜	⊖	
Brakes	●	●	◒	⊖	⊖	⊖	⊜	
Exhaust	●	●	●	⊖	⊜	⊜	⊜	
Body rust	◒	○	⊖	⊜	⊜	⊜	⊜	
Paint/trim	○	○	○	○	⊖	⊖	⊖	
Integrity	◒	○	○	⊖	⊖	⊖	⊖	
Hardware	○	○	○	⊖	⊖	⊖	⊖	

Volkswagen Golf, GTI, Golf III 4

TROUBLE SPOTS	88	89	90	91	92	93	94	95
Engine	○	◒	Insufficient data	Insufficient data	Insufficient data	Insufficient data	⊜	⊜
Cooling	●	●					⊜	⊜
Fuel	◒	◒					⊜	⊖
Ignition	○	⊖					⊜	⊜
Auto. trans.	*	*					⊜	*
Man. trans.	⊖	⊖					⊜	⊜
Clutch	○	⊖					⊜	⊖
Electrical	●	●					◒	○
A/C	○	◒					⊖	⊖
Suspension	⊖	◒					⊜	⊖
Brakes	◒	◒					⊜	⊜
Exhaust	●	●					⊜	⊜
Body rust	○	○					⊜	⊜
Paint/trim	○	◒					⊖	⊖
Integrity	◒	●					○	⊖
Hardware	●	●					●	◒

Volkswagen Jetta, Jetta III 4

TROUBLE SPOTS	88	89	90	91	92	93	94	95
Engine	◒	○	○	○	○	Insufficient data	⊜	⊜
Cooling	●	◒	◒	○	⊖		⊜	⊜
Fuel	◒	◒	○	○	⊖		⊜	⊖
Ignition	○	⊖	⊖	○	○		⊜	⊜
Auto. trans.	*	*	*	*	*		⊜	*
Man. trans.	⊖	⊖	⊖	⊖	*		⊜	⊜
Clutch	○	○	⊖	⊖	*		⊜	⊖
Electrical	●	●	●	●	●		◒	○
A/C	●	◒	◒	⊖	○		⊖	⊖
Suspension	○	○	◒	○	⊖		⊜	⊖
Brakes	●	◒	◒	○	○		⊜	⊜
Exhaust	●	●	◒	○	⊖		⊜	⊜
Body rust	○	○	⊖	⊜	⊖		⊜	⊜
Paint/trim	○	◒	⊖	○	○		⊖	⊖
Integrity	●	◒	◒	●	◒		○	⊖
Hardware	●	●	◒	●	●		●	◒

Volkswagen Passat

TROUBLE SPOTS	88	89	90	91	92	93	94	95
Engine			◒	◒	Insufficient data	Insufficient data	Insufficient data	⊜
Cooling			◒	◒				⊜
Fuel			○	○				⊜
Ignition			⊖	○				⊜
Auto. trans.			*	*				*
Man. trans.			*	*				*
Clutch			*	*				*
Electrical			●	●				○
A/C			◒	⊖				⊜
Suspension			◒	⊖				⊜
Brakes			○	●				⊜
Exhaust			●	○				⊜
Body rust			⊖	⊜				⊜
Paint/trim			⊖	⊖				⊜
Integrity			⊖	◒				⊖
Hardware			●	●				⊖

Volvo 240 Series

TROUBLE SPOTS	88	89	90	91	92	93	94	95
Engine	⊖	⊖	⊖	⊜	⊜	⊜		
Cooling	◒	○	○	◒	○	⊖		
Fuel	○	○	⊖	⊖	⊖	⊖		
Ignition	⊖	⊖	⊖	⊖	⊖	⊖		
Auto. trans.	○	⊖	⊖	⊜	○	⊜		
Man. trans.	⊜	*	*	*	*	*		
Clutch	⊖	*	*	*	*	*		
Electrical	●	●	●	●	◒	●		
A/C	●	●	○	⊖	⊜	⊖		
Suspension	○	○	⊖	⊖	⊖	⊜		
Brakes	●	●	●	●	●	◒		
Exhaust	◒	◒	○	⊖	⊖	⊜		
Body rust	⊜	⊖	⊜	⊜	⊜	⊜		
Paint/trim	○	⊖	⊖	⊖	⊖	⊜		
Integrity	○	⊖	⊖	⊖	○	⊖		
Hardware	○	○	◒	○	⊜	○		

Volvo 740 Series

TROUBLE SPOTS	88	89	90	91	92	93	94	95
Engine	⊖	○	⊖	⊖	⊜			
Cooling	○	○	○	◒	○			
Fuel	⊖	○	○	○	⊖			
Ignition	⊖	⊖	⊖	⊜	⊜			
Auto. trans.	⊖	⊖	⊖	⊜	⊜			
Man. trans.	*	*	*	*				
Clutch	*	*	*	*				
Electrical	●	●	◒	◒	◒			
A/C	●	◒	○	⊖	⊖			
Suspension	○	⊖	⊖	⊖	⊖			
Brakes	●	●	●	◒	◒			
Exhaust	◒	○	○	○	⊜			
Body rust	⊜	⊜	⊜	⊜	⊜			
Paint/trim	⊖	⊖	⊖	○	⊖			
Integrity	◒	○	○	○	⊖			
Hardware	●	◒	◒	◒	○			

Volvo 760 Series

TROUBLE SPOTS	88	89	90	91	92	93	94	95
Engine	◒	○	Insufficient data					
Cooling	●	●						
Fuel	○	○						
Ignition	⊖	⊖						
Auto. trans.	⊖	⊖						
Man. trans.								
Clutch								
Electrical	●	●						
A/C	●	●						
Suspension	○	○						
Brakes	●	●						
Exhaust	○	○						
Body rust	⊖	⊜						
Paint/trim	○	⊖						
Integrity	◒	◒						
Hardware	●	●						

Volvo 850 Series

TROUBLE SPOTS	88	89	90	91	92	93	94	95
Engine						⊜	⊜	⊜
Cooling						⊜	⊜	⊜
Fuel						⊖	⊖	⊜
Ignition						⊜	⊜	⊜
Auto. trans.						⊖	⊜	⊜
Man. trans.						⊖	⊜	*
Clutch						⊜	⊖	*
Electrical						○	○	⊖
A/C						⊖	⊜	⊜
Suspension						⊖	⊖	⊜
Brakes						⊜	⊜	⊜
Exhaust						⊜	⊜	⊜
Body rust						⊜	⊜	⊜
Paint/trim						⊖	○	⊜
Integrity						○	○	⊖
Hardware						○	○	⊖

Volvo 940 Series

TROUBLE SPOTS	88	89	90	91	92	93	94	95
Engine				○	⊜	⊜	⊜	Insufficient data
Cooling				○	●	○	⊜	
Fuel				⊖	⊖	⊖	⊖	
Ignition				⊜	⊜	⊖	⊖	
Auto. trans.				⊜	⊜	⊖	⊜	
Man. trans.								
Clutch								
Electrical				○	○	⊖	○	
A/C				○	⊖	⊖	⊖	
Suspension				⊖	⊖	⊖	⊜	
Brakes				◒	◒	○	⊜	
Exhaust				⊖	⊜	⊜	⊜	
Body rust				⊜	⊜	⊜	⊜	
Paint/trim				⊜	⊜	⊖	⊜	
Integrity				⊖	⊖	○	⊖	
Hardware				○	○	⊖	○	

Volvo 960 Series

TROUBLE SPOTS	88	89	90	91	92	93	94	95
Engine					Insufficient data	⊜	⊜	⊖
Cooling						⊖	⊜	⊜
Fuel						⊖	⊜	⊜
Ignition						⊜	⊜	⊜
Auto. trans.						⊖	⊜	⊜
Man. trans.								
Clutch								
Electrical						○	○	⊖
A/C						○	⊜	⊜
Suspension						⊖	⊖	⊖
Brakes						○	⊜	⊖
Exhaust						⊜	⊜	⊜
Body rust						⊜	⊜	⊜
Paint/trim						⊖	⊖	⊜
Integrity						◒	⊖	⊜
Hardware						◒	○	⊖

12

MANUFACTURERS' TELEPHONE NUMBERS

Want more information? Can't find a particular model? Call the car manufacturers directly for additional product material and dealer locations. Most manufacturers have full-color brochures and comprehensive lists of features, color combinations, and technical data on all available models—from economy cars to sport-utility vehicles. Although all of our information was current at press time, model specifications, prices, and optional equipment may have changed. Plus, some models may have been dropped from a manufacturer's roster since the publication of this book. Your best bet is to call these numbers and get the latest information.

Acura	800-862-2872
Audi	800-822-2834
BMW	800-831-1117
Buick	800-521-7300
Cadillac	800-458-8006
Chevrolet	800-222-1020
Chrysler	800-992-1997
Dodge	800-992-1997
Eagle	800-992-1997
Ford	800-392-3673
Geo	800-222-1020
GMC	800-462-8782
Honda	310-783-2000
Hyundai	800-633-5151
Infiniti	800-662-6200
Isuzu	310-699-0500
Jaguar	800-544-4767
Jeep	800-992-1997
Lexus	800-872-5398
Lincoln	800-392-3673
Mazda	800-222-5500
Mercedes-Benz	800-222-0100
Mercury	800-392-3673
Mitsubishi	800-222-0037
Nissan	800-647-7261
Oldsmobile	800-442-6537
Plymouth	800-992-1997
Pontiac	800-762-2737
Saab	800-955-9007
Saturn	800-553-6000
Subaru	800-782-2783
Suzuki	714-996-7040
Toyota	800-331-4331
Volkswagen	800-822-8987
Volvo	800-458-1552

Index